THE ACHIEVEMENTS OF INTERNATIONAL LAW

The aim of this collection of essays in Robin Churchill's honour is to discuss key examples of the achievements of international law – with the express aim of exploring both what it has achieved and also its limits. This will serve as a response to the two popular but opposite misconceptions about the role of international law. One view is that international law is too weak to improve the world in any significant way. The other view is that international law is a panacea that can be used to rid the world of many of its ills.

The book is divided into four distinct parts, each reflecting on what international law has achieved within broadly defined substantive areas. It opens with a discussion on general international law and international human rights law, before exploring the law of the sea and fisheries. It then looks at international environmental law before finally examining the use of force and international criminal law. The collection will provide a contrast to the popular misconceptions about international law by offering examples of both its successes and limitations as a system.

The Achievements of International Law

Essays in Honour of Robin Churchill

Edited by
Jacques Hartmann
and
Urfan Khaliq

•HART•
OXFORD • LONDON • NEW YORK • NEW DELHI • SYDNEY

HART PUBLISHING

Bloomsbury Publishing Plc

Kemp House, Chawley Park, Cumnor Hill, Oxford, OX2 9PH, UK

1385 Broadway, New York, NY 10018, USA

29 Earlsfort Terrace, Dublin 2, Ireland

HART PUBLISHING, the Hart/Stag logo, BLOOMSBURY and the Diana logo are trademarks of Bloomsbury Publishing Plc

First published in Great Britain 2021

A catalogue record for this book is available from the British Library.

Library of Congress Cataloging-in-Publication data

Names: Churchill, R. R. (Robin Rolf), honouree. | Hartmann, Jacques (Law professor), editor. | Khaliq, Urfan, 1970- editor.

Title: The achievements of international law : essays in honour of Robin Churchill / edited by Jacques Hartmann and Urfan Khaliq.

Description: Oxford ; New York : Hart Publishing, an imprint of Bloomsbury Publishing, 2021. | Includes bibliographical references and index.

Identifiers: LCCN 2021018044 (print) | LCCN 2021018045 (ebook) | ISBN 9781509917372 (hardback) | ISBN 9781509950560 (paperback) | ISBN 9781509917389 (pdf) | ISBN 9781509917396 (Epub)

Subjects: LCSH: International law. | Law of the sea. | Environmental law, International. | International criminal law. | Jus cogens (International law) | Churchill, R. R. (Robin Rolf)

Classification: LCC KZ3410 .A2825 2021 (print) | LCC KZ3410 (ebook) | DDC 341—dc23

LC record available at https://lccn.loc.gov/2021018044

LC ebook record available at https://lccn.loc.gov/2021018045

ISBN: HB: 978-1-50991-737-2
ePDF: 978-1-50991-738-9
ePub: 978-1-50991-739-6

Typeset by Compuscript Ltd, Shannon

FOREWORD

DAVID ANDERSON*

As the present volume testifies, Robin Churchill has made many important contributions to international law, especially the international Law of the Sea. He has done so in several ways: teaching, writing, editing and consulting.

Professor Churchill has taught at different university law schools, notably Cardiff and later Dundee, over a long and distinguished career. In addition to his two principal universities, at different times he has also joined the academic staff of universities as far apart as Tromsø and Wollongong. Many students of international law, the international protection of human rights and the settlement of international disputes have benefited from his pedagogic skills.

A worldwide audience know Professor Churchill from his published works and those he has edited: he can truly be said to be a leading scholar and publicist. For 30 years, he has been well known to students and practitioners of the Law of the Sea as the co-author (with Professor Vaughan Lowe) of the leading textbook on the topic, *The Law of the Sea.*[1] This single volume addresses all the key issues and adopts moderate stances on controversial issues: it is frequently cited and thus retains its place as the leading single-volume work, notwithstanding the recent appearance of similar monographs by other experts.

Professor Churchill is also well known as the author of annual surveys of the various dispute settlement mechanisms applicable to the Law of the Sea. Since 2001, these surveys have been published regularly in the *International Journal of Marine and Coastal Law*, on the advisory board of which he serves as a member.[2] They now form a comprehensive and systematic record of decisions and advisory opinions concerning the law of the sea given by the International Court of Justice, the International Tribunal for the Law of the Sea, arbitrations and conciliation commissions. These surveys also point to shortcomings and inconsistencies (fortunately rare) in the reasoning of the many different international courts and tribunals charged with applying and interpreting the modern Law of the Sea.

* Judge, International Tribunal for the Law of the Sea (1996–2005).

[1] RR Churchill and AV Lowe, *The Law of the Sea*, 3rd edn (Manchester, Manchester University Press, 1999). A fourth edition is expected shortly.

[2] See, eg, the survey for 2016–17 in R Churchill, 'Dispute Settlement in the Law of the Sea: Survey for 2015, Part II and 2016' (2017) 32 *International Journal of Marine and Coastal Law* 379.

Apart from writing studies in his own name, Professor Churchill has served as a member of research teams convened by learned bodies, such as the British Institute of International and Comparative Law. A recent example is the Institute's *Report on the Obligations of States under Articles 74(3) and 83(3) of UNCLOS in Respect of Undelimited Maritime Areas*,[3] to which he made significant contributions concerning the relevant law and State practice. He has also acted as a consultant to governments, European institutions, international organisations and non-governmental organisations.[4] During the 1970s, *New Directions in the Law of the Sea*,[5] a compilation of treaties, national legislation and other materials, edited by Professor Churchill and others, was of great help to delegates to the Third United Nations Conference on the Law of the Sea.

As well as the Law of the Sea, Professor Churchill is a leading authority in at least two other related fields: first, the EU's Fisheries Policy, the subject of his monograph (published with Daniel Owen) entitled *The EC Common Fisheries Policy*;[6] and, second, the law and politics of the Arctic region, a topic addressed in his monograph (with Geir Ulfstein) entitled *Marine Management in Disputed Areas: The Case of the Barents Sea*.[7]

A recent example of Professor Churchill's standing as a leading authority is provided by the *Report of the International Law Association on Baselines in the Law of the Sea*.[8] This Report, drafted by a group of maritime experts drawn from many different countries, addressed the highly controversial question whether the practice of States in drawing straight baselines had produced a new rule of customary international law, departing from the terms of Article 7 of the United Nations Convention on the Law of the Sea. After much internal discussion, the experts decided the question by citing with approval the following assessment made in 2005 by Professor Churchill:

> Although the amount of non-conforming state practice is substantial, it still represents no more than about a quarter of coastal States parties to the Convention. It is also quite diverse, in the sense that it does not point to any particular way in which straight

[3] British Institute of International and Comparative Law, *Report on the Obligations of States under Articles 74(3) and 83(3) of UNCLOS in Respect of Undelimited Maritime Areas* (London, British Institute of International and Comparative Law, 2016).

[4] RR Churchill, *The Meaning of the 'Genuine Link' Requirement in Relation to the Nationality of Ships* (2000) remains one of the best surveys of the topic. It appears to have been produced as part of a consultancy for the International Seafarers Union, available at https://orca.cf.ac.uk/45062/1/ITF-Oct2000.pdf.

[5] SH Lay, R Churchill and M Nordquist (eds), *New Directions in the Law of the Sea, vols I and II* (London, British Institute of International and Comparative Law and Oceana Publications, 1973) and later volumes.

[6] RR Churchill and D Owen, *The EC Common Fisheries Policy* (Oxford, Oxford University Press, 2010).

[7] RR Churchill and G Ulfstein, *Marine Management in Disputed Areas* (Dartmouth, Routledge, 1992).

[8] International Law Association, *Report of the International Law Association on Baselines under the International Law of the Sea* (International Law Association, 2018), available at https://www.ila-hq.org/images/ILA/DraftReports/DraftReport_Baselines.pdf.

> baselines should be drawn: in reality, it seems to suggest no more than that a coastal State may draw straight baselines however it likes. All this, coupled with the fact that at least eight different States and the EU have protested to one or more baseline claims, leads to the conclusion that practice relating to the drawing of straight baselines does not amount (yet) either to an agreed interpretation of the Convention or a new rule of customary international law.[9]

This passage brings out the author's strengths as an international lawyer. The facts are noted and analysed. A cautious, balanced conclusion is drawn. Indeed, the qualities of Professor Churchill's published work can best be summed up as clear, sensible and moderate, but also as advancing interesting ideas. It is a pleasure to add my words of appreciation to those of the authors and editors of the present volume.

[9] RR Churchill, 'The Impact of State Practice on the Jurisdictional Framework Contained in the LOS Convention' in AG Oude Elferink (ed), *Stability and Change in the Law of the Sea: The Role of the LS Convention* (Leiden, Martinus Nijhoff, 2005) 108.

ACKNOWLEDGEMENTS

Given the standing and regard in which Robin is held, it was only natural that a collection in his honour would be published. Both of us have known Robin for a good number of years and our lives have been significantly enriched as a result of his friendship. We each worked with Robin as more junior colleagues – at Cardiff and Dundee respectively – with he the more senior, established and respected colleague. We each benefitted enormously from his generosity in terms of his time and advice: be it to negotiate a Board of Studies with a proposal for a new module, pitching lectures on a notoriously difficult topic or which journal to send a draft article to. You could ask Robin to read a draft of anything you had written and it would come back full of comments, suggestions, some rewriting and a commentary at the end as to how it could be improved upon. Barely a sentence would go without comment or suggestion. The comments were in immaculate even handwriting and always written in ink. Also, the text of the draft would be printed on one side, and on the other side was something entirely unrelated. In the days before duplex printers, Robin – the ever-conscious environmentalist – would ensure that every piece of paper had both sides fully used, so as not to waste paper. Similar was his approach to expression in draft articles, it was through him that one of us learnt that less is often more – one of his more common hand-written comments in the margin being 'tautology!'. The extent of the comments were met with a sense of trepidation upon receipt but everything by Robin was done with care, affection, respect and selflessness, on the one hand, and, on the other hand, intellectual robustness. It goes without saying, the quality of the draft was always vastly improved as a result of Robin's guidance. Co-authoring with Robin was simply a masterclass in how to write an academic piece. The clarity of thought, the efficiency, the precise mapping of the scope of the discussion, the attention to detail – the skills of a master craftsman at the height of his powers – all wonders to behold. Many of today's so-called 'academic coaches' who promise to reveal the secrets of successful writing and publishing would themselves learn a great deal by spending just a few hours with Robin. Working with younger colleagues, so as to nurture them to find their own voices, was something Robin has always taken very seriously. It is part of his DNA to share, guide and to assist so that future generations of scholars can also make their way. Testimony to this fact is that five of the contributors to this collection, each very well established and regarded academics in their own right, are Robin's former students. The British higher education landscape has changed enormously in recent decades but Robin's kindness, generosity and commitment to excellence are timeless, universal qualities and unfortunately increasingly rare. When the idea was first mooted with him some years ago that there should be a collection in Robin's honour, the only impediment was his humility – Robin was not sure he was worthy. It is a mark of the man. He took persuading but we were honoured when he eventually did so but also somewhat daunted. Writing to those involved in the project and those few who had to decline, it is obvious that it is not only respect in which Robin is held, it is also great affection. That made our lives as editors easier as each of the contributors agreed to scope their discussions within the framework of the 'Achievements of International Law' as the theme of this collection. We wish to thank each of them.

As is inevitable in projects of this sort it took us longer than we planned to get all submissions together. Covid-19 was also an unwelcome consideration to be negotiated. Notwithstanding this, all contributors responded as we requested, to our queries and comments. Stephanie Theophanidou and Samuel White provided assistance at various times for which we are grateful. The Cardiff University School of Law and Politics, Research Support Scheme provided funding to assist with some of the research assistance we benefited from. At Hart, we had the pleasure to work with Sinead Moloney and her team. As always, working with Hart was a seamless and enjoyable experience from start to finish. We are grateful to all of the above.

Shortly after submission of the manuscript we learnt that Professor Robert Cryer, a friend, colleague and contributor to this collection had passed away. Rob had been unwell for a while but was adamant that he would complete his chapter, which he duly did. It is an especial privilege and honour to have that essay as part of this collection.

Jacques Hartmann and Urfan Khaliq – January 2021.

CONTENTS

PART III
THE LAW OF THE SEA AND FISHERIES

PART IV
INTERNATIONAL ENVIRONMENTAL LAW

PART V
INTERNATIONAL CRIMINAL COOPERATION

LIST OF CONTRIBUTORS

David Anderson CMG was a Judge of the International Tribunal for the Law of the Sea between 1996 and 2005, after serving as a legal adviser at the UK Foreign and Commonwealth Office for many years. For over 20 years, he played an active part in the Third UN Conference on the Law of the Sea, the Secretary-General's Consultations about Part XI and the Straddling Fish Stocks Conference. He has negotiated over a dozen maritime boundary treaties in several different seas and oceans.

Richard Caddell is Senior Lecturer in Law at Cardiff University. He was awarded a PhD on the Law of the Sea from Cardiff University in 2009, where he studied under Professor Robin Churchill. His main research interests engage the Law of the Sea, international environmental law, wildlife conservation, fisheries and polar law. He regularly acts as a legal adviser to national governments, intergovernmental bodies and non-governmental organisations on environmental and marine issues, and is also an academic member of Francis Taylor Building, Inner Temple, London.

Robert Cryer was Professor of International and Criminal Law at the University of Birmingham and Extraordinary Professor of Law at the University of the Free State, South Africa. He had previously held academic positions in Nottingham and Manchester. His first academic job was as a research assistant on Robin Churchill and Vaughan Lowe, *The Law of the Sea*, 3rd edn (Manchester, Manchester University Press, 1999). He was author, amongst other works, of *The Tokyo International Military Tribunal: A Reappraisal* (Oxford, Oxford University Press, 2008) (with Neil Boister) and *An Introduction to International Criminal Law and Procedure*, 4th edn (Cambridge, Cambridge University Press, 2019) (with Darryl Robinson and Sergey Vasiliev). Rob passed away during the publication process at the end of 2020; as editors, we dealt with all copy-editing queries and very much hope we addressed them in a way that would have been agreeable to him.

Erdem Denk is Professor of International Law at the Faculty of Political Science, Ankara University. He studied international relations and international law at the Faculty of Political Science, Ankara University. He then wrote his PhD thesis entitled 'Relative Sovereignty over International Watercourses: Rights and Obligations of Watercourse States' at Cardiff University under the supervision of Professor Robin Churchill. His main interest areas are the theory and history of international law, international organisations and legal issues of Turkish foreign policy, on which he has authored and edited several books and articles. He is currently writing a book on the history of 'international' law and order since the Palaeolithic.

Sir Malcolm Evans KCMG OBE is Professor of Public International Law at the University of Bristol. He was a member of the UN Subcommittee for Prevention of Torture from 2009 to 2020 and Chair of the Subcommittee from 2011 to 2020. He has also served as Chair of the Meeting of Chairs of UN Human Rights Treaty Bodies.

Duncan French is Professor of International Law and Pro Vice Chancellor at the University of Lincoln. He previously worked at the Universities of Reading and Sheffield. He was a doctoral student of Professor Robin Churchill's during the late 1990s at Cardiff University, researching international environmental law and developing countries. His recent work has variously focused on the Sustainable Development Goals, the International Seabed Authority, planetary boundaries and international law, and the interactions between public and private international law.

Jacques Hartmann is Reader in Law at Dundee Law School, Dundee University.

Tore Henriksen is Professor and Director of the Norwegian Centre for the Law of the Sea at the Arctic University of Norway, Tromsø.

Urfan Khaliq is Professor of International and European Laws at Cardiff University and Head of the School of Law and Politics.

Dino Kritsiotis is Professor of Public International Law at the University of Nottingham.

Vaughan Lowe QC, Bencher of Gray's Inn, is Emeritus Chichele Professor of Public International Law and Emeritus Fellow of All Souls College at the University of Oxford.

Daniel Owen is a barrister at Fenners Chambers, Cambridge. He specialises in the law that governs our use of the world's seas and oceans. He and Robin Churchill are the co-authors of *The EC Common Fisheries Policy* (Oxford, Oxford University Press, 2010).

Catherine Redgwell is Chichele Professor of International and Fellow of All Souls College at the University of Oxford.

Geir Ulfstein is Professor of International Law at the Department of Public and International Law, University of Oslo and co-director of PluriCourts – Centre for the Study of the Legitimate Roles of the Judiciary in the Global Order, University of Oslo.

Introduction

There are two popular but opposing misconceptions about the role of international law.[1] One group cynically views international law as too weak to improve the world in any significant way. Its members see international law as a system that primarily reflects the interests of powerful States.[2] At the other extreme, there are those who perhaps view international law rather too optimistically. They see international law almost as a magic cure-all that might rid the world of its ills.[3]

The aim of this collection is to reply to both groups – the cynics and the idealists – and in turn to celebrate Professor Robin Churchill's extensive contribution to international law. By discussing key examples of the achievements of international law, the authors seek both to explore what international law has achieved and also to exemplify its limitations. Thus, each chapter reflects on the achievements within specific areas of the law. The authors are leading authorities within their fields, all of whom have worked with Professor Churchill and many of whom owe him much in terms of the development of their academic career.

As noted in the foreword by David Anderson, Professor Churchill has himself made many important contributions to international law. David Anderson rightly highlights the Law of the Sea, the European Union's Common Fisheries Policy, and the law and politics of the Arctic region as areas in which Professor Churchill is an undisputed authority. There are other areas too, notably international human rights law. But Professor Churchill's contributions are not limited to his academic output or influence on the development of aspects of international law. He has also nurtured talent and tirelessly shared his wide knowledge and experience with generations of established and budding scholars, students and practitioners alike. As the contributions to this collection testify, Professor Churchill's influence and work covers many other areas of international law and extends across all parts of the globe. The contributions are divided into five parts: I. General International Law; II. Human Rights Law; III. Law of the Sea and Fisheries; IV. International Environmental Law; and V. International Criminal Cooperation.

The first part of this collection focuses on general international law. It contains three chapters, all drawing on historical lessons. In 'Less is More: Rules and

[1] *cf* A Clapham, *Brierly's Law of Nations: An Introduction to the Role of International Law in International Relations*, 7th edn (Oxford, Oxford University Press, 2012) 503.

[2] *cf* JL Goldsmith and EA Posner, *The Limits of International Law* (Oxford, Oxford University Press, 2007).

[3] A Cassese (ed), *Realizing Utopia: The Future of International Law* (Oxford, Oxford University Press, 2012).

Principles in International Law-Making', Vaughan Lowe considers two styles of international law-making: those which create detailed, precise provisions (rule-based) and those which simply set out the principle without going into further depth (principle-based). Through the lens of the United Nations Convention on the Law of the Sea (UNCLOS) and building on his long experience as both a practising international lawyer and distinguished academic, Lowe argues that the rule-based provisions in UNCLOS have not fared as well as the principle-based provisions. At the same time, he notes that the principle-based rules have allowed States to develop State practice more organically, building on the high-level principles. Lowe concludes that a key lesson from UNCLOS is that in the law, as in life, it is often the case that 'less is more'. In 'An Amodernist Approach to International Law: The Case of Law of the Sea in the Amarna Letters', Erdem Denk challenges the common assumption that international law is one of the unique achievements of modern (Western) society. Denk contests what he terms the 'civilisation-based/centric' approaches and suggests that 'international law' has been created whenever and wherever two or more mutually recognising polities have existed and governed their interactions. Using the Amarna letters from several thousand years ago, Denk provides an example for his argument relating to marine matters. In 'The Sources of Public International Law Historically Considered', Dino Kritsiotis provides a historic consideration of the sources of international law, a topic which understandably continues to be at the centre of international law as a discipline. Kritsiotis principally focuses on the relationship between treaties and customary international law, going back in time to the eve of the exponential rise of treaties in their multilateral form, and continuing right through to the seminal decision of the International Court of Justice in the *North Sea Continental Shelf* cases. In doing so, he charts the changes that have occurred over time in the main sources of public international law.

The second part of this collection contains three chapters focusing in different ways on the individual and their rights as part of international law. In the first of these ('The UN and Human Rights: Reform through Review?'), Malcolm Evans considers the 2020 review of the United Nations (UN) treaty body system. Evans explains the background of that process, its outcome, and analyses how defensive preparations for the 2020 Review, which have oscillated between poles of idealism and political reality, have generated the most comprehensive and ambitious reform proposals of the UN treaty body system in recent times. In 'United Nations Human Rights Treaty Bodies: Universality and National Implementation', Geir Ulfstein considers the challenges facing the UN human rights treaty bodies, looking at the same 2020 Review. He discusses whether the treaty bodies should defer to decisions made by national organs by applying different standards of review, concluding that these bodies should apply a selective, conditional and cautious deference to national decisions. In the final chapter in this part ('International Parental Child Abduction and the Need for Alternative Regimes?'), Urfan Khaliq looks at how nations have sought to cooperate in order to tackle a particular international and individual rights-related issue: international parental child abduction.

This is an issue that relates to individual rights, but Khaliq examines this in the context of public and private international law regimes and argues that the existing treaty regimes are not capable of being universal, as routinely claimed. Rather, he seeks to illustrate that the law in this area is based upon assumptions and premises that reflect a Eurocentric perspective, which will not permit universally inclusive regimes or solutions. He proposes some possible solutions whilst highlighting the shortcomings of the alternatives.

The third part of this collection focuses on the achievements of an area of law, where Professor Churchill has made numerous contributions, namely the law of the sea and fisheries. The first chapter in this part ('Coastal State Jurisdiction in Ice-Covered Areas: The Impacts of Climate Change and the Polar Code') is by Tore Henriksen. In line with other chapters of this book, Henriksen illustrates that the law is not static. He investigates if and how the changes in sea ice coverage and the legislative initiative taken through the International Maritime Organization affect the extended environmental jurisdiction of the coastal State under Article 234 of the 1982 UN Convention on the Law of the Sea (UNCLOS). He argues that the effect of climate change, and of the recent Polar Code, is the narrowing of the margin of appreciation of the coastal States under that provision. The reference to the margin of appreciation in this context is important, as that term is used far more often in the context of human rights law, yet the concept is one that allows States to more readily accept obligations and more easily abide by them. The following chapter ('Responsibility and Liability of Flag States in the Context of Fisheries') by Daniel Owen seeks to bring renewed attention to the responsibility and liability of flag States in the context of fisheries. Focusing on an Advisory Opinion of the International Tribunal for the Law of the Sea, Owen highlights the failure as well as several achievements of international law that flow from the failure. He goes on to propose how the failure of flag States might be remedied through litigation, concluding that although this method has not yet been tried, the Advisory Opinion provides an impetus to reassess the possibility. In the final chapter in Part III ('Compulsory Inter-State Adjudication in the Anthropocene: Achieving the Paradoxical?'), Duncan French likewise considers the role of adjudication, albeit in relation to resolving disputes within international environmental law. French especially explores the underlying principle of consensual jurisdiction and the opportunities for so-called compulsory jurisdiction. He concludes that there is a need for further research in this area, in particular with regard to what form a *lex anthropocene* might take.

Part IV of the volume focuses on the achievements in international environmental law. In the first chapter in this part ('The Challenge of Effective Compliance and Enforcement of International Environmental Law'), Catherine Redgwell picks up from the previous two chapters by considering the inadequacies of traditional dispute settlement for enforcement of international environmental law obligations. After having explained the existing inadequacies, Redgwell focuses on the innovative role of implementation monitoring and compliance under multilateral environmental agreements, with particular reference to biodiversity-related treaties.

She concludes that notwithstanding some innovative compliance approaches and rare success stories, the failure to comply with procedural and substantive environmental treaty obligations continues to undermine efforts at nature conservation. In the following chapter ('Where's the Catch? Shifting Stocks, International Fisheries Management and the Climate Change Conundrum') Richard Caddell focuses on how international law has responded to a new threat, namely the impact of global climate change. Focusing on fisheries, Caddell considers whether current regulatory trends and philosophies are sufficient to address the future problems posed by the changing distributions of valuable marine living resources. He concludes that although there have been recent innovations, such as the novel approach which has been adopted to frame future fisheries management in the Arctic, these developments represent an exception to the rule and that much work remains to be done.

The final part of this book contains two chapters focusing on the achievements of international law in criminal cooperation. In the first of these ('The Influence of *Jus Cogens* on International Crimes: Have They Made Any Difference?'), Robert Cryer analyses the influence of *jus cogens* in international criminal law. Through an evaluation of the jurisprudence of the International Court of Justice and the International Criminal Tribunal for the former Yugoslavia, Cryer argues that for the most part, no real additional consequences have been seen to flow from the *jus cogens* nature of violations of international criminal law. In the final chapter ('The Achievements and Limits of Global Counter-terrorism Cooperation'), Jacques Hartmann investigates the importance of domestic law for international counter-terrorism cooperation. Hartmann highlights both the achievements on the global terrorism regime as well as its inherent limitations, arguing that by its very nature, any response to terrorism requires action by State organs, which are limited in their actions by national law.

In light of the 13 substantive chapters, it is apt to ask the following question: what are the achievements of international law? There are simply only a few clear answers to this question and that is probably as it should be. Fundamentally, it needs to be borne in mind that there are swathes of substantive international law – for example, the global rules relating to trade, finance, immunity and intellectual property – that this collection has not even attempted to touch upon. But even if we had, we strongly suspect that there still would be few clear answers. This lack of clarity is indicative of the complexity and breadth of the body of rules and how they are simultaneously highly sophisticated, rudimentary and somewhere in between depending on the matter at hand. In some instances, the very existence of a body of rules can be considered an achievement. Erdem Denk, however, warns us to note that the existence of international laws is a given wherever and whenever polities have interacted and recognised each other. Other chapters – all of those on human rights matters in one way or another – remind us that aspects of international law (even if the adoption of rules is in itself an achievement) are still strongly contested. The chapter by Malcolm Evans on the reform of the UN human rights treaty bodies, for example, is indicative of the surprising robustness of the institutions and systems that have been established, but also the peril they are in. Geir Ulfstein sees a domestic margin of appreciation as having a greater role to play to ensure compliance with such norms. Urfan Khaliq, by contrast, highlights achievements (the adoption of a treaty on parental child abduction) while also noting the existence of competing assumptions, making the supposed global regime effectively regional and perhaps the need for rival regimes to address the mischief in question on a global level.

In other chapters, particularly those in Parts III and IV (all of which relate to or discuss climate change in one way or another), it is again clear that the rules are probably achievements in their own right, but here the rules can bear little relation to the environmental challenges we undoubtedly face. In terms of the enforcement of environmental rules (which vary significantly), the chapters by Daniel Owen, Duncan French and Catherine Redgwell note the importance of adjudication and methods of enforcement, but, of course, the rules need to be fit for purpose when being adjudicated upon. This relates back to the argument made by Vaughan Lowe in the opening chapter that, certainly when it is comes to UNCLOS, those treaty provisions which set out principles have fared better over time than those which set out detailed rules. This theme, of the need for flexibility in provisions to have lasting value, is common to other discussions too. A number of chapters – including those by Richard Caddell and Tore Henriksen – note how the situation is not static and thus if the law is to achieve its objectives, it cannot be either. But we come back to the following question: how do we ensure that the law evolves over time so that it meets the societal need that has arisen? In different ways, the chapters by Dino Kritsiotis, Robert Cryer and Jacques Hartmann all address this. These three chapters consider how the law has developed over time. In the chapter by Kritsiotis, this is via a detailed analysis of the relationship between treaties and customary international law in general terms. In relation to the development over time of international criminal law, which is analysed by Cryer and Hartmann in their chapters, the rise of the sub-discipline is probably in itself an achievement. Cryer highlights how *jus cogens* has in substantive terms added little to international criminal law, whereas Hartmann's analysis illustrates the tension between, on the one hand, domestic norms and, on the other, international rules, and how when they interact, one can potentially undermine the other.

The chapters as a whole clearly recognise the interests and perspectives of States, but also to what extent and how international law can and does limit States' interests. Equally, they all appreciate the role of power and understand the limitations of international law. For us, what these chapters all highlight is that between the cynics and optimists, there is a clear middle ground – fittingly, it is the same middle ground that Professor Robin Churchill's scholarship has also fallen squarely into and to which we have all sought to pay tribute.

PART I

General International Law

1

Less is More

Rules and Principles in International Law-Making

VAUGHAN LOWE

Abstract: This chapter considers styles of international law-making: those which create detailed, precise provisions (rule-based) and those which simply set out the principle without going into further depth (principle-based). It does so through the lens of UNCLOS and argues principles are often preferable to detailed provisions in seeking to address pressing global problems.

I. Introduction

Robin Churchill and I were colleagues teaching law in Cardiff in the 1970s. In those days we waited keenly for the latest drafts from UNCLOS III, parsing each sentence and watching the architecture of what became the 1982 UN Convention on the Law of the Sea (hereinafter UNCLOS or 'the Convention')[1] emerge. Some of the main lines were more or less clear from the outset. Provisions on the territorial sea and contiguous zone and the high seas were practically unchanged from the 1958 Geneva Conventions and even from the drafts of the League of Nations codification conferences. Other provisions, such as those on the control of fishing and marine pollution, and the regime for the deep seabed, were new and even startling, sounding in the same register as the writings of jurists such as Bedjaoui and Bencheikh and others who were then starting to promote the ideas of the

[1] In our book *The Law of the Sea*, (Manchester, Manchester United Press, 1983, subsequent editions published in 1988 and 1999) we decided to use the abbreviation 'UNCLOS' to refer to the United Nations Conference on the Law of the Sea, as in UNCLOS III, UNCLOS I etc. We abbreviated the United Nations Convention on the Law of the Sea (adopted 10 December 1982, entered into force 16 November 1994) 1833 UNTS 3 to 'LOSC'. One can only swim against the tide of history for so long. Here, 'UNCLOS' refers to the 1982 Convention on the Law of the Sea, the Conference itself fast fading from memory and now in less need of an abbreviation.

New International Economic Order. It was a time when everything appeared to be possible, if only the sufficient political will could be found to reach the agreements that seemed to be not only economically and environmentally sustainable, but also morally and politically necessary.

Imagination and moral ambition are admirable qualities in a lawyer – particularly in legal scholars, whose independence of the awkward idiosyncrasies and ambiguities of concrete situations allows the development of a more abstract, generalised view of legal rules and principles. But a lawyer whose imagination and ambition lose sight of the hard realities of the world to which those rules and principles must apply is of limited use: too impractical to be a good lawyer and too dependent upon the tools of the lawyer's trade to be a good idealist. That is a trap that Robin Churchill has never been in in danger of falling into. Of his many qualities as a scholar, perhaps that which makes him most exceptional and truly invaluable as a colleague is his encyclopaedic knowledge of what is going on in the world of the law of the sea. In the days before the internet, detailed news of the latest developments had to await the arrival, by surface mail, of the latest edition of *International Legal Materials* or the *International Law Reports*, unless one was lucky enough to come across a rare copy of a cyclostyled text of the latest treaty or judgment. Yet, somehow, Robin was always up to date, knowing not only what legal developments were arising but also what technical developments – in fishing techniques, ship design and so on – underpinned them. He was a fount not only of knowledge, but also of understanding.

The need for this kind of detailed knowledge and understanding is great, and enduring. For all its length, UNCLOS leaves many questions of the law of the sea unanswered, and all of its provisions are susceptible to further refinement. The Convention is something of a stylistic hybrid, reflecting two very different approaches to treaty drafting. While some of its provisions are immensely detailed, others are terse, often vague, generalisations – not to mention the questions that UNCLOS does not even purport to address. This short tribute to Robin Churchill considers these two styles of law-making, which focus on the roles of text and practice in the development of the law of the sea.

II. The Two Styles of Law-Making

The first style is the elaboration of very detailed rules that attempt to provide precise guidance for all situations that are likely to arise in the ordinary course of events. In UNCLOS, this approach is epitomised by the provisions of Part XI, on the deep seabed, but it also characterises many other provisions, such as Article 62 on the utilisation of living resources, Article 76 on the definition of the continental shelf and Article 111 on hot pursuit, along with other sets of provisions such as Part XII on the protection and preservation of the marine environment.

In each of these instances, there is a basic principle, such as the 'common heritage of mankind', or the principle that 'surplus' fish stocks (the portion of the total allowable catch that a State cannot take in its own exclusive economic zone (EEZ) should be made available to neighbouring States, or the principle that the continental shelf is the natural prolongation of the land territory of a coastal State. That principle is then elaborated in a set of detailed rules set out in the Convention that stipulate how the principle is to be applied.

The second style simply sets out the basic principle, stopping short of an attempt to stipulate in detail how the principle should be applied in practice. Article 88 on the reservation of the high seas for peaceful purposes, Article 100 on the duty to cooperate in the repression of piracy and Part IX on enclosed or semi-enclosed seas are clear cases of this, but there are other examples that may not be so immediately obvious. For instance, Article 33 may at first glance appear to say all that needs to be said about the contiguous zone (apart from its 'appendix' in Article 303 on archaeological and historical objects found at sea, which appears at the end of UNCLOS as the afterthought that it was).[2] But when it is compared with the provisions in Part II section 3 on the territorial sea, with Article 111 on hot pursuit, and with the provisions of Part XII on the enforcement of environmental laws and regulations, its skeletal nature becomes clearer.

These two contrasting approaches can be described as 'rule-based' and 'principle-based' approaches, respectively. Of course, most of UNCLOS lies somewhere along the scale between those two polar concepts, but the contrast is nonetheless a useful tool for examining the law-making process in the law of the sea.

III. The Detailed Rule-Based Approach

There appears to be a significant difference in the fate of the Articles that exemplify the two styles. Those that exemplify the 'rule-based' approach have, in general, not fared well. Part XI of UNCLOS is the most notorious example. UNCLOS steered, on the one hand, between Scylla and Charybdis: the twin fears of the power of capital, which was seen by some as a threat to the principle of the common heritage of mankind and the likely instrument for the seizure of the wealth of the deep ocean by the most highly developed industrialised States, and, on the other hand, the fear of the effects of the one State-one vote principle, which some thought would place the industrialised States in thrall to a permanent majority of developing States in any democratic institutions established to govern the international seabed area. Great efforts were put into attempts to find a robust consensus in support of a detailed regime that explicitly spelled out the rights and duties of States in great detail, so that the need and opportunity for future decision-making in relation to the deep seabed regime would be minimised. But the effort was ultimately unsuccessful, for all its carefully constructed detail and checks and balances: Part XI of UNCLOS was not acceptable to some of the key western States and they declined

[2] The topic emerged late in the conference, at the ninth session in 1980.

to ratify the Convention as it stood. Part XI was, in effect, dismantled and replaced by the provisions of the 1994 Agreement relating to the Implementation of Part XI of the Convention, which materially changed the decision-making mechanisms for the International Seabed Authority.

The lesson is plain: detailed legal regimes are potentially valuable as means of assuaging mistrust, but their usefulness in practice depends very much on getting the formula right. The more detail that is included in the treaty provisions, the more confident States can be that they understand the full implications of the agreement that they are invited to make; however, equally, the more detail that is included, the more likely it is that any particular State will find something in the text with which it disagrees sufficiently strongly to make it decide not to ratify the agreement at all.

That is not the only weakness of the 'rule-based' approach to law-making. Article 111 UNCLOS, on hot pursuit, illustrates another problem. This sets out the rules that govern the circumstances in which a foreign ship may be seized by a coastal State on the high seas when the foreign ship has fled the coastal State's maritime zones after committing an offence against the coastal State laws in those zones. The Article was built upon a settled body of State practice, stretching back into the early nineteenth century and beyond, which had already been codified, in terms substantially identical to those in Article 111, in Article 23 of the 1958 Geneva Convention on the High Seas. This State practice evidenced the wide acceptance of specific rules, such as those requiring that the pursuit must 'only be commenced after a visual or auditory signal to stop has been given at a distance which enables it to be seen or heard by the foreign ship' (Article 111(4) UNCLOS) and must not thereafter be interrupted before the pursued vessel is seized.

The requirements made good sense in the nineteenth century, when practically the only way to be certain that the ship seized on the high seas was the ship that had been spotted breaking the law was to keep the ship constantly in sight. But those requirements make little or no sense today.

Intelligence may have come from State A that a ship flying the flag of State B has set off carrying a cargo of narcotic drugs with the intention of smuggling them into State C. In order to identify and apprehend as many of the participants in the smuggling operation as possible, the authorities of States A and C may wish not to arrest the ship immediately, but instead to track its progress and identify boats coming from ports in State C to meet up with it in order to offload the illegal cargo, and then to identify those on land in State C who meet up with those boats and start distributing the drugs within the State. State C may wish to allow the ship to sail out of its waters and arrest it only some hours after unloading its illegal cargo, by which time the ship is on the high seas. All of this can be done perfectly easily with radar and with drones, in a manner that leaves no doubt that the ship arrested is the one whose progress has been tracked throughout the voyage. The ship would not have been warned by giving it an auditory or visual signal to stop, but if such a signal had been given, the ship could have warned those at sea and on land complicit in the smuggling plan and thereby defeated the purpose of the exercise. And quite why an 'auditory or visual signal' rather than, say, a wireless signal[3] should be required is similarly unclear.

As a result of these (and other) difficulties[4] with the wording of the Article on hot pursuit, States have naturally tended to stretch the Convention rules and adopt a more pragmatic approach. A drug smuggler arrested on the high seas by a State Party to UNCLOS cannot in practice assume that a domestic court will find that the arrest was unlawful because it did not follow an auditory or visual signal or because the ship, while continuously tracked, was not continuously 'pursued'.

This is an instance where the rule-based approach to law-making is shown to be defective not because the rules were unacceptable, but because the detailed rules are recognised to be plainly impracticable in certain respects.

The examples illustrate the range of the weaknesses of the rule-based approach. Part XI of UNCLOS, as initially drafted, failed because it was too ambitious and, in the eyes of the industrialised States, too idealistic to serve as a model for the management of what was ultimately a commercial and industrial activity competing for investment capital and resources with any number of other opportunities. The hot pursuit provision failed for a quite different reason. States were perfectly happy to agree upon the wording; indeed, they had done so not long before when a substantially identical provision appeared in the High Seas Convention. Article 111 failed because it was insufficiently flexible to be responsive to changing demands – changing technology, changing patterns of criminal activity, and changing policing policies and practices.

These defects are inherent in 'rule-based' law-making. They constitute a weakness that attends all attempts to move the law forward by the prescription of detailed rules. The problem is particularly evident in the field of environmental law, where it is common to assume that the adoption of a detailed and tightly drafted international agreement is a rational and useful response to what may be undeniably pressing moral and political imperatives.

In some circumstances, this approach may indeed be very well suited to the problem addressed. A good example can be seen in the work of the International Maritime Organization (IMO) on the Safety of Life at Sea (SOLAS) and marine pollution treaties. There, detailed rules are laid down, some applicable only to newly built ships, others requiring the retrospective fitting of new equipment to older vessels. The detailed rules are amended from time to time to keep up with changes in technology and regulatory demands, just as national regulatory

[3] The initial drafters of the provision in its incarnation as art 23 of the Convention on the High Seas (adopted 29 April 1958, entered into force 30 September 1962) 450 UNTS 11 apparently intended to exclude the possibility of sending the signal by wireless means: see S Nandan and S Rosenne, *United Nations Convention on the Law of the Sea 1982: A Commentary*, vol III (Leiden, Brill Nijhoff, 1995) 258.

[4] See, eg, the cases discussed in WC Gilmore, 'Hot Pursuit and Constructive Presence in Canadian Law Enforcement: A Case Note' (1988) 12 *Marine Policy* 105; WC Gilmore, 'Hot Pursuit: The Case of *R v Mills and Others*' (1995) 44 *International and Comparative Law Quarterly* 949; W Gilmore, 'Drug Trafficking at Sea: The Case of *R v Charrington and Others*' (2000) 49 *International and Comparative Law Quarterly* 477.

legislation would be amended. Several factors contribute to the success and efficacy of this system. First, the rules serve to apply a common standard to what is essentially a single industry– the international shipping industry – which operates on a truly global scale. There are shared objectives. Everyone – from shipowners to insurers to shippers of goods, and from port States at the ends of voyages to coastal States washed by the waters through which the vessels transit – wants safe, non-polluting ships. Powerful as tax advantages may be as a factor influencing the flagging of vessels, there is little pressure to maintain a competitive edge by operating sub-standard ships: shipowners and port and flag States have an interest in maintaining a level playing field so that competing ships and ports do not unfairly undercut prices by lowering their safety and environmental standards. The system of coordinated inspections of ships in ports[5] and the practice of port authorities in detaining (or refusing entry to) ships not equipped to international standards, together with the requirements of insurers and ship classification societies, greatly reduce any temptation to flout the international rules. The economics of shipping are also very important. Shipping costs generally represent only a small percentage of the price of a product, and compliance with international standards does not have economic consequences on the scale of, for instance, compliance with measures to reduce greenhouse gases on land. Further, the IMO itself has largely succeeded in maintaining its position as an expert technical agency, seeking practical solutions to immediate problems rather than pursuing long-term political objectives.

Combinations of circumstances such as these can enable rule-based approaches to law-making to succeed. But in many areas of international life, the factors do not align in this way. In those areas, the scope for successful action by rule-making is reduced.

IV. The General Principle-Based Approach

What is the alternative? As mentioned above, UNCLOS itself adopts a different approach to some problems. The concise statement in Article 88 of the principle that 'the high seas shall be reserved for peaceful purposes' is a good example of this. The principle could not be stated in more general terms and the terms could barely be more open to a wide range of interpretations. What is 'peaceful'? What constitutes the 'purpose' of an action? What is the significance of the fact that 'peaceful purposes' are phrased in the plural? What is required by the duty to 'reserve' the high seas for peaceful purposes? UNCLOS gives no answer to these questions. The questions are not only so wide, but are so fundamental that one might think that Article 88 has very little value as a principle of international law.

[5] See International Maritime Organization, 'Port State Control', available at: www.imo.org/en/OurWork/MSAS/Pages/PortStateControl.aspx.

However, this would overlook an important role played by statements of principle such as Article 88 UNCLOS. While they are not framed in a way that clearly restrains or clearly authorises any specific State conduct or provides a precise rule which can be readily applied to decide a dispute, they do serve as a focus for discussion of specific activities at sea. Thus, questions of the legality of activities such as weapons testing and naval manoeuvres on the high seas can be couched not only in terms of their compatibility with the requirement that high seas users have 'due regard for the interests of other States in their exercise of the freedom of the high seas' (Article 87(2) UNCLOS), but also in terms of their 'peacefulness' and consonance with Article 88. Article 88 identifies a particular value against which any specific activity is to be measured, even though the Article itself does not establish a test of legality or a precise criterion. What is and is not compatible with Article 88 will gradually become clearer as States decide what activities they will assert the right to engage in on the high seas and which activities on the high seas they will protest against.

Plainly, Article 33 on the contiguous zone is drafted in more detailed terms than Article 88. It makes clear where the contiguous zone is and, in broad terms, the specific purposes for which the jurisdiction of the coastal State may exercise 'control' therein, thereby indicating that the contiguous zone, unlike the territorial sea, is not a zone over which the coastal State enjoys sovereignty or plenary jurisdiction. But it does not clearly indicate whether the list of purposes is exhaustive, or what precisely 'control' means and how it differs from 'jurisdiction', or how contiguous zone rights inter-relate with concepts such as hot pursuit and constructive presence, or whether contiguous zone rights of neighbouring States may overlap or must be delimited between them. In addition, it has none of the detail relating to rights of arrest and so forth that are spelled out in relation to the territorial sea and in Article 111.

Has Article 33 UNCLOS been any the less 'successful' for this lack of detail? I think that the answer is that it has not. The impression from reported State practice is that States have accepted the principle that they may exercise jurisdiction for the purposes of securing compliance with their customs, fiscal, immigration and sanitary laws out to 24 nautical miles (NM) from the shore, and whatever the precise manner in which they have exercised that jurisdiction in practice, it appears to have evoked very little in the way of protest from third States.

True, there have been claims to contiguous zones extending beyond the limits of Articles 33 and 303 UNCLOS. Several States have claimed the right to enforce controls for security purposes within contiguous zones, and there have been occasional claims to exercise control for customs, fiscal, immigration or sanitary purposes at distances greater than the 24 NM stipulated by Article 33. Examples are recorded in works such as Roach and Smith's classic *Excessive Maritime Claims*,[6] along with information on the responses (notably from the US) to such claims.

[6] JA Roach and RW Smith, *Excessive Maritime Claims*, 3rd edn (Leiden, Martinus Nijhoff, 2012).

Such excessive claims are tested out in the international marketplace: some attract protests from other States and others do not. The claims to exercise jurisdiction beyond the 24 NM limit seem to have been abandoned in the face of protests,[7] whereas the claims to exercise control for security purposes within a 24 NM zone appear to have been maintained, despite objections being made to them by some States, for example.[8] In this way, State practice builds upon the basic principles set out in the Convention.

V. Subsequent Practice and the Elaboration of General Principles

In legal terms, this State practice in the application of UNCLOS might be relevant as 'subsequent practice' under the Vienna Convention on the Law of Treaties (VCLT). Article 31(3)(b) VCLT refers to 'any subsequent practice in the application of the treaty which establishes the agreement of the parties regarding its application' as something that must be taken into account when interpreting a treaty; and difficult as it may be to establish an 'agreement' on the basis of practice – particularly an agreement among all or most of the parties to a widely ratified international convention such as UNCLOS – there has been increasing recognition that Article 31(3)(b) must be applied pragmatically, giving weight to 'a 'concordant, common and consistent' sequence of acts or pronouncements which is sufficient to establish a discernible pattern implying the agreement of the parties regarding its interpretation',[9] even if evidence of any actual 'agreement' is sparse or practically non-existent. Nonetheless, it is more likely that this practice of UNCLOS parties will be taken into account as a 'supplementary means of interpretation' under Article 32 VCLT.[10]

Where does this practice leave UNCLOS? Except in cases of genuine consensus among States Parties on its application – such as the undoubted rule, arising from State practice, that naval manoeuvres on the high seas are compatible with the 'peaceful purposes' principle in Article 88 UNCLOS – there is plainly a real possibility, perhaps even a likelihood, that practice in the application of UNCLOS will diverge, differing from State to State. An UNCLOS provision might be interpreted and applied (or, more likely in my view, applied and interpreted: people usually

[7] See, eg, the 200 NM claim made by Namibia in 1990, which was revoked in 1991: *ibid* 159.
[8] ibid 154–58.
[9] World Trade Organization, *Japan: Alcoholic Beverages II – Report of the Appellate Body* (4 October 1996) WT/DS8/AB/R, ET/DS10/AB/R and WT/DS11/AB/R, 13; *cf* C McLachlan, 'The Evolution of Treaty Obligations in International Law' in G Nolte (ed), *Treaties and Subsequent Practice* (Oxford, Oxford University Press, 2013).
[10] See Conclusion 4 of the International Law Commission, 'Draft Conclusions on Subsequent Agreements and Subsequent Practice in Relation to the Interpretation of Treaties, with Commentaries' (2018) UN Doc A/73/10, 27–37.

tend to get on with their jobs in matters that lawyers subsequently categorise as falling under a particular treaty or rule of customary international law, rather than first conducting legal analyses in order to decide precisely how they will carry out their jobs) in one way by one group of States and in another way by another group. The groups may be associated by geography, such as the group of Latin American States whose practice in relation to 200 NM claims was highly influential in the early years of the Third UN Conference on the Law of the Sea, or be linked by political or other factors, such as the group of NATO States and their 'Partners across the globe',[11] which tend to take similar positions on many questions relating to the law applicable to non-nuclear military activities at sea. Does this mean that there is not one UNCLOS, but several versions of UNCLOS, the choice between which depends upon the interpretations of unclear or unspecific UNCLOS provisions adopted by the particular States involved in a given situation?

At one level, the answer must be 'no': there is not a multiplicity of forms of UNCLOS, the precise content of whose provisions varies according to the practice and positions on detailed questions of UNCLOS interpretation of the States concerned in any specific situation. Article 309 UNCLOS stipulates that: 'No reservations or exceptions may be made to this Convention unless expressly permitted by other articles of this Convention.' The creation of 'variable geometry' within UNCLOS by means of agreed, or concurrent but not agreed, interpretations and applications of its provisions is not consonant with Article 309.

No international court or tribunal, faced with two cases giving rise to precisely the same question of interpretation, would be likely to say that the meaning of the relevant UNCLOS position would vary according to the positions of the States concerned on that question. It would surely consider that UNCLOS has one meaning, applicable equally to all UNCLOS States Parties. While the principle that decisions of international courts and tribunals have no binding force except between the parties and in respect of the particular case impedes a formal system of binding judicial precedents in international law, the thoroughness of pleadings before and deliberations of international tribunals, and the self-evident desirability of consistency in judicial decision-making, in fact produce a high level of consistency and certainty in judicial interpretations of the Convention.

This is not to say that the actual outcomes of concrete cases (in contrast to the interpretations of the underlying UNCLOS provisions) will necessarily be equally consistent. For example, a tribunal might decide that State A is precluded or estopped by its prior conduct or statements from denying in a particular case that certain conduct is compatible with the Convention.[12] But that is not the same as saying that the meaning of the Convention itself varies from case to case.

[11] See the North Atlantic Treaty Organization homepage: www.nato.int.

[12] *cf* the importance attached to British acquiescence as an independent basis for the decision of the International Court of Justice in the *Anglo-Norwegian Fisheries Case* [1951] ICJ Reports 116, 137.

The meaning of Convention provisions is, in theory, in principle uniform and autonomous: one meaning is correct and other meanings are not.

However, the practicalities are rather different. Definitive interpretations of treaty provisions arise only when they are the subject of a determination by a court or tribunal having the status of *res judicata*. By definition, such determinations arise only in circumstances where there is a question over the correct legal interpretation of a provision. If there is no such question, the matter will not be submitted to a court or tribunal for a decision. It is naturally improbable that States that adopt similar interpretations and positions on a question of interpretation will put the question forward for judicial interpretation. There may be apparent exceptions – for example, in maritime boundary cases – where the parties may agree on the legal rules, but not on the result that the application of those rules produces in the particular case. There may also be differences over questions of fact, such as the precise location of an arrested vessel, or over questions of characterisation, such as the question whether the conduct of a particular passage through the territorial sea was or was not a 'threat to the peace, good order or security of the coastal State' within the meaning of Article 19(1) UNCLOS – in these cases too, the parties may agree upon the legal rules, but disagree on the result of their application. But in the present context, such differences concerning the result of the application of rules should be regarded as differences over the precise meaning of the rules. Such cases are only apparent, and not real, exceptions to the general point that States that adopt similar interpretations and positions on a question of interpretation do not litigate that question.

The consequence is that as between like-minded States, applications of their shared interpretation of a provision will not be challenged and the Convention will be applied in line with that interpretation. As between States adopting a different interpretation, that different interpretation will be adopted. Only when an incident arises involving States adopting different interpretations will an occasion for litigation, and the determination of the 'definitive interpretation', present itself. This situation is far from unusual. The question of the right of warships to exercise innocent passage without prior notification or authorisation is a good and very long-standing instance of the more or less peaceful coexistence of different interpretations of the law.

The answer to the question of whether there is one UNCLOS or many accordingly depends on what 'UNCLOS' is seen to be. On the one hand, as a text, obviously there is only one UNCLOS. That text is liable to be the subject of a series of interpretations, gradually refining its precise meaning. One can answer the question of how a law-abiding State ought to behave by referring to that text. Yet, as a legal regime, and in answering the question 'how *do* law-abiding States behave?', it appears that there is more than one UNCLOS. The variations resulting from unresolved differences in the interpretation of the general provisions of UNCLOS – either from the use of the wiggle room that persists around the edges of the core of certainty in provisions or from the adoption of practices that appear to contradict the express terms of the Convention – create a situation in which there are in fact competing versions of UNCLOS in operation, rather like competing versions of a play script or a musical score.

In this 'multiple UNCLOS' scenario, in addition to the agreed common core of the Convention, there is a blurred grey area around the edges of interpretations adopted by some (but not all) States Parties.

The propensity of convention texts to give rise to such grey areas is reinforced by another problem: that of characterisation. It can be remarkably difficult to assign instances of State practice to the neat legal categories established by convention texts and academic analyses. At what point does a 'temporary' claim to a maritime zone or a claim explicitly motivated by a local emergency cease to be a temporary suspension of the normal rules and become a claim to a permanent zone? If a small vessel is arrested in the contiguous zone because it is believed to be carrying people intent on attacking a coastal facility, is that the expression of a claim to exercise control for security purposes or for immigration purposes? Or is it perhaps a claim to exercise a right of anticipatory self-defence? The coastal State itself may not know the answer to this. It may know nothing apart from the fact that a small ship is near its coast and acting suspiciously and is perhaps not responding to radio messages. It may also have intelligence, not linked to that particular vessel, about the possibility of an imminent attack upon it. How is such practice to be factored into the legal analysis of the incident?

Of course, any or all of these questions might be answered by express statements or explanations given by the State concerned. In relation to questions of major importance, such as the status of particular straits and of passage rights through them, such statements are not uncommon. For example, declarations that the Straits of Dover or the Straits of Hormuz are regarded as international straits through which a right of transit passage exists are made because the States making the declaration wish to leave their position on the question in no doubt, in case they should feel the need to take serious steps, perhaps even involving the use of force, to assert the rights in question. But the vast majority of activity at sea – routine law-enforcement, fishing regulation, navigation, scientific research and so on – proceeds without any such explicit pronouncements. The implicit interpretation of the UNCLOS provisions must be inferred from the practice, and that may be a difficult exercise.

Indeed, the ambiguities of practice may conceal, or deliberately obscure, divergent interpretations of a convention text. A well-known example concerns the passage of warships, where it is common practice for a ship to send an informal message, purely as a matter of professional courtesy, to a local coastguard that the warship is travelling through the area. The coastguard may be instructed to regard such a message as a 'prior notification' or a request for 'prior authorisation' of the passage, though the warship may in turn recall that its flag State considers that there is no need for any such notification or authorisation. There will be two interpretations of a single episode, and the difference over the interpretation of the law can be pushed out of sight into the grey zone of interpretation without the question of which is correct ever being forced to a definitive conclusion.

VI. Conclusion

To those who see international law primarily as a normative system prescribing how States should act, all of this uncertainty may appear untidy and undesirable – as a sign of weaknesses or defects in the system that are, even if practically unavoidable, to be regretted. To those who see international law primarily as a mechanism for the peaceful adjustment of international disputes, these ambiguities and fudges are valuable parts of the system, securing the application of the rule of law up to a tolerable level of compliance and consistency of conduct, but avoiding the doctrinaire imposition of complete uniformity that would be considered the unachievable and destructive ambition of the zealot.

The world faces challenges whose seriousness and urgency can barely be comprehended. In the face of these challenges, the temptation to work towards the solemn adoption of a sonorous, platitudinous text – on the environment, human rights, or the right to development or self-determination – is often irresistible. Moving beyond the platitudes, those who best understand the problems may spend many years trying to create effective legal regimes to implement the vague general principles, and to do so in a context where international mistrust and rivalry obstruct genuinely collaborative solutions. One lesson from UNCLOS is that it can be better not to try to get everything written down, but to work with a framework of legal principles that States can adopt and adapt to their own situations. It was the wise observation of Immanuel Kant that of the crooked timber of humanity, no straight thing was ever made. Better for international law to work with the grain and not to seek to provide answers to every question: in the law, as in life, it is often the case that less is more.

2

An Amodernist Approach to International Law

The Law of the Sea in the Amarna Letters

ERDEM DENK

Abstract: It is a widely held assumption that international law is one of the unique achievements of modern society. This modern(ist) paradigm postulates that international law is a product of the European/Western civilisation that has flourished in recent centuries. Even 'critical scholars' of international law only suggest that it was discovered in the sixteenth century. The present chapter challenges these 'civilisation-based/centric' approaches and suggests that 'international law' has existed whenever and wherever two or more mutually recognising polities existed and governed their interactions. As is demonstrated with the example of the Law of the Sea in the Amarna letters, each and every epoch came with its own peculiarities, customs, formalities and scale.

I. Introduction: Modern Approaches to International Law

The achievements of international law have been an attractive topic for international law scholars, most of whom also tend to see international law as an achievement. Despite the many debates concerning its main features, sources, methodology, function, development, goals and even history, mainstream approaches assume that the 1648 Westphalian Agreements of Munster and Osnebok signed between European States represent the starting point of international law. The establishment of the League of Nations and the United Nations (UN) have been the true milestones in constituting *the* international law that applies and is relevant to all.

Notwithstanding studies loosely referring to ancient practices that pioneered or heralded practices which have parallels in modern international law, such samples are usually ignored. It would not be incorrect to argue that, as will be expanded upon below, only ancient Greece and the Roman Empire escape this blinkered disdain.

Whereas their contemporaries in, say, Ancient China, let alone older ones that existed millennia before and embodied even more detailed rules and procedures, are lost in the shuffle, the relevance of *polis* and *ius gentium* is pretty much readily acknowledged, highlighted and appreciated.[1] This self-proclaimed universalist approach, in a quite particularistic fashion,[2] points at Thucydides as the founding father of Realpolitik, Stoics and Sophists as the founding fathers of legal philosophy[3] and *ius gentium* as the very origin of international law. So, certain spatial moments are focused on selectively and are constructed and then instrumentalised as the inspirational origins of today's international law to such an extent that even the 'history of international law is confused with the history of Roman law',[4] and thus the contemporary needs of the field and the discipline are secured.

This approach is endemic in mainstream English-language textbooks. Shaw, for example, refers to treaties from ancient Mesopotamia, China and India, yet still refers to their 'geographical and cultural *restrictedness*', as 'the notion of a universal community with its ideal of world order was not in evidence' (emphasis added).[5] This could well be seen as a simple factual finding if the means and conditions of those ages that also 'restricted' all contemporaries were all duly and fairly taken into account, and if the author did not immediately and enthusiastically emphasise that 'the role of ancient Israel must also be noted. A *universal* ethical stance coupled with rules relating to warfare were handed down to other peoples and religions and the demand for justice and a fair system of law founded upon strict morality permeated the thought and conduct of subsequent generations' (emphasis added).[6] Accordingly, these philosophical and legal conceptions were then fermented in the Roman Empire's *ius gentium* and were then discovered, polished, reinforced and mobilised by 'Renaissance Europe', which made, inter alia, international law possible.[7] The progressive development of international law is considered to go hand in hand with the progress of humanity. The more enlightened humanity becomes, the more sophisticated and well-ordered international law will be.

In short, the widespread self-proclaimed universalist approach reminds us that enlightened modernism put an end to the darkness of the Middle Ages. So, international law as such, by its very nature, was itself an achievement. This also provides a template for all sorts of academic writing: in addressing any (contemporary)

[1] See also O Butkevych, 'History of Ancient International Law: Challenges and Prospects' (2003) 5 *Journal of the History of International Law* 189, 193 and 227.

[2] For a study that, albeit unconvincingly, hunts for a non-Orientalist essentialist particularism, see I Wallerstein, *European Universalism: The Rhetoric of Power* (New York, New Press, 2006) 31ff.

[3] For all its problems, Bernal's book still exposes how the ancient Greek roots of modern Europe were discovered and constructed in the nineteenth century. See M Bernal, *Black Athena: The Archaeological and Documentary Evidence* (New Brunswick, NJ, Rutgers University Press, 1987).

[4] Butkevych (n 1) 193.

[5] MN Shaw, *International Law*, 6th edn (Cambridge, Cambridge University Press, 2008) 15–16.

[6] ibid 15.

[7] ibid 16ff.

legal issue, first refer to the Greco-Roman origins of the topic and/or the concept in question; then focus primarily on the pioneering ancient and medieval practices of the European/Western world; finally, elaborate on the modern developments, never forgetting that every single nuance ('progress') deserves our utmost attention.

There have, of course, been critical voices occasionally raised, or tuned, in line with (potential) power shifts. Alternative narratives have occasionally been proffered by those who are uncomfortable with, or suffer from, this Euro/West-centric paradigm. For example, Persian, Indian, Islamic-Arabic, Turkish-Ottoman, Japanese, African, Latin, Soviet and Chinese-centric approaches have all argued in an essentially identical way that modern (positive and normative) sciences in general and (international) law in particular had in fact been, or may only be, developed by *their* respective civilisations[8] as the genuine cradle of humanity: 'What you had in Europe in the 16th–18th centuries, we had had several hundreds (or thousands) years [*sic*] before.'[9] While some claimed their legitimate, honourable and dignified place back in the family of (the law of) nations, some argued that a just and fair legal order could only be developed by their egalitarian ideology and people, whether Marxist-Leninism[10] in the mid-twentieth century or (a revived) Confucianism now.[11] Such views also either retrospectively or futuristically believe in the idea that international law is in fact a (potential) achievement – an achievement of their own. Yet such radical criticisms have a rather 'ontological' problem: they criticise and seek to replace selective, particularistic and European/Western civilisation-centric approaches with another, namely their own selective, particularistic and civilisation-centric approach, be it 'Americocentrism, Afrocentrism, Cino- or Indocentrism'.[12] A solipsistic and particularistic narration of a field and a discipline of law cannot (and at least for epistemological consistency concerns should not) be falsified by another solipsist and particularistic narration. In other words, universalist essentialism cannot be purified by another form of universalist essentialism.

Be that as it may, this achievement-oriented, not to say achievement-obsessed, attitude is so insidious and infectious that even seemingly fully equipped critical

[8] For a study which urges that modern international law 'was just one of many normative systems which existed in various regions of the globe' and that a truly international law in our globalising world may only be accomplished with an 'intercivilizational perspective', see O Yasuaki, 'When was the Law of International Society Born: An Inquiry of the History of International Law from an Intercivilizational Perspective' (2000) 2 *Journal of the History of International Law* 1. Yasuaki's Hague lectures do this in significant detail.

[9] Butkevych (n 1) 213. For a book that focuses on *Siyar*, see M Khadduri (trans), *The Islamic Law of Nations: Shaybani's Siyar* (Baltimore, Johns Hopkins University Press, 1966).

[10] For a recent article that examines how 'Soviet international law was based on two conflicting ideas – the idea of universal peace and the idea of world revolution', see A Cherviatsova and O Yarmysh, 'Soviet International Law: Between Slogans and Practice' (2017) 19 *Journal of the History of International Law* 296.

[11] For a historical account of China's attitude to international law and its relationship with the Chinese philosophy, see P Junwu, 'Chinese Philosophy and International Law' (2011) 1 *Asian Journal of International Law* 233.

[12] Butkevych (n 1) 213.

approaches are also contaminated. The so-called Third World Approaches to International Law (TWAIL), which have gained and lost currency over time, with their shared counter-hegemonic political economy approach is the most striking example in this context.

In fact, notwithstanding the fact that they do not coherently and convincingly clarify whether they problematise international law as a scientific discipline or as an artefact/instrument of Western States (or both), 'TWAILers', as they are known, claim that the Eurocentric 'regime of international law is illegitimate'[13] and that is why they claim to raise 'a distinctive voice in the field of international law'.[14] Accordingly, international law is 'a predatory system that legitimises, reproduces and sustains the plunder and subordination of the *Third World* by the *West*' (emphasis added).[15]

As international law is 'a medium for the creation and perpetuation of a racialized hierarchy of international norms and institutions that subordinate *non-Europeans to Europeans*' (emphasis added),[16] the 'discipline's supposedly formally universalizable doctrines are the product of European imperialism (e.g., the desire of cultural expansion through the cost and oppression to other peoples)'.[17]

Be that as it may, TWAILers also 'recognize that international law is not always an instrument of colonial or post-colonial opposition, [as] it can under certain circumstances be an instrument for or a site of liberation'.[18] That is why 'a systematic process of resistance to the negative aspects of international law is accompanied with continuous claims for reform'[19] and the tasks before TWAILers are portrayed as the 'democratic shaping of international law', exploring 'the relationship between international law and global justice' and ensuring that 'alternative conceptions of the 'good life' are safeguarded by international law'.[20] International law should accordingly be transformed 'from being a language of oppression to a language of emancipation –a body of rules and practices that reflect and embody the struggles and aspirations of peoples from the Third World and which, thereby, *promotes truly global justice*' (emphasis added).[21]

[13] M Mutua, 'What is TWAIL?' (2000) 94 *Proceedings of the Annual Meeting (American Society of International Law)* 31.

[14] A Anghie, 'What is TWAIL: Comment' (2000) 94 *Proceedings of the Annual Meeting (American Society of International Law)* 40.

[15] Mutua (n 13) 31 (footnotes omitted).

[16] ibid.

[17] JD Haskell, 'TRAIL-ing TWAIL: Arguments and Blind Spots in Third World Approaches to International Law' (2014) 27 *Canadian Journal of Law & Jurisprudence* 391.

[18] JT Gathii, 'The Agenda of Third World Approaches to International Law (TWAIL)' in J Dunoff and M Pollack (eds), *International Legal Theory: Foundations and Frontiers* (Cambridge, Cambridge University Press, forthcoming, 2021) 30–31.

[19] ibid 31 (footnotes omitted).

[20] BS Chimni, 'The Past, Present and Future of International Law: A Critical Third World Approach' (2007) 8 *Melbourne Journal of International Law* 511.

[21] A Anghie and BS Chimni, 'Third World Approaches to International Law and Individual Responsibility in Internal Conflicts' (2003) 2 *Chinese Journal of International Law* 77, 79. See also JT Gathii, 'TWAIL: A Brief History of its Origins, its Decentralized Network, and a Tentative Bibliography' (2011) 3 *Trade, Law and Development* 43.

Therefore, TWAIL scholars 'have argued in favor of a more inclusive international law that would overcome its Eurocentric origins and colonial and imperial legacies'.[22] A 'postmodern doctrine' of international law, for example, developed from a Third World perspective would arguably 'help bring about modifications that lend it stability and legitimacy' and thus better serve the needs of all in the 'postcapitalist global order', which will be 'more humane and respectful of nature'.[23] For there is a 'a need to build a movement that cuts across space and time … to form a global opposition force that can challenge those transnational social forces which bolster the regime of capital at the expense of peoples interests'.[24]

Candidly, the need for a genuine manifestation of 'global justice' is obvious. Yet 'this Third Worldist futurism'[25] ironically leans on ideas and movements that cut 'across space and time', despite the historicist methodology of its Marxist roots, which postulates that everything is structurally determined and no notion can be ahistorical and universal.

Chimni, who acknowledges the 'complexities of international politics', 'the realities of power' and 'dominant/hegemonic ideas and beliefs tend to carry the day', therefore notes rather reticently, if not apologetically, that his 'stress on deliberative reason is to be seen as a procedural ideal'.[26] He further notes that it is the 'universal juridical conscience' instead of the '"will" of a handful of privileged States' and the resolutions of international organisations and the practices of civil society that would review, revise and revive international law.[27] Undoubtedly, having a pluralistic and participatory democracy at all levels is certainly an important issue. But the question is who actually represents and/or will represent the wisdom and will of the governmental and non-governmental organisations. Hoping that such governance-friendly chairs would/could be occupied by the subalterns rather than, for example, Third World elites is not realistic.

Be that as it may, neither 'Third World' nor 'the West' is clearly defined and framed by TWAILers. TWAILers are, to say the least, imprecise in fine-tuning their terminological toolkit and conceptual framework. It is common to come across expressions that reproduce or regenerate binary oppositions such as East–West and Europeans–non-Europeans.[28] It is not clear whether 'Third World'

[22] Gathii (n 18) 30–31.

[23] In a more recent article, Chimni apparently prefers to use 'postmodern doctrine' instead of 'TWAIL', at least in a context that ponders on how to reconceptualise the doctrine of customary international law from a Third World perspective. See BS Chimni, 'Customary International Law: A Third World Perspective' (2018) 112 *American Journal of International Law* 1, 37 and 41. Still, Chimni notes that 'a full account of an alternative doctrine would have to await another essay' (at 38).

[24] BS Chimni, 'Third World Approaches to International Law: A Manifesto' (2006) 8 *International Community Law Review* 3, 21.

[25] SG Sreejith, 'An Auto-critique of TWAIL's Historical Fallacy: Sketching an Alternative Manifesto' (2017) 38 *Third World Quarterly* 1511, 1519.

[26] Chimni (n 23) 38.

[27] See ibid 38ff.

[28] It would certainly be quite unfair to criticise TWAIL for being essentialist in the conventional sense of the word. As is best seen in Rajagopal's analyses of different essentialist models of Third World

includes 'rising powers' like China and India, whose domestic orders are at least as hierarchical as any capitalist State and that (particularly China) have recently geared up their expansionist policies.[29] More importantly, albeit stated in a context where the effects of the colonial encounter are deciphered, talking about 'a collective conscience and a feeling of oneness in the minds of *the peoples of the Third World*, which prepares them for a collective resistance against all forms of marginalisation' (emphasis added)[30] is also problematic. The 'peoples of the Third World' consist of many components, each of which had/has its own reasons and roles in the colonisation process. In order to unveil the realities, the 'colonial encounter' should be deciphered in many ways, aspects, terms and means. In this context, notwithstanding all the asymmetries they enjoyed, especially in the Americas and Africa, Europeans could not and in fact did not colonise on or for their own. The active role of local collaborators and compradors who had already held hierarchical positions should also be duly taken into account. It is quite tricky whether such can, and should, be seen a part of 'Third World' on the spot. At least Third World people cannot be romanticised as egalitarian societies, assuming that unequal, pyramidal and hierarchical orders alien to them were brought in from abroad. The reshuffling effect of the colonial encounter is one thing; its categorical novelty of, say, bringing in hierarchy, subordination, slavery, exploitation, plunder and so on is another. This point is particularly important with regard to current and oncoming issues and positions. For the present purposes, it will suffice to conclude that Third World would certainly be a good idea.[31]

Looked at from this point of view and, in particular, noting that 'contributionist TWAILers'[32] have invited 'the peoples of the Third World' to study the ancient practices of *non-European/Western (other) civilisations*,[33] the irony is clear. First,

categorisation, ideological, geopolitical or historical deterministic models that put the narrative of the 'nation' at the centre in an essentialist manner are in fact rejected. Instead, a non-essentialist 'cultural' model that makes it possible to 'expos[e] the myriad ways in which power is exercised by the dominant groups to the detriment of the disempowered' is preferred as it opens up 'creative possibilities of decentring the category "Third World" from its geographical moorings'. See B Rajagopal, 'Locating the Third World in Cultural Geography' (1998) 15 *Third World Legal Studies* 1, 2–3. So, the otherness of 'Third World' is obviously conceived as a constructed political reality. But it is hard to make a similar comment regarding the term 'civilisation' often used by the TWAILers.

[29] In a more recent article, Chimni indicated in a footnote that 'for the purpose of this article, no distinction is made between emerging powers such as Brazil, China, and India and other third World states.' See Chimni (n 23) 38, fn 16.

[30] Sreejith (n 25) 1513.

[31] This is just a reminder to Gandhi's brilliant answer ('I think it would be a good idea') to a journalist who asked: 'What do you think of Western civilization?'

[32] Gathii argues that there are two major trends in TWAIL studies. Whereas the 'contributionists' emphasise Africa's (the Third World's) contributions to international law, the 'critical theorists' examine its 'subordination in its international relations as a legacy that is traceable to international law'. See JT Gathii, 'Africa and the History of International Law' (2012) Legal Studies Research Paper Series No 48 of 2011–12, 1.

[33] For an account of the 'contributionist generation' within the context of shifting attitudes in the literature, see I de la Rasilla del Moral, 'The Shifting Origins of International Law' (2015) 28 *Leiden Journal of International Law* 419.

this 'third Worldisation' implicitly turns the fiction generated against those labelled as 'third world' into reality. Talking about a historical-political and therefore *constructed* reality and its enduring effects is one thing, but taking it for granted is another. To borrow a term from Marxist political economy that apparently inspires TWAILers, no historical fact or concept can be seen as an a priori truth. Conceptual categories can certainly be traced back for genealogical purposes. But taking some concepts for granted and retroactively assuming that they meant what we conceive them now to mean would be contrary, at the very least, to what TWAIL supposedly stands for. In other words, there was no 'West/Europe' or 'Third World' whatsoever before 1492 and even until the nineteenth century, when 'the West/Europe' as such was eventually conceptualised and constructed. So, implying reconcilable Western and non-Western civilisations simply means to certify, in a rather self-Orientalist fashion,[34] the modernist Orientalist approach that fixes East and West as distinct and homogeneous epistemological worlds which, *by their very nature*, do indeed inevitably conflict. Even the history of international law is usually revisited within this context and to this end. Most studies focus on the 'civilisations' (such as the 'Asian', 'African' and 'European') that existed prior to the European colonial encounter.[35]

Second, be that as it may, setting one of the objectives of TWAIL as exploring 'how third world peoples and countries can overcome these challenges'[36] is even more problematic. This compels 'the peoples of the Third World' to put their full effort into demonstrating *their* abilities and capabilities.

At this very point, one cannot help but recall Fanon's diagnosis: why should 'black men want to prove to white men, at all costs, the richness of their thought, the equal value of their intellect'? Surely because 'the native is an oppressed person whose permanent dream is to become the persecutor.' But the point is that 'the man who adores the Negro is as "sick" as the man who abominates him'.[37] In short, TWAIL puzzlingly, if not mimetically, seeks to restore, renovate and legitimise modern international law.[38] It longs to make international law a success story.

However, rightfully deciphering that contemporary international law is shaped in line with the agenda of capitalism and imperialism is one thing, but championing the adjustment and calibration of this law with the needs of a post-capitalist

[34] An article exploring 'the validity of Muslim claims for a particularistic Islamic law of nations' concludes that 'irrespective of its geographic origin and alleged normative shortcomings, international law is primarily a modern phenomenon serving functional needs not attainable by pre-modern precursors'. See E Afsah, 'Contested Universalities of International Law: Islam's Struggle with Modernity' (2008) 10 *Journal of the History of International Law* 259.

[35] A glance at the titles in a tentative bibliography of TWAIL studies speaks for itself. See Gathii (n 21) 49ff.

[36] Gathii (n 18) 3.

[37] For quoted excerpts, see F Fanon, *Black Skin, White Masks*, CL Markmann (trans) (London, Pluto Press, 1986) 12, 53 and 10, respectively.

[38] See also Afsah (n 34), who problematises whether the ancient practices of the rest of the world do fit into the accomplishments of the modern West.

and postmodernist global order is another. The Westphalian system that both reflected and served the needs of the capitalist division of labour among nation-States is now simply being transformed into a global law that seeks to keep pace with the new phase of capitalism. This would-be legal order is open to the contributions/participation of all individuals from all civilisations, just like the flexible post-Fordist production system which requires a rather heterogeneously intermingled world and labour market. Assuming that having all peoples on board would automatically result in a much more comprehensive and fair legal order would not be realistic at all. The wrongs of a modernist *mission civilisatrice* cannot be compensated by a postmodernist *mission des civilisations*. A categorically new look, and, in fact, a paradigm shift are called for.

Taking this opportunity, as well as taking advantage of the proliferation of studies on the history of international law that mostly focus on a specific region or period,[39] I will suggest a new holistic approach to international law, namely an *amodernist* approach to international law (AMAIL). Having made the foregoing criticism of critical as well as mainstream scholarship, I will first lay out my basic arguments, then I will elaborate on a brief account of the history of international law from this perspective and finally I will focus on a specific period, namely the Amarna Age, to figure out how an ancient international law system developed its own Law of the Sea, the modern version of which has been outstandingly studied by Professor Robin Churchill.

II. An Amodernist Approach to International Law

A. Paradigmatic Illusions

To start with, the reason why I stay away from prefixes such as 'post-', 'pre-' or 'anti-' and prefer 'a-' indicates a modernism-free approach.[40] The intention behind this is very simple. I will not engage in an in-depth discussion of what concepts like the Enlightenment or the Scientific Revolution mean for social sciences in general. Rather, I will simply diverge from what I call the modernist paradigm shared (in the Kuhnian sense)[41] by international law scholars, including those studying the history of international law and those deciphering its colonial origins such as the TWAILers. Generally speaking, the distinguishing feature of the modernist paradigm adopted by all for their own good reasons is that it,

[39] In addition to those quoted throughout the study, see also DJ Bederman, *International Law in Antiquity* (Cambridge, Cambridge University Press, 2001); and A Altman, *Tracing the Earliest Recorded Concepts of International Law: The Ancient Near East (2500–330 BCE)* (Leiden, Martinus Nijhoff, 2012).

[40] For another call for amodern studies, see B Latour, 'Postmodern? No, Simply Amodern! Steps towards an Anthropology of Science' (1990) 21 *Studies in History and Philosophy of Science* 145.

[41] Kuhn defines 'paradigm' as 'what members of a scientific community, and they alone, share'. See TS Kuhn, *The Essential Tension* (Chicago, University of Chicago Press, 1977) 294.

albeit claiming ahistoricism, presupposes 'a break in the regular passage of time … [that] designates a combat in which there are victors and vanquished'.[42] This break, assuming that it occurred not in 1648, but in 1492, as the TWAILers also suggest, signals that things have changed categorically. This sense of uniqueness is embedded even in the studies of the TWAILers who see international law as a 'product of European imperialism'.[43] They assert that international law has 'been *developed* in the Western World and then *exported to* other places, above all Asia … in the nineteenth century to provide the ideological legitimacy to the agenda of colonisation' (emphasis added).[44] Accordingly, international law is 'premised on Europe as the centre, Christianity as the basis for civilization, capitalism as innate in humans, and imperialism as a necessity'.[45] Moreover, even 'an important strand of this TWAIL scholarship traces the origins of the state as a product of European colonialism and imperialism and examines the consequences of its adoption in the non-European world'.[46] In this context, it is argued that crucial modern concept(ion)s such as border, law, positivism, the balance of power and even Statehood/sovereignty that give international law its unprecedented unique character are also modern in nature.

Leaving aside the Orientalist tone that becomes even more obvious, particularly recalling the precedential examples provided by Ancient Greece,[47] these modernist illusions are groundless. It is undeniable, and in fact inevitably natural, that modernism has geographical, historical, cultural and terminological features that are peculiar to it. However, surplus value, exploitation and imperialism are not inventions of capitalism or of Europe/the West, and nor is the State. Moreover, if law is an apparatus that is, inter alia, meant to compensate and/or cast a veil over inequalities and injustices, its contemporary sophistication is more normal, as sociopolitical life becomes more unequal by the day.

As will be elaborated upon below, human beings have organised themselves into polities since time immemorial. They not only developed their respective mechanisms, authorities, rules, institutions and statecraft, but also engaged with 'others'. As is eloquently noted in a detailed and pioneering study on the Amarna records, although 'concepts such as the national interest or balance of power

[42] B Latour, *We Have Never Been Modern*, C Porter (trans) (Cambridge, MA, Harvard University Press, 1993) 10.

[43] Haskell (n 17) 391.

[44] A Orakhelashvili, 'The Relevance of Theory and History: The Essence and Origins of International Law' in A Orakhelashvili (ed), *Research Handbook on the Theory and History of International Law* (Cheltenham, Edward Elgar, 2011) 19.

[45] Mutua (n 13) 33. See also Gathii, who notes that what the newly decolonised States found in front of them was 'an international law that was Eurocentric in its geographic origin, Christian in its religious basis, imperial in its political objectives and mercantilist in its material underpinnings'. JT Gathii, 'International Law and Eurocentricity' (1998) 9 *European Journal of International Law* 184, 187–88.

[46] Gathii (n 18) 16.

[47] See nn 50–53 below and the accompanying text. For a similar criticism of a study which argues that 'we do not find such clear manifestation of the principle of balance of power as in the case of the Hellenic communities', see Butkevych (n 1) 216.

would not be articulated for centuries', it is clear that 'balances of power regularly formed, dissipated, and reformed during the Amarna era'.[48] Determining that such concepts do not naturally appear by name in ancient records does, and in fact should, not necessarily mean that such concepts did not exist.[49] Similarly, three key strands of international law – namely, the law of diplomacy, the law of war and the law of treaties – were well established. In short, the solipsistic attitude of modern(ist) international law scholarship is incorrect, inaccurate, ill-founded and, most of all, misleading in five senses.

First, time of international law, in the strict sense of the word, does not flow linearly. Second, structural conditions that led to and characterised the Westphalian legal order have occurred several times before and *thus* did so in similar international law systems. Third, such legal orders ceased to exist as a result of changes in these structural conditions and were replaced by another order, ie, imperial law(s) of whatever ilk. Fourth, the mainstream argument claiming that the modern(ist) international law is an unprecedented and unique discipline can only be accepted as far as its terminological toolkit is concerned. Nevertheless, the novelty of a discipline per se is quite different from the novelty of the field or area in which it is working. The characteristics or features that are claimed or presumed to 'formally' make the Westphalian incarnation of international law unique are not substantially or conceptually unique to it, although terminologically they are. It is just the latest, not *the* only or *the* last international law system. Last but not least, all these are in fact problems that pertain not only to international law in particular, but to all modern(ist) social sciences in general.

B. International Law as a Modern(ist) Social Science?

To start in reverse order, it is worth briefly recalling that the quest since time immemorial to gain a better grasp of human behaviour over time led to specialisation, which in turn fragmented 'humanities' into 'social sciences' in the nineteenth century. This departmentalisation was welcomed due to the diversification of means, capabilities and demands that required a much more detailed and unprecedented understanding of society. It also coincided with the paradigm shift compelled by the rise of capitalism and modernism. Having said that, the fragmentation resulting from specialisation led to the situation where disciplines, sub-disciplines and even areas of interest led to a siloing of thought and intellectual isolationism. This has been the case for the contemporary discipline of international law since the very beginning.

[48] SR David, 'Realism, Constructivism, and the Amarna Letters' in R Cohen and R Westbrook (eds), *Amarna Diplomacy: The Beginnings of International Relations* (Baltimore, Johns Hopkins University Press, 2000) 62.

[49] David's expression appears improperly formulated: 'The ancients may not have known the term "balance of power", but they acted as if they did.' See ibid.

This point becomes even more critical given the fact that the earliest treatises of international law written during the course of the nineteenth century did not refer to numerous ancient documents – including the Amarna letters, which will be discussed below – that had then recently been discovered. It may be that such developments were not widely known in intellectual circles, but intellectual isolationism certainly played a role. For example, Oppenheimer starts his chapter on the 'Development of the Law of Nations before Grotius' with a sub-chapter entitled 'No Law of Nations in antiquity' and states that 'International Law as a law between Sovereign and equal States based on the common consent of these States is a product of modern Christian civilisation, and may be said to be hardly four hundred years old'. Despite acknowledging that 'the roots of this law go very far back into history', he underlines that such 'rules and usages which were observed by the different nations of antiquity with regard to their external relations' still does not amount to an international law system as 'the conception of a Family of Nations did not arise in the mental horizon of the ancient world. Each nation had its own religion and gods, its own language, law, and morality'.[50] One could be charitable and consider that he and his contemporaries did not have a grasp of ancient practices. Yet he quite self-assuredly noted that 'it will be of interest to throw a glance at the respective rules and usages of the Jews, Greeks, and Romans'.[51] Cultural myopia and no doubt an Orientalist perspective play a central role in such an approach.[52] Likewise, as is clearly seen from, inter alia, studies on the 'epochs of international law', whereas the last five centuries were carefully examined and divided into decades, if not years, ancient or primitive samples actually correspond to millennia, if they are lucky enough to be mentioned, but are still only entitled to a couple of paragraphs or pages if that. The most striking example is Grewe's *The Epochs of International Law*. Although duly aware of at least some of the ancient systems thanks to Preiser's pioneering study written in German,[53] Grewe dedicates only three pages to 'Early International Legal Orders in Occidental Antiquity and in the Non-European World' in the introduction. The six main parts of the study include several chapters dedicated to the Roman, Spanish, French and British eras, and then the epochs of the League of Nations and the UN.

Interestingly enough, such approaches quite overconfidently assert that: 'International law as such could not have emerged in antiquity.'[54] There are even

[50] L Oppenheim, *International Law: A Treatise, Vol I: Peace*, 2nd edn (London, Longmans, Green & Co, 1912) 45–46. See also Butkevych (n 1) 210.

[51] Oppenheim (n 50) 46.

[52] E Said, *Orientalism* (New York, Pantheon, 1978).

[53] Having 'examined the origins of modern international law, the law of pre-classical Antiquity, the historical epochs of the law of nations in Antiquity, and early international legal orders in the non-European world', Preiser points at 'a structurally unchanged European law of nations spanning two and a half millennia' and yet notes that 'only from the late Middle Ages is it possible to find consistent traces of an international legal order which combines the international legal phenomena of all epochs into a reasonably functional system'. See WG Grewe, *The Epochs of International Law*, trans and revised by M Byers (Berlin, Walter de Gruyter, 2000) 8.

[54] Butkevych (n 1) 193.

historical studies that in a rather methodologically ill-founded and self-Orientalist fashion compare the imperial tributary system of ancient China to the Westphalian order[55] (not, say, with Christendom or the Holy Roman Empire as should be the case).

So, as Lindqvist notes: 'It is not knowledge we lack. What is missing is the courage to understand what we know and draw conclusions.'[56] This is particularly the case if the writings of some authors who are overlooked are taken into account. Korff, for example, wrote in 1924 that 'we know now that it is not our civilization that created these institutions, but that every civilization possessed whole systems of them; that they are first a necessary product of social life, and secondly, that they had everywhere many traits in common and do not belong exclusively, as was formerly supposed, to Europe. It is to be regretted that these first attempts have not yet been followed by a general treatise'.[57] Even TWAILers bring the starting point back from 1648 to 1492 and more often than not focus on issues, people or *civilisations* that prevailed at the time of the European colonial encounter. As far as is known, no TWAILer has ever scrutinised, inter alia, Mesopotamia, Amarna, ancient India or ancient China.

A key accomplishment of capitalist-imperialist modernism is thus not solely its ability to engineer a Eurocentric international law, but also its skill to portray Europe as *the* founder of *the* international law. This international law, as a modern achievement, simply ignored the findings of archaeologists, prehistorians, ethnologists and anthropologist (who of course were usually equally clouded in their views) on the practices of the 'barbarians'. Said noted that such disciplines and scholars were busily using different sets of tools, methodologies and paradigms.[58] Whereas international law was a product of 'civilised nations',[59] the practices of the 'other' were either considered unworthy or formed part of the scope of other disciplines.

However, as will be argued below, modern ('Westphalian') international law is just the *latest*, not the only or the last, international law system the world has known. International law continually evolves and there have been several eras where there have been competing notions of what it is. Wherever the relevant structural conditions have existed, international law has flourished. Yet whenever these conditions changed and the given system was absorbed within another polity, the 'pre-existing' international law was substituted by an imperial legal system that prevailed until the cycle repeated itself.

The structural conditions for the existence of an international law system are relatively few. First, polities that we today call 'sovereign and independent States'

[55] See Y Zewei, 'Western International Law and China's Confucianism in the 19th Century: Collision and Integration' (2011) 13 *Journal of the History of International Law* 285, 295.

[56] S Lindqvist, *Exterminate All the Brutes*, J Tate (trans) (New York, New Press, 1996) 2 and 172.

[57] SA Korff, 'Introduction to the History of International Law' (1924) 18 *American Journal of International Law* 246, 247.

[58] See generally Said (n 52).

[59] GW Gong, *The Standard of 'Civilization' in International Society* (Oxford, Clarendon Press, 1984).

should exist. Second, at least two such polities should coexist, mutually recognise and respect each other's existence. Third, the polities should engage in relations with one another. Fourth, the polities should comply with principles and rules that are based on shared and common values. Last but not least, the shared values should lay the foundations not only of the system and govern the inter-relations of the polities in question, but also of their joint stance against the common others beyond. It therefore goes without saying that, notwithstanding the claim of the modernists, the existence of an international law system is not a result and/or product of modernism. Several international law systems have existed so far and will also do so wherever or whenever the said structural conditions prevail.

Taking these foundational conditions into account and slightly adjusting the famous maxim 'where there is a society, there is law (*ubi societas, ibi ius*)', it will be suggested that 'where there are polities, there is international law (*ubi politie, ibi ius gentium*)'.[60] Hence, the history of inter-polity ('international') relations and the body of rules that govern such relations, namely international law, is as old as human history.[61]

III. A Brief Amodernist Account of the History of International Law

As has been convincingly highlighted by archaeological and ethnographic studies, hunter-gatherers developed their own rules and customs that ensured social cohesion and control. They did not have central authorities in the conventional sense of the term and some of them decisively and 'actively resisted' any sort of concentration of power.[62] Most hunter-gatherer polities were regulated by all on behalf of all. Within this framework, they obviously had a social control system that secured order and thus performed the function of 'law' as we would recognise it now.[63] Such societies had a wide range of dispute settlement mechanisms,

[60] This argument is developed and extensively studied in my forthcoming book (in Turkish) on the history of international law and order since the Palaeolithic.

[61] Despite taking civilisations as the main agents of history, Korff also notes that 'as soon as there developed a cultural center of a certain level of civilization, a state of some prominence, there grew up simultaneously relations with the outside world that soon took the shape of a whole system of institutions. In other words, such a system was the necessary consequence of any civilization and was as old as human culture in general'. Furthermore, 'different ancient civilizations reveal a remarkable similarity in their main lines of development. Take, for example, the history of ambassadorial missions, the question of extradition of fugitive criminals, the protection of certain classes of foreigners, and, above all, the sanctity of international contracts. In the growth of all these institutions identical principles prevail everywhere, in Sumer or Thebes, in Nineveh or Athens, and down to Rome'. See Korff (n 57) 246–47.

[62] See M Finnegan, 'The Politics of Eros: Ritual Dialogue and Egalitarianism in Three Central African Hunter-Gatherer Societies' (2013) 19 *Journal of the Royal Anthropological Institute* 697, 699.

[63] See B Malinowski, *Crime and Custom in Savage Society* (London, Kegan Paul Trench, Trubner & Co Ltd, 1926). For a study which argues that accepting the method of Malinowski 'would be to disregard entirely the formal structure of law in modern society in favour of the study of the social processes

which aimed to prevent and reduce conflict.[64] Furthermore, wherever and whenever autonomous socio-political units situated beside or close to each other within a single geographical region[65] existed, 'peer polity interaction' in terms of a 'full range of interchanges took place'.[66] Such interactions had repercussions at the 'local, regional, national and supranational' levels and in turn led to 'supra-regional networks' of 'information, political competition, and exchange'[67] that even crystallised into features such as Göbeklitepe and Stonehenge. As Numelin notes, 'as long as human conditions have existed side by side without living in a permanent state of enmity – and sometimes even then – there have evolved certain rudimentary forms of diplomatic usage. It has been necessary for the leaders or primitive societies (kings, chiefs, councils of elders) to maintain some sort of mutual relations, first through occasional messengers, later through envoys and other suchlike representatives'.[68] This in turn means that polities that existed side by side developed rules that governed their external relations.

As there were a number of disconnected political interactions in distinct parts of the world, it would not be wrong to assume that there were different (inchoate) international law systems existing simultaneously at any given time. These systems separately developed apparently shared certain basic features. As demonstrated by Numelin, they duly hosted, exchanged gifts and negotiated with the envoys of their counterparts. They developed rules and procedures such as the waving of white objects (for example, cotton) to signal peaceful envoys or, conversely, pointing a spear upwards or downwards to signal intent in terms of hostilities, whereas customs securing the regular exchange of goods confirm the existence and effectiveness of a principle that is today referred to as *pacta sunt servanda*.[69]

Sumerian city-States that took shape around five millennia ago are the forerunners of a series of States that were later established in the wider region from (today's) Anatolia to Egypt and Persia for approximately 1,000 years. These territorial polities consisting of a wider network of villages that were clustered around a capital were ruled by kings who had titles such as chief commander, chief priest,

from which they derive … Forms have a function, too. In neglecting them the functionalist betrays his own cause', see W Seagle, 'Primitive Law and Professor Malinowski' (1937) 39 *American Anthropologist* 275, 290.

[64] See generally S Roberts, *Order and Dispute: An Introduction to Legal Anthropology*, 2nd edn (New Orleans, Quid Pro Books, 2013).

[65] C Renfrew, 'Introduction: Peer Polity Interaction and Socio-political Change' in C Renfrew and JF Cherry (eds), *Peer Polity Interaction and Socio-Political Change* (Cambridge, Cambridge University Press, 1986) 1.

[66] ibid.

[67] T Watkins, 'Supra-regional Networks in the Neolithic of Southwest Asia' (2008) 21 *Journal of World Prehistory* 139, 163, 171 and 145, respectively.

[68] R Numelin, *The Beginnings of Diplomacy* (New York, Philosophical Library, 1950) 13. Troublesome remarks such as 'rudimentary' and 'primitive societies' are ignored. See also Renfrew and Cherry (n 65); EM Schortman, 'Interregional Interaction in Prehistory: The Need for a New Perspective' (1989) 54 *American Antiquity* 52.

[69] For relevant examples, see Numelin (n 68) 146, 181, 217, 254–55, 263 and 268.

chief tax-collector and chief justice. Such actors had apparently risen above and among many in the struggle to consolidate and centralise power and eventually had secured political, economic, military, ideological and religious domination in their respective terrains. Dyakov,[70] who examined the estate records of the period, noted that even the largest temple in Lagash – unlike the widespread misconception in the literature – owned relatively little real estate and the Sumerian kings had clearly secured their 'secular power' over their this closest rivals.[71] Coupled with practices such as annihilating the 'unmerciful debts' owed to the corrupt temple, the kings obviously had a legitimate ideological monopoly of their own.[72]

The manner in which a monopoly over the base metals needed for weaponry was secured is also illustrative of the accumulation of power. Bronze is an alloy of copper and tin or arsenic. Since these (and the latter in particular) were rare raw materials in Mesopotamia, they could only be sourced from remote areas.[73] So, only actors who had appropriated copper deposits and also sponsored and guarded the trade routes could commission, patronise and even monopolise bronze goods. Possession and control over bronze was directly related to power. The greater the quantity of bronze, the greater the military power and the greater the wealth. The value of bronze weaponry was such that legal codes ordered that those who stole a bronze spear from the palace should be sentenced to death.[74]

Although some scholars have argued that the kings were simply 'big men' acting in their personal capacity and interest,[75] such 'big men' were symbolically and effectively representing and protecting the unity and integrity of the socio-economic and political order ensconced behind well-fortified walls. The kings were shepherds of their respective flocks,[76] making their kingdoms the forerunners of the modern regulatory State.

It is well documented that the kings stood for the good of and in the name of wider society.[77] They were the face of a ruling historical bloc in the Gramscian sense. The Epic of Gilgamesh, one of the oldest surviving works of literature,

[70] IM Diakonoff, *Society and State in Ancient Mesopotamia – Sumer – Summary* (St Petersburg, Institute of Oriental Manuscripts, RAS, 1959).

[71] SN Kramer, *History Begins at Sumer* (Philadelphia, University of Pennsylvania Press, 1956) 45.

[72] Urukagina, King of Lagash, declares in his famous codes that 'the orphan did not fall a prey to the wealthy' and 'the widow did not fall a prey to the powerful'. See SN Kramer, *The Sumerians* (Chicago, University of Chicago Press, 1963) 84.

[73] F Briquel-Chatonnet, C Michel and P Bordreuil, *Tarihin Başlangıçları – Eski Yakındoğu Kültür ve Uygarlıkları*, L Başaran (trans) (Delhi, Alfa, 2015) 56.

[74] Article 126 of the Hittite Laws. See MT Roth, *Law Collections from Mesopotamia and Asia Minor* (Atlanta, Scholars Press, 1995) 231.

[75] For relevant scholarly debates, see J Zollmann, 'African International Legal Histories: International Law in Africa: Perspectives and Possibilities' (2018) 31 *Leiden Journal of International Law* 897, 907.

[76] This concept (today mostly associated with Christian theology) was more often than not used by almost all Mesopotamian kings from Gilgamesh to Hammurabi, particularly in the preambles of their legal codes. See, eg, Kramer (n 71) 328.

[77] See generally ibid 33ff. For a study from a legal perspective, see C Wilcke, *Early Ancient Near Eastern Law – A History of its Beginnings: The Early Dynastic and Sargonic Periods* (Ann Arbor, Eisenbrauns, 2003).

depicts the socio-political life of the period and clearly reveals that even the most powerful kings consulted the (houses of) elders and young men.[78]

As noted earlier, the basic condition and indicator of the availability of an international legal system is having two or more mutually recognising polities that enter into relations with one another in accordance with the principles and rules that are based on shared and common values and that govern not only 'internal' relations of these mutually recognised counterparts, but also their 'external' dealings with others. The Mesopotamian pantheon seem to satisfy these conditions. Sumerian kings, representing the will of the supreme gods, maintained law and order not only in their relations with each other but also collectively against 'mountainous outsiders'. Nomadic peoples were considered a common threat to urbanised peoples – for example, the nomadic Gutian people were seen as 'an unbridled people, with human intelligence but canine instincts and monkeys' features'.[79] Enslaving nomadic people was commonplace, so much so that the term used for mountainous groups had the same etymological root as the word 'slave'.[80] Most strikingly, the name of the Amorite/Amurru nomads who raided Sumerian cities from the western flank of Mesopotamia also meant both 'west(erner)' and 'slave'.[81] So, the Sumerians, who called themselves the 'black heads',[82] clearly had a sense of common identity built on common values that others did not share.

All of the above means that the polities in question were, at least on paper, 'peace-loving' in the sense that the UN Charter requires. Equally, the UN Charter does not expressly refer to a balance of power, but this is inherent in the rules relating to the working of the UN Security Council and was the fundamental basis for the avoidance of armageddon during the height of the Cold War. The balance of power was equally known in the Sumerian system and is not peculiar to the current incarnation of international law.

In the Sumerian system, the parties were sensitive about the exact extent and scope of their domains relating to, for example, determining the taxable population and the limits of the public order to be safeguarded. They each marked their respective borders with specific boundary stones called *kudurru* that, with legal codes inscribed on them, also signalled the beginning of the respective jurisdictions of the parties. Furthermore, there are various samples of clay documents and agreements which demonstrate that the city-States and their successor States had in fact developed elementary juridical cooperation in criminal matters in order to address matters that might endanger their common orders and effectively adopted

[78] Kramer (n 71) 74 and 77.

[79] MR Bachvarova, 'The Destroyed City in Ancient "World History": From Agade to Troy' in MR Bachvarova, D Dutsch and A Suter (eds), *The Fall of Cities in the Mediterranean* (Cambridge, Cambridge University Press, 2016) 44.

[80] Kramer (n 71) 303.

[81] J Oates, *Babylon* (London, Thames & Hudson, 2015) 55–56; *cf* Kramer (n 71) 287.

[82] Kramer (n 71) 285. These examples also demonstrate how historically constructed and variable our political concepts are.

a system that required either the handing over or trying of fugitives (*aut dedere aut judicare* as we call it today).[83]

In summary the Sumer city-States are clearly prototypes of territorial States, the latest iteration of which is the modern nation-State. Various treaties starting from the Treaty of Mesilim (circa 2500 BCE) and other documents illustrate there were duly observed customs and compliance with rules that governed relations vis-a-vis other Sumerian city-States or others. This equilibrium could not be changed meaningfully until a recruited nomadic warrior called Sargon who combined and harmonised the social-economic-military dynamics of Sumerian urban and Semitic rural areas.[84] He conquered the whole wider Mesopotamia region in between high mountains, deserts and seas, and thus established the first known empire – the Akkadian Empire – in circa 2350 BCE. As 'kings of the four corners' and 'king of the kings', Sargon and his successors did not enter into relations with anyone on earth on an equal footing, which means that the international law system of the Sumerian city-States was replaced by a monist and universalist imperial law system. The Akkadian Empire indeed sowed the seeds of the imperial administration system based on decentralisation, integrating the transportation and communication systems of wider Mesopotamia, standardising the units of measurement and even replacing the Sumerian language with their Semitic Akkadian – what became the *lingua franca* of a region covering today's Anatolia, Egypt, Mesopotamia and Iran for almost a millennium.[85] Although the gods and goddesses of the places conquered were incorporated into a pantheon headed by the chief god, a novel and all-encompassing universal ideology was not forthcoming.[86] Therefore, it could not institutionalise its system and thus

[83] For relevant examples, see VM Sánchez, 'Political Refugees, Captives, Slaves and Other Migrants in International Law of Ancient Near East (2nd Millennium BC)' (2015) 13ff, available at https://www.semanticscholar.org/author/V.-M.-Sánchez/145587301.

[84] For Sargon's 'autobiographies' and his rise to power, see JG Westenholz, *Legends of the Kings of Akkade: The Texts* (Ann Arbor, Eisenbrauns, 1997) 33ff.

[85] R Cohen and R Westbrook (eds), *Amarna Diplomacy: The Beginnings of International Relations* (Baltimore, Johns Hopkins University Press, 2000) 9–10.

[86] The first genuine empire in this sense was arguably established by the Achaemenids in Persia in around 550 BCE. See generally MA Deadname, *A Political History of the Achaemenid Empire*, WJ Vogelsang (trans) (Leiden, Brill, 1989); J Wiesehöfer, 'The Achaemenid Empire' in I Morris and W Scheidel (eds), *The Dynamics of Ancient Empires: State Power from Assyria to Byzantium* (Oxford, Oxford University Press, 2009) 66. They not only conquered vast areas but also, thanks to their first ever monotheist State religion, Zoroastrianism, demonstrated that a true empire/emperor should also have an all-encompassing ideology. This universalistic model adopted mutatis mutandis by subsequent empires such as the Romans and Ottomans best manifests itself in the Cyrus Cylinder, which is labelled as 'the first declaration of Human Rights' by contemporary Iran. See A Kuhrt, 'Cyrus the Great of Persia: Images and Realities' in M Heinz and MH Feldman (eds), *Representations of Political Power: Case Histories from Times of Change and Dissolving Order in the Ancient Near East* (Ann Arbor, Eisenbrauns, 2007) 173, fn 20. Written in the Akkadian cuneiform script apparently for Mesopotamian subjects, the Achaemenid rulers were trying to assure once-strangers that all those belonging to heterogeneous backgrounds would live (and trade) in peace as long as they remain loyal, just like the *ius gentium* of Roman law and the rules applied to *dhimmis* (The People of Book) by the Ottomans.

collapsed soon after it ceased to conquer and grow in size. Its dissolution gave way to various polities that kept effective hold of certain territories. The so-called Third Dynasty of Ur (circa 2112–2004 BCE)[87] had sought to revive the system of city-States, whereas other powers claimed that they inherited the imperial legacy of the Akkadians. The balance of power reached between such actors created a system between the so-called Great Powers of the Amarna Age in the thirteenth century BCE. The marine rules of this age will be examined in more detail below. For the present purposes, it is only necessary to note that the aforementioned powers treated each other broadly as more or less equal, whereas their vassals were treated as 'equal subjects'. Nomadic groups and, in particular, land and sea bandits were common 'others'. This distinction confirms the thesis of the present study, which suggests that mutually recognising polities throughout history have developed their own international law.

In short, an international law has flourished wherever and whenever two or more polities have mutually recognised each other and entered into relations on an equal footing. So, despite the claims of the modernists, several international law systems have existed and two or more systems have existed simultaneously in different corners of the world.[88] As and when conditions changed and the given system was absorbed into another polity, the 'pre-existing' international law was substituted by an imperial legal system that prevailed until the cycle repeated itself, usually on an ever-enlarging scale, in the same way that Westphalian European public law transformed into the system now known as international law.

The above discussion on the pre- and post-factual and conceptual effects of the Sumerian city-States clearly highlights the rich history of international law outside of the Westphalian system. Regrettably, it is a history that has been largely ignored in the literature. Having revisited the history of international law from an amodernist perspective, this chapter will now endeavour to highlight the practices, rules and customs of a specific international law system developed and observed in what we would now call the Law of the Sea.

[87] Kramer (n 71) 68ff.

[88] Coexisting international law systems in Ancient Greece and China are good examples in this respect. Both the Greek city-States (c 650–323 BCE) and the kingdoms of the so-called Warring States Period (c 475–221 BCE) shared a sense of identity symbolised/provided respectively by the mythological Mount Olympus and the *Tian* ('Heaven') reigning over all those beneath. Both 'family of nations' developed various practices, principles and rules that govern their mutual relations and even convened special truce, peace, non-aggression and disarmament meetings, and made agreements duly sealed in special ceremonies. Furthermore, both were ended by powers that had imperial ambitions, ie, Alexander the Great and Shi Huang-di, respectively. Whilst the former failed to establish his empire (which would be achieved by the Romans), the latter, as the Son of Heaven (*Tian-zhu*) who had been given the Mandate of Heaven (*Tian-ming*), founded the first Chinese empire (*Zhōngguó* – 'central/middle state') in 221 BCE that would endure until 1911 CE. For a relatively early modern account, see WAP Martin, *Traces of International Law in Ancient China* (New York, Industrial Review Publishing Company, 1883). See also RL Walker, *The Multi-State System of Ancient China* (Hamden, Shoe String Press, 1953). For the Ancient Greek system, see C Phillipson, *The International Law and Custom of Ancient Greece and Rome* (London, Macmillan, 1911).

IV. The First Law of the Sea: The Amarna Letters

In their seminal study on the Law of the Sea, Robin Churchill and Vaughan Lowe note that:

> The development of the law of the sea is inseparable from the development of international law in general. While there have over the centuries been many documented systems of relations between independent polities, in Africa and Asia and Europe, the 'international law' as it exists today is the body of law initially generated by the relations between the European States during the period known as 'modern' (i.e., post-medieval) history. Cultural imperialism that may be; but it is an inescapable fact.[89]

Before proceeding further and examining the relevant passages from the 'Amarna letters', a brief note is necessary on the period which produced them.

A. The Amarna Letters

Briefly, the Amarna Age is a post-empire period that apparently reached its zenith in the second half of the second millennium before the Common Era. Assyria, Babylon, Egypt, the Hittites and Mitanni, known as the Great Powers, all flourished in the Levant, Mesopotamia and Anatolia, and a balance of power existed between them.

Interaction between these 'Great Powers' naturally led to, inter alia, conflict, negotiations, peace agreements and trade in the wider region. The Amarna cuneiform tablets 'shed light on the affairs of the late Eighteenth Dynasty in the fourteenth century BCE'[90] and comprise the 'diplomatic archive' of Ancient Egypt. The tablets seem to have been deposited in the then capital el-Amarna and were unearthed in the late nineteenth and early twentieth centuries. The tablets essentially consist of around 382 letters. Among these are diplomatic correspondence between the 'Great Kings'. It is this correspondence that will be considered in the remainder of this chapter.

From this correspondence, it is clear there is enough material to explore the three basic pillars of (modern) international law, namely the law of treaties, the law of war and the law of diplomacy more broadly. It is striking that the correspondence illustrates that the Great Kings entered into relations with each other on an equal footing, as they always referred to each other as 'brother'. Equally, there are also letters to and from more subordinate local rulers, but these do not usually

[89] RR Churchill and AV Lowe, *The Law of the Sea*, 3rd edn (Manchester, Manchester University Press, 1999) 3–4.

[90] WM Schniedewind (ed), *The El-Amarna Correspondence: A New Edition of the Cuneiform Letters from the Site of El-Amarna Based on Collations of all Extant Tablets*, vol 1 (Leiden, Brill, 2015) xi. An earlier compilation is WL Moran (ed and trans), *The Amarna Letters* (Baltimore, Johns Hopkins University Press, 1992).

communicate directly with the Egyptian king (pharaoh), but with his officials. Despite apparently being the Egyptian versions of the correspondence, the letters are mostly written in Akkadian, which was the *lingua franca* for over a millennia of an extensive area covering (today's) Anatolia, Mesopotamia, Persia and Egypt. In other words, Amarna States had a common and standardised medium of interaction, which is a *sine qua non* for any international law system.[91]

The remaining analysis will explore only one of the fundamental substantive fields of international law, namely 'the law of the sea' as revealed in the Amarna letters. The choice of topic requires little justification in this volume. Furthermore, it is an area of substantive law which, with regard to this era, has been underexplored in the legal literature. Finally, it highlights the method, social and political necessity and nature of the development of international rules in a historical context.

B. Letters That Relate to Marine Customs and Rules

It is clear that there was intense and complex interaction between the kings, each of whom sought to expand the economic and political influence of their State.[92] Although most of these States were essentially terrestrial polities and communities, the 'zones of transference' among them also included trade routes via the sea, namely the Mediterranean and the Aegean.[93] Moreover, as will be discussed below, some of the nomadic and semi-nomadic groups that not only interacted but also traded with various States and thus provided 'bridges' between settled polities were quite literally 'floating' ones. In short, a remarkable portion of interaction was via the seas, which prompted the kingdoms to develop the principles and rules that were relevant to this context.

[91] 'The existence of a neutral language, Akkadian – like English today – helped to integrate the system.' Furthermore, as 'most correspondents are non-native speakers', this system also produced 'a cosmopolitan elite conversant with the same classical canon … who was also responsible … for managing relations and resolving conflicts between members of the system'. See R Cohen and R Westbrook, 'Conclusion: The Beginnings of International Relations' in R Cohen and R Westbrook (eds), *Amarna Diplomacy: The Beginnings of International Relations* (Baltimore, Johns Hopkins University Press, 2000) 235–36.

[92] See J Emanuel, 'Differentiating Naval Warfare and Piracy in the Late Bronze–Early Iron Age Mediterranean: Possibility or Pipe Dream?' in Ł Niesiołowski-Spanò and M Węcowski (eds), *Change, Continuity, and Connectivity: North-Eastern Mediterranean at the Turn of the Bronze Age and in the Early Iron Age* (Wiesbaden, Harrassowitz Verlag, 2018) 269–71.

[93] Without doubt, the Uluburun is the most famous shipwreck which constitutes a 'fundamental indicator of a sea route' of the Amarna Age and gives clear and ample evidence of late Bronze Age trade patterns. The Uluburun ship that sank 'in the Amarna period or soon thereafter' had 'a Levantine origin and an Aegean destination'. But as the Amarna letters do not include even 'a single epistle … exchanged between the Egyptian king and any Aegean ruler', the contacts were mostly of an economic nature rather than diplomatic ones. See F Zangani, 'Amarna and Uluburun: Reconsidering Patterns of Exchange in the Late Bronze Age' (2016) 148 *Palestine Exploration Quarterly* 230, 232, 234, 241 and 242.

i. Ships

There is no doubt that 'along with fishing, navigation is the oldest use of the sea … and ships are … the most important means of transporting goods'.[94] Contemporary international law does not provide a legal definition of the term 'ship'. It is generally accepted that 'a ship can be described as a vessel used or capable of being used as a means of transportation on water … whether self-propelled or not'.[95] Although it is impossible to determine and confirm the exact time and place of the invention of simple rafts and boats, all such vessels that have clearly been used since time immemorial may be defined as and considered to be 'ships'. It is clearly visible in the Amarna letters that ships formed 'an extremely cohesive class of craft'[96] and were used extensively. Further, there was not only a 'public (war)ship-private ship' distinction but also a rudimentary concept of what we would now consider to be a 'flag State'.

There are, for example, letters which read as follows: 'my brother, these men [and] this ship *belong to the king [my lord]*. So you, the ship [of the king, my lord] quickly (and) [safe]ly send [me] (back)' (emphasis added).[97] Likewise, letters that signify trade and aid relations between kings also include passages such as 'my merchant(s) (and) *my ship*' (emphasis added)[98] and 'for my brother [I have prepared] a great shipment and Keliya [I will] send … a great shipment will I send to my bro[ther]'.[99]

These excerpts clearly demonstrate that kings owned 'public vessels'. Indeed, it is well documented that ships were visibly separable due to their decoration and the symbols (presumably including emblems and flags) that appeared on them, as well as due to their construction techniques. Such distinguishing marks, which were also meant to show off the 'frightening and irresistible might'[100] of the kings, were also necessary and functional in light of the prevalence of piracy in the region. The ships had a 'dual charge of defending the coastal waters against pirates and invaders and escorting shipments of particular value or import to foreign ports'.[101]

It should be noted that one letter refers to the term 'navy': 'May the king speak to the three cities and to the *ships of the navy*' (emphasis added).[102] Although the term 'navy' is translated as 'ships of the army' in Moran's earlier translation,[103]

[94] Churchill and Lowe (n 89) 255.

[95] R Lagoni, 'Merchant Ships' in *Max Planck Encyclopedia of Public International Law*, vol 11 (Amsterdam, North-Holland, 1989) 228.

[96] For a detailed analysis of the then-used ships, see S Wachsmann, 'The Ships of the Sea Peoples' (1981) 10 *International Journal of Nautical Archaeology and Underwater Exploration* 187, 191ff.

[97] EA 40, lines 16–20. A total of 382 Amarna letters are classified and cited with the abbreviation EA, which is short for 'El Amarna'.

[98] EA 39, lines 17–20.

[99] EA 29, lines 166–72.

[100] Wachsmann (n 96) 191. For the transference and rapid spread of maritime technology across the Mediterranean and the Aegean Seas, see Emanuel (n 92) 242.

[101] Emanuel (n 92) 245.

[102] EA 101, lines 1–10.

[103] See Moran (n 90) 174.

the term ‘regular armies’ is often used in the Amarna letters. Based on this, it can be stated that some public vessels were either continuously or temporally used in naval warfare. The construction techniques and operation styles of the ships suggest that much of the naval warfare would have occurred in coastal areas, such as the entrance to the Nile Delta, rather than the open sea.[104] This is simply because naval wars were primarily man to man and ships were not heavily armed, except for rams, during the Amarna Age.[105]

Thus, ‘State’ and king-owned vessels were not only in use but also enjoyed a special status during times of war and peace.

ii. Maritime Zones

It would be stretching credibility to suggest that the modern notion of maritime zones were known in the Amarna Age. However, if we consider the matter from a different conceptual vantage point, things may appear differently. In a complaint letter written to the King of Egypt, a local ruler noted that another ruler ‘has seized my ship and behold now he is likewise going out in the *high sea* to seize my ships’ (emphasis added).[106] In Moran’s earlier compilation, this is translated as ‘going to sea’, not ‘going out in the high sea’. Yet the context, object and purpose of the letter suggests that the ordinary meaning of this term can legitimately be interpreted as parts of the sea which are not adjacent to the coast. A contextual interpretation taking into account the general spirit of Amarna letters also suggests this. The land territories of the kingships were conceived together with the adjacent coastal belts and possibly ‘inland waters’ as distinct from the ‘high’ seas.[107] For example, in a letter relating to ‘Egyptian ships … anchored at Beirut’,[108] there is a notion of ‘coastal waters’. Further, there is recognition of the ‘ports’ of others and, by implication, the rights of others over those waters. Alongside this, there are several letters that point to customs procedures and confirm that customs inspections for ships were well established. For example, in his letter to the King of Egypt, the Alashian King asks ‘his brother’ whether ‘as for my merchant(s) (and) my ship, may your customs’ inspector not draw near to them’.[109] In what seems to be related correspondence between the official commissioners of the parties, the Alashian letter also emphasises that ‘these men are the servants of the king, [my] lo[rd]. So may your customs inspector not draw near to them. And you, my brother, safely (and) quickly send (them back to me)’.[110]

[104] Wachsmann (n 96) 188.
[105] ibid 216.
[106] EA 114, lines 15–20.
[107] See also Emanuel’s quoted piece in Emanuel (n 92) 245, which talks about coastal waters and foreign ports.
[108] See Commentary to EA 143 in Schniedewind (n 90) 1495. The relevant part of the letter (lines 18–31) is as follows: ‘now with the arrival of the ships of the king, my lord, which are anchored at Beirut, the handmaiden of the king’.
[109] EA 39, lines 17–20.
[110] EA 40, lines 24–28.

In another exchange, a local ruler urges the King of Egypt that 'hostile … *ships of the navy do not enter the land of Amurru*' and asks 'whose ships have been hostile to me … seize the *ships* of the men of the city of Arwad *which are in the land of Egypt* … whose cities are these? Not the king's? Place one man in each city and *let him not permit the ships of the land of Amurru (to go forth)* … May the king speak to the three cities and to the ships of the navy, and no sooner will they go to *the land of Amurru*' (emphasis added).[111]

This excerpt brings to mind debates and practice relating to the breadth of the territorial sea. It is clear that the underlying rationale is assuaging the security concerns of coastal States by providing them with a safe zone of sorts within the vicinity of their immediate coast which is essentially considered to be an integral part of their (land) territories.

This allows us to conclude that, conceptually speaking, there were notions of maritime zones and that the sea was divided into two basic regions: 'no man's sea' and those parts of it adjacent to the coast that were part of the domain of the kings.

iii. Piracy and Privateering

Professors Churchill and Lowe have emphasised that 'to act against piracy' is a 'long established right – and, indeed, the duty … of every State'.[112] As they further note, the 1982 United Nations Convention on the Law of the Sea and the 1958 Convention on the High Seas that purport to codify the customary law state that 'piracy includes any illegal act of violence, detention or depredation committed for private ends by the crew or passengers of a private ship … against another ship … or person or property on board it, on (or over) the high seas'. As incidents that take place in the territorial sea 'are not, as a matter of international law, piracy',[113] it is clear that piracy includes incidents that occur 'outside the jurisdiction of any State'.[114] Privateering, on the other hand, might be defined as almost identical acts committed not (solely) for private ends, but on behalf of a commissioning State. Privateering has now been abandoned and piracy has been considered since at least the Middle Ages by Western powers at least to be *hostis humani generis*. Furthermore, as the modern literature (largely based on the accounts of Herodotus and Roman law) highlights, the pre-medieval versions of privateering and piracy are well known. It is clear that banditry, piracy and privateering were pressing issues during the Amarna Age. As Artzy notes:

> [T]he symbiotic relationship of the greater powers with military or economic mercenaries or with smaller, militarily weaker groups bound by treaties and alliances could

[111] EA 101, lines 18–33.

[112] Churchill and Lowe (n 89) 209.

[113] ibid 209–10. See the Convention on the High Seas (adopted 29 April 1958, entered into force 30 September 1962) 450 UNTS 11, art 15(1)(a); United Nations Convention on the Law of the Sea (adopted 10 December 1982, entered into force 16 November 1994) 1833 UNTS 3, art 101(a)(i).

[114] 1958 Convention on the High Seas, art 15(1)(b); 1982 Convention on the Law of the Sea, art 101(a)(ii).

> easily be broken. A dependency of the economic powers on others was a sure way for destabilization and disaster. The international economic system of the Late Bronze Age demanded security for the merchants and their merchandise for a profitable trade.[115]

Conditions existed which have been described as 'shiploads of freebooting' people 'trawling the Mediterranean in search of either plunder or military service in the hire of a foreign king'.[116] Consequentially, 'in many places … there were regular fortified harbours and signal stations for the use of the pirates, and the fleets which put in at these places were admirably equipped for their own work with fine crews, expert pilots, and light, fast ships'.[117] Such groups, which are referred to as 'Sea Peoples' by Wachsmann[118] and 'nomads of the sea' by Artzy, were then, just as is the case now, 'similar in behaviour as in their escape from socially established norms in their dress'.[119] The most notorious were the 'apiru', who have been subject to academic debate regarding, for example, their name and origin.[120]

Such groups can best be considered to be pirates or privateers, as it is hard to accurately discern the changing political situation and alliances. This is in part because of the unstable, unpredictable and ever-changing attitude adopted by their leaders. As has been noted:

> '[N]omads of the sea' were fringe groups employed as economic mercenaries within established, yet varied political and economic systems of the Bronze Age. They became an essential part of a trade network, a position obtained because of their peculiar expertise: knowledge in navigation and prerequisites for successful maritime trade plus capital in the form of a boat. They served as intermediaries and brought their traditions to coastal settlements and along land routes of the economic hinterland. Thus, those who started as hirelings carried out, in time, their own 'sailors' trade' and the natural evolution was no longer favorable, the 'Nomads of the Sea' (who, in the process, became merchants of the sea), reverted to marauding practices: they joined forces with pirates, and the image of 'Sea Peoples' familiar to us from the Egyptian sources emerged.[121]

It can therefore be concluded that both piracy and privateering were a social, political and legal fact in the Amarna Age. There are numerous examples of these recorded in the Amarna letters. For example, in his letter to an Egyptian official,

[115] M Artzy, 'Nomads of the Sea' in S Swiny, RL Hohlfelder and HW Swiny (eds), *Proceedings of the Second International Symposium 'Cities on the Sea', Nicosia, Cyprus, October 18–22, 1994* (Atlanta, Scholars Press, 1997) 2.

[116] Emanuel (n 92) 275.

[117] Artzy (n 115) 6.

[118] Wachsmann (n 96); S Wachsmann, 'The Ships of the Sea Peoples (IJNA, 10.3: 187–220): Additional Notes' (1982) 11 *International Journal of Nautical Archaeology and Underwater Exploration* 297. This might be an adjusted version of the famous 'who live on the ships' description of the Hittite king (at 297). The author points at the Sekel/Sikila people and compares their 'seasonal raidings' and 'commonda tactics' with those of the Vikings.

[119] Artzy (n 115) 6.

[120] See, eg, R Borger, 'Das Problem der 'apīru ("Ḫabiru")' (1953) 74 *Zeitschrift des Deutschen Palästina-Vereins* 2, 121. I am grateful to my PhD student Bihter Çarhoğlu for translating this article from German into Turkish.

[121] Artzy (n 115) 1.

a local ruler complained about the capital's silence concerning attacks by foreigners and asked the official to convince the king to 'send you at the head of regular troops that you may drive off the "*apiru* men"'. He is threatening enough to urge that: 'If this year the regul[ar tro]ops do not come forth, then all the territories will join the [*apîru* men].'[122] The tensions and problems which piracy and privateering led to can clearly be seen in another letter written by a local ruler to the King of Egypt. The King is informed that another local ruler released a defeated ruler and 'took his ransom money from his hand', despite his earlier commitment that 'in a ship I will send him to the King'.[123]

In sum, while it can be seen that piracy and privateering were a recurring problem in the Amarna Age, rules existed which demonstrate the prohibited nature of such activity.

iv. Blockade

The final example to be considered from the Amarna letters in this context is that of blockade. Most commentators discussing the Law of the Sea do not define 'blockade', presumably because it is part of the rules governing the use of force. However, such a disciplinary distinction is irrelevant in this context and the Amarna letters refer to the issue on a number of occasions. Contemporary international law defines blockade as 'an operation used in war aimed at preventing ingress and egress of all vessels, regardless of nationality or type of cargo, to and from part or all of the coast of an enemy State by the use of – warships and other means'. Blockade basically aims at interrupting 'all seaborne transportation links to and from the blockaded coast or port, particularly the passage of neutral vessels'. There should be a state of war between the blockading and the blockaded, the blockade must have been duly declared and notified, and the blockade must be effective.[124] Perhaps somewhat surprisingly, the Amarna letters provide evidence to suggest that these criteria were recognised in some form even during the era in question.

In a letter to the King of Egypt, a local ruler wrote that he cannot send the requested goods (boxwood) simply because 'I am unable to send my ships there because Aziru *is at war with me* and all the city rulers are *at peace with him*. Their ships *go about as they please* and they *bring whatever they need*' (emphasis added).[125] From this, it can be suggested that rules relating to a state of war, including the rights and duties of neutral parties, were known during the Amarna Age. Likewise, in another letter previously discussed in the context of marine zones, a

[122] EA 77, lines 18–25 and 26–29.

[123] EA 245, lines 24–35.

[124] L Weber, 'Blockade' in *Max Planck Encyclopedia of Public International Law*, vol 11 (Amsterdam, North-Holland, 1989) 47. In a way that confirms the Eurocentric modernist approach, it is noted that the 'Dutch conducted *for the first time* a permanent siege-like maritime operation in 1584 against the ports of Flanders, then under Spanish rule' (emphasis added).

[125] EA 126, lines 4–13.

local ruler wrote to the King of Egypt that 'whose cities are these? Not the king's? *Place one man in each city and let him not permit the ships of the land of Amurru (to go forth)*' (emphasis added).[126] Most strikingly, the contemporary assumption that the effectiveness of the blockade is to be ensured and secured by naval vessels is also seemingly met. In a letter to the King of Egypt, a ruler complains about another who '*does not let my ships (go)* to the land of Yarimuta and to send them to Ṣumur *I am not able [bec]ause of the ships of the city* of Arvad. Behold, he says t[o him] '[R]ib-[Hadda] has taken it. [Th]us he is against me' (emphasis added).[127]

Consequently, the Amarna letters provide ample evidence that the States of the time understandably attached considerable importance to marine areas for security and economic reasons. They not only regulated their interactions in terms of trading, customs and so on, but also developed measures against, for example, privateering by others. Therefore, they offer conceptual precedents for the contemporary Law of the Sea.

V. Conclusions

In the introduction to this volume, Urfan Khaliq and Jacques Hartmann draw attention to the fact that 'there are two popular but opposite misconceptions about the role of international law'. The cynics assert that international law primarily reflects the interests of powerful States and is therefore 'too weak to improve the world in any significant way'. The optimists, on the other hand, see international law 'almost as a magic cure that might rid the world of all its ills'. Yet Professor Robin Churchill's scholarship, like that of some others, appreciates 'the role of power but also understand the limitations of international law'. So, the achievements as well as the limitations of international law as such are to be discussed and elaborated upon.

This chapter aimed to do so admittedly in a rather uncommon fashion. First, it is demonstrated that, contrary to what modernism postulates, international law is itself a true achievement of 'sovereign and independent' polities ('States') that consented to coexist and interact on an equal footing at any given time. The (legal) solutions and answers of each era do, and will, certainly change historically. Yet the (legal) issues, problems and questions concerning inter-polity relations are quite ahistorical. There is not a radical rupture. Nor is there a continuity in the strict sense of the word. Similar structural conditions produce, not to say necessitate and even dictate, similar conceptual tools. The (sovereigns of the) polities of all such times simply seek to protect their borders, maintain the balance of power, and regulate and foster their mutual interactions. In doing so, they create, develop and observe rules which constitute three of the key strands of international law, namely

[126] EA 101, lines 18–33.
[127] EA 105, lines 83–88. See also letter EA 110 for a similar blockade complaint.

the law of diplomacy, the law of war and the law of treaties. Such laws certainly limit the discretion and sovereignty of the very powers consenting to them. That is why States more often than not tend to comply with such rules. Nevertheless, yielding to temptation against the limitations of international law also has its limits. For any power that redraws its boundaries by absorbing another – becoming an empire – effectively brings an end to the international law system that existed between it and the other power. Borders not only represent but also effectively ensure the existence of all. Moreover, dealing with 'common others' also necessitates cooperation. So, it may be suggested that not being able to 'improve the world in any significant way' is not a weakness. As per all legal systems, its main 'mission and vision' is to protect the status quo of society, ie, the relevant 'family of nations' that made it possible. No doubt, the more sophisticated the family becomes, the more elegant the toolkit is. This certainly demonstrates that international law cannot be seen 'almost as a magic cure that might rid the world of all its ills'. Nonetheless, it is equally true that modern international law, leaving aside the unrealistic expectations of some, is slowly providing solutions to some pressing problems. However, the argument that international law addresses and orders matters in an unprecedented way is misconceived; it is simply the latest in a long line of iterations and none has previously provided a cure for the world's ills.

3

The Sources of Public International Law Historically Considered

DINO KRITSIOTIS

Abstract: This chapter argues for a broader historical consideration of the sources of public international law, one that pre-dates the preoccupation with Article 38(1) of the 1945 Statute of the International Court of Justice. It recentres custom as 'the older and the original source of International Law' (Lassa Oppenheim), taking the reader back to a period of the 'necessity' of natural law (Emer de Vattel) and the first articulation of the Martens Clause (in the preamble to the 1899 Hague Convention (II) with respect to the Laws and Customs of War on Land). Also under consideration is the relationship between bilateral treaties and custom (seen through the prism of the decision of the US Supreme Court in *Paquette Habana* (1900)) as well as multilateral treaties and custom (as discussed by the International Court of Justice in the *North Sea Continental Shelf Cases* (1969)), as foretold through the processes of codification, crystallisation and progressive development.

I. Introduction

This chapter presents a most welcome opportunity to reconnect with my very first and much-admired teacher and mentor in the field of public international law, Professor Robin Churchill, who led the tutorials in the year-long course offered on that subject at the University of Wales College of Cardiff when I studied there as an undergraduate.[1] Robin's deep dedication to his students, his remarkable patience

[1] Now Cardiff University (where he also acted as my personal tutor during my three years of undergraduate study). The lectures for that course were then delivered by Professor ED Brown, author of (amongst other things) *The International Law of the Sea* (Aldershot, Dartmouth Publishing, 1994). One of the prescribed texts for our classes was that of G Schwarzenberger (1908–91), *A Manual of International Law*, 6th edn (Milton, Professional Books Ltd, 1976), which had in fact been co-authored with Brown for its sixth edition – though I had apparently developed something of an early fixation for I Brownlie, *Principles of Public International Law* (Oxford, Clarendon Press, 1990), then in its fourth edition.

with their first faltering steps and various foibles with the discipline were known to all – and now, an entire generation or so later, I am placing on record my personal debt to him for his quietly rigorous instruction as well as his many acts of kindness and encouragement throughout the years. I am most thankful, too, to Professor Urfan Khaliq and Dr Jacques Hartmann, the editors of this volume, for their warm invitation to contribute to this collection. It is an immense delight for me to be in the company of those offering this rich and rightful tribute to so outstanding an educator and jurist of our discipline.

It is not often that students come by an opportunity of this kind, still less that they are able to seize it in any meaningful or sustained way. For this chapter, I have decided to return to one of the fundamentals of the discipline – namely, the sources of public international law – as they were first imparted to me all those years ago now and provide some of my own thoughts and impressions as they have gathered form over the span of my own academic career. The chapter has therefore been composed in the form of a continuation of those early classroom conversations, neither teacher nor student aware that their fortnightly exchanges would be the subject of a much-delayed rejoinder of this kind. Yet, it seemed to me that my own research specialisations of the international law on the use of force and armed conflict could provide a useful angle to refract the material and ideas from those very first lessons, since they really are quite different to the specialisations of my once instructor.[2]

It is in this sense, then, that the sources of public international law are 'historically considered', for the chapter involves a deliberate return to a topic at the very centre of our discipline – the rules governing the formal validation of all laws that bear its actual name. It has been composed as a prolonged meditation of sorts, principally on the relationship between treaties and custom, but it has also proved useful to pry a little more deliberately than usual into the past, the period before that which delivered our reigning orthodoxy (or set of orthodoxies). There is, then, an additional sense in which things are 'historically considered', for the chapter goes further back in time, taking us from the eve of the exponential rise of treaties in their multilateral form right through to the decision of the International Court of Justice in the *North Sea Continental Shelf Cases* in February 1969.[3] For me, it is

[2] Professor Churchill's interests in those – his first – years of an academic career centred on the Law of the Sea (especially in respect of fisheries) and international environmental law. See G Ulfstein, P Andersen and R Churchill, *The Regulation of Fisheries: Legal, Economic and Social Aspects: Proceedings of a European Workshop, University of Tromso, Norway, 2–4 June 1986* (Strasbourg, Council of Europe, 1987); R Churchill and D Freestone (eds), *International Law and Global Climate Change* (London, Graham and Trotman, 1991); R Churchill, J Gibson and LM Warren (eds), *Law, Policy and the Environment* (Oxford, Basil Blackwell, 1991). He was also interested in – and taught – the law of the European Economic Community (as it was then known). See RR Churchill, *EEC Fisheries Law* (Dordrecht, Martinus Nijhoff, 1987), although there is also evidence of the interface between these two disciplines. See RR Churchill, 'The EEC's Contribution to the "State" Practice in the Field of Fisheries' in ED Brown and RR Churchill (eds), *The UN Convention on the Law of the Sea: Impact and Implementation. Proceedings of the Nineteenth Annual Conference of the Law of the Sea Institute* (Honolulu HI, Law of the Sea Institute, 1985).

[3] *North Sea Continental Shelf Cases (Federal Republic of Germany/Denmark; Federal Republic of Germany/Netherlands)* [1969] ICJ Rep 3.

a meditation that could not have occurred at the time of those first lessons, yet it is also a meditation that could not have occurred but for those lessons, so it has been as much a pleasure for me to devise as it has been to write.

II. Before Article 38(1) of the 1945 Statute of the International Court of Justice

That Article 38(1) of the 1945 Statute of the International Court of Justice does not announce any 'hierarchy' for the formal sources of public international law is not a matter of any doubt, and this fact – this absence of a hierarchy – has been taken to express '[t]he unbridled freedom of States' in the making of the law: '[b]oth systems [of treaty and custom] possessed equal rank and status', where '[t]he complete interchangeability of the two sources plainly sanctioned the wish of sovereign States to regulate international relations as they thought best, without any obligation being imposed from outside'.[4] Historically, then, the very structure and authority of the law has been such as to inflict no permanent effect on relations between States that, it has been said, 'did not tie their hands for good; they were able to get rid of [obligations] by mutual agreement as soon as their understanding proved contrary to their interests'[5] – with their freedom of action kept secure in accordance with the positivist refrain that '[r]estrictions upon the independence of States cannot ... be presumed.'[6]

In truth, it will be appreciated that Article 38(1) of the Statute makes reference to judicial decisions and the teachings of the most highly qualified publicists, but it does so in the context of articulating 'subsidiary means for the determination of rules of law' – clear evidence if it were needed that some hierarchy had been implicated after all, for this formulation intimates that, in addition to these subsidiary means, there must also exist primary means for the determination of rules of public international law (otherwise known as the material sources of that law).[7] Whereas the formal sources of law *create* or make the law, material sources are there to help *determine* what that law is, assuming of course that it has been created in the first place. The Statute is not forthcoming on what the primary material sources of the law are or might be, although it is not difficult to imagine some

[4] A Cassese, *International Law in a Divided World* (Oxford, Clarendon Press, 1986) 169. This provision is 'taken over nearly verbatim' from art 38 of the 1920 Statute of the Permanent Court of International Justice: J Crawford, *Brownlie's Principles of Public International Law*, 8th edn (Oxford, Oxford University Press, 2012) 21.

[5] ibid. It is in this context that the 'attempt' of general principles of law has been described as 'revolutionary', for this was 'the first time an international heteronomous law ... was to be created': ibid 171. For further discussion of this dynamic in respect of custom, see P Weil, 'Towards a Relative Normativity of International Law?' (1983) 77 *American Journal of International Law* 413, 433–34.

[6] *The Case of the SS Lotus (France v Turkey)* [1927] PCIJ Rep Series A No 10, 18.

[7] See RY Jennings, 'The Progressive Development of International Law and its Codification' (1947) 24 *British Yearbook of International Law* 301, 303 (emphasising the dimension of the 'ascertainment' of the law as opposed to the 'source of its validity').

coincidence with the formal sources of the law themselves – that is to say that, in addition to the formal sources of law serving as law-creating process, to greater or lesser degrees of effect, they may also act as their own law-determining agencies.[8]

Alongside treaties and custom, 'general principles of law recognized by civilized nations' are announced as one of the other 'formal sources' – or 'modalities'[9] – of public international law, and the inclusion of such general principles in the Court's Statute has an important and interesting history: in no way was this intended to convey the impression of the empirical equality of significance with treaties and custom,[10] even though their presence in the Statute means that they are now spoken in very much the same breath as part and parcel of the 'official creed' of international law.[11] Still, the fact that we find treaties and custom taking pride of place in positivism's constellation is not necessarily indicative of earlier periods of the history of international law: in his (remarkably short) chapter on the sources and principles of public international law published in 1904, John Westlake had written that: 'Custom and reason are the two sources of international law.'[12] And it is from this iteration – relating to the question of the evidences of custom – that mention was made of treaties, for, Westlake claimed: 'The best evidence of the consent which makes international law is the practice of states appearing in their actions, in the treaties they conclude, and in the judgments of their prize and other courts.'[13] Hidden in this statement is, perhaps, an early imperative for clarifying the source of law by virtue of its function (validation *versus* evidentiary) or functions (validation *and* evidentiary).

Be that as it may, the general position of Westlake was not shared by Lassa Oppenheim, who took issue with it in the first edition of his treatise that was published in 1905, the year after the appearance of Westlake's volume, where he identified just two sources of international law: express consent ('given when States conclude a treaty stipulating certain rules for the future international conduct of the parties')[14] and tacit consent ('given through States having adopted the custom

[8] Terminology from Schwarzenberger and Brown (n 1).

[9] RR Churchill and AV Lowe, *The Law of the Sea*, 3rd edn (Manchester, Manchester University Press, 1999) 6. See also V Lowe, 'The Politics of Law-Making: Are the Method and Character of Norm Creation Changing?' in M Byers (ed), *The Role of Law in International Politics: Essays in International Relations and International Law* (Oxford, Oxford University Press, 2000) 212 (referring to 'the "normal" processes for the validation of putative norms and institutions').

[10] Note Cassese's observation that the proposition of 'general principles of law' constituted an 'attempt' to 'create a new, albeit secondary, source of international law': Cassese (n 4) 172. This was also referred to as a 'third source' (at 173).

[11] Churchill and Lowe (n 9) 6.

[12] J Westlake, *International Law*, Part I: Peace (Cambridge, Cambridge University Press, 1904) 14. Westlake was not alone in this regard. See J Kent, *Commentaries on American Law*, vol 1, 12th edn, OW Holmes Jr (ed) (Boston, MA, Little, Brown & Co, 1873) 1–2, who had written that: 'When the United States ceased to be a part of the British Empire, and assumed the character of an independent nation, they became subject to that system of rules which reason, morality, and custom had established among civilized nations of Europe, as their public law.'

[13] Westlake (n 12) 16.

[14] L Oppenheim, *International Law: A Treatise*, Vol I: Peace (London, Longmans, Green & Co, 1905) 22 (§16).

of submitting to certain rules of international conduct').[15] It is from this premise that Oppenheim then went on to conclude that '[t]reaties and custom are, therefore, exclusively' – he very much emphasised that reference to exclusivity – 'the sources of the Law of Nations'.[16] And that insistence was entered specifically by reference to Westlake: 'Why he does not recognise treaties as a source, I cannot understand, and I cannot agree to reason being a source. Reason is a means of interpreting law, but it cannot call law into existence.'[17]

III. The Necessity of Natural Law

While it may be true that custom 'is the older and the original source of International Law' when set against or compared with treaties,[18] for many centuries, the authority of public international law as told in successive histories seemed to reside or unite its fate with natural law, which, quite evidently, commanded a 'vital historical role in the emergence of the European states-system'.[19] And it is telling that, in his *The Law of Nations or Principles of the Law of Nature Applied to the Conduct and Affairs of Nations and Sovereigns*, which appeared in 1758, Emer de Vattel distinguished between the 'necessary law of nations' ('the application of the law of nature to *Nations*')[20] and the 'positive law of nations' (which comprised three kinds of normativity: voluntary law, which was based on presumed consent; conventional law, which originated in express consent; and customary law, which derived from tacit consent).[21] The association with the dispensations set forth by both Westlake and Oppenheim over a century-and-a-half later cannot be missed, but what is calling out for our attention is the very idea of a *necessary* law of nations: '[i]t is *necessary*', maintained Vattel, 'because the nations are *absolutely* bound to observe it',[22]

[15] ibid.

[16] ibid.

[17] ibid. For Westlake (n 12) 15, there were 'two causes' that underpinned recourse to reason: 'First, the rules already regarded as established, whatever their source, must be referred to their principles, applied, and their principles extended to new cases, by the methods of reasoning proper to jurisprudence, enlightened by a sound view of the necessities of international life. Secondly, the rules as yet established, even when so applied and extended, do not cover the whole field of international life, which is constantly developed in new directions. Therefore from time to time new rules have to be proposed on reasonable grounds, acted on provisionally, and ultimately adopted or rejected as may be determined by experience, including the effect, not less important in international than in national affairs, of interest coupled with preponderating power.'

[18] Oppenheim (n 14) 22 (§17).

[19] H Bull, 'Natural Law and International Relations' (1979) 5 *British Journal of International Studies* 171, 171. See also M García-Salmones Rovira, *The Project of Positivism in International Law* (Oxford, Oxford University Press, 2013) 31 (on the 'fall' of natural law); Crawford (n 4) 7 (on 'the wider intellectual history of the field or its normative underpinnings').

[20] E de Vattel, *Le droit des gens, ou principes de la loi naturelle appliqués à la conduit et aux affaires des nations et des souverains* (Amsterdam, E van Harrevelt, 1758), Preliminaries (§7).

[21] ibid.

[22] ibid.

standing in marked contrast to the optionality of all three kinds of positive law that Vattel had identified.

Natural law thus carried with it a series of rather forbidding and even timeless connotations,[23] for it 'encompassed and regulated the natural and social life of the universe in all its infinite variety – from the movements of the stars in their courses to the gurgling of the four humours through the veins and arteries of the human body, from the thoughts and deeds of all of the creatures of land, sea, and air, to those of human beings and the angels in the heavens. Its strictures applied universally to all cultures and civilizations, past, present, and future'.[24] Not much fell outside its sweep, or so it would appear. How natural law – or, more properly, its legions of adherents – set about that task of regulation depended, of course, on how one *understood* what natural law was about or what it stood for, with Jackson H Ralston observing in his *International Arbitration from Athens to Locarno* (1929) that 'if we mean by natural law that in each instance a special providential interference determines the course of events, the vast majority of intelligent people will reject the idea. If, on the other hand, by the term we mean that certain governing principles which control the action of men in their individual relations still rule when they are aggregated into nations, the evidence in its favour seems overwhelming'.[25] Still, these reflections and refinements notwithstanding, even the very early decades of the twentieth century witnessed the decrying of any ongoing significance of natural law and so-called natural rights, their dethronement secured by the forward march of positivist thinking and of positivist law:

> The law of nature may have been helpful, some three centuries ago, to build up a new law of nations, and the conception of inalienable rights of men and nations may have exercised a salutary influence, some one hundred and fifty years ago, on the development of modern democracy and on both sides of the ocean; but they have failed as a durable foundation of either municipal or international law and can not be used in the present day as substitutes for positive municipal law, on the one hand, and for positive international law, as recognized by nations and governments through their acts and statements, on the other hand.[26]

[23] For Cicero, natural law consisted of 'right reason in agreement with nature[,] … of universal application, unchanging and everlasting'. MT Cicero, *De Re Publica*, bk II, §33, 210–11.

[24] SC Neff, 'A Short History of International Law' in MD Evans (ed), *International Law*, 5th edn (Oxford, Oxford University Press, 2018) 6.

[25] JH Ralston, *International Arbitration from Athens to Locarno* (Stanford, Stanford University Press, 1929) 3. Hence Neff's identification of the 'dominant approach' of natural law as 'rationalist in outlook, holding the content of natural law to be susceptible of discovery and application by means of human reason rather than of revelation': ibid. See further RH Helmholz, *Natural Law in Court: A History of Legal Theory and Practice* (Cambridge, MA, Harvard University Press, 2015).

[26] *North American Dredging Company of Texas (USA) v United Mexican States* [1926] 4 RIAA 26, 29–30 (§12).

IV. Thinking through the Contents and Relevance of the Martens Clause

The possibilities of plotting a certain historical moment of clean and convenient rupture in the changing authority of public international law is difficult to maintain, for, it has been observed, '[s]chools of legal thought do not have the coherence and defined life-spans of movements in fields such as art history',[27] and it is perhaps more rewarding of an exercise to examine how these schools of thought – that is, how their respective imperatives or normative dynamics – came to interact with one another over time. It is also instructive to consider how the various stipulations of positive law came to realise their own limits or limitations, which is nowhere more apparent than in the famous Martens Clause of the preamble to the 1899 Hague Convention (II) with respect to the Laws and Customs of War on Land,[28] which provided that: 'Until a more complete code of the laws of war is issued, the High Contracting Parties think it right to declare that in cases not included in the Regulations adopted by them, populations and belligerents remain under the protection and empire of the principles of international law, as they result from the usages between civilized nations, from the laws of humanity, and the requirements of public conscience.'

This asseveration has been regarded as 'an ingenious blend of natural law and positivism',[29] preceded as it was in the preamble by the statement that 'it could

[27] Churchill and Lowe (n 9) 5. Consider in this respect the assessment of O Schachter, *International Law in Theory and Practice* (Dordrecht, Martinus Nijhoff, 1991) 36: 'It had become evident to international lawyers as it had to others that the States that made and applied law were not governed by morality or "natural reason"; they acted for reasons of power and interest. It followed that law could only be ascertained and determined through the actual methods used by States to give effect to their political wills.'

[28] Convention (II) with Respect to the Laws and Customs of War on Land and its annex: Regulations concerning the Laws and Customs of War on Land (signed 29 July 1899, entered into force 4 September 1900) 187 CTS 429. Alongside the Martens Clause, it is worth considering art 227(1) of the Treaty of Versailles (signed 28 June 1919, entered into force 20 January 1920) 225 CTS 188, where the Allied and Associated Powers publicly arraigned William II of Hohenzollern, or the former German Emperor, 'for a supreme offence against international morality and the sanctity of treaties'. Article 227(3) of that treaty went on to specify that the special tribunal created to try the accused – which never came to pass – 'will be guided by the highest motives of international policy, with a view to vindicating the solemn obligations of international undertakings and the validity of international morality'. Apparently, these words were 'crafted rather casually' by Robert Lansing, the US Secretary of State, who 'never thought he was drafting a legal instrument or treaty provision': WA Schabas, *The Trial of the Kaiser* (Oxford, Oxford University Press, 2018) 4.

[29] A Cassese, 'The Martens Clause: Half a Loaf or Simply Pie in the Sky?' (2000) 11 *European Journal of International* Law 187, 189. For Oppenheim (n 14) 93 (§59), FF Martens 'intends to be a real Positivist, but traces of Natural Law are nevertheless now and then to be found in his [*Völkerrecht. Das Internationale Recht der civilisirten Nationen* (Weidmann, 1883)]'. On the 'inherent tension' of Martens as an independent international law expert and 'dependent' State representative, consider L Mälksoo, 'Friedrich Fromhold von Martens (Fyodor Fyodorovich Martens) (1845–1909)' in B Fassbender and

not be intended by the High Contracting Parties that the cases not provided for should, for want of a written provision, be left to the arbitrary judgment of the military commanders'.[30] Several observations do seem to be in order from these formulations contained in the Hague Convention. First, the reference to the 'want' of a written provision suggests that the Martens Clause might have been conceived within the context of custom, for it calls to mind the classic differentiation made in the literature between *lex scripta* and *lex non scripta* and, at least on an initial approach, intimates that we are not too far away from the law's positivist moorings; it is simply a question of shifting between the said 'modalities'.[31] However, as my second observation, the Martens Clause does go on to relate how the 'principles of international law' result from – how they are the product of – three specific but undefined propositions or imperatives: usages between civilised nations, the laws of humanity and the requirements of public conscience. We are given nothing other than this, but it is notable that the focal point is cast in terms of *principles* rather than *rules* of international law,[32] though it is left to the imagination what these principles are or could be – as well as how, indeed, they may be said to relate to the 'general principles' of law known today.[33]

The third observation to make is perhaps a statement of the obvious, but it is one that should not be overlooked, and it is that these principles can derive from not one but a multiplicity of imperatives – of usages between civilised nations, the laws of humanity and, finally, the requirements of public conscience. According to the positive law as expressed in the preamble to the Hague Convention,[34] then,

A Peters (eds), *The Oxford Handbook of the History of International Law* (Oxford, Oxford University Press, 2012) 1150.

[30] Though consider the claim that the Clause 'had no true practical weight before 1945' and that '[i]t became a part of the positive law in 1949, but is still not as much taken seriously as it could and should'. See R Kolb, 'The Protection of the Individual in Times of War and Peace' in Fassbender and Peters (n 29) 327.

[31] Churchill and Lowe (n 9) 6.

[32] In its Advisory Opinion in *Legality of the Threat or Use of Nuclear Weapons* [1996] ICJ Rep 226, 256 (§74), the International Court of Justice made reference to 'the principles and rules of international humanitarian law applicable in armed conflict'. The 'cardinal' principles were announced to be the principles of distinction and unnecessary suffering, and it is in this context that the Court 'would likewise refer, in relation to these principles' to the Martens Clause: ibid 257 (§78).

[33] Where, it has been said, they 'do not have just a supplementary role, but may give rise to rules of independent legal force': R Jennings and A Watts (eds), *Oppenheim's International Law*, Vol I: Peace, 9th edn (London, Longman, 1992) 40 (§12). It may be relevant to this analysis that, in announcing the Martens Clause, the Protocol Additional to the Geneva Conventions of 12 August 1949, and Relating to the Protection of Victims of International Armed Conflicts (Protocol I) (adopted 8 June 1977, entered into force 7 December 1979) 1125 UNTS 3 does so under the rubric of 'General Principles and Scope of Application'. In the context of custom, the International Committee of the Red Cross (ICRC) has invoked 'general principles' in reference to the protection of the natural environment (the principle of distinction, the principle of military necessity and the principle of proportionality) and the use of weapons (the principle of unnecessary suffering and the principle against indiscriminate attacks): J-M Henckaerts and L Doswald-Beck (eds), *Customary International Humanitarian Law*, Vol I: Rules (Cambridge, Cambridge University Press, 2005) 237 and 244.

[34] See further J Klabbers, 'Treaties and Their Preambles' in MJ Bowman and D Kritsiotis (eds), *Conceptual and Contextual Perspectives on the Modern Law of Treaties* (Cambridge, Cambridge University Press, 2018) 172.

each of these imperatives on its own is capable of yielding principles that were somehow to be regarded as binding in law. And it is here that we might want to depart from the dialectic between treaty and custom because the reference to 'usages between civilised nations' was to usages *simpliciter* and not to custom *stricto sensu*, with the understanding of that time that '[u]sage is an international habit of action that has not yet received full legal attestation'.[35] To be sure, the language of 'custom' has surfaced in one of the subsequent iterations of the Clause,[36] but it has been said that this 'may have deprived the Martens [C]lause of its intrinsic coherence and legal logic' because that iteration of the First Additional Protocol to the Geneva Conventions 'conflates the emerging product (principles of international law) with one of its component factors (established custom) and raises questions about the function, role, and necessity of the uncodified principles of humanity and dictates of public conscience. The original wording has a coherence that the Protocol lacks'.[37]

As for the 'laws of humanity'[38] and the apparent 'requirements'[39] of public conscience,[40] the Hague Convention (II) leaves us none the wiser as to what these

[35] See Crawford (n 4) 23 ('"custom" and "usage" are terms of art with different meanings'). See also I Shearer, *Starke's International Law*, 11th edn (London, Butterworths, 1994) 31. This distinction would have been known at that time: Oppenheim (n 14) 25 distinguished between 'legally binding rules' and 'such rules as have the character of usages, but also rules of politeness, convenience, and good-will'.

[36] Protocol I (n 33) art 1(2). This is in contrast to the preamble to the Protocol Additional to the Geneva Conventions of 12 August 1949, and Relating to the Protection of Victims of Non-international Armed Conflicts (Protocol II) (adopted 8 June 1977, entered into force 7 December 1978) 1125 UNTS 609, which recalls 'that, in cases not covered by the law in force, the human person remains under the protection of the principles of humanity and the dictates of the public conscience'. The omission of any reference to custom in this formulation arose because '[i]t was apparently felt that the regulation of non-international armed conflicts was too recent a matter of State practice to have sufficiently developed in this field': Y Sandoz, C Swinarski and B Zimmermann (eds), *Commentary on the Additional Protocols of 8 June 1977 to the Geneva Conventions of 12 August 1949* (Geneva, International Committee of the Red Cross, 1987) 1341.

[37] T Meron, 'The Martens Clause, Principles of Humanity, and Dictates of Public Conscience' (2000) 94 *American Journal of International Law* 78, 81. To this extent, the Martens Clause would appear to be doing something different from – something more than – the final preambular recital of the Vienna Convention on Diplomatic Relations (adopted 18 April 1961, entered into force 24 April 1964) 500 UNTS 95 ('Affirming that the rules of customary international law should continue to govern questions not expressly regulated by provisions of the present Convention') and to the penultimate preambular recital of the United Nations Convention on the Law of the Sea (adopted 10 December 1982, entered into force 16 November 1994) 1833 UNTS 3 ('Affirming that matters not regulated by this Convention continue to be governed by the rules and principles of general international law'). However, consider Y Dinstein, *The Conduct of Hostilities under the Law of International Armed Conflict*, 3rd edn (Cambridge, Cambridge University Press, 2016) 14 ('The Martens Clause should merely serve as a reminder that the adoption of a treaty does not preclude the continued existence of customary international law').

[38] Note, specifically, Cassese (n 29) 188 on this proposition: 'The principal – and general – merit of the clause … is that it approached the question of the laws of humanity for the first time not as a *moral* issue but from a *positivist* (or, to put it more accurately, from an *apparently positivist*) perspective. Previously, international treaties and Declarations had simply proclaimed the importance of such laws or humanitarian considerations [where] states had not been enjoined to abide by any strict legal standard upholding the laws of humanity, *qua moral principles*, while acting in the course of a war.' Compare the final preambular recital of the Constitution of the International Labour Organization (1919) 203 CTS 12: 'The High Contracting Parties, moved by sentiments of justice and humanity as well as by the desire

propositions and their ensuing principles – principles of law no less[41] – would or could be; however, for our penultimate observation, it is instructive to learn what kind of traction they have acquired in the intervening decades and how little we still know about their scope or content.[42] By way of example, with its 'overtones' of the Martens Clause,[43] the judgment of the International Court of Justice in the *Corfu Channel Case* of April 1949 is often cited as an instance of the Clause in action,[44] though there 'humanity' was invoked in order to replicate those laws of war as announced in the 1907 Hague Convention (VIII) Relative to the Laying of Automatic Submarine Contact Mines[45] for the laws of peace. As the Court reasoned:

> The obligations incumbent upon the Albanian authorities consisted in notifying, for the benefit of shipping in general, the existence of a minefield in Albanian territorial waters and in warning the approaching British warships of the imminent danger to which the minefield exposed them. Such obligations are based, not on the Hague Convention of 1907, No. VIII, which is applicable in time of war, but on certain general and well-recognized principles, namely: elementary considerations of humanity, even more exacting in peace than in war; the principle of the freedom of maritime communication; and every State's obligation not to allow knowingly its territory to be used for acts contrary to the rights of other States.[46]

And this brings us to the fifth and final observation regarding the Martens Clause, which questions why the principles admitted into or recognised by public international law by some 23 States[47] only found such expression with regard to the conduct of warfare,[48] but not, apparently, to other realms of human conduct or

to secure the permanent peace of the world, and with a view to attaining the objectives set forth in this Preamble, agree to the following Constitution of the International Labour Organization.'

[39] Or 'dictates' of public conscience in subsequent iterations: see common arts 63/62/142/158 of the Geneva Convention (I) for the Amelioration of the Condition of the Wounded and Sick in Armed Forces in the Field (adopted 12 August 1949, entered into force 21 October 1950) 75 UNTS 31; Geneva Convention (II) for the Amelioration of the Condition of Wounded, Sick and Shipwrecked Members of Armed Forces at Sea (adopted 12 August 1949, entered into force 21 October 1950) 75 UNTS 85; Geneva Convention (III) Relative to the Treatment of Prisoners of War (adopted 12 August 1949, entered into force 21 October 1950) 75 UNTS 135; Geneva Convention (IV) Relative to the Protection of Civilian Persons in Time of War (adopted 12 August 1949, entered into force 21 October 1950) 75 UNTS 287. See also Protocol I (n 33) art 1(2).

[40] Which, taken together, form the 'core' of the Martens Clause: Dinstein (n 37) 13.

[41] Cassese (n 29) 188. Though consider ibid 14 ('principles of humanity' and 'the dictates of the public conscience' do 'not constitute additional strata of the law').

[42] See further M Salter, 'Reinterpreting Competing Interpretations of the Scope and Potential of the Martens Clause' (2012) 17 *Journal of Conflict & Security Law* 403.

[43] Dinstein (n 37) 13.

[44] Indeed, Cassese (n 29) 213 posits the view that the Court 'codified' the Clause in the *Corfu Channel Case (United Kingdom v Albania) (Merits)* [1949] ICJ Rep 4.

[45] Hague Convention (VIII) Relative to the Laying of Automatic Submarine Contact Mines (signed 18 October 1907, entered into force 26 January 1910) 205 CTS 331.

[46] *Corfu Channel Case* (n 44) 22.

[47] At least initially, as they were eventually joined by 28 other States.

[48] So that the first preambular recital of the Geneva Protocol for the Prohibition of the Use in War of Asphyxiating, Poisonous or Other Gases, and of Bacteriological Methods of Warfare (adopted

activity: even the *Corfu Channel Case* was an attempt to expand the humanity of warfare to times of peace and the laws of peace; it did not constitute an explication of how the laws of humanity might be defined beyond the condition of warfare itself. So what of 'the protection and empire' of these 'principles of international law' more generally? What work, what function or functions, can be claimed for these principles when they are read in a more historical vein? And with what voice – and to what ends – did either the laws of humanity or the requirements of public conscience speak on matters such as slavery and the slave trade,[49] genocide,[50] colonisation and relations with indigenous peoples in the absence of written provisions or *lex scripta*?[51]

V. Treaties, Custom and *Paquette Habana* (1900)

Let us now try to make some headway on the relationship or, better, configurations of relationship between the two principal (formal) sources of public international law known today – treaties and custom – especially in the context of the reversal of the prevalence of these two sources when considered more generally.[52] And this change has undoubtedly occurred because the overwhelming concentration of practice tended to be of the treaty in its bilateral rather than multilateral form – a phenomenon that was supposedly punctuated by the Peace of Aachen of October 1748 that ended the War of the Austrian Succession.[53]

We can appreciate more fully this significance of custom – and also, more generally, of bilateral treaties within the international legal order – from the judgment

17 June 1925, entered into force 8 February 1928) 94 LNTS 65 stated that 'the use in war of asphyxiating, poisonous or other gases, and of all analogous liquids, materials or devices, has justly been condemned by the general opinion of the civilized world'.

[49] See, eg, *The Antelope*, 23 US 66 (1825).

[50] In the preamble to UNGA Res 96(I) (11 December 1946) UN Doc A/RES/96(I), it was stated that 'such denial of the right of existence shocks the conscience of mankind, results in great losses to humanity in the form of cultural and other contributions represented by these groups, and is contrary to moral law and to the spirit and aims of the United Nations'. On the general significance of this development, see WA Schabas, *Genocide in International Law: The Crime of Crimes*, 2nd edn (Cambridge, Cambridge University Press, 2009) 55–57.

[51] Note in this respect the observation made by Judge Shahabuddeen in *Legality of the Threat or Use of Nuclear Weapons* (n 32) 408: 'the Martens Clause provided its own self-sufficient and conclusive authority for the proposition that there were already in existence principles of international law under which considerations of humanity could themselves exert legal force *to govern military conduct in which no relevant rule was provided by conventional law*' (emphasis added).

[52] Jennings and Watts (n 33) 31 (on treaties as 'the second source' of international law historically). See also P Alston and R Goodman, *International Human Rights: Text and Materials* (Oxford, Oxford University Press, 2013) 72 (on custom as 'the oldest and original source of international law').

[53] Where '[t]he multilateral character of the treaty was considered a novelty': R Lesaffer, 'The Peace of Aachen (1748) and the Rise of Multilateral Treaties' available at: http://opil.ouplaw.com/page/Peace-Aachen/the-peace-of-aachen-1748-and-the-rise-of-multilateral-treaties. Lesaffer also states that: 'The actual peace treaty … was styled as a true multilateral peace treaty between eight equal treaty partners all of which were fully bound to the treaty in its entirety.' See further JM Sosin, 'Louisburg and the Peace of Aix-la-Chapelle, 1748' (1957) 14 *William and Mary Quarterly* 516.

of the United States Supreme Court in *Paquette Habana* in January 1900.[54] There, contending with 'no treaty and no controlling executive or legislative act or judicial decision' to apply to the facts before it,[55] the Supreme Court set out 'to trace the history of the rule' that fishing vessels have been recognised as exempt from capture as prize of war 'from the earliest accessible sources, through the increasing recognition of it, with occasional setbacks, to what we may now justly consider as its final establishment in our own country and generally throughout the civilized world'.[56] Among those 'accessible sources', the Court cited sovereign orders to admirals (such as from Henry IV and Louis XVI), legislative or governmental decrees, military proclamations and diplomatic correspondence, as well as standing orders of the admiralty – but it also made mention of certain bilateral treaties (eg, those between Great Britain and France, the Holy Roman Empire and France, and the US and Prussia).[57]

And this marshalling of proofs by the Court was not only directed towards the *fact* of the relevant rule as the Court saw it, but to its overall contours as well: we learn that the exemption for fishing vessels did not apply 'to coast fishermen or their vessels, if employed for a warlike purpose, or in such a way as to give aid or information to the enemy; nor when military or naval operations create a necessity to which all private interests must give way' and nor had it been 'extended to ships or vessels employed on the high sea in taking whales or seals, or cod or other fish which are not brought fresh to the market, but are salted or otherwise cured and made a regular article of commerce'.[58] In dissent, Chief Justice Fuller, who had been joined by Justices Harlan and McKenna, seized on these considerations to claim that the 'supposed rule' had been confined 'to very narrow limits' which were then applied to the facts as presented to the Court:

> [These two vessels] were of twenty-five and thirty-tons burden respectively. They carried large tanks, in which the fish taken were kept alive. They were owned by citizens of Havana, and the owners and the masters and crew were to be compensated by shares of each … They belonged, in short, to the class of fishing or coasting vessels of from five to twenty tons burden, and from twenty tons upwards, which … are declared to be vessels of the United States, and the shares of whose men, when the vessels are employed in fishing are regulated by statute. They were engaged in what were substantially commercial

[54] *Paquette Habana*, 175 US 677 (1900).

[55] ibid 700.

[56] ibid 686.

[57] Reference was also made to the works of jurists. As the Supreme Court maintained, 'where there is no treaty, and no controlling executive or legislative act or judicial decision, resort must be had to the customs and usages of civilized nations; *and, as evidence of these, to works of jurists and commentators, who by years of labor, research and experience, have made themselves peculiarly well acquainted with the subjects of which they treat. Such works are resorted to by judicial tribunals, not for the speculations of their authors concerning what the law ought to be, but for trustworthy evidence of what the law really is*' (ibid 700, emphasis added). The Court later wrote in terms of 'the precedents and authorities on the subject' (ibid 708).

[58] ibid 708. Hence, the Court remarked of both the *Paquette Habana* and the *Lola*, 'we cannot doubt that each [vessel] was engaged in the coast fishery, and not in a commercial adventure, within the rule of international law' (at 714).

> ventures, and the mere fact that the fish were kept alive by contrivances for that purpose – a practice of considerable antiquity – did not render them any the less an article of trade than if they have been brought in cured.[59]

Most crucially, however, and more fundamentally, the dissent reserved its chief criticism for the 'supposed rule' itself: 'the exemption of fishing craft', Chief Justice Fuller and his colleagues maintained, 'is essentially an act of grace, and not a matter of right, and it is extended or denied as the exigency is believed to demand'.[60] Indeed, the very first page of their dissent takes issue with 'any such established international rule' and with whether 'this court can properly revise action which must be treated as having been taken in the ordinary exercise of discretion in the conduct of war'.[61] On this reading of the relevant practice, any exemption according to fishing vessels had not occurred 'as a matter of law',[62] but, rather, by way of grace or discretion, and there was no question that the captures had taken place in disregard of 'established international law'.[63]

What is of interest to us here is the invocation of bilateral treaties in the Court's analysis and in the context of its discussion of custom: we learn that an order of Henry IV ('Concerning Safety for Fisherman – *De Securitate pro Piscatoribus*'), dated 26 October 1403, was adopted pursuant to a treaty between himself and Charles VI, King of France.[64] On 2 October 1521, a further treaty was concluded between Emperor Charles V and Francis I of France when 'a suitable time for the herring fishery was at hand', where it was agreed 'that the subjects of each sovereign, fishing in the sea or exercising the call of fishermen, could and might, until the end of next January, without incurring any attack, depredation, molestation, trouble, or hindrance soever, safely and freely, everywhere in the sea, take herrings and every other kind of fish, the existing war by land and sea notwithstanding'.[65] And, then, in 1675, Louis XIV of France and the States General of Holland entered a mutual agreement granting to Dutch and French fisherman 'the liberty, undisturbed by their vessels of war, of fishing along the coasts of France, Holland, and England'.[66] Almost a century later in September 1785, Prussia and the US

[59] ibid 718–19.

[60] ibid 719 (with Harlan and McKenna JJ).

[61] ibid 715.

[62] ibid 721. In his view, 'the rule is that the exemption from the rigors of war is in the control of the Executive. He is bound by no immutable rule on the subject. It is for him to apply, or to modify, or to deny altogether such immunity as may have been usually extended' (at 720).

[63] ibid 717.

[64] Also an order dated 5 October 1406, Henry IV taking into 'his safe conduct and under his special protection, guardianship, and defense all and singular the fishermen of France, Flanders, and Brittany, with their fishing vessels and boats, everywhere on the sea': ibid 687.

[65] ibid 687–88 (with a recital appearing in the treaty of 'a great and fierce war [that] had arisen between them' (ibid 687)).

[66] ibid 689. See also at 688: 'The herring fishery was permitted, in time of war, by French and Dutch edicts in 1536.' This practice was discontinued by virtue of ordinances of 1681 and 1692 because of 'the faithless conduct of the enemies of France, who, abusing the good faith with which she had always observed the treaties, habitually carried off her fishermen, while their own fished in safety' (at 689).

concluded a treaty of amity and commerce which provided that 'all women & children, scholars of every faculty, cultivators of the earth, artizans, manufacturers and fishermen unarmed and inhabiting unfortified towns, villages or places, & in general all others whose occupations are for the common subsistence & benefit of mankind, shall be allowed to continue their respective employments, & shall not be molested in their persons, nor shall their houses or goods be burnt, or otherwise destroyed, nor their fields wasted by the armed force of the enemy, into whose power, by the events of war, they may happen to fall; but if any thing is necessary to be taken from them for the use of such armed force, the same shall be paid for at a reasonable price'[67] – a provision that was repeated in two later bilateral treaties between these two countries, one in 1799[68] and the other in 1828.[69] It also featured in the treaty reached between the US and Mexico in February 1848.[70]

Do these conventional developments necessarily spell out an (or any) equivalent rule for custom? Or do they mark out a particular provenance for fishing vessels aside from, or as interruptions to, the then prevailing rule as it then stood in custom? It is interesting to observe that in the judgment, the Supreme Court made reference to Lord Stowell's judgment of November 1798 in *The Young Jacob and Johanna*, in which he had written:

> In former wars, it has not been usual to make captures of these small fishing vessels; but this rule was a rule of comity only, and not of legal decision; it has prevailed from views of mutual accommodation between neighboring countries, and from tenderness to a poor and industrious order of people. In the present war, there has, I presume, been sufficient reason for changing this mode of treatment, and as they are brought before me for my judgment, they must be referred to the general principles of this Court; they fall under the character and description of the last class of cases – that is, of ships constantly and exclusively employed in the enemy's trade.[71]

For the Supreme Court, the telling element in this passage of analysis was the idea of 'legal decision' as a quantifier of the practice presented before Lord Stowell: 'Assuming the phrase "legal decision" to have been there used, in the sense in which courts are accustomed to use it, as equivalent to "judicial decision", it is true that, so far as appears, there had been no such decision on the point in England. The word "comity" was apparently used by Lord Stowell as synonymous with courtesy or good will.'[72] Yet the Supreme Court went on to form the view in January 1900

See further RJ Valin, *Nouveau Commentaire sur l'Odonnance de la Marine, du Mois d'Août 1681*, vol II (La Rochelle, Legier et Mesnier, 1776) 689–90.

[67] 8 Stat 96, art 23.

[68] 8 Stat 174.

[69] 8 Stat 384.

[70] The Treaty of Peace, Friendship, Limits, and Settlement between the United States of America and the Mexican Republic (Treaty of Guadalupe Hidalgo) 9 Stat 922, art XXII(1). Inserted into that treaty were 'the very words of earlier treaties with Prussia … forbidding the hostile molestation or seizure in time of war of the persons, occupations, houses, or goods of fishermen' (at 699).

[71] *The Young Jacob and Johanna* (1798) 1 C Rob 20 (cited in *Paquette Habana* (n 54) 693).

[72] *Paquette Habana* (n 54) 694.

that 'the period of a hundred years which has since elapsed is amply sufficient to have enabled what originally may have rested in custom or comity, courtesy or concession, to grow, by the general assent or civilized nations, into a settled rule of international law'.[73] In its assessment, then, the quality and presumably the quantum of practice[74] in the intervening years was of an order to persuade it that 'a settled rule of international law' had indeed come into being – although 'custom' and 'comity' are unfortunately run together in the analysis when, in truth, they are not comparable propositions: custom concerns those rules that are regarded as legally binding; rules of comity, on the other hand, are not and derive instead from 'politeness, convenience, and good will'.[75]

For the Court, there had therefore come a moment – inexplicitly disposed, but nevertheless occurring at some point over the previous 10 decades or so – where 'custom' had undergone some form of change, and this accords with what the Court had intimated at the very outset of its ruling ('By an ancient usage among civilized nations, beginning centuries ago and gradually ripening into a rule of international law').[76] Ultimately, the Court seems to have been levered into this conclusion by the position of France, which, through its prize tribunals, had taken 'a wholly different view of the question' from that of Lord Stowell – and had done so both before and after the decision in *The Young Jacob and Johanna*.[77] Reflecting on these divergent approaches, the Court paused to acknowledge an excerpt from Henry Wheaton's *A Digest of the Law of Maritime Captures and Prizes* published in 1815 – where, apparently, '[t]his custom, so honourable to the humanity of civilized nations has fallen into disuse … and it is remarkable that both France and England mutually reproach each other with that breach of faith which has abolished it'.[78] It did so both to confirm 'Wheaton's opinion that the custom had been a general one, as well as that it ought to remain so', but also to impugn the 'assumption' that it had been 'abolished by the differences between France and

[73] ibid. The Supreme Court cited Sir J Mackintosh in its aid (ibid): 'In the present century a slow and silent, but very substantial mitigation has taken place in the practice of war; and in proportion as that mitigated practice has received the sanction of time, it is raised from the rank of mere usage, and becomes part of the law of nations.' See J Mackintosh, *A Discourse on the Study of the Law of Nature and Nations*, 2nd edn (London, T Cadell, Jun & W Davies, 1799) 29.

[74] Later in its judgment, the Supreme Court referred to 'precedents and authorities on the subject' which appear 'to us abundantly to demonstrate that at the present day' the existence of an established rule of international law: *Paquette Habana* (n 54) 708.

[75] Jennings and Watts (n 33) 51 (concluding that '[t]he comity of nations is not a source of international law'). See also H Lauterpacht, 'Allegiance, Diplomatic Protection and Criminal Jurisdiction over Aliens' (1947) 9 *Cambridge Law Journal* 330, 331 (on comity as 'considerations of courtesy, amity, neighbourly feeling and reciprocity'), also referring to 'the current laxity of terminology' (at 332).

[76] *Paquette Habana* (n 54) 686. Note, too, how France, 'from remote times … set the example of alleviating the evils of war in favor of all coast fishermen' (at 688).

[77] ibid 694, with the pointed reminder that Louis XVI was 'our ally in [the] war' of Independence (at 689).

[78] According to Wheaton, the exemption from capture of fishing boats and their cargoes was achieved 'both from views of mutual accommodation between neighbouring countries, and from tenderness to a poor and industrious order of people': H Wheaton, *A Digest of the Law of Maritime Captures and Prizes* (New York, Forbes & Co Printers, 1815) 60–61 (§18).

England at the close of the last century' ('hardly justified', the Court thought, 'by the state of things when [Wheaton] wrote, and has not since been borne out').[79]

We can now appreciate that the initial invocation of bilateral treaties in the judgment of the Supreme Court was intended as an illustration of this 'usage':[80] the undated treaty between Henry IV and Charles VI explains the adoption of an order of October 1403 by the former to his admirals and other officers for fishermen to 'carry on their industry';[81] the second treaty mentioned above, between Emperor Charles V and Francis I of France of October 1521, was also directed towards 'the grave detriment and intolerable injury of the innocent subjects', so that it, too, is indicative of this usage.[82] We may also form the same impression of the mutual agreement between Louis XIV and the States General of Holland of 1675,[83] as well as the treaty between the US and Prussia of September 1785. As has been mentioned, the relevant provision from that latter treaty – according to the Court, 'the clearest exemption from hostile molestation of seizure of the persons, occupation, houses, and goods of unarmed fishermen inhabiting unfortified places'[84] – was repeated in subsequent treaties between these two countries of 1799 and 1828 and between the US and Mexico in 1848. Yet, when the last of these treaties is mentioned towards the very end of the judgment, it is in the context of demonstrating the generalised 'state of things' as a matter of custom.[85]

Whereas the full consequence of bilateral treaties on custom remains rather unclear from these pronouncements,[86] the extent to which such treaties can and

[79] *Paquette Habana* (n 54) 696.

[80] Notably, it has been observed that '[c]ustom must not be confused with usage', for usage occurs 'when a habit of doing certain actions has grown up without their being a conviction that these actions are, according to International Law, obligatory or right. Some conduct of States concerning their international relations may therefore be usual without being the outcome of customary International Law'. See L Oppenheim, *International Law: A Treatise*, Vol I: Peace, 8th edn, H Lauterpacht (ed) (London, Longmans, 1955) 26–27. However, note the Supreme Court's reference to 'the customs and usages of civilized nations' in *Paquette Habana* (n 54) 700.

[81] *Paquette Habana* (n 54) 687.

[82] ibid 687–88.

[83] ibid 698 (although here the Court made reference to the 'same custom' when, it is clear, it was addressing usages as contained in the 'compilation' of É Cleirac, *Us et Coutumes de la Mer* (Bordeaux, Jacques Mongiron Millanges, 1661) 544).

[84] As described by the Supreme Court: *Paquette Habana* (n 54) 691.

[85] With a particular focus on the experiences of the French Empire, including the 1854–56 Crimean War, the 1859 war with Italy and the 1870 war with Prussia: ibid 696 and 699. See further DJ Bederman, 'The Feigned Demise of Prize' (1995) 9 *Emory International Law Review* 31.

[86] Though consider JL Goldsmith and EA Posner, 'Understanding the Resemblance between Modern and Traditional Customary International Law' (1999–2000) 40 *Virginia Journal of International Law* 639, 667 (regarding a rule that '[i]n reality … was based on unrelated bilateral agreements scattered over centuries', amongst other things). For an assessment of this question in the wholly separate sub-discipline of international investment law – where, as of 2006, at least 177 States were parties to bilateral investment treaties (BITs) – consider JE Alvarez, 'A BIT on Custom' (2009) 42 *New York University Journal of International Law and Politics* 17 (concluding (at 77) that the 'two elements of custom are demonstrated by the conclusion of investment treaties by the full diversity of nations, by the enactment of national laws (including many promulgated with the obligations of BITs and FTAs in mind), and by the practice of states in both defending investor-state disputes and generally acquiescing in arbitral outcomes which not infrequently rely on both treaty and non-treaty sources of law').

do influence custom is an open and complex question:[87] they are, after all, legal relationships deliberately formed *inter partes* and, presumably, their contents are designed for application *inter partes* and strictly *inter partes*.[88] Still, one can also begin to appreciate how, as a matter of principle, the patterning effect of identical or near-identical provisions appearing in an extensive swathe of bilateral treaties can be said to produce rules of a more general or generalised significance,[89] and it is for this very reason that it has been claimed that '[b]ilateral consular treaties have exercised a most important influence on the development of customary international law on consuls, now codified in the Vienna Convention on Consular Relations'.[90] That said, it is difficult to follow how instances of isolated treaty action – specifically, bilateral treaty action – can be considered without more to be actual *evidence* of custom, and still less any domestic measures adopted pursuant to those treaty ends.[91]

VI. Multilateral Treaties: On Codification and Progressive Development

The advent and subsequent multiplication of treaties in their multilateral form[92] began to focus attention on the species of treaty in terms of its intended or projected relationship with the arrangements of custom, with treaties often making explicit at their outset what their precise ambitions were or were intended to be: the preamble to the 1899 Hague Convention (II), for instance, expressed the

See also SM Schwebel, 'The Influence of Bilateral Investment Treaties on Customary International Law' (2004) 98 *Proceedings of the American Society of International Law* 27 (making reference to 'a cascade of parallel treaties' and reporting that more than 2,000 BITs have been concluded in the last quarter of a century or so).

87 See RR Baxter, 'Multilateral Treaties as Evidence of Customary International Law' (1965–66) 41 *British Yearbook of International Law* 275, 276.

88 The operational premise of Schwebel's analysis (n 86) 29 (concluding that '[t]he process by which provisions of treaties binding only the parties to those treaties may seep into general international law and thus bind the international community as a whole is subtle and elusive' and that '[i]t is nevertheless a real process known to international law').

89 Note the reference to the 'remarkably widespread basis' of bilateral investment relations observed in *Mondev International Ltd v United States of America* (11 October 2002) ICSID Case No ARB(AF) 99/2, para 117. See also Crawford (n 4) 24 (regarding 'an extensive pattern of treaties in the same terms' as a material source of custom).

90 RR Baxter, 'Treaties and Custom' (1970-I) 129 *Recueil des Cours* 25, 87.

91 Some of which is at work in the *Paquette Habana* judgment itself (n 54).

92 Including treaties that had begun life as bilateral initiatives: the 1928 Kellogg-Briand Pact, or Pact of Paris, had originated as 'Draft of Pact of Perpetual Friendship between France and the United States' (1927), but, following representations by the US, was expanded beyond this immediate circle. US Secretary of State Frank B Kellogg had expressed the view that: 'American public opinion would not view such a treaty with favor because it looks too much like a treaty of alliance and too short a step toward universal peace.' See JV Fuller (ed), *Papers Relating to the Foreign Relations of the United States, 1927*, Vol II (Washington DC, US Government Printing Office, 1942), Document 687 (Telegram from the Secretary of State to the Chargé in France: 30 December 1927).

importance of its task 'to revise the laws and general customs of war, either with the view of defining them more precisely, or of laying down certain limits for the purpose of modifying their severity as far as possible'.[93] A preliminary provision appearing at the tail-end of the preamble of the London Declaration Concerning the Laws of Naval War specified that '[t]he Signatory Powers are agreed that the rules contained in the following Chapters correspond in substance with the generally recognized principles of international law', with the language of codification evidently avoided.[94]

Then again, it was not always immediately clear what these ambitions were: for instance, the Paris Declaration Respecting Maritime Law of April 1856[95] announced in its preamble that the plenipotentiaries had deemed it 'advantageous to *establish* a uniform doctrine' on maritime law in time of war 'by seeking to *introduce* into international relations fixed principles in this respect' (emphasis added).[96] And yet, the first of these principles provided that privateering '*is, and remains*, abolished' (emphasis added).[97] To take yet another example: did the public condemnation of the use of asphyxiating, poisonous or other gases, and of all analogous liquids, materials or devices in warfare – as recognised in the preamble to the 1925 Geneva Gas Protocol – mean that the Protocol was engaging in the *codification* of 'the general opinion of the civilized world'[98] or of some *change* to the overall content of public international law as it stood at that point in time? And when the Contracting Parties to the 1948 United Nations Convention on the Prevention and Punishment of the Crime of Genocide confirmed that genocide 'is

[93] This formulation was repeated in the preamble to the Convention (IV) Respecting the Laws and Customs of War on Land (signed 18 October 1907, entered into force 26 January 1910) 187 CTS 227.

[94] Perhaps because this was more than an exercise in the 'mere codification of custom': IV Hull, *A Scrap of Paper: Breaking and Making International Law during the Great War* (Ithaca, NY, Cornell University Press, 2014) 143. The idea of relating the Declaration's 'rules' to the 'generally recognized principles of international law' was conceivably one way of uniting the codificatory and progressive components of the Declaration. Most notably, in its preparations for the London Conference, the British government had concluded in a note dated 10 November 1908 that 'the main task of the Conference will not … be to deliberate de lege ferenda [but] should … place on record that those Powers which are best qualified and most directly interested, recognize, as the result of their common deliberations, that there exists in fact a common law of nations of which is the purport of the Declaration, in the common interest, to set out the principles'. See Misc No 4 (1909), Cd 4554, 19.

[95] Though framed in terms of a 'Declaration', the Declaration (adopted 16 April 1856, entered into force 16 April 1856) 115 CTS 1 was reached after 'agreement' among its plenipotentiaries (fifth preambular recital) whose contents 'is not and shall not be binding, except between those Powers who have acceded, or shall accede, to it'.

[96] ibid.

[97] However, see Baxter (n 87) 278; and Jennings (n 7) 307 (on the Declaration as 'a statement of what the law ought to be'). It is of course entirely possible that the 'fixed principle' on privateering was but one element of this 'uniform doctrine' and might explain why '[t]he Governments of the undersigned Plenipotentiaries engage to bring the present declaration to the knowledge of the States which have not taken part in the Congress of Paris, and to invite them to accede' (ibid). See further HW Malkin, 'The Inner History of the Declaration of Paris' (1927) 8 *British Yearbook of International Law* 1, 2 (on the settlement of 'the age-long controversy as to the position of enemy goods on a neutral ship and neutral goods under an enemy flag').

[98] To be usefully contrasted with the language of the Martens Clause (n 39).

a crime under international law which they undertake to prevent and to punish',[99] did that confirmation speak to an earlier normative pedigree of *either* or *both* the notion of criminalisation as well as the undertakings formulated there?[100]

To be sure, treaties are now wreathed in claims of their animating cause or endeavour: there is now no shortage of references to codification in the preambular recitals of treaties, and this is either done on singular terms (the 1958 Geneva Convention on the High Seas '[d]esiring to codify the rules of international law relating to the high seas')[101] or combined with other considerations (as with the States Parties to the 1969 Vienna Convention on the Law of Treaties '[b]elieving that the codification and progressive development of the law of treaties achieved in the present Convention will promote the purposes of the United Nations set for in the Charter').[102] These incantations are of course good as far as they go,[103] but they ought to be treated with the utmost caution lest they serve as routinised platitudes

[99] United Nations Convention on the Prevention and Punishment of the Crime of Genocide (adopted 9 December 1948, entered into force 12 January 1951) UN Doc A/RES/3/260, art 1.

[100] After all, the General Assembly had already affirmed that genocide 'is a crime under international law' in UNGA Res 96(I) (n 50) at the same time that it invited Member States of the United Nations 'to enact the necessary legislation for the prevention and punishment of this crime'. The preamble to the Convention emphasised the General Assembly's position that genocide is 'contrary to the spirit and aims of the United Nations and condemned by the civilized world'. Consider too the idea of the actual prohibition of genocide: R Higgins, *Problems and Process: International Law and How We Use it* (Oxford, Clarendon Press, 1994) 29. Baxter (n 87) 284 considered that the Convention 'carries internal evidence' that 'it was intended to declare existing customary law', but it was declaring laws on many fronts (on criminality, on the jurisdictional infrastructure, on dispute settlement etc) and it is difficult to discern *which* of these laws was in existence when the Genocide Convention was adopted. See further Schabas (n 50) 648–49.

[101] Geneva Convention on the High Seas (adopted 29 April 1958, entered into force 30 September 1962) 450 UNTS 11. No preamble was included for the 1958 Geneva Convention on the Territorial Sea and Contiguous Zone (adopted 29 April 1958, entered into force 10 September 1964) (516 UNTS 205) or for the 1958 Geneva Convention on the Continental Shelf (adopted 29 April 1958, entered into force 10 June 1964) (499 UNTS 311). The 1958 Geneva Convention on Fishing and Conservation of the Living Resources on the High Seas (adopted 29 April 1958, entered into force 20 March 1966) (559 UNTS 285) did contain a preamble, but made no reference to codification or, indeed, to progressive development ('there is a clear necessity that [problems] be solved, whenever possible, on the basis of international cooperation through the concerted action of all the States concerned').

[102] Vienna Convention on the Law of Treaties (adopted 23 May 1969, entered into force 27 January 1980) 1155 UNTS 331. To similar effect, see the penultimate preambular recital of the United Nations Convention on the Law of the Sea (n 37): 'Believing that the codification and progressive development of the law of the sea achieved in this Convention will contribute to the strengthening of peace, security, cooperation and friendly relations among all nations in conformity with the principles of justice and equal rights and will promote the economic and social advancement of all peoples of the world, in accordance with the Purposes and Principles of the United Nations as set forth in the Charter.' It is a formulation that has also appeared in General Assembly Resolutions, eg, UNGA Res 2625 (XXV) (24 October 1970) UN Doc A/RES/2625 (XXV) ('Considering that the progressive development and codification of the following principles'). See V Lowe, *International Law* (Oxford, Oxford University Press, 2007) 118.

[103] Though not all treaties are susceptible to them – Jennings (n 7) 307 wrote of 'the baneful influences of a misunderstanding of the rubric of codification'. Also, '[t]he Chicago Civil Aviation Conference of 1944 was not called a codification conference, nor is the word code mentioned in any one of the ninety-six articles of the resulting Convention; yet can it be doubted that this Treaty, which provides a single set of rules covering every aspect of aviation law and replacing the two great regional systems which

that tell us very little about the status of specific propositions contained within those very treaties: the *desire* to codify does not necessarily entail the *success* of an exercise of codification; the successful codification of one proposition does not mean that all propositions contained within the same treaty have been duly codified; an effort committed to the codification *and* progressive development of the law does not tell us which provision[104] – indeed, which parts of which provisions[105] – are codifications and which are otherwise.[106]

It is interesting that in Article 15 of the 1947 Statute of the International Law Commission, the expression 'codification of international law' is used to mean 'the more precise formulation and systemization of rules of international law in fields where there already has been extensive State practice, precedent and doctrine'. Note how the emphasis here is very much on the *rules* themselves, in contrast to what is necessarily meant by the 'progressive development of international law' ('used for convenience as meaning the preparation of draft conventions on subjects which have not yet been regulated by international law or in regard to which the law has not yet been sufficiently developed in the practice of States'). Progressive development can therefore relate to entire 'subjects' or fields of study awaiting legal regulation, though, at the same time, it was also contemplated that it could encompass innovation in 'the law' – that is, 'rules' – that had 'not yet been sufficiently developed in the practice of States'.

From this, it would appear that the crucial difference – the crucial distinguishing factor – between codification and progressive development rests on the fact that codification assumes that there is some pre-existing normative activity that is

had hitherto divided the world between them, is any less a code of international law in every proper sense of the word?' (ibid).

[104] Note how the preamble to the 1907 Hague Convention (IV) (n 93) spoke in terms of the *revision* of the general laws and customs of war, 'either with the view to defining them with greater precision or to confining them with such limits as would mitigate their severity as far as possible'.

[105] Compare, for instance, the first sentence of art 44(3) of Protocol I (n 33) ('In order to promote the protection of the civilian population from the effects of hostilities, combatants are obliged to distinguish themselves from the civilian population while they are engaged in an attack or in a military operation preparatory to an attack') with the second sentence of that provision ('Recognising, however, that there are situations in armed conflicts where, owing to the nature of the hostilities an armed combatant cannot so distinguish himself, he shall retain his status as a combatant, provided that, in such situations, he carries his arms openly: (a) during each military engagement, and (b) during such time as he is visible to the adversary while he is engaged in a military deployment preceding the launching of an attack in which he is to participate'). The former sentence has been regarded as 'a long-standing rule of customary international law', a form of words not applied to the second sentence (or 'exception') to the general rule contained in the first sentence: Henckaerts and Doswald-Beck (n 33) 384 and 387–89. See also M Bothe, KJ Partsch and WA Solf, *New Rules for Victims of Armed Conflicts: Commentary on the Two 1977 Protocols Additional to the Geneva Conventions of 1949*, 2nd revised edn (Leiden, Martinus Nijhoff, 2013) 285–89.

[106] Hence Draft Conclusion 12 of Sir Michael Wood, Special Rapporteur of the International Law Commission (2013–18) on 'Identification of Customary International Law': 'A treaty provision may reflect or come to reflect a rule of customary international law if it is established that the provision in question: (a) at the time when the treaty was concluded, codifies an existing rule of customary international law; (b) has led to the crystallization of an emerging rule of customary international law; or (c) has generated a new rule of customary international law, by giving rise to a general practice accepted as law.' Note, too, how Baxter (n 87) 278 makes reference to 'the treaty or the individual clause of a treaty'.

calling out for the formalised expression of some sort;[107] the law already presents itself as a going concern such that, as Judge Max Sorensen put it in his dissenting opinion in the *North Sea Continental Shelf Cases* in February 1969: 'There are treaty provisions which simply formulate rules of international law which have already been generally accepted as part of international customary law, and it is beyond dispute that the rules embodied and formulated in such provisions are applicable to all States, whether or not they are parties to the treaty'.[108] And as for the progressive development of the law as steered by any treaty, 'it is equally clear that there are treaty provisions which are intended to modify the existing legal situation, whether they change the content of existing rules or regulate matters which have not been previously regulated by international law. Rules set forth in such treaty provisions are neither binding upon nor can be invoked by non-contracting States'.[109]

While this framework might seem clear and uncontroversial,[110] Judge Sorenson did go on to admit that 'this distinction between codification and progressive development may be difficult to apply rigorously to the facts of international legal relations',[111] setting out his thinking in the following terms:

> Although theoretically clear and distinguishable, the two notions tend in practice to overlap or to leave between them an intermediate area in which it is not possible to indicate precisely where codification ends and progressive development begins. The very act of formulating or restating an existing customary rule may have the effect of defining its contents more precisely and removing such doubts as may have existed as to its exact scope or the modalities of its application. The opportunity may also be taken of adapting the rule to contemporary conditions, whether factual or legal, in the international community. On the other hand, a treaty purporting to create new law may be based on a certain amount of State practice and doctrinal opinion which has not yet crystallized into customary law. It may start, not from *tabula rasa*, but from a customary rule *in statu nascendi*.[112]

[107] Though see Jennings (n 7) 302 (on 'codification' as 'any systematic statement of the whole or part of the law in written form, and that it does not necessarily imply a process which leave the main substance of the law unchanged, even though this may be true of some cases'). This is to be distinguished from 'codification' in its ordinary meaning, where it 'certainly indicates a written form of law' as 'codification in this very strict sense, however useful it may be in consolidating the already developed rules of a mature system, can have little place in a comparatively undeveloped system like international law' (ibid). Also, '[t]he whole point of traditional codification is not only to create a new source of law but also to sweep away the old' (at 306).

[108] *North Sea Continental Shelf* (n 3) 242. See further Higgins (n 100) 28–29 (and the reference to 'what is already customary international law'; 'pre-existing customary law'; 'already customary law'; '[t]he prohibition against genocide clearly pre-existed the Convention as a prohibition of customary international law'; 'a repetition of existing customary international law').

[109] Again, *per* Judge Sorenson in *North Sea Continental Shelf* (ibid). Judge Sorenson's point of focus is on treaty provisions, although it should not go unnoticed how closely his formulation bears on the Statute of the International Law Commission (ie, 'or regulate matters which have not previously been regulated by international law').

[110] Making it difficult to accept the notion of 'actual or prospective codifications': Lowe (n 102) 86.

[111] *North Sea Continental Shelf* (n 3) 242.

[112] ibid 242–43. As evidence of this overlapping or 'intermediate area', Judge Sorensen cited the following passage from the International Law Commission, 'Report of the International Law Commission

There is in this statement a recognition of the virtues of codification, but, more especially, there is also a clear nod to the complexities associated with or even inherent in that undertaking: effectively, the unmarked boundary between codification and progressive development and the existence of 'an intermediate area' that, for better or worse, counts as neither one thing nor the other.[113] It is instructive that, in articulating his general scepticism towards the idea of codification several decades earlier,[114] Lassa Oppenheim had described himself as 'decidedly not a blind and enthusiastic admirer of codification in general',[115] and we find in his work perhaps an even deeper equivocation about the overall merits of codification at the very moment he was tilting towards its inevitability:[116]

> Codification certainly interferes with the so-called organic growth of the law through usage into custom. It is true that a law, once codified, cannot so easily adapt itself to the merits of the individuality of single cases which come under it. It is further a fact, which cannot be denied, that together with codification there frequently enters into courts of justice and into the area of juridical literature a hair-splitting tendency and an interpretation of the law which clings often more to the letter and the word of the law than to its spirit and principles. And it is not at all a fact that codification does away with controversies altogether. Codification certainly clears up many questions of law which have been hitherto debatable, but it creates at the same time new controversies. And, lastly, all jurists know very well that the art of legislation is still in its infancy and not at all highly developed. The hands of legislators are very often clumsy, and legislation does often more harm than good.[117]

VII. On the *North Sea Continental Shelf Cases* (1969)

A closer understanding of the relationship between treaties – multilateral treaties specifically – and customary international law emerged following the judgment

Covering the Work of its Eight Session' (23 April–4 July 1956) UN Doc A/3159, para 26: 'Not only may there be wide differences of opinion as to whether a subject is already "sufficiently developed in practice", but also several of the provisions adopted by the Commission, based on a "recognized principle of international law", have been framed in a such a way as to place them in the "progressive development" category. Although it tried at first to specify which Articles fell into one and which into the other category, the Commission has had to abandon the attempt, as several do not wholly belong to either.'

[113] However, consider Jennings (n 7) 302 ('it is assumed that "codification" means any systematic statement of the whole or part of the law in written form, and that it does not necessarily imply a process which leaves the main substance of the law unchanged, even though this may be true of some cases. In other words, codification properly conceived is itself a method for the progressive development of the law').

[114] Perhaps counter-intuitively given the 'improvement' this could entail for the 'science' of international law: L Oppenheim, 'The Science of International Law: Its Task and Method' (1908) 2 *American Journal of International Law* 313, 356.

[115] Oppenheim (n 14) 39 (§34) (while accepting that a 'movement for … codification' had arisen against '[t]he lack of precision which is natural to the majority of the rules of the Law of Nations on account of its slow and gradual growth' (ibid 35 (§30))).

[116] '[O]n the other hand', he wrote, 'the fact must be recognized that history has given its verdict in favour of codification' (ibid 40 (§34)).

[117] ibid 39–40 (§34).

of the International Court of Justice in the *North Sea Continental Shelf Cases* in February 1969. Denmark and the Netherlands were parties to the 1958 Geneva Convention on the Continental Shelf, whereas the Federal Republic of Germany was not.[118] At issue in this case on the delimitation of the continental shelf between these three countries was the so-called equidistance rule appearing in Article 6 of the Convention: the claim presented by Denmark and the Netherlands to the Court was that, though not 'contractually bound' by the 1958 Convention, that Convention 'or the régime of the Convention, and in particular Article 6 has become binding on the Federal Republic in another way – namely because, by conduct, by public statements and proclamations, and in other ways, the Republic has unilaterally assumed the obligations of the Convention; or has manifested its acceptance of the conventional régime; or has recognized it as being generally applicable to the delimitation of continental shelf areas'.[119] This aspect of the unilateral assumption of obligations is one that has often been elided in the literature or has come to be overshadowed by the much more prominent and well-rehearsed dialectic between treaty and custom,[120] but it is one that is truly deserving of greater attention because of the fertile ground supplied by the context of a multilateral treaty – any multilateral treaty for that matter – for 'acts performed by a single state' that have legal consequences for that State and, indeed, in turn, for other States.[121]

What is significant for our purposes is the shape that the Court gave to the evidential burden for this category of commitment in public international law; 'it is clear', concluded the Court, that 'only a very definite consistent course of conduct on the part of a State in the situation of the Federal Republic could justify the Court in upholding [these contentions].'[122] And, in its view, that course of

[118] Denmark since 10 June 1964 and the Netherlands since 20 March 1966. The Federal Republic had signed the Convention on the Continental Shelf (n 101) on 30 October 1958, but had never ratified it. The Convention entered into force on 10 June 1964.

[119] *North Sea Continental Shelf* (n 3) 25 (§27). Especially as the Court then went on to refer to the suggestion that 'the Federal Republic had held itself so assuming, accepting or recognizing, in such a manner as to cause other States, and in particular Denmark and the Netherlands, to rely on the attitude thus taken up' (at 25). The Court subsequently made reference to 'a situation of estoppel' where the Federal Republic would be 'precluded from denying the applicability of the conventional régime, by reason of past conduct, declarations, etc., which not only clearly and consistently evidenced acceptance of that régime, but also had caused Denmark and the Netherlands, in reliance on such conduct, detrimentally to change position or suffer some prejudice', but the Court found 'no evidence whatsoever' of this in the instant case (at 26 (§30)).

[120] Most classically O Schachter, 'Entangled Treaty and Custom' in Y Dinstein and M Tabory (eds), *International Law at a Time of Perplexity: Essays in Honour of Shabtai Rosenne* (Dordrecht, Martinus Nijhoff, 1989) 717. Though see KN Guernsey, 'The North Sea Continental Shelf Cases' (2000) 27 *Ohio Northern University Law Review* 141, 145–46.

[121] Jennings and Watts (n 33) 1187–88 (§576). Note how the International Law Commission referred to 'unilateral behaviour on the international plane' in the first preambular recital to its 'Guiding Principles applicable to unilateral declarations of States capable of creating legal obligations' (58th session in 2006) UN Doc A/61/10. For Brownlie, although an unratified treaty has no 'binding force either in the law of treaties or otherwise', he regarded such instruments as 'candidates for public reaction, approving or not, as the case may be: they may stand for a threshold of consensus and confront states in a significant way'. See I Brownlie, *Principles of Public International Law*, 2nd edn (Oxford, Clarendon Press, 1973) 2.

[122] *North Sea Continental Shelf* (n 3) 25 (§28).

conduct had to be directed towards demonstrating 'a real intention to manifest acceptance or recognition of the applicability of the conventional régime' which, the Court maintained in the absence of becoming a party to a given treaty, 'is not lightly to be presumed'.[123] In the end, though, after reviewing all of the evidence before it, the Court considered that 'none of the elements invoked' by Denmark and the Netherlands had been 'decisive', for 'each is ultimately negative or inconclusive; all are capable of varying interpretations or explanations'.[124] A normative possibility had thus been thwarted on account of insufficient proofs of intention that had been presented to the Court.

It was then and only then that the Court attended to the claim of Denmark and the Netherlands that the identified method of maritime delimitation was not confined to 'a merely conventional obligation' since it 'is or must now be regarded as involving a rule that is part of the *corpus* of general international law [which] is binding on the Federal Republic automatically and independently of any specific assent, direct or indirect'.[125] It was at this moment that custom entered the reckoning, with the Court adhering to the view that a given rule could command support from more than one of the formal sources of law.[126] Importantly, the Court observed that, in the course of their oral presentations before the Court, Denmark and the Netherlands had claimed that it had not been their contention that Article 6 of the Geneva Convention 'embodied already received rules of customary law in the sense that the Convention was merely declaratory of existing rules'; apparently, '[t]heir contention was, rather, that although prior to the Conference, continental shelf law was only in the formative stage, and State practice lacked uniformity, yet "the process of the definition and consolidation of the emerging customary law took place through the work of the International Law Commission, the reaction of governments to that work and the proceedings of the Geneva Conference";

[123] ibid. It is then that the Court moved on to consider the 'situation of estoppel' (n 119). However, the Federal Republic of Germany was a signatory to the Convention and, even at that point in time, that status carried with it certain legal implications: AD McNair, *The Law of Treaties* (Oxford, Oxford University Press, 1961) 199.

[124] *North Sea Continental Shelf* (n 3) 26 (§32). Of the 'various acts' presented to the Court 'as being indicative of the Federal Republic's acceptance of the régime of Article 6', it is worthwhile recalling those mentioned by the Court in this passage from its judgment: 'that at the Geneva Conference the Federal Republic did not take formal objection to Article 6 and eventually signed the Convention without entering any reservation in respect of that provision; that it at one time announced its intention to ratify the Convention; that in its public declarations concerning its continental shelf rights it appeared to rely on, or at least cited, certain provisions of the Geneva Convention. In this last connection a good deal has been made of the joint Minute signed in Bonn, on 4 August 1964, between the then-negotiating delegations of the Federal Republic and the Netherlands. But this minute made it clear that what the Federal Republic was seeking was an agreed division, rather than a delimitation of the central North Sea continental shelf areas, and the reference it made to Article 6 was specifically to the first sentence of paragraphs 1 and 2 of that Article, which speaks exclusively of delimitation by agreement and not at all of the use of the equidistance method' (§31).

[125] ibid 28 (§37).

[126] An approach it has embraced in its subsequent jurisprudence – in particular, *Military and Paramilitary Activities in and against Nicaragua (Merits)* [1986] ICJ Rep 14, 94 (§176) ('customary international law continues to exist alongside treaty law').

and this emerging customary law became "crystallized in the adoption of the Continental Shelf Convention by the Conference"'.[127]

Most crucially, this introduction of the phenomenon of crystallisation of an emerging custom was given a specific chronological imprimatur – that is, a certain identifiable point in time – in terms of the lifespan of the respective norm: at this point in its judgment, note how the Court makes reference to what it calls 'continental shelf law' or 'the' and 'this emerging customary law' as opposed to the entire Convention itself (which was its wont at a previous point in the judgment ('or the régime of the Convention, and in particular Article 6')).[128] Later in its ruling, the Court concluded that 'the Geneva Convention did not embody or crystallize any pre-existing or emergent rule of customary law, according to which the delimitation of continental shelf areas between adjacent States must, unless the Parties otherwise agree, be carried out on an equidistance–special circumstances basis'.[129] We are thus being invited to inform a sense as to the precise moment that this law – this rule on continental shelf delimitation between adjacent States – had come into being where it is intricately, intimately associated with the moment of the adoption of the 1958 Geneva Convention.[130]

Contrast the invocation of crystallisation by the Court in the later decision of the *Fisheries Jurisdiction Case* between the UK and Iceland,[131] which concerned the Second United Nations Conference on the Law of the Sea in Geneva in March and April 1960 and its impact on custom. There the Court had said that:

> [A]fter that Conference the law evolved through the practice of States on the basis of the debates and near-agreements at the Conference. Two concepts have crystallized as customary law in recent years arising out of the general consensus revealed at that Conference. The first is the concept of the fishery zone, the area in which a State may claim exclusive fishery jurisdiction independently of its territorial sea; the extension of that fishery zone up to a 12-mile limit from the baselines appears now to be generally accepted. The second is the concept of preferential rights of fishing in adjacent waters in favour of the coastal State in a situation of special dependence on its coastal fisheries, this preference operating in regard to other States concerned in the exploitation of the same fisheries.[132]

What is of particular interest to us here is the timing of the crystallisation of custom: while the Court does not commit to the identification of any actual or explicit point in time ('in recent years') for the emergence of the customs with which it is engaged, it is clear that the 'general consensus' of the Second Conference

[127] *North Sea Continental Shelf* (n 3) 38 (§61).

[128] (n 119).

[129] *North Sea Continental Shelf* (n 3) 41 (§69).

[130] See further RK Gardiner, *International Law* (London, Longman, 2003) 115: 'Crystallisation signifies the case where the act of making the treaty fixes a proposition sufficiently for it to become a rule of customary law at that moment, some variance of practice or divergence of *opinio* [*juris*] having prevented its earlier emergence.'

[131] *Fisheries Jurisdiction Case (United Kingdom of Great Britain and Northern Ireland v Iceland) (Merits)* [1974] ICJ Rep 3.

[132] ibid 23 (§52).

was indispensable to the formation of *both* of these customs, and it is in this more general sense that the Court has recourse to the idiom of *crystallisation*.[133] The crystallisation occurs – indeed, the *crystallisations* occur – after the Conference is over; they post-date that Conference and are independent of any treaty adoption or development, so that crystallisation is used in a more general sense to depict the emergence of a given custom norm outside or beyond the treaty context.[134]

Having established that there had been no crystallisation of custom as a result of the adoption of the 1958 Geneva Convention on the Continental Shelf in the *North Sea Continental Shelf Cases*, the Court then went on to consider whether crystallisation had occurred after the adoption of that treaty, for, as claimed by Denmark and the Netherlands:

> [E]ven if there was at that date of the Geneva Convention no rule of customary international law in favour of the equidistance principle, and no such rule was crystallized in Article 6 of the Convention, nevertheless such a rule has come into being since the Convention, partly because of its own impact, partly on the basis of subsequent State practice – and that this rule, being now a rule of customary international law binding on all States, including therefore the Federal Republic, should be declared applicable to the delimitation of the boundaries between the Parties' respect continental shelf areas in the North Sea.[135]

The Court evidently had no principled objection to adopting this line of analysis for, as it said, 'this process is a perfectly possible one and does from time to time occur: it constitutes indeed one of the recognized methods by which new rules of customary international law may be formed',[136] but it was equally of the view that 'this result is not lightly to be regarded as having been attained'.[137] It could not therefore be gainsaid that the Convention had had such an impact in practice and, again, the marshalled evidence was found wanting by the Court. And it is from this passage that we can discern the two senses of crystallisation: a more specific sense in which a rule is crystallised in – or by virtue – of a treaty; and another, more general, sense where crystallisation occurs beyond the adoption of that treaty.[138]

[133] See also Henckaerts and Doswald-Beck (n 33) 523 (Rule 147), 525, 572 (Rule 156) and 590 (ibid) (on the crystallisation of a customary rule). See, however, ibid xlix (on the International Law Association's position on multilateral treaties and the crystallisation of emerging custom). Crystallisation is notably not mentioned in the Statute of the International Law Commission.

[134] To be contrasted again with the stance of the Court in respect of the Draft Convention on the Law of the Sea of 28 August 1981, where 'it could not ignore any provision of the draft convention if it came to the conclusion that the content of such provision is binding upon all members of the international community because it embodies or crystallizes a pre-existing or emergent rule of customary law'. See *Case Concerning the Continental Shelf (Tunisia/Libyan Arab Jamahiriya)* [1982] ICJ Rep 18, 38 (§24). This is precisely the approach of the Court in *North Sea Continental Shelf Cases*, which the Court referred to in its February 1982 judgment (ibid 46 (§42)).

[135] *North Sea Continental Shelf* (n 3) 41 (§70).

[136] ibid 41 (§71).

[137] ibid.

[138] Gardiner (n 130) 115 refers to this latter process as 'consolidation' or 'subsequent consolidation' ('where practice and *opinio* [*juris*] converge upon a treaty *after* the treaty has been adopted'). He observes that this term is a 'convenient label' rather than a 'term of art' and 'does not describe the process alone but also the result'.

And, as an additional matter for the Court, for Article 6 of the Geneva Convention to be seen in this light would involve 'treating that Article as a norm-creating provision which, while only conventional or contractual in origin, has since passed into the general *corpus* of international law, and is now accepted as such by the *opinio juris*, so as to have become binding even for countries which have never, and do not, become parties to the Convention'.[139] The focus of the Court, then, was on the specific content of the relevant rule, and the formulation presented here is interesting because its implication is that not all provisions contained within a treaty are necessarily 'norm-creating';[140] for the Court, it was necessary that 'the provision concerned should, at all events, be of a fundamentally norm-creating character such as could be regarded as forming the basis of a general rule of law'.[141]

Set against this standard and '[c]onsidered *in abstracto*[,] the equidistance principle might be said to fulfil this requirement'.[142] Yet, the Court continued:

> [I]n the particular form in which it is embodied in Article 6 of the Geneva Convention, and having regard to the relationship of that Article to other provisions of the Convention, this must be open to some doubt. In the first place, Article 6 is so framed as to put second the obligation to make use of the equidistance method, causing it to come after a primary obligation to effect delimitation by agreement. Such a primary obligation constitutes an unusual preface to what is claimed to be a potential general rule of law. Without attempting to enter into, still less to pronounce upon any question of *jus cogens*, it is well understood that, in practice, rules of international law can, by agreement, be derogated from in particular cases, or as between particular parties – but this is not normally the subject of any express provision, as it is in Article 6 of the Geneva Convention. Secondly the part played by the notion of special circumstances relative to the principle of equidistance as embodied in Article 6, and the very considerable, still unresolved controversies as to the exact meaning and scope of this notion, must raise further doubts as to the potentially norm-creating character of the rule. Finally, the faculty of making reservations to Article 6, while it might not of itself prevent the equidistance principle being eventually received as general law, does add considerably to the difficulty of regarding this result as having been brought about (or being potentially possible) on the basis of the Convention.[143]

Before we close this section, it is worth emphasising that, having identified the relevant rule for its analysis, the Court did not then immediately launch into an empirical investigation in order to ascertain where the treaty rule stands as a matter of custom; rather, it trained its focus inward by considering the rule itself to see whether it possessed what the Court had labelled a 'fundamentally norm-creating character'.[144] We can perhaps appreciate why this formed the structure of the Court's thinking: the Court wanted to be clear for itself what the (treaty)

[139] *North Sea Continental Shelf* (n 3) 41 (§71).
[140] ibid.
[141] *North Sea Continental Shelf* (n 3) 41–42 (§72).
[142] ibid 42 (§72).
[143] ibid. See further Higgins (n 100) 30.
[144] (n 141).

rule demanded as the preface to its enquiries into the state of the (customary) rule. Note, though, how, in setting to this task, the Court initially refers to 'the equidistance principle',[145] but then – almost immediately – goes on to speak of 'the particular form in which it is embodied in Article 6 of the Geneva Convention'.[146] It is here that the Court opens up in a much deeper way about the 'fundamentally norm-creating character'[147] of a given rule, and it does so precisely because of the proclaimed transposition from treaty to custom ('such as could be regarded as forming the basis of a general rule of law').[148] We learn that it matters a great deal how a given rule is designed or articulated, we learn of the importance of the determinacy of that rule and, finally, we learn of the significance of the permissibility of reservations in respect of that same rule.[149] Let us deal with each of these considerations in turn.

First, the design of the rule: the Court observed how Article 6 of the Geneva Convention is 'framed' such that it enlists the equidistance method as a 'second' obligation, 'causing it to come after a primary obligation to effect delimitation by agreement'.[150] In relevant part, Article 6 of that Convention provides as follows: 'Where the same continental shelf is adjacent to the territories of two adjacent States, the boundary of the continental shelf shall be determined by agreement between them. In the absence of agreement, and unless another boundary line is justified by special circumstances, the boundary shall be determined by application of the principle of equidistance from the nearest points of the baselines from which the breadth of the territorial sea of each State is measured.'[151] While the Court was keen to emphasise the essential relation between the primary obligation and second obligation in its identification of the relevant rule,[152] it is clear from this formulation that there is a further factor that enters this mix – Article 6's reference to 'special circumstances'. To be sure, the Court did touch upon this point when it turned to deal with its second consideration (mentioning 'the part played by the notion of special circumstances relative to the principle of equidistance as

[145] (n 135 and n 143).

[146] (n 143). Also note the Court's reference to '[t]he status of the rule in the Convention [that] depends mainly on the processes that led the Commission to propose it'. *North Sea Continental Shelf* (n 3) 38 (§62).

[147] (n 141).

[148] ibid.

[149] art 12(1) of the Convention on the Continental Shelf (n 101) provided that '[a]t the time of signature, ratification or accession, any State may make reservations to articles of the Convention other than to articles 1 to 3 inclusive'.

[150] (n 143).

[151] art 6(2). art 6(1), on the delimitation of the continental shelf for opposite States, is structured along similar lines (though the Convention refers to this as the median line): 'Where the same continental shelf is adjacent to the territories of two or more States whose coasts are opposite each other, the boundary of the continental shelf appertaining to such States shall be determined by agreement between them. In the absence of agreement, and unless another boundary line is justified by special circumstances, the boundary is the median line, every point of which is equidistant from the nearest points of the baselines from which the breadth of the territorial sea of each State is measured.'

[152] Captured by the elegant expression of the primary obligation as 'an unusual preface to what is claimed to be a potential general rule of law': (n 143).

embodied in Article 6'),[153] but since the Court was concerned at that very moment with the operational logic of the rule,[154] it is incumbent to ask whether the presence of 'special circumstances' forms part of the second obligation contained in Article 6[155] or whether it might constitute an exception to that obligation.[156]

More problematically still is the precise relation between primary and second obligations. Above all, this has to do with their timing or temporal association. According to Article 6, the secondary obligation becomes active '[i]n the absence of agreement': when or where there is an absence of agreement, 'the boundary shall be determined by application of the principle of equidistance from the nearest points of the baselines from which the breadth of the territorial sea of each State is measured'.[157] The Court rightfully had concerns with 'the very considerable, still unresolved controversies as to the exact meaning and scope of [the] notion' of special circumstances,[158] but there is a prior and indispensable question of when it can be said that an 'absence of agreement' had come to pass. In other words, the problem of 'exact meaning' would appear to pervade other aspects of Article 6 as well, including the hinge connecting the first and second obligations – at least as viewed by the Court. Crucial though this matter may have been,[159] it is separate to the question of who decides – and who decides conclusively – on this notion of *absence*: is it to be one or other or both of the parties, operating as they are in a decentralised legal order?

Turning to the second consideration on the mind of the Court, here the Court moved to the 'still unresolved controversies' of the 'exact meaning and scope' of 'special circumstances', but, as has been noted, this concern has more general application for Article 6 all told ('agreement' versus 'absence of agreement', 'shall be determined' etc). At issue here is what might be termed the *determinacy* of the rule or '[t]he pre-eminent literary property [of] the rule text', essentially 'that which makes its message clear'.[160] And, in a rather brief refrain, the Court made reference to 'the potentially norm-creating character of the rule' in order to convey the broad thrust of its concern.[161] We can begin to appreciate why the Court may

[153] ibid.
[154] Hence: 'Without attempting to enter into, still less to pronounce upon any question of *jus cogens*, it is well understood that, in practice, rules of international law can, by agreement, be derogated from in particular cases, or as between particular parties – but this is not normally the subject of any express provision, as it is in Article 6 of the Geneva Convention' (ibid).
[155] Note the Court's reference to 'an equidistance–special circumstances basis' earlier in its judgment (n 129).
[156] Note the construction of Jennings and Watts (n 33) 777 (§323) (the Geneva Convention 'provides … that the continental shelf boundaries shall be determined by agreement between the parties; and then provides, "in the absence of agreement", for the application of the equidistance principle, "unless another boundary line is justified by special circumstances"').
[157] art 6(2) of the Convention on the Continental Shelf (n 101).
[158] (n 143).
[159] For example, is it altogether conceivable when an absence of an agreement might be said to occur: how is this to be distinguished from protracted/prolonged negotiations as prefatory/preparatory to any such agreement?
[160] TM Franck, *The Power of Legitimacy among Nations* (New York, Oxford University Press, 1990) 52.
[161] (n 143).

have done so; in a way that custom simply does not, treaties afford opportunities for high rhetorical indulgences, diplomatic compromises and drafting ambiguities such that it should not be supposed that these are easily translatable into actionable legal propositions as a matter of custom.[162] There is the additional point of how a treaty rule may be conceived on the basis of certain assumptions or apparatuses stemming from that same treaty such that the 'norm-creating character' of the rule – what the Court had in much the same breath characterised as 'a potential general rule of law'[163] – is somehow stifled: it complicates the transposition from treaty to custom as a matter of principle, and perhaps fatally so.[164] As the Court advised in the *Nicaragua Case* in June 1986, 'a principle enshrined in a treaty, if reflected in customary international law, may well be so unencumbered with the conditions and modalities surrounding it in the treaty'.[165]

It is this notion of encumbering – or conventional encumbering, if we are to be more precise[166] – that usefully captures the point at hand. In a judgment otherwise given to the closeness (one might even say mirroring) of treaty and custom,[167] the Court could not find that a customary equivalent for the 'reporting requirement' for the right of self-defence as contained in Article 51 of the Charter of the United Nations.[168] And it did so precisely because this requirement was attended by such conventional encumbering: 'Whatever influence the Charter may have had on customary international law it is not a condition of the lawfulness of the

[162] Consider, for instance, art I of the Treaty of Amity, Economic Relations, and Consular Rights between the United States of America and Iran (signed 15 August 1955, entered into force 16 June 1957) 8 UST 900: 'There shall be firm and enduring peace and sincere friendship between the United States of America and Iran.'

[163] (n 143).

[164] Note, eg, C Ryngaert, *Jurisdiction in International Law*, 2nd edn (Oxford, Oxford University Press, 2015) 124: 'The operation of the *aut dedere* requirement is indeed limited to States Parties, which pool their sovereignty and explicitly authorize each other to exercise jurisdiction over crimes committed by their nationals in their territory.' This should be contrasted with the arrangements for the prosecution of war crimes: note how, in their joint separate opinion in *Case Concerning the Arrest Warrant of 11 April 2000 (Democratic Republic of Congo v Belgium)* [2002] ICJ Rep 3, 75 (§42), Judges Higgins, Kooijmans and Buergenthal considered '[w]hether this obligation … is an obligation only of treaty law, *inter partes*, or whether it is now, *at least as regards the offences articulated in the treaties*, an obligation of customary international law' (emphasis in original).

[165] *Nicaragua Case* (n 126) 105 (§200).

[166] See also the Court's observation that '[i]t would … seem apparent that the attitude referred to expresses an *opinio juris* respecting such rule (or set of rules), *to be thenceforth treated separately from the provisions, especially those of an institutional kind, to which it is subject on the treaty-law plane of the Charter*' (ibid 100 (§188), emphasis added). What the Court evidently had in mind was a 'rule or set of rules' – twice referred to by the Court in this very paragraph – which were of general application, and not 'merely that of a "reiteration or elucidation" of the treaty commitment undertaken in the Charter'. And, earlier in its judgment, the Court had noted how '[a] State may accept a rule contained in a treaty not simply because it favours the application of the rule itself, but also because the treaty establishes what the State regards as desirable institutions or mechanisms to ensure implementation of the rule' (ibid 95 (§178)).

[167] In the *Nicaragua Case* the Court more than once referred to the 'identical' nature of treaty and customary rules, or of a treaty rule that 'parallels a rule of customary international law': ibid 95 (§178).

[168] This appears in the second sentence of art 51 of the Charter (signed 26 June 1945, entered into force 24 October 1945) 1 UNTS XVI: 'Measures taken by Members in the exercise of this right of self-defence shall be immediately reported to the Security Council and shall not in any way affect the

use of force in self-defence that a procedure so closely dependent on the content of a treaty commitment and of the institutions established by it, should have been followed.'[169] In this assessment, it may be advisable, too, to reflect on *how* a conventional rule conceives of any intended general reach: note how in the United Nations Convention of the Law of the Sea, some of the provisions are actually addressed to *every* State,[170] as opposed to merely its State or States Parties.[171] This might be taken to suggest that, as far as the treaty is concerned and as a matter of legislative principle, the rule is amenable to customary iteration – that if this has not already happened by the time of the treaty, then there is no reason why this cannot so transpire in the future.[172] By way of further example, Article VI of the Genocide Convention is notably not framed in terms of States Parties and States Parties alone;[173] 'a competent tribunal of the State in the territory of which the act was committed' has all the hallmarks of speaking beyond the conventional paradigm and may well implicate the 'universal reach' of that particular obligation.[174]

authority and responsibility of the Security Council under the present Charter to take at any time such action as it deems necessary in order to maintain or restore international peace and security.'

[169] *Nicaragua Case* (n 126) 105 (§200). See, too, the discussion in DW Greig, 'Self-Defence and the Security Council: What Does Article 51 Require?' (1991) 40 *International & Comparative Law Quarterly* 366, 369, 379–86; and, more recently, JA Green, 'The Article 51 Reporting Requirement for Self-Defense Actions' (2015) 55 *Virginia Journal of International Law* 563.

[170] Such as art 3 on the 'breadth of the territorial sea' ('Every State has the right to establish the breadth of its territorial sea up to a limit not exceeding 12 nautical miles, measured from baselines determined in accordance with this Convention'). The other provisions to do so are art 90 (right of navigation); art 91 (nationality of ships); art 94 (duties of the flag State); art 98 (duty to render assistance); art 99 (prohibition of the transport of slaves); art 105 (seizure of a pirate ship or aircraft); art 113 (breaking or injury of a submarine cable or pipeline); art 114 (breaking or injury by owners of a submarine cable or pipeline of another submarine cable or pipeline); art 115 (indemnity for loss incurred in avoiding injury to a submarine cable or pipeline); art 211 (pollution from vessels). Consider, too, the references to 'all States' in the Convention: arts 17 and 52 (right of innocent passage); art 58 (rights and duties of other States in the exclusive economic zone); art 79 (submarine cables and pipelines on the continental shelf); art 86 (application of the provisions of Part VII on the high seas); art 87 (freedom of the high seas); art 100 (duty to cooperate in the repression of piracy); art 108 (illicit traffic in narcotic drugs or psychotropic substances); art 109 (unauthorised broadcasting from the high seas); art 112 (right to lay submarine cable and pipelines); art 116 (right to fish on the high seas); art 117 (duty of States to adapt with respect to their nationals measures for the conservation of the living resources of the high seas); art 141 (use of the Area exclusively for peaceful purposes); art 205 (publication of reports); art 217 (enforcement by flag States); art 238 (right to conduct marine scientific research); art 256 (marine scientific research in the Area); art 257 (marine scientific research in the water column beyond the exclusive economic zone); art 260 (safety zones); art 274 (objectives of the Authority) and art 305 (signature). *cf* art 61 (conservation of the living resources) and art 119 (conservation of the living resources of the high seas) – which refers to 'all States concerned'. art 276 (establishment of regional centres) refers to '[a]ll States of a region'.

[171] As in the reference to 'all States Parties' in art 144 (transfer of technology); art 150 (policies relating to activities in the Area); art 151 (production policies); art 155 (the Review Conference); art 156 (establishment of the Authority); art 312 (amendment); art 313 (amendment by simplified procedure); art 314 (amendments to the provision of this Convention relating exclusively to activities in the Area); art 316 (entry into force of amendments); and art 319 (depositary).

[172] See further Crawford (n 4) 24 (where 'recitals in treaties and other international instruments (especially when in "all states" form)' is analysed as a material source of custom).

[173] As is done, for instance, with art V ('The Contracting Parties undertake to enact, in accordance with their respective Constitutions, the necessary legislation to give effect to the provisions of the present Convention, and, in particular, to provide effective penalties for persons guilty of genocide or any of the other acts enumerated in article III') and art XII ('Any Contracting Party may at any time,

And now for the final consideration of the Court: 'the faculty of making reservations to Article 6, while it might not of itself prevent the equidistance principle being eventually received as general law, does add considerably to the difficulty of regarding this result as having been brought about (or being potentially possible) on the basis of the Convention'.[175] Set against the two earlier considerations of the Court, this statement edged the Court closer towards the space of its empirical investigation of the acceptance of the principle of equidistance 'as general law',[176] but the Court did so in such a way that it was sounding an audible note of scepticism about the *possibility* of this acceptance ever occurring over time.[177] For the Court, this fact of 'the faculty of making reservations' to the rule enjoined an already troublesome history of the provision, where the formulation of the International Law Commission had been accepted 'almost unchanged', said the Court, at the Geneva Conference.[178] And that principle of equidistance 'as it now figures in Article 6 of the Convention, had been proposed by the Commission with considerable hesitation, somewhat on an experimental basis, at most *de lege ferenda*, and not at all *de lege lata* or as an emerging rule of customary international law. This is clearly not the sort of foundation on which Article 6 of the Convention could be said to have reflected or crystallized such a rule'.[179]

Yet, as keen as the Court was to delve into and consider the relevance of aspects of the Convention other than Article 6, its approach does raise the urgent question of what considerations in their totality can and should be taken into account in arguing for a direct *equation* of custom.[180] For example, and most

by notification addressed to the Secretary-General of the United Nations, extend the application of the present Convention to all or any of the territories for the conduct of whose foreign relations that Contracting Party is responsible'). See also art I; art VI; art VII; art VIII; art IX; and art XV.

[174] CJ Tams, L Berster and B Schiffbauer, *Convention on the Prevention and Punishment of the Crime of Genocide: A Commentary* (Munich/Oxford/Baden-Baden, CH Beck/Hart/Nomos, 2014) 241. See also at 245 (Art VI as 'the only provision addressing literally every state in the world').

[175] (n 143).

[176] ibid.

[177] To similar effect, consider the reasoning of the UN Human Rights Committee in its General Comment No 24 (52): 'General comment on issues relating to reservations made upon ratification or accession to the Covenant or the Optional Protocols thereto, or in relation to declarations under article 41 of the Covenant' (11 November 1994) UN Doc CCPR/C/21/Rev.1/Add.6 (§8).

[178] *North Sea Continental Shelf* (n 3) 38 (§62).

[179] ibid.

[180] Reservations were entered to the 1925 Geneva Protocol (n 48) and these have been regarded as 'persuasive evidence that a number of the parties did not initially regard the Protocol as declaratory of a rule of customary international law placing an unqualified obligation upon all States to refrain from the use of such methods of warfare' (Baxter (n 87) 284). It is interesting that Rule 74 of the ICRC Study on Customary International Humanitarian Law is categorical in its sweep – '[t]he use of chemical weapons is prohibited' – and it is a rule established for both international and non-international armed conflicts; Henckaerts and Doswald-Beck (n 33) 259. Yet, the Study also speaks of 'increasing evidence' – not necessarily conclusive evidence it must be said – 'that it may now be unlawful to retaliate in kind to another state's use of chemical weapons', and it does so on the basis that there are still 21 ('first-use') reservations to the Geneva Protocol, though 16 of these States are parties to the 1993 Chemical Weapons Convention (which contains a categorical prohibition). As the ICRC Study (at 260) concludes: 'This leaves only five States (Angola, Iraq, Israel, North Korea and Libya) which, under treaty law, could avail themselves of their reserved right to retaliate in kind to the first use of chemical weapons.'

famously, an integral component of the United Nations Convention on the Law of the Sea was that it was concluded as a 'package deal',[181] reached on a consensus basis and mindful 'that the problems of the ocean space are closely related and need to be considered as a whole'.[182] Most significantly, this meant a holistic outlook for the ocean space beyond the divisibility of regimes set out in the four Geneva Conventions in April 1958, an 'all-embracing package that incorporates the subject matter of all four of the Geneva Conventions into a single Convention'.[183] And, for the Court in *Case Concerning Continental Shelf* in June 1985, where both Libya and Malta had participated in the negotiations of the United Nations Convention on the Law of the Sea but had not become parties to it by the time of the judgment,[184] 'it cannot be denied that the 1982 Convention is of major importance, having been adopted by an overwhelming majority of States; hence it is clearly the duty of the Court, even independently of the references made to the Convention by the Parties, to consider in what degree any relevant provisions are binding upon the Parties as a rule of customary international law'.[185] The ambitious design of the Convention meant 'that consequential changes in the customary law of the continental shelf resulted' from the endorsement of the law on the exclusive economic zone in practice,[186] with the Court fully conscious of the connectedness of these two institutions.[187]

[181] H Caminos and MR Molitor, 'Progressive Development of International Law and the Package Deal' (1985) 79 *American Journal of International Law* 871, 873–74 (on the background of 'an interrelated package'). See further RY Jennings, 'Law-Making and the Package Deal' in *Le droit international, unité et diversité: Mélanges offerts à Paul Reuter* (Paris, A Pedone, 1981) 347.

[182] As it is put in the preamble to the United Nations Convention on the Law of the Sea (n 37). art 309 of this Convention makes clear that '[n]o reservations or exceptions may be made … unless expressly permitted by other articles of this Convention'.

[183] This is the first signal of the 'package concept' or 'package grounds' as discussed by P Allott, 'Power Sharing in the Law of the Sea' (1983) 77 *American Journal of International Law* 1, 12. Additionally, the Convention integrated 'what is in effect a major pollution convention and a major piece of international economic legislation (the deep seabed regime)'; Allott proceeds to consider three main parts of the Convention 'as subordinate integrated packages' (the general Law of the Sea, deep seabed, and pollution and marine scientific research) as well as 'some more recherché packages': the relationship between the territorial sea, the exclusive economic zone and transit passage through straits used for international navigation; the relationship between art 55 (the legal regime of the exclusive economic zone) and art 86 (the high seas); the relationship between the delimitation provisions (arts 15, 74 and 83) and art 298 (optional exception for delimitation disputes); and the relationship among arts 76 (definition of the continental shelf), art 134(4) (limits of the international seabed area) and Annex II of the Convention (Commission on the Limits of the Continental Shelf).

[184] Nor was the Convention yet in force. Libya had signed the Convention on 3 December 1984, but has never ratified it. Malta had the Convention signed on 10 December 1984, but only ratified it on 20 May 1993.

[185] *Case Concerning the Continental Shelf (Libyan Arab Jamahiriya/Malta)* [1985] ICJ Rep 13, 30 (§27). This is the same paragraph that contained the following observation: 'That the questions of entitlement and of delimitation of [the] continental shelf, on the one hand, and of delimitation of [the] continental shelf on the other, are not only distinct but are also complimentary is self-evident.'

[186] See AE Boyle, 'Reflections on the Treaty as Law-Making Instrument' in A Orakhelashvili and S Williams (eds), *40 Years of the Vienna Convention on the Law of Treaties* (London, British Institute of International and Comparative Law, 2010) 6. As the Court concluded in *Case Concerning the Continental Shelf* (n 185) 33 (§33): 'even though the present case relates only to the delimitation of the continental shelf and not to that of the exclusive economic zone, the principles and rules underlying

VIII. Final Reflections

This chapter has sought to chart the changes that have occurred over a much broader span of time in two of the formal sources of public international law – namely, treaties and custom as forms of authority that have been established by the discipline. As we have seen, our analysis has also broached the Martens Clause, or 'the principles of international law' as derived from 'the usages between civilized nations, from the laws of humanity, and the requirements of public conscience', although we have probed why these imperatives have not yielded results beyond the condition of war or armed conflict. There is also the question of how these 'principles' – or 'principles of international law',[188] as it is put in the original version of the Clause – cohere with or relate to the 'general principles of law recognized by civilized nations' as mentioned in the Statute of the International Court of Justice, the third formal source known to public international law.[189] For the most part, however, the interest of the chapter has been defined by the relationship between treaties and custom in the context of the expanded recourse to the instrument of the multilateral treaty and as foretold through the idioms of codification, crystallisation and progressive development. The meaning and significance of each of these notions have come into much starker relief with the social shift from custom to convention and from bilateral to multilateral treaties, though this to not to decry the irrepressible relevance that custom still manages to assert today.[190] There is considerable merit in our appreciation of the formal sources of public international law when focusing on the context or contexts in which laws are actually made,[191] but, as this chapter has hopefully shown, it is especially rewarding, too, to locate those discussions within a much broader historical canvas.

the latter concept cannot be left out of consideration. As the 1982 Convention demonstrates, the two institutions – continental shelf and exclusive economic zone – are linked together in modern law'.

[187] *Case Concerning the Continental Shelf* (n 185) 33 (§34): 'Although the institutions of the continental shelf and the exclusive economic zone are different and distinct, the rights which the exclusive economic zone entails over the sea-bed of the zone are defined by reference to the régime laid down for the continental shelf. Although there can be a continental shelf where there is no exclusive economic zone, there cannot be an exclusive economic zone without a corresponding continental shelf. It follows that, for juridical and practical reasons, the distance criterion must now apply to the continental shelf as well as to the exclusive economic zone; and this quite apart from the provision as to distance in paragraph 1 of Article 76.'

[188] Vattel (n 20).

[189] See further Cassese (n 12).

[190] Consider, eg, A Perreau-Saussine and JB Murphy (eds), *The Nature of Customary Law: Legal, Historical and Philosophical Perspectives* (Cambridge, Cambridge University Press, 2009).

[191] One of the intellectual inspirations behind Bowman and Kritsiotis (n 34).

PART II

Human Rights Law

4

The United Nations and Human Rights

Reform through Review?

MALCOLM EVANS

Abstract: The UN human rights system is routinely described as being at some form of crossroad. The most recent crossroad is the 2020 Review of the treaty body system, foreseen by the 'treaty strengthening process' initiated in 2012 and that culminated in 2014 with UNGA Resolution 68/268. This chapter will look at the background to that process, its outcome, and how defensive preparations for the 2020 Review, which have oscillated between poles of idealism and political reality, have in fact generated the most comprehensive and ambitious reform proposals of recent times.

I. Introduction

In the cautionary tale of 'Matilda', written by Hilaire Belloc: 'Matilda told such dreadful lies, it made one gasp and stretch one's eyes.' So when her aunt went out to see 'that very interesting play, the second Mrs Tanquery', leaving Matilda at home by herself and a fire broke out, Matilda called for help, but although the neighbours heard her, 'every time she shouted "fire", they only answered "little liar"' and she died in the flames.[1] This cautionary tale can be transposed to the current situation of the United Nations (UN) human rights treaty body system.

This system comprises the 10 committees established by the core UN human rights treaties, the members of which are independent experts elected by the States Parties to the treaty concerned in accordance with the provisions of each convention.[2] Though serviced by the UN Office of the High Commissioner (OHCHR), they are not a part of that Office, nor are they a creation of the Human

[1] H Belloc, 'Matilda' in *Cautionary Tales for Children* (London, Basil Blackwood, 1907).

[2] See section II below for details of each convention.

Rights Council, as are the UN Special Procedures.[3] Each is a legally autonomous entity, mandated to act in accordance with the provisions of the treaties by which they are each established. Nine of the 10 human rights treaty bodies work in a largely similar fashion.[4] They have two principal roles. The first is to receive reports submitted by the States Parties concerning the manner in which they are implementing their treaty obligations and which are then discussed with the State Party concerned, following which the Committee issues 'concluding observations' to the State concerning its compliance with its convention obligations. All States Parties are to submit an initial report within a fixed period after the treaty enters into force in respect of them and then subsequent reports on a periodic basis. This 'reporting procedure' is the chief means of oversight.[5]

In addition, all these nine treaties have (some only very recently) an optional procedure whereby communications can be submitted to the Committees, on which they may express 'views'.[6] Though carefully couched in non-judicial language, these communications procedures are widely seen as the closest that the UN has come to generating quasi-judicial determinations concerning alleged

[3] See generally A Nolan, R Freedman and T Murphy (eds), *The United Nations Special Procedures System* (Leiden, Brill, 2017).

[4] The exception is the Optional Protocol to the Convention against Torture and Other Cruel, Inhuman or Degrading Treatment or Punishment (adopted 18 December 2002, entered into force 22 June 2006) 2375 UNTS 237 (OPCAT), whose work is focused on visiting places of detention and assisting States in the establishment of 'National Preventive Mechanisms'. For this reason, and although it is recognised as a 'core convention' as it establishes its own treaty monitoring body, the Subcommittee on Prevention of Torture and Other Cruel, Inhuman or Degrading Treatment or Punishment (SPT), its work will not be addressed in this chapter. For background, see R Murray et al, *The Optional Protocol to the UN Convention against Torture* (Oxford, Oxford University Press, 2012).

[5] For a succinct general overview, see N Rodley, 'The Role and Impact of Treaty Bodies' in D Shelton (ed), *The Oxford Handbook of International Human Rights Law* (Oxford, Oxford University Press, 2013) 621; J Connors, 'United Nations' in D Moeckli, S Shah and S Sivakumaran (eds), *International Human Rights Law*, 3rd edn (Oxford, Oxford University Press, 2017) 387–99.

[6] Currently eight of the nine treaty bodies may receive communications from individuals (the relevant mechanism for the Convention on Migrant Workers (CMW) is not yet in force). Most also make provision for States Parties to bring communications too, although the procedures vary somewhat. The inter-State procedure had been considered something of a dead letter. It was, however, utilised for the first time in 2018 when Qatar lodged communications in respect of Saudi Arabia and the United Arab Emirates (declared admissible in August 2019) (see CERD/C/99/6 (Saudi Arabia) and CERD/C/99/3 and CERD/C/99/4 (United Arab Emirates). On 15 March 2021 both procedures were suspended at the request of the parties, following the Al Ula Declaration of 5 January 2021 and it is unlikely that they will be revived. The State of Palestine lodged a communication in respect of Israel (over which the CERD decided it has jurisdiction in December 2019 (see CERD/C/100/3-5) – at the time of writing, it is still considering the question of admissibility). For further information, see Office of the High Commissioner for Human Rights (OHCHR), 'Inter-State Communications' available at www.ohchr.org/EN/HRBodies/CERD/Pages/InterstateCommunications.aspx. These communications may well have been inspired by the judgment of the International Court of Justice (ICJ) in the *Application of the International Convention on the Elimination of All Forms of Racial Discrimination (Georgia v Russian Federation)* (Preliminary Objections, Judgment of 1 April 2011) [2011] ICJ Rep 70, para 141, where it was determined that in order for it to have jurisdiction to hear a case concerning the interpretation and application under art 22 of the Convention, it was necessary for the dispute not to have been settled either through negotiation or by the procedures provided for in that Convention for the settlement of disputes. On one reading, this required the use of the inter-State procedure before a dispute can be taken to the ICJ. Be that as it may, this added to the workload of the treaty body system in a way that had not been previously anticipated.

violations of human rights by States Parties.[7] Six treaties also have 'inquiry' procedures permitting them to conduct investigations in situations where they believe there to be systematic violations of the convention in question.[8]

For many years now, it has been trite to say that the system is on the brink of collapse.[9] Yet it has not collapsed and it continues to function much as before. As a result, claims that the system is failing have a 'Matilda-like' quality to them: even if they are heard and understood, they are increasingly just not really believed. But the system is nevertheless in crisis and there are two dimensions to this. The first concerns the effectiveness of the treaty body system understood in terms of its day-to-day operational practice: is it working well for States, for the OHCHR and for the treaty bodies themselves? The second, which has received less consideration, concerns the effectiveness of the treaty bodies in securing better protection of rights holders – this being what the system is intended to achieve. Section II of this chapter outlines the nature of the 'crisis' facing the treaty body system and section III provides a brief overview of the responses to this by the OHCHR, by the treaty bodies and by States acting through the UN and culminating in UNGA Resolution 68/268 adopted in April 2014. Section IV looks at that Resolution and considers its impact on the working the treaty body system. As will be seen, the Resolution mandated a 'review' of the system in 2020 and section V looks at the preparations for this. It is in this preparatory work that the faultlines concerning the question of the 'effectiveness' of the system have become most apparent and, as will be seen, the positions and proposals advanced have had the practical effect of generating proposals for the most radical overhaul of the operational practice of the human rights treaty body system in 25 years. Moreover, this has happened not by design or even by stealth, but as a by-product of attempts to forge consensus positions which became crystallised into reform packages in advance of the review itself. The chapter will conclude with a short reflection on the prospects for change and the significance of the process.

II. The Treaty Body Crisis

In 2012 Navi Pillay, the UN High Commissioner for Human Rights, produced a major report on the future of the treaty body system which outlined the crisis

[7] The work of the treaty bodies is considered to be 'authoritative' rather than legally binding. See generally G Neuman, 'The Functions of the Human Rights Committee' in D Moeckli, H Keller and C Heri (eds), *The Human Rights Covenants at 50* (Oxford, Oxford University Press, 2018) 34.

[8] The Committee against Torture (CAT), the Committee on Enforced Disappearances (CED), the Committee on the Elimination of Discrimination against Women (CEDAW), the Committee on Economic, Social and Cultural Rights (CESCR), the Committee on the Rights of the Child (CRC) and the Committee on the Rights of Persons with Disabilities (CRPD) are able to undertake confidential inquiries, the CAT and the CED by virtue of the Convention texts, and the others as a result of subsequent Optional Protocols.

[9] Indeed, as far back as 1989, Philip Alston was referring to the system being at 'a critical crossroads' and at 'a time of crisis'. See 'Effective implementation of international instruments on human rights,

that it was then facing[10] and that was largely projected as a crisis of capacity to handle the growing workload of the Committees, the number of which had grown incrementally over time. The first of the human rights treaty bodies to be established was the Committee on the Elimination of Racial Discrimination (CERD), which commenced working in 1970.[11] This was followed by the Human Rights Committee (HRC) in 1977,[12] the Committee on the Elimination of Discrimination against Women (CEDAW) in 1982,[13] Committee against Torture (CAT) in 1988[14] and the Committee on Rights of the Child (CRC) in 1991[15] In addition, in 1985 the Committee on Economic, Social and Cultural Rights (CESCR) was established by United Nations Economic and Social Council (ECOSOC) Resolution 1985/17 in order to undertake the monitoring functions which had originally been assigned to the ECOSOC under the Covenant on Economic, Social and Cultural Rights.[16] There then followed a period of some 14 years before the next treaty body came into being: the Committee on Migrant Workers (CMW) in 2004.[17] This was followed by the Subcommittee on Prevention of Torture (SPT), in 2007,[18] the Committee on the Rights of Persons with Disabilities (CRPD) in 2009[19] and, most

including reporting obligations under international instruments on human rights' (8 November 1989) UN Doc A/44/668.

[10] N Pillay, *Strengthening the United Nations Human Rights Treaty Body System: A Report by the United Nations High Commissioner for Human Rights* (Geneva, Office of the High Commissioner for Human Rights, 2012). For an analysis of this report, see S Egan, 'Strengthening the Human Rights Treaty Body System' (2013) 13 *Human Rights Law Review* 209.

[11] The CERD was established by the International Convention on the Elimination of All Forms of Racial Discrimination (adopted 21 December 1965, entered into force 4 January 1969) 660 UNTS 195. The CERD held its first session in January 1970.

[12] The HRC was established by the International Covenant on Civil and Political Rights (adopted 16 December 1966, entered into force 23 March 1976) 999 UNTS 171. The HRC met for the first time in March 1977.

[13] The CEDAW was established by the Convention on the Elimination of All Forms of Discrimination against Women (adopted 18 December 1979, entered into force 3 September 1981) 1249 UNTS 13. The CEDAW met for the first time in October 1982.

[14] The CAT was established by the Convention against Torture and other Cruel, Inhuman and Degrading Treatment or Punishment (adopted 10 December 1984, entered into force 26 June 1987) 1465 UNTS 85. The CAT met for the first time in April 1988.

[15] The CRC was established by the Convention on the Rights of the Child (adopted 20 November 1989, entered into force 2 September 1990) 1577 UNTS 3. The CRC met for the first time in September 1991.

[16] The United Nations Economic and Social Council (ECOSOC) had originally been tasked with overseeing the reporting procedures provided for in the International Covenant on Economic, Social and Cultural Rights (adopted 16 December 1966, entered into force 3 January 1976) 993 UNTS 3. The CESCR first met in March 1987.

[17] The CMW was established by the International Convention on the Protection of the Rights of All Migrant Workers and Members of their Families (adopted 18 December 1990, entered into force 1 July 2003) 2220 UNTS 3. The CMW met for the first time in March 2004.

[18] The SPT was established by the Optional Protocol to the Convention against Torture and Other Cruel, Inhuman and Degrading Treatment or Punishment (adopted 18 December 2002, entered into force 22 June 2006) 2375 UNTS 237. The SPT met for the first time in February 2007.

[19] The CRPD was established by the Convention on the Rights of Persons with Disabilities (adopted 13 December 2006, entered into force 3 May 2008) 2515 UNTS 3. The CRPD met for the first time in February 2009.

recently, the Committee on Enforced Disappearances (CED) in 2011.[20] Following a period of relative stability, it is likely that the number of treaty bodies will again start to increase, as there are currently a number processes taking place which may result in additional human rights treaty bodies coming into being.[21] The growth of the system has therefore been 'linear' and the implications of that growth for the system as a whole have not really been taken into consideration along the way. Indeed, it is only relatively recently that the treaty bodies have come to be seen as a 'system' at all.[22]

Inevitably, the number of States bound by the treaties has also increased over time. In 2000 there were a total of 927 ratifications of the six UN human rights treaties then in force; by 2012, this had risen to 1,586 ratifications of the then 10 core treaties and associated instruments.[23] By the end of 2018, there were 1,703 ratifications, a figure that will continue to rise.[24] Moreover, in 2000, only three

[20] The CED was established by the International Convention for the Protection of All Persons from Enforced Disappearances (adopted 20 December 2006, entered into force 23 December 2010) 2716 UNTS 3. The CED met for the first time in November 2011.

[21] In 2014 a process was commenced to draft a legally binding convention on business and human rights. See 'Elaboration of an international legally binding instrument on transnational corporations and other business enterprises with respect to human rights' (25 June 2014) UN Doc A/HRC/26/L.22. A 'Zero Draft' was circulated in 2018, which was revised in July 2019. It envisages a committee of up to 18 members who will consider reports on compliance by States Parties. There will also be an optional protocol providing for individual and group communications to that committee. These proposals continue to be refined. For the latest information, see the United Nations Human Rights Council, 'Open-Ended Intergovernmental Working Group on Transnational Corporations and Other Business Enterprises with Respect to Human Rights', available at www.ohchr.org/EN/HRBodies/HRC/WGTransCorp/Pages/IGWGOnTNC.aspx. There are also ongoing discussions concerning the possibility of a Convention on the Rights of Older Persons, on which subject the UN established an open-ended working group some 10 years ago. For details, see the United Nations Department of Economic and Social Affairs, 'OHCHR – Rights of Older Persons', available at https://social.un.org/ageing-working-group/unohchr.shtml. For more background on this and a rather negative assessment, see L Poffe, 'Towards a New United Nations Convention for Older Persons?' (2015) 15 *Human Rights Law Review* 591. The recently adopted United Nations Declaration on the Rights of Peasants and Other People Working in Rural Areas, UNGA Res 73/165 (17 December 2018) may yet lead to calls for another Convention process. Additionally, in 2018 the Human Rights Council in its Resolution 36/11 established an open-ended working group with a mandate 'to elaborate the content of an international regulatory framework, without prejudging the nature thereof, to protect human rights and ensure accountability violations and abuses relating to the activities of private military and security companies'. As the title makes clear, it is not apparent what the nature of this framework might yet be, but another human rights treaty is certainly a possibility. The overarching point is that the trend towards establishing processes which may have a human rights-style treaty as their outcome shows no signs of abating. The author is aware that other, more embryonic developments to establish such processes are also taking place. Back in 2012, however, the High Commissioner said it was 'absolutely … clear … that the approach of absorbing new mandates within existing resources is not sustainable. See Pillay (n 10) 9.

[22] At the time of her report, the High Commissioner found it necessary 'to highlight the importance of viewing treaty bodies as a system, including by the treaty bodies themselves': Pillay (n 10) 9. It remains the case that treaty bodies still find it difficult to think of themselves a part of a broader system.

[23] ibid 17.

[24] For statistical information, see 'Compliance by States parties with their reporting obligations to international human rights treaty bodies', a document produced annually for the meeting of Chairs of the human rights treaty bodies. The latest publicly available version is UN Doc HRI/MC/2020/4, which sets out the position as at 6 March 2020. This is updated on the OHCHR website from time to time.

treaties had an individual communication procedure,[25] whereas today all except the SPT (whose mandate is very different) do so and, as a result, the number of communications submitted will continue to rise. The resulting problem is quite simple: the system is unable to cope with the rising number of States Parties and the work this will generate. The only reason the system had not collapsed already, the High Commissioner argued, was 'because of the dedication of the experts, who are unpaid volunteers, the support of Staff in the OHCHR and States' non-compliance with reporting obligations'.[26]

The High Commissioner's Report concluded that only about 16 per cent of reports were actually submitted on time and at the time of the Report, some 315 initial reports and 311 periodic reports – a total of 626 – were overdue.[27] However, if these were to be submitted, this would only add to the backlog of 281 reports that had been submitted but were still waiting to be considered by the relevant treaty body.[28] In 2012 the High Commissioner concluded that if States did as they ought, the system could not cope and that 'it is unacceptable that the system can only function because of non-compliance'.[29] By the end of 2018, the position had barely changed, with 261 initial and 325 periodic reports yet to be submitted, a total of 586 and some 34 per cent of all reports due.[30] The system still survives due to non-compliance. Why is this so?

Committees meet for varying numbers of weeks each year, in 2012 ranging from two to nine weeks,[31] and now spend two half-day sessions questioning each State Party about its report and receiving answers. It must also prepare, deliberate, determine and adopt its 'concluding observations'. As a result, when working at 'full stretch', a treaty body cannot consider more than the equivalent of 2–3 State reports per week. In 2012 the relatively newly established CRPD was allocated only three weeks of meeting time, yet it already had a backlog of submitted initial reports which would have taken it over seven years to clear, and another 50 State reports were overdue.[32] What would be the point of discussing the situation in a country which, by the time it is considered, would be so completely out of date? And

This chapter draws on a version correct as of 31 December 2018, made available for reference at the 2019 Chairs Meeting, but which was not issued as a separate public document. It is referred to as the 'Reporting Compliance Report 2019'.

[25] These being the HRC, the CAT and the CERD.

[26] Pillay (n 10) 9.

[27] ibid 21.

[28] ibid 19.

[29] ibid 9.

[30] Reporting Compliance Report 2019 (n 24) 8.

[31] In 2012 the HRC, the CEDAW and the CRC met for nine weeks, the CERD and the CAT for eight weeks, the CESCR for seven weeks, the CED for four weeks, and the CMW and the CRPD (and the SPT) for three weeks. See UN Doc HRI/MC/2018/2 (n 24) 12. Some committees also have pre-sessional working groups.

[32] Pillay (n 10) 19, 23. The General Assembly's response to such situations was to grant individual Committees some extra meeting time in order to address their backlogs. Nevertheless, there is something profoundly problematic in treaty bodies having to come 'cap in hand' to the General Assembly for additional funds in order to allow them to consider the compliance record of those self-same States.

what would be the incentive for other States to comply with their commitments, knowing that it would be many years indeed before they would be examined? At the time of the High Commissioner's Report, if all States submitted their reports as they ought, then across the system[33] as a whole, about 320 reports would have needed to be considered each year, whereas the treaty bodies were only able to schedule 120–40 per year into their respective sessions. As a result, non-compliance by States was indeed essential in relation to the ability of the treaty body system to function, and this remains the case today.

The problems, however, concerned much more than the backlog of State reports waiting to be considered. There was a similar backlog of individual communications. At the end of 2011, a total of 480 communications were pending, and the HRC, the body to which most communications are currently submitted, had a backlog of over 330, which would have taken some 3–4 years to deal with.[34] The position has continued to worsen, with the HRC now having a backlog of over 700 cases.[35] The CAT also has a backlog of some 148 cases,[36] up from 115 at the time of the High Commissioner's Report.[37] Moreover, it would be far too simplistic to think that the problems could be solved by only allocating more meeting time to the Committees. Expert members are not paid and there are finite limits to the amount of time which members can spend in Geneva away from their sources of employment, income and (it is rarely added) family and friends. The Chairs of treaty bodies have recently declared their belief that spending 12 weeks per year in formal session is the maximum that can be expected of a member.[38]

The mechanics behind the reporting processes are also rarely thought about. If Committees are to meet more often, there must be more secretariat staff available to service this increased level of activity. There need to be more conference room interpreters, precis writers and conference room support staff. Indeed, there needs to be an adequate number of meeting rooms that are properly equipped and available to be used. Moreover, reports (and treaty body outputs) must be translated into the working languages of the Committees: number of pages to be translated had rocketed from about 4,500 in 2000 to 13,500 in 2011.[39] The time required is considerable and the cost is eye-watering.[40]

[33] It should be noted that the actual position varies from treaty to treaty, as each will have different backlogs and numbers of reports to be submitted. However, for the present purposes, it is the overall position which is of importance when assessing the situation of the system as a whole.

[34] Pillay (n 10) 23.

[35] See 'Report of the Human Rights Committee' (2018) UN Doc A/73/40, para 29.

[36] See 'Report of the Committee against Torture' (2018) UN Doc A/73/44, para 61.

[37] Pillay (n 10) 23.

[38] *Treaty Body Chairpersons Position Paper on the Future of the Treaty Body System* adopted at the 31st Meeting of Chairpersons (24–28 June 2019), available at www.ohchr.org/Documents/HRBodies/TB/AnnualMeeting/31Meeting/ChairpersonsPositionPaper_July2019.docx. This Position Paper is discussed in detail in section V below.

[39] Pillay (n 10) 24. In 2011 the treaty bodies themselves generated an additional 5,000 pages to be translated.

[40] ibid 54, fn 38 records that the average cost of translating one page of a document into the other five official UN languages was at that time (2012) between $1,900 and $2,000, meaning that a 300-page

If the system presented problems for the treaty bodies and the OHCHR, it also presented problems for States. As the number of treaties and treaty bodies has increased, the reporting obligations of States have grown in number and in complexity. Some treaties have fixed reporting periods, ranging from two to five years, whilst for others it is flexible.[41] Given that there are separate reporting obligations under the two Optional Protocols to the Convention on the Rights of the Child, in general terms, if a State is a party to the nine treaties with reporting obligations, then it would be expected to produce about 10 reports over a five-year period – an average of two per year (though they might be concentrated at particular points in time). Since each treaty body not only has its own reporting requirements but also its own processes and procedures, the requirements on States can be complex and confusing. Indeed, from a State's perspective, the system can appear to lack focus, consistency and coherence.

At one level, the answer might seem simple: more money. It is true that the amounts of money spent on the system were, and remain, comparatively modest. At the time of the High Commissioner's Report, the estimated cost of the treaty bodies' work to the UN was $56.4 million (about 10 per cent of which was extra-budgetary funding from States),[42] a not insignificant sum. This, however, is by no means the end of the calculation. To this needs to be added the very considerable sums which are spent by States on the preparation of reports, their presentation in Geneva and their follow-up. There is then the very considerable amounts spent by civil society – and by governments, philanthropic bodies and the general public in supporting them – in raising issues, producing materials for the Committees, lobbying and following up on their work. The costs of this are rarely estimated or factored into the overall 'costs' of the system. Whilst it is routinely said that very little is spent on human rights protection by the UN – and this is true – it is also true that a great deal more than this is spent on the system taken as a whole.

If even more money is to be spent on the system, then it is important that it is spent well. This brings us back to the purpose of the system, which is to better protect rights holders by monitoring the compliance of States with their international obligations as set out in the treaties. Geneva-based reporting processes may indeed result in better compliance and better protection, though this is more often assumed than demonstrated. What is incontestable is that if the reporting processes provided for in the treaties are to achieve their overall objective, then States need to report, and those reports need to be considered by the Committees in a timely fashion through processes which are fair, efficient, collaborative and

report would cost well over half a million dollars to translate. These figures will not have decreased in the meantime.

[41] Periodic reports are to be submitted to the CAT, the CEDAW and the CRPD every four years. For the CERD, the period is two years, but States have long been permitted to consolidate two reports, so the de facto period is also four years. For the CMW and the CRC, the period is five years. There is no fixed period set for the CED, the CESCR and the HRC. The HRC uses a range of three to six years and the CESCR five years. For details, see UN Doc HRI/MC/2018/2 (n 24) Table 1.

[42] Pillay (n 10) 95–96.

constructive. They also need to result in clear practical outcomes that States can realistically be expected to engage with.

The 'crisis' within the treaty body system, then, was a crisis at several levels. Most obviously, there was a straightforward crisis of capacity: the system could not cope with the volume of work that it had on its plate, what might be called a 'backlog' crisis. There was also a 'structural crisis': if all States abided by their treaty obligations, then the treaty body system could not function. Both crises concern the 'effectiveness' of the system and these were the aspects of the crisis which has been the focus of attention in the 'treaty-strengthening process'. But there is another crisis of effectiveness, which is whether this system,[43] originally devised in the 1960s, is delivering optimal human rights protection for rights holders in the twenty-first century.[44] This crisis has not yet been seriously considered by the General Assembly.

III. Addressing the Crisis: The 'Treaty-Strengthening Process'

A. The Road to UNGA Resolution 68/268

Whilst the problems facing the treaty bodies have become more acute in recent years, they are not new, and virtually nothing said by the High Commissioner in her 2012 report had not already been said of the system by Philip Alston in a series of reports on the treaty body system from 1989 to 1997.[45] As Sir Nigel Rodley

[43] Discussions concerning the effectiveness of the system should be distinguished from discussions concerning the impact of participation of States within the system. Much recent scholarship has sought to explain the positive impact of the system as being not so much due to the monitoring and other work of the treaty bodies per se, but because of other factors resulting from ratification and participation. See, eg, A Hathaway, 'Do Human Rights Treaties Make a Difference?' (2002) 111 *Yale Law Journal* 1935; T Risse, S Ropp and K Sikkink (eds), *The Persistent Power of Human Rights* (Cambridge, Cambridge University Press, 2013); R Goodman and D Jinks, *Socialising States: Promoting Human Rights through International Law* (Oxford, Oxford University Press, 2013). For an interesting approach which places more importance on the working methods (though not necessarily the concrete outputs) of the treaty bodies in enhancing compliance, see G de Burca, 'Human Rights Experimentalism' (2017) 111 *American Journal of International Law* 277.

[44] See, eg, K Boyle, *New Instruments for Human Rights Protection* (Oxford, Oxford University Press, 2009); R Freedman, *Failing to Protect: The UN and the Politicisation of Human Rights* (London, Hurst & Co, 2014); S Subedi, *The Effectiveness of the UN Human Rights System* (Abingdon, Routledge, 2017).

[45] See UN Doc A/44/668 (n 9); 'Interim report on enhancing the long-term effectiveness of the United Nations human rights treaty system' (26 April 1993) A/CONF.157/PC/62/Add.11/Rev.1, this being a paper submitted to the 1993 World Conference on Human Rights; 'Final report on enhancing the long-term effectiveness of the United Nations human rights treaty system' (27 March 1997) E/CN.4/1997/74. For a representation of the problems identified and reflections on them, see P Alston and J Crawford, *The Future of Human Rights Treaty Monitoring* (Cambridge, Cambridge University Press, 2000). Other influential analyses at that time setting out the nature of the problems to be faced and offering potential solutions included AF Beyefsky (ed), *The UN Human Rights System in the 20th Century* (Leiden, Kluwer, 2000); AF Bayefsky, *The UN Human Rights Treaty System: Universality at the Crossroads* (Leiden, Martinus Nijhoff, 2001).

stated, with his customary directness and economy, 'the longstanding and intensifying challenge confronting the system is that there is too much work to be done, in too short a time, with inadequate resources. It is not a new problem'.[46] Indeed, a series of significant initiatives have taken place over the last 15 years which have sought to address them,[47] but these various processes have in some ways become a part of the problem, not least because it has been unclear 'whose crisis' it is to solve, and they have had little positive impact.

The most ambitious reform proposals were those advanced in 2006 by High Commissioner Louise Arbour, who sought to abandon altogether the current system of each treaty having its own monitoring body and to replace the existing bodies with a single, full-time body which would exercise their functions.[48] This proved completely unworkable and has not been returned to in the latest round of discussions within the UN concerning institutional development, although it is still floated as an idea from time to time.[49]

Each treaty body has its own autonomous treaty basis, its differing sets of States Parties, its own history and its own trajectory. The treaty bodies have different focuses of work, reflecting the specific treaty obligations and the competencies of their membership. As has been seen, States continue to draft treaties which will create additional treaty bodies[50] and it is unlikely that the idea of establishing a unified treaty body will be returned to in the foreseeable future. The proposal for a unified treaty body was, in effect, an example of the High Commissioner presenting 'top-down' reform proposals which both treaty bodies and States considered to be unacceptable.[51] However, there was a view that similar outcomes might be achieved by seeking to 'harmonise' to the processes of the treaty bodies[52] – a form of 'soft merger'.

This meant that the baton passed to the treaty bodies themselves in what became known as the Dublin Process. The 'Dublin Process' was launched in 2009 and was designed to facilitate the closer working of the treaty bodies, whilst respecting

[46] Rodley (n 5) 642.

[47] For a succinct and insightful overview, see FD Gaer 'The Institutional Future of the Covenants' in Moeckli, Keller and Heri (n 7) 334.

[48] 'Concept paper on the High Commissioner's proposal for a unified standing treaty body' (22 March 2006) UN Doc HRI/MC/2006/2. For comment on these proposals, see M O'Flaherty and C O'Brien, 'Reform of the UN Human Rights Treaty Monitoring Bodies: A Critique of the Concept Paper of the High Commissioner's Proposal for a Unified Standing Treaty Body' (2007) 7 *Human Rights Law Review* 141.

[49] For a recent call for a single unified treaty body, see Subedi (n 44) 97–99, 245–46.

[50] See above n 21.

[51] See 'Report of a brainstorming meeting on reform of the human rights treaty body system, "Malbun II", Liechtenstein' (16 September 2006) UN Doc A/61/351. This echoed the negative outcome of the earlier 'Malbun I' meeting in 2003, which had been called to consider proposals to streamline reporting processes made by Kofi Annan, the UN Secretary General, in 'Strengthening the United Nations: an agenda for further change' (9 September 2002) UN Doc A/57/387, paras 52–54. See M O'Flaherty, 'The High Commissioner and the Treaty Bodies' in FD Gaer and CL Broecker (eds), *The United Nations High Commissioner for Human Rights: Conscience for the World* (Leiden, Martinus Nijhoff, 2014) 101, 108; Gaer (n 47) 341–42.

[52] 'Malbun II' report (n 51) para 35.

their diversity.[53] Rather than seeking to replace the treaty bodies, the idea was to bring them closer together – possibly in the hope that one day they might arrive at a point at which their uniting could be contemplated. This coming together could take a variety of forms. At its most maximal, it could involve the Chairs of the treaty bodies agreeing on common working practices which would be implemented within the various committees. The high water mark of this approach was the so-called 'Poznan Formula', adopted at the meeting within the framework of the Dublin Process which vested Chairs with the authority to make decisions on matters of process, albeit that those treaty bodies which had not previously had the opportunity to discuss and mandate their Chair prior to such decisions would be free to reject them.[54] The very weakness of this attempt to introduce a form of 'centralised' harmonisation even from within the treaty body system underscored the power and autonomy of the individual treaty bodies and their unwillingness to surrender decision-making over their individual processes.

As a result, the outcome of the Dublin Process was a much weaker form of coming together, being little more than a sharing of best practices and a willingness to consider the advantages of adopting common approaches.[55] Rather than the treaty bodies taking control of their collective destiny and agreeing upon a system-wide change to their practices, the result was that each treaty body was to undertake its work with better knowledge and understanding of what the others were doing and reflecting on whether there were advantages *for it* in terms of doing as others did. It remained an essentially atomised approach. This ultimately found reflection in the emergence of the word 'alignment' as a favoured way of describing the process. This might best be described as a 'bottom-up' process in which each treaty body considered how it might align its work with that of others, in ways which would help address at least some of the problems within the system.

This, however, proved to be just too small-scale and incremental. Indeed, it would be fair to say that the treaty bodies working within the Dublin Process had become so fixated on preserving their autonomy that they lost sight of the problems which the process was intended to address. Having rejected an 'external' solution to the crisis of capacity facing the system, they manifestly failed to generate an 'internal solution'. Worse, they gave the impression that they were not willing to accept that they too had a responsibility for the problems which needed to be addressed.

[53] This was launched with a meeting in Dublin, leading to the 'Dublin Statement on the Process of Strengthening of the United Nations Human Rights Treaty Body System' (Dublin, 19 November 2009) available at www2.ohchr.org/english/bodies/HRTD/docs/DublinStatement.pdf. On the background to the Dublin Process see M O'Flaherty, 'Reform of the UN Human Rights Treaty Body System: Locating the Dublin Statement' (2010) 10 *Human Rights Law Review* 319; O'Flaherty (n 51).

[54] *The Poznan Statement on the Reforms of the UN Human Rights Treaty Body System* (Poznan, 28–29 September 2010) para 17, available at www2.ohchr.org/english/bodies/HRTD/docs/PoznanStatement.pdf.

[55] *Strengthening the United Nations Human Rights Treaty Body System, Dublin II Meeting* (Outcome Document) (Dublin, 10–11 November 2011), available at www2.ohchr.org/english/bodies/HRTD/docs/DublinII_Outcome_Document.pdf.

At the end of the day, if more resources needed to be allocated within the UN budget to service an expanded treaty body system – and they were – then this was always going to need the approval of the UN 5th Committee. This meant that, ultimately, the baton was always going to have to pass to UN Member States. The outcomes of the Dublin Process were presented to States at a meeting in Sion in 2011 and were not well received.[56] A series of consultations between States then took place in which the treaty bodies were increasingly marginalised,[57] during which a group of States which came to be known within the process as the Cross Regional Group (the CRG) seized the initiative. In February 2012 the General Assembly established an intergovernmental process which sought to impose the views of States on how the treaty body system should function as the 'price to pay' for additional resources – a process rather euphemistically referred to as the 'treaty strengthening process'.[58] This process culminated in General Assembly Resolution 68/268, adopted in April 2014,[59] and it was into that process that both the OHCHR and the treaty bodies needed to inject their views. What had previously been a 'top-down'/'bottom-up' issue between the OHCHR and the treaty bodies became a process in which the OHCHR and the treaty bodies were seeking to influence the outcome of a State-led process which was, in many ways, 'top down' to both of them.

B. The OHCHR and the Treaty Strengthening Process

The question of 'ownership' of the process – or even of inputs into the process – quickly assumed significance. In June 2012 Navi Pillay, the High Commissioner, issued her major Report, *Strengthening the United Nations Human Rights Treaty System*, which was discussed above. This landmark document helped benchmark the nature of the crisis facing the system at that time and offered a range of suggestions for addressing them. It is worth noting that although the Report stressed that it was the product of series of stakeholder engagements,[60] including with the treaty bodies themselves, the Chairs of the treaty bodies were unaware of its detailed proposals until the published report was presented to them at their annual meeting in Addis Ababa a few days after its publication.

The Report acknowledged both the systemic nature of the crisis facing the treaty bodies and the more immediately pressing problem of addressing the

[56] See *Report of the Informal Technical Consultation for States Parties on Treaty Body Strengthening (Sion, Switzerland, 12–13 May 2011)*, available at www.ohchr.org/Documents/HRBodies/TB/HRTD/Sion/Sion_report_final.pdf.

[57] These consultations were held in Geneva (February 2012) and New York (April 2012).

[58] UNGA Res 66/254, 'Intergovernmental process of the General Assembly on strengthening and enhancing the effective functioning of the human rights treaty body system' (23 February 2012) UN Doc A/Res/66/254 (hereinafter 'UNGA Res 66/254').

[59] UNGA Res 68/268, 'Strengthening and enhancing the effective functioning of the human rights treaty body system' (9 April 2014) UN Doc A/Res/68/268 (hereinafter 'UNGA Res 68/268').

[60] Pillay (n 10) 9.

substantial backlogs facing the system. Its central recommendation was the introduction of a 'Comprehensive Reporting Calendar' (more usually referred to as a 'Master Calendar'), which would allow for a predictable schedule of reviews that would be of benefit to all.[61] Reports are scheduled for consideration by each treaty following their receipt in accordance with each treaty's own programme of work. This means that even if a State submits a report on time, it cannot be sure when it will be considered by the relevant committee and, as each committee determines its own schedule, a State may find that a number of committees are considering its reports in a short space of time. It also means that if a State does not submit a report at all, its record of compliance might not be scrutinised. Working on the basis that, if a State had ratified all treaties and optional protocols, it would have 10 reports to submit, the Report argued that reporting under all treaties should take place over a five-year cycle, with a State submitting a maximum of two reports per year.[62] Significantly, it also allowed for scheduling reviews of States in the absence of a report.[63] Each State would therefore appear before two committees each year and the goals of predictability and regularity of review would be achieved.

Inevitably, so appealingly simple a scheme had what proved to be some fatal flaws. As far as States were concerned, the first was cost. The Report acknowledged that the Master Calendar approach would require a near-doubling of the existing budget,[64] even when taking into account a range of cost-saving measures such as reducing the length of documentation and reduced translation.[65] Cost increases on this scale were never realistic, yet the process of offering cost savings by changing existing practices suggested to States that such savings might be possible. Predictably, States seized on this in the discussions that followed. A second concern was the suggestion that States' compliance should be considered irrespective of whether they had submitted a report. This would mean that the many States that failed to do so could no longer evade the expert scrutiny which they had – by and large – so far managed to avoid with little difficulty.

As regards the treaty bodies, the proposals were problematic for other reasons. It meant increasing the number of weeks spent in total on reviewing reports from 73 to 108, with an additional 16 weeks needed to consider individual communications, as well as time needed for other regular activities.[66] The feasibility of this from a member perspective had never really been explored and it posed near-intolerable burdens on members of some committees, as well as on the Secretariat

[61] ibid 37–45.

[62] ibid 37.

[63] ibid 39. This terminology was preferred to that of 'in absentia' consideration, since it was hoped that the State representatives would attend an oral dialogue even if there were no report. A number of Committees already schedule such reviews from time to time, and experience suggests that doing so tends to prompt States to provide a report.

[64] ibid 42, 95–96, the cost rising from the then current estimate of $56 million to $108, an additional $52 million.

[65] ibid 53–54, 57–58. The cost implications of all proposals are clearly indicated throughout the report, inviting a focus on this aspect of the strengthening process.

[66] ibid 42.

and the infrastructure of the OHCHR in Geneva. The proposal for a five-year cycle also failed to respect the periodicity for reporting set out in several of the treaties, which some Committees felt very strongly about. The Report underscored the need for the treaty bodies to adopt not only common working practices, but new working practices in the form of a 'Simplified Reporting Procedure' (SRP)[67] which had first been championed by the CAT, but which few others were prepared to adopt on a wholesale basis, as well as common structures for the dialogues with States Parties[68] and concluding observations,[69] limits on the numbers of questions asked with the SRP[70] and recommendations made in concluding observations[71] – and much else besides. It was as if the treaty bodies were again to be subject to a 'dictat' as regards how they undertook their work, and the threat of a return to the unified single treaty body once again seemed to loom large. Moreover, it alerted States to the possibility of dictating the minutiae of the treaty bodies' working methods – running the risk of undermining their ability to determine their own rules of procedure, and their independence. In short, the High Commissioner had succeeded in producing a set of proposals which, for different reasons, became anathema both to States and to the treaty bodies, both procedurally and substantively.[72]

C. The Treaty Bodies and the Treaty Strengthening Process

The treaty bodies had been wrong-footed by UNGA Resolution 66/254 establishing the intergovernmental process. They were also wrong-footed by the High Commissioner's Report offering proposals for the future of the treaty body system, from which they felt excluded[73] and which were far removed from the rather

[67] ibid 47–50.

[68] ibid 55–57.

[69] ibid 60–62, suggesting a limit of six pages or 3,300 words. This was at the lowest end of the spectrum of practice, with the CRC concluding observations averaging 20–21 pages.

[70] ibid 55, suggesting a maximum of 25 questions.

[71] ibid, suggesting a maximum of 20 recommendations.

[72] A further exacerbating factor in the toxic mix concerned the suggestion made by the CRG that the independence of the treaty body members needed to be policed by making them subject to a code of conduct. In 2006 the newly constituted Human Rights Council had imposed such a code on its Special Procedures mandate holders, but it did not have the authority to do so in respect of treaty body members. The idea of independently elected members being answerable for their conduct to the very States whose conduct they are charged with scrutinising is obviously a bad one and should have been easy to dismiss. The Chairs, however, came under intense pressure from the OHCHR to adopt its own Guidelines, the 'Guidelines on the independence and impartiality of members of the human rights treaty bodies ("the Addis Ababa Guidelines")' (2 August 2012) UN Doc A/67/222, Annex I as a counterbalance to the threat of Guidelines being imposed on them by States. Despite the obvious merits of the Addis Ababa Guidelines, the process by which they were adopted at the Chairs Meeting (which ran close to bullying) once again reinforced the impression that the High Commissioner and the OHCHR were again seeking to direct the future of the system.

[73] This also had overtones of other previous reform attempts. In 2002 the UN Secretary-General's 'Strengthening the United Nations' (UN Doc A/57/387 (n 51)) included proposals for standardising

introspective, self-centred and self-important product of the Dublin Process, the concrete proposals of which were quickly lost to history.[74] In short, the Chairs of the treaty bodies felt that they had been left without a position. Worse, it also appeared that they had also been left without a voice and had been excluded from the process altogether.

GA Resolution 66/254 established an 'intergovernmental process' that was 'to conduct open, transparent and inclusive negotiations on how to strengthen and enhance the effective functioning of the human rights treaty body system'.[75] In doing so, it was required to take into consideration 'relevant proposals on strengthening and enhancing the effective functioning of the human rights treaty body system', including those of the Secretary-General, and invited the High Commissioner to present a 'compilation report' by June 2012,[76] this being the report discussed in the previous section. It then 'reaffirmed' that the discussions were to be open to 'all Member States of the UN, observer States, relevant intergovernmental organisations and relevant United Nations Bodies'.[77] The treaty bodies are, of course, none of these. They were, however, addressed in the final paragraph of the Resolution, which, in rather dismissive language, requests the President of the General Assembly:

> [T]o work out separate informal arrangements, after consultation with Member States, that would allow the open-ended intergovernmental process to benefit from the inputs and expertise of the human rights treaty bodies, national human rights institutions and relevant non-governmental organisations, bearing in mind the intergovernmental nature of the process referred to in paragraph 1.[78]

In other words, the General Assembly had decided that the process of addressing the crisis in the treaty body system would exclude any form of formal engagement with the very addressees of their work. Rather, alongside non-governmental organisations (NGOs) and others, some informal way should be found to let States have the benefit of their thoughts. Moreover, and as previously mentioned, the High Commissioner's Report had offered a template for discussion that included very granular details addressed by the rules of procedure of the treaty bodies and of which, in theory, the Committees were masters. The result was that the General

reporting procedures and a single report to be submitted to the treaty bodies, which according to O'Flaherty (n 51) 108 had caught the treaty bodies by surprise. Writing in 2014, J Connors and M Schmidt, 'United Nations' in D Moeckli, S Shah and S Sivakumaran (eds), *International Human Rights Law*, 2nd edn (Oxford, Oxford University Press, 2014) 387 claim that the proposals were 'well received' by treaty body members. This does not accord with the recollection of this author of the response to them following their presentation to the Chairs (of which he was one) at their Annual Meeting in Addis Ababa in June 2012.

[74] O'Flaherty (n 51) 117 argues that the Dublin Outcome Statement was in fact fully reflected in the High Commissioner's Report. Assuming this to be the case, this Report also fell from view in the processes which followed.

[75] UNGA Res 66/254 (n 58) operative para 1.

[76] ibid operative para 3.

[77] ibid operative para 4.

[78] ibid operative para 6.

Assembly was set to embark on the task of rewriting how the human rights treaty bodies fulfilled their convention mandates of holding States to account. The High Commissioner had managed to put the very heart of the treaty body system on the General Assembly's dissection table with the patient fully sedated[79] – but the patient finally woke up during the operation.

By the following year, the Chairs had met informally and were able to ensure that their Annual Meeting would be held in New York in May 2013, where they could have greater contact with States and the intergovernmental process. Their annual meeting was dominated by 'informal-informal' meetings with those involved in the process. Wisely, under the circumstances, they refrained from making detailed proposals, but focused on setting out a series of principles which, in their view, should underpin the process. As recorded in the Report of its meeting and in passages that are worth quoting at some length, Claudio Grossman, the Chair of the Chairpersons Meeting, summed up their approach in the following terms:

> The Chairperson then proceeded to enumerate the principles and benchmarks which the Chairpersons considered fundamental in relation to the treaty body-strengthening process. As these principles were rooted in human rights treaty law, as elaborated and ratified by States, the Chairpersons expected them to be faithfully reflected in the process and outcome of the treaty body strengthening process. The first principle was that any outcome of the inter-governmental process should strengthen the human rights protection that the treaty body system offers. The second principle was the independence and impartiality of the treaty bodies and their members. At the 2012 annual meeting of Chairpersons of treaty bodies, the Chairpersons had endorsed the Addis Ababa Guidelines which interpreted the concepts of independence and impartiality for treaty body members. The Chairperson added that these Guidelines were based on pre-existing guidelines of the Human Rights Committee, relevant rules of procedure, and decisions of other treaty bodies relating to independence. Less than a year later, the Addis Ababa Guidelines had been incorporated, in one way or another, in either the rules of procedure or the working practices of all Committees, as documented in the report on the implementation by the treaty bodies of the recommendations contained in the report of the High Commissioner on strengthening the treaty body system (HRI/MC/2013/4). This had given the Addis Ababa Guidelines tremendous weight. Third, any outcome of the inter-governmental process should be comprehensive and sustainable, meaning that treaty bodies should be equipped with the proper material and human resources from the regular budget to adequately carry out their responsibilities under the respective treaties. The fourth principle was the principle of efficiency and needed to be tested in light of the goal of the system to respect, protect and promote human rights. In this context, all cost-saving measures needed to be fully re-invested in a system that dramatically suffered from a lack of resources. Valuable capacity-building initiatives should therefore not be undertaken at the expense of the scarce resources of

[79] For a more positive assessment of the impact of the Report, see O'Flaherty (n 51) 116, admittedly written before the final outcome of the process was known.

> the treaty bodies, but additional resources should be made available for this purpose. Fifth, the inter-governmental process provided member States and treaty bodies with a unique opportunity to modernize the work of treaty bodies by fully benefitting from opportunities created by technological development, while at the same time making it universally accessible for persons with disabilities, and to honour the principle of reasonable accommodation.
>
> The Chairperson further highlighted that the strengthening process was by definition a multi-stakeholder process in which both States and treaty bodies had specific competencies. The Chairpersons very much valued the dialogue in each committee as well as the informal consultation which was a permanent feature of the annual meeting of Chairpersons. The treaties, however, provided for the rules of procedure and the working methods of treaty bodies to be determined by the treaty bodies themselves. The Chair highlighted that the treaty bodies were committed to the continued harmonization of their working methods and in this context welcomed the report of the High Commissioner on treaty body strengthening. He concluded by stating that the treaty bodies had already greatly invested in coming up with possible solutions for a crisis that, if unattended to, could seriously weaken a system already under stress.[80]

Though measured, the underlying message was not subtle. The treaty bodies are creations of law, independent, autonomous and masters of their own procedure. They exist to serve the interests of rights holders, and any changes in their work and practice must reflect this. Undeniably, they face a crisis and additional resourcing is required to meet this – and savings resulting from procedural change must be re-invested in the system itself. The independence of that system is paramount and has been effectively safeguarded by the treaty bodies themselves. The treaty bodies are not blind to the need for change and are anxious to do so – but it is they which should drive the process. The treaty strengthening process allows States the opportunity to assist the treaty bodies in doing so. In short, it was a carefully crafted rebuke to those who sought to instrumentalise the crisis to weaken the system – and to all of those, States and officials alike, who had sought to exclude the treaty bodies from the process and impose solutions upon them.[81] That said, although the treaty bodies continued to be actively engaged with the process right up until its conclusion in April 2014, it was not a negotiation and in the final analysis, the treaty bodies were in effect subjected to 'external decision-making' as regards their future work and practice.

[80] 'Report of the Chairs of the Human Rights Treaty Bodies on Their Twenty-Fifth Meeting' (19 August 2013) UN Doc A/68/334, paras 28–29.

[81] For the full text of the statement of the Chairs (which had been discussed in great detail at the meeting prior to delivery), see 'Human Rights Treaty Bodies and the Inter-governmental Process on Treaty Body Strengthening: Informal Consultation with States', Statement by Mr Claudio Grossman, Chairperson-Rapporteur, 25th Meeting of the UN human rights treaty bodies chairpersons (New York, 21 May 2013), available at https://tbinternet.ohchr.org/_layouts/15/treatybodyexternal/Download.aspx?symbolno=INT%2fCHAIRPERSONS%2fSTA%2f25%2f19774&Lang=en.

IV. Strengthening the Treaties: Resolution 68/268

A. Resolution 68/268

When in April 2014 the UN General Assembly adopted Resolution 68/268 on 'Strengthening and enhancing the effective functioning of the human rights treaty body system', it was greeted with sighs of relief by the treaty bodies and most observers, as much as for what it did not contain as for what it did.[82] During the intergovernmental process, numerous States had advanced various proposals which would have seriously undermined the integrity of the system. Space constraints preclude a full presentation and analysis, but a flavour of the nature and intensity of the challenge can be gauged from the letter sent by the Russian Federation to the UN in September 2012 setting out its approach to 'enhancing' the human rights treaty bodies.[83]

The Russian Federation claimed that 'the treaty bodies … often face justifiable critic for overstepping their mandates'[84] and that the 'principal aim' of the process was to 'strengthen the capacity of the human rights treaty bodies to assist States parties in complying with their human rights obligations'.[85] Thus, for Russia, the treaty bodies were there to assist not rights holders, but States. To that end, it had objections to the SRP in which the treaty body asks questions of the State rather than receiving a report from the State on which it might raise issues. Russia thought the treaty bodies using this process asked too many questions, including questions on matters beyond their mandate. It objected to the idea of a 'Master Calendar' since this ignored the treaty provisions on periodicity of reporting,[86] but also, more importantly, because it 'undermined the basic principle … [of] constructive dialogue', since this could result in a situation in which a country could be considered in the absence of a report, or even of a governmental delegation.[87] It objected to the practices of the treaty bodies in appointing country rapporteurs[88] and using parallel chambers,[89] and – most importantly – it

[82] For an analysis of the outcome, see C Broecker and M O'Flaherty, *The Outcome of the General Assembly's Human Rights Treaty Strengthening Process: An Important Milestone on a Longer Journey* (Versoix, Universal Rights Group, 2014). As the title suggests, the authors accepted that this was a 'sticking plaster' and that it would be necessary to return to the 'more fundamental reforms of the system once again' (ibid 27). For a less positive reaction, see Subedi (n 44) 96–97, who lamented that the Resolution 'did not contain any significant measures to strengthen the treaty bodies, let alone overhaul the system' and who thought its proposals were 'mundane, technical, timid and cosmetic'. His assessment of the nature of the measures is almost certainly correct: but for the treaty bodies, this was considered a positive outcome, not a lost opportunity.

[83] 'Letter dated 21 September 2012 from the Permanent Representative of the Russian Federation to the United Nations addressed to the Secretary-General' (25 September 2012) UN Doc A/67/390.

[84] ibid para 2.

[85] ibid para 6.

[86] ibid para 21.

[87] ibid para 19.

[88] ibid para 24.

[89] ibid para 25.

insisted that 'the practice of conducting "closed" meetings of committee experts and various stakeholders must cease'[90] – in other words, the Committees should not receive private briefings from NGOs, and any material received from NGOs should be given publicly. Concluding observations should be shorter[91] and there should be no follow-up mechanisms since implementation falls 'exclusively within the competence of States parties',[92] and it was not the role of the treaty bodies 'to engage in monitoring and oversight'.[93] General Comments should be drafted 'in close collaboration with the States parties'[94] and there was a need to 'depoliticise' the treaty bodies by making 'experts more objective and … truly independent, not only of States parties but also of other groups seeking to exert influence, including civil society institutions, the academic community and United Nations system entities'.[95] To that end, there should be a code of conduct and the establishment of 'an appropriate accountability mechanism'.[96]

Whilst this was clearly an extreme position, it was not an outlier. The core position was that there should be no master calendar or consideration of States in the absence of a report, that treaty body mandates were to be strictly construed, and that experts should be subjected to codes of conduct and be accountable to States for their behaviour. Since the purpose of the system was to assist States, not rights holders, it was for States to determine what assistance was required and how it should be offered to them. It was this letter from the Russian Federation, as much as anything else, which had alerted the Chairs of the treaty bodies to the dangers to be faced and prompted them to make their robust response which was outlined above. What remained to be seen was how these tensions would play out. Against this intensely hostile background, the general view that they played out relatively well was entirely justified.

A major positive feature of the Resolution was its 'reaffirmation of the independence of the human rights treaty bodies',[97] something which has to be read in the light of nearly 30 years' worth of reports and proposals from independent experts, the UN Secretary-General and UN High Commissioners, as well as academics and others, calling for the very existence of the independent treaty bodies to be ended in favour of a new single body. Importantly, this independence is also reflected by the operative paragraphs 'encouraging' the treaty bodies to act in certain ways, rather than the Resolution making 'decisions' in respect of matters concerning

[90] ibid para 27.
[91] ibid para 34.
[92] ibid para 35.
[93] ibid para 38.
[94] ibid para 47.
[95] ibid para 50.
[96] ibid.
[97] UNGA Res 68/268 (n 59) para 9 of the Preamble. See also para 35 of the Preamble, which stressed that those involved in the process had 'different legal competencies in accordance with the Charter and the international human rights instruments establishing the treaty bodies, and recognizing in this regard the ongoing efforts of different treaty bodies towards strengthening and enhancing their effective functioning'. This amounts to a further acknowledgement of the autonomous nature of the human rights treaty bodies.

their working practices.[98] The status of the treaty bodies was further reflected in the references to the Resolution being the product of a 'multi-stakeholder approach' and noting the 'participation … of the treaty bodies' in the process – this being a far cry from the language of Resolution 66/254, which had sought to sideline them. Attempts to impose a code of conduct on members were turned on their head, the Resolution reaffirmed 'the importance of the independence and impartiality of the members of the human rights treaty bodies' and underlined the importance of all stakeholders of the treaty body system, as well as the Secretariat, respecting fully the independence of treaty body members and the importance of avoiding any act that would interfere with the exercise of their functions'.[99] It also noted the adoption of the Addis Ababa Guidelines, and encouraged their implementation,[100] whilst seeking the views of States on their development and 'inviting' the Chairs to keep States updated on their implementation.[101] The Resolution, then, largely respects the autonomy and integrity of the treaty bodies and their members, a positive outcome which could not have been assumed in advance.[102]

From a practical perspective, the Resolution was also largely positive in its impact, although it fell far short of the ambitious vision set out in the High Commissioner's Report. The idea of a 'Master Calendar' based on a fixed reporting cycle in which all States would be considered irrespective of whether they had submitted a report vanished without trace. Instead, the Resolution decided on a complex formula to determine the amount of meeting time to be made available to the treaty bodies based on the average number of reports submitted over a given period and on an assumption that 2.5 reports could be considered per week. Additional time was allocated for other activities as well as for individual communications.[103] It should be stressed that this was not an instruction to the treaty bodies on how to spend their time, but an instruction concerning the amount of time which was to be put at their disposal. Since this had previously been subject to ad hoc requests and rather unseemly haggling, the formulaic nature of this new approach had considerable merit as well as flexibility. It provided a significant increase in their meeting time which could be used, over time, to eliminate the backlog and move towards sustainability.

Inevitably, there was some bad news too. As foreshadowed by the High Commissioner's Report, significant cost-cutting measures were also introduced –

[98] See also Gaer (n 47) 345.

[99] UNGA Res 68/268 (n 59) para 35.

[100] ibid para 36.

[101] The closest the Resolution comes to seeking to exert a form of oversight is in para 39, when it encourages the Chairs to hold their annual meeting in either Geneva or New York so that there could be 'an open and formal interactive dialogue in which all issues, including those related to independence and impartiality of treaty body members, may be raised by states in a constructive manner'.

[102] See also Gaer (n 47) 345, who cautiously refers to the Resolution 'technically respecting' the independence of the treaty bodies.

[103] UNGA Res 68/268, para 26. Paragraph 27 also provided for a review of the numbers of weeks allocated biennially, but with a guarantee that the total allocation would not be less than that enjoyed at the time of the Resolution.

again, not by telling the treaty bodies what to do, but by placing limits on what the various branches of the UN were permitted to provide in support of their work. It was decided that summary records (as had been suggested by the High Commissioner) would only be issued in one working language (in practice, almost always either English of French) and not translated.[104] Potentially more significantly, a word limit on treaty body documentation of 10,700 words was imposed (though this was not without precedent within the system).[105] In reality, few treaty body outputs exceeded that length, and it was probably beneficial, encouraging concise and precise writing in place of the florid, verbose and often otiose language commonly found in UN documentation.

If the aim of this was to save translation costs, the decision to impose word limits on State Party reports and associated documentation was far more significant.[106] State Party reports can ramble inconsequentially through hundreds of pages of sometimes largely pointless material, doing little other than costing the UN huge sums of money for their translation.[107] This is possibly the most wasteful element of the entire system and is largely in the hands of States themselves to solve, though it is also important that the treaty bodies do not ask States to submit material which is not necessary or to ask so many questions that they cannot realistically be answered within the agreed word limits.[108] Bearing in mind the limited time that is devoted to the dialogue, this is a useful discipline for both sides, as well as saving significant sums of money.

However, one cost-saving measure was most unwelcome – the decision to allocate only three official working languages, with the possibility of the use of a fourth on an exceptional basis.[109] Given the importance placed on geographical representation and multi-lingualism within the UN, and that experts are drawn from all regions of the world, this has meant that some experts are not able to work in even their second languages.

Another feature of the Resolution is that not all the savings introduced by these cost-cutting measures have been used to support the treaty bodies directly. Rather, it has been channelled into increased capacity building and technical assistance for States, largely in the preparation of their reports.[110] This plays directly into

[104] ibid para 24. It is, however, important to note that verbatim records are also kept of meetings and so a record of meetings continues to exist. In addition, summary records of meetings between treaty bodies and States Parties could be translated into the official UN language used by a State Party at its request: ibid para 25.

[105] ibid para 15.

[106] ibid para 16. Documentation submitted by States to treaty bodies was to be limited to 31,800 words for initial reports, 21,200 for periodic reports and 42,000 for core documents.

[107] See n 40 above.

[108] UNGA Res 68/268 alludes to this, with para 16 'calling upon' the treaty bodies to set limits to the number of questions in order to ensure States might meet the word limits. This is entirely reasonable.

[109] ibid para 30. For those States seeking to restrict the effectiveness of the treaty bodies, this measure has largely backfired as most committees now work in English, French and Spanish, and the languages most commonly dropped have been Russian, Chinese and (to a lesser extent) Arabic.

[110] ibid paras 17–20. This is not to suggest that those who undertake technical assistance in accordance with the Resolution do not do good work do – they do. The point is that it really should not

the trope so often – and so disingenuously – advanced by States that they find the process of reporting to human rights treaty bodies to be particularly complicated and difficult for them, both to understand what is required and to execute it.[111] For most, this is of course complete nonsense, as they routinely engage in international processes which are far more complex and demanding. But it proved necessary to waste considerable sums of money to address the alleged incompetence and/or inadequacy of States, which are, in truth, neither.

Finally, for the current purposes,[112] the Resolution 'encouraged' the treaty bodies to consider a broad range of measures which will be considered in the following section. What can be said at this point is that, in terms of its overall approach and content, the outcome of the treaty strengthening processes was considerably more positive than had been feared, helped to address the immediate crisis concerning the lack of capacity to address the backlog of reports, but avoided the more systemic questions concerning the shape, structure and sustainability of the human rights treaty body system. This was largely put on hold by the final paragraph of the Resolution, which:

> Decides to consider the state of the human rights treaty body system not later than six years from the date of adoption of the present resolution, to review the effectiveness of the measures taken in order to ensure their sustainability and, if appropriate, to decide on further action to strengthen and enhance the effective functioning of the human rights treaty body system.[113]

The sting is in the word 'decides'. The Resolution held open the threat of returning to an 'external top-down' approach, in which the General Assembly instructs the treaty bodies how to go about their business, if it was not persuaded by the manner in which the treaty bodies have responded to the Resolution. It is this realisation – this Sword of Damocles – which coloured that response, and to which we now turn.

B. The Initial Response of the Treaty Bodies

Resolution 68/268 expressly encouraged the treaty bodies to undertake a range of tasks. A first 'basket' largely relates to internal organisational matters, these being

be necessary as States ought to be able to do this for themselves rather than taking resources out of the OHCHR (and the treaty body system). For an example of work funded through the Treaty Body Capacity Building Programme see 'OHCHR Training Package on Reporting to the United Nations Human Rights Treaty Bodies' (2017) funded through UNGA Res 68/268, available at www.ohchr.org/EN/PublicationsResources/Pages/TrainingPackage.aspx.

[111] Gaer (n 47) 346 pithily sums it all up: 'Pocketing these savings, the UNGA authorized additional meeting time for the treaty bodies to address the reporting backlog and increase the review of reports, and allocated some five million dollars previously used for Secretariat expenses for "capacity" building to assist states in preparing their reports to the treaty bodies.'

[112] UNGA Res 68/268 also addresses other important issues which cannot be addressed within the confines of this chapter.

[113] ibid para 41.

to continue to review the Addis Ababa Guidelines,[114] to enhance the role of the Chairs in relation to procedural matters,[115] and to 'strengthen the interaction' between the Chairs and States Parties to all human rights treaties.[116] A second 'basket' relates to matters concerned with the work of the treaty bodies with States and includes offering the 'SRP' to States,[117] developing aligned approaches to the 'constructive dialogue',[118] concluding observations,[119] working methods and rules of procedure[120] and the drafting of general comments.[121] Finally, it 'invites' them to work towards achieving a 'clear and regularized schedule for reporting by States parties'.[122]

Regarding the first 'basket' of issues, the response regarding the Addis Ababa Guidelines is easily dealt with. At each of its subsequent meetings, the Chairs have a standard agenda item in which they review the experience of each Committee concerning the Guidelines, sharing any issues faced concerning their interpretation and application in order to foster a better system-wide understanding of them.[123] The question of enhanced interaction with States is also easily addressed. In 2014 the Annual Meeting of the Chairs was held in Geneva and in 2015 in Costa Rica, but since 2016 they have all taken place in New York. This allows for an afternoon to be spent in a joint meeting with all UN Member States discussing matters of generic significance to the working of the treaty body system. Though some questioning is hostile in tone, most is constructive and supportive, and the Chairs tend to view these meetings as a positive opportunity rather than as a moment of accountability (as was doubtless the intention of some).[124] Meeting in New York

[114] ibid para 36. For the Addis Ababa Guidelines, see n 72 above.
[115] UNGA Res 68/268, para 38.
[116] ibid para 39.
[117] ibid para 1. It is significant that this is the very first recommendation.
[118] ibid para 5.
[119] ibid para 6.
[120] ibid para 9.
[121] ibid para 1.
[122] ibid para 34.
[123] This happened for the first time the following year. See 'Provisional agenda and annotations' for the twenty-seventh meeting of chairpersons of the human rights treaty bodies (San José, 22–26 June 2015) UN Doc HRI/MC/2015/1, Item 4(a). A similar discussion has taken place at all subsequent meetings of the Chairs. That said, there is a degree of disparity in the approach of the Committees to the Guidelines. Several Committees have formally endorsed them, while others have not done so but have expressly amended their rules of procedure to reflect them. One committee, the CESCR, for reasons which remain entirely opaque, has done neither, but argues that its practice is fully in accordance with them. For a summary, see the paper submitted to the 30th Session of the Chairs Meeting in 2018, 'Identifying progress achieved in aligning the working methods and practices of the treaty bodies' (23 March 2018) UN Doc HRI/MC/2018/3, paras 51–56. This is not the place to delve further into the detail of the practical application of the Guidelines, but what is clear is that the treaty bodies do regularly consider and review their practice under the Guidelines, but that their practice, whilst faithful to the spirit of the Guidelines, is not uniform.
[124] See, eg, 'Report of the Chairs of the human rights treaty bodies on their 30th meeting' (11 July 2018) UN Doc A/73/140, paras 33–40. A total of 85 States and other observers attended the annual consultation, and the record gives a good flavour of the general approach and atmosphere.

has also allowed the Chairs to meet directly with the UN Secretary-General and has done much to enhance the overall visibility of the treaty body system.[125]

The issue of 'enhancing the role of the Chairs in procedural matters' is more complex. In essence, this reflects the idea that the Chairs collectively ought to be able to decide upon procedural matters which would then be implemented by the Committees. It has already been seen that this proposal failed to gain traction within the Dublin Process, and the so-called 'Poznan Formula',[126] which contains a weak version of this approach, remains the dead letter it has always been.[127] What the Chairs can do well is to agree upon system-wide approaches which they endorse as Chairs collectively, and then take to their individual committees for their consideration and, hopefully, acceptance. Nevertheless, there is an increasingly strong pressure on Committees to justify why they are not following a position which has been endorsed by the Chairs and it is increasingly the case that they do.[128] However, to suggest that the Chairs can collectively impose change on the Committees is simply unrealistic.[129] To that extent, the philosophy of the 'bottom-up' Dublin Process remains intact – though there has undoubtedly been an important shift towards the Chairs Meeting being the place which generates and legitimates new procedural thinking, even if it cannot require it.[130] Moreover, a Chair whose committee tried to initiate change without taking into account the impact on the system as a whole would certainly now be asked to provide an explanation by other Chairs. It is, then, fair to say that there has been an enhancement of the role of the Chairs, albeit probably not in the manner and to the extent that had been hoped for by some.

For many, it was the second basket of issues which were the most contentious since, no matter how one might seek to present it, they represented a fairly clear set of expectations that the treaty bodies would introduce the simplified reporting

[125] The most recent meeting between the Secretary-General and the Chairs took place during the 31st meeting of the Chairs (New York, 24–28 June 2019). See the press release available at www.un.org/sg/en/content/sg/note-correspondents/2019-06-25/note-correspondents-%E2%80%93-secretary-general%E2%80%99s-meeting-chairs-of-the-human-rights-treaty-bodies.

[126] See the *Poznan Statement* (n 54).

[127] O'Flaherty (n 51) 114 suggests that the Addis Ababa Guidelines were recommended to the treaties on the basis of the Poznan formula, but that is not the recollection of this author (who was present at the time of their endorsement by the Chairs) and is consistent with the tendency of those who favour a stronger Chairs Meeting to overstate the content of the formula.

[128] See generally the paper submitted to the 30th Session of the Chairs Meeting in 2018, UN Doc HRI/MC/2018/3 (n 123), which sets out in detail the extent to which the various Committees have moved towards aligned procedures in the wake of UNGA Res 68/268.

[129] It might also be undesirable. Sir Nigel Rodley, who was Chair of the HRC at the time of the treaty strengthening process, wrote (also at that time) that 'attempts to give the chairpersons' meeting decision-making power … need to be treated with caution' due to dampening impact that this might have on their creativity. See Rodley (n 5) 647.

[130] See, eg, UN Doc A/73/140 (n 124) para 64, which, as regards the role of Chairs and Vice Chairs, merely noted that: 'The Chairs reiterated the encouragement by the General Assembly to the treaty bodies to continue to enhance the role of the Chairs in relation to procedural matters.' This wording suggests that the Chairs have little belief that this will happen.

system and adopt common working methods. The challenge of responding[131] to the 'encouragements' of the General Assembly was taken up immediately at the Annual Meeting of the Chairs of Treaty Bodies held in Geneva in June 2014.[132] The Chairs endorsed a series of suggestions which, if adopted by the respective treaty bodies, would result in aligned approaches to the reporting process, to the structure of the dialogue with States Parties and to concluding observations.[133] At their Annual Meeting in 2015, the Chairs endorsed an aligned approach to the process for adopting General Comments.[134] Within little over a year, then, the Chairs had responded to the Resolution by endorsing common approaches to all of the matters that they had been encouraged to address. This appeared to be a swift and comprehensive response.

However, appearances can be deceptive. The agreed aligned processes, when looked at in detail, often amount to little more than a series of exhortations to the treaty bodies to consider adopting various measures, or are framed in such general terms that they more or less permit the continuation of existing practices with relatively little alteration. It is fair to say that these documents were drafted in such a way as to allow most committees to be able to 'locate' their existing practices within them, rather than to require change. The one area in which substantial change was called for related to the use of the SRP, but this, again, was in the most half-hearted of terms. The Report says:

> 1. The Chairpersons draw the Committees' attention to the call by the General Assembly in resolution 68/268, paragraph 1, to make available to States a simplified reporting procedure.
> 2. The Chairs also recognise that as of 1 January 2015, periodic reports will be subject to the word length set out in paragraph 16 of GA resolution 68/268. In response to this changed situation, the Chairpersons endorse the view that committees which examine periodic reports should consider making such a procedure available after 1 January 2015.
> 3. They further endorse the view that Committees might consider making a simplified process available for the consideration of initial reports in those specific instances where they believe this would enhance the constructive dialogue.

As this makes clear, the Chairs sought to excuse themselves for having to make the suggestion at all, claiming it was a result of changed circumstances brought on by

[131] The use of the word 'responding' is significant. The Chairs consciously rejected the idea that they were 'implementing' the recommendations of the General Assembly in order to underline their autonomous standing. It is a fine point, and the very need to insist on it says something about how precarious they felt that independence to be.

[132] The author of this chapter was the Chair of that meeting, leading the discussions which resulted in the documents which were adopted.

[133] See 'Report of the Chairs of the human rights treaty bodies on their 26th Meeting' (11 August 2014) UN Doc A/69/285, paras 28–54 and 86–93, Annex I and Annex II. It also has to be said that they did not do so with any obvious enthusiasm, observing that: 'The Chairpersons consider it necessary to place before their Committees a series of proposals for alignments' (para 83).

[134] See 'Report of the Chairs of the human rights treaty bodies on their 27th Meeting' (7 August 2015) UN Doc A/70/302, paras 21–25 and 91(a)–(h) for an aligned approach to the consultation process in the elaboration of General Comments.

the decision of the General Assembly on word length. The Report then says that the Committee 'should' consider its introduction for periodic reports and 'might' consider its use for initial reports if they think it beneficial. This is not exactly a call to action and is a good example of the overall approach that was initially taken. It is not difficult to 'align' around the existing lowest common denominators and agreements to consider whether to consider a course of action. The initial response is best described as 'grudging'.

C. The Practical Impact of Resolution 68/268

Over time, this attitude has changed and the practical impact of Resolution 68/268 has proven to be both significant and generally positive. Although some of the cost-cutting measures have been regrettable, they have not had a serious impact upon the work of the treaty bodies.[135] The major achievement has been the expansion of meeting time that has allowed the Committees to largely eliminate the backlog of submitted reports and the numbers currently 'in the pipeline' are now consonant with sustainability. The working practices of the treaty bodies have changed as a result of the Resolution, though not as significantly as might have been expected. Most significantly, and despite initial hesitations, more and more Committees have moved towards offering the SRP, but the pattern remains mixed. All now offer it for periodic reports (albeit subject to a variety of different conditions) and some for initial reports.[136] Paradoxically, if the aim of 'alignment' was to bring about a simpler and more consistent system, it has had the opposite effect, with each committee offering the simplified process to different categories of States, which may or may not accept it.[137] In order to address this, in 2019 the Chairs endorsed a series of further suggestions aimed at aligning and coordinating the reporting processes which may or may not be accepted by each Committee.[138] Without doubt, the system has become more rather than less complex, though it may be more effective as a result.

As far as the reporting system is concerned, it has indeed been a crisis averted. However, this has masked other equally important problems. First, the capacity

[135] Perhaps the most damaging was the unforeseen consequence of reducing the volume of material to be translated, which seemed to result in greater bureaucracy and delays in securing translations, for reasons which are not entirely obvious.

[136] See UN Doc HRI/MC/2018/3 (n 123) paras 4–9. Of the eight treaty bodies receiving initial reports, only two offer the SRP and both only for those which are long overdue (the CAT and the CMW). All seven treaty bodies receiving periodic reports now offer the SRP, but each Committee has different criteria for determining those States to which it is offered.

[137] Of the 657 States that have been offered the SRP since its inception, only 203 have opted to use it. See ibid para 8.

[138] See 'Simplified reporting procedure: possible elements of a common aligned procedure' (15 April 2019) UN Doc HRI/MC/2019/3 and the resulting 'Possible elements for a common aligned procedure for the simplified reporting procedure' endorsed by the Chairs at their 31st meeting (New York, 24–28 June 2019). See 'Report of the Chairs of the human rights treaty bodies on their thirty-first annual meeting' (30 July 2019) UN Doc A/74/256, Annex II.

crisis has largely been transferred to the number of individual communications which are waiting to be considered – the numbers of which continue to rise annually.[139] There is currently no solution to this problem in sight. Second, the sustainability of the reporting system remains premised on the fact that many States do not report and most States do not do so on time. Third, and most dramatically, due to general shortfalls in the UN budget brought about by Member States delaying their contribution, in May 2019 it was decided to cancel many treaty body sessions in the second half of 2019. This undid much of the work achieved in reducing the backlog at a stroke. Although this decision was ultimately rescinded,[140] the situation repeated itself in 2020, masked only partially by the need to move most sessions online as a result of the COVID-19 pandemic.

The system remains in crisis. Relatively little has changed. The basic structural problems within the system remain unaddressed, funding remains as precarious as ever and whilst the treaty bodies under pressure have managed to stave off an assault on their independence, they have not yet cohered as a system and still tend to see themselves as a loose affiliation of autonomous entities. This, then, formed the background to the 2020 Review.

V. The Road to the 2020 Review

A. The Problem to be Addressed

The 2020 Review was known about from the moment Resolution 68/268 was adopted. What was – and still remains – unclear was how this review would be undertaken. It had generally been assumed that it would not be so intensive as the previous intergovernmental process, but that it would result in another General Assembly resolution, though at the time of writing, this remains speculation. More importantly, it was entirely unclear what would be looked at. Would it be limited to the implementation of and response to Resolution 68/268 or would it return to the fundamentals of the system? As a result, it was a difficult review to prepare for. Nevertheless, preparations were made.

At a dinner held during the 2015 Chairs Meeting, the President of Costa Rica announced an intention to support a study into the future of the treaty body system and, with Swiss funding, an independent study was commissioned by the

[139] See nn 34–37. For a fuller analysis, see M Limon, *Reform of the UN Human Rights Petitions Systems: An Assessment of the UN Human Rights Communications Procedures and Proposals for a Single Integrated System* (Versoix, Universal Rights Group, 2018) 20–28.

[140] This was communicated to the Chairs just before the start of their Annual Chair in New York in June 2019. It was, however, made clear that funding problems were likely to return in 2020. This was indeed the case, though the impact of this was, in part, lost from view due to the cancellation of sessions in Geneva as a result of the Covid-19 pandemic. The only treaty body whose work was, in the end, curtailed was the SPT, whose final two visits of 2019 were postponed for financial reasons.

OHCHR to be undertaken by the Geneva Academy of International Humanitarian Law and Human Rights. An 'Academic Platform on the 2020 Treaty Body Review' was established and its Report was published in May 2018.[141] This Report drew on a series of consultations held with a broad range of actors and offers a radical model for the future functioning of the treaty body system, which is considered below.

From early on in the process, aspects of the emergent findings caused concern among some of the treaty body Chairs, who convened a series of informal meetings with interested parties to scope potential alternative models for its future working. Following a major meeting in Wilton Park in March 2017,[142] these ideas were refined into a series of questions which at their 2018 meeting, the Chairs agreed to put to the treaty bodies.[143] The responses to these questions were considered at a meeting in Copenhagen in February 2019[144] and were further refined into a series of practical proposals which formed the basis of the document entitled *Treaty Body Chairpersons Position Paper on the Future of the Treaty Body System*, which was endorsed by the Chairs at their Annual meeting in June of that year.[145]

In the meantime, as a position endorsed by the Chairs, the document had an autonomous existence as well as forming a contribution by the Chairs in their own capacity to the 2020 Review process and was presented as such both to the UN Secretary-General and to Member States in the course of the Annual Meeting of the Chairs that year.[146] Therefore, in addition to the views of States, there were two significant inputs – one based on what might be called 'external' appraisal and the other on 'internal reflection'. What both had in common is that they did not shy away from the basic structural problems which the treaty body system faces, which need to be faced up to and which were lost from view in 2014.

It is worth recalling the nature of the problem and it is embarrassingly simple to do so. In general terms, there are nearly 200 States in the world today. There are currently 10 sets of reporting obligations under human rights treaties. The aim of universal ratification of the UN human rights treaties means that there will be in the region of 2,000 reports to be considered within a reporting cycle. If that cycle is four years, then that means an average of 500 reports per year, or about 10 per week. A single committee can currently handle 2.5 reports a week, so that means four committees would need to be in continuous session – over 200 weeks of meetings a year – just to consider reports alone. A committee with 200 States

[141] C Callejon et al, *Optimizing the UN Treaty Body System: Academic Platform Report on the 2020 Review* (Geneva, Geneva Academy, 2018).

[142] 'Towards a 21st Century Treaty Body System' Report No 1574 (Wilton Park conference, 28 February–2 March 2017) available at www.wiltonpark.org.uk/event/wp1574.

[143] UN Doc A/73/140 (n 124) para 61 and Annex III, requesting each Committee to appoint a Focal Point for this purpose.

[144] See 'Outcome Document: Meeting of Treaty Body Members' (Copenhagen, Denmark, 26–27 February 2019), available at https://tbinternet.ohchr.org/_layouts/15/treatybodyexternal/Download.aspx?symbolno=INT/CHAIRPERSONS/CHR/31/28550&Lang=en.

[145] *Treaty Body Chairpersons Position Paper on the Future of the Treaty Body System* adopted at the 31st Annual Meeting of Chairpersons (New York, 24–28 June 2019).

[146] See n 125 above.

Parties would need to consider 50 reports a year, requiring it to be in session for 25 weeks for just that purpose. Yet the common consensus among the treaty bodies is that unpaid experts simply cannot give more than 12 weeks of the year to the role.

As a result, the current system of unpaid independent experts meeting in Geneva to consider State reports in full plenary sessions simply cannot work. Something must change: the Committees must be able to meet for much longer; or they need to be able to consider more than one report at once; or they need to consider reports much less frequently. Everyone has an objection to every one of these options and so the system continues as it is, and it is only able to do so only because so many States do not fulfil their reporting obligations and so avoid scrutiny. This remains a fundamental flaw in the system which must also be addressed and which can only be remedied by the consideration of States in the absence of a report, which, as we have seen, States are reluctant to agree to, unsurprisingly enough. Nothing has changed since the High Commissioner presented her suggestion for the Master Calendar in 2012 or, indeed, Philip Alston his Independent Expert Reports in 1989 and 1997.[147] The problem is the same and the issues are the same. So what was now being suggested?

B. The Geneva Academy Proposals

Reduced to its basics, the solution to the problems proposed by the Geneva Academy was both simple and radical. One of the recurring criticisms which States have of the current system is that it is unduly burdensome, requiring them to produce reports and send delegations to Geneva to engage in the 'constructive dialogues' several times a year. The High Commissioner's Master Calendar proposal meant that each State might be required to do so twice a year in perpetuity. The Geneva Academy proposals took a very different approach. Each State would produce a 'Single State Report', addressing lists of issues prepared by each of the relevant treaty bodies which would be considered in a 'Single Consolidated Review' held once every seven or eight years. A State would come to Geneva for a week, during which time it would meet with each of the treaty bodies on different days and would discuss with them the relevant parts of its report.[148]

This, at a stroke, changes the entire dynamic of the system. Rather than having up to 500 reports to consider each year, there would only be 25–30 consolidated reports to consider. If each took a week, then only 25–30 weeks of meeting time would be necessary. However, and as the Report accepts, 'this option would require nine committees to sit simultaneously in Geneva in different meeting rooms during the same week. States under review would meet each relevant TB in turn'.[149]

[147] See section III.A above.
[148] Callejon et al (n 141) 19–20.
[149] ibid 20.

The downside is, of course, obvious. Rather than being scrutinised every four years by each Committee, scrutiny would take place only every seven or eight years. Recognising this, the Geneva Academy suggested a variant of the proposal – that once every four years, each State would be required to be in Geneva for a period of a week, when it could meet with a 'cluster' of treaty bodies.[150] This would mean that although each treaty body would meet with the State every eight years, once every four years the State would be examined by at least some treaty bodies, thus mitigating that problem to some extent. The Report then considers how the treaty bodies ought to be 'clustered' for the purposes of review, one option being that the two 'generalist' Covenant Committees meet with the State in year one in the cycle and the others in year five and so on. Another would be for the 10 Committees to be divided equally (or more equally) between the two cycles, ideally five in each.[151]

This suggestion was attractive to neither States nor treaty bodies. For States, not only did it mean they would be considered even in the absence of a report,[152] but the idea of sending expert teams capable of addressing such a broad range of issues over such a short period of time would also be extremely burdensome indeed; for most treaty bodies, not only did it fail to address the problem or their meeting each State only once every eight years, but it is also almost impossible to imagine how it could work in practice. If one of the constraints is the availability of members, then on one reading, this proposal – which envisages 25 States meeting each year for a day with all members of each committee each week – would either require all 172 experts to be either available for about six months of the year or in constant transit, which would be as eye-wateringly expensive as it would be physically impossible. Another option would be for several States to be considered in the same week: for example, five States meeting each of five committees per day over a five-week period. Such an intensive roundabout, whilst theoretically feasible, is difficult to imagine working effectively in practice. Nor is it clear when and how the Committees would be able to undertake the rest of their work.

More generally, the Geneva Academy proposals appeared to privilege the concerns of the State over the effectiveness of the treaty body system, that system being required to reshape itself in order to reduce its burdens on States. But where is the voice of the rights holder? The terms of reference of the Geneva Academy study did not include an evaluation of whether the system delivered optimal outcomes for rights holders; its focus was primarily on the effectiveness and efficiency of the machinery of protection.[153] This was an important omission, once

[150] ibid 21–22, described as 'Clustered Reviews'.

[151] ibid 22, the suggestion being that those monitoring individuals (the HRC, the CESCR, the CERD, the CAT and the CED) be in one cluster, whilst those addressing specific groups (CEDAW, the CRC, the CMW and the CRPD) be in another. This division into individual and group-focussed treaties is conceptually difficult to grasp as all conventions address the rights of individuals.

[152] ibid 23.

[153] ibid 15, setting out the scope of the report, which is limited to '(1) TB functions; (2) synergies that could be developed inside and outside the TB system; (3) the system's accessibility; and (4) the system's structure'.

again reflecting the failure of so many reform proposals which consider effectiveness to mean 'well operating' processes, not whether these processes deliver better human rights protection.

C. The Chairs' Process

The origins of what is here called 'the Chairs' Process' have already been outlined. Like all processes, it absorbed and responded to many of the ideas which were circulating while it was taking place, whilst also generating new ideas and approaches. The single most important element of the *Treaty Body Chairpersons Position Paper on the Future of the Treaty Body System* is that it seeks to move beyond the so-called 'harmonisation' (or even alignment) agenda which had dominated discussions over the last 10 years. As the response by the treaty body Chairs to Resolution 68/268 clearly demonstrated, harmonisation ran the risk of becoming little more than a quest for inclusive language.[154] Other, more practical matters, such as the adoption of the Addis Ababa Guidelines, were less the result of harmonisation and more an act of collective self-defence. As one colleague pithily and memorably put it at the Copenhagen consultation in February 2019: 'Harmonisation has seen better days.'

Instead, the Chairs embraced diversity, believing that a coherent, predictable system does not necessarily require uniformity. More prosaically, it was clear that there was not going to be a consensus on the single best way of addressing the systemic structural crisis facing the treaty body system and that different treaty bodies favoured tackling it in very different ways. So rather than seek to agree upon a single solution and to impose it on others – which in practice would be near-impossible to do – why not facilitate a common framework which achieved the same goals, but in different ways?

The starting point was to identify new common practices which did have consensus support. Importantly, this includes making the SRP available for all periodic reports and accepting its being offered in respect of initial reports by those treaty bodies that wish to do so.[155] The use of the SRP involves States being sent 'Lists of Issues Prior to Reporting' (ie, questions to answer), and it was also agreed that these should be limited to 25–30 and be coordinated in order to avoid unnecessarily raising similar questions at similar times. They also agreed to endorse a

[154] Indeed, the theory that the work of the treaty bodies would be enhanced by them all working in the same way was always an entirely unproven hypothesis. It may be presumed that it would make the task of serving the treaty bodies by the OHCHR simpler and would make it easier for States, and indeed civil society, if there was only one common process to get to grips with. But there was never any evidence that it would improve the protection of rights holders if CEDAW, for example, conducted its reviews of State reports in exactly the same way as the CERD, or vice versa.

[155] 'Treaty body Chairpersons Position Paper on the future of the treaty body system' adopted at the 31st Meeting of Chairpersons (New York, 24–28 June 2019): 'All treaty bodies agree to offer the SRP to all States parties for periodic reports and may do so for initial Reports. All treaty bodies offering the SRP for initial reports will develop a standard list of issues prior to reporting (LOIPR).'

common framework for reviews, comprising two sessions of three hours (and potentially by videoconference in exceptional circumstances), resulting in concluding observations, and follow up to concluding observations, which adhered to previously agreed aligned methodologies. In essence, the Chairs' position paper offers a substantially aligned, or common, methodology for the consideration of reports. The variations which it permits are relatively inconsequential.

Turning to the reporting cycle, matters were very different: if there was a high degree of consensus on what should be done, there was less consensus on when it should be done.

The first goal had to be to construct a system in which it would be possible for the compliance of all States Parties to be considered in an orderly, predictable timeframe, irrespective of whether they had submitted a report, in a relatively similar manner. This inevitably required calendars but it does not require a single calendar, and if there are several calendars they do not require a common reporting cycle. During discussions, it became clear that whilst the HRC and the CESCR had little objection to an eight-year reporting cycle, other Committees did. Rather than seek to 'harmonise' and impose a common solution, it was agreed that:

> The Covenant Committees (CESCR and CCPR) will review countries on an 8-year cycle and will synchronize the timing of their reviews.
>
> The Convention Committees will review countries on a 4-year cycle, unless the provisions of a particular Convention provide otherwise.[156]

In order to ensure that these separate cycles do not rub against each other, it was further agreed that, as regards the timing of reviews:

> The treaty bodies will ensure that should a State party be scheduled for review by a number of treaty bodies within a relatively short period, the scheduling of the reviews in question shall be altered to ensure an appropriate period elapses between reviews by convention committees. Covenant Committees may wish to conduct back to back reviews.[157]

In addition:

> A single consolidated report may be submitted to both Covenant Committees if they choose to offer this option to States parties. The Convention Committees may wish to continue to receive separate reports in order not to dilute the Convention-specific focus.[158]

De facto, this permits the 'Covenant Committees' to forge a close relationship, or even a common process, built around an eight-year reporting cycle, whereas the 'Convention Committees' would continue to work on the basis of their own reporting cycles, but in a much more coordinated and structured fashion – in effect, each would have its own tailored 'treaty calendar' rather than a common 'master calendar'.

[156] ibid.
[157] ibid.
[158] ibid.

This allows for another piece of the jigsaw to be put into place: 'All treaty bodies will schedule reviews with State parties in accordance with the reporting cycle. The review will take place as scheduled irrespective of whether a report has been submitted (ie review in the absence of a report). This will ensure the regularity of reviews as provided for in the treaties.'[159] This, then, finally permits the achievement of a predictable review cycle which includes all States Parties, coordinated in a way which respects the differing mandates and independence of the treaty bodies, but which also seeks to ensure that the reporting burden on States is spread out across the reporting cycles.

The final element of the jigsaw is how up to 200 States can be considered across the reporting cycles. For the Covenant Committees, it is solved by moving to the eight-year cycle. For the others: 'All treaty bodies agree to increase their capacity to review state party reports and individual communications, for example by working in chambers, working groups or country teams. This will facilitate the need to review up to 50 reports per year for Convention Committees, and 25 reports per year for Covenant Committees.' In other words, each Committee is to find its own solution, but it will have to adopt a solution which coheres with the system-wide approach.

That such a solution might be quite radical is also foreseen in what is, without doubt, the most far-reaching suggestion, this being that:

> All treaty bodies agree that there are considerable benefits in conducting dialogues with States parties concerning their reports at a regional level, and that this should be offered to states on a pilot basis by those committees wishing to do so, with a view to permanent implementation. Such dialogues may be conducted by a delegation of the treaty body, with Concluding Observations being adopted by the Committee as a whole.[160]

This means that for those treaty bodies and States that are prepared to try, the entire experience of the reporting procedure could be transformed from a 'Geneva-based' meeting with a full plenary into a regionally, or even nationally, based discussion with a delegation. This draws some inspiration from the fieldwork model of the SPT.

Although motivated in part by concerns at the emerging direction of the Geneva Academy's proposals, the proposals made by the Chairs are not entirely dissimilar in some respects, notably a willingness to consider extended reporting cycles, but only for those who wish to do so. The key difference is that the Chairs' proposals seek to balance the benefits of a common overarching framework with diverse approaches reflecting the dynamics of each Convention and Committee.[161] Whilst they reject the idea of the Committees 'coming to the State' in Geneva,

[159] ibid.

[160] ibid.

[161] This also reflects the wisdom of the observation made by Sir Nigel Rodley during the strengthening process that: 'Rigid harmonization could entail the sort of sclerosis that would prevent the kind of experimentation that has led to improving methodology.' See Rodley (n 5) 647.

they also embrace the idea of the Committees 'coming to the State' in the region, thus taking the protection of human rights by the treaty bodies closer to the rights holders, with the aim of increasing the impact and effectiveness of their work and of the system as a whole. This is something which had also been suggested by the Geneva Academy[162] and it is an idea whose time may be coming.

VI. Conclusion: Reform by Review

Writing in 1997, Philip Alston noted:

> In light of current trends the existing reporting system is unsustainable ... Four options are available to States: (a) to dismiss the concern as alarmist and take no action; (b) to urge the treaty bodies to undertake far-reaching reforms and adapt to cope with existing and new demands from within existing resources; (c) to provide greatly enhanced budgetary resources to sustain the status quo; (d) to combine some elements of (b) and (c) with the adoption of some far-reaching reforms.[163]

Nearly 25 years on, the situation is basically unchanged, and the systemic crisis facing the treaty body system as a result of its growth and the growth in the numbers of States within the international community continues to be compounded, but the system has survived. The crisis is now a real crisis, but, recalling our cautionary tale mentioned at the outset, is it still not too late to rescue 'Matilda'. This chapter was written in the midst of the 2020 Review, which, as the postscript sets out, more or less evaporated (or, perhaps, disappeared from view). The various proposals and positions were put forward in ignorance of how it would be conducted or, indeed, what were its aims. In all probability, they still remain to be decided, and the nature of the proposals that have been generated have undoubtedly influenced the nature of the process. What is clear enough is that the shadow of the process leading up to Resolution 68/268 has loomed large: States have been unwilling to commit themselves to undertaking so intensive (and expensive) a process; the OHCHR has refrained from directly imputing into the process as it did in 2012; and the Chairs of the treaty bodies have been anxious to avoid being caught out again by having a process imposed on them at short notice and for which they were ill-prepared.

More positively, the failure of Resolution 68/268 to address the systemic problems which faced the treaty bodies left a space which other could fill. Though flawed, the proposals of the Geneva Academy were a vital catalyst, reinforcing the need to return to the idea of fixed and regular reviews of all States within an order system which was capable of coping with universal participation and universal compliance. The idea of perpetuating a system of international human rights

[162] Callejon et al (n 141) 35–36. However, it is difficult to see how this would be reconcilable with many of their other proposals concerning consolidated or clustered reviews.

[163] 'Final report on enhancing the long-term effectiveness of the United Nations human rights treaty system' (27 March 1997) UN Doc E/CN.4/1997/74, para 120.

protection which could only function on the assumption of mass non-compliance had to be rejected. If their solutions were flawed, the direction was correct. The crucial addition brought by the Chairs' Process was to re-imagine the role of harmonisation and alignment as being a tool of coherence rather than compulsion. It offers a vision that respects the mandates and independence of the treaty bodies, whilst, it is hoped, respecting and responding to the perfectly rational criticisms of States concerning the current system and whilst also, crucially, exploring new and innovative means of protecting the interests of the rights holders.

Above all else, however, almost the entirety of the proposals endorsed by the Chairs can be achieved by the Committees themselves through changes to their rules of procedure. They do not need an intergovernmental review or another General Assembly Resolution in order to bring them about. They would certainly need the goodwill of the OHCHR to embrace changes to established working practices, but that ought not be a constraint. The process of review has generated the most ambitious set of reform proposals of the treaty body system in 25 years. It is now up to the Committees to be bold enough to seize the initiative that the Chairs have handed them, for the OHCHR to support them and for States to refrain from frustrating them. And even if this all proves too ambitious for today, at least there is a vision which can be returned to tomorrow.

In his preface to the 2012 High Commissioner's Report, Ban Ki-moon, the UN Secretary-General, described the UN human rights treaty body system as 'one of the greatest achievements in the history of the global struggle for human rights'.[164] The 'problems' posed by near-universal ratification of the human rights treaties are problems flowing from the success of the system. When in 1944 Hersch Lauterpacht wrote his visionary work *An International Bill of Rights*, he accepted that 'the International Bill of Rights of Man … cannot be accepted without a substantial sacrifice by States of their freedom of action' and that the first main obstacle to be overcome 'is the probably disinclination of governments to submit to the restrictions of sovereignty implied in the Bill of Rights'.[165] He might barely have hoped to foresee that nearly all sovereign States might commit themselves to so extensive a series of binding legal obligations concerning the manner in which they treat those subject to their domestic jurisdictions, as is currently the case. Nor even 30 years ago might it have been guessed that the oversight of such obligations would be as rigorous as it has become. If, through the treaty strengthening process, States are reacting against these developments, then it demonstrates the potency of what has been created: States do not put such efforts into contesting matters which do not trouble them. That so many States in the twenty-first century seem troubled by being held to account for the manner in which they ill-treat those over whom they exercise authority should be seen as a shocking indictment of

[164] Pillay (n 10) 7.

[165] H Lauterpacht, *An International Bill of Rights* (Oxford, Oxford University Press, 2013 [1945]) 82, 222.

their stewardship of their sovereign prerogatives. That they have to do so through subterfuge rather than through an assertion of right should be seen as a triumph for the normative international legal order.

VII. Postscript

Did the 2020 Review happen? Perhaps – and perhaps not. As with so much else, COVID-19 hugely impacted on the process, moving most consideration online and significantly reducing the 'discursive space'. Morocco and Switzerland were appointed co-facilitators of the process and, following rounds of online meetings in June and July, produced their Report to the Chair of the UN General Assembly in September 2020, just a little later than planned.[166] That Report has been duly noted to the General Assembly,[167] and that, currently, appears to be that. It remains as unclear at the start of 2021 what is, formally speaking, going to happen. The '2020 Review' has become (at least for now) something of a chimera. Doubtless it will raise its head again, but in what form and to what end is a mystery.[168]

What is clear, however, is that COVID-19 has had a major effect on the future of the treaty body system and the review. In-person treaty body sessions in Geneva were put on hold in March 2020 and are yet to resume. The first ever online session of a human rights treaty body took place in June 2021, the 41st session of the Subcommittee for the Prevention of Torture. Suddenly, and after years of procedural caution, radically different ways of working have come to the fore. This was swiftly reflected in the Report of the co-facilitators, which advocates a 'digital shift' in the working methods of the Committees.[169] The Committees themselves have become increasingly nervous of the implications of this, based on six months of experience struggling with problems of online access, inadequate platforms, limited interpretation facilities and vastly reduced online meeting times, and backlogs in the consideration of State Reports and Individual Communications have soared. In some ways, the gains of the last six years have already been wiped out.

Yet, in other ways, there has been major progress. The Co-Facilitators' Report endorses the premises of Resolution 68/268 and urges the OHCHR to work with the treaty bodies to bring about further enhancements to their working methods.[170] It also recognises the benefits of coordinated calendars for both the States and the treaty bodies.[171] In short, it seems to allow the space for the treaty bodies to adopt

[166] See UN Doc A/75/601 (14 September 2020) Annex, 'Report on the process of the consideration of the state of the United Nations human rights treaty body system' (hereinafter 'Co-Facilitators' Report').

[167] See UNGA Doc A/75/478/Add 1 and UNGA Res 75/174 (16 December 2020), para 2.

[168] The co-facilitators recommend that there be some form of follow-up process (Co-Facilitators' Report (n 166) para 83), but it is not clear what has become of that suggestion.

[169] ibid paras 12–19, making it clear that this is very much inspired by the experience of online working during the COVID-19 pandemic.

[170] ibid paras 35–36.

[171] ibid paras 55–56.

the approaches set out in the Chairs' Position Paper, with longer reporting cycles, but with lighter touch intermediate reviews, which, for practical purposes, restore the regulatory of review to something akin to previous practice. The benefits of such intermediate reviews taking place at a regional or country level, involving delegations of the Committees, is also acknowledged.[172] If these approaches can be operationalised and funded (which is a big 'if'),[173] there is cause for cautious optimism that a more positive future is potentially within view, prompted by, but not necessarily the product of, the 2020 Review. The treaty bodies and their Chairs may well have finally taken hold of their own destiny and reversed the most negative aspect of Resolution 68/268 – the idea that it was for States to decide what they could or could not do.

[172] ibid paras 67–69.

[173] The co-facilitators called for appropriate levels of funding, and revised and improved funding formulas (ibid paras 74–77), but this has already been rebuffed by the General Assembly when it reaffirmed its support for the formulas in Res 68/268 when adopting Res 75/174, para 5, which is not an encouraging sign.

5

United Nations Human Rights Treaty Bodies

Universality and National Implementation

GEIR ULFSTEIN

Abstract: This chapter considers the challenges facing the UN human rights treaty bodies, looking at the 2020 Review. It considers whether the treaty bodies should defer to decisions made by national organs by applying different standards of review. It does so through a discussion of a number of international organisations and bodies, not just those concerned with human rights matters, and argues that UN human rights treaty bodies should consider a selective, conditional and cautious deference to national decisions.

I. Introduction[1]

The United Nations (UN) human rights treaty bodies shall oversee national implementation of international human rights obligations. There are now 10 committees of independent experts, including the Human Rights Committee, the Committee against Torture and the Committee on the Rights of the Child. The Committees examine reports by the States Parties on their implementation of the relevant human rights obligations and adopt general comments on the interpretation of the rights. Several of them are also delegated the court-like function of deciding cases on individual complaints.[2] These international organs have been a success in the

[1] This chapter was supported by the Research Council of Norway through its Centres of Excellence Funding Scheme, project number 223274 PluriCourts–The Legitimacy of the International Judiciary. I am grateful for insightful comments by Andreas Follesdal and Matthew Saul, PluriCourts.

[2] On treaty bodies, see generally R Churchill and G Ulfstein, 'Autonomous Institutional Arrangements in Multilateral Environmental Agreements: A Little-Noticed Phenomenon in International Law' (2000) 94 *American Journal of International Law* 623. On the human rights treaty bodies, see H Keller and G Ulfstein (eds), *UN Human Rights Treaty Bodies: Law and Legitimacy* (Cambridge, Cambridge University Press, 2012). On the complaints mechanism, see G Ulfstein, 'Individual Complaints' in H Keller and G Ulfstein (eds), *UN Human Rights Treaty Bodies: Law and Legitimacy* (Cambridge,

sense that they have increasingly extended their importance. As stated by former UN Secretary-General Ban Ki-moon: they are 'one of the greatest achievements in the history of the global struggle for human rights'.[3]

International courts and tribunals (ICs) have been seen as essential mechanisms for increasing respect for the international rule of law. However, they have recently been criticised for their composition and procedures, as well as for their too extensive intrusions into national sovereignty.[4] Some of the critique is based on narrow nationalism and populism, and can be seen as threats to international cooperation. However, other aspects of the criticism may be justified and give reason to reforms.

One way of responding to the critique is that ICs defer to decisions by national organs by applying different standards of review. The European Court of Human Rights (ECtHR) is well known for its use of a margin of appreciation. Also, other ICs increasingly apply forms of deference.[5] However, the Inter-American Court of Human Rights (IACtHR) has been reluctant to apply deference in the form of the margin of appreciation.[6] This reluctance is shared by the human rights treaty bodies.[7] But to what extent should the treaty bodies defer to national decision-making, not for strategic reasons, but because the international system for human rights would become more legitimate?

ICs should, arguably, defer to decisions by national organs on three different grounds. First, there may be epistemic reasons for deference if national organs better secure relevant knowledge to render credible decisions.[8] Second, the

Cambridge University Press, 2012); G Ulfstein, 'The Human Rights Treaty Bodies and Legitimacy Challenges' in N Grossman et al (eds), *Legitimacy and International Courts* (Cambridge, Cambridge University Press, 2018).

[3] Office of the High Commissioner of Human Rights, 'Strengthening the United Nations Human Rights Treaty Body System. A Report by the United Nations High Commissioner for Human Rights' (2012), 7.

[4] P Sands, 'Judicialization and its Challenges' in A Follesdal and G Ulfstein (eds), *The Judicialization of International Law: A Mixed Blessing?* (Oxford, Oxford University Press, 2018); M Madsen, P Cebulak and M Wiebusch, 'Special Issue: Resistance to International Courts Introduction and Conclusion' (2018) 14 *International Journal of Law in Context* 193; J Pauwelyn and RJ Hamilton, 'Exit from International Tribunals' (2018) *Journal of International Dispute Settlement* 1; E Voeten, 'Populism and Backlashes against International Courts' (2018), available at www.ssrn.com/abstract=3255764.

[5] Y Shany, 'Toward a General Margin of Appreciation Doctrine in International Law?' (2005) 16 *European Journal of International Law* 907; L Gruszczynski and WG Werner, 'Introduction' in L Gruszczynski and WG Werner (eds), *Deference in International Courts and Tribunals: Standard of Review and Margin of Appreciation* (Oxford, Oxford University Press, 2014).

[6] P Contreras, 'National Discretion and International Deference in the Restriction of Human Rights: A Comparison between the Jurisprudence of the European and the Inter-American Court of Human Rights' (2012) 11 *Northwestern Journal of International Human Rights* 28, 28; J Contesse, 'Contestation and Deference in the Inter-American Human Rights System' (2016) 79 *Law and Contemporary Problems* 123, 141.

[7] D McGoldrick, 'A Defence of the Margin of Appreciation and an Argument for its Application by the Human Rights Committee' (2016) 1 *International and Comparative Law Quarterly* 21, 22; V Engström, 'Deference and the Human Rights Committee' (2016) 34 *Nordic Journal of Human Rights* 73, 77; Y Shany, 'All Roads Lead to Strasbourg?: Application of the Margin of Appreciation Doctrine by the European Court of Human Rights and the UN Human Rights Committee' (2017) *Journal of International Dispute Settlement* 1, 1–2.

[8] Gruszczynski and Werner (n 5) 2.

principle of subsidiarity – in the protection of national autonomy – establishes a rebuttable presumption that decision-making should be taken at the domestic level, unless it is more effectively or efficiently performed by international organs.[9] Finally, separation of powers may be taken as an argument for restricting the judicial powers of ICs when they unduly interfere with legislative and executive functions.[10] However, these grounds may not be easily distinguished from each other in practice. Furthermore, they can be mutually reinforcing or they may point in opposite directions.

In the field of human rights protection, it can be argued that a State should be accorded considerable freedom in deciding the rights and obligations of individuals. On the other hand, States may not be trusted when it comes to controlling restrictions in relation to their own governmental powers. This is of special concern regarding the protection of the most fundamental rights of individuals, especially in non-democratic States with insufficient rule of law protection. Therefore, permitting national discretion in the implementation of their international obligations may lead to abuse and the undermining of effective human rights protection. Furthermore, such discretion may threaten the sovereign equality of States and the universality of human rights.

In the ongoing reform process of the ECtHR, the principle of subsidiarity and the use of the margin of appreciation have been essential elements. However, despite the concern about the treaty bodies' intrusion into national sovereignty, deference was not part of the treaty body reform process, which culminated in adoption of General Assembly Resolution 68/268 'Strengthening and enhancing the effective functioning of the human rights treaty body system' in 2014.[11] Yet, this issue may become relevant when the General Assembly again considers the state of the treaty body system in 2020, as envisaged by Resolution 68/268. In this chapter I propose that these bodies should – under specified conditions – defer to national decisions when deciding individual complaints.

The chapter proceeds as follows. First, I present the practice of the ECtHR with respect to the margin of appreciation (section II). Then I discuss comparable standards of review as applied by other ICs (section III). I use these practices as

[9] See A Føllesdal, 'Survey Article: Subsidiarity' (1998) 6 *Journal of Political Philosophy* 190; PG Carozza, 'Subsidiarity as a Structural Principle of International Human Rights Law' (2003) 97 *American Journal of International Law* 38; I Feichtner, 'Subsidiarity' *Max Planck Encyclopedia of Public International Law* (2009); GL Neuman, 'Subsidiarity' in D Shelton (ed), *The Oxford Handbook of International Human Rights Law* (Oxford, Oxford University Press, 2013); A Follesdal, 'Subsidiarity and International Human Rights Courts: Respecting Self-Governance and Protecting Human Rights – or Neither? (2016) 79 *Law and Contemporary Problems* 147, 148; M Jachtenfuchs and N Krisch, 'Subsidiarity in Global Governance' (2016) 79 *Law and Contemporary Problems* 1, 6.

[10] J Waldron, 'Separation of Powers in Thought and Practice' (2013) 54 *Boston College Law Review* 433, 438. See also G Ulfstein, 'A Transnational Separation of Powers?' in M Saul, A Follesdal and G Ulfstein (eds), *The International Human Rights Judiciary and National Parliaments* (Cambridge, Cambridge University Press, 2017).

[11] UNGA Res 68/L.37 'Strengthening and enhancing the effective functioning of the human rights treaty body system' (9 April 2014) UN Doc A/RES/68/L.37.

a basis for discussing whether similar standards should be applied by the human rights treaty bodies (section IV). Finally, I present some conclusions (section V).

II. Deference by the ECtHR

A. Introduction

The ECtHR has developed practices concerning deference to domestic decisions relating to facts, the interpretation and application of national law, as well as the interpretation and application of the European Convention on Human Rights (ECHR). The first two elements – facts and the interpretation and application of national law – are covered by what the courts has called 'the fourth instance' doctrine, whereas implementation of the ECHR is dealt with as an aspect of the margin of appreciation. In this section I discuss how deference based on epistemic reasons, subsidiarity and separation of powers is applied by the ECtHR with respect to the fourth instance doctrine and the margin of appreciation. I also examine how these standards of review relate to comparable standards known from the domestic context. Finally, I present the Court's limits for use of such standards to prevent abuse by the Member States.

B. Fourth Instance

The Copenhagen Declaration, adopted by the Member States in 2018, situates the fourth instance doctrine as part of the principle of subsidiarity. It is dealt with in the context of the requirement of exhaustion of local remedies.[12] But this doctrine also establishes a standard of review with respect to assessment of facts and the interpretation and application of domestic law.

National courts are closer to the facts of the cases than the ECtHR. This means that they have a potential epistemic advantage. Furthermore, national courts are experts on domestic law and, under domestic law, they have the function of finally determining the interpretation of national law. The ECtHR is an international organ and shall determine the international obligations, not the content of domestic law. Therefore, the principle of subsidiarity calls for wide discretion for such courts in interpreting and applying domestic law. However, a caveat is that national courts may be myopic and have a domestic bias in their dealing with facts as well as national law.

[12] Copenhagen Declaration on the Reform of the European Convention on Human Rights System (adopted 13 April 2018), para 28(c), available at www.coe.int/en/web/human-rights-rule-of-law/events/-/asset_publisher/E5WWthsy4Jfg/content/copenhagen-declaration-on-the-reform-of-the-european-convention-on-human-rights-system?inheritRedirect=false.

The ECtHR has reiterated that 'it is not its task to substitute itself for the domestic courts as regards the assessment of the facts and their legal classification, provided that these are based on a reasonable assessment of the evidence'.[13] This means that the Court allows wide discretion to domestic courts in the assessment of facts and the interpretation and application of domestic law.

C. Margin of Appreciation

The margin of appreciation has been practised by the ECtHR since the classic *Handyside* case in 1976, with roots going back to the *Cyprus* case in 1958.[14] It was recognised by Member States in the Brighton Declaration, which '[w]elcomes the development by the Court in its case law of principles such as subsidiarity and the margin of appreciation, and encourages the Court to give great prominence to and apply consistently these principles in its judgments'.[15] The margin has also been acknowledged in the subsequent Brussels[16] and Copenhagen Declarations. Furthermore, the new Protocol 15 expressly supports the margin of appreciation.[17]

The margin of appreciation is a standard of review applied by the ECtHR in its examination of decisions taken at the national level.[18] The Copenhagen Declaration sets out that 'national authorities are in principle better placed than an international court to evaluate local needs and conditions'.[19] The reference to local needs and conditions indicates that the function of the margin of appreciation is not seen primarily as an epistemic reason for deference, but rather as based on subsidiarity, in the sense of respecting national autonomy. This is in accordance with the functional division of responsibilities: domestic courts are superior at the national level, while the ECtHR is entrusted with the final responsibility to interpret the ECHR.

It is essential that the margin is relevant for the application of the ECHR in a national context, not for the interpretation of the Convention. The ECtHR may take

[13] *Rohlena v The Czech Republic* App No 59552/08 (ECtHR, 27 January 2015), para 51.

[14] Y Arai-Takahashi, 'The Margin of Appreciation Doctrine: A Theoretical Analysis of Strasbourg's Variable Geometry' in A Føllesdal, B Peters and G Ulfstein (eds), *Constituting Europe: The European Court of Human Rights in a National, European and Global Context* (Cambridge, Cambridge University Press, 2013) 65–66.

[15] Brighton Declaration (adopted 20 April 2012), para 12(a), available at http://www.echr.coe.int/Documents/2012_Brighton_FinalDeclaration_ENG.pdf.

[16] Brussels Declaration (adopted 27 March 2015), available at www.echr.coe.int/Documents/Brussels_Declaration_ENG.pdf.

[17] Article 1 of Protocol No 15 amending the Convention for the Protection of Human Rights and Fundamental Freedoms (CETS No 2013) (not yet in force).

[18] G Letsas, *A Theory of Interpretation of the European Convention on Human Rights* (Oxford, Oxford University Press, 2007) 80–81; A Legg, *The Margin of Appreciation in International Human Rights Law: Deference and Proportionality* (Oxford, Oxford University Press, 2012). See also G Letsas, 'Two Concepts of the Margin of Appreciation' (2006) 26 *Oxford Journal of Legal Studies* 705.

[19] Copenhagen Declaration on the Reform of the European Convention on Human Rights System (adopted 13 April 2018), para 28(b).

into account the general practice of Member States as an expression of 'European consensus' and may even be persuaded by specific domestic courts about the best interpretation of the ECHR as part of a 'judicial dialogue'. But the interpretation of the Convention will apply for all Member States, whereas the margin of appreciation is only relevant for the application of the ECHR in the instant case.

The margin allowed by the Court to the domestic application of the ECHR is governed by several factors. First, it depends on the right under examination. The Court will allow discretion in respect of Articles 8–11 ECHR, which expressly permit a balancing between the right in question and other interests, such as allowing respect for private and family life if necessary in a democratic society. Other articles, such as Article 3 on torture, allow no such balancing.

The permissible freedom of choice may also vary between the rights where interference is expressly allowed. For example, restrictions on the freedom of expression 'must be established convincingly'.[20] On the other hand, the Court has allowed a wide margin when it comes to the choice of 'general measures of economic or social strategy'.[21]

The breadth of the margin may depend on the general international legal obligations in the area,[22] as well as on whether there a European consensus exists on the issue.[23] In the Court's practice, a European consensus can have a double function: it can provide a basis for evolutive interpretation that is binding on all Member States, or, alternatively, it can provide one of the factors in determining the margin of appreciation in relation to an individual State in its application of Convention rights.

National decision-making organs may enjoy a wider margin of appreciation if they are able to convince the ECtHR that they have taken into account the relevant principles of interpretation, such as the principle of proportionality, as applied by the ECtHR. For example, the Court stated in the *Von Hannover (No 2)* case (2012) that: 'Where the balancing exercise has been undertaken by the national authorities in conformity with the criteria laid down in the Court's case-law, the Court would require strong reasons to substitute its view for that of the domestic courts.'[24] This has been called a 'procedural turn' or a 'process-based' review of national decision-making.[25]

[20] *Pentikäinen v Finland* App No 11882/10 (ECtHR, 20 October 2015), para 87.

[21] *Biao v Denmark* App No 38590/10 (ECtHR, 24 May 2016), para 93.

[22] *Naït-Liman v Switzerland* App No 51357/07 (ECtHR, 15 March 2018), para 173.

[23] See, eg, *Bayatyan v Armenia* App No 23459/03 (ECtHR, 7 July 2011), para 122: 'The Court may also have regard to any consensus and common values emerging from the practices of the States Parties to the Convention.'

[24] *Von Hannover v Germany (No 2)* App Nos 40660/08 and 60641/08 (ECtHR, 7 February 2012), para 107.

[25] E Brems, 'Procedural Protection: An Examination of Procedural Safeguards Read into Substantive Convention Rights' in E Brems and J Gerards (eds), *Shaping Rights in the ECHR: The Role of the European Court of Human Rights in Determining the Scope of Human Rights* (Cambridge, Cambridge University Press, 2013); R Spano, 'Universality or Diversity of Human Rights?: Strasbourg in the Age of Subsidiarity' (2014) 14 *Human Rights Law Review* 487; M Saul, 'The European Court of Human Rights' Margin of Appreciation and the Processes of National Parliaments' (2015) 15 *Human Rights*

We also find reflections of the separation of powers approach in the Court's margin of appreciation practice. The margin applies to all constitutional organs, but the margin is not necessarily the same for the national legislature, the executive and the domestic courts. For example, the Court stated in the *İzzettin Doğan and Others* case (Grand Chamber) (2016) that: 'In matters of general policy, on which opinions within a democratic society may reasonably differ widely, the role of the *domestic policymaker* should be given special weight' (emphasis added).[26] Such deference is based on the democratic character of decision-making in the Member States, but it may also be grounded in other advantages of legislative decision-making.[27]

D. Standards of Review

The margin of appreciation has similarities to standards of review applied by domestic courts in their administrative review of acts from the executive, and even constitutional review of legislative acts. But the margin as applied by the ECtHR has distinct features compared to standards of review applied by domestic courts, reflecting its application to the field of human rights in the context of European democracies. In *A and Others* (2009), the Court expressly distinguished the deference represented by the margin of appreciation from standards of review applied in a domestic setting:

> The doctrine of the margin of appreciation has always been meant as a tool to define relations between the domestic authorities and the Court. It cannot have the same application to the relations between the organs of State at the domestic level.[28]

As we have seen, the standard of review is wider when it comes to review of facts and national legislation under the fourth instance doctrine.

However, it should be kept in mind that the use of standards of review does not pre-empt review of national decisions by the Court. As stated in the Copenhagen Declaration, the 'margin of appreciation goes hand in hand with supervision under the Convention system, and the decision as to whether there has been a violation of the Convention ultimately rests with the Court'.[29]

Law Review 745; OM Arnardottir, 'The "Procedural Turn" under the European Convention on Human Rights and Presumptions of Convention Compliance' (2017) *International Journal of Constitutional Law* 9; P Popelier and C van de Heyning, 'Subsidiarity Post-Brighton: Procedural Rationality as Answer?' (2017) 30 *Leiden Journal of International Law* 5; R Spano, 'The Future of the European Court of Human Rights: Subsidiarity, Process-Based Review and the Rule of Law' (2018) 18 *Human Rights Law Review* 1.

[26] *İzzettin Doğan and Others v Turkey* App No 62649/10 (ECtHR, 26 April 2016), para 112.

[27] Saul (n 25) 762–68.

[28] *A and Others v United Kingdom* App No 3455/05 (ECtHR, 19 February 2009), para 184.

[29] Copenhagen Declaration on the Reform of the European Convention on Human Rights System (adopted 13 April 2018), para 28(d).

E. Abuse of Powers

It is of importance that the Court in its recent case law has also designated instances of bad faith implementation of ECHR standards. In such instances, the need for ensuring the effective implementation of the international obligations means that relevant States will not benefit from the deference represented by the margin of appreciation. However, a challenge is how to apply a differentiation based on good or bad faith implementation, without well-founded accusations that the Court applies double standards between Member States.[30]

F. Conclusions

The practice of the ECtHR demonstrates the different standards of review applied in the fourth instance (facts and domestic law) and the margin of appreciation (international obligations) situations. The assessment of facts primarily reflects epistemic concerns, whereas the application of domestic law and the ECHR is essentially a matter of protecting national autonomy.

The great advantage of the margin of appreciation is that it allows for different national decisions and traditions to be taken into account, and allows for national democratic decision-making. It may also build trust between the ECtHR and national decision-making – to the extent that national decision-making respects the methodology applied by the Court. The margin is flexible in the Court's approach to different aspects of national discretion, such as the difference between protecting freedom of expression and the protection of economic and social rights. Furthermore, separation of powers can be taken into account by applying different standards to decisions taken by, respectively, domestic courts, the executive and the legislature.

However, the use of the margin also involves some dangers and risks. First of all, it is important that the Court's deference does not undermine the need for 'practical and effective' protection under the ECHR. This is of particular importance for core human rights, such as protection against torture, but also for the protection of minorities and vulnerable groups against decisions by the majority.[31] The need for effective protection also means that the margin is not applied in bad faith implementation by Member States.

Second, the use of the margin – and thereby different modes of implementation in different States – could, arguably, threaten the consistent application of

[30] B Çalı, 'Coping with Crisis: Whither the Variable Geometry in the Jurisprudence the European Court of Human Rights?' (2018) 35 *Wisconsin International Law Journal* 237, 269–70. See also Spano, 'The Future of the European Court of Human Rights' (n 25) 20–22.

[31] A Follesdal, 'Appreciating the Margin of Appreciation' in A Etinson (ed), *Human Rights: Moral or Political?* (Oxford, Oxford University Press, 2018) 281.

the international obligations, and thereby also predictability and the rule of law. However, it is essential to distinguish between interpretation and application of the ECHR. The margin concerns the application of the Convention in the domestic context and will not have consequences for its general interpretation.

Moreover, it may be questioned what expertise the Court has when it comes to reviewing the procedures applied by national constitutional organs and how far it should go in imposing certain standards, especially to what extent it should determine that some procedures are more democratic than others. The Court's concern should be to ensure processes that are more likely to protect the ECHR rights, even if they may conflict with domestic views on what might be the most democratic procedures. Finally, the use of the margin of appreciation may challenge the general international law principle of the sovereign equality between States to the extent that the Court applies different margins to different States.[32]

III. Deference by Other International Courts

A. Introduction

International courts and tribunals vary widely in terms of whether they exercise general and special jurisdiction, which subject areas they cover and whether they are inter-State or allow access for non-State actors. Still, there is an emerging practice with deference more generally. As we will see, the distinctions applied by different ICs are based on epistemic reasons, subsidiarity and separation of powers as bases for the use of deference.

B. The International Court of Justice

The International Court of Justice (ICJ) is an inter-State court dealing with inter-State cases. Shany argues that there are statements both by the majority and in separate opinions in several cases by the ICJ that could support some standard of review.[33] Cannizzaro is of the opinion that a margin of appreciation has been applied both by the Permanent Court of International Justice (PCIJ) and the ICJ in selected cases.[34]

[32] For critical comments, see E Benvenisti, 'Margin of Appreciation, Consensus and Universal Standards' (1998–99) 31 *New York University Journal of International Law and Politics* 842.

[33] Shany (n 5) 931–39.

[34] E Cannizzaro, 'Proportionality and Margin of Appreciation in the Whaling Case: Reconciling Antithetical Doctrines?' (2016) 27 *European Journal of International Law* 1061, 1065–67.

However, the *Oil Platforms* case (2003) has been seen as a clear rejection by the ICJ of any deference to the discretion applied by national authorities. The Court stated:

> [T]he United States claims that it considered in good faith that the attacks on the platforms were necessary to protect its essential security interests, and suggests that 'A measure of discretion should be afforded to a party's good faith application of measures to protect its essential security interests' ... The Court does not however have to decide whether the United States interpretation of Article XX, paragraph 1*(d)* [of the applicable Friendship, Navigation and Commerce Treaty] on this point is correct, since the requirement of international law that measures taken avowedly in self-defence must have been necessary for that purpose is *strict and objective, leaving no room for any 'measure of discretion'*. (Emphasis added)[35]

Yet, it has been argued that the ICJ applied a form of deference in the *Whaling* case (2014). The ICJ stated:

> 61. The Court considers that Article VIII gives *discretion* to a State party to the ICRW [International Convention for the Regulation of Whaling] to reject the request for a special permit or to specify the conditions under which a permit will be granted. However, whether the killing, taking and treating of whales pursuant to a requested special permit is for purposes of scientific research cannot depend *simply* on that State's perception. (Emphasis added)

The ICJ distinguished under the heading 'The Standard of review' between review of whether the catch *involved scientific research* and whether it was *for purposes of* scientific research:

> 67. When reviewing the grant of a special permit authorizing the killing, taking and treating of whales, the Court will assess, first, whether the programme under which these activities occur involves scientific research. Secondly, the Court will consider if the killing, taking and treating of whales is 'for purposes of' scientific research by examining whether, in the use of lethal methods, the programme's design and implementation are *reasonable* in relation to achieving its stated objectives. This standard of review is an *objective one*. (Emphasis added)

This distinction is of importance to the Court as the *reasonable* test only applies to the question of whether the catch was for purposes of scientific research. The elements of this test are thus defined:

> 88. ... In order to ascertain whether a programme's use of lethal methods is for purposes of scientific research, the Court will consider *whether the elements of a programme's design and implementation are reasonable in relation to its stated scientific objectives* ... As shown by the arguments of the Parties, *such elements may include*: decisions regarding the use of lethal methods; the scale of the programme's use of lethal sampling; the methodology used to select sample sizes;

[35] *Case Concerning Oil Platforms (Islamic Republic of Iran v United States of America)* [2003] ICJ Rep 161, para 73.

> a comparison of the target sample sizes and the actual take; the time frame associated with a programme; the programme's scientific output; and the degree to which a programme co-ordinates its activities with related research projects. (Emphasis added)

That the 'reasonable' test is said to be objective militates against a deference to the national decision. However, the ICJ, arguably, allowed Japan some discretion in terms of how the research programme should be designed by distinguishing between 'involves' and 'for purposes of' scientific research; use of the term 'reasonable; and presenting a non-exhaustive list of elements that can be taken into account in the Court's review. The reasonableness test would seem to allow considerably more discretion than a necessity test.

The deference applied is assumedly based on epistemic reasons rather than subsidiarity in the form of protecting national autonomy, since the domestic authority should be considered to possess greater scientific expertise than the ICJ.

C. The International Tribunal for the Law of the Sea

Like the ICJ, the International Tribunal for the Law of the Sea (ITLOS) is also an inter-State court dealing with inter-State cases. There is some practice from ITLOS on the appropriate standard of review concerning the prompt release of vessels, demonstrating that also this court may be open to allowing some discretion to national authorities. Article 73(2) of the United Nations Law of the Sea Convention (UNCLOS) establishes that: 'Arrested vessels and their crews shall be promptly released upon the posting of a reasonable bond or other security.' Rayfuse explains that two different approaches have emerged in the practice by ITLOS:

> Two approaches to determining the standard of reasonableness, or the 'margin of appreciation', have emerged in the Tribunal's jurisprudence; one of *strong deference* to the regulations and decisions of the coastal State and another that seeks to assess *reasonableness by reference to some sort of international standard*. Essentially these approaches mirror those taken in the trade and human rights situations … Thus, it is hardly surprising that the notion of an international standard of reasonableness of bond appears to be that which has won favour in the Tribunal … This does not, however, mean that national law is irrelevant. On the contrary, the Tribunal has made it clear that in assessing the reasonableness of the bond the laws of the detaining State and the decisions of its courts are relevant. However … they are to be treated only as relevant facts to be considered in the context of all the information provided by the parties in arriving at an objective assessment of the reasonableness of the bond. (Emphasis added)[36]

[36] R Rayfuse, 'Standard of Review in the International Tribunal for the Law of the Sea' in Gruszczynski and Werner (eds) (n 5) 344–45. See also J-P Cot, 'The Law of the Sea and the Margin of Appreciation' in C Kojima et al (eds), *Law of the Sea, Environmental Law and Settlement of Disputes* (Leiden, Martinus Nijhoff, 2007) 399.

Another issue concerned whether confiscation of a bunker vessel and the gas oil on board, as a result of violation of fisheries regulations, was 'necessary' under Article 73(1) UNCLOS. Paik, one of the ITLOS judges, argues that the Tribunal in this case, ie, *M/V Virginia G* (2014), 'adopted a relatively high standard of review' when it found that the confiscation was not necessary.[37]

The basis for deference in both the prompt release cases and the confiscation of the bunker vessel case may either be seen as epistemic or based on subsidiarity in the sense of protecting national autonomy.

D. The WTO Appellate Body

The World Trade Organization (WTO) is also an inter-State dispute settlement system dealing with inter-State obligations. Article 3.2 of the Dispute Settlement Understanding (DSU), in its reference to the need for security and predictability in trade relations and to preserve the balance of WTO members' rights and obligations, has been seen as the framework for the applicable standard of review. The Appellate Body has foremost used Article 11 DSU, stating that 'a panel should make an objective assessment of the matter before it, including an objective assessment of the facts'. But 'the standard of an "objective assessment" is couched in rather broad terms that do very little to provide substantive guidance on the nature and intensity of the scrutiny that panels should apply in reviewing national measures'.[38]

The Appellate Body distinguishes between its review of interpretative issues and assessment of facts. While it said in the *EC-Hormones* case that it will undertake a *de novo* review of interpretation, the review of facts is 'neither *de novo* as such, nor total' deference.[39] Article 17.6(ii) of the Anti-Dumping Agreement is special in terms of stating that 'where the panel finds that a relevant provision of the Agreement admits of more than one permissible interpretation, the panel shall find the authorities' measure to be in conformity with the Agreement if it rests upon one of those permissible interpretations'. This explicitly leaves some room for domestic discretion.

Article XX of the General Agreement on Tariffs and Trade (GATT) has the title 'General Exceptions'. It allows for exceptions for explicitly listed purposes as long as the measures would not 'constitute a means of arbitrary or unjustifiable discrimination' or 'a disguised restriction on international trade'. For example, litra (a) allows measures '*necessary* to protect public morals' (emphasis added). However, it has been argued that 'an Article XX review largely boils down to assessing the *overall reasonableness* of the Member choosing the measure that it uses

[37] J-H Paik, 'Standard of Review and the Law of the Sea' in C Espósito et al (eds), *Ocean Law and Policy. Twenty Years of Development under the UNCLOS Regime* (Leiden, Brill, 2016) 365.

[38] J Bohanes and N Lockhart, 'Standard Review in WTO Law' in D Bethlehem et al (eds), *The Oxford Handbook of International Trade Law* (Oxford, Oxford University Press, 2009) 382–83 at 383.

[39] ibid 385.

to achieve its objective, given the trade restrictiveness of that measure' (emphasis added).[40]

The freedom of the members can be illustrated by the *Seals* case (2014). This case concerned a prohibition against the importation from Canada and Norway of seal products to the European Union (EU), based on the protection of animal welfare. The Appellate Body rejected 'Canada's argument that the Panel was required to assess whether the seal welfare risks associated with seal hunts exceed the level of animal welfare risks accepted by the European Union in other situations such as terrestrial wildlife hunts'.[41] It further concluded that 'the Panel did not err in concluding that the EU Seal Regime "is capable of making and does make some contribution" to its objective, or that it does so "to a certain extent". We further consider that the Panel did not err in concluding that, although the alternative measure was less trade restrictive than the EU Seal Regime, it was not reasonably available'.[42] This means that the EU had considerable discretion both in determining the level of protection of animals and determining which measures should be applied for this purpose.

It is interesting to note that the Appellate Body's deference in the *Seals* case related to a national law-making decision concerning morally sensitive issues. This supports subsidiarity in the form of autonomy rather than epistemic reasons – here in a regional organisation rather than a State – as well as separation of powers in terms of decisions by the regional legislature. The issue of democratic decision-making was not a criterion, which would have been difficult to apply for decisions by the EU as an organisation and due to the varied democratic credentials of the WTO membership.

E. Investment Arbitration

Unlike the inter-State ICJ, the ITLOS and the WTO dispute settlement system, investment treaties (BITs) typically give individuals and companies the right to take the host State to an arbitration tribunal (ISDS). An ISDS is special in the sense that it is based on bilateral treaties. Furthermore, it provides for ad hoc tribunals rather than permanent ICs.

BITs 'tend to say nothing, or only very little, about the appropriate standard of review for arbitrating disputes between sovereign states and foreign investors … They are simply silent, and their silence has been interpreted in innumerable ways by different tribunals'.[43] These tribunals have referred to different standards

[40] R Howse, 'The World Trade Organization 20 Years On: Global Governance by Judiciary' (2016) 27 *European Journal of International Law* 9, 50.

[41] WTO, *European Communities – Measures Prohibiting the Importation and Marketing of Seal Products – Reports of the Appellate Body* (22 May 2014) WT/DS400/AB/R and WT/DS401/AB/R [5.201].

[42] ibid [5.289].

[43] C Henckels, *Proportionality and Deference in Investor-State Arbitration: Balancing Investment Protection and Regulatory Autonomy* (Cambridge, Cambridge University Press, 2015) 7.

of review, but 'they have only infrequently articulated the rationale for their approaches or the reasons why it might be appropriate for a tribunal to afford a measure of deference in the determination of liability'.[44] The standards of review 'can range from complete deference under non-justiciability doctrines resulting in an absence of arbitral review to reconsidering any factual or legal determinations made at the domestic level de novo. Investment treaty tribunals are aware of the task they face and, to a large extent, are receptive to granting deference to host state institutions. Yet, to the extent they invoke the notion of deference, they attribute different meanings to it'.[45]

In the academic literature, there has been discussion of what should be an appropriate standard of review to be applied in investment arbitration. Burke-White and von Staden have proposed the use of the margin of appreciation as developed by the ECtHR.[46] However, this approach has been criticised with reference to the dual function of investment arbitration as having 'both a domestic public law function and a function for international investment law as a whole'. Therefore, '[d]etermining the precise degree of deference in investment arbitration, in turn, must take account of the dual function arbitral tribunals have as public bodies at the domestic and the international level'.[47]

ISDS mechanisms are examples of ICs dealing with issues that can have important effects beyond the regime and can interfere with domestic governmental politics – ie, reduce the sovereign regulatory space, including what has been called 'regulatory chill'. In this sense, they are comparable to the morally sensitive WTO cases referred to above. The ISDS cases do not necessarily deal with morally sensitive cases, but their relevance for the domestic legislative freedom may be a basis for practising deference with respect to domestic decision-making. Thus, their deference should hardly be seen as an aspect of epistemic reasons, but rather as a combination of subsidiarity in the form of respect for national autonomy, as well as an expression of the separation of powers.

F. The Inter-American Court of Human Rights

The IACtHR has been sceptical of the use of the margin of appreciation – at least so far. It seems that it has used the margin in some cases, but inconsistently. There are also examples of support for the fourth instance doctrine.[48]

[44] ibid.

[45] SW Schill, 'Deference in Investment Treaty Arbitration: Re-conceptualizing the Standard of Review' (2012) 3 *Journal of International Dispute Settlement* 577, 579.

[46] WW Burke-White and A von Staden, 'Private Litigation in a Public Law Sphere: The Standard of Review in Investor-State Arbitrations' (2010) 35 *Yale Journal of International Law* 283, 286.

[47] Schill (n 45) 580.

[48] Contesse (n 6) 141. See also B Duhaime, 'Subsidiarity in the Americas. What Room is There for Deference in the Inter-American System?' in Gruszczynski and Werner (eds) (n 5) 301.

The reluctance by the IACtHR to use the margin of appreciation has been explained by the facts that the cases before the Court have traditionally related to State violence in the form of torture, forced disappearances and extra-judicial killings, and that the domestic regimes have been military dictatorships and authoritarian regimes.[49]

However, there are calls for taking into account national decision-making in view of the changing political landscape in Latin America towards less State violence and more democracy.[50] It has been pointed out that, like the ECtHR, there is no need for the IACtHR to distinguish between more or less developed democracies. The Court can examine the instant case and ask whether this case has been treated according to the standards required by the Court's practice rather than ask about the democratic credentials of the relevant State.[51]

G. Conclusions

We have seen that there is an embryonic practice and debate about the use of deference in national decisions by several ICs. The use of deference may be based on epistemic reasons. The ICJ arguably applied deference to national decisions about scientific issues – an area where it does not have special professional competence. Epistemic reasons may also be the basis for ITLOS's deference to cases of prompt release and confiscation of a vessel, but it may also be seen as an aspect of subsidiarity.

The *Seals* case by the WTO Appellate Body and the practice by investment tribunals concern deference to the national legislature on issues that are of moral or political sensitivity. This lends support to separation of powers in favour of domestic legislative organs as a basis for deference. However, there is no requirement that the legislature is of a democratic character.

In addition to the ECtHR, the IACtHR is the only IC among the examined courts with a special mandate to protect human rights, and is in this sense more comparable to the human rights treaty bodies. This court has been sceptical to the use of a margin of appreciation. However, the context of the IACtHR is different from that of the ECtHR, since the Latin American continent has a history of authoritarian States and grave human rights violations. In these circumstances, the

[49] Contreras (n 5) 29. See also Contesse (n 6) 123; L Burgorgue-Larsen, '"Decompartmentalization": The Key Technique for Interpreting Regional Human Rights Treaties' (2018) 16 *International Journal of Constitutional Law* 187, 208.

[50] See Contesse (n 6) 144; PG Carozza and P González, 'The Final Word? Constitutional Dialogue and the Inter-American Court of Human Rights: A Reply to Jorge Contesse' (2017) 15 *International Journal of Constitutional Law* 436, 441.

[51] N Tsereteli, 'Emerging Doctrine of Deference of the Inter-American Court of Human Rights?' (2016) 20 *International Journal of Human Rights* 1097, 1106; A Follesdal, 'Exporting the Margin of Appreciation: Lessons for the Inter-American Court of Human Rights' (2017) 15 *International Journal of Constitutional Law* 359, 369–71.

IACtHR has prioritised upholding the effective protection of human rights over allowing national autonomy.

However, we have seen a tendency towards more use of a margin of appreciation by the IACtHR and active support for such use by academic authors in a context of more democratic States in Latin America. It has also been pointed out that the Court need not distinguish between democratic and non-democratic States, or States with more or less democratic credentials. Instead, the Court could ask whether the relevant case has been treated according to the standards required by the IACtHR.

IV. Deference by Human Rights Treaty Bodies

A. Introduction

The ECtHR as well as other ICs apply forms of deference. However, the IACtHR has been reluctant to use a margin of appreciation. What can this diverse practice teach us with respect to possible deference applied by the UN human rights treaty bodies?

There are good reasons for claiming that the use of deference is even more relevant for the treaty bodies than for the ECtHR. First, these global bodies are even further away from national decision-making than the regional ECtHR. Furthermore, the social, cultural and political conditions are more diverse at the global level than in Europe.

On the other hand, several arguments against deference may be adduced. In a world of numerous undemocratic States with little respect for the rule of law and the protection of human rights, there is a special need to ensure the effective protection of such rights. The existence of authoritarian States has been a main concern for the IACtHR's rejection of the use of a margin of appreciation. Second, the universality of the rights may be at more risk in a diverse world. Third, there is also the need to respect the sovereign equality of States. Fourth, it is necessary to discuss the relevance of two aspects that are of special interest for the treaty bodies, ie, that these bodies render non-binding decisions rather than binding judgments and that they are composed differently and have different procedures from ICs.

I first examine to what extent the use of deference by the treaty bodies is called for in their assessment of, respectively, facts, the interpretation and application of national law, and the interpretation and application of international law. I discuss whether deference based on epistemic reasons, subsidiarity and separation of powers may threaten the effective protection of human rights. Then I ask whether such deference is inconsistent with either the sovereign equality of States or the universality of human rights. Finally, I ask whether it makes a difference that the treaty bodies render non-binding decisions and that their composition and procedures are different from those of ICs.

B. Assessment of Facts

The assessment of facts is seen by the ECtHR as covered by its insistence that it is not a fourth instance court. This means that domestic courts are accorded considerable discretion in establishing the relevant facts. This is consistent with their presumed epistemic advantage in assessing the facts. On the other hand, one should keep in mind possible deficiencies in national authorities' ability and willingness to conduct unbiased assessment of the facts. The ICJ *Whaling* case is also an example of reliance on the special expertise of national authorities. Deference by the ITLOS in cases of prompt release and confiscation of a vessel may either be seen as based on epistemic reasons or on subsidiarity.

The treaty bodies will rarely be exposed to scientific issues comparable to the *Whaling* case. However, the potential advantage of local authorities in assessing the facts of a case is also relevant in relation to the treaty bodies. These bodies may even be less capable than the ECtHR of addressing the facts of the case if one takes into consideration their distance to such facts as global bodies and their limited secretarial capacity. Yet, the need to ensure effective protection of human rights in a world with considerable variations in democratic protection and rule of law guarantees means that the treaty bodies should be cautious in terms of relying too much on the assessment of the facts by domestic authorities.

C. Interpretation and Application of National Law

Interpretation and application of national law is also covered by the fourth instance doctrine practised by ECtHR, which means that the Court accords wide discretion to domestic courts. This could be seen as based on epistemic grounds, as national courts would presumably have greater expertise in applying domestic law. Furthermore, such deference is supported by subsidiarity considerations: national law should primarily be interpreted by domestic organs.

These subsidiarity considerations are even more relevant for the treaty bodies since the global treaty bodies are further away for domestic decision-making than regional courts, suggesting relatively extensive deference.

D. Interpretation and Application of International Law

The treaty bodies shall resolve disputes on the implementation of international human rights obligations. While the function of domestic courts is to interpret domestic law, the treaty bodies shall interpret international law. This means that interpretation of the international obligations is at the core of the functions of the treaty bodies. The treaty bodies are, through their professional composition and practice, generally also in a better epistemic position to interpret international obligations than national courts. However, the principle of subsidiarity suggests a presumption that decision-making should be taken at the national level unless it is better performed by the treaty bodies. How should these concerns be weighed against the need to ensure the effective protection of international human rights?

i. Deference Should Not be Applied to Interpretation, Only to Application

It is important to distinguish between the interpretation and application of international obligations. While the treaty bodies have special professional competence and responsibility concerning the interpretation of the conventions, the application of the rights raises issues involving appreciation of the local context. The ECtHR's margin of appreciation concerns the application of human rights rather than their interpretation.

ii. Deference Should Not be Applied for Core Human Rights

Deference should not be applied to the implementation of core human rights, such as the prohibition against torture. These rights are of special international concern. However, the existence of violations of such rights should not be taken as a ground for denying deference to review of all human rights – which the IACtHR seems to do. Such differentiation between the rights is also in accordance with the practice by the ECtHR. The treaty bodies should undertake a *de novo* review of the core rights. But this prevents deference with respect to other human rights.

iii. Deference Should Depend on Whether the Treaty Bodies' Methodology is Respected

Deference by the treaty bodies should be conditional in the sense that it should depend on whether national authorities have respected the treaty bodies' legal methodology. Also here, the approach by the ECtHR may provide guidance. The practice built on the *Von Hannover (No 2)* case (2012) establishes that the Court would require 'strong reasons' for reviewing domestic organs if they have applied the legal methodology following from the Court's practice. This would also work as an incentive towards embedding international human rights in national law and practice.

iv. Deference Should be Narrower than the Margin of Appreciation

It should be kept in mind that the 'thickness' of the treaty bodies' practice is not as extensive as the practice of the ECtHR. This means that domestic organs are given less guidance about the proper implementation of the international obligations. What is more, the obligations contained in the global human rights conventions are generally not as extensively embedded in national legislation and practice.[52] While the standard of review may vary between different rights along the lines practised by the ECtHR, for instance, leaving more discretion to the protection of economic and social rights, these factors militate in favour of a generally narrower deference to domestic implementation than the one applied by the ECtHR. This means that even if States Parties apply the treaty bodies' legal methodology, review should not require 'strong reasons'. Finally, in the absence of a world of democracies and rule of law-abiding States, the treaty bodies should not apply a parallel to European consensus, ie, global consensus as a basis for deference.

v. Separation of Powers Should be Taken into Account

The separation of powers argument – in the sense of protecting legislative freedom – should also be accorded weight. The treaty bodies have the main responsibility for considering violations. But the judicial function should be balanced against the legislative prerogative of States Parties. The ECtHR has stated that decisions by the legislator should be given special weight 'in matters of general policy, on which opinions within a democratic society may reasonably differ widely'.[53] This is comparable to the practice of the WTO Appellate Body in the *Seals* case where the standards among States may reasonably differ. It is worth mentioning that such deference to the legislator by the Appellate Body is, unlike the ECtHR, not dependent on the democratic character of the domestic organs. However, in a human rights context, it is important to be aware that morally and politically sensitive issues may also involve concerns about the protection of vulnerable groups, for example, ethnic or sexual minorities. Therefore, the treaty bodies need to keep an eye on the protection of such groups, particularly against democratic majorities. Furthermore, the treaty bodies should also require that the legislature is able to demonstrate that the methodology of these bodies is respected if deference to the national legislature is accorded.

vi. Abuse of Powers

But even if it seems that the methodology of the treaty bodies is applied, there are limits to how far treaty bodies should go in their use of deference. The principle of effective interpretation of treaties means that the treaty bodies should ensure that the commitments of the international obligations are respected and not abused. A parallel can be drawn with the ECtHR's rejection of the use of the margin of appreciation in cases of bad faith implementation of ECHR obligations.

[52] On the 'thickness' and the embeddedness of the ECtHR's practice, see R Spano, 'The Future of the European Court of Human Rights' (n 25).

[53] *İzzettin Doğan and Others v Turkey* (n 26) para 112.

E. Sovereign Equality

McGoldrick argues that to apply the margin of appreciation in the practice of the treaty bodies 'on the precondition of a functioning democracy would be problematic. It is Eurocentric and rather condescending'.[54]

The general international law principle of the sovereign equality between States should be respected. This would exclude differentiation based on whether a State is democratic or not. But such differentiation is neither practised by the ECtHR nor by the IACtHR or by any IC. The differentiation suggested in this chapter is based on whether domestic organs apply the same legal methodology as the treaty bodies, not on their democratic attributes. One may assume that democratic States more often tend to respect this methodology. But this would be an outcome of a differentiation which does not violate the principle of sovereign equality.

F. Universality

The human rights conventions establish universal human rights, in the sense that all States Parties have the same obligations. But the proposed differentiation based on the application of human rights in the domestic context rather than their general interpretation would strike a compromise between universality and diversity based on different national, political and cultural contexts. Yet, there is a fine line between interpretation and application. The treaty bodies should ensure that respect for different national circumstances should not undermine a common interpretation of the human rights obligations.

G. Non-binding Status

It could be argued that the treaty bodies should not apply deference since their findings are legally non-binding. This means that their findings are not as intrusive as the binding judgments by ICs. On the other hand, the treaty bodies may be concerned that applying deference could undermine the effective implementation of their non-binding findings.

But the ICJ concluded in the *Diallo* case (2010) that the practice of the Human Rights Committee should be given 'great weight' because the Committee 'was established specifically to supervise the application of that treaty'. The Court also referred to the need for promoting 'the necessary clarity', 'the essential consistence' and 'legal security' for both individuals and the State.[55] Thus, although not legally

[54] McGoldrick (n 7) 57.

[55] *Ahmadou Sadio Diallo* (*Republic of Guinea v Democratic Republic of Congo*) (Merits, Judgment) [2010] ICJ Rep 639, para 66.

binding, States have an obligation to take the treaty bodies' findings seriously by ascribing them 'great weight'.[56] It follows that the treaty bodies should act as if national organs would consider their findings in good faith, in the sense that the domestic organs have the intention of implementing such findings. Therefore, the treaty bodies should apply deference as if their findings were legally binding.

H. Composition and Procedures

McGoldrick argues that the treaty bodies 'are more politicized in their composition than the ECtHR. This could be the underlying reason why there is a reluctance to create space for MoA [margin of appreciation] reasoning since it is more liable to be abused'.[57]

In our context, the question is whether the composition and procedures of the treaty bodies *should* be an argument against the use of deference. Some of the treaty bodies may be lacking some of the fact-finding abilities and legal expertise and culture that we find in an international court. This may represent epistemic deficiencies at the international level. On the other hand, they may include professional expertise that may be lacking in domestic courts, for instance, child psychology in cases involving minors. This may be an argument for differentiation in the application of deference by different treaty bodies – or in the content of the standard of review. The treaty bodies should ensure the effective implementation of their respective conventions. This means that each treaty body should only allow deference to national decision-making to the extent that it is capable of ensuring that the international obligations are effectively implemented at the domestic level.

V. Conclusions

In this chapter I have argued that the treaty bodies should apply a selective, conditional and cautious deference to national decisions. Such deference can draw on experiences from the ECtHR as well as other ICs. The reluctance by the IACtHR to use a margin of appreciation has not been found to be a decisive argument against the use of deference by the treaty bodies.

A differentiation should be made between different bases for deference: epistemic reasons, subsidiarity and separation of powers. Furthermore, it should be distinguished between assessment of facts, the interpretation and application of national law, and the interpretation and application of international law.

[56] Ulfstein, 'The Human Rights Treaty Bodies and Legitimacy Challenges' (n 2) 292–93.
[57] McGoldrick (n 7) 60.

The following propositions are put forward:

- Wide discretion should be given to domestic authorities in their interpretation and application of national law, whereas the treaty bodies should be cautious in relying too much on their assessment of the facts.
- Deference should not be applied to interpretation of the international obligations, but only to the domestic application of these obligations.
- Deference should not be applied for core human rights.
- Deference should depend on whether the treaty bodies' methodology is respected.
- Deference should be narrower than the margin of appreciation.
- Separation of powers should be taken into account in relation to the domestic legislature.
- Treaty bodies should ensure that domestic authorities do not abuse their powers.

Such deference can be applied without compromising the effectiveness and universality of human rights or the sovereign equality of States. Neither the non-binding status of the treaty bodies' findings nor their composition and procedures prevent the use of deference. The suggested use of deference by the treaty bodies should be seen as a further improvement of the system rather than an aspect of its failure.

6

International Parental Child Abduction and the Need for Alternative Regimes?

URFAN KHALIQ

Abstract: International parental child abduction is an issue that nation-States have sought to tackle. The existing treaty regimes, however, are not capable of being universal as is claimed. Rather, it is the argument of this chapter that the law is based upon assumptions and premises that reflect a Eurocentric perspective and this will not permit a universal inclusive regime. It proposes some possible solutions which may be considered, but also highlights the shortcomings of such alternatives.

I. Introduction

In a collection examining the achievements of international law, it is apt to examine where the law is not quite what one might hope for and the reasons for this. The international law on parental child abduction is such a field. It is an area where domestic and international politics, legal cultures and traditions coincide in ways that make international law-making laden with difficulties and intrigue. What might broadly be construed as public international law, private international law, international human rights law and Islamic family law intersect here and are relevant in different ways. The aim of this chapter is to provide a broad overview of some of the pertinent issues and how they interrelate to one another. This chapter will argue that in the key global convention that governs international parental child abduction, which had an ambition of universal collaboration, there is a presumption of cultural (Eurocentric) norms. However, the participation of States that do not share these norms challenges the framework. Clearly the many issues cannot be fully explored in a chapter of this length, but it is hoped that the issues in question highlight some of the occasionally seemingly intractable issues that are faced in international law-making.[1] The chapter sets out by examining broadly

[1] This chapter is drawn from several years working with a number of governments and organisations in trying to address the issue of parental child abductions. A far lengthier exposition of

the international law relating to parental child abductions. It then highlights some of the problems of expanding the existing legal regime to a more universal one. Finally, it sets out what may be a way forward, but does so in the context of the 'politics' of doing so and the potential problems with creating what may be considered 'alternative regimes'.

II. Parental Child Abduction and International Law

Parental child abduction is a global problem. The ease of international travel and the establishment of millions of 'transnational' families, especially since the end of the Second World War, mean that when relationships break down, as some invariably do, children may be taken across borders by one parent or the other. This will always be without the consent and usually the knowledge of the other parent. Furthermore, such acts may be designed to evade any existing court decisions about custody. It is simply impossible to know how many children are abducted by their parents and taken to another country in any one year. By the 1970s, the problem was deemed pressing enough for the Hague Conference on Private International Law to propose a convention addressing the matter. This led to the adoption of the Hague Convention on International Child Abduction, 1980 (hereinafter '1980 Hague Abduction Convention').[2] The Hague Conference is not alone in adopting a treaty on the issue. Adopted under the auspices of the Organization of American States, there is also the 1989 Inter-American Convention on the International Return of Children (hereinafter 'the OAS Convention').[3] The OAS Convention is in force between 14 Latin American and Caribbean States. The US and Canada are notably not parties to it.[4] The OAS Convention, as a regional convention, is not open to States that are not members of the OAS and thus cannot provide a global

that work is to be published as A Emon and U Khaliq, *Jurisdictional Exceptionalisms: Islamic Law, International Law & International Child Abduction* (Cambridge, Cambridge University Press, 2021). I am grateful to my friend, colleague and co-author Anver Emon for permission to draw from our joint venture for the purposes of this chapter. I am also very grateful for the detailed comments and suggestions from Dr Rachel Cahill O'Callaghan and Jacques Hartmann on an earlier draft. Needless to say, I am solely responsible for the errors or inaccuracies in this chapter.

[2] More accurately, Convention of 25 October 1980 on the Civil Aspects of International Child Abduction, entered into force 1 December 1983, available at: https://www.hcch.net/en/instruments/conventions/full-text/?cid=24.

[3] B-53: Inter-American Convention on the International Return of Children (adopted 15 July 1989, entered into force 4 November 1994) OAS Treaty Series No 70, available at: www.oas.org/juridico/english/treaties/b-53.html

[4] See www.oas.org/juridico/english/sigs/b-53.html for States Parties. A total of 17 Latin American and Caribbean States are currently parties to the 1980 Hague Child Abduction Convention (Hague Convention on the Civil Aspects of International Child Abduction (adopted 25 October 1980, entered into force 1 December 1980) Hague XXVII), while the Inter-American Convention is in force between 14 States from the Americas (including Bolivia and Antigua & Barbuda, which are not yet parties to the 1980 Hague Child Abduction Convention).

solution to the problem of parental child abductions.[5] This chapter will, therefore, only deal with the 1980 Hague Abduction Convention.

A. The 1980 Hague Convention on International Child Abduction

At the outset, it is key to stress that notwithstanding the ambiguity in its title, the 1980 Hague Abduction Convention is concerned with the matter of parental (not stranger) child abductions and seeks to address the civil (not criminal) implications of such incidents – where one parent crosses an international border with a child without the permission or knowledge of the other parent. The Convention was adopted under the auspices of the Hague Conference on Private International Law. Currently, the Conference has 85 members – 84 States and the European Union (EU).[6] The Hague Conference is an 'intergovernmental organisation' and according to Article 1 of the Statute of the Hague Conference on Private International Law (1951), its sole aim is to 'work for the progressive unification of the rules of Private International Law'.[7] The Conference considers that due to its reputation and influence, its conventions are suitable for global participation, referring to itself as 'the World Organisation for Cross-border Co-operation in Civil and Commercial Matters'.[8] The Hague Conference as an organisation draws a distinction between those States that are members of it and those that are not.[9] While (regional) international organisations, such as the Council of Europe, the African Union or the Organization of American States, only allow Member States to become party to conventions adopted under their auspices, the Hague Conference allows non-Member States (known as either non-Hague States or connected States) to also become party to its conventions.[10] At the time of writing, around

[5] Inter-American Convention on the International Return of Children, art 38. It is worth noting that by virtue of art 34 of the Inter-American Convention, among States that are parties to that Convention and to the 1980 Hague Abduction Convention, the OAS Convention prevails. However, States Parties may enter into bilateral agreements to give priority to the application of the Hague Convention in relations between them. On the OAS Convention, there is a relative paucity in the English-language literature. However, for a useful overview, see H Jiménez, 'Inter-American Convention on the International Return of Children' (1990) 29 *International Legal Materials* 63.

[6] See https://www.hcch.net/en/states/hcch-members.

[7] Statute of the Hague Conference on Private International Law (adopted 31 October 1951, entered into force 15 July 1955), available at: https://www.hcch.net/en/instruments/conventions/full-text. On the history of the Conference, see K Lipstein, 'One Hundred Years of Hague Conferences on Private International Law' (1993) 42 *International and Comparative Law Quarterly* 553.

[8] See also further on this point W Reese, 'The Hague Conference on Private International Law: Some Observations' (1985) 19 *The International Lawyer* 881.

[9] See https://www.hcch.net/en/states/other-connected-parties for those States considered 'connected'.

[10] The Statute of the Council of Europe (adopted 5 May 1949, entered into force 3 August 1949) ETS No 1, notes, for example, that: 'Any European State may become a member of the Council of Europe as far as it accepts the principles of the rule of law and of the enjoyment by all persons within its jurisdiction of human rights and fundamental freedoms.' Article 59(1) of the European Convention for the Protection of Human Rights and Fundamental Freedoms (adopted 4 November 1950, entered into

70 States are 'connected' in that they are party to at least one of the 40 or so conventions adopted under the auspices of the Conference.[11] Examining which States have become party and when to the Conference system as a whole, its Eurocentric cultural origins are apparent. This is notwithstanding the fact that its membership has become geographically broader in recent years. Turkey joined in 1955, whereas Japan was the first non-European Member State becoming party to the Conference in 1957, shortly followed by Egypt in 1961. The Hague Conference's membership has grown by just under half in the last 20 years, with 38 new members since 2000. Although membership of the Hague Conference is now genuinely geographically diverse, it is worth emphasising that strikingly, only six African States out of the 55 members of the African Union are members of the Conference,[12] while only 13 out of the 57 Member States of the Organization of the Islamic Conference are also members of the Hague Conference.[13]

Moving on to the 1980 Hague Abduction Convention, it is considered by the Hague Conference to be its most successful Convention and if success is measured solely in terms of the number of Contracting Parties to a Convention, then that is certainly true. As of the time of writing, there are 101 Contracting Parties to it.[14] While the Hague Conference, as a whole, draws a distinction between Member States and connected States, the 1980 Hague Abduction Convention draws a distinction which is unconventional, if not unique. The Convention differentiates between those States that ratified the 1980 Hague Abduction Convention when it was first adopted[15] and those that, thereafter, can only accede to the Abduction Convention.[16] The consequence of this is laid out in Article 38, where in the relevant part it is noted:

> The accession will have effect *only* as regards the relations between the *acceding* State and such Contracting States as will have *declared their acceptance of the accession*. Such a declaration will also have to be made by any Member State ratifying, accepting or approving the Convention after an accession. (Emphasis added)

This does not apply to ratifying States, which are all deemed to owe obligations to each other. However, States that subsequently accede only owe obligations to those other pre-existing Contracting States that have recognised their accession.

force 3 September 1953) 213 UNTS 22, notes that: 'This Convention shall be open to the signature of the members of the Council of Europe.'

[11] There are also seven 'older' Conventions adopted prior to 1945. The 40 Conventions being referred to are the post-1945 Conventions.

[12] Egypt, Tunisia, Morocco, South Africa, Zambia and Burkina Faso.

[13] Although, of course, of these, Egypt, Tunisia, Burkina Faso and Morocco are also members of the African Union. The others are Azerbaijan, Albania, Turkey, Uzbekistan, Saudi Arabia, Malaysia, Jordan, Kazakhstan and Suriname.

[14] https://www.hcch.net/en/instruments/conventions/status-table/?cid=24

[15] 1980 Hague Abduction Convention, art 37.

[16] ibid art 38. Member States of the Conference who did not ratify the Convention at the time of its adoption will also accede to it. However, the distinction is critical, in that Contracting States that did not ratify the Convention (although Member States at the time of its negotiation) still played a role in its negotiation, whereas non-Member States could not.

In essence, the 1980 Hague Abduction Convention creates a series of bilateral treaties within it. Under the law of reservations, as codified in Articles 19–21 of the Vienna Convention on the Law of Treaties, all multilateral treaties which permit reservations lead to bilateral relations between reserving States and others. Here the distinction is that two States can be party to the 1980 Hague Abduction Convention, yet owe no legal obligation whatsoever to one another.[17] Twenty-seven States ratified the 1980 Hague Abduction Convention and all of those can be described as 'traditional' Hague Conference States.[18]

With 101 Contracting States, the 1980 Hague Abduction Convention is more 'global' than the Conference as a whole, but that does not mean the regime created by the Convention is capable of functioning effectively between many Contracting States. Further, it is the contention of this chapter that the 1980 Hague Abduction Convention cannot function effectively as a global treaty to address parental child abductions. That is the crux of the issue here. What happens when States – those with non-Western religious and cultural norms – join the Convention? Second, how should parental child abductions between States that are party to the 1980 Hague Child Abduction Convention and those that are not be addressed? Third, how should parental child abductions between States that are not party to the 1980 Hague Abduction Convention, in particular Muslim (majority) family law States, be addressed? Before answering these questions, it is apt to set out the basic premise of the 1980 Hague Abduction Convention.

Any convention that aimed to maximise international cooperation on parental child abduction could not afford to pass judgement (inadvertently or otherwise) on the approach of a State's domestic family law regime. Therefore, a fundamental feature of the 1980 Hague Abduction Convention was to presume that parental abductions of children are per se contrary to the 'best interests' of children.[19] The presumption is especially important since the Convention, as is the case with all international conventions dealing with children, does not define what the 'best interests' of a child actually are.[20] What is deemed in the 'best interests' of a child is actually heavily dependent upon the approach of the society in question. The 1980 Hague Abduction Convention is not alone in leaving the term undefined;

[17] Vienna Convention on the Law of Treaties (adopted 23 May 1969, entered into force 27 January 1980) 1155 UNTS 331. In the context of the 1980 Hague Abduction Convention, practice differs significantly between States. New Zealand is noteworthy as an acceding State, in that it clearly has a policy of recognising every other State's accession to the 1980 Hague Abduction Convention.

[18] See https://www.hcch.net/en/instruments/conventions/status-table/?cid=24.

[19] See A Dyer, 'Report on International Child Abduction by One Parent ("Legal Kidnapping")', A&D14 de la Quatorzième session: Tome III Elèvement d'enfants, Child Abduction (Hague Conference on Private International Law 1982) 22.

[20] In a similar vein, see art 3 of the Convention on the Rights of the Child (adopted 20 November 1989, entered into force 2 September 1990) 1577 UNTS 3, 1989, where in all actions 'the best interests of the child shall be a primary consideration'. For an insightful attempt to articulate what this means, see M Freeman, *A Commentary on the Convention on the Rights of the Child: Article 3, The Best Interests of the Child* (Leiden, Martinus Nijhoff, 2007).

nevertheless, *the* underlying assumption of the entire Convention is that abduction is per se against the child's best interests. Of course, it was recognised at the time that:

> [A] large number of countries retain the more traditional legal standards for assignment of custody, which range from establishment of a presumption or an irrefutable right in favour of the parent of one sex or the other to systems where the legal dispute over custody centres around the 'fitness' or 'unfitness' of one of the parties, usually the mother, based on allegations of sexual conduct which may have little or nothing to do with the actual suitability of the parent to exercise the custody over the care of the child.[21]

Assuming without explaining 'best interests of the child', the 1980 Hague Abduction Convention's central feature is the automatic return of the child. The automatic return feature operates between States that are parties to the Convention and recognise each other as such. This feature of the Convention requires judges in a State Party to which a child was abducted ('refuge states') to order the automatic return of the child to the State from where the child was abducted – what the Convention calls the child's 'habitual residence'.[22] The automatic return is not a determination of who is best suited to exercise custody over the abducted child; the Convention does not decide the substantive merits of a custody dispute. Rather, the automatic return deems that courts in the child's habitual residence are the *jurisdictionally* appropriate venue to address the underlying custodial contest. Courts in refuge States are not to engage in any substantive analysis of the doctrines or standards by which the court in the child's State of habitual residence would adjudicate the issue of custody.[23] Such standards and approaches, by their very nature, are subject to considerable variation across cultures, traditions, peoples and States, and would require considerable judicial time and commitment, both of which would operate against the best interests of the child in being returned hastily to his or her 'habitual residence'.

As such, the Convention does not offer rules governing jurisdiction, provide standards of analysis or guide judicial determination of the merits of the case. The automatic return mechanism simply requires, under certain circumstances, a court to order the return of the child to his or her habitual residence. This mechanism is embedded in Article 3 of the Convention. Articles 3 and 12 outline when an abduction is wrongful and set forth the conditions under which automatic return is required. For our purposes, there are two key exceptions to this: the Article 13 'grave risk' provision and the 'public policy' provision in Article 20.[24] These carefully crafted, narrow exceptions were subject to extensive debate among

[21] Dyer (n 19) 22.

[22] 1980 Hague Abduction Convention, art 3(a).

[23] For statistics of the number of children returned, see https://www.hcch.net/en/publications-and-studies/details4/?pid=6598&dtid=32.

[24] Article 12 is the other exception, where more than a year has elapsed from the date of the wrongful removal.

the delegates. Article 20 was hotly debated during the Convention's drafting. It reads as follows:

> The return of the child under the provisions of Article 12 may be refused if this would not be permitted by the fundamental principles of the requested State relating to the protection of human rights and fundamental freedoms.[25]

Though Article 20 found its way into the body of the Convention, it has nonetheless been shown to have few, if any, teeth. Beaumont and McEleavy, writing decades after the Convention was finalised, argued that Article 20 has 'nearly faded without trace'.[26] In the subsequent years, as far as is known, no national court has interpreted Article 20 in an expansive manner so as to refuse to return abducted children.[27] Despite Article 20's subsequent history, it nonetheless remains an ever-present exception that may be resorted to as new States –with legal systems and cultures different from the Eurocentric context that inspired the Convention – are pressed to accede to the 1980 Hague Abduction Convention. Indeed, scholarly writings on Article 20 suggest as much. Beaumont and McEleavy speculated that Article 20 may be of 'greater importance if the Convention succeeds in gaining further ratifications among countries which enforce laws or traditions found unacceptable in modern Western democracies'.[28] Schuz, commenting much more recently than Beaumont and McEleavy, indicated that there were already 'indications that courts might become more willing to use the Article 20 defence if countries with non-Western religious and cultural norms join the Convention'.[29]

The discussion now moves on to Muslim family law States and the Hague Conference system, and then specifically the 1980 Hague Child Abduction Convention. There are a number of key considerations here. First, the 'best interests of the child' determination is different – including religion and gender. Second, the role of religion is central and the role that religion plays is a dominant consideration in the legal questions at stake.

III. Muslim Family Law States and the Hague Conference System

In academic and more general literature, the media and popular parlance are replete with references to, inter alia, Muslim States,[30] Islamic States,[31] the Islamic

[25] 1980 Hague Abduction Convention, art 20.

[26] P Beaumont and P McEleavy, *The Hague Convention on International Child Abduction* (Oxford, Oxford University Press, 1999) 16.

[27] Although see the Grand Chamber of the European Court of Human Rights in Application No 27853/09 *X v Latvia*, judgment 26 November 2013, which is critical in this regard.

[28] Beaumont and McEleavy (n 26) 76.

[29] R Schuz, *The Hague Child Abduction Convention: A Critical Analysis* (Oxford, Hart Publishing, 2013) 355. Equally, however, they may not accept the accession of such States.

[30] See, for example, N Abaid, *Sharia, Muslim States and International Human Rights Treaty Obligations: A Comparative Study* (London, British Institute of International and Comparative Law, 2008).

world,[32] the Muslim world[33] and Islamic civilisation.[34] Scholars and commentators use such terms interchangeably, but also adopt different methodologies to identify them. Here reliance is placed on the useful, though imperfect, correlation between 'Muslim family law States' and membership in the Organisation of Islamic Cooperation (OIC). The correlation is imperfect because a number of OIC Member States do not have Muslim family law and some non-OIC Member States with Muslim minorities – for example, Israel, India, the Philippines, Singapore, Sri Lanka, and Trinidad and Tobago – have separate legal codes regulating the marriages and divorces of their respective Muslim populations.[35] Nonetheless, the strong correlation allows the discussion in this chapter to remain focused on the legal issues at the heart of parental child abduction.

It is important to explain the approach adopted. There are few sustained methodological attempts to identify 'Muslim States', but whatever methodology is used is open to differing degrees of objection.[36] For example, what makes a modern nation-State 'Islamic'? There is substance to the argument that as post-Westphalian nation-States did not exist during the era of Islamic empires, and 'empire' is the default Islamic jurisdictional paradigm, 'Islamic State' is a misnomer despite groups such as ISIS – the *Islamic State* of Iraq and Syria – claiming the moniker of statehood for itself.[37] Nation-States, however, provide the contemporary framework for political organisation on a global level, so for these purposes it is essential

[31] See, for example, J Rehman, *Islamic State Practices, International Law and the Threat from Terrorism: A Critique of the 'Clash of Civilizations' in the New World Order* (Oxford, Hart Publishing, 2005).

[32] P Adamson, *Philosophy in the Islamic World: A History of Philosophy without Any Gaps*, vol 3 (Oxford, Oxford University Press, 2016).

[33] See, for example, the Wiley journal *The Muslim World* published in association with the Hartford Seminary.

[34] See, for example, I Netton (ed), *Encyclopaedia of Islamic Civilisation and Religion* (Abingdon, Routledge, 2009). In terms of public international law, reference to the 'civilisation' is, of course, replete with the connotations of colonialism and notions of the barbarian. See also and more broadly N Tzouvala, *Capitalism as Civilisation: A History of International Law* (Cambridge, Cambridge University Press, 2020).

[35] Primarily, the Muslim Marriage and Divorce Act, Chapter 45:02, 1961 (Trinidad and Tobago); the Muslim Personal Law (Shariat) Application Act 1937, the Dissolution of Muslim Marriages Act 1939 and the Muslim Women (Protection of Rights on Divorce) Act 1986 (India); the Muslim Marriage and Divorce Act 1951 (Sri Lanka); Presidential Decree No 1083 (1977) and the Code of Muslim Personal Laws (the Philippines); and the Administration of Muslim Law Act 1966 (Singapore). Israel still relies on the Ottoman law, which pre-dates the British mandate. In Greece, in Western Thrace, as a part of the Ottoman legacy there was also a separate legal system for Muslims, but the vestiges of that system have been increasingly limited in recent years and it can now be opted out of.

[36] A sustained attempt to define 'Islamic Statehood' is I Rauf, *Defining Islamic Statehood: Measuring and Indexing Contemporary Muslim States* (London, Palgrave Macmillan, 2015). The book is the outcome of a global project to identify what makes a State's institutions and laws 'Islamic' and to then map contemporary nation-States onto the index to see how 'Islamic' they are. See also E Justyna Powell, *Islamic Law and International Law: Peaceful Resolution of Disputes* (Oxford, Oxford University Press, 2020), who also attempts to define Islamic/Muslim States in a great deal of detail.

[37] W Hallaq, *The Impossible State: Islam, Politics, and Modernity's Moral Predicament* (New York, Columbia University Press, 2012). See also M Berger, 'Sharia and the Nation State' in R Peters and P Bearman (eds), *The Ashgate Research Companion to Islamic Law* (London, Routledge, 2014) 223.

to move beyond this objection.[38] In short, there is simply no one (or indeed any satisfactory) methodology for identifying 'Muslim' or 'Islamic' States. This absence of any meaningful standard explains the plurality (if not cacophony) of approaches adopted by States that are perceived as or consider themselves to be Islamic in some sense or other. Yet, for the purposes of this chapter, this absence is not an impediment. In the narrowly defined context of parental child abduction, the standard by which States are identified as 'Muslim' requires identifying the presence of some form of Islamically inspired family law (eg, Muslim family law or Islamic family law) or what is often termed in legislative codes as personal status law and the associated jurisdictional rules. For this reason, the phrase 'Muslim family law States' calibrates the scope of this chapter. Most States with a majority population who are identified or identify themselves as Muslim regulate 'personal status laws' to some degree by reference to Islamic practices and beliefs. This is the case notwithstanding the colonial encounter in those territories. European colonialists in areas with sizeable Muslim populations certainly took aim at a range of legal fields to maximise commerce and economic development with European-inspired conditions of legality transplanted in newly acquired colonial possessions.[39] However, for various reasons, European colonial administrators pursued a policy of enabling and preserving to varying degrees the laws and practices by which colonised persons conducted and regulated their marriages, divorces, deaths and inheritance.[40] This effort, of course, led to some practices and rules mutating or being reformed, and ultimately the creation of 'personal status law' statutes for Muslim populations.[41] The British in India, for example, sought to understand 'Islamic law', which led to the commissioning and publishing of Charles Hamilton's *Hedaya*, a groundbreaking work and one that still influences, to varying degrees, the approach towards aspects of 'Muslim family law' in contemporary India, Pakistan and Bangladesh.[42] Works such as the *Hedaya* underline the continuing importance and irony of the colonial encounter for many contemporary States with Muslim majorities; that which is considered by many to be 'religiously ordained' and thus legitimate is in actual fact the outcome and product of the colonial encounter.[43]

[38] This is notwithstanding the fact that the 'Empire prism' is still pervasive in certain substantive legal subjects when it comes to the assertion of jurisdiction by courts and other public authorities in many 'Muslim States'. See further the discussion below.

[39] For the most succinct general overview, see L Buskens, 'Sharia and the Colonial State' in R Peters and P Bearman (eds), *The Ashgate Research Companion to Islamic Law* (London, Routledge, 2014) 209.

[40] For a comparative historical account of colonial practices in Muslim majority States that now utilise some version of Muslim family law, see I Hussin, *The Politics of Islamic Law: Local Elites, Colonial Authority, and the Making of the Muslim State* (Chicago, University of Chicago Press, 2016).

[41] For a fascinating historical analysis of how this takes shape, see S Ghabrial, 'Le "fiqh francisé"?: Muslim Personal Status Law Reform and Women's Litigation in Colonial Algeria (1870–1930)' (PhD dissertation, McGill University, 2014).

[42] C Hamilton, *The Hedaya or Guide: A Commentary on the Mussulman Laws*, 2nd edn (updated by S Grady, Lahore, Premier Book House, 1870).

[43] Some such as An-Na'im have argued that the very act of setting out positivist rules by the State ceases to make Sharīʿa what it is supposed to be. See A An-Na'im (ed), *Islamic Family Law in a Changing World: A Global Resource Book* (London, Zed Books, 2002) 18.

Consequently, in Muslim family law States, the prevailing law governing parental responsibility and child custody draws upon an Islamic historical tradition that survived the European colonial encounter and thereby represents in these post-colonial societies the kernels of local, regional authenticity and contributes to the nationalising narrative of newly formed States.[44] Of particular importance to Muslim family law States in the parental abduction context are the grounds of sex and religion, as both often feature in domestic considerations on custodial fitness and the best interests of the child. Reform of family law in many Muslim family law States takes on a political dimension and sensitivity which simply does not extend or apply to other areas of law in these States. In societies where 'Islam' is an integral and important part of the broader political, cultural and social landscape, to amend any positivist laws deemed 'religious' will necessarily consume substantial political capital, if such amendments are deemed contrary to the interests and views of the 'religious' constituency. Methodologically, it is still important to clarify the range of States being referred to when using the term 'Muslim family law States'. First, Muslim family law States are not only those with a majority Muslim population. In some States, such as Singapore, Muslims are a minority. While the broader political dynamics on Islamic family law may be different from its neighbour Malaysia, with its majority Muslim population, Singapore's Muslim minority nonetheless can regulate its family law matters according to religiously inspired laws under the Administration of Muslim Law Act, 1966. These States are not a focus of the discussion. Second, such States do not include only those that proclaim themselves to be Islamic. Turkey provides a good example of this. While Turkey is constitutionally secular, Muslim family laws continue to regulate family matters that touch upon international parental child abduction.[45]

A. Muslim Family Law States and the Hague Conference System

With regard to the 57 OIC Member States, it is clear that a country's status as secular or religious will not predict whether it joins the Hague Conference or participates in the Hague Children Conventions.[46] Albania,[47] Azerbaijan,[48] Burkina Faso,[49]

[44] See, generally, the special issue of (2010) 58(4) *American Journal of Comparative Law*.

[45] While domestically secular, the nature and scope of Turkish secularism is increasingly contested. At the same time, Turkey considers itself an important and influential player in the Muslim world. See further the discussions on secularism and political identity in A Kuru and A Stepan (eds), *Democracy, Islam, and Secularism in Turkey* (New York, Columbia University Press, 2012); and MH Yavuz, *Islamic Political Identity in Turkey* (Oxford, Oxford University Press, 2003). On the role of Islam in Turkish family law, see I Yilmaz, 'Semi-official Turkish Muslim Legal Pluralism: Encounters between Secular Official Law and Unofficial Shari'a' in A Possamai, J Richardson and B Turner (eds), *The Sociology of Shari'a: Case Studies from around the World* (New York, Springer, 2015) 51.

[46] The other key 'Children's Convention' adopted under the auspices of the Hague Conference, which is not the focus of this chapter, is the Convention Jurisdiction, Applicable Law, Recognition, Enforcement and Co-operation in Respect of Parental Responsibility and Measures for the Protection of Children (adopted 19 October 1996, entered into force 1 January 2002) Hague XXXIV.

Kazakhstan[50] and Turkey,[51] all of which are members of both the OIC and the Hague Conference, are constitutionally secular, but not all have acceded to the 1980 Hague Abduction Convention.[52] Saudi Arabia, Jordon, Malaysia, Morocco, Tunisia and Egypt are not constitutionally secular States, yet States such as Morocco and Tunisia have played a leading role with respect to the Hague Conference and its Children's Conventions. Egypt,[53] despite joining the Hague Conference in 1961, has become party to only three Conventions, with the last of its accessions being in 1981.[54] Saudi Arabia joined the Hague Conference in 2016 and to date has not acceded to any conventions.[55] Whether it will do so and to which Conventions remains to be seen. Moreover, it is worth noting that Jordon[56] became party to the Hague Conference in 2001 and Malaysia[57] did so in 2002, and to date neither has acceded to any conventions. Morocco and Tunisia are members of the OIC and the Hague Conference system, and have become party to a number of conventions adopted under the auspices of the latter. Morocco, for instance, joined the Hague Conference in 1993 and is party to seven conventions, including the 1980 Hague Abduction Convention. Tunisia joined the Hague Conference in 2014 and has since become party to three conventions, including the 1980 Hague Abduction Convention.[58]

[47] Article 10 of the 1998 Constitution of the Republic of Albania as amended on 13 January 2007 declares that 'there is no official religion' and that the 'State is neutral on questions of belief'.

[48] Article 7(1) of the Constitution of the Republic of Azerbaijan declares that the 'Azerbaijani state is [a] democratic, legal, secular, unitary republic'.

[49] Article 31 of the 1991 Constitution of Burkina Faso as amended declares that 'Burkina Faso is a democratic, unitary and secular State'.

[50] Article 1 of the Constitution of the Republic of Kazakhstan 'proclaims itself a democratic, secular, legal and social state whose highest values are an individual, his life, rights and freedoms'.

[51] Article 2 of the 1982 Constitution of the Republic of Turkey states: 'The Republic of Turkey is a democratic, secular and social state governed by rule of law.'

[52] Azerbaijan is not party to the Convention.

[53] Article 2 of the 2014 Constitution of the Arab Republic of Egypt states: 'Islam is the religion of the State and Arabic is its official language. The principles of Islamic Sharia are the main source of legislation.'

[54] It is party to the Convention on the Recognition of Divorces and Legal Separations (adopted 1 June 1970, entered into force 24 August 1975) Hague XVIII, accession 21 April 1980; the Convention on Civil Procedure (adopted 1 March 1954, entered into force 12 April 1957) Hague II, accession 4 November 1981; and the Convention on the Service Abroad of Judicial and Extrajudicial Documents in Civil or Commercial Matters (adopted 15 November 1965, entered into force 10 February 1969) Hague XIV, accession 12 December 1968. In 1978, it signed the Convention on Celebration and Recognition of the Validity of Marriages (adopted 14 March 1978, entered into force 1 May 1991) Hague XXVI.

[55] As noted above, Saudi Arabia has no formal constitution; it has a Basic Law that might be considered constitutional and that defines Saudi Arabia as an Islamic State. See, for example, Ali M Al-Mehaimeed, 'The Constitutional System of Saudi Arabia: A Conspectus' (1993) 8 *Arab Law Quarterly* 30.

[56] Article 2 of the 1952 Constitution of The Hashemite Kingdom of Jordan states: 'Islam is the religion of the State and Arabic is its official language.'

[57] Article 3(1) of the Federal Constitution of Malaysia, 1957 (as amended), which is entitled 'Religion of the Federation', states: 'Islam is the religion of the Federation; but other religions may be practised in peace and harmony in any part of the Federation.'

[58] With the other two being the Convention Abolishing the Requirement of Legalisation for Foreign Public Documents (adopted 5 October 1961, entered into force 24 January 1965) Hague XII and the Convention of 15 November 1965 on the Service Abroad of Judicial and Extrajudicial Documents in Civil or Commercial Matters.

With regard to the 1980 Hague Abduction Convention, only 12 out of the OIC Member States, less than one-fifth, are party to the 1980 Hague Abduction Convention: Albania, Burkina Faso, Gabon,[59] Guinea,[60] Iraq, Kazakhstan, Morocco, Pakistan, Tunisia, Turkey, Turkmenistan[61] and Uzbekistan.[62] Of this group, only four are avowedly Islamic in their constitutional design – Iraq, Morocco, Pakistan and Tunisia – and are thus noteworthy not only because of their constitutional design but also due to the differential evidence to support their national commitment to the enforcement of their treaty obligations.

Iraq became party to the 1980 Hague Abduction Convention in June 2014. It is not party to any other Hague Convention and is not a member of the Hague Conference. The 2005 Iraqi Constitution is unambiguous in that Islam is the official faith and a central tenet of the State. Article 2 notes: 'Islam is the official religion of the State and is a foundation source of legislation … No law may be enacted that contradicts the established provisions of Islam.' Moreover, while the Iraqi Law of Personal Status, 1959 broke the stranglehold of clerics on family law, nonetheless the law is informed by Islamic legal doctrines and principles.[63] Iraq is unusual in that it is an OIC Member State that proclaims Islam as the formal State religion, has joined the 1980 Hague Abduction Convention, but has not joined the Hague Conference as a Member State.[64] Iraq's accession to the Convention is noteworthy in that further to the US-led invasion of Iraq in 2003, the size of the Iraqi diaspora has increased significantly, creating the conditions for parental child abduction, especially *from* Iraq. It is difficult, however, on every level to conceive how Iraq can accede to the 1980 Hague Abduction Convention *and* comply with its requirements in good faith.[65] Iraq's accession to the 1980 Hague Abduction Convention

[59] Article 2 of the 1991 Constitution of the Gabonese Republic states: 'Gabon is an indivisible, secular, democratic and social Republic.'

[60] Article 1 of the Constitution of Guinea states: 'Guinea is a unitary republic, indivisible, secular, democratic and social.'

[61] Article 1 of the 2008 Constitution of Turkmenistan states 'Turkmenistan is a democratic, legal and secular state in which the government takes the form of presidential republic.'

[62] Uzbekistan has no clear constitutional position on faith and in practice seeks to exert extreme control it. Article 1 of the 1992 Constitution notes: 'Uzbekistan is a sovereign democratic republic.' Article 12 notes: 'In the Republic of Uzbekistan, public life shall develop on the basis of a diversity of political institutions, ideologies and opinions. No ideology may be established as the state.' J Fox, *Political Secularism, Religion, and the State: A Time Series Analysis of Worldwide Data* (Cambridge, Cambridge University Press, 2015) 45, identified it as a State having a 'negative attitude' towards religion. This rather understates the position. Human Rights Watch and the US Commission on International Religious Freedom (USCIRF) have for many years considered Uzbekistan to be one of the more repressive regimes in the context of religious freedom. See Human Rights Watch, Annual Report, 2017, available at: https://www.hrw.org/world-report/2017/country-chapters/uzbekistan; and USCIRF at www.uscirf.gov/countries/uzbekistan#annual-reports.

[63] Law No 188 of 1959, Personal Status Law. On the history of the legislation, see N Efrati, 'Negotiating Rights in Iraq: Women and the Personal Status Law' (2005) 59(4) *Middle East Journal* 577.

[64] Article 2 of the 2005 Iraqi Constitution states: 'Islam is the official religion of the State and is a foundation source of legislation … No law may be enacted that contradicts the established provisions of Islam.'

[65] The principle is referred to in both the preamble and substantively in art 26 of the Vienna Convention on the Law of Treaties 1969.

was not accompanied by any domestic law reform in Iraq, as would be necessary. Nevertheless, while Iraq's accession to the Hague Abduction Convention need not be recognised due to the discretion other Contracting States to the Convention have to recognise others or not under Article 38, 16 contracting States have recognised Iraq's accession.[66]

The position with regard to Morocco is not unlike Iraq's. Islam is constitutionally the faith religion of the State in Morocco.[67] As a constitutional monarchy, Morocco's King also claims as an honorific title *amīr al-mu'minīn* or 'Commander of the Faithful', a title which conveys: (a) the royal family's claim to descent from the Prophet Muhammad; (b) a capacity to stand 'above the ethnic, social and political factions' of the country; and (c) a discretionary prerogative, the legitimacy of which derives from the King's religious commitments.[68] In the context of international parental child abduction, Morocco is unique in that it is an 'Islamic State' that is both a member of the Hague Conference and a party to both the 1980 Hague Abduction Convention and the 1996 Protection Convention. Morocco acceded to the 1980 Hague Abduction Convention in 2010 and its accession was widely accepted within a relatively short period of time.[69] The widespread acceptance by other States Parties of Morocco's accession is no doubt significantly influenced by the substantial reforms in 2004 of its Personal Status Law,[70] as well as its proximity to Europe and demographic movements across the Mediterranean.

Tunisia is also, as noted above, a party to the 1980 Hague Abduction Convention, having acceded to it in 2017. Tunisia has long been considered by various United Nations (UN) treaty bodies as an exemplar for other Muslim family law States as far as 'progressive' law reform in this area is concerned. After the 2011 Arab Spring, which began in Tunisia and then spread across the Arab world, Tunisia underwent substantial reforms, including to its Constitution. In this contest of populist agitation, formerly suppressed voices rose to the surface, including Islamist ones. While there was considerable debate about the role of Islam in any new Tunisian Constitution, the 2014 Tunisian Constitution is careful to reflect

[66] As of April 2020: Japan, China, Argentina, Mexico, Serbia, Venezuela, Peru, the Russian Federation, Ukraine, Moldova, Chile, New Zealand, Andorra, Brazil, Georgia and Uruguay. It seems highly unlikely that any of these States hosts a sizeable Iraqi diaspora. Iraq has not responded to the January 2017 questionnaire concerning the practical operation of the Hague Abduction Convention. See Preliminary Document No 2 of January 2017, available at: https://www.hcch.net/en/publications-and-studies/details4/?pid=6548&dtid=33.

[67] Article 3 of the 2011 Constitution states: 'L'Islam est la religion de l'Etat, qui garantit à tous le libre exercice des cultes.'

[68] F Alicino, 'Morocco: An Islamic Globalizing Monarchy within the Elusive Phenomenon of Arab Spring' (2015) 95(1–2) *Oriente Moderno* 145, 146.

[69] As of the end of 2020, Morocco's accession has been accepted by over 50 other Contracting States.

[70] Official Gazette General Provisions Sherifyan Dahir (Royal Edict) no 1.04.22 issued on 12 Dou Al Hijja 1424 (3 February 2004) to Implement Law No 70.03 as the Family Code Al-Moudawana. For commentary on the 2004 reforms, see Z Mir-Hosseini, 'How the Door of Ijtihad was Opened and Closed: A Comparative Analysis of Recent Family Law Reforms in Iran and Morocco' (2007) 69(4) *Washington and Lee Law Review* 1499.

Tunisia's Islamic character while preserving certain long-standing commitments to secularity in government. For instance, while the constitution recognises Islam as the religion of the State, Islam and Islamic law are not formal sources of legal obligation. Rather, as Article 2 expressly states: 'Tunisia is a civil state based on citizenship, the will of the people and the supremacy of law.' To emphasise this commitment to popular sovereignty, Article 2 concludes: 'This article may not be amended.'[71] Following the 2014 Constitution, Tunisia acceded to the 1980 Hague Abduction Convention. However, it is noteworthy that at the time of writing, only eight States have accepted Tunisia's accession; this general non-responsiveness displays a current lack of confidence in Tunisia being able to uphold its obligations.

Pakistan's accession to the 1980 Hague Abduction Convention in 2016 was perhaps surprising, but less so than that of Iraq. Pakistan had been engaging with some Hague Conference States over a period of time with regard to the return of children who had been abducted by one of their parents and taken to Pakistan. Pakistan's accession has at the time of writing not been widely accepted by other States Parties to the 1980 Hague Abduction Convention.[72] This may be explained in part by Pakistan's failure to amend its relevant domestic legislation. Pakistan's family law rules are heavily influenced by religious rules concerning matters of personal status such as marriage, divorce, custody and inheritance.[73] Pakistan's accession to the 1980 Hague Abduction Convention confronts many of the 'traditional' Hague Conference States with difficult questions and uncomfortable issues.

B. Muslim Family Law States, Politics and the Integration of Non-signatory States: Bilateral Arrangements and the UN Convention on the Rights of the Child

A second key question is how to address parental child abductions between States that are party to the 1980 Hague Child Abduction Convention and those that are not. While it is tempting to reduce the challenge of international parental child abduction and Muslim family law States to the narrow issue of Islam and Islamic law, the scope of parental abductions from one State to another reflects regional

[71] Constitution of the Republic of Tunisia, 2014. Available at: https://wipolex.wipo.int/en/text/335069 (Arabic version); www.lse.ac.uk/GranthamInstitute/wp-content/uploads/laws/4808.pdf (English translation).

[72] Three years after its accession took effect, only eight other States had accepted the accession of Pakistan. These were New Zealand, Ukraine, Andorra and five Latin American States. At the end of 2020, however, the United States of America recognised Pakistan's accession. This is noteworthy but it is far too early to ascertain the practical difference this will make. At the time of writing, Pakistan had not responded to the January 2017 questionnaire concerning the practical operation of the 1980 Hague Child Abduction Convention. Preliminary Document No 2 of January 2017, available at: https://www.hcch.net/en/publications-and-studies/details4/?pid=6548&dtid=33.

[73] For a Pakistani decision that recounts the legal topography in the case of international child abduction, see *Louise Anne Fairley v Sajjd Ahmed Rana*, PLD 2007 Lahore 300 (decided 29 November 2006).

developments, trade networks and associated demographic movements. In each case, the issue boils down to whether the States in question have arrangements between themselves, such as being party to the 1980 Hague Abduction Convention, to resolve the conflict. For example in 2012–13, according to the UK Foreign and Commonwealth Office's statistics, the 'top ten Hague countries' to which 179 children were abducted from the UK were respectively the US, Poland, Ireland, Germany, France, Canada, South Africa, Spain, Australia and Turkey.[74] Poland was not a major destination for children abducted from the UK before 2004, when Poland joined the EU. After 2004, as significant numbers of Polish nationals exercised their EU law rights to migrate to the UK, cases of children abducted from the UK to Poland increased. Non-signatory States to the 1980 Hague Abduction Convention, by contrast, are considered 'safe havens' for parents who abduct their children from a signatory State. Such States, such as Muslim family law States, represent a veritable legal black hole vis-a-vis left-behind parents seeking redress. Equally, it is the case that where both States are not party to the 1980 Hague Convention, there is no multilateral treaty (or as far as known bilateral treaty) in force that seeks to address the issue of parental child abduction on a regional or local level that encompasses the OIC States.[75] Some States that are signatories to the 1980 Hague Abduction Convention have sought to engage on a bilateral basis with certain non-signatories so as to affect the returns of some abducted children outside of the Convention framework. These arrangements have the advantage of providing a workable solution for the return of children abducted and taken to or from a non-signatory State. For non-signatory States, such arrangements also avoid the need to navigate many of the deeper and more turbulent political and legal currents involved in reforming their relevant domestic rules. As far as can be ascertained, existing bilateral arrangements to date have been between, on the one hand, States that are members of the Hague Conference and party to the 1980 Hague Abduction Convention, and, on the other hand, Muslim family law States that are not (or were not at the time of agreement) party to the Convention.[76] However, it is equally worth noting that some Hague Conference Member States do not enter into bilateral agreements as a matter of policy. Such States prefer a multilateral, overarching framework and view bilateral agreements as undermining more inclusive efforts to resolve such problems.[77] Finally, some Muslim family law States have acceded to the Hague Abduction Convention after earlier entering into bilateral arrangements. For example, Morocco entered into agreements with France (1983) and Belgium (1981) before acceding to the Convention in 2010.[78]

[74] With 32, 29, 28, 18, 12, 11, 10, 10, 9 and 8 recorded abductions respectively.

[75] At the regional level, there is the OAS treaty – see the discussion above.

[76] See below for examples.

[77] For example, the Federal Republic of Germany does not enter into such bilateral agreements for precisely such reasons. This is based on personal discussions and correspondence by the author with representatives of the Federal Republic. France, by contrast, in the past has had over 20 bilateral agreements dealing with such matters. See the statement by B Biondi in (2004) *The Judges' Newsletter* 22, available at: https://assets.hcch.net/docs/d2d27e41-5e46-4573-b8b4-b452811ca2b9.pdf.

[78] Both France and Belgium have recognised Morocco's accession.

Pakistan and the UK negotiated a Protocol on child abduction in 2003, yet, as noted above, Pakistan has been a party to the 1980 Hague Abduction Convention since 2016.[79] Such bilateral agreements or protocols presumably continue to operate if the accession of one party to the Convention is not recognised by the other. For instance, because the UK has not accepted Pakistan's accession to the Convention, the Protocol continues to operate between the two countries in cases of child abduction. In this complex diplomatic context, these bilateral arrangements are, inter alia, recognition that the 1980 Hague Abduction Convention, with its background, history, assumptions and exceptions, is stymied as a global convention for the return of abducted children.

One common legal denominator across these bilateral agreements is Article 11 of the UN Convention on the Rights of the Child (UNCRC).[80] While the contracting parties to these bilateral agreements do not work within the Hague Conference system, their agreements are nonetheless construed, in part, as ensuring compliance with the UNCRC. In contrast to the diplomatic tensions over the 1980 Hague Abduction Convention, the negotiating history of Article 11 UNCRC did not evince remotely the same level of dispute and thus became the foundation of non-convention agreements.[81] Article 11 of the UNCRC provides:

> 1. States Parties shall take measures to combat the illicit transfer and non-return of children abroad.
> 2. To this end, States Parties shall promote the conclusion of bilateral or multilateral agreements or accession to existing agreements.[82]

There are many reasons why Article 11 UNCRC may enjoy such broad acceptance. The UNCRC was the first occasion on which a significant number of Muslim family law States actively took part in negotiations of a global human rights instrument. Furthermore, those negotiations took place well after certain significant political events, specifically the 1979 Iranian Revolution and the Soviet invasion of Afghanistan, both of which have substantively contributed to an assertive and transnational 'Islamic identity' in the modern era. The fact that the UNCRC was to be a global treaty dealing with, in part, the issue of parental child abduction was not lost on the French representative, who emphasised early on in the negotiations that the UNCRC's proposed provision on child abduction should not 'take second place' to existing conventions such as the 1980 Hague Abduction Convention.[83] The UNCRC provision was thus to be the primary basis for global efforts to tackle parental child abduction. To that end, several non-governmental organisations (NGOs) emphasised the use of bilateral agreements to supplement multilateral

[79] See further J Young, 'The Constitutional Limits of Judicial Activism: Judicial Conduct of International Relations and Child Abduction' (2003) 66 *Modern Law Review* 823; and Emon and Khaliq (n 1) ch 3.

[80] For examples of these bilateral agreements, see the selection provided on the Hague Conference's website: www.hcch.net/index_en.php?act=publications.details&pid=5215&dtid=28.

[81] The *travaux préparatoires* refer to art 6 in the first and second readings.

[82] For the text of the treaty, see www.ohchr.org/en/professionalinterest/pages/crc.aspx.

[83] See E/1982/12/Add.1,C, 49–55.

ones as a route to satisfying Article 11 UNCRC,[84] and this was subsequently clarified in one of the French drafts for part of the provision.[85]

Two things are apparent from Article 11's negotiating history, which was neither particularly difficult nor drawn out. First, Article 11 UNCRC was intended to stand *apart* from the Hague Conference approach to international parental child abduction. For example, the French proposals for the text of Article 11 were directly drawn from the French-language version of the 1980 Hague Abduction Convention. Thus, terms such as 'déplacement illicite' were in the French proposals for Article 11. Other State representatives, such as those from Finland, successfully protested against the importation of words from the 1980 Hague Abduction Convention, which have specific meanings in that context. They were adamant *against* transplanting the Hague Conference system's set of approaches and assumptions to the UNCRC's new regime.[86] The objective was to facilitate to return of abducted children, but without being the same as the 1980 Hague Abduction Convention.

Second, it is clear from the Working Group's records that cultural and religious considerations were not a ground of contention during the negotiation.[87] Government representatives from all parts of the world expressed their views on the proposals. This is unlike the negotiation of the 1980 Hague Abduction Convention. In the context of Article 11 UNCRC, Muslim family law States, such as Kuwait, Pakistan and Qatar, made their views known, and nothing in their remarks suggested that Islam or Muslim family law posed obstacles to agreement. Qatar simply noted that 'Islamic law recognizes the need to protect children'.[88] The Pakistani representative made no reference to Islam, but noted: 'The Government supports the proposal that all countries should cooperate closely through accession to the Hague Convention on Civil Aspects of International Child Abduction of 25 October 1980, which is open to all States.'[89] The published *travaux préparatoires* do not refer to any specific proposal during the negotiation on Article 11. However, the Economic and Social Council referred to the 1980 Hague Abduction Convention in a resolution that opened negotiations on the Children's Convention.[90] Kuwait did hint at difficult challenges facing the negotiation, but nothing in the published *travaux préparatoires* suggests that these hints were a source of substantive contention. There is no other substantive reference to Islamic or Muslim family law in the *travaux préparatoires* for Article 11 UNCRC; no State, whether a Muslim family law State or otherwise, seems to have considered it an obstacle to agreement. This

[84] ibid.

[85] E/CN.4/1983/62, para 47.

[86] E/CN.4/1989/48, 40–41.

[87] See United Nations, *Legislative History of the Convention on the Rights of the Child*, vol I (New York, United Nations, 2007) 426–36.

[88] ibid.

[89] ibid.

[90] Economic and Social Council Resolution 1982/39 on the 'Protection of the Rights of Children and Parents in Cases of Removal or Retention of Children', 7 May 1982, 2.

absence is telling, given that cultural and religious differences were overt bones of contention concerning other provisions of the UNCRC.[91]

However, it should be stressed that States Parties always had the option of entering a reservation to all or part of Article 11 if they found any part of it objectionable. This may explain the lack of contention over Article 11. Importantly, while a significant number of Muslim family law States have entered 'Islamic reservations' to some UNCRC provisions, none specifically refers to Article 11.[92] The Committee on the Rights of the Child has not issued a General Comment on Article 11, nor has it been a consistent focus of discussion under the State reporting system.[93]

Nevertheless, without an express mechanism – domestic or international – for resolving international parental child abduction cases, Article 11 does not constitute a sufficient basis, despite global agreement, for addressing parental child abduction. That is why, in the absence of consensus on the 1980 Hague Abduction Convention, bilateral agreements remain an important alternative. These agreements, which refer to the broader principles of the UNCRC in addition to Article 11, try to ensure the return of abducted children outside the Hague Abduction Convention framework.[94] Yet none of the bilateral agreements provides for the automatic return of the child who has been abducted – the central tenet of the 1980 Hague Abduction Convention.[95]

[91] S Harris-Short, 'International Human Rights Law: Imperialist, Inept and Ineffective? Cultural Relativism and the UN Convention on the Rights of the Child, (2003) 25(1) *Human Rights Quarterly* 130.

[92] The reservations of Muslim family law States to certain UN human rights treaties are well documented and there is an extensive literature on this. The saga relating to what became the Report of the ILC on the Work of its 63rd Session, GA, Official Records, 66th Session, Supplement No 10, Addendum 1, UN Doc A/66/10/Add. 1 is well known and in part relates to the difficulty and contention of the issue of reservations to human rights treaties. For an overview by the Special Rapporteur himself see A Pellett, 'The ILC Guide to Practice on Reservations to Treaties: A General Presentation by the Special Rapporteur' (2013) 24(4) *European Journal of International Law* 1061.

[93] The Committee has issued 'General Comment No 6 (2005) Treatment of Unaccompanied and Separated Children Outside Their Country of Origin' (1 September 2005) UN Doc CRC/GC/2005/6, but in this General Comment it defines such children as those separated from both parents (7) and thus it does not deal with children abducted by one parent. For detailed discussion of art 11 and its interpretation and application, see, Tobin, N Lowe and E Luke, 'Article 11: Protection against the Illicit Transfer and Non-return of Children Abroad' in J Tobin (ed), *The UN Convention on the Rights of the Child: A Commentary* (Oxford, Oxford University Press, 2019) 370.

[94] For examples of bilateral agreements between Contracting States and non-Contracting States, see the Hague Conference's website: www.hcch.net/index_en.php?act=publications.details&pid=5215&dtid=28. Moreover, for a useful but now dated analysis of some agreements, see the Hague Conference's Preliminary Document No 7 of August 2002 on the issue, prepared for the Special Commission of September/October 2002: C Gosselain, 'Child Abduction and Transfrontier Access: Bilateral Conventions and Islamic States: A Research Paper', available at: www.hcch.net/upload/abd2002_pd7e.pdf. E Schnitzer-Reese, 'International Child Abduction to non-Hague Convention Countries: The Need for an International Family Court' (2004) 2(1) *Northwestern Journal of International Human Rights*, available at: http://scholarlycommons.law.northwestern.edu/njihr/vol2/iss1/7 argues for an international family law court; such an option was debated and dismissed in the early history leading up to the 1980 Hague Abduction Convention.

[95] Notably the Australia–Egypt bilateral agreement does in art 6(c) provide for a cooperative mechanism for encouraging and facilitating 'agreement by the parents on the access by a parent to the child

While such bilateral agreements offer potential alternative approaches or channels of cooperation, they have had limited success at best. Indeed, it is the view of representatives from almost all Hague Conference Member States that have such agreements that they have simply not worked as envisaged or hoped.[96] William Duncan, then Deputy Secretary General of the Hague Conference, noted that the mechanisms of cooperation created by these bilateral agreements have often been ineffective and inefficient. This is further reinforced by the fact that no bilateral agreements have been adopted since 2005.[97] Moreover, in the case of countries applying Muslim family law, provisions for enforcing foreign decisions did not work well, 'one of the reasons being a tendency in certain States of the Islamic tradition to invoke public policy, based on Koranic law, as a basis for refusing recognition'.[98] While the UNCRC has been an impetus for these bilateral agreements, these agreements have not been successful. In many cases, their limits reflect the ongoing place of Muslim family law in one of the contracting States Parties. In such cases, domestic legal regimes, and the central role of religion in those societies and its reflection in the law and practice, have served as a hindrance to the effective operation of bilateral agreements on parental child abduction. Consequently, as much as Article 11 UNCRC might be seen as opening a door to more cooperation on international child abduction, there remains an underlying issue concerning the impact of Sharīʿa on the scope of cooperation Muslim family law States can offer on the international plane. While there are a number of spheres in which this manifests itself, in this chapter I wish to pick out one: jurisdiction.

C. The Centrality of Jurisdiction in Parental Child Abduction

Jurisdiction is a lawyer's term par excellence. Perhaps, indeed probably, because of this, it is not always clear what it is meant by it. It was apt not so long ago for Vaughan Lowe – a scholar forever closely associated with Robin – to note that there were few general treatises devoted to the topic.[99] The practice, primarily, of various human rights courts and tribunals in more recent years put paid to

or return of the child to the territory of the other Party'. But the cooperation anticipated is principally persuasive through diplomatic channels. For the text, see www.hcch.net/index_en.php?act=publications.details&pid=5215&dtid=28.

[96] This is based on personal discussions and correspondence with representatives of those Hague Conference States with such bilateral agreements.

[97] The last two such agreements are between the US and Egypt in 2003 and Switzerland and Lebanon in 2005. The texts of the agreements can be found at: www.hcch.net/index_en.php?act=publications.details&pid=5215&dtid=28.

[98] W Duncan, 'Toward the Malta Process' *The Judges' Newsletter* 8 (Autumn 2004) 5, available at: www.hcch.net/upload/autumn2004.pdf. For more detailed analysis, see Gosselain (n 94).

[99] V Lowe and C Stalker, 'Jurisdiction' in M Evans (ed), *International Law*, 3rd edn (Oxford, Oxford University Press, 2010) 314, 315.

that and there has been an enormous amount written on the topic since then.[100] Notwithstanding this, there is little of any systematic depth written at all – let alone in recent years – on the notion of jurisdiction in private international law.[101] In terms of jurisdiction under Islamic law, there is next to nothing in the literature.[102] Yet, there is a fundamental difference in approach here vis-a-vis jurisdiction in terms of personal matters and conceptions of territory. In general terms, most States do not by and large assume jurisdiction over individuals – whether civil or criminal – due to faith as a basis for that exercise of jurisdiction. That is exactly what is done in cases of child abduction that come before many courts in Muslim family law States. The nexus is often nothing other than religion – namely, one of the parties to the parental child abduction identifies as, or is identifiable as, a Muslim. While courts in many States struggle, on substantive matters, with what is appropriate to be considered by them in terms of jurisdiction, none other than courts in Muslim family law States seem to routinely have reference to religion as a relevant – indeed, critical – factor in that jurisdictional determination.[103] While this approach to religion is unusual, it is this method in conjunction with the approach to 'territory' that is critical. For in Muslim family law States in disputes over child custody, in the context of parental child abduction, reference is not normally to other States as distinct territorial units, but whether or not those territories are a part of the *dominion of Islam*, as per the classic or premodern Islamic legal sources.[104] This is the prism of empire being used to assume the acceptability of the culture and norms in other (Muslim majority) nation-States, notwithstanding substantial differences between them. The empire prism – with those outside of it deemed less acceptable than those within – is a form of exceptionalism and a value judgement about the (inappropriate) mores of the 'other'. The central objective of the 1980 Hague Abduction Convention is to speedily return the child wrongly removed to his or her country of habitual residence. This is precisely in order to avoid substantive determination of the custody of the child by the courts of the State to which the child has been abducted and such value judgements about the approach adopted in other States. In Muslim family law States, the approach adopted by the 1980 Hague Abduction Convention cannot apply in the absence of substantial domestic law reform, indeed a fundamental rewriting of parts of it. Domestic law reform in Muslim majority States in the field of family law is infused

[100] The literature is now enormous, so much so that Oxford University Press has published a handbook devoted solely to the issue: S Allen, D Costelloe, M Fitzmaurice, P Gragl and E Guntrip (eds), *The Oxford Handbook of Jurisdiction in International Law* (Oxford, Oxford University Press, 2019).

[101] There is notably J Fawcett (ed), *Declining Jurisdiction in Private International Law* (Oxford, Oxford University Press, 1995), but this was published over 25 years ago. A number of other monographs have examined aspects of jurisdiction in the context of private international law, but always with a focus on one substantive issue or other.

[102] In Allen et al (n 100), for example, two pages are devoted to the topic. In Emon and Khaliq (n 1), we cover the topic in far more detail.

[103] For a recent example before the UK Supreme Court, see *Villiers* v *Villiers* [2020] UKSC 30. Rabbinic courts in Israel may also do so.

[104] For a detailed discussion, see Emon and Khaliq (n 1).

with all the politics of the post-colonial polity, which is normally closely interconnected with notions of national identity. These are turbulent, precarious and deep waters in which to tread, and normally it is only the despotic or the foolhardy who venture there.

Equally, courts in non-Muslim family law States may also need to consider their jurisdiction over matters that may occur in Muslim family law States. Extra-territorial jurisdiction under human rights treaties may oblige a State's courts to not send a child abducted from a Muslim family law State back to that State, even if obliged to do so under the 1980 Hague Abduction Convention where both are parties.[105] The crux of the issue is as follows. Under certain human rights treaties, a State that is refuge to an abducted child cannot return that child to its habitual residence if, due to conditions in the latter (legal and otherwise), doing so would violate the refuge State's obligations under human rights treaties. For example, suppose a mother abducts her child from Bahrain and both migrate to Germany. The father subsequently petitions a German court to return the child to Bahrain. The German authorities may be prohibited from doing so due to Germany's treaty obligations, based on certain conditions in Bahrain that invoke obligations under global instruments such as the International Covenant on Civil and Political Rights (ICCPR) or regional ones such as the European Convention on Human Rights (ECHR). This situation is analogous to the Article 20 exception in the 1980 Hague Abduction Convention, though broader and wider because it affects all States Parties and not just those that are parties to the Hague Abduction Convention.[106]

D. Jurisdiction under the ICCPR

To illustrate the implications of human rights instruments on parental abduction issues in the context of jurisdiction, I will briefly examine the situation under the ICCPR with regard to extra-territoriality, namely the extent to which a State Party to the ICCPR must restrict the possibility of return when the destination country's conditions potentially violate ICCPR provisions. As noted above, national courts have on the whole taken a restrictive approach to Article 20 of the 1980 Hague Abduction Convention, as the Pérez-Vera Report advised.[107] However, the Pérez-Vera Report clearly now reads as being from a different era, when human rights considerations were not quite the leitmotif of international relations that

[105] This will be the case where both Contracting States recognise the other as party to the 1980 Hague Abduction Convention and one is a Muslim family law State and the other is not: New Zealand and Iraq, for example.

[106] Article 11 of the Children's Convention obliges States Parties to 'take measures to combat the illicit transfer and non-return of children abroad' and to 'promote the conclusion of bilateral or multilateral agreements or accession to existing agreements'. Article 11 has been under-utilised by the Committee on the Rights of the Child (CRC). For a detailed discussion, see Tobin, Lowe and Luke (n 93) 370.

[107] See, E Pèrez-Vera, 'Report of the Special Commission' A&D14, 113–18.

they have since become. As a consequence of subsequent jurisprudential developments, human rights considerations will have a far greater impact on returns than was envisaged when the Hague Abduction Convention was drafted and has hitherto been the case. Article 2(1) ICCPR sets out the jurisdictional scope of its obligations on States Parties:

> Each State Party to the present Covenant undertakes to respect and to ensure to all individuals *within its territory and subject to its jurisdiction* the rights recognized in the present Covenant, without distinction of any kind, such as race, colour, sex, language, religion, political or other opinion, national or social origin, property, birth or other status. (Emphasis added)

The reference to territory and jurisdiction implies that the ICCPR extends to everyone within a State's territory or before its agencies, regardless of his or her nationality.[108] All who come before the national courts of States Parties are thus entitled to rights that are protected by the ICCPR.[109] Moreover, those rights are to be enjoyed without discrimination on the basis of any of the listed prohibited grounds. Of particular importance to Muslim family law States in the parental abduction context are the grounds of sex and religion, as both feature in Muslim family law State domestic considerations on custodial fitness and the best interests of the child. Finally, the most obvious reading of the provision is that for a State Party to owe an obligation under the ICCPR, the individual must be both 'within its territory' and 'subject to its jurisdiction'. On this reading, though, jurisdiction is always territorial, thereby forestalling extra-territorial considerations as a feature of the obligation.[110] Notably, the Human Rights Committee in General Comment No 31 departed from the obvious literal meaning of Article 2.[111] While a State's territory and jurisdiction will by and large coincide, the approach taken by the Committee means that *there are now circumstances where they will not and where a State Party will owe obligations outside its territory*. This disjunctive reading of the wording of the Covenant has been supported by the International Court of Justice in the *Wall Opinion.*[112] The Human Rights Committee's approach in General Comment No 31 applies to its entire practice and thus reflects its position regardless of which aspect of its supervisory functions (State reporting or petition) it is undertaking. In 2009, in a factually complex Communication which concerned the limits of the Covenant's jurisdictional application, the Committee

[108] This has been subject to a General Comment from the HRC: General Comment No 15.

[109] There are limited exceptions to this: arts 24 (children's rights) and 25 (right to vote), and art 13, which applies only to aliens.

[110] The French version of the Covenant similarly notes, 'Les Etats parties au présent Pacte s'engagent à respecter et à garantir à tous les individus se trouvant sur leur territoire et relevant de leur compétence les droits reconnus dans le présent Pacte.'

[111] Human Rights Committee, 'General Comment 31: Nature of the General Legal Obligation on States Parties to the Covenant, Adopted 29 March 2004' para 10, available at: https://www.unhcr.org/4963237716.pdf.

[112] *Advisory Opinion, Legal Consequences of the Construction of a Wall in the Occupied Palestinian Territory* [2004] ICJ Reports 136, paras 109–11.

further noted that for a State Party to be responsible for extra-territorial violations of the Covenant, there must be 'a link in the causal chain that would make possible violations *in another jurisdiction*' (emphasis added).[113] Although 'another jurisdiction' is used, this was in the context of the particular facts of the Communication – more generally, the principle is best understood as referring to violations of the Covenant outside of a State's territory. Even though jurisdiction and responsibility are not the same thing, without the causal link, jurisdiction in some circumstances cannot exist.[114]

In the context of parental child abduction, Muslim family law States and the ICCPR, extra-jurisdictional considerations will revolve around two related issues. The first is discrimination on the basis of sex against men and women, depending upon the age of the child(ren) or the marital status of the mother, when awarding of custody. The second is discrimination on the basis of religion, which becomes relevant in Muslim family law jurisdictions when one of the parents seeking custody of the child is not Muslim. These domestic legal practices in Muslim family law States pose challenges for States Parties to the ICCPR when exercising jurisdiction in cases seeking to return a child to his or her habitual residence in which ICCPR rights may not be as robustly protected. If an individual brought this issue before the Human Rights Committee (HRC), three considerations would prevail in assessing the extra-territorial application of the ICCPR: (1) is the individual within the power or effective control of a State Party?; (2) what is the (jurisdictional) relationship between the individual and the State Party in relation to a violation of any of the rights set forth in the Covenant?; and (3) is there a causal link between the State Party's exercise of jurisdiction over the individual and violations of ICCPR obligations?

It is not difficult to imagine how the ICCPR could be invoked. Imagine the following hypothetical. A marital relationship breaks down in the context of a discovered infidelity in, for example, Saudi Arabia, and the mother (who engaged in the infidelity) flees with her children to the Netherlands. The husband petitions the Dutch courts for the return of his children. If the children are returned, the mother cannot return with them to fight for custody as she will face the threat of capital punishment for her infidelity in a criminal trial in which evidential rules are discriminatory on the basis of gender. This example is not far-fetched. Such a

[113] Communication No 1539/2006, *Mohammad Munaf v Romania* (21 August 2009) UN Doc CCPR/C/96/D/1539/2006, 4.2; see in particular the Dissenting Opinion of W Kälin, where the issue is discussed in detail.

[114] Although see M Scheinin, 'Just Another Word? Jurisdiction in the Roadmaps of State Responsibility and Human Rights' in M Langford, W Vandenhole, M Scheinin and W van Genugten (eds), *Global Justice, State Duties: The Extraterritorial Scope of Economic, Social, and Cultural Rights in International Law* (Cambridge, Cambridge University Press, 2013) 212–32, who argues that 'jurisdiction in the context of human rights treaties is used to describe aspects of either the state responsibility regime or the admissibility criteria under human rights treaties'. There is something to this in the context of the jurisprudence of the European Court of Human Rights, but while courts and tribunals may compound the issues, jurisdiction and responsibility are related but distinct concepts.

threat was precisely part of the broader context of *Re J* in the House of Lords.[115] However, it should be stressed that under the ICCPR framework, the return of the abducted child does not trigger the application of the ICCPR, but rather the mother's access to justice and rights to life and freedom from torture. Nevertheless, if this hypothetical occurred between States Parties to the 1980 Hague Abduction Convention, the ICCPR could be invoked to overturn the operating assumptions in the Convention.

IV. Mapping a Route Forward: Rival Regimes?

The discussion above has argued that the 1980 Hague Abduction Convention is not suited to being a universal treaty that can address the problem of parental child abduction on a global scale. The absence of accessions to the Convention from many African, Middle East and Asian States is noteworthy – the particular gap in coverage is from those States that may be considered Muslim family law States. As has been highlighted, even when there are accessions from these States to the 1980 Hague Abduction Convention, it does not lead to an effectively functioning regime for one of a host of reasons. Notwithstanding the assertions and views of the Hague Conference and those associated with it, the facts speak for themselves – the 1980 Hague Abduction Convention is, culturally speaking, a Eurocentric regime. In those cases where Muslim family law States do accede to the Convention, their accessions are generally not widely recognised and this is in large part because they are not considered to have the domestic legislative framework to give effect to the key principle of the Convention – the speedy return of the abducted child. This is because religious principles are a central element of the decision-making process and this was not a consideration when the 1980 Hague Abduction Convention was negotiated. In the absence of significant domestic law reform – which is simply untenable in many Muslim family law States – any routes forward seem intractable. There is also no reason why it should be the standard and approaches of 'traditional' Hague Conference States that should prevail. It is important to stress that this is not a zero-sum game, with 'this' system or 'that' prevailing; rather, the ideal objective should be to have regimes in place which provide legal solutions to the predicaments in which children unwittingly find themselves when they become pawns in the breakdown of the relationship of their parents. It is possible to contemplate a few routes forward; each is laden with difficulties.

First, the Hague Conference could acknowledge that the States negotiating the 1980 Hague Abduction Convention ensured through the inclusion of Article 38 that they retained discretion as to whether to return children to States that subsequently acceded to it. This provision – which as far as is known is unique – ensures

[115] *Re J* [2005] UKHL 40.

there is no legal obligation upon a ratifying State to return a child to any State that has acceded to the Convention. In reality, this ensures that the 1980 Hague Abduction Convention provides a template for a series of bilateral relations between States, within the institutional framework established by the Convention. The Hague Conference could as a strategy seek to explicitly encourage States that accede to the 1980 Hague Abduction Convention to use it as the basis for returning abducted children, but to pragmatically encourage that only where the legal relationship will be between States where the Convention's operative assumptions are acceptable. There is no legal reason why a child abducted by his or her mother from, for example, Dubai and taken to Malaysia cannot be returned, but there are legal impediments for the child's return to, for example, Denmark. There is currently no regime in place that would create such an obligation between the United Arab Emirates and Malaysia, but using the 1980 Hague Abduction Convention in the way suggested would do so. The downside, of course, for the Hague Conference is that such an approach would – in the eyes of its Secretariat – 'undermine' the integrity of the Convention and further require the Conference to acknowledge that the Convention is not suited to being a universal treaty. The Article 20 public order exception is unlikely to be an issue in requested returns between Muslim family law States. This approach would effectively organise the States Parties to the 1980 Hague Abduction Convention into a two-tier system. Presenting such an initiative as a stepping-stone to 'full accession' would be disingenuous as Contracting States from Europe, North America and Australia will most likely withhold acceptance of such accessions. But at the very least, this approach would create a legal regime where there currently is not one and would facilitate the return of some children abducted by a parent.

A second approach would be for the Hague Conference to work with all Muslim family law States to facilitate the drafting of a Protocol based upon the 1980 Hague Abduction Convention, but with the aim of it only operating between Muslim family law States acknowledging the central role of religion in the decision-making process. This would have the advantage of not undermining the 1980 Hague Abduction Convention and its effective operation among States that share a similar European heritage in their legal orders. Such a Protocol would only facilitate the return of children between Muslim family law States. The 'imperial prism of jurisdiction' can be circumvented and there would be no need to address the current assumptions informing what is in the best interests of the child. Such an exercise would also allow the Hague Conference to engage with many States that are currently non-members and this may over time lead to closer relations with regard to other Hague Conference Conventions. However, it is highly questionable whether this would be a priority for the Hague Conference and there may be very little return for a significant investment of time and resources, both of which may be unaffordable. Further, the Hague Conference likely does not have the expertise or the confidence of Muslim family law States, many of which may already perceive it as laden with certain European cultural ideals about law and governance. Additionally, for the Hague Conference, this would be a significant departure from its past practice and may be seen as undermining the standing and strength of its most successful Convention.

Finally, the OIC may consider drafting its own version of a parental child abduction convention that would operate between its Member States. Such a precedent exists in the form of the 1989 Inter-American Convention on the International Return of Children, noted above. For the OIC to organise a process with a view to drafting such a convention would create a 'rival' to the 1980 Hague Abduction Convention. The politics of treaty-making and rival legal orders would come to the fore, and competing exceptionalisms would be brought into stark contrast. However, for two organisations that have little in common, the political and institutional costs are not so great. After all, there are numerous regional mechanisms for the protection of human rights. Although these regional treaties do not compete with each other, they do have a complex relationship with the core UN human rights treaties. Still the regional human rights treaties do not undermine the UN human rights treaties, despite existing in the same legal universe. If the OIC were to propose a parental child abduction convention, it could muster the necessary expertise and would have the political traction amongst its membership. But whether the substantive matter would be of interest to it is another matter entirely. The OIC is hardly renowned for its dynamism in any substantive area of law, let alone such a potentially contentious and difficult one as international parental child abduction.[116]

V. Conclusions

The creation of a societal phenomenon – international parental child abductions – has led to legal developments. It is clear that the 1980 Hague Abduction Convention establishes a basis upon which States agree to return abducted children to their State of habitual residence, without consideration of what is deemed in the host State to be in the child's best interests. There are clear limits to the 1980 Hague Abduction Convention. Many States have not acceded to it and, furthermore, the 1980 Hague Abduction Convention relies on a domestic legal framework and institutions to enforce and give effect to it. Participation in the 1980 Hague Abduction Convention is particularly problematic for Muslim family law States, where variants of Islam are central to the legal framework in this field, and where considerations of a child's 'best interests' do not align with the culturally Eurocentric approach which underpins the Convention. Therefore, even when and if such States do accede, the domestic legal framework does not lend itself to

[116] Over the course of its history, the OIC has adopted 17 conventions under its aegis. Few, if any have made a substantive contribution and most are not in force. On the OIC and its contributions to international law and legal development, see S Farrar, 'The Organisation of Islamic Cooperation: Forever on the Periphery of Public International Law?' (2014) 13 *Chinese Journal of International Law* 787.

compliance (without significant legislative change) with the obligations under the 1980 Hague Abduction Convention.

The aim of this chapter was not to evaluate the efficacy of the 1980 Hague Abduction Convention per se, but rather to illustrate that in this field (like all others), the law cannot provide the solutions some wronged parents seek and that there are major lacunas in the practical application of the law. To address this, it needs to be recognised that religion plays a key role in some jurisdictions and for Muslim family law States, another framework needs to exist which considers the cultural and legal differences at play. There are no easy or perfect solutions. Complementary, conflicting or even regimes which rival the 1980 Hague Abduction Convention all have a potential role to play. Returning to the theme of this volume and the 'achievements' of international law, it is clear that the law relating to international parental child abduction is currently not what one would hope for. If the objective of the law is to address the problem of international parental child abduction on a far more inclusive and universal basis, then once we have established the shortcomings of the existing regime, we can move forward. More can be achieved – in time, it is hoped it will be.

PART III

The Law of the Sea and Fisheries

7

Coastal State Jurisdiction in Ice-Covered Areas

The Impacts of Climate Change and the Polar Code

TORE HENRIKSEN

Abstract: Law is not static and neither is the Law of the Sea. An example is the legal framework for international shipping in Arctic waters. The 1982 UN Convention on the Law of the Sea (UNCLOS) provides the coastal State with extended environmental jurisdiction over international shipping in ice-covered waters under their jurisdiction. This jurisdiction is now challenged by factual and legal developments. As the extended jurisdiction is dependent on the coverage of sea ice creating 'obstructions or exceptional hazards', its thinning and withdrawal as a result of climate change may affect the extent of this jurisdiction. The regulation of international shipping is normally adopted through the competent international organisation – the International Maritime Organization (IMO). This chapter investigates if and how the changes in sea ice coverage and the legislative initiative taken through the IMO affect the extended environmental jurisdiction of the coastal State. It provides an overview and an insight into Article 234 UNCLOS. The main findings of the investigation of the effects of climate change and of the Polar Code is the narrowing of the margin of appreciation of the coastal States under Article 234.

I. Introduction

This chapter investigates the environmental jurisdiction of coastal States. More specifically, the objective is to investigate the unique jurisdiction coastal States are provided in regulating navigation in the Arctic Ocean and to discuss the implications of climate change and the increasingly legislative activities of the international community for this role. This study provides an example of how a norm in international law is faced with new factual and legal developments that may restrict its applicability or even make it redundant. It is not necessarily an example of a failure or inadequacy of international law, but rather of how the international Law of the Sea is able to adapt to external and internal changes. The passage in 1969 of the US flagged oil tanker *SS Manhattan* through the Northwest Passage provided the background for the negotiations of and the adoption of what became Article 234 of the UN Convention on the Law of the Sea (UNCLOS).[1] The incident confirmed the inadequacy of the contemporary Law of the Sea in addressing environmental threats from international navigation. Shortly afterwards, Canada adopted the Arctic Waters Pollution Prevention Act (AWPPA),[2] which facilitated the extended environmental jurisdiction over foreign flagged vessels.[3] The motive was to prevent pollution by vessels in marine ecological vulnerable areas of the Canadian Arctic region.[4] Canada was successful in providing an international legal basis for the AWPPA through the adoption of Article 234. It is a unique provision, in reality negotiated by the US, Canada and the Soviet Union.[5] It provides a right for the coastal State to adopt and enforce national measures on a unilateral basis applicable to foreign flagged vessels in ice-covered areas within its 200 miles exclusive economic zone (EEZ).[6] UNCLOS strikes a balance between international navigational rights and the rights of coastal States.[7] The International Maritime Organization (IMO) is recognised by UNCLOS as the competent international organisation to provide for universe and uniform shipping regulations.[8] The reason for States accepting an exemption from the general norm – a *lex specialis* norm – was probably that the IMO had just recently amended its mandate to include prevention of vessel-source pollution. The prevailing climatic conditions, the extensive sea-ice coverage and other harsh conditions in the marine Arctic, combined with small numbers of international navigation, suggested that it was not a priority area for special IMO regulations.

Now, again, it is the prospect of increased international shipping with subsequent threats to the marine environment that challenges the contemporary Law

[1] United Nations Convention on the Law of the Sea (adopted 10 December 1982, entered into force 16 November 1994) 1833 UNTS 3 (UNCLOS).

[2] Arctic Waters Pollution Prevention Act (RS 1985, c A-12).

[3] D Pharand, 'The Northwest Passage in International Law' (1979) 17 *Canadian Yearbook of International Law* 99, 120–21.

[4] R Bilder, 'The Canadian Arctic Waters Pollution Prevention Act: New Stresses on the Law of the Sea' (1970) 69 *Michigan Law Review* 1, 3–4.

[5] S Rosenne and A Yankov (eds), *United Nations Convention on the Law of the Sea 1982. A Commentary. Volume IV: Articles 192 to 278, Final Act and Annex VI* (Leiden, Martinus Nijhoff, 1990) 393.

[6] UNCLOS, art 234: 'Coastal States have the right to adopt and enforce non-discriminatory laws and regulations for the prevention, reduction and control of marine pollution from vessels in ice-covered areas within the limits of the exclusive economic zone, where particularly severe climatic conditions and the presence of ice covering such areas for most of the year create obstructions or exceptional hazards to navigation, and pollution of the marine environment could cause major harm to or irreversible disturbance of the ecological balance. Such laws and regulations shall have due regard to navigation and the protection and preservation of the marine environment based on the best available scientific evidence.'

[7] A Chircop, 'Jurisdiction over Ice-Covered Areas and the Polar Code: An Emerging Symbiotic Relationship?' (2016) 22 *Journal of International Maritime Law* 275, 277–78.

[8] UNCLOS, art 211(1).

of the Sea. The melting and thinning of the sea ice as a consequence of climate change raises the prospect of increased access to and use of Arctic waters for resource extraction and transportation. The Arctic Ocean may be open during the summer months during the next few decades. The IMO has responded to and acknowledged the need to regulate the extra hazards of Arctic shipping through the adoption of the Polar Code.

What are the implications of these developments for the extended jurisdiction of Arctic coastal States, which may be separated into two sub-questions: first, will the withdrawal and thinning of the sea ice at some stage make Article 234 inoperable?;[9] and, second, to what extent do the recent legislative activities of the IMO (and more specifically the Polar Code) affect the extended jurisdiction? As pointed out by Chircop,[10] the rules and standards adopted under the instruments of the IMO provide the baseline for Article 234, as its added value is where the coastal State adopts stricter regulations. What happens when the Polar Code raises such a baseline? These questions cannot be properly addressed without an in-depth analysis of the provision itself.

The environmental and legal developments raise a more general question about the present and future role of coastal States in the governance of Arctic shipping. Is it moving towards the normal role it has been designated under the Law of the Sea? The adoption of the Polar Code can be viewed a move by the international community to bring the governance of Arctic shipping under the more generally applicable rules and standards. There, the flag State has the main responsibility for ensuring that vessels flying its flag comply with its international obligations through the effective exercise of jurisdiction.[11] The coastal State has normally limited environmental jurisdiction over foreign-flagged vessels exercising navigational rights through its 200 miles EEZ and territorial sea. Or will these developments instead facilitate a combination of national coastal State and international regulations, where the coastal State jurisdiction provides a level of flexibility and control that the international community cannot provide? The relationship between national regulations and international regulations should then rather be described as 'complementary'.[12]

The investigation of a possible development of the role of the coastal State is necessarily based on Article 234 and other relevant UNCLOS provisions. This chapter is divided into six sections, including the Introduction. Section III includes an overview of the main criteria for the application of Article 234. In section IV, the consequences of climate change for the future applicability of Article 234 is addressed. This is primarily done by investigating the meaning of the 'ice-cover

[9] See E Franckx, 'Should the Law Governing Maritime Areas in the Arctic Adapt to Changing Climatic Circumstances?' in T Koivurova et al (eds), *Climate Governance in the Arctic* (Dordrecht, Springer, 2009) 119, 135.

[10] Chircop (n 7) 281.

[11] UNCLOS, arts 94 and 211(2).

[12] Chircop (n 7) 283.

areas' criterion and how it may be affected by sea ice melting. Different impacts of the Polar Code on the extended jurisdiction are assessed in section V. These range from a radical to a modest impact. A radical impact implies that Article 234 in effect has been amended by the three IMO Conventions. This would limit the right of the coastal States to adopt stricter regulations. A modest impact is that the Polar Code affects the prescriptive and enforcement rights under Article 234 through interpretation and/or as relevant considerations in the balancing of interests as proscribed by its due regard duty.[13] Conclusions are drawn in section VI. But first a presentation is given in section II of the factual and legal developments that may affect coastal State jurisdiction.

II. Factual and Legal Developments: Climate Change and the Polar Code

A. Climate Change

The Arctic is probably the region of the world that is most disproportionally affected by the impacts of climate change. One of the major impacts is the retreat and thinning of the sea ice.[14] The annual mean sea-ice area is estimated to shrink by 56,000 km^2 a year.[15] It is estimated that the ice thickness of the central Arctic Ocean has declined to an average of 1.3 metres in 2012.[16] Large areas have changed from being dominated by multi-year sea ice to mostly consisting of first-year sea ice. It is estimated that largely ice-free summers will occur by the end of the 2030s.[17]

As a consequence of the retreat and thinning of the Arctic sea ice, the maritime area is being opened up to new and to extended human activities such as fishing, bioprospecting, petroleum activities, maritime tourism and transport.[18] By sailing through the Arctic Ocean and the adjacent seas, the distances between ports in Europe and in East Asia may be drastically reduced, described as trans-Arctic

[13] Under art 31(3)(c) of the Vienna Convention on the Law of Treaties (adopted 23 May 1969, entered into force 27 January 1980) 1155 UNTS 331, any relevant rule of international law applicable between the parties shall be taken into account in the interpretation of a treaty. The argument is that the regulations of the Polar Code are relevant rules as they, like art 234 UNCLOS, aim at protecting the polar marine environment, inter alia by addressing the hazards posed by the presence of sea ice. Further, the Polar Code regulations are in practice applicable between the parties to UNCLOS and the relevant IMO conventions. The latter have approximately 150–60 contracting parties, amounting to between 96 and 99 per cent of global commercial tonnage. See IMO, 'Status of Treaties', available at www.imo.org/en/About/Conventions/StatusOfConventions/Documents/StatusOfTreaties.pdf.

[14] D Barber et al, 'Arctic Sea Ice' in Arctic Monitoring and Assessment Programme (AMAP), *Snow, Water, Ice and Permafrost in the Arctic (SWIPA)* (AMAP, 2017) 104–36.

[15] ibid 105.

[16] J Overland, J Walsh and V Kattsov, 'Trends and Feedbacks' in AMAP (n 14) 12.

[17] Barber et al (n 14) 109.

[18] O Young, 'Governing the Arctic Ocean' (2016) 72 *Marine Policy* 271, 271.

shipping. The two main routes include the waters north of Canada (the Northwest Passage) or of Russia (the Northern Sea Route), which lie within the jurisdiction of these two coastal States.[19] A third trans-Arctic shipping route is envisaged through the Central Arctic Ocean (known as the Transpolar Sea Route), mainly located in waters beyond national jurisdiction.[20] However, large parts of the Arctic Ocean will be covered by sea ice for extensive periods of the year (the winter season) in the foreseeable future. It is likely that the maritime activities in Arctic waters during the nearest decades will predominantly be destinational or regional, involving the transport of extracted terrestrial or marine natural resources from the region, marine tourism, community resupply and fisheries.[21]

B. Addressing the (In)Adequacy of Arctic Ocean Shipping Governance: The Polar Code

With the prospect of increased human activities, the focus has been on the adequacy of the governance regimes applicable to the Arctic Ocean.[22] The five Arctic coastal States have argued that the Law of the Sea provides a solid foundation for responsible management and that there is no need for any new comprehensive legal regime for the Arctic Ocean.[23] However, they have recognised the need for collaboration, including through the IMO, to strengthen existing measures to adopt new measures in order to improve maritime safety and to prevent or reduce the risk of ship-based pollution.

In 2009, the IMO amended its Guidelines on Shipping in Arctic Ice-Covered Waters[24] to make them applicable to Antarctic waters.[25] Shortly afterwards, initiatives were taken by several States to negotiate a mandatory Polar Code.[26] After several years of negotiations, the Maritime Safety Committee (MSC) and the Marine Environment Protection Committee (MEPC) of the IMO adopted the International Code for Ships Operating in Polar Waters (the Polar Code).[27]

[19] A Buixadé Farré et al, 'Commercial Arctic Shipping through the Northeast Passage: Routes, Resources, Governance, Technology, and Infrastructure' (2014) 37 *Polar Geography* 298, 301.

[20] M Humpert and A Raspotnik, 'The Future of Arctic Shipping along the Transpolar Sea Route' (2012) 1 *Arctic Yearbook* 281.

[21] Arctic Council, *Arctic Marine Shipping Assessment 2009 Report*, 2nd printing (April 2009) 91 and 121 available at www.pame.is/index.php/projects/arctic-marine-shipping/amsa.

[22] See, eg, Young (n 18) 272.

[23] Ilulissat Declaration (adopted 28 May 2008) 48 ILM 370 (2009).

[24] International Maritime Organization (IMO), 'Guidelines for ships operating in arctic ice-covered waters' (23 December 2002) MSC/Circ.1056 and MEPC/Circ.399.

[25] IMO, 'Guidelines for ships operating in polar waters' (2 December 2009) Res A.1024(26).

[26] Ø Jensen, 'The International Code for Ships Operating in Polar Waters: Finalization, Adoption and Law of the Sea Implications' (2016) 7 *Arctic Review on Law and Politics* 60, 63.

[27] IMO, 'International Code for Ships Operating in Polar Waters (Polar Code)' (21 November 2014) Res MSC.385 (94) and (15 May 2015) Res MEPC.264 (68), available at www.imo.org/en/MediaCentre/HotTopics/polar/Documents/POLAR%20CODE%20TEXT%20AS%20ADOPTED.pdf.

The Polar Code is applicable both to Antarctic and Arctic waters.[28] Arctic waters basically include the marine waters north of 60°N, within and beyond areas under national jurisdiction, which traditionally have been ice-covered throughout the year. The goal of the Polar Code is 'to provide for safe ship operation and the protection of the polar environment by addressing risks present in polar waters and not adequately mitigated by other [IMO] instruments'.[29] IMO instruments are generally applicable to all maritime waters, including Arctic waters. The background for the negotiation and adoption of the Polar Code was that navigation in polar waters 'impose[s] additional demands on ships, their systems and operation beyond the existing [IMO] requirements'.[30] The Polar Code consists of two main parts: maritime safety measures (Part I) and pollution prevention measures (Part II).[31] Interestingly, the Polar Code acknowledges the link between the two parts, as applying the safety measures will reduce the risk of accidents, with subsequent consequences for the environment.[32] Both parts include legally binding measures (Parts I-A and I-B) and recommendations (Parts II-A and II-B), involving three IMO Conventions (SOLAS 74,[33] MARPOL 73/78[34] and the STCW Convention).[35] Parts I-A and I-B of the Polar Code are made legally binding through amendments of these conventions.[36] The Polar Code entered into force on 1 January 2017.[37]

In addition to operational requirements, the maritime safety measures include what is traditionally described as construction, design, equipment and manning

[28] See SOLAS, regs XIV/1.2 and XIV/1.3 respectively; and MARPOL Annex I, regs 1.11.7 and 46.2; Annex II, regs 13.8.1 and 21.2; Annex IV, regs 17.2 and 17.3; and Annex V, regs 1.14.7 and 13.2.

[29] Polar Code, Introduction, s 1.

[30] ibid Preamble, Item 2.

[31] The Polar Code includes a Preamble, Introduction, Part I (Safety Measures of the Polar Code), Part II (Pollution Prevention Measures) and Appendices.

[32] Polar Code, Preamble, Item 5.

[33] International Convention for the Safety of Life at Sea (adopted 1 November 1974, entered into force 25 May 1980) 1184 UNTS 278 (SOLAS 74).

[34] International Convention for the Prevention of Pollution from Ships, as modified by the Protocol of 1978 (adopted 2 November 1973 and 17 February 1978, entered into force 2 October 1983) 1340 UNTS 62 (MARPOL 73/78).

[35] International Convention on Standards of Training, Certification and Watchkeeping for Seafarers (adopted 1 December 1978, entered into force 28 April 1984) 1361 UNTS I-23001 (STCW Convention). Its annex has been amended. See Adoption of Amendments to the Annex to the International Convention on Standards of Training, Certification and Watchkeeping for Seafarers 1978 (adopted 24 June 2010) STCW/CONF.2/DC/1, available in 'Meeting Documents' of IMODOCS at http://docs.imo.org.

[36] The Introduction and Part I-A Safety Measures of the Polar Code are made legally binding through adding Chapter XIV 'Safety Measures for Ships operating in Polar Waters' to SOLAS 74; see Res MSC.386(94) of the 'Report of the Maritime Safety Committee on its Ninety-Fourth Session' (27 November 2014) MSC 94/21/Add.1, Annex 7. The Introduction and Part II-A Pollution Prevention Measures of the Polar Code are made legally binding through amendments of relevant annexes of MARPOL 73/78; see Res MEPC.265(68) of the 'Report of the Marine Pollution Prevention Committee on its Sixty-Eighth Session' (15 May 2015) MEPC 68/21/Add.1, Annex 11. In addition, Chapter 12 'Manning and Training' of Part I-A of the Polar Code became legally binding through amendments to the STCW; see Res MSC.416(97) of the 'Report of the Maritime Safety Committee on its Ninety-Seventh Session' (2 December 2016) MSC 97/22/Add.1, Annex 8.

[37] Chapter 12 of the Polar Code 'Manning and Training' of Part I-A became legally binding in July 2018. The recommendations are found in Parts I-B and II-B respectively.

(CDEM) regulations. The CDEM regulations include requirements on ship structure, requiring vessels to be ice-strengthened depending on the areas in which they are to be operated, as well as to have fire safety systems that are functional under expected environmental conditions. The safety measures are goal-based, providing the flag State (and thus the ship-owner) with some discretion in relation to fulfilling the functional requirements.[38] This approach is chosen due to the fact that the level of risk varies depending on different factors, such as geographical location, the time of year and ice coverage.[39] The pollution prevention measures address different types of vessel-source pollution, in parallel to the MARPOL 73/78 annexes. In contrast to the safety measures, the pollution prevention measures are formulated as prescriptive rules. They include a ban on any discharge of oil or oily mixture into the sea.[40] Consequently, Arctic waters are for practical purposes equivalent to a special area under MARPOL 73/78 Annexes I–II. A phase 2 of the Polar Code has been initiated as the MSC is considering expanding it to include non-SOLAS vessels (eg, fishing vessels and yachts) and the MEPC is contemplating different means to restrict the risks of use and carriage of heavy fuel oil in the Arctic, including a ban.[41] There is already such ban in Antarctic waters.[42] In the Polar Code, the flag States are recommended to apply the same ban in relation to vessels operating in Arctic waters.[43]

III. The Criteria for Extended Environmental Jurisdiction under Article 234

A. Introduction

Only one provision of UNCLOS – Article 234 – is specifically designed for the protection of the Arctic marine environment.[44] It provides the coastal State with

[38] Polar Code, Part I-A, s 1.1.

[39] ibid Introduction, s 3.2.

[40] ibid Part II-A, s 1.1.

[41] 'Report of the Maritime Safety Committee on its Ninety-Eighth Session' (30 June 2017) MSC 98/23, para 10.29; and 'Report of the Marine Environment Protection Committee on its Seventy-Second Session' (18 May 2018) MEPC 72/17, para 11.9.

[42] MARPOL 73/78, Annex I, reg 43.

[43] Polar Code, Part II-B, para 1.1.

[44] On the background of art 234 UNCLOS, see inter alia DM McRae and DJ Goundrey, 'Environmental Jurisdiction in Arctic Waters: The Extent of Article 234' (1982) 16 *University of British Columbia Law Review* 197, 210–15; JN Moore, 'The UNCLOS Negotiations on Ice-Covered Areas' in M Nordquist, JN Moore and TH Heidar (eds), *Changes in the Arctic Environment and the Law of the Sea* (Leiden, Brill Nijhoff, 2010) 17, 19–20; A de Mestral, 'Article 234 of the United Nations Convention on the Law of the Sea: Its Origins and its Future' in S Lalonde and TL McDorman (eds), *International Law and Politics of the Arctic Ocean: Essays in Honor of Donat Pharand* (Leiden, Brill, 2015) 111, 111–19; L Boone and E Franckx, 'Ice-Covered Areas' in A Proelss (ed), *United Nations Convention on the Law of the Sea: A Commentary* (Munich, Verlag CH Beck, 2017) 1566, 1571–73.

the right to prescribe and enforce legislation to prevent, reduce and control marine pollution from vessels in ice-covered areas within the limits of its 200 nautical miles EEZ. In the following discussion, it will be described as 'extended' jurisdiction. This is because the scope of the prescriptive and enforcement rights are broader than is the case under the otherwise applicable rules. Article 234 has been described as one of the most ambiguous provisions of UNCLOS.[45] It consists of two sentences filled with several, vague and interconnected criteria on the geographical, temporal and substantial scope of the jurisdiction. As the coastal State is provided with a certain level of discretion as to the exercise of its jurisdiction under Article 234, it was essential that the exercise of this jurisdiction was subjected to the compulsory dispute settlement procedures of UNCLOS.[46]

The ambiguous character of the provision has not prevented Arctic coastal States from invoking the provision when regulating navigation through their arctic waters. Canada and Russia have adopted legislation based partly on Article 234.[47] A third Arctic coastal State was added to the list in 2017 – Denmark in respect of Greenland. The Greenland EEZ Marine Environment Protection Act provides a legal basis for adopting regulations to protect the environment in ice-covered areas.[48] Some examples of the practice of the coastal States are provided to illustrate how the conditions of the provisions have been read. With the exception of the US, all the Arctic coastal States are States Parties to UNCLOS.[49] The US has explicitly accepted that Article 234 is part of customary international law.[50]

Located in a separate section 8 of Part XII of Article 234 UNCLOS may be described as lex specialis in relation to the general provisions on vessel-source pollution.[51] It may be argued the exceptional character of the provision has implications on its reading. Still, it is an integrated part of Part XII on the protection and preservation of marine environment.[52] Article 234 does not include or refer to the

[45] C Lamson, 'Arctic Shipping, Marine Safety and Environmental Protection' (1987) 11 *Marine Policy* 3, 4.

[46] Moore (n 44) 22. *cf* arts 286, 297 and 298 UNCLOS, setting out the limitations and optional exceptions to the compulsory procedures.

[47] Boone and Franckx (n 44) 1580–84.

[48] Act No 1534 of 19 December 2017 on the Protection of the Marine Environment of the Greenlandic EEZ, s 7 (in Danish: Lov nr 1534 af 19/12/2017 om beskyttelse af havmiljøet i den eksklusive økonomiske zone ved Grønland), available at www.retsinformation.dk/eli/lta/2017/1534.

[49] An overview of the States Parties to UNCLOS is available at www.un.org/depts/los/convention_agreements/convention_overview_convention.htm.

[50] Reference given by T McDorman, 'A Note on the Potential Conflicting Treaty Rights and Obligations between the IMO's Polar Code and Article 234 of the Law of the Sea Convention' in Lalonde and McDorman (n 44) 141, 143.

[51] Committee on Coastal State Jurisdiction Relating to Marine Pollution of the International Law Association, 'Final Report London Conference (2000)' in Erik Franckx (ed), *Vessel-Source Pollution and Coastal State Jurisdiction: The Work of the ILA Committee on Coastal State Jurisdiction Relating to Marine Pollution (1991–2000)* (The Hague, Kluwer Law International, 2001). See also McRae and Goundrey (n 44) 197–228; Rosenne and Yankov (n 5) 393.

[52] Chircop (n 7) 280.

restrictions on the prescriptive jurisdiction of coastal States found in Article 211 or on the enforcement jurisdiction of Article 220. These provisions provide for the general jurisdiction of coastal States on vessel-source pollution. In essence, the environmental jurisdiction of a coastal State under Article 211 is normally restricted to adopting legislation consistent with the regulations adopted through generally accepted IMO instruments. Its enforcement jurisdiction under Article 220 does not necessarily coincide with the prescriptive jurisdiction of Article 211. A coastal State may only undertake physical enforcement in the EEZ when violations of regulations have or may have serious consequences for the marine environment. Conversely, in adopting and enforcing measures under Article 234, the coastal State is not restricted to applying the regulations under the different IMO instruments. It is competent to adopt unilateral national legislation that is applicable and enforceable against foreign-flagged vessels. As formulated by Chircop, the provision provides 'additional powers to coastal states in marine regions with ice-covered waters not enjoyed by coastal states of other marine regions'.[53] However, Article 234 is of practical use when the coastal State is considering adopting regulations, which involve other or stricter measures than those that are applicable under Article 211.[54]

Article 234 stipulates that the coastal State has the right to adopt and enforce non-discriminatory legislation for preventing, reducing and controlling pollution from vessels in ice-covered areas within the limits of the EEZ. This right is subject to several conditions.

The combination of particularly severe climatic conditions and the presence of ice covering such areas for most of the year create obstructions or exceptional hazards to navigation. Pollution of the marine environment could cause major harm to or irreversible disturbance to the ecological balance. The legislation adopted under Article 234 shall have due regard to navigation and the protection and preservation of the marine environment, and shall be based on the best scientific evidence.

Consequently, the coastal State does not enjoy carte blanche jurisdiction. The provision includes criteria setting out the geographical and environmental scope (where), as well as the substantive scope (what and how) of the extended jurisdiction. These criteria will be further presented below. The extended environmental jurisdiction is not directly applicable to naval vessels or to other vessels owned or operated by States and used for non-commercial purposes.[55]

Sections III.B and III.C investigate the geographical, environmental and substantive scope of the provision.

[53] A Chircop, 'Climate Change and the Prospects of Increased Navigation in the Canadian Arctic' (2007) 6 *World Maritime University Journal of Maritime Affairs* 193, 200–01.

[54] ibid.

[55] UNCLOS, art 236.

B. Geographical and Environmental Scope

The area of the provision's application is restricted to:

- areas within the limits of the EEZ;
- ice-covered areas; and
- areas where pollution of the marine environment may cause major harm or irreversible disturbance to the ecological balance.

The reference to 'within the limits of' the EEZ' – the geographical scope of the provision – has been the subject of extensive academic debate.[56] A literal reading implies that the jurisdiction may only be exercised in the EEZ, as the 'limits' refer to the inner and outer limits of the maritime zone as described in Articles 55 and 57 UNCLOS. The alternative reading is that the reference is to the outer limits of the EEZ, meaning that Article 234 also applies to the territorial sea.[57] If Article 234 is applicable to the territorial sea, there is also a question as to whether it is applicable to the straits therein recognised that are used for international navigation where there is right of transit passage.[58]

This chapter does not aim to answer the questions on the geographical scope. As this chapter investigates the impact of the Polar Code on the jurisdiction of the Arctic coastal State, it should be noted that its CDEM and operational discharge regulations may well have status as general accepted international rules and standards (GAIRAS) under Article 21(2) UNCLOS and as applicable international regulations under Article 42. Even if Article 234 is not applicable to the territorial sea and to straits, such status would provide the coastal State with a legal basis to adopt and enforce legislation addressing the hazards of navigating in these parts of its Arctic waters. On the ice-cover criterion, not all forms of ice coverage qualify – the relevant area needs to be covered by ice for 'most of the year' and the ice cover must present an obstacle or a hazard to navigation. The hazard must be exceptional, meaning that it must be of a different character from and/or higher than the conditions in waters where the vessel normally operates.[59] Navigating in ice-covered areas and under particular severe climatic conditions clearly expose vessels to such hazards. This criterion will be further addressed in section IV below.

The marine environment of the relevant area is required to have a certain degree of sensitivity. The object of environmental protection (ecological balance) seems to have been formulated in order to highlight the need to protect a vulnerable or sensitive marine environment. The wording is similar to 'rare and fragile

[56] See an overview over the arguments in Franckx and Bone (n 44) 1573–75.

[57] See Rosenne and Yankov (n 5) 397, who refer to 'that part of the sea extending from the outer limits of the coastal State's exclusive economic zone to that State's coastline'.

[58] UNCLOS, art 38.

[59] SP Fields, 'Article 234 of the United Nations Convention on the Law of the Sea: The Overlooked Linchpin for Achieving Safety and Security in the US Arctic?' (2015–16) 7 *Harvard National Security Journal* 55, 89.

ecosystems' of Article 194(5) UNCLOS.[60] This is confirmed by the fact that the criterion is premised on the effects of and not the scope of the discharges. If discharges from one vessel may inflict such harms or disturbance, the number of vessels navigating the area is not decisive.[61] A probability of negative effects on the environment is sufficient.[62] As the risk needs to be of major harm or irreversible disturbance, not all forms of risk will justify the adoption of measures under Article 234. Harm and disturbance are relative concepts and have to be read within their respective context.

C. Substantive Scope

Within the geographical and environmental/temporal scope of Article 234, the coastal State has the right to adopt and enforce legislation with the purpose of preventing, reducing and controlling pollution from vessels. The enforcement jurisdiction is concurrent with the legislative jurisdiction. The coastal State may in principle board and inspect vessels at sea and even arrest a vessel and institute criminal proceedings if it has grounds for believing that it has committed violations of regulations adopted under Article 234. This right applies irrespective of whether it concerns discharges, routeing measures or violations of CDEM requirements and even if the violation has not caused discharges. The enforcement jurisdiction is subjected to the same restrictions as the prescriptive jurisdiction. Further, the safeguards stipulated in Articles 223–33 are applicable. The exercise jurisdiction is subject to several restrictions:

- to prevent, reduce and control pollution from vessels;
- to be non-discriminatory;
- to have due regard to navigation and to environmental protection; and
- to be based on the best scientific evidence.

i. Prevent, Reduce and Control Pollution

The substantive scope of Article 234 corresponds to that of Article 211 and should be read in conjunction with it. The measures that may be taken by the coastal State may range from precautionary and proactive measures to reparation measures. Legislation on oil pollution preparedness and response and liability schemes may be part of the latter. The preventive measures obviously provide for the regulation of operational discharges from vessels, which may cause environmental

[60] Rosenne and Yankov (n 5) 393.

[61] See also A Chircop, 'The Growth of International Shipping in the Arctic: Is a Regulatory Review Timely?' (2009) 24 *International Journal of Marine and Coastal Law* 355, 370.

[62] K Bartenstein, 'The "Arctic Exception" in the Law of the Sea Convention: A Contribution to Safer Navigation in the Northwest Passage?' (2011) 42 *Ocean Development & International Law* 22, 38–39.

damage and disturbances. The legal debate has primarily focused on whether the jurisdiction also includes what has traditionally been regarded as maritime safety measures.[63] These include CDEM rules and standards, and ships' routeing measures. Importantly, Article 211(1) UNCLOS suggests that there are no fixed boundaries between these two objectives: routeing measures, principally aimed at maritime safety, may be adopted under Part XII as they reduce the risk of accidents and subsequent pollution. Ringbom[64] argues that prevention of pollution not only includes operational discharges, but also regulation of navigation as well as CDEM rules and standards.[65] This question will be further investigated in section V.C below.

Other impacts of shipping than operational and accidental pollution include the release of toxic antifouling paint, emissions of pollutants to air (nitrogen oxide, sulphur dioxide and carbon dioxide), underwater noise, strikes of marine mammals, the introduction of non-indigenous species through ballast water, and physical damage or disturbances.[66] In relation to the latter, the navigation of vessels through ice-covered waters may interfere with and disrupt the traditional livelihood of indigenous communities such as hunting and fishing.[67] It is doubtful whether Article 234 provides a legal basis for measures to prevent such impacts. It clearly includes measures to prevent the release of toxic antifouling, which could cause major harm and disturbances to the marine environment. Although emissions of pollutants to air from vessels qualify as marine pollution under Article 212 UNCLOS, it is questionable Article 234 provides a basis for regulating air pollution. It is not very likely that such marine pollution – unless the emission was radioactive – could cause major harm or irreversible disturbance to the marine environment of a specific area. Underwater noise qualifies as pollution.[68] It is more doubtful that it is capable of inflicting the harm and disturbances required. Ship strikes of marine mammals, the introduction of non-indigenous species through ballast water and physical damage to the seabed may cause harm or irreversible disturbance to the marine environment. However, these impacts do not qualify as pollution under UNCLOS.[69] Recent case law suggests that the environmental jurisdiction of the

[63] ibid 37–38; Chircop (n 7) 283–84.

[64] H Ringbom, *The EU Maritime Safety Policy and International Law* (Leiden, Martinus Nijhoff, 2008) 390.

[65] Similarly, see B Kwiatkowska, *The 200 Mile Exclusive Economic Zone in the New Law of the Sea* (Leiden, Martinus Nijhoff, 1989) 176–77.

[66] OSPAR Commission, *Assessment of the Impacts of Shipping on the Marine Environment*, No 440 (OSPAR Commission, 2009) 16–27.

[67] Inuit Circumpolar Council, 'The Sea Ice Never Stops: Circumpolar Inuit Reflections on Sea Ice Use and Shipping in Inuit Nunaat' (December 2014), available at https://oaarchive.arctic-council.org/handle/11374/410.

[68] The Joint Group of Experts on the Scientific Aspects of Marine Environmental Protection (GESAMP), *Pollution in the Open Oceans: A Review of Assessments and Related Studies, No 79* (GESAMP Reports & Studies Series, 2009) 39. GESAMP contributed to the definition of pollution in art 1(1)(4) UNCLOS. *cf* RR Churchill and AV Lowe, *The Law of the Sea*, 3rd edn (Manchester, Manchester University Press, 1999) 328; J Firestone and C Jarvis, 'Response and Responsibility: Regulating Noise Pollution in the Marine Environment' (2007) 10 *Journal of International Wildlife Law and Policy* 109, 126–27.

[69] UNCLOS, art 1(1)(4).

coastal State under Part XII UNCLOS may extend beyond preventing pollution of the marine environment. The tribunal in the Chagos Marine Protected Area Arbitration stated that Article 194 is 'not limited to measures aimed strictly at controlling pollution and extends to measures focussed primarily on conservation and the preservation of eco-systems'.[70] This suggests that Article 234 may provide a legal basis for taking measures to prevent the other types of impacts. However, even if the scope of marine environmental protection obligations has evolved and expanded in recent years, the jurisdiction under Article 234 is still to prevent pollution of the marine environment. Consequently, the coastal State may not base legislation to prevent the introduction of non-indigenous species or physical damage to the marine environment on Article 234. In section V below, the question on the impact of the Polar Code on the substantive scope of Article 234 will be further examined.

ii. Non-discrimination

The non-discrimination requirement must be read in conjunction with Article 227, which sets out the general obligation of non-discrimination under Part XII.[71] It prescribes that when exercising environmental jurisdiction, a State 'shall not discriminate in form or fact against vessels of any other state'. Thus, there is a ban on discrimination against all vessels, irrespective of the identity of the flag State.

iii. Due Regard

The legislation shall have 'due regard to navigation and to the protection and preservation of the marine environment'. Importantly, the due regard requirement does not only relate to navigation but also the protection and preservation of the marine environment. Some authors have only focused on the navigational element and subsequently argued that the coastal State may not adopt legislation that in effect ban navigation.[72] As due regard is to be given both to navigation and to the environment, it is better read as a requirement to balance between the two interests.[73] Thus, it is not excluded that environmental interests may be given greater weight under certain circumstances.[74] This interpretation is supported by

[70] In the Matter of the Chagos Marine Protected Area Arbitration, before an Arbitral Tribunal Constituted under Annex VII of the United Nations Convention on the Law of the Sea, between the Republic Of Mauritius and the United Kingdom of Great Britain and Northern Ireland. *Award in the Arbitration Regarding the Chagos Marine Protected Area between Mauritius and the United Kingdom of Great Britain and Northern Ireland* (18 March 2015) 31 RIAA 359, 580 (para 538).

[71] Rosenne and Yankov (n 5) 396–97; Bartenstein (n 62) 40–41.

[72] McRae and Goundrey (n 44) 220–21; LC Williams, 'An Ocean between Us: The Implications of Inconsistencies between the Navigational Laws of Coastal Arctic Council Nations and the United Nations Convention on the Law of the Sea for Arctic Navigation' (2017) 70 *Vanderbilt Law Review* 379, 405.

[73] J Attenhofer, 'Navigation Along Precedence: How Arctic Sovereignty Melts with the Ice' (2011) 54 *German Yearbook of International Law* 125, 152; Chircop (n 7) 280.

[74] Bartenstein (n 62) 45.

use of 'navigation' and not navigational rights. Navigation is merely a reference to a maritime activity. If 'rights' have been included, it would provide them with stronger protection. Therefore, the balancing of the two legitimate interests does not exclude the coastal State from taking decisions that may effectively ban navigation within an area if there are legitimate reasons for such decision.[75] Furthermore, both Articles 21 (1) and 56 (1) (b) (iii) of UNCLOS presume that the competence of the coastal State to regulate international navigation in the territorial sea and exclusive economic zone is supplemented by Article 234. Consequently, flag States are required under Articles 21 (4) and 56 (3) to comply with legislation adopted by the coastal State in accordance with UNCLOS. The due regard duty, combined with the other criteria means that the coastal State effectively is charged with undertaking risk assessments; the risk related to shipping through ecological vulnerable areas, a risk particularly affected by the combination of presence of sea ice and severe climatic conditions. The implications of the due regard criterion will be further discussed below, in particular in section 5.4.

iv. Best Scientific Evidence

The legislation is to be based on 'best available scientific evidence'. In contrast to Article 61 regarding the obligation to conserve living marine resources, the coastal State is not merely to take into account scientific evidence – it is to base its legislation on such evidence. The requirement is meant to prevent arbitrary decisions or decision serving purely national self-interests.[76] Consequently, the coastal State has the burden of proof or the duty to document that the regulations considered for adoption are necessary to prevent major harm or irreversible disturbance to the marine environment from the impacts of vessels. The requirement is inherently dynamic, requiring the coastal State to ensure that the legislation is adapted to developments in science and technology.[77]

IV. Climate Change and Article 234

A. Introduction

This section addresses the question of whether the retreat and thinning of sea ice will affect the right of the coastal State to exercise the extended environmental jurisdiction of Article 234. The presence of sea ice cover and particularly severe

[75] P Luttman, 'Ice-Covered Areas under the Law of the Sea Convention: How Extensive are Canada's Coastal State Powers in the Arctic?' (2015) 29 *Ocean Yearbook* 85, 96.
[76] Bartenstein (n 62) 40.
[77] ibid.

climatic conditions constitute cumulative criteria as together they either create 'obstructions' or 'exceptional hazards' to navigation in the area. In addition, the area must be ice-covered for 'most of the year' in order for Article 234 to be applicable. The focus here will be on the criterion of sea ice coverage and the implications of existing and predicted sea ice melting (see section IV.D below). Before investigating the ice coverage criterion in light of the impacts created by climate change, it is worth paying attention to the first very extensive and complicated sentence of Article 234. Its wording raises question whether it is sufficient that an area is ice-covered for most of the year or whether there has to be actual ice cover for the coastal State to exercise jurisdiction under Article 234. The impact of climate change on the extended jurisdiction is significantly different depending on which alternative is applied. If it is sufficient that the area is ice-covered for most of the year, the fact that the area is becoming ice-free and navigable for longer periods does not affect the jurisdiction directly. The critical point is that the area remains ice-covered for most of the year. With the other alternative, the melting and withdrawal of sea ice means a parallel temporal restriction on the application of Article 234. This will be discussed further in section IV.B below.

B. Ice-Covered Areas: Actual Presence of Ice Cover or Ice-Covered for Most of the Year?

The first sentence of Article 234 stipulates that the right to adopt and enforce legislation for the prevention of vessel-source pollution is applicable to navigation 'in ice-covered areas … where particular severe climatic conditions and the presence of ice covering such areas most of the year', McRae and Goundrey[78] in their seminal work on Article 234 suggested two possible interpretations of this sentence: a narrow and a broad interpretation. Under the narrow interpretation, the jurisdiction is applicable to areas where the combination of sea ice and particularly severe climatic conditions creates obstacles or exceptional hazards to navigation. Consequently, the extended jurisdiction may only be exercised during the periods of the year and in areas where the combination of ice and climatic conditions poses obstacles or hazards to navigation. The criterion under the narrow interpretation is then more of a temporal than a geographical character. Under the broad interpretation, which according to McRae and Goundrey is the more literal one, the coastal State may adopt and enforce legislation in areas where these (ice and climatic) conditions prevail for most of the year. Thus, 'where' is a reference to the geographical area.[79] It is sufficient for the right to exercise extended jurisdiction that areas within the limits of the EEZ are ice-covered for 'most of the year'. This means that the coastal State enjoys the extended jurisdiction throughout the year,

[78] McRae and Goundrey (n 44) 216–20.
[79] Bartenstein (n 62) 30.

irrespective of whether the sea ice and climatic conditions create an obstruction or exceptional hazards.[80] McRae and Goundrey as well as Bartenstein admit that this interpretation renders the combined sea ice and climatic conditions criteria unnecessary.[81] They even argue that the legislation does not need to address 'pollution likely to cause major harm to or irreversible disturbance of the ecological balance'.[82] Such an interpretation is questionable, as there is a presumption that all parts of a treaty provision have a meaning, under the so-called rule of non-redundancy.[83] The preparatory works of Article 234 do not shed much light on which of the alternatives is to be preferred.[84] A very early text seems to explicitly require actual presence of sea ice.[85] In the following negotiations, the text was further developed, specifying the special characteristics of the marine environment of ice-covered areas.[86] This did not help clarify the requirement of the presence of ice cover – quite the reverse. However, as noted by Bartenstein,[87] the international community accepted the extended jurisdiction in order to empower the coastal State to address the obstacles to and hazards to navigation under sea ice and severe climatic conditions.

As observed, the consequences of the two alternatives may be significant, particularly in relation to the impacts of climate change. Under the narrow interpretation, the coastal State would have to operate with a 'twin set of measures' or two legal regimes:[88] extended jurisdiction (Article 234) during the period where areas are ice-covered (the winter season) and normal environmental jurisdiction (Articles 211 and 220) during the ice-free period (the summer season). The problem is that there is no clear transition from an ice-covered to an ice-free season, particularly due to uncertainties as to what is meant by 'ice-covered'. Further, the ice and climatic conditions may shift from year to year, from area to area and within a season. The broad interpretation provides the coastal State with more flexibility in terms of addressing such unstable conditions. State practice seems to be consistent with this alternative.[89] The consequence of applying the broad interpretation is that the coastal State may exercise extended jurisdiction throughout the year. The practical difference between the two interpretations would be during the ice-free season. The exercise of jurisdiction during this period would not be unrestricted. The duty to have 'due regard to navigation and the protection and preservation of the marine environment' will restrict the exercise of the jurisdiction in relation to

[80] McRae and Goundrey (n 44) 218–19.
[81] ibid 217; Bartenstein (n 62) 30.
[82] McRae and Goundrey (n 44) 218–19.
[83] A Orakhelashvili, *The Interpretation of Acts and Rules in Public International Law* (Oxford, Oxford University Press, 2008) 422–25.
[84] McRae and Goundrey (n 44) 218–19.
[85] Rosenne and Yankov (n 5) 395.
[86] ibid.
[87] Bartenstein (n 62) 30.
[88] McRae and Goundrey (n 44) 218–19; Bartenstein (n 62) 30–31.
[89] Bartenstein (n 62) 31.

when, where and which measures the coastal State may take.[90] If a shipping lane is not 'ice-covered', the coastal State will under neither alternative be competent to require vessels transiting the area to have an ice-strengthened hull. The adoption of such requirements would be contrary to the requirement under Article 234 of having due regard of navigation and of the protection of the environment. Therefore, there might not be any difference in substance between the two alternative interpretations. For more on the substance of the due regard duty, see section V.D below.

Still, it is worthwhile to investigate the meaning of the ice coverage criterion and the implications of climate change. Irrespective of an alternative, the criterion has a direct bearing on the geographical application (most of the year) and on the substantive limitations on the exercise of discretion (the due regard requirement) under Article 234.

C. Ice Coverage

The presence of sea ice is an important environmental factor that controls weather and climate, ecology and human activities in the Arctic region.[91] Sea ice is a significant natural hazard, both directly and indirectly. A primary objective of Article 234 is to prevent the obstacles and hazards that the presence of sea ice poses to international shipping from materialising. Before investigating the impacts of climate change, the thresholds of Article 234 are examined. If the sea ice falls under these thresholds, the future of Article 234 is in question.

i. Ice-Covered for Most of the Year

The right of the coastal State to legislate and enforce relates to navigation through 'ice-covered areas', which have to be present for 'most of the year'.[92] Thus, the criterion involves quantitative, qualitative and temporal components: the ice has to have a certain spatial coverage or concentration (quantity), composition or characteristics (quality), and duration (temporal).

ii. Quantitative and Qualitative Components

It is not a requirement that all waters within the EEZ are ice-covered. The sea ice does not have to be perennial. The coverage must have such an extent and

[90] See McRae and Goundrey (n 44) 220.

[91] H Eicken and AR Mahoney, 'Sea Ice: Hazards, Risks and Implications for Disasters' in JT Ellis, DJ Sherman and JF Schroder (eds), *Coastal and Marine Hazards, Risks, and Disasters* (Amsterdam, Elsevier, 2015) 381, 382.

[92] It should be noted that the investigation of the ice-cover criterion does address the question of whether the sea ice actually must be present for the coastal State to exercise jurisdiction under art 234 UNCLOS.

characteristics that it may either hinder vessels from navigating through a specific area or subject them to 'exceptional hazards'. As noted by the Canadian Coast Guard, sea ice poses an obstacle to any ship, even icebreakers.[93] Navigating in ice-covered areas involves challenges to both the structure of the vessel and how it is operated. As sea ice is an environmental phenomena, it is natural to use its scientific understanding when interpreting it as a legal term.[94] The Sea Ice Nomenclature as developed by the World Meteorological Organization (WMO) provides a scientific categorisation on which this chapter will be based.[95] The relevance of the Sea Ice Nomenclature is strengthened by the fact that Polar Code incorporates and refers to its concepts in the regulations addressing the hazards of sea ice.[96]

The Sea Ice Nomenclature defines sea ice as frozen sea water.[97] The sea ice grows during the autumn and the early winter months, and starts melting depending on the sea water temperature during the summer months. The annual cycle of sea ice formation in the Arctic Ocean traditionally reaches a maximum extent at the end of the winter season (March) and a minimum extent at the end of the summer season (September).[98] Sea ice is categorised according to its stage of development (age), mobility and concentration; all these characteristics have implications for the navigability through the sea ice.[99]

Sea-ice thickness is the main feature of the different ages, which include inter alia new ice, young ice, first-year ice and old ice.[100] First-year ice is from one winter's growth, ranging from 30 centimetres to over 2 metres in thickness. Old ice may extent to 3 metres or even more, and it is denser or harder than the younger sea ice. A vessel will obviously encounter greater resistance when attempting to navigate through old ice than through young ice. As a vessel attempts to manoeuvre through the ice, this may inflict damage to its hull, propeller and rudder.[101] The mobility of the sea ice adds a second layer to the obstacles and hazards to navigation. Sea ice is either fast ice or drift ice.[102] Drift ice is mobile, drifting in response to winds and currents, depending on its age and concentration. Consequently, the ice-cover may not be homogeneous, but may consist of separate floes, cracks or leads of open waters.[103] The obstacles or hazards to navigation under such circumstances may include vessels becoming beset or trapped where the pack ice

[93] Canadian Coast Guard, *Ice Navigation in Canadian Waters* (Minister of Fisheries and Oceans Canada, 2012) 81, available at http://www.ccg-gcc.gc.ca/folios/00913/docs/ice-navigation-dans-les-galces-eng.pdf.

[94] See also Rosenne and Yankov (n 5) 397.

[95] 'WMO Sea-Ice Nomenclature' (WMO No 259) vols III and III, available at http://jcomm.info/index.php?option=com_oe&task=viewDocumentRecord&docID=14598.

[96] Polar Code Introduction, s 2.

[97] 'WMO Sea-Ice Nomenclature' (n 95) Terminology – Vol I, App 1, para 1.1.

[98] Barber et al (n 14) 106.

[99] 'WMO Sea-Ice Nomenclature' (n 95) Vol 1, App 1, paras 2, 1 and 4.

[100] ibid para 2.

[101] A Kendrick, 'Operating in Ice' (*Gard News*, February/April 2012), available at http://www.gard.no/web/updates/content/20650915/operating-in-ice.

[102] 'WMO Sea-Ice Nomenclature' (n 95) Vol I, App 1, paras 1.1.1 and 1.1.2.

[103] ibid Vol I, App 1, para 4.

is compacting or the vessel is being hit by large and mobile floes or subjected to pressure on its hull.[104]

The concentration of sea ice adds the third layer to obstacles and hazards to navigation. This is the ratio of an area covered by ice and the type or form of the ice therein.[105] This ranges from compact ice, where the ice covers the whole area, to open water and bergy water. Obviously, an area of compact multi-year sea ice poses greater obstacles and exceptional hazards than an area of predominantly first-year sea ice where the coverage is 40 per cent. As noted above, waters with lower ice concentration may have more dynamic and unpredictable ice conditions. Bergy bits and growlers, and pieces of floating glacier ice that are difficult to detect on radar may pose serious threats to vessels.[106]

To sum up the *quantitative and qualitative components*: individually or in combination, the composition, characteristics and concentration of sea ice may pose an obstacle to navigation by preventing shipping through and area, and even a hazard as vessels may be beset, damaged or lost after the impact of the sea ice.

iii. The Temporal Component

The areas within the limits of the EEZ must be ice-covered 'for most of the year'. Ice coverage for shorter periods of the year, such as in the Baltic Sea, would not qualify. Further, the ice coverage has to be an annual phenomenon; the irregular presence of ice would not suffice. Consistently with the purpose of the provision to prevent vessel-source pollution, the ice coverage of an area must have such duration that there cannot be any regular shipping through it without special measures to prevent the sea ice (in combination with climatic conditions) from causing obstacles or hazards. As referred to above, the sea ice of the Arctic Ocean traditionally reaches its maximum extent in March and its minimum extent in September.[107] Consequently, ice coverage of at least six months will qualify as 'most of the year'.[108]

D. Climate Change and Ice Coverage

The 2004 Arctic Climate Impact Assessment (ACIA) Report to the Arctic Council was the first to highlight the effects of climate change in the Arctic region.[109]

[104] I Kubat, D Fowler and M Sayeed, 'Floating Ice and Ice Pressure Challenge to Ships' in JF Shroder, W Haeberli and C Whiteman (eds), *Snow and Ice-Related Hazards, Risks, and Disaster* (Amsterdam, Elsevier, 2015) 647, 650.

[105] 'WMO Sea-Ice Nomenclature' (n 95) Vol I, App 1, para 4.

[106] Canadian Coast Guard (n 93) 104-06.

[107] See Barber et al (n 14).

[108] EJ Molenaar, *Coastal State Jurisdiction over Vessel-Source Pollution* (The Hague, Kluwer Law International, 1998) 420.

[109] ACIA, *Impacts of a Warming Arctic: Arctic Climate Impact Assessment* (Cambridge, Cambridge University Press, 2004).

One of its key findings was that reduced sea ice is likely to increase marine transport in the region.[110] The navigational season of the Northern Sea Route was estimated to be extended by 100 days by 2080. Subsequent reports, as referred to in section II above, suggest that the melting of the sea ice is continuing at a greater pace. Sea-ice extent continues a long-term downward trend, both in the winter and summer seasons. Importantly, older ice is rapidly disappearing and most sea ice in the Arctic is 'first-year' ice. The Arctic is projected to be largely free of sea ice in late summer during the next few decades, possibly as early as the 2030s.[111] The winter ice will be thinner, more salty, less rigid and more mobile than the present sea ice.

The thinning and retreat of sea ice will not only be beneficial to shipping, but may expose it to other hazards. More open water may affect the climate. Notably, the combination of ice coverage and particularly severe climatic conditions are the main criteria for the extended jurisdiction. The climate is the weather conditions of a particular area over a period of time.[112] Factors that affect the climate in the Arctic include sea and air temperatures, geography, latitude, wind strength and direction, precipitation, air pressure, humidity, clouds (including fog) and not least variations in these.[113] More open waters affect the temperatures and the exchange of moisture between the atmosphere and the ocean, which may lead to more extreme weather locally and at lower latitudes. One of the findings of the Intergovernmental Panel on Climate Change (IPPC) climate assessment is that there is a 'possibility of increasingly unpredictable extreme weather events, storms, and inundation by large storm surges'.[114]

These climatic conditions, combined with the increased mobility of sea ice, as well as the increased movement of land ice into the ocean (ie, bergy bits and growlers), may increase the hazards relating to navigation.[115] Even if the thickness is reduced from 3–5 metres to 1–2 metres (first-year ice) in more areas, the sea ice will still be an obstacle or even a hazard inter alia to vessels with or without minimum ice-strengthened hulls. Under the Polar Code, vessels designed to operate in sea ice are required to have ice-strengthened hulls. It operates with three categories of vessels, depending on their capabilities to navigate through different thicknesses of sea ice.[116] Vessels designed to operate in at least first thin first-year

[110] ibid 84-86, key finding No 6.

[111] 'Extract from the Snow, Water, Ice and Permafrost in the Arctic: Summary for Policy-Makers' in AMAP (n 14) xi.

[112] *Lexico's Dictionary*, available at https://en.oxforddictionaries.com/definition/climate.

[113] Norwegian Polar Institute, 'Research on Climate', available at http://www.npolar.no/en/research/climate; National Snow & Ice Data Center, 'All about Arctic Climatology and Meteorology', available at www.nsidc.org/cryosphere/arctic-meteorology/factors_affecting_climate_weather.html.

[114] JN Larsen et al, 'Polar Regions' in VR Barros et al (eds), *Climate Change 2014: Impacts, Adaptation, and Vulnerability. Part B: Regional Aspects. Contribution of Working Group II to the Fifth Assessment Report of the Intergovernmental Panel on Climate Change* (Cambridge, Cambridge University Press, 2014) 1567, 1581.

[115] AMAP (n 14) xii.

[116] Polar Code, Introduction, ss 2.1, 2.2 and 2.3.

ice are required to have ice-strengthened hulls.[117] Consequently, the Polar Code confirms the need for special regulations of navigation even under the predicted ice conditions.

The Arctic Ocean, including areas within the limits of the 200 nautical-mile EEZs, will (with variations) continue to be ice-covered for most of the year in the decades to come. Some of the adjacent sub-Arctic seas such as the Barents Sea may become permanently ice-free during this century, making Article 234 UNCLOS inapplicable.[118] However, this provision will not necessarily become redundant in other areas. The thinning and retreat of the sea ice will make areas even more accessible to commercial shipping and thus increase the risks. As pointed out above, thinner and more fragmented sea ice in motion combined with harsh climatic conditions constitute hazards such as besetment and physical impacts, which may be addressed by measures adopted under Article 234. However, the changes in sea-ice cover do have implications for the required due regard assessments/risk assessment to be undertaken by the coastal State, based on the best scientific evidence. This will further restrict the discretion of the coastal State in relation to the types of and duration of measures and their geographical scope. If the whole sea route a vessel is planning to use is ice-free, then the coastal State can hardly require the vessel to be ice-strengthened.[119]

V. The Polar Code and Article 234

A. Introduction

This section deals with the second stream of research questions – the possible impacts or recent legal developments (more specifically brought about by the Polar Code) on the extended jurisdiction under Article 234 UNCLOS. The obvious impact, as stated by Chircop[120] and referred to above, is that rules and standards adopted under the Polar Code provide the baseline for Article 234. Its added value lies where the coastal State adopts stricter or other types of regulations.

In this section other impacts of the Polar Code are investigated through three sub-questions. As the Polar Code regulates navigation in ice-covered waters that are also within areas that fall under national jurisdiction, the first question to be addressed in section V.B is whether it effectively amends Article 234 and thereby restricts the extended jurisdiction. The second sub-question addressed in section V.C relates to the impact of the Polar Code as part of the context of relevant rules

[117] ibid Part I-A, s 3.3.2.2. *cf* Introduction, s 2.2.

[118] IH Onarheim and M Årthun,' Toward an Ice-Free Barents Sea' (2017) 44 *Geophysical Research Letters* 8387, 8392–93.

[119] See the definition of 'ice-free' in 'WMO Sea Ice Nomenclature' (n 95) Vol I, App 1, para 4.2.8.

[120] Chircop (n 7) 281.

of international law within which Article 234 is to be interpreted. The third sub-question investigated in section V.D is whether the Polar Code regulations may be characterised as balancing navigational and environmental interests, and thus impact on the due regard duty or risk assessment of the coastal State. This could potentially restrict the discretion of the coastal State.

The last question on the relationship between the Polar Code and Article 234 to be addressed in section V.E concerns enforcement. As noted in section III.A above, the enforcement jurisdiction of Article 234 coincides with the legislative jurisdiction, in contrast to the normal environmental jurisdiction. Even if the coastal State does not adopt its national measures, is it competent to enforce compliance with the Polar Code regulations on the basis of Article 234?

The Polar Code, which is the subject of the investigation in this part of the chapter, is directed at the 'internal' aspects of vessels: how they are to be constructed, designed and equipped, how their crew should be trained and how they should be operated within their capabilities, as well as restrictions on their operational discharges in polar waters. It does not regulate what may be described as 'external' conditions of the operation of vessels. Measures to regulate such conditions may include ships' routeing measures (eg, mandatory sea lanes), prior notification/permission requirements before entering the waters, duty to report positions during the voyage and a duty for vessels to use ice-breaker assistance. Article 234 may arguably provide a legal basis for these requirements. As the focus of this section is on the Polar Code, these measures will not be discussed further here. However, the requirements of due regard and that the measures be based on the best available scientific evidence are applicable to such measures.

B. Does the Polar Code Amend Article 234?

During the negotiations, it was agreed that Polar Code regulations be made legally binding through amendments of SOLAS 74 and MARPOL 73/78 and the STCW. As they would be applicable to international shipping in Arctic waters, there were questions on the legal relationship between the Polar Code regulations and Article 234.[121] Would the amendments of the IMO Conventions have priority over Article 234 as newer treaties (*lex posterior*)? Or, as stipulated in Article 311 UNCLOS, would Article 234 have priority over them?

Both Russia and Canada were active during the negotiations to ensure that the Polar Code would not restrict their rights under Article 234.[122] They were successful in including a savings clause in SOLAS 74.[123] MARPOL 73/78 and the STCW

[121] See McDorman (n 50) 144–50; Chircop (n 7) 281–82.
[122] McDorman (n 50) 156–57; JA Roach, 'The Polar Code and its Adequacy' in RC Beckman et al (eds), *Governance of Arctic Shipping Balancing Rights and Interests of Arctic States and User States* (Leiden, Brill Nijhoff, 2017) 144, 165.
[123] SOLAS 74, Chapter XIV, reg 2.

already included similar clauses.[124] The saving clause of the new Chapter XIV of SOLAS 74 states: 'Nothing in this chapter shall prejudice the rights or obligations of States under international law.'[125] The conclusion is that Article 234 is not amended by the Polar Code.[126] However, this does not exclude the relevant Polar Code regulations from being relevant factors in the interpretation of the provision.

C. The Polar Code as a Relevant Legal Context in Interpreting Article 234

Section III.C above includes examples on how the Polar Code may contribute to the interpretation of Article 234. Through the inclusion and reference to the WMO Sea Ice Nomenclature, there is a common understanding of the concept of 'ice cover'. The Polar Code provides a nuanced understanding of sea-ice cover and the hazards to navigation posed by ice alone and in combination with climatic conditions. This contributes to clarifying the scope of the extended jurisdiction.

This sub-section investigates how Polar Code may affect the substantial scope of Article 234, as was introduced in section IV.C above. The background is the question whether the coastal State has jurisdiction to adopt maritime safety measures on the basis of Article 234. According to its wording, the jurisdiction involves the prevention, reduction and control of vessel-source pollution. Pharand[127] argued that the preventive character of the jurisdiction implied an extensive reading. Necessarily, measures to prevent the risks posed by sea ice in combination with severe climate conditions from materialising would include safety measures like requirements of ice strengthening and ships' routeing measures.[128] The decisive criterion is whether the measure contributes to preventing pollution (given that the other criteria of Article 234 are present). The purpose here is to assess whether the Polar Code strengthens or weakens such a reading of Article 234. The Polar Code clearly distinguishes between maritime safety measures and pollution prevention measures, locating them in separate parts. One reason for this distinction is that the measures have legal bases in different IMO Conventions (SOLAS 74, MARPOL 73/78 and the STCW). These conventions are administered by each of the two main committees of the IMO. However, the preamble identifies a key principle of the Polar Code, which is to apply 'a holistic approach in reducing the identified risks'.[129] It is acknowledged that there is a direct relationship

[124] MARPOL 73/78, art 16; SOLAS Chapter XIV, reg 2; STCW Convention, art V(4).

[125] Res MSC.386(94) on 'Amendments to the International Convention for the Safety of Life at Sea (SOLAS), 1974, as Amended' of the 'Report of the Maritime Safety Committee on its Ninety-Fourth Session' MSC 94/21/Add.1, Annex 7.

[126] Similar;y, see McDorman (n 50) 159; Chircop (n 7) 283; Roach (n 122) 166.

[127] D Pharand, 'The Arctic Waters and the Northwest Passage: A Final Revisit' (2007) 38 *Ocean Development & International Law* 3, 47.

[128] Bartenstein (n 62) 37.

[129] Polar Code, Preamble, Item 7.

between maritime safety and the protection of the marine environment as a 'safety measure taken to reduce the probability of an accident will largely benefit the environment'.[130] Therefore, it is safe to conclude that the Polar Code confirms the expanding reading of Article 234 and that it includes traditional safety measures to the extent that they contribute to preventing pollution. Most of the safety measures regulations of the Polar Code will reduce the probability of accidents or prevent sea ice from blocking navigation, and thus the risks of pollution. These include the requirements of structure (ice strengthening), stability (maintain stability even if damaged by ice), water-tight integrity, machinery, fire safety, navigational equipment and communication equipment and training (training requirements of key crew members). Similar measures could be adopted under Article 234. However, other Polar Code requirements such as those on life-saving appliances and arrangements are for the safety of the crew and of passengers. The coastal State would not be competent to adopt such requirements under Article 234.[131] Further, coastal States may adopt other types of maritime safety measures than those included in the Polar Code, such as ships' routeing and prior notification, as they may assist in preventing accidents resulting in pollution.

D. The Due Regard Duty and the Polar Code: Balancing Navigational and Environmental Interests

i. General

This sub-section investigates the possible role of the Polar Code regulations in the balancing act proscribed by the due regard duty. As discussed in section III.C.iii above, the duty of due regard – one of the restrictions on the jurisdiction – should be read as a requirement of the coastal State to balance between navigational and environmental interests. The duty of due regard entails risk assessment. A due regard requirement is included in other provisions of UNCLOS as a restriction on a right or a freedom to prevent it from being exercised at the expense of the rights and freedoms of other States in the same area.[132] The obligation is formulated somewhat differently in Article 234, where it does not refer to rights. This suggests that facilitating for navigation is not an absolute requirement under Article 234. It is legitimate for the coastal State to restrict navigation within an area for environmental protection purposes. Therefore, Bartenstein[133] is correct in arguing that the due regard duty implies other types of considerations – that it is a distinctive (*sui generis*) duty.

[130] ibid Preamble, Item 5.
[131] See also Chircop (n 61) 371.
[132] UNCLOS, arts 56(2), 58(3) and 87.
[133] Bartenstein (n 62) 45.

In the Chagos Marine Protection Area Arbitration, the Tribunal offered an interpretation of the due regard duty under Article 56(2) UNCLOS.[134] Although not of direct relevance in this case, the award's reading of the due regard concept may still be useful. The Tribunal concludes that the concept does not include a 'universal rule of conduct'.[135] It is more of a relational requirement:

> Rather, the extent of the regard required by the Convention will depend upon the nature of the rights held by … their importance, the extent of the anticipated impairment, the nature and importance of the activities contemplated by the … and the availability of alternative approaches.[136]

In the context of Article 234, the Tribunal's approach calls for an overall assessment of factors, including the importance of the navigational interests in the relevant areas, how they may be restricted by the planned measures, the type of measures considered, the necessity of the measures to protect and preserve the environment from the impacts of shipping under the prevailing sea ice and climatic conditions, as well as alternative measures. In short, the duty of due regard requires the State to undertake proper consideration in the planning of and the adoption of measures to ensure that they are relevant, reasonable and necessary in relation to the actual risks.[137] As formulated by Zhang: 'Its basic concept is to balance the interests of the States in their use of the sea and those of the entire international community.'[138] Further, taken together with the obligation to base its legislation on the best scientific evidence available, the decision-making is to build on the factual circumstances.[139] The due regard duty is therefore dynamic and not static.[140] Consequently, the balancing under the due regard duty and thus the discretion of the coastal State will be affected by the retreat and thinning of sea ice as well as the changing climate.

ii. *Due Regard in Respect of Whom?*

The duty to have due regard compels the coastal State to balance between the interests of navigation and of the protection and preservation of the marine environment. Neither of them are exclusively interests of the coastal State; they are interests of the international community. All States enjoy rights of navigation from the territorial sea to the high seas. The protection and preservation of the marine environment – which is not geographically defined – suggests that more than

[134] Chagos Marine Protected Area Arbitration (n 70).
[135] ibid 571, para 519.
[136] ibid.
[137] McRae and Goundrey (n 44) 220; Bartenstein (n 62) 41.
[138] Z Guobin, 'A Discussion on "Due Regard" in the United Nations Convention on the Law of the Sea' (2014) *China Oceans Law Review* 70, 77.
[139] McRae and Goundrey (n 44) 221–22; Bartenstein (n 62) 39–41; Chircop (n 61) 392.
[140] Franckx (n 9) 134.

purely coastal State interests should be included in the balancing. It can be read as a reference to the general *erga omnes* obligation under Article 192 to protect and preserve the marine environment. Thus, the international community of States have a legitimate interest in its definition and implementation. The fact that the coastal State is required to balance interests of the international community may influence how the discretion under Article 234 is exercised.

With the decreasing and thinning of sea ice as described in section IV above, alternative routes (at least for ice-strengthened vessels) may be developed through areas of the Arctic Ocean beyond national jurisdiction. Then, as correctly pointed out by Chircop,[141] the unilateral set measures of the coastal State may not be adequate to protect the marine environment. The duty to have due regard for navigation and protection of the marine environment may then be even stronger in favour of coordinating national legislation with the international rules and standards. Different and incompatible regulations may hinder international shipping or lead to inappropriate cooperation where less attention is paid to environmental considerations. A duty to coordinate measures may be derived from the obligation under Article 197 UNCLOS to cooperate on developing rules and standards to protect the marine environment, which is further specified in Article 211(1). Under the latter provision, States are required to cooperate through competent international organisations to establish international rules and standards to prevent vessel-source pollution. This duty is also applicable to Arctic waters.

iii. The Polar Code and the Due Regard Duty

Therefore, the question is whether the Polar Code regulations may be viewed as reflecting the balance between navigational and environmental protection interests. This would constrain the extended jurisdiction of the coastal State. Franckx[142] has described the duty to have due regard for navigation and protection of the marine environment as flexible, making the provision adaptable. Writing before the adoption of the Polar Code, he considered the 2009 IMO Guidelines for Ships Operating in Polar Waters to be a multilateral attempt to give concrete content to the due regard duty. In the report of the Committee on Coastal State Jurisdiction established under the International Law Association, it was argued what became the 2002 IMO Guidelines on Arctic Shipping 'might well prove an important element in the future application of this article [Article 234]'.[143]

The due regard concept is necessarily flexible as it requires the coastal State to adopt measures that are relevant, reasonable and necessary to address the obstacles and hazards to navigation under the factual (eg, geographical and climatic) circumstances. As described above in section III.C.iii, the due regard duty compels

[141] Chircop (n 61) 372.
[142] Franckx (n 9) 134.
[143] Committee on Coastal State Jurisdiction (n 51) 131–32 (Conclusion No 14).

the coastal State to base its regulations on risk assessments. The Polar Code is based on balancing between navigational and environmental interests, as its regulations includes requirements for vessels navigating in Arctic waters when encountering sea ice and other navigational hazards. Vessels are to navigate in areas within their operational limits.

It is challenging to transform a general framework such as the Polar Code into a due regard duty to be applied in different and specific circumstances. The Polar Code itself recognises that: 'The risk level within polar waters may differ depending on the geographical location, time of the year with respect to daylight, ice-coverage, etc. Thus, the mitigating measures required to address the above specific hazards may vary within polar waters.'[144] In the following text, the question of whether and how the Polar Code may affect the due regard obligation of the coastal State will be addressed by investigating examples from the safety measures (section V.D.iii.a) and the pollution prevention measures (section V.D.iii.b) of the Polar Code.

a. Safety Measures

Following the acknowledgement that the risk levels vary over time as well as geographically, the safety measures are designed using a goal-based approach.[145] Thereby, the requirements are tailored to the hazards under which the vessel is anticipated to operate. The regulation on ice strengthening operates with three categories of structural strengths: A, B and C vessels. The construction and design of the vessels are to be approved by the flag State or a recognised classification society, taking into account standards that are acceptable to the IMO.[146] Category A includes vessels designed to operate in at least medium first-year ice, while Category C vessels are designed to operate in open water or less severe ice conditions. While Category A vessels are required to have an ice-strengthened hull adequate to withstand these sea-ice conditions, Category C vessels may not be ice-strengthened. The operational limitations of the vessel (including ice strengthening) shall be stipulated in the Polar Ship Certificate.[147]

Therefore, it may prove be difficult to apply such goal-based norms directly in the balancing act of the due regard requirement. The two coastal States in question (Canada and Russia) have adopted regulations that set out operational limitations for vessels operating within specific areas and/or during periods based on the prevailing ice conditions and ice classification of the vessels.[148] The Polar

[144] Polar Code, Part I-A, s 3.2.

[145] ibid Part I-A, s 1.1.

[146] ibid Part I-A, s 3.3.2. Alternative structural arrangements and designs are acceptable, provided that these meet the goals and functional requirements and provide a level of safety equivalent to the requirements of Chapter 3. *cf* SOLAS Chapter XIV, reg 4; Polar Code, Part I-A, s 1.1.2.

[147] Polar Code, Introduction, s 1.3 and App 1.

[148] Canada, 'Arctic Shipping Safety and Pollution Prevention Regulations' (2017) SOR/2017-286, s 8(1); *cf* sch 1 and s 8(2), 151 *Canada Gazette* (1 July 2017) 2867–89; Russia, 'Rules of Navigation in

Code aims to bridge the potential different operational limitations requirements for ice-covered areas between the flag States under the Polar Code and the coastal States under Article 234. It aims to do this first through the harmonisation of the different ice classification rules. The ice classification of a vessel is decided by its classification society, normally according to its own ice classification rules.[149] Consequently, vessels navigating through Arctic waters may have different ice classifications, which are not necessarily those used by the coastal States in their regulations. This would complicate the process of deciding whether they may sail through their planned routes. The reference to the Polar Class[150] developed by the International Association of Classification Societies, as a standard acceptable to the IMO, is aimed at harmonising the different ice classification rules.[151] The Polar Class includes seven classes spanning from vessels operating year-round (P1) to vessels operating in the summer season in thin first-year ice (P7). The guidelines under the Polar Code for determining equivalence with the Polar Class may assist the coastal States and the flag States in deciding whether the vessel is or will be operating within its limitations sailing in the planned routes, and the requirements set by the coastal State.[152] Second, the Polar Code includes a recommendation that an 'appropriate methodology' is applied in determining the operational limitations of the vessel in sea ice.[153] As both Canada and Russia have developed their own methodologies, one purpose of this is to ensure harmonisation. It is not a legally binding norm. One of the reasons for this may be to avoid direct impact on the extended jurisdiction. The IMO has recommended an 'appropriate methodology' – more specifically, the Polar Operational Limit Assessment Risk Indexing System (POLARIS).[154] The POLARIS was developed using the practice of Canadian and Russian methodologies, which involves a calculation of the risks based inter alia on the prevailing ice conditions (concentration and age of ice) and the ice class of the vessel.[155] Whether a vessel may operate or navigate within the relevant areas

the Water Area of the Northern Sea Route' approved by the order of the Ministry of Transport of Russia No 7 of 17 January 2013, para II.10; *cf* Annex 2 'Criteria of the admission of ships to the Northern Sea Route in compliance with category of their ice strengthening'. An English translation is available at www.nsra.ru/en/ofitsialnaya_informatsiya/pravila_plavaniya.html.

[149] See, eg, Revised HELCOM Recommendation 25/7 'Safety of Winter Navigation in the Baltic Sea Area' (2 May 2004), Annex 'Approximate Correspondence between Ice Classes of the Finnish-Swedish Ice Class Rules (Baltic Ice Classes) and the Ice Classes of Other Classification Societies'.

[150] International Association of Classification Societies (IACS), Unified Requirements for Polar Class Ships (UR I), available at www.iacs.org.uk/publications/unified-requirements/ur-i.

[151] According to IACS decisions, the Unified Requirements relate to specific requirements and practices of classification societies. If accepted by a Member Society, Unified Requirements shall be incorporated in its rules and practices. The Unified Requirements are the minimum requirements.

[152] Polar Code Part I-B, para 4, 'Method for determining equivalent ice class'.

[153] Ibid Part I-A, Chapter 1, para 1.3.7, specified in Polar Code, Part I-B, para 1.2.

[154] IMO, 'Guidance on Methodologies for Assessing Operational Capabilities and Limitations in Ice' (6 June 2016) MSC.1/Circ.15, Appendix, 'Methodology for Assessing Operational Capabilities and Limitations in Ice: Polar Operational Limit Assessment Risk Indexing System (POLARIS)'.

[155] ibid POLARIS, para IV.

depends on the level of the calculated risk.[156] If the calculated risk is at the highest level, the vessel should avoid the area. Under Article 234, the coastal State is competent to restrict the vessels from navigating through this area. Canada has recognised the POLARIS as an alternative methodology.[157] Vessels applying for permission to sail the Northern Sea Route shall submit a copy of their Polar Ship Certificate.[158] This may suggest that Russia also seeks to harmonise its regulations with the Polar Code. Even if it is not legally binding, the POLARIS may prove to be important in harmonising the international (ie, the Polar Code) and national legislation on operational limits for vessels operating in ice-covered areas.

By applying these non-binding guidelines, the coastal State may be viewed as having paid due regard to navigation and the protection of the marine environment. Article 234 provides an added value as the coastal State is competent to adopt legislation consistent with these guidelines, stipulating more specific requirements for vessels sailing through the ice-covered waters within their 200-mile EEZs. It is more doubtful whether the normal environmental jurisdiction under Article 211 provides for such a right.

b. Pollution Prevention Measures

The pollution prevention measures of the Polar Code may more easily be aligned with the due regard duty as they are designed as prescriptive norms. Chapter 1 on prevention of pollution by oil includes a general ban on operational discharges of oil and oily mixtures.[159] The pollution prevention measures includes further bans or restrictions on operational discharges of substances and structural requirements regulated by MARPOL 73/78 Annexes II, IV and V.[160] These measures can be regarded as the international community balancing between navigational and the marine environment protection interests. Consequently, they have implications for the exercise of jurisdiction under Article 234 and the alternatives open to the coastal State: whether the coastal State may adopt more stringent or weaker regulations, or whether these must conform to the Polar Code regulations. Obviously, it would be challenging to adopt weaker regulations based on the extended environmental jurisdiction of Article 234. This would mean permitting operational discharges prohibited by the Polar Code. In any case, the flag contracting States Parties to MARPOL 73/78 annexes, including the coastal State, would still be required in relation of vessels flying their flag operating in Arctic waters to comply

[156] 'Guidance on Methodologies for Assessing Operational Capabilities and Limitations in Ice' (n 154), appendix, paragraph 1.2.3

[157] 'Arctic Shipping Safety and Pollution Prevention Regulations' (n 148) s 8(2)(b) and (c).

[158] Amendments to 'Rules of Navigation in the Water Area of the Northern Sea Route' approved by the order of the Ministry of Transport of the Russian Federation No 7 of 17 January 2013, Order of the Ministry of Transport No 5 of 9 January 2017, available at http://www.nsra.ru/en/ofitsialnaya_informatsiya /pravila_plavaniya/f122.html.

[159] Polar Code, Part II-A, s 1.1.1 with some specifications in ss 1.1.2–1.1.4.

[160] ibid Part II-A, Chapters 2, 4 and 5 respectively.

with the mandatory bans introduced by the Polar Code.[161] As the bans probably qualify as GAIRAS under Article 211(2) UNCLOS, all contracting flag States Parties are required to implement the ban. The added value of the jurisdiction of the coastal State under Article 234 is probably in situations where it considers adopting stricter regulations or other types of regulations than the Polar Code, such as a ban on the use and transport of heavy fuel oil or stricter regulations on discharges of sewage or garbage. Under the Arctic Waters Pollution Prevention Act of Canada, there is a general ban on deposits of waste from vessels in its Arctic waters.[162] In order to maintain this ban, Canada has incorporated selected operational and structural measures of the Polar Code.[163] Overall, Canada seeks to maintain more stringent regulations than the Polar Code. For example, the exceptions on the discharge of clean or segregated ballast and the transitional period for Category A vessels built before 1 January 2017 are not made applicable.[164] Vessels are not permitted to discharge cargo residues in Canadian Arctic waters.[165] With reference to the requirement of measures to be based on the best scientific evidence available, it is interesting to note that Canada has not provided any reasons for maintaining stricter regulations. However, by incorporating the Polar Code regulation of discharges of sewage, the Canadian regulations are in fact tightened.[166]

c. Assessment

As underlined in the Polar Code, the risk level of polar waters may differ geographically and over time, including in relation to the sensitivity of the marine environment.[167] The adoption of more stringent pollution prevention measures may be consistent with the due regard requirement. However, with the measures of Part II-A of the Polar Code made legally binding through the amendments of the MARPOL annexes, the duty of the coastal State to scientifically document the necessity of more stringent measures becomes more evident.

E. The Polar Code and Enforcement

The Polar Code redefines the baseline according to which the substantive scope of the extended jurisdiction will be assessed.[168] This is reflected by the fact that coastal States seem to harmonise their legislation with the Polar Code regulations.

[161] MARPOL 73/78, Annex I, regs 15 and 34. *cf* Annex I, reg 2(1).
[162] Arctic Waters Pollution Prevention Act (RSC 1985, c A-12), s 4(1); *cf* s 2 (definition of waste).
[163] 'Regulatory Impact Analysis Statement' 151 *Canada Gazette* (1 July 2017) 2877–78.
[164] Polar Code, Part II-A, ss 1.1.2 and 1.1.3.
[165] ibid Part II-A, s 5.2.1.5. *cf* 'Arctic Shipping Safety and Pollution Prevention Regulations' (n 148) s 26.
[166] 'Regulatory Impact Analysis Statement' (n 163) 2879.
[167] Polar Code, Introduction, s 3.2.
[168] Chircop (n 7) 283.

The next question is whether coastal States have a role in ensuring that the Polar Code is complied with. This is primarily the role and duty of the flag State. Chircop argues that Article 234 in fact 'enhances the prospects of the Polar Code being enforced against rogue vessels'.[169]

The extended jurisdiction does include a right to enforce the legislation that the coastal State adopts under Article 234. The scope of the enforcement jurisdiction corresponds to the scope of the prescriptive jurisdiction. The coastal State may take enforcement measures to ensure compliance with the legislation. There are no limitations on the enforcement jurisdiction as regards requirements of environmental impacts from non-compliance or on which types of enforcement measures should be taken. Therefore, in contrast to the normal enforcement jurisdiction, the coastal State seems to be competent to enforce violations of CDEM requirements, even if they do not cause or threaten to cause pollution. This could include measures ranging from inspection and detention of the vessels to criminal prosecution. Furthermore, the coastal State may undertake physical enforcement measures in relation to a vessel navigating through its EEZ, irrespective of the seriousness of the violation. Bartenstein argues that the seemingly more expansive enforcement jurisdiction is more psychological than real.[170] This is because the enforcement jurisdiction is also subjected to the duties not to discriminate and to have due regard for navigation and protection of the marine environment.

Having due regard means that the exercise of jurisdiction is to be reasonable and necessary. The coastal State is clearly competent to physically intervene in respect of vessels navigating in or into areas in which sea ice and climatic conditions exceed their operational capacity. The requirement of reasonableness and necessity means that the use of physical enforcement measures are less likely where the vessel has violated regulations, but which has not caused any discharges or risks of discharges.

VI. Conclusions

This chapter has illustrated how UNCLOS may adapt to changing legal and factual circumstances in order to address risks to the marine environment. These circumstances include the possible impacts of climate change and of the Polar Code on the extended environmental jurisdiction of Arctic coastal States. As shown above (see section IV), climate change has not made Article 234 redundant and it is difficult to predict if and when that will happen. During the next few decades, the sea ice and climatic conditions will most likely be of a character that justifies measures under Article 234. Scientific reports suggest that the ice cover in combination with the climatic conditions will become more dynamic, exposing vessels to hazards

[169] ibid 283.
[170] Bartenstein (n 62) 39.

or risks. Still, the changes in sea-ice cover is likely to affect the substantive scope of the jurisdiction. The due regard duty – that the measures taken are reasonable and necessary as documented by scientific evidence – will play a more prominent role, restricting the discretion of the coastal State. This will become evident as the summer season is extended, limiting the right, for example, to require vessels to be ice strengthened or to sail through designated sea lanes.

The most apparent impact of the Polar Code is that it redefines the baseline for the application of Article 234. The added value of Article 234 is where the coastal State aims at establishing stricter or other regulations than those adopted by the IMO. The baseline provided by the Polar Code is distinct in relation to its pollution prevention measures, as they include prescriptive rules on operational discharges. An adoption by the coastal State of stricter requirements (for example, on discharges of sewage) than the Polar Code for vessels navigating within its EEZ would not be unproblematic. The due regard requirement will require it to document that the requirement is reasonable and necessary as verified by scientific evidence in the context in question. It is not equally apparent that the safety measures of the Polar Code will impact coastal State jurisdiction under Article 234. Importantly, the reference to and the use of the Sea Ice Nomenclature of the WMO add to and develop the reading of the concept as used in Article 234. This contributes to a more diversified understanding of 'ice-covered areas' and how, in combination with climatic conditions, sea ice may pose obstacles and hazards to navigation. The goal-based character of the maritime safety measures provides the flag States with discretion in terms of operationalising them, making their baseline quality less apparent. The consequence could be incompatible requirements restricting navigation. Therefore, it is important that the requirements on the operational limitations as set by the coastal States and those applicable to the flag States through the Polar Code are harmonised. This chapter has argued that the due regard obligation implies that the coastal States are required to take measures to ensure equivalence between the operational limits set by the coastal State and those established under the Polar Code. The POLARIS recommendation may be regarded as such an attempt. The coastal State is competent under Article 234 to incorporate the POLARIS into its legislation. This may enhance the maritime safety and environmental protection of the region.

This chapter has documented that coastal States still have a unique role to play in the governance of Arctic shipping. The description of Article 234 as ambiguous and controversial hides the fact that the provision explicitly provides them with exceptional discretion in regulating international shipping in waters under their jurisdiction. Historically, providing the coastal State with extended jurisdiction over its Arctic waters was understandable as the IMO instruments did not address the exceptional hazards of operating in Arctic waters. This is still the case to some degree. Perhaps more important as shipping activities intensify is the fact that Article 234 provides the regulatory regime of Arctic shipping with more flexibility than is possible through the IMO and as recognised by the Polar Code. The regulations may be adapted to the real-time hazards and to the changing and different conditions within Arctic waters. Not least, it provides a right of the coastal State to monitor, control and enforce the compliance of vessels navigating with the legislation adopted under Article 234. This discretion is not unrestricted and may not be used arbitrarily, as the coastal State is subject to non-discrimination, due regard and scientific documentation requirements.

More controversial are the measures adopted under Article 234, which are not included in the toolbox of the Polar Code. These include prior notification and permission schemes coupled with reporting obligations, ships' routeing, and requirement of using ice-breaker assistance or pilotage coupled with fees. Both Russia and Canada have established a scheme of mandatory prior notification and permission and position reporting, which has raised concerns amongst several flag States.[171] Singapore asked for scientific documentation for the need of the Canadian regulation (NORDREG) and further questioned how NORDREG demonstrated due regard to navigation. These measures are probably more controversial as they are applicable year-round, irrespective of ice coverage and particularly severe climatic conditions. This would also be the case if the coastal State adopts routeing measures to prevent vessels from navigating through shallow waters or to protect vulnerable habitats or species. The controversies will probably increase as the impacts of climate change become more widespread and as more questions on the legitimacy of adopting measures under Article 234 may be raised. In order to reduce conflicts, the coastal State should at least consult with other States through the IMO before adopting such measures.

A final point to note is that most of the shipping activities in Arctic waters are likely to remain destinational in the years to come. The Polar Code is, with some exceptions, applicable to destinational shipping, as is Article 234. However, recent amendments of Russian legislation may have an impact on the governance of Arctic shipping, as all transport of oil, natural gas and coal from ports in the Russian Arctic is to be undertaken by Russian-flagged vessels.[172] This nationalisation of the transport of natural resources, which is the dominant use of the Northern Sea Route, may reduce the international character of the navigation through the Northern Sea Route. A consequence may be a weakening of the relevance of Article 234.

[171] K Bartenstein, 'Navigating the Arctic: The Canadian NORDREG, the International Polar Code and Regional Cooperation' (2011) 54 *German Yearbook of International Law* 77, 94.

[172] 'Russian Legislators Ban Foreign Shipments of Oil, Natural Gas and Aoal along Northern Sea Route' *Barents Observer* (26 December 2017), available at www.thebarentsobserver.com/en/arctic/2017/12/russian-legislators-ban-foreign-shipments-oil-natural-gas-and-coal-along-northern-sea; 'Amendments to Merchant Shipping Code of Russia' *President of Russia Official Website* (29 December 2017), available at www.en.kremlin.ru/acts/news/56546. The amendments of the Russian Merchant Shipping Code are available in an English translation at www.global-regulation.com/translation/russia/2946018/amending-the-merchant-shipping-code-of-the-russian-federation.html.

8

The Responsibility and Liability of Flag States in the Context of Fisheries

DANIEL OWEN*

Abstract: This chapter considers the obligation of due diligence of flag States in the context of fisheries, with reference to the Advisory Opinion of the International Tribunal for the Law of the Sea (ITLOS) in Case No 21. In particular, it looks into whether State-against-State litigation could be used to enforce that obligation.

I. Introduction[1]

The purpose of this chapter is to bring renewed attention to the responsibility and liability of flag States in the context of fisheries. It focuses, in particular, on the Advisory Opinion of the International Tribunal for the Law of the Sea in Case No 21. The chapter relates to vessels that undertake fishing either in the waters of a State other than their flag State (ie, vessels flagged to State X fishing in the waters of State Y) or on the high seas.

The chapter highlights both a failure of international law and several achievements of international law that flow from this failure. The failure in question is that of many flag States having not met their international obligations. The achievements are those of States, acting in capacities other than as flag States, stepping in to mitigate this failure. The chapter goes on to propose how the failure of flag States might be remedied more directly, namely through litigation.

* The author would like to thank the following people who provided comments on an earlier draft of this chapter: Stella Bartolini Cavicchi; Jessica Battle; Professor Robin Churchill; Alistair Graham; and the co-editors of this book.

[1] Sections V and VI of this chapter are based on material used in a written briefing prepared by the author for WWF International ('The ITLOS Advisory Opinion in Case No 21: Introductory briefing on the due diligence obligation of flag States regarding their fishing vessels, the liability for breach of this obligation and the possibilities for litigation', WWF International, February 2016). Nonetheless, the contents of this chapter represent the author's own perspective. The manuscript for this chapter was submitted in February 2019.

The term 'fishing' will be used broadly here to mean not just the activity of catching fish but also activities related to catching, including activities of carrier vessels (such as refrigerated cargo vessels, also known as 'reefers'), resupply vessels (whether resupplying consumables or crew) and support vessels (used in some fisheries, for example, purse seine fisheries that use fish aggregating devices).

In turn, the term 'fishing vessel' will be employed here to mean any vessel used, or intended for use, for 'fishing', and so will include the various categories of vessel referred to above. This inclusive approach is increasingly common in contemporary treaties, both regional and global, on fisheries conservation and management.[2]

II. IUU Fishing

This chapter will refer at various points to 'IUU fishing'. The term 'IUU fishing', which stands for 'illegal, unreported and unregulated fishing', first arose within the Commission for the Conservation of Antarctic Marine Living Resources (CCAMLR).[3] It was subsequently used in the Food and Agriculture Organization (FAO)'s 'International Plan of Action to Prevent, Deter, and Eliminate Illegal, Unreported and Unregulated Fishing' adopted in 2000.[4]

'IUU fishing' is defined in paragraph 3 of the FAO's International Plan of Action. That definition will not be considered in detail here. However, it is relevant to point out that each of the three words 'illegal', 'unreported' and 'unregulated' has a separate sub-definition. The definition in paragraph 3 has been reproduced or cross-referred to in several fisheries-related instruments.[5]

Examples of IUU fishing in the waters of a coastal State could include fishing without the permission of that State or fishing in contravention of that State's laws and regulations (both of these would be 'illegal' fishing). Examples of IUU fishing on the high seas could include, for a vessel flagged to a member of a regional fisheries management organisation (RFMO), fishing in contravention of that RFMO's binding conservation and management measures (which would be 'illegal' fishing) or, for a vessel flagged to a State that is not a member of an RFMO, fishing in a

[2] See, eg, Convention on the Conservation and Management of Highly Migratory Fish Stocks in the Western and Central Pacific Ocean (adopted 5 September 2000, entered into force 19 June 2004) 2275 UNTS 43, art 1(d) and (e); Convention on the Conservation and Management of High Seas Fishery Resources in the South Pacific Ocean (adopted 14 November 2009, entered into force 24 August 2012) 2899 UNTS, art 1(1)(g) and (h); and Agreement on Port State Measures to Prevent, Deter and Eliminate Illegal, Unreported and Unregulated Fishing (adopted 22 November 2009, entered into force 5 June 2016), art 1(c), (d) and (j).

[3] FAO Fisheries Department, *The State of World Fisheries and Aquaculture 2000* (Rome, FAO, 2000) 58 (Box 13).

[4] Available at www.fao.org/fishery/ipoa-iuu/en.

[5] See, for example, (and sometimes with some variations): 2009 Agreement on Port State Measures to Prevent, Deter and Eliminate Illegal, Unreported and Unregulated Fishing, art 1(e); 2010 Convention on the Conservation and Management of High Seas Fishery Resources in the South Pacific Ocean, art 1(1)(j); IUU Regulation (n 25) art 2(1)–(4).

manner that is not consistent with or contravenes that RFMO's binding conservation and management measures (which would be 'unregulated' fishing).

IUU fishing is a global problem. It occurs in waters under national jurisdiction and in waters beyond national jurisdiction. It can be perpetrated by vessels of any size. So it is certainly not exclusive to vessels undertaking fishing activities in the waters of States other than their flag State or on the high seas. However, as already stated, such vessels are the focus of this chapter.

III. The Role of the Flag State

Very briefly, a flag State is a State that entitles a vessel to fly its flag and, by doing so, confers its nationality on that vessel. In turn, as a general proposition, the law of the flag State is the law that governs the vessel – although in certain circumstances, the law of the coastal State or the port State will also be relevant, to varying degrees, depending on where the vessel is and what it is doing.[6]

The 1982 United Nations Convention on the Law of the Sea (UNCLOS)[7] sets out some basic propositions on flag States, including that '[e]very State shall fix the conditions for the grant of its nationality … and for the right to fly its flag',[8] '[e]very State shall effectively exercise its jurisdiction and control in administrative, technical and social matters over ships flying its flag'[9] and '[s]hips shall sail under the flag of one State only'.[10]

If a vessel operating on the high seas has no flag State, it lays itself open to direct intervention there by warships, irrespective of its activity.[11] It is not unknown for there to be vessels operating on the high seas without a flag State (or with more than one flag State at once, which has the same effect),[12] but the risks of intervention are ever-present for such vessels.

In principle, the law of the flag State will vary from one flag State to another. However, there are several treaties in force that establish duties applicable to flag States. Where a flag State is a party to such a treaty, the duties established by that treaty become applicable to that State; these duties may in turn require the flag State to ensure that vessels flying its flag meet certain standards (on which, see below).

[6] For a definition of 'coastal State' and 'port State', see R Churchill and V Lowe, *The Law of the Sea*, 3rd edn (Manchester, Manchester University Press, 1999) 344: 'A coastal State is the State in one of whose maritime zones a particular vessel lies' and 'A port State is the State in one of whose ports a particular vessel lies'.

[7] 1982 United Nations Convention on the Law of the Sea (adopted 10 December 1982, entered into force 16 November 1994) 1833 UNTS 3 (UNCLOS).

[8] ibid art 91(1).

[9] ibid art 94(1).

[10] ibid art 92(1).

[11] ibid art 110(1)(d).

[12] ibid art 92(2).

The material scope of the treaties referred to above varies. Some of the treaties relate to merchant shipping; key amongst these are global treaties on ship safety and marine pollution.[13] To the extent that merchant ships covered by such treaties are involved in activities related to catching fish (eg, reefers – see above), there may be scope for these treaties to have some bearing, indirectly, on fishing.

However, there are other treaties establishing duties applicable to flag States that, in whole or in part, relate directly to fishing. The binding standards that they establish about fishing relate mainly to fisheries conservation and management. (There are also treaties establishing binding standards on other aspects of fishing, including the International Labour Organization (ILO)'s 2007 Work in Fishing Convention (C188),[14] the International Maritime Organization (IMO)'s 1995 STCW-F Convention[15] and the IMO's 2012 Cape Town Agreement.[16] These three treaties are likely to play an increasingly important role, but will not be discussed further here.)

The principal legal frameworks enabling or establishing standards on fisheries conservation and management are found in UNCLOS[17] and in the 1995 United Nations Fish Stocks Agreement (UNFSA).[18] UNCLOS and UNFSA are global rather than regional in their geographical scope.

However, in international fisheries, the regional level is very important too. At that level, duties on flag States may be created by treaties establishing RFMOs or, in turn, by binding measures adopted by RFMOs. RFMOs' measures are given major prominence by, for example, UNFSA.[19]

Even though a treaty, or a binding measure adopted by an RFMO, may establish duties applicable to a flag State, this does not necessarily mean that a flag State will implement those duties. It is well known that some flag States, whether in the context of merchant shipping or fisheries, do not implement their duties, whether due to lack of capacity (including financial capacity) or lack of intention.

Such States are attractive to those vessel owners and operators that, on the one hand, seek a flag State for their vessel(s), but, on the other hand, do not want that

[13] The International Maritime Organization (IMO)'s International Convention for the Safety of Life at Sea (adopted 1 November 1974, entered into force 25 May 1980) 1184 UNTS 2, as amended (SOLAS Convention); the IMO's Protocol of 1978 relating to the International Convention for the prevention of pollution from ships, 1973 (adopted 17 February 1978, entered into force 2 October 1983) 1340 UNTS 61, as amended (MARPOL 73/78).

[14] The International Labour Organization (ILO)'s 2007 Work in Fishing Convention (C188) (adopted 14 June 2007, entered into force on 16 November 2017). See further the ILO website: www.ilo.org.

[15] International Convention on Standards of Training, Certification and Watchkeeping for Fishing Vessel Personnel (adopted 7 July 1995, entered into force 29 September 2012).

[16] Cape Town Agreement on the Implementation of the Provisions of the 1993 Torremolinos Protocol relating to the 1977 International Convention for the Safety of Fishing Vessels (adopted 11 October 2012, not yet entered into force).

[17] See especially UNCLOS, arts 61–64 and 116–19.

[18] Agreement for the Implementation of the Provisions of the United Nations Convention on the Law of the Sea of 10 December 1982 relating to the Conservation and Management of Straddling Fish Stocks and Highly Migratory Fish Stocks (adopted 4 August 1995, entered into force 11 December 2001) 2167 UNTS 3 (UNFSA).

[19] ibid arts 8(3) and 17, for example.

State to implement its duties too vigorously, because doing so could create financial burdens for the owner or operator, or practical constraints on the operation of the vessels in question.

Over the decades, hope has been held out that flag States will fulfil their obligations. In some cases, this is not a false hope: there are certainly many flag States that take their obligations seriously. But in many other cases, it has indeed become a false hope.

At more than one point there was a move to develop and enforce a concept known as 'genuine link', whereby it was said that there should be a genuine link between a vessel and its flag State. However, and despite the existence in UNCLOS of a requirement for a genuine link,[20] this move largely failed in that, today, although some flag States do require a strong and meaningful link, many others do not.[21]

IV. The Response to Failures by Flag States

Faced with a widespread non-application of the concept of 'genuine link', the international community has developed other ways to try to ensure compliance by flag States with their duties or compliance by vessels with the relevant standards. Those other ways initially consisted of States acting as 'port States', whereby States with ports enforce the standards concerned against foreign-flagged vessels using those ports.

The use of port States evolved first in the context of merchant shipping.[22] However, its use has since spread, firmly and irreversibly, into the realm of fisheries. Indeed, there is now a fisheries treaty in force precisely on this subject, namely the 2009 Port State Measures Agreement.[23]

Within the realm of fisheries, States also act in other capacities to ensure compliance with international standards. Those other capacities include acting as market States and as States of nationality.

The capacity of 'market State' involves a State acting by virtue of the fact that it imports, exports or re-exports products arising from fishing. An example of a State operating actively as a market State is the European Union (EU). (The EU will be regarded as a State for the present purposes.)[24] The EU's role as a market State has become well known through the implementation of the EU's IUU Regulation.[25] Under that Regulation, one of the tools available to the EU is that non-EU Member

[20] Article 91(1) UNCLOS states, amongst other things, the following: 'There must exist a genuine link between the State and the ship.'

[21] There is an extensive literature on 'genuine link'. See, eg, Churchill and Lowe (n 6) 257–63; Y Tanaka, *The International Law of the Sea* (Cambridge, Cambridge University Press, 2015) 162–64.

[22] See further Churchill and Lowe (n 6) 274–76. See also, eg, the Paris MoU website: www.parismou.org.

[23] See n 2 above for the full name of this treaty. See also www.fao.org/port-state-measures.

[24] Further consideration of the EU as a 'State' in the context of fisheries is beyond the scope of this chapter. However, on the competence of the EU in the field of fisheries, see R Churchill and D Owen, *The EC Common Fisheries Policy* (Oxford, Oxford University Press, 2010) 129–31 and 301–13.

[25] Council Regulation (EC) No 1005/2008 of 29 September 2008 establishing a Community system to prevent, deter and eliminate illegal, unreported and unregulated fishing, amending Regulations (EEC)

States, including flag States, can be identified as 'non-cooperating', whereupon certain measures will apply in respect of those States.[26]

The capacity of 'State of nationality' involves a State acting by virtue of the fact that it provides nationality to a natural or legal person involved in fishing in cases where the fishing concerned takes place in waters beyond the jurisdiction of that State or by means of a vessel that is not flagged to that State (or both).[27] An example of a State operating actively as State of nationality is Spain. Its operations in that respect include, amongst others, Operation Sparrow and Operation Sparrow II.[28]

RFMOs, which were pioneers in developing the use of port States in a fisheries context, are increasingly adopting measures that require their Member States to act as market States and States of nationality.[29] However, it must be said that activity of States in these two latter capacities has yet to become mainstream.

Over the decades, the role of the flag State, as the State with primary responsibility for enforcing international standards in fisheries, has diminished and the role of other States – particularly port States – has increased. This has undoubtedly had an effect in terms of achieving successes in enforcement, but it has allowed flag State responsibility to somewhat slip into the shade.

An attempt to counter this was an FAO initiative to develop 'Voluntary Guidelines for Flag State Performance' (hereinafter 'the Guidelines'). The initiative originated in 2007,[30] but the Guidelines were not adopted until 2014. They are reasonably detailed[31] and in principle several of their provisions may become relevant as components of the due diligence obligation of flag States – an obligation which is discussed in section V below.

The Guidelines state that: 'All flag States are encouraged to have performance assessments conducted periodically.'[32] However, the provisions on the procedure for such assessments are lamentably sparse.[33] In addition, the page of the FAO website that deals with the Guidelines is silent as to whether any such performance assessments have been carried out to date.[34]

No 2847/93, (EC) No 1936/2001 and (EC) No 601/2004 and repealing Regulations (EC) No 1093/94 and (EC) No 1447/1999 [2008] OJ L286/1, as amended (IUU Regulation).

[26] ibid arts 31–36 and 38. States currently identified as 'non-cooperating' are listed on the DG Mare website: www.ec.europa.eu/fisheries.

[27] The term 'involved in' is not a term of art. See, eg, art 39 of the IUU Regulation on nationals, which uses 'support' and 'engage in' instead; and CCAMLR Conservation Measure 10–08 (2017) on nationals, which uses 'responsible for', 'benefiting from', 'supporting' and 'engaging in'.

[28] See, eg, IUU Watch, 'Learning Lessons from Spain's Experience of Prosecuting Nationals for Involvement in Illegal, Unreported and Unregulated (IUU Fishing)' (April 2017), available at www.iuuwatch.eu/2017/04/learning-lessons-spains-experience-prosecuting-nationals-involvement-illegal-unreported-unregulated-iuu-fishing.

[29] See, eg, CCAMLR Conservation Measure 10–05 (2017) and CCAMLR Conservation Measure 10–08 (2017) respectively.

[30] FAO, *Report of the Twenty-Seventh Session of the Committee on Fisheries*, Rome, 5–9 March 2007, FAO Fisheries Report No 830 (Rome, FAO, 2007), para 71.

[31] For the text of the Guidelines, see FAO, 'The Voluntary Guidelines for Flag State Performance, the 2009 FAO Agreement on Port State Measures and other Instruments Combating IUU Fishing' (March 2014) COFI/2014/4.2/Rev.1, App II.

[32] ibid para 44. See also para 56.

[33] ibid paras 45 and 46.

[34] See www.fao.org/fishery/topic/16159/en.

If performance assessments are an indicator of implementation by flag States of the Guidelines, the apparent lack of evidence of the existence of any assessments is of some concern. The overall impression created by the long gestation period of the Guidelines, followed by the apparent lack of response, is that political initiatives to galvanise flag States into taking their responsibilities seriously continue to exhibit a lack of practical effect.

In April 2015, there was a development that may help move the responsibility of flag States, in the context of fisheries, back into the light and generate some practical outcomes. This development was the delivery by the International Tribunal for the Law of the Sea of an Advisory Opinion on, amongst other things, the responsibility and liability of flag States in the context of fisheries. The Advisory Opinion is discussed in section V below.[35]

V. The ITLOS Advisory Opinion in Case No 21

A. Introduction

In April 2015, the International Tribunal for the Law of the Sea (ITLOS or 'the Tribunal') delivered an Advisory Opinion (AO), in Case No 21, in response to four questions posed to it by the West African Sub-Regional Fisheries Commission (SRFC).[36] The SRFC is an intergovernmental organisation for

[35] For journal articles on the subject of flag State obligations in a fisheries context published since 2005 and prior to the delivery of the AO, see, eg, G Xue, 'China's Distant Water Fisheries and its Response to Flag State Responsibilities' (2006) 30 *Marine Policy* 651; T Zwinge, 'Duties of Flag States to Implement and Enforce International Standards and Regulations – and Measures to Counter their Failure to Do So' (2011) 10 *Journal of International Business and Law* 297 (on fisheries, see specifically 305–09 and 313–17); Y Takei, 'Assessing Flag State Performance in Legal Terms: Clarifications of the Margin of Discretion' (2013) 28 *International Journal of Marine & Coastal Law* 97; K Erikstein and J Swan, 'Voluntary Guidelines for Flag State Performance: A New Tool to Conquer IUU Fishing' (2014) 29 *International Journal of Marine & Coastal Law* 116; G Handl, 'Flag State Responsibility for Illegal, Unreported and Unregulated Fishing in Foreign EEZs' (2014) 44 *Environmental Policy and Law* 158; V Schatz, 'Combating Illegal Fishing in the Exclusive Economic Zone: Flag State Obligations in the Context of the Primary Responsibility of the Coastal State' (2016) 7 *Goettingen Journal of International Law* 383 (with an addendum on the Advisory Opinion).

[36] *Request for an advisory opinion submitted by the Sub-Regional Fisheries Commission (SRFC)* (Advisory Opinion of 2 April 2015) ITLOS Reports 2015, 4. For additional analyses of the AO, see, eg, J Gao, 'The ITLOS Advisory Opinion for the SRFC' (2015) 14 *Chinese Journal of International Law* 735; M Gavouneli, 'Request for an Advisory Opinion Submitted by the Sub-Regional Fisheries Commission (SRFC) (ITLOS)' (2015) 54 *International Legal Materials* 890; Y Tanaka, 'Reflections on the Advisory Jurisdiction of ITLOS as a Full Court: The ITLOS Advisory Opinion of 2015' (2015) 14 *Law and Practice of International Courts and Tribunals* 318; E van der Marel, 'ITLOS Issues its Advisory Opinion on IUU Fishing' *The JCLOS Blog* (21 April 2015); V Ventura, 'Tackling Illegal, Unregulated and Unreported Fishing: The ITLOS Advisory Opinion on Flag State Responsibility for IUU fishing and the Principle of Due Diligence' (2015) 12(1) *Brazilian Journal of International Law* 50, 60–63 and 64; D Freestone, 'Case 21: Request for an Advisory Opinion Submitted by the Sub-Regional Fisheries Commission (SRFC)' (2016) 1(1) *Asia-Pacific Journal*

fisheries cooperation, established by a treaty adopted in 1985, with a membership consisting of seven West African coastal States.[37]

The SRFC had been concerned about the impact of IUU fishing, including by foreign-flagged vessels, in its Member States' waters, and was seeking the Tribunal's advice. In its request for advice, the SRFC invoked the so-called 'MCA Convention'. This is one of the treaties concluded by the seven Member States of the SRFC and is referred to below.[38]

The SRFC's four questions to ITLOS addressed flag State obligations and liability (Questions 1 and 2), obligations and liability of international organisations in certain circumstances (Question 3) and coastal State obligations (Question 4). In its AO, ITLOS answered all four questions. However, this chapter is concerned with the content of the AO regarding Questions 1 and 2 only.

The Tribunal limits its jurisdiction to the exclusive economic zones (EEZs) of SRFC Member States.[39] This approach may be seen as a measured response to the fact that the Tribunal's jurisdiction to deliver any AO at all in answer to the SRFC's questions was contested by several States.[40]

The Tribunal states that its AO 'has no binding force and is given only to the SRFC', though it adds that it is 'mindful of the fact that … it will … contribute to the implementation of [UNCLOS]'.[41] The AO's contribution to the implementation of UNCLOS is considered further below.

B. Question 1: Introduction

Question 1 (Q1), as posed by the SRFC, reads as follows: 'What are the obligations of the flag State in cases where illegal, unreported and unregulated (IUU) fishing activities are conducted within the [EEZs] of third party States?'[42]

of Ocean Law and Policy 131; M Lando, 'The Advisory Jurisdiction of the International Tribunal for the Law of the Sea: Comments on the Request for an Advisory Opinion Submitted by the Sub-Regional Fisheries Commission' (2016) 29 *Leiden Journal of International Law* 441; V Schatz, 'Fishing for Interpretation: The ITLOS Advisory Opinion on Flag State Responsibility for Illegal Fishing in the EEZ' (2016) 47 *Ocean Development & International Law* 327; A Telesetsky, 'The Global North, the Global South, and the Challenges of Ensuring Due Diligence for Sustainable Fishing Governance' (2017) 26 *Transnational Law and Contemporary Problems* 435.

[37] The Member States are: Cape Verde, Gambia, Guinea, Guinea-Bissau, Mauritania, Senegal and Sierra Leone.

[38] For more information on the Convention on the Determination of the Minimal Conditions for Access and Exploitation of Marine Resources within the maritime areas under jurisdiction of the Member States of the SRFC (signed 8 June 2012, entered into force 16 September 2012) (MCA Convention) and its relevance in Case No 21, see SRFC's 'Technical Note' (March 2013), www.itlos.org/en/cases/list-of-cases/case-no-21.

[39] See, amongst others, paras 69, 87 and 89 of the Advisory Opinion (n 36).

[40] On jurisdiction, see ibid paras 37–69.

[41] ibid paras 76 and 77.

[42] ibid para 85.

In answering Q1, the Tribunal takes, amongst other things, the following steps: it defines the geographical scope of Q1; it states that the flag State is not absolved of responsibility in the EEZ; it sets out the relevant provisions of UNCLOS; it identifies the flag State obligation arising from these provisions; it identifies two categories of actions by which the flag State must meet its obligation; it states that the flag State obligation is one of conduct and, in turn, one of due diligence; and it identifies elements of the due diligence obligation.

Regarding the statement by ITLOS that the flag State is not absolved of responsibility in the EEZ, ITLOS is careful first to point out that 'in light of the special rights and responsibilities given to the coastal State in the [EEZ] under [UNCLOS], the primary responsibility for taking the necessary measures to prevent, deter and eliminate IUU fishing rests with the coastal State'.[43] However, ITLOS goes on to make clear that this coastal State responsibility 'does not release other States from their obligations in this regard'[44] and that the reference to 'other States' includes flag States.[45]

The provisions of UNCLOS considered by the Tribunal are as follows: the preamble;[46] Articles 91, 92 and 94,[47] but with special focus on Articles 92 and 94;[48] Articles 192 and 193,[49] with the Tribunal citing[50] its finding in another case that 'the conservation of the living resources of the sea is an element in the protection and preservation of the marine environment';[51] and Articles 58(3) and 62(4).[52]

In brief, Articles 91, 92 and 94 relate to flag States.[53] Article 192 and 193 relate to protection and preservation of the marine environment. Article 58(3) requires States, such as flag States, '[i]n exercising their rights and performing their duties under [UNCLOS] in the [EEZ]', to (a) have 'due regard to the rights and duties of the coastal State' and (b) comply with the coastal State's (UNCLOS-consistent) laws and regulations. Article 62(4) makes it clear that foreign-flagged fishing vessels are subject to the coastal State's (UNCLOS-consistent) laws and regulations.

C. Question 1: The Nature of the Obligation

The Tribunal reaches various conclusions from its analysis of the above provisions and it expresses its conclusions in various ways.[54] However, this chapter focuses

[43] ibid para 106.
[44] ibid para 108.
[45] ibid paras 134 and 135.
[46] ibid para 102.
[47] ibid para 111.
[48] ibid paras 115 and 116–19.
[49] ibid paras 111 and 120.
[50] ibid para 120.
[51] *Southern Bluefin Tuna Cases (New Zealand v Japan; Australia v Japan)* (Provisional Measures, Order of 27 August 1999) ITLOS Reports 1999, 280, para 70.
[52] Advisory Opinion (n 36) paras 111, 121–24 and 127. See also paras 134–40.
[53] Some of their provisions are referred to in section III above.
[54] See, eg, Advisory Opinion (n 36) paras 102, 119, 120, 124 and 127.

on the form of words used by the Tribunal in paragraph 127 of the AO, namely the following:

> [T]he flag State has the 'responsibility to ensure', pursuant to [Articles 58(3) and 62(4) UNCLOS], compliance by vessels flying its flag with the laws and regulations concerning conservation measures adopted by the coastal State. The flag State must meet this responsibility by taking measures defined in paragraphs 134 to 140 [of the AO] as well as by effectively exercising its jurisdiction and control in 'administrative, technical and social matters' over ships flying its flag in accordance with [Article 94(1) UNCLOS].

As can be seen, two categories of actions are referred to by the Tribunal. First, the flag State is to take the measures defined in paragraphs 134–40 of the AO. Second, the flag State is to effectively exercise its jurisdiction and control in 'administrative, technical and social matters' over ships flying its flag in accordance with Article 94(1) UNCLOS. These two categories are considered further below.

In paragraph 129 of the AO, the Tribunal adds that the obligation of the flag State, such as that referred to in paragraph 127 of the AO, is an obligation of conduct and, in turn, an obligation of 'due diligence':

> In the case of IUU fishing in the [EEZs] of the SRFC Member States, the obligation of a flag State not party to the MCA Convention to ensure that vessels flying its flag are not involved in IUU fishing is … an obligation 'of conduct'. In other words, as stated in the [ITLOS Advisory Opinion in Case No 17], this is an obligation 'to deploy adequate means, to exercise best possible efforts, to do the utmost' to prevent IUU fishing by ships flying its flag. However, as an obligation 'of conduct' this is a 'due diligence obligation', not an obligation 'of result'. This means that this is not an obligation of the flag State to achieve compliance by fishing vessels flying its flag in each case with the requirement not to engage in IUU fishing in the [EEZs] of the SRFC Member States. The flag State is under the 'due diligence obligation' to take all necessary measures to ensure compliance and to prevent IUU fishing by fishing vessels flying its flag.

So, as can be seen, the Tribunal concludes that: 'The flag State is under the "due diligence obligation" to take all necessary measures to ensure compliance and to prevent IUU fishing by fishing vessels flying its flag.'

It is beyond the scope of this chapter to explain how the Tribunal reaches its conclusion that the flag State's obligation is one of 'due diligence' rather than being one of result.[55] However, put very briefly, that conclusion is not derived from UNCLOS directly, but from broad principles and the findings of international courts and tribunals.

[55] On obligations of conduct (including obligations of due diligence) compared to obligations of result, see, eg, R Wolfrum, 'Obligations of Result versus Obligations of Conduct: Some Thoughts about the Implementation of International Obligations' in MH Arsanjani et al (eds), *Looking to the Future: Essays on International Law in Honor of W Michael Reisman* (Leiden, Martinus Nijhoff, 2010).

The Tribunal, in identifying the nature of the obligation on flag States, focuses on EEZ fisheries. Indeed, regarding Q1, the Tribunal states clearly that Q1 'does not relate to the obligations of flag States in cases of IUU fishing in other maritime areas [ie, in maritime areas other than the EEZs of SRFC Member States], including the high seas'.[56]

Questions therefore remain about the application of a due diligence obligation to fisheries on the high seas. In that regard, Articles 58(3) and 62(4) UNCLOS – which are amongst the provisions relied upon by the Tribunal – relate only to the EEZ. However, the failure by the Tribunal to consider the high seas may be seen as a reflection of its measured approach to jurisdiction (see above).

At first glance, it would be surprising if a flag State's obligation to be duly diligent should not also apply to fisheries conducted on the high seas, where the context would be adherence to the conservation and management measures of relevant RFMOs. In that context, the provisions of section 2 of Part VII of UNCLOS and the provisions of UNFSA would be relevant, amongst other things.

D. Question 1: Content of the Obligation

As already noted above, two categories of actions are referred to by the Tribunal when stating how the flag State must meet its obligation. One of these is put in rather general terms: the flag State is to effectively exercise its jurisdiction and control in 'administrative, technical and social matters' over ships flying its flag in accordance with Article 94(1) UNCLOS. The other category is more specific: the flag State is to take the measures defined in paragraphs 134–40 of the AO.

The Tribunal prefixes the measures listed in paragraphs 134–40 with the following statement:

> The Tribunal holds that, in the present case, [UNCLOS] is the key instrument which provides guidance regarding the content of the measures that need to be taken by the flag State in order to ensure compliance with the 'due diligence' obligation to prevent IUU fishing by vessels flying its flag in the [EEZs] of the SRFC Member States.[57]

The measures defined in paragraphs 134–40 of the AO will not be set out here. But, in summary, they relate to the following: 'necessary measures, including those of enforcement, to ensure compliance'; authorisation to fish; 'necessary measures' to ensure compliance with 'protection and preservation measures'; vessel marking (in particular); 'enforcement mechanisms', including sanctions; investigation of reports; and cooperation.

[56] Advisory Opinion (n 36) para 89.
[57] ibid para 133.

E. Question 2: Introduction

Question 2 (Q2), as posed by the SRFC, reads as follows: 'To what extent shall the flag State be held liable for IUU fishing activities conducted by vessels sailing under its flag?'[58]

The Tribunal notes that 'neither [UNCLOS] nor the MCA Convention provides guidance on the issue of liability of the flag State for IUU fishing activities conducted by vessels under its flag'.[59] It adds that in answering Q2, it 'will therefore be guided by relevant rules of international law on responsibility of States for internationally wrongful acts'.[60]

It identifies three rules of 'general international law' relevant to Q2, namely Articles 1, 2 and 31(1) of the International Law Commission's Articles on Responsibility of States for Internationally Wrongful Acts.[61]

F. Question 2: The Existence of Liability

As to when the flag State is liable, the Tribunal concludes that it is 'of the view that the SRFC Member States may hold liable the flag State of a vessel conducting IUU fishing activities in their [EEZs] for a breach, attributable to the flag State, of its international obligations referred to in the reply to [Q1]'.[62]

As to when the flag State is not liable, the Tribunal concludes that 'the flag State is not liable if it has taken all necessary and appropriate measures to meet its "due diligence" obligations to ensure that vessels flying its flag do not conduct IUU fishing activities in the [EEZs] of the SRFC Member States'.[63]

The Tribunal is clear about the relevance of the behaviour of vessels and about the frequency of IUU fishing activities, stating that:

> In the present case, the liability of the flag State does not arise from a failure of vessels flying its flag to comply with the laws and regulations of the SRFC Member States concerning IUU fishing activities in their [EEZs], as the violation of such laws and regulations by vessels is not per se attributable to the flag State.[64]
>
> The Tribunal also wishes to address the issue as to whether isolated IUU fishing activities or only a repeated pattern of such activities would entail a breach of 'due diligence' obligations of the flag State … the frequency of IUU fishing activities by vessels in the [EEZs] of the SRFC Member States is not relevant to the issue as to whether there is a breach of 'due diligence' obligations by the flag State.[65]

[58] ibid para 141.
[59] ibid para 142.
[60] ibid para 143.
[61] ibid para 144.
[62] ibid para 147. The Tribunal cites paras 109–40 of the Advisory Opinion and para 170 of its own judgment in *The M/V 'Saiga' (No 2) Case (Saint Vincent and the Grenadines v Guinea)* ITLOS Reports 1999, 10.
[63] Advisory Opinion (n 36) para 148.
[64] ibid para 146 (reproduced here in part).
[65] ibid para 150.

VI. Applying the ITLOS Advisory Opinion to Litigation

As noted in section IV above, the rise of the role of port States in enforcing international standards in fisheries has allowed flag State responsibility to somewhat slip into the shade. Yet it is very clear from the AO of ITLOS that flag States do have a responsibility and, what is more, that they are liable if they are found to be in breach of that responsibility.

This raises the question of whether one way to bring flag State responsibility back into the light would be State-against-State litigation for breach of that responsibility, thus starkly reminding flag States of the obligation they take on, and the potential liability they accept, when they place fishing vessels on their registers.

The Tribunal, in answering Q1 and thereby setting out the due diligence obligation of flag States, uses a rationale that is based on the provisions of UNCLOS, as well as on broad principles and the findings of international courts and tribunals (see section V above).

In turn, in answering Q2 on the liability of flag States, the Tribunal uses a rationale that is based on the International Law Commission's Articles on Responsibility of States for Internationally Wrongful Acts (again, see section V above).

In other words, the Tribunal does not rely on any regional treaties, such as the SRFC's MCA Convention, to derive its conclusion about the due diligence obligation of flag States or its conclusion about the liability of flag States. In principle, as a result, its conclusions have applications beyond the narrow jurisdictional confines of the AO, ie, to flag States in general and to coastal States in general.

As mentioned above, one potential application is litigation. Let us suppose that a coastal State Party to UNCLOS wishes to bring a flag State Party to UNCLOS before an international court or tribunal, alleging a breach by the flag State of the latter's due diligence obligation. In principle, the Tribunal's conclusions from the AO about the due diligence obligation of flag States and about the liability of flag States could be invoked by the coastal State, irrespective of whether that coastal State is a Member State of the SRFC. That is because of the rationale of the Tribunal's conclusions, as noted above.

A coastal State, in litigation against a flag State, would need to demonstrate a breach by the flag State of the latter's due diligence obligation. However, as a crucial prerequisite, it would also need to be able to bring the flag State concerned before an international court or tribunal. UNCLOS, in Part XV, contains important provisions on dispute settlement in that respect, although these provisions only apply as between the States Parties to UNCLOS.[66]

As various provisions of Part XV of UNCLOS make clear, Part XV relates (only) to disputes 'concerning the interpretation or application' of UNCLOS (see, for example, Article 286). On the assumption that any dispute between a coastal

[66] It is beyond the scope of this chapter to consider litigation involving one or more non-parties to UNCLOS.

State Party to UNCLOS and a flag State Party to UNCLOS concerning adherence by the flag State to the latter's due diligence obligation would be a dispute 'concerning the interpretation or application' of UNCLOS, Part XV would apply to that dispute.

Part XV of UNCLOS has three sections. Section 2, entitled 'Compulsory procedures entailing binding decisions', is the core of Part XV and is sandwiched between sections 1 and 3. Section 3 sets out various limitations and exceptions to section 2.[67] Section 1, amongst other things, sets out procedures that either must be or may be followed by States when they first become engaged in a dispute.

Section 1 of Part XV also includes a provision, Article 282, which precludes resorting to Part XV if the parties to a dispute concerning the interpretation or application of UNCLOS 'have agreed, through a general, regional or bilateral agreement or otherwise, that such dispute shall, at the request of any party to the dispute, be submitted to a procedure that entails a binding decision'.[68]

Further consideration of Article 282 is beyond the scope of this chapter, but its potential relevance should not be overlooked. For example, a flag State might seek to rely on it where a fisheries access agreement exists between the two States in dispute. Its relevance in any given case would depend on the terms of the agreement in question.

As noted above, section 2 is the core of Part XV of UNCLOS and is entitled 'Compulsory procedures entailing binding decisions'. It starts with Article 286, which reads as follows:

> Subject to section 3, any dispute concerning the interpretation or application of this Convention shall, where no settlement has been reached by recourse to section 1, be submitted at the request of any party to the dispute to the court or tribunal having jurisdiction under this section.

Thus, if State Party 'A' to UNCLOS (eg, a coastal State Party) wants to take State Party 'B' to UNCLOS (eg, a flag State Party) to an international court or tribunal, State 'A' can do so without needing the dispute-specific consent of State 'B': State 'B' has already given its consent by virtue of its being a party to UNCLOS.

The coastal State would then need to demonstrate to the court or tribunal concerned that the flag State was in breach of the latter's due diligence obligation. As noted in section V above, two categories of actions are referred to by the Tribunal when stating how the flag State must meet its obligation. One of these is put in quite general terms (a reference to Article 94(1) UNCLOS) and one is more specific (a list of measures set out in paragraphs 134–40 of the AO).

In principle, a failure by a flag State to adhere to one or more of the measures set out in paragraphs 134–40 of the AO (or to adhere to Article 94(1) UNCLOS) should be sufficient to constitute a breach. In practice, the measures referred to in

[67] One of the limitations set out in s 3 of Part XV is in art 297(3)(a) UNCLOS. This relates to disputes concerning certain fisheries matters in the EEZ. However, it only comes into play when a coastal State is the respondent in a dispute; it does not prevent a coastal State from initiating a dispute.

[68] The parties can, by consensus, agree to disregard art 282 UNCLOS.

paragraphs 134–40 are quite broadly worded (as is Article 94(1) UNCLOS) and so there is clearly some room for interpretation.

If the coastal State were to be successful in demonstrating a breach by the flag State of the latter's due diligence obligation, the Tribunal's conclusion in the AO about flag State liability flowing from such a breach would in turn become relevant – for example, by the coastal State requesting an award of compensation. Indeed, it would seem unlikely that a coastal State would take the trouble to bring an action against a flag State without invoking the liability of the flag State.

Article 296(1) UNCLOS, at the end of section 2 of Part XV of UNCLOS, states that any decision of a court or tribunal having jurisdiction under section 2 'shall be final and shall be complied with by all parties to the dispute'. In other words, the decision is binding on the parties concerned.

Within section 2 of Part XV, there are rules, set out in Article 287, for the choice of dispute settlement forum. Because of the way these rules work and because of the choices made, or indeed not yet made, under Article 287 by States Parties, it is currently the case that the most likely forum in a dispute between any two States Parties to UNCLOS would be an Annex VII arbitral tribunal.[69]

However, an Annex VII arbitral tribunal is not the only possible outcome. What is more, the parties could, by consensus, potentially choose one of the other forums listed in Article 287(1) (for example, ITLOS) as an alternative (see Article 287(4) and (5)). Questions arise as to what weight a court or tribunal other than ITLOS would give to the AO, but that is beyond the scope of this chapter.

Litigation on this matter (other than the Philippines–China case, on which see section VII below) has not occurred yet. The reasons for that may include, amongst other things, politics or constraints on capacity (including financial capacity).

Of course, ideally, a test case would involve the 'right' coastal State against the 'right' flag State. In practice, the existence of the factors referred to above may lead to a sub-optimal combination of claimant and respondent. However, in view of uncertainties about the application of the due diligence obligation to the high seas (see section V above), coupled with questions about which State(s) would have standing to bring an action in respect of the high seas, it does seem likely that any test case would involve EEZ fisheries rather than high seas fisheries.

It must be emphasised that before any coastal State were to commence proceedings against a flag State, it would be very important for that coastal State to take legal advice on, amongst other things, the following: (a) the jurisdiction of relevant courts and tribunals; (b) the merits of the case; (c) the potential remedies that might be awarded by the court or tribunal concerned; and (d) the potential costs of litigation.

The term 'the merits of the case' as used in (b) above means the chances of the coastal State being successful, including, in particular, the chances of it being able to demonstrate successfully a breach by the flag State concerned of the latter's due

[69] An Annex VII arbitral tribunal was the relevant forum in *The Republic of the Philippines v The People's Republic of China* (Award of 12 July 2016) PCA Case No 2013-19, available at https://pca-cpa.org/en/cases/7, on which see section VII below.

diligence obligation. Outside the purely legal sphere, the political risks of litigation would also be a factor to be taken into account.

VII. The Philippines–China Case

A. Introduction

On 12 July 2016, an arbitral tribunal (hereinafter 'the Arbitral Tribunal') established under Annex VII of UNCLOS, in a case brought by Philippines against China, delivered its Award.[70] The case concerned the South China Sea. The very lengthy award covers multiple issues.[71] However, its consideration of Submission Nos 9, 10 and 12(b) of the Philippines addresses flag State responsibility. The following account of that consideration will focus on general points rather than on what the Arbitral Tribunal finds in respect of either China or Philippines specifically.[72]

B. Submission No 9

In addressing Submission No 9 of the Philippines,[73] the Arbitral Tribunal refers to the AO of ITLOS.[74] It sets out the final part of paragraph 129 of the AO, which, as noted in section V above, concludes that: 'The flag State is under the "due diligence obligation" to take all necessary measures to ensure compliance and to prevent IUU fishing by fishing vessels flying its flag.' The Arbitral Tribunal continues:

> The [Arbitral] Tribunal agrees with the [AO] in this respect. Given the importance of fisheries to the entire concept of the [EEZ], the degree to which [UNCLOS] subordinates fishing within the [EEZ] to the control of the coastal State, and the obligations expressly placed on the nationals of other States by Article 62(4) of [UNCLOS], the [Arbitral] Tribunal considers that anything less than due diligence by a State in preventing its nationals from unlawfully fishing in the [EEZ] of another would fall short of the regard due pursuant to Article 58(3) of [UNCLOS].[75]

It can be seen that, in justifying the existence of an obligation of due diligence on flag States, the Arbitral Tribunal focuses on Articles 58(3) and 62(4) UNCLOS.[76]

[70] ibid.
[71] ibid iii–viii.
[72] For a more detailed analysis of the Arbitral Tribunal's Award in relation to flag State responsibility, see E van der Marel, 'The Due Diligence Obligations of the Flag State with Respect to its Fishing Vessels and the Environment' *The NCLOS Blog* (18 October 2016), https://site.uit.no/nclos/2016/10/18/the-due-diligence-obligations-of-the-flag-state-with-respect-to-its-fishing-vessels-and-the-environment.
[73] The part of the Award dealing with Submission No 9 is entitled 'Alleged failure to prevent Chinese nationals from exploiting the Philippines' living resources' (*The Republic of the Philippines v The People's Republic of China* (n 69) 287).
[74] ibid para 743.
[75] ibid para 744.
[76] See further van der Marel (n 72) 'Commentary'.

ITLOS, in its AO, does likewise; however, it also gives Articles 91, 92 and 94 UNCLOS a prominent role.[77] In any event, what is clear is that the Arbitral Tribunal agrees with the AO about the existence of the due diligence obligation. In addition, its apparent reliance on Articles 58(3) and 62(4) may include a degree of implication about the role Articles 91, 92 and 94, and, in any case, it does not undermine that role.

However, a note of uncertainty does arise in the Arbitral Tribunal's Award, which states:

> In many cases, the precise scope and application of the obligation on a flag State to exercise due diligence in respect of fishing by vessels flying its flag in the [EEZ] of another State may be difficult to determine. Often, unlawful fishing will be carried out covertly, far from any official presence, and it will be far from obvious what the flag State could realistically have done to prevent it.[78]

It is not clear to this author what the Arbitral Tribunal means when it refers to 'the precise scope and application' of the due diligence obligation being 'difficult to determine' in 'many cases'. Assuming that by 'many cases', it means the instances where 'unlawful fishing will be carried out covertly, far from any official presence', it seems to suggest that the existence of IUU fishing in waters 'far from any official presence' renders the obligation's 'scope and application' in some doubt.

This author considers that the scope and application of flag States' due diligence obligation is the same irrespective of the vessels' distance from any 'official presence'. Indeed, it is a feature of fishing that much of it takes place far from any 'official presence'. Contemporary methods of monitoring, control and surveillance (MCS) take that distance into account. Such methods include, amongst other things, the following: satellite-based vessel monitoring systems (VMS); automatic identification systems (AIS); observers; remote electronic monitoring (REM); and electronic logbooks with frequent reporting. All of these methods are imposable by the flag State. What is more, their efficacy can be enhanced by routine cooperation between the flag State and States geographically closer to the vessel (notably coastal States and port States). In this author's view, the deployment of contemporary MCS methods and routine cooperation at the State level are among several measures that lie at the heart of the scope and application of flag States' due diligence obligation.

C. Submission Nos 11 and 12(b)

As noted above, ITLOS, in its AO, elaborates the content of the flag State's obligation of due diligence. It does that, in part, by stating that the flag State is to take

[77] The Arbitral Tribunal does consider art 94 in relation to Submission No 13 on safety of navigation (*The Republic of the Philippines v The People's Republic of China* (n 69) paras 1082, 1083, 1090, 1109. See also para 1060 on the Philippines' submissions.

[78] ibid para 754.

the measures defined in paragraphs 134–40 of the AO. Of these, paragraph 136 states that:

> Pursuant to articles 192 and 193 of the Convention, the flag State has the obligation to take the necessary measures to ensure that vessels flying its flag comply with the protection and preservation measures adopted by the SRFC Member States.

Therefore, in the view of ITLOS, the duty 'to take the necessary measures to ensure that vessels flying its flag comply with the protection and preservation measures adopted by the SRFC Member States' is a part of the flag State's obligation of due diligence. Furthermore, as discussed in section VI above, this duty should be applicable to coastal States in general rather than only to SRFC Member States.

The matter of protection and preservation of the marine environment is considered by the Arbitral Tribunal in its Award in the Philippines–China case in response to Submission Nos 11 and 12(b) of the Philippines.[79] In its findings, the Arbitral Tribunal interprets Part XII of UNCLOS, which deals with the protection and preservation of the marine environment, and finds several duties of due diligence.

First, it holds that 'the general obligation to "protect and preserve the marine environment" in Article 192 includes a due diligence obligation to prevent the harvesting of species that are recognised internationally as being at risk of extinction and requiring international protection'.[80] Second, with reference to Article 194(5) UNCLOS, it holds that 'Article 192 imposes a due diligence obligation to take those measures "necessary to protect and preserve rare or fragile ecosystems as well as the habitat of depleted, threatened or endangered species and other forms of marine life"'.[81] Third, it states that 'the obligation to ensure that … fishing vessels do not take measures to pollute the marine environment' (such as cyanide fishing) is a due diligence obligation for the flag State of those vessels.[82]

To attempt to integrate the Award of the Arbitral Tribunal with the AO of ITLOS, it could be said that where the activities of fishing vessels are relevant to any of the effects described in the previous paragraph and where those effects would be in breach of coastal State laws, the due diligence obligation of flag States 'to take all necessary measures to ensure compliance and to prevent IUU fishing by fishing vessels flying its flag' (see section V above) includes, at a general level, the duty to take the necessary measures to ensure that vessels flying its flag comply with the protection and preservation measures adopted by coastal States (as per paragraph 136 of the AO) and, more specifically, the duty to comply with the three due diligence obligations described in the previous paragraph.

[79] The part of the Award dealing with Submission Nos 11 and 12(b) is entitled 'Alleged failure to protect and preserve the marine environment' (*The Republic of the Philippines v The People's Republic of China* (n 69) 319).

[80] ibid para 956.

[81] ibid para 959.

[82] ibid para 971.

D. Relevance of the Award

The Philippines–China case can, in part, be seen as a case brought by an aggrieved coastal State against a flag State in the context of fisheries. It is the first such case since the delivery by ITLOS of its AO in 2015.

The Arbitral Tribunal was supportive of the conclusion by ITLOS in its AO that the flag State is 'under the "due diligence obligation" to take all necessary measures to ensure compliance and to prevent IUU fishing by fishing vessels flying its flag' (although there was a note of uncertainty about 'the precise scope and application' of the obligation).

In addition, the Arbitral Tribunal identified some due diligence obligations in Part XII of UNCLOS, on protection and preservation of the marine environment, that apply to the flag State, and these can be seen as an elaboration, or a reflection, of the finding by ITLOS in paragraph 136 of its AO.

Overall, in the view of this author, the Philippines–China case is a helpful development in terms of progressing the implementation of flag State obligations in the context of fisheries.

VIII. Conclusion

A newcomer to the scene of international fisheries could be forgiven for thinking that the obligations of certain flag States in the context of fisheries have somehow been transferred to port States, market States and States of nationality.

The reality, of course, is that these obligations still rest firmly with the flag States concerned and that what we see – in terms of the elaborate 'work-around' arrangements in law and policy that have evolved – is a response by the international community to a failure by some of its members to fulfil their obligations when acting as flag States.

That ongoing failure by some flag States represents a failure of international law, in that the international obligation exists, but it remains unenforced. In contrast, the work-arounds – and in particular the development of the role of port States, including the growth of regional and global cooperation in that respect – are important achievements that help to mitigate that failure.

However, is it right that certain States should benefit financially from offering their flags to vessel owners and operators, and yet do very little in return for that benefit in terms of meeting their obligations, especially when the burden is then shouldered by other States and, through IUU fishing, by society in general? Assuming it is indeed not right, what are the options to bring home to flag States their obligations?

One option that has not been tried to date, other than tangentially in the Philippines–China case, is litigation by a coastal State against a flag State. Some of the relevant considerations are explored above. The route has its challenges, including political constraints, constraints on capacity (including financial capacity), identifying the content of the due diligence obligation and collecting the requisite evidence.

However, the AO delivered by ITLOS in Case No 21 is an impetus to look at the litigation option. ITLOS has provided its interpretation of the law and, what is more, has made it clear that liability exists for breach of the due diligence obligation. Is that where things will now rest? Or, slowly and carefully, could a test case be developed that would – without prejudice to the role of port States, market States and States of nationality (and coastal States) – remind flag States of the consequences for them of a failure to fulfil their obligations?

9

Compulsory Inter-State Adjudication in the Anthropocene

Achieving the Paradoxical?

DUNCAN FRENCH

Abstract: The object of this chapter is to consider the future role of international, specifically inter-State, adjudication in resolving disputes within international environmental law, with a particular focus on the emerging challenges of the Anthropocene. The Anthropocene – still in many ways a controversial concept – nonetheless reflects an emerging view that the planet has entered a new geological epoch; one characterised by anthropogenic-induced planetary shifts. This chapter explores just one theme in international adjudication, namely the underlying principle of consensual jurisdiction and the opportunities for so-called compulsory jurisdiction. Is compulsory jurisdiction either a political or a practicable way forward; an absolute necessity in the light of the Anthropocene or a false panacea?

'With infinite complacency men went to and fro over this globe about their little affairs, serene in their assurance of their empire over matter' (HG Wells, *The War of the Worlds* (1897))

'Only within the moment of time represented by the present century has one species – man – acquired significant power to alter the nature of his world' (Rachel Carson, *Silent Spring* (1962))

I. Introduction

The object of this chapter is to consider the future role of international, specifically inter-State, adjudication in resolving disputes within international environmental law, with a particular focus on the emerging challenges of the Anthropocene. The Anthropocene – still in many ways a controversial concept – nonetheless reflects an emerging view that the planet has entered a new geological epoch; one characterised by anthropogenic-induced planetary shifts. Climate change is the most obvious, and discussed, of these changes, but the scale and scope of the challenges are much more diverse and most are as equally systemic in terms of their nature and consequence.[1] Others discount the Anthropocene as scientifically unproven and inaccurate.[2] In any event, and if only partially accurate, the Anthropocene also raises enormous technical, political, cultural and socio-economic decisions for future generations.

Within this debate on what humanity can do to prepare for the Anthropocene, it is a truism that law will play a fundamental role, though the precise contours of what that will be are understandably contested. Broadly, however, it is likely to be framed – positively – in terms of how the law can be changed so that governance (both global and domestic) be made more receptive to dramatically altered planetary conditions, and that regulation be updated, and amended, to be made more effective and adaptive. But it could also be negatively framed in recognising the continuing powerful interests that law often represents, and seeks to protect, and which are capable of obstructing necessary legal reform. In considering the achievements of international law, as this collection does, this chapter throws out the challenge of whether our current structure is fit for purpose going forward. The law is only as good as the next challenge it has to meet.

However, the focus of this chapter is narrower than a general review of the emerging law and Anthropocene literature,[3] and in two principal ways. First, the chapter centres upon international adjudication – and inter-State adjudication at that – rather than broader issues of law-making, regime-building, inducements to compliance etc. This is itself rather novel in many respects, as much of the current literature has so far focused on how to respond proactively to the Anthropocene through the development of new rules and institution-building. There has been much less attention on dispute settlement,[4] despite the central role this has proved to have within international governance and, over the last three decades especially, international environmental law.

Second, and more nuanced, this chapter does not consider what international dispute settlement will, or should, be like once the Anthropocene has fully presented itself. The general risk here is how to talk about normative change in the future tense with little true understanding of how the challenges will ultimately evidence themselves. Thus, to avoid this methodological challenge, the objective

[1] W Steffen et al, 'The Trajectory of the Anthropocene: The Great Acceleration' (2015) 2 *The Anthropocene Review* 81.

[2] J Westcott, 'Written in Stone', available at https://aeon.co/essays/is-rushing-to-declare-the-anthropocene-also-human-error: 'the Anthropocene is a neologism that attempts to pin down a lot of free-floating anxiety'.

[3] See, eg, R Kim and K Bosselmann, 'International Environmental Law in the Anthropocene: Towards a Purposive System of Multilateral Environmental Agreements' (2013) 2 *Transnational Environmental Law* 285; L Kotzé (ed), *Environmental Law and Governance for the Anthropocene* (Oxford, Hart Publishing, 2017).

[4] On the relevance of the judiciary and the Anthropocene, see L Collins, 'Judging the Anthropocene: Transformative Adjudication in the Anthropocene Epoch' in Kotzé (n 3) 309–27.

of the chapter is to consider potential developments in international adjudication, as we enter the *transition* to the Anthropocene. There is no doubt that in many experts' minds we are now transitioning to the Anthropocene. Whether that can be halted, or reversed, is one of the big questions of our time. For law, transition also reflects a period where the status quo and future realities begin to meet and cross over, and opportunities for institutional and normative change can be explored and, with the appropriate political will, tested.

The chapter therefore explores the role of inter-State adjudication in the period of transition: what can be done to prepare for the greater – global – challenges ahead? What prevents further, seemingly more ambitious change? And can one think about fundamental reform without either succumbing to utopian ideals of a planetary political community or regressing to dystopian apathy as to our future inability to adapt? The chapter explores just one theme in international adjudication, namely the underlying principle of consensual jurisdiction and the opportunities for so-called compulsory jurisdiction. Is compulsory jurisdiction, whatever that is taken to mean (and there are various shades that might be given to it), either a political or a practicable way forward? Is it an absolute necessity in the light of the Anthropocene or is it a false panacea? This is, of course, just one issue that international courts and tribunals currently, and will continue to, face. Other issues include – amongst many others – the continued development of environmental principles, the treatment of scientific evidence, the need for increased flexibility in ancillary measures, and the possibilities for effective reparation for harm done and to prevent future harm. One should also not neglect Judge Weeramantry's words on the wisdom of legal civilisations past and present,[5] and thus the corresponding need for broad representation on the bench.

And yet, there is a paradox within the debate on law and the Anthropocene. The current approach to dispute resolution, as with almost every other legal field of endeavour, is firmly embedded within present normative and political structures. Change is possible, but is invariably incremental and subject to various constraints. Dramatic reform of inter-State adjudication, like most areas, is both unlikely and simultaneously its value is inevitably overstated. This would certainly seem to be the case with the notion of compulsory jurisdiction, where compulsion, though alluring, masks not only normative and political complexities but also false hope. This chapter will therefore conclude, if rather counter-intuitively, that despite the narrowing down of the issue to inter-State adjudication as an exemplar of possible reform, the issue points to a much wider question, moving forward. Namely, that if our planetary reality is to change to an extent unforeseen, do we need to make a more radical shift in our thinking? Perhaps to a *lex anthropocenae* – an Anthropocene law?

[5] *Gabčíkovo-Nagymaros Project (Hungary/Slovakia)* [1997] ICJ Rep 7, 96–97.

II. The Anthropocene, International Law and Inter-State Adjudication

International adjudication has shown itself to be an increasingly fundamental feature of international environmental law.[6] Long gone is the time when the only cases to be referenced were *Trail Smelter Arbitration*[7] (admittedly still the only fully decided international adjudication on transboundary atmosphere pollution),[8] *Behring Fur Seals Arbitration*[9] (rarely properly understood), snatched sentences of *Nuclear Tests Cases*[10] and, even more obliquely, the *Corfu Channel* case.[11] The increasing number of international environmental case law now in existence, especially since 1995 – and even more so in the last decade – and, just as important, the broad range of courts and tribunals now dealing with such disputes are more than enough evidence of a maturing discipline, though admittedly one still with incoherencies, both internal to itself and external to other bodies of law.[12] Moreover, while this chapter focuses on inter-State dispute resolution, one should not ignore the environmental disputes arising before a wide array of other tribunals and forums, including human rights courts[13] (and treaty committees), the (admittedly still-mixed) story of environmental matters before investor-State arbitral tribunals,[14] the role of regional courts (eg, the Court of Justice of the European Union) and the increasingly important role played *globally* by domestic courts.[15] It is this panoply which has made environmental dispute resolution such a rich field of enquiry. In addition, and inserted for much more than for the sake of

[6] See generally T Stephens, *International Courts and Environmental Protection* (Cambridge, Cambridge University Press, 2009); J Harrison, 'Reflections on the Role of International Courts and Tribunals in the Settlement of Environmental Disputes and the Development of International Environmental Law' (2013) 25 *Journal of Environmental Law* 501.

[7] *Trail Smelter Case (United States v Canada)* (16 April 1938 and 11 March 1941) 3 RIAA 1905–82.

[8] See D French, 'Trail Smelter (United States of America/Canada) (1938 and 1941)' in C Miles and E Bjorke (eds), *Landmark Cases in Public International Law* (Oxford, Hart Publishing, 2017) 159–88.

[9] *Great Britain v United States* (1893) Moore Intl Arbitrations 755.

[10] *Nuclear Tests (Australia v France)* [1974] ICJ Rep 253, 270; *Nuclear Tests (New Zealand v France)* [1974] ICJ Rep 457, 475. See especially the dissenting opinion of Judge de Castro in *Nuclear Tests (Australia v France)* at 372, 389.

[11] *Corfu Channel Case (United Kingdom v Albania)* [1949] ICJ Rep 4, 22: 'every state's obligation not to allow knowingly its territory to be used for acts contrary to the rights of other states'.

[12] A Boyle, 'Relationship between International Environmental Law and Other Branches of International Law' in D Bodansky et al (eds), *Oxford Handbook of International Environmental Law* (Oxford, Oxford University Press, 2008) 125–46.

[13] See, eg, the 7 February 2018 Advisory Opinion of the Inter-American Court of Human Rights on the environmental obligations of States Parties. For an English summary, see G Vega-Barbosa and L Aboagye, 'Human Rights and the Protection of the Environment: The Advisory Opinion of the Inter-American Court of Human Rights', available at www.ejiltalk.org/human-rights-and-the-protection-of-the-environment-the-advisory-opinion-of-the-inter-american-court-of-human-rights.

[14] M-C Cordonier Segger, M Gehring and A Newcombe (eds), *World Investment Law and Sustainable Development* (The Hague, Kluwer Law International, 2011).

[15] J Peel and H Osofsky, *Climate Change Litigation: Regulatory Pathways to Cleaner Energy* (Cambridge, Cambridge University Press, 2015).

mere completeness, one must mention the putative role of international criminal tribunals in being able to hold those to account who have committed either the recognised 'environmental' war crime[16] or, in light of changes to International Criminal Court (ICC) prosecutorial guidance,[17] where established crimes are evidenced or are exacerbated by environmental-destructive actions. One might also note the broader campaigns to expand environmental consciousness through the establishment of new environmental crimes (most notably ecocide).[18]

Of course, theories of transnational law and polycentric governance have helped,[19] in part, to explain and to provide a descriptive framework for the rise of such a rich array of courts and tribunals, as well as hoping aspirationally that over time, they might lead to a body of unified and challenging case law. Nevertheless, behind this plurality of mechanisms, inter-State dispute resolution remains steadfastly at the core of international adjudication.[20] States continue – and it is to be hoped will continue – to look to independent third-party courts and tribunals to resolve their transboundary and international disputes (environmental or otherwise) with other States. The rise of human rights actions, mixed claims and the like are, of course, not to be in any way discounted; they are fundamental (perhaps even more so) to holding States to account by a wide array of internationally engaged actors[21] – as are such processes as compliance committees in multilateral environmental agreements.

Nevertheless, the focus of this chapter is very much on disputes brought before the International Court of Justice (ICJ), the International Tribunal for the Law of the Sea (ITLOS) and internationally constituted arbitrations as forums for *inter-State* disputes. Equally, as will be noted below, matters of environmental law have also found their way into a broad array of other inter-State proceedings, notably under the World Trade Organization (WTO), and there is always possibility for further developments; one reflects in particular on the inter-State jurisdiction regional human rights courts possess as well as hearing individual claims.[22]

Without seeking to provide a summary of the recent case law, one might note the diversity of inter-State environmental disputes over the last 25 years, both

[16] Rome Statute of the International Criminal Court (adopted 17 July 1998, entered into force 1 July 2002) 2187 UNTS 3, art 8(2)(b)(iv).

[17] ICC Office of the Prosecutor, 'Policy Paper on Case Selection and Prioritisation' (15 September 2016), especially paras 40 and 41.

[18] For general information on this campaign, see the Ecocide Law website: www.eradicatingecocide.com.

[19] See, eg, D Bodansky, 'Climate Change: Transnational Legal Order or Disorder' in T Halliday and G Shaffer (eds), *Transnational Legal Orders* (Cambridge, Cambridge University Press, 2015) 287–308.

[20] This chapter does not consider the role played by Advisory Opinions; nevertheless, it is important to recognise their global normative significance. As the International Court of Justice has made clear, its role in responding to a request for an Opinion is to serve the international community: see *Legal Consequences of the Construction of a Wall in the Occupied Palestinian Territory (Advisory Opinion)* [2004] ICJ Rep 136, 157–58.

[21] Harrison (n 6) 503.

[22] See generally S Prebensen, *Inter-State Complaints under Treaty Provisions: The Experience under the European Convention on Human Rights* (Leiden, Brill, 2009).

in terms of geographical coverage – eg, Europe, South and Latin America, and Asia-Pacific – and subject matter, often raising a broad array of general questions of pollution control and natural resource (mis)use. Of course, it is notable that the geographical coverage is far from universal and that there are certain environmental issues – at least as regards inter-State adjudication – that remain noticeably under-argued. Mention has already been made of the paucity of case law on trans-boundary atmospheric harm and much has been written, for instance, on climate change in this regard.[23] Moreover, the old jurisdictional divides between what is considered a domestic environmental issue, what concerns a shared resource and what relates to a global commons remain a key determinant not only of the existence and extent of international political action, but also of the possibilities of formal legal redress.[24]

Of course, what is an environmental dispute is itself a rightly contested issue[25] and, rightly or wrongly, a specialist environmental tribunal at the international level remains without general support.[26] Preference is still given to bestowing the traditional mechanisms with the opportunity to decide on disputes with an environmental component.[27] Moreover, we have seen environmental issues arising as an important, yet secondary, focus in many of the most recent high-profile 'non-environmental' cases. Perhaps the most notable of these is the *South China Sea Arbitration* (2016) between the Philippines and China.[28] As will be discussed below, that arbitration provides an interesting perspective on the advantages and limitations of how adjudication between States might contribute to effective relations during challenging times.

Nevertheless, this prompts an initial question; why the particular focus on dispute settlement in the *transition* to the Anthropocene? It is impossible within this chapter to do justice to the history of, and the complexity around the debates on, the Anthropocene, and how this will affect human society and the economy. The term 'Anthropocene' is usually attributed to a 2000 article by Crutzen and Stoermer in the International Geosphere-Biosphere Global Change newsletter.[29] At its core, it is the belief that the Earth is now entering a new, disruptive and dangerous phase – and one that humanity, despite initiating it, may not fully understand and may not be able to address or ameliorate. Moreover, despite its inherently

[23] See, eg, P Sands, 'Climate Change and the Rule of Law: Adjudicating the Future in International Law' (2016) 28 *Journal of Environmental Law* 19.

[24] D French, 'Common Concern, Common Heritage and Other Global(-ising) Concepts: Rhetorical Devices, Legal Principles or a Fundamental Challenge?' in M Bowman et al (eds), *Research Handbook on Biodiversity and Law* (Cheltenham, Edward Elgar, 2016) 335–37.

[25] See D French, 'Environmental Dispute Settlement: The First (Hesitant) Signs of Spring?' (2006) 19 *Hague Yearbook of International Law* 3.

[26] See O Pedersen, 'An International Environmental Court and International Legalism' (2012) 24 *Journal of Environmental Law* 547.

[27] A Boyle and J Harrison, 'Judicial Settlement of International Environmental Disputes: Current Problems' (2013) 4 *Journal of International Dispute Settlement* 245.

[28] *The Republic of the Philippines v The People's Republic of China* (Award of 12 July 2016) PCA Case No 2013-19.

[29] P Crutzen and E Stoermer, 'The "Anthropocene"' (2000) 41 *IGBP Newsletter* 17.

scientific focus, the concept has a broader relevance and systemic impact; as Kotzé has noted, 'the term "Anthropocene" is rapidly transcending its initial use as a mere rhetorical device, permitting deeper epistemological and ontological enquiries into regulatory interventions that govern human behaviour on Earth'.[30]

Thus, in answering why this chapter focuses on dispute settlement as we transition towards the Anthropocene, the answer would seem to be both obvious in one sense and perhaps not so in another. As regards the obvious response, it is clear that the environmental challenges going forward will present significant challenges for the global community, and dispute resolution will not be immune from what many might perceive as a governance gap. In particular, there is somewhat of a division between evolutionary and revolutionary thought as to how far the old paradigms will have to adapt to respond to the Anthropocene.[31] And the challenges to general international relations and international law – participation, consent, inducements against free-riding, compliance etc (in other words, effective governance) – is applicable mutatis mutandis to the particularities of international adjudication.

Such reasoning starts from the question as to how far will the 'old ways' of working be effective in tackling the potential shifts – environmental and correspondingly socio-political – ahead? Will change be (too) slow, reactive and incrementally undertaken, or will a constitutional moment arise,[32] linked to dramatic geopolitical change, that will concentrate and refocus minds; that nothing short of a fundamental shift in the normative and governance tectonic plates will be necessary to prevent future crises? Such sweeping considerations are as applicable to international adjudication as they are to other institutional features of the system.

And yet, to understand the likelihood and success of such reform, it must be located within the process of wider systemic change. Indeed, State practice over the centuries would reveal that developments are often grindingly slow. Change has happened, but it has always built on previous and incremental steps. To take the Law of the Sea, for instance – the expertise for which Professor Robin Churchill is renowned[33] – both in terms of the substantive law and, of particular relevance here, the dispute resolution system put in place under the 1982 United Nations Convention on the Law of the Sea (UNCLOS), the law has evolved gradually rather than dramatically. Despite its ambitious scope – categorised later as 'comprehensive' in nature – the rules on dispute resolution in UNLCOS do not dramatically depart from earlier principle, namely that of State consent (at ratification), the right of a State to exempt itself from jurisdiction (when permitted by

[30] Kotzé (n 3) vii.

[31] T Stephens, 'Reimagining International Environmental Law in the Anthropocene' in Kotzé (n 3) 50–51.

[32] ibid.

[33] R Churchill and V Lowe, *The Law of the Sea*, 3rd edn (Manchester, Manchester University Press, 1999).

the treaty) and reliance on traditional models of dispute resolution.[34] It bears all the hallmarks of the strengths and weakness of the general international law from whence it came. Of course, the system has rightly been heralded as one of the most complex in international treaty law,[35] and it certainly is, and yet there is nothing ultimately radical or revolutionary about it.

At the same time, if it is seen over a longer period of time, change can be viewed as much more dramatic. From this perspective, the laissez-faire notion of Grotius' *mare liberum* – at best constrained by the broadest of principles of good neighbourliness – which governed maritime matters since the latter part of the Middle Ages has now been supplanted by a much denser regulatory and adjudicatory framework that seeks to hold even the most powerful States to account for their actions on the seas. It is far from perfect, but the scale of its success is much more impressive when placed within a longer span of time and perspective.

There is another, integrally linked reason for why focusing on dispute resolution is as obvious within this wider debate. As has long been known, dispute resolution can send normative signals to the international community as to what is important, what is a global priority and how States – generally – should act.[36] This includes, but extends beyond, a tribunal's (most particularly the ICJ's)) ability to declare what is and what is not customary international law, or to provide an authoritative interpretation of a treaty provision (or for the ICJ and ITLOS in some situations to provide an advisory opinion). These are all important, but norm-signalling is broader than this; it helps shape a much wider normative debate. The ICJ did not have to endorse sustainable development as a concept in *Gabčíkovo-Nagymaros Project (Hungary/Slovakia)* (1997)[37] and then repeat it in *Pulp Mills on the River Uruguay (Argentina v Uruguay)* (2010),[38] and yet it did. And before that, it certainly did not have to recognise environmental protection in such strident terms as it did in its 1996 *Advisory Opinion on Legality of the Threat or Use of Nuclear Weapons*,[39] but again it did. In part, no doubt, this was to justify

[34] See ibid ch 19, which rightly positions the UNCLOS provisions within the wider context of international dispute settlement.

[35] Y Tanaka, *The International Law of the Sea* (Cambridge, Cambridge University Press, 2012) 390: 'the [Law of the Sea Convention] establishes a unique mechanism combining the voluntary and compulsory procedures for dispute settlement'.

[36] A von Bogdandy and I Venzke, 'On the Functions of International Courts: An Appraisal in Light of Their Burgeoning Public Authority' (2012) *Amsterdam Centre for International Law Research Paper* No 2012-10, 9: 'international courts perform a critical function in signalling credible commitments and thus help to overcome collective action problems'.

[37] *Gabčíkovo-Nagymaros Project (Hungary/Slovakia)* [1997] ICJ Rep 7, 78: 'This need to reconcile economic development with protection of the environment is aptly expressed in the concept of sustainable development.'

[38] *Pulp Mills on the River Uruguay (Argentina v Uruguay)* [2010] ICJ Rep 14, 74: 'the need to strike a balance between the use of the waters and the protection of the river consistent with the objective of sustainable development'.

[39] *Legality of the Threat or Use of Nuclear Weapons (Advisory Opinion)* [1996] ICJ Rep 226, 241: 'The Court also recognizes that the environment is not an abstraction but represents the living space, the quality of life and the very health of human beings, including generations unborn.'

its own reasoning and conclusions, but beyond that to send an important normative signal.

Such a role for international courts and tribunals will become ever more pivotal moving forward into the Anthropocene. This goes beyond the rather sterile debate on international judicial law-making, but is in fact a much more dynamic and fluid example of the positive role that courts and tribunals play in international affairs.[40] Judicial reasoning, when appropriately phrased and timed, can directly impact international negotiations and the mindset of international negotiators. I would go further: it can also aid in setting the parameters of acceptable political discourse on a particular topic. Time and again in international law – and there are examples in environmental law – judicial decisions have shaped the limitations of acceptable normative debate.

As for the particular interest in the *transition* to the Anthropocene and the role of dispute settlement within that, transition suggests a reasonably identifiable temporal period of time between the status quo and the Anthropocene fully realised.[41] I use transition here in a broader sense, it being used as a metaphor for the parallel political imagination necessary to tackle the Anthropocene, as it is for identifiable *real* periods of deteriorating ecological harm. We do not yet see the full consequences of the Anthropocene. We have yet to cross all planetary boundaries. We see some disturbing signs in patterns that we have previously taken for granted – ocean currents, polar ice, coral death and the regularity of seasonal changes – and yet the long-term trend of these changes, whilst almost certainly negative, is not fully ascertained. Moreover, the Anthropocene is not a single moment, but itself will occur over a period of time, at different rates and differently in different global regions, and at different speeds on different environmental matters. The human and economic impact may precede the actual force of the environmental change or we may build up some resilience and manage to not be affected until sometime afterwards (and, on some matters, technology may provide longer-term respite). The speed and endurance of human adaptation will, of course, also be a matter of intragenerational equity between peoples.[42]

Thus, transition is both a physical reality and a political/normative construct. Recognising the duality of this concept is important for this chapter. Legal reform, and in particular in relation to dispute resolution, will need to reflect the importance of finding new ways of doing things moving forward, usually one hopes (though it cannot be guaranteed) progressively. But what should that look like? What changes are necessary? And how should institutional reform be matched with the emerging socio-ecological reality? This is what a period of transition

[40] See C Tams and A Tzanakopoulos, '*Barcelona Traction* at 40: The ICJ as an Agent of Legal Development' (2010) 23 *Leiden Journal of International Law* 781.

[41] Within the debate on the Anthropocene, transition is considered both as a verb ('transitioning' – be it to a sustainable future or towards further planetary damage) and as a noun (as the transition – see, eg, www.ageoftransition.org/the-anthropocene).

[42] C Gonzalez, 'Global Justice in the Anthropocene' in Kotzé (n 3) 234.

allows – if properly utilised – as it can permit experimentation and the testing of new ideas and new ways of doing things. It can trial change, sense-check State willingness to endorse it, and provide an opportunity for reform before reform itself comes too late. This, of course, is rarely how law works; it is often post hoc and thereby struggles to catch up with modern phenomena, be that cultural shifts in gender and sexual equality, the regulation of the internet and social media or tackling new terrorist threats. We see this all the time. But with the potential scale and scope of environmental change predicted, not only must old ways be increasingly subjected to contestation, but so too must the mentality of how (and when) to challenge them.

This chapter will now turn to the issue of consensual jurisdiction as the specific area of inter-State dispute resolution identified in order to consider what reform might look like, what obstacles to reform exist and whether change, however remote, is likely. It can but scratch the surface of a much larger conversation, but it highlights key themes. Though trite, it also warns against easy and populist solutions. There are those that would seem to be solutions and yet when placed within the broader political and legal context will rarely operate as hoped. This is not to be unduly pessimistic of change, but to be realistic as to what can be achieved.

III. Consensual Jurisdiction: Consistency in Principle, Diversity in Practice

One of the perennial questions in international adjudication – other than perhaps the difficulty of enforcement of inter-State awards[43] – is the principle of consent, referred to here as consensual jurisdiction. Other than Article 2(3) of the UN Charter, which mandates the peaceful settlement of all international disputes, the requirement of consensual jurisdiction is undoubtedly the overarching constitutional principle of inter-State dispute resolution. As the Permanent Court of International Justice memorably said: 'No state can, without its consent, be compelled to submit its disputes with other states either to mediation or arbitration, or to any other kind of dispute settlement.'[44] The principle thus provides the basic building block for the system as a whole. As Merrills notes: 'The principle of consensuality is as fundamental to adjudication … as to arbitration.'[45]

While it is a truism to note that States retain a high – though by no means absolute – degree of control over how a dispute is resolved and, in particular, a recalcitrant State can often prevent (or at least delay) dispute resolution, when that dispute is to be resolved through a formal adjudicatory mechanism, legal as well

[43] A Llamzon, 'Jurisdiction and Compliance in Recent Decisions of the International Court of Justice' (2007) 18 *European Journal of International Law* 815.

[44] *Advisory Opinion on the Status of Eastern Carelia* [1923] PCIJ Rep Series B No 5, 27.

[45] J Merrills, *International Dispute Settlement*, 6th edn (Cambridge, Cambridge University Press, 2017) 124.

as political considerations come into play. From a legal perspective, the first and overarching question is whether consent has been given by the States involved. And this is determined by both general, customary norms and the *lex specialis* of the governing treaties, the plurality here recognising that the scope and resolution of the dispute are determined by both the substantive law and the procedural 'adjudicatory' law, which are often not contained within the same texts.[46] Much will, of course, depend on the nature of the dispute, the parties to it and the specificity of the legal rules likely to determine its resolution, as well as (especially important for the purposes of this chapter) what might be termed the wider normative context, ie, whether or not it falls within a legal regime that provides for (obligatory) dispute resolution. Of course, though trite to say, formal adjudication is but one – and not necessarily the most effective – way to resolve international (environmental) disputes. Nevertheless, inter-State adjudication remains, rightly or wrongly, perceived as being at the very top of the dispute resolution pyramid, and an undue amount of political and legal attention is given to it.

One of the preliminary challenges for inter-State environmental dispute resolution is thus whether the States involved are willing, and have consented, to have resolved their dispute by third-party settlement. Of course, willingness and consent are not invariably the same,[47] and indeed often they are not. Whereas consent is a matter of formality – a question of law – and so long as consent can be identified as having been bestowed at some point, it is therefore a static criterion, willingness indicates a broader and more dynamic political acceptance to seek to utilise third-party mechanisms to argue (and settle) the dispute. It often reflects a view – if frequently left implicit – that resolution of the dispute is more important than the dispute itself. Willingness, as broadly understood, therefore captures a range of legal, political and pragmatic elements, many of which are beyond the scope of this chapter. Nevertheless, the two are inextricably linked. A challenge by a State to a tribunal's jurisdiction would generally – though certainly not always – indicate a broader unwillingness to engage, whereas if a State wishes to resolve the dispute through a third-party mechanism, a challenge to consent is much less likely.

As is well understood, formal consent to jurisdiction over a dispute can be granted by States in several ways. First, consent may be granted ad hoc in a legally binding *compromis* between the States Parties involved (once a dispute has arisen and the States can settle on the legal and factual issues that need to be resolved). In those cases where adjudication is to be utilised outside the context of a pre-established court, the *compromis* will also provide the constitutional basis for the establishment of a tribunal, either created from 'scratch' (rare these days) or by reference to an international court or an arbitral tribunal established under the auspices ordinarily of the Permanent Court of Arbitration. There are several instances of environmental disputes reaching international courts or tribunals by

[46] See Harrison (n 6) 504.
[47] B Zangl et al, 'Between Law and Politics: Explaining International Dispute Settlement Behavior' (2011) 18 *European Journal of International Relations* 369.

virtue of a *compromis*, such as *Gabčíkovo-Nagymaros Project (Hungary/Slovakia)* (1997) (namely the ICJ) and *In the Arbitration Regarding the Iron Rhine ('Ijzeren Rijn') Railway (Belgium/The Netherlands)* (2005)[48] (namely arbitration).

Second, consent may be given ante hoc (for instance, ratifying or acceding to a dispute settlement treaty (eg, Article XXXI of the 1948 American Treaty on Pacific Settlement, otherwise known as the Pact of Bogotá as, for instance, relied on in *Aerial Herbicide Spraying (Ecuador v Colombia)* (discontinued))[49] or to a treaty that has a compromissory dispute settlement clause within it, such as the 1975 Statute of the River Uruguay, which provided the basis for the *Pulp Mills* dispute).[50] Such clauses may be obligatory – that is, allowing for the unilateral initiation of a dispute settlement mechanism without the need for further consent by any other party – as was the case in *Pulp Mills*, or be of a voluntary nature, as many are within multilateral environmental agreements (MEAs) where such clauses in fact exist. Article 27 of the 1992 Convention on Biological Diversity, for instance, is wholly permissive:

> 3. When ratifying, accepting, approving or acceding to this Convention, or at any time thereafter, a State or regional economic integration organization may declare in writing to the Depositary that for a dispute not resolved in accordance with paragraph 1 or paragraph 2 above, it accepts one or both of the following means of dispute settlement as compulsory:
>   (a) Arbitration in accordance with the procedure laid down in Part 1 of Annex II;
>   (b) Submission of the dispute to the International Court of Justice.

In contrast, one might compare Article IX of the 1948 Convention on the Prevention and Punishment of the Crime of Genocide on dispute settlement:

> Disputes between the Contracting Parties relating to the interpretation, application or fulfilment of the present Convention, including those relating to the responsibility of a State for genocide or for any of the other acts enumerated in article III, shall be submitted to the International Court of Justice at the request of any of the parties to the dispute.

The ability of a State Party under the Genocide Convention for unilateral initiation of the dispute settlement provision thus generates – perhaps understandably, if not altogether accurately – the sense that it has created a form of compulsory jurisdiction (inaccurate in the sense that it is compulsory only *inter partes* and not as a matter of general law, which the notion of compulsion might ordinarily imply). Nevertheless, in contrast to the open and flexible nature of the use of the formal methods of dispute settlement contained in Article 27(3) of the

[48] *In the Arbitration Regarding the Iron Rhine ('Ijzeren Rijn') Railway between the Kingdom of Belgium and the Kingdom of the Netherlands* (Award of 24 May 2005) 27 RIAA 35.

[49] *Case Concerning Aerial Herbicide Spraying (Ecuador v Colombia)* (Application Instituting Proceedings) General List No 138 [2008] para 7; (Order of 13 September 2013) [2013] ICJ Rep 278 (removal from list). Despite its discontinuance, its relevance was noted by French (n 8) 184.

[50] Harrison (n 6) 503–04.

Biodiversity Convention, the clause in the Genocide Convention noticeably and significantly creates an important secondary obligation, from which States Parties cannot exclude themselves. As of yet, States Parties under MEAs have not utilised formal dispute settlement procedures via such provisions, in part because alternative, more effective non-compliance regimes have been put in place,[51] but also undoubtedly because there is simply not the political interest to hold each other to account through such provisions.[52] Indeed, looking at the ratifications of the Biodiversity Convention, it would appear that less than half-a-dozen States have formally accepted 'compulsory' jurisdiction under Article 27.[53] When an MEA has been the subject of a legal dispute – which so far has been rare (see *Whaling in the Antarctic* below) – or has, slightly less rarely, been argued as applicable law,[54] it has so far come to the attention of courts via other routes.[55]

Third, Article 36(2) of the Statute of the International Court of Justice permits a State to consent to the jurisdiction of the Court in advance '*ipso facto* and without special agreement, in relation to any other state accepting the same obligation, the jurisdiction of the Court in all legal disputes'. Such consent may be unconditionally or conditionally given.[56] Of course, in many ways this system of 'optional declarations' is simply an enhanced variation of an ante hoc compromissory clause, in this case permissively given not by ratification of the ICJ Statute, but by a further legal act. As is well known, this is as close as the negotiators could secure, when establishing the Permanent Court of International Justice after the close of the First World War, a form of compulsory international jurisdiction.[57] It is noticeable that Australia successfully brought its claim against Japan for alleged violations of the

[51] KN Scott, 'Non-compliance Procedures and Dispute Resolution Mechanisms under International Environmental Agreements' in D French et al (eds), *International Law and Dispute Settlement: New Problems and Techniques* (Oxford, Hart Publishing, 2010) 225–70.

[52] See generally Harrison (n 6) 503: 'litigation is considered to entail a number of disadvantages when it comes to environmental disputes, largely because of its predominantly bilateral character and its focus on compensation and restitution, as opposed to prevention'.

[53] Namely (presently) Austria, Cuba, Georgia, Latvia and the Netherlands.

[54] See, eg, *Certain Activities Carried out by Nicaragua in the Border Area (Costa Rica v Nicaragua) and Construction of a Road in Costa Rica along the San Juan River (Nicaragua v Costa Rica)* [2015] ICJ Rep 665, which included, inter alia, interpretation of the 1971 Ramsar Convention on Wetlands of International Importance Especially as Waterfowl Habitat and the 1992 Convention on Biological Diversity.

[55] See also D French, 'Treaty Interpretation and the Incorporation of Extraneous Legal Rules' (2006) 55 *International and Comparative Law Quarterly* 281, with particular reference to the discussion on art 31(3)(c) of the 1969 Vienna Convention on the Law of Treaties ('There shall be taken into account, together with the context … (c) any relevant rules of international law applicable in the relations between the parties'). See also the narrow reading of art 31(3)(c) by the WTO panel in *EC – Approval and Marketing of Biotech Products* (29 September 2006) WT/DS291/R, WT/DS292/R and WT/DS293/R.

[56] Some of these declarations expressly contain conditions excluding environmental and natural resource disputes, including, for instance, that of Canada's declaration ('disputes arising out of or concerning conservation and management measures taken by Canada with respect to vessels fishing in the NAFO Regulatory Area … and the enforcement of such measures'), on which see below.

[57] P-M Dupuy, 'The Danger of Fragmentation or Unification of the International Legal System and the International Court of Justice' (1998–99) 31 *New York University Journal of International Law and Politics* 791.

1946 International Convention for the Regulation of Whaling, decided as *Whaling in the Antarctic (Australia v Japan; New Zealand Intervening)* (2014),[58] under their respective Article 36(2) optional declarations, as the Convention itself had no dispute settlement clause. Similarly, Naura raised its complaints about Australia in *Certain Phosphate Lands in Nauru (Nauru v Australia)* (discontinued)[59] by virtue of their respective optional declarations, as did Spain (unsuccessfully) against Canada in *Fisheries Jurisdiction (Spain v Canada)* (1998).[60]

Unsurprisingly, challenges by the respondent State to the ICJ's jurisdiction have often accompanied a claim unilaterally initiated by virtue of Article 36(2), and a rich jurisprudence has arisen.[61] The way in which the Court has approached such challenges, and especially separate and dissenting opinions of individual judges, has helped develop a more general view as to the relationship between consensual jurisdiction and the necessity of enforcing international law. For some, a narrow reading of consent is essential to preserve respect for State sovereignty[62] and, indeed, State willingness to engage.[63] Others, however, see a wider principle at work. As Judge Weeramantry noted in *Fisheries Jurisdiction (Spain v Canada)* (1998), a case in which the majority ruled against finding jurisdiction:

> Much was made in argument of the negative effects that would ensue to the optional jurisdictional system if the Court were to hold that the reservations clause does not exclude the matter in question from the jurisdiction of the Court. It seems to me, however, that apart from the non-judicial nature of this argument, it is the Court's mission to uphold the integrity of its jurisdiction so far as has been entrusted to it by the optional clause system … It is within this seamless fabric of international law that the entire optional clause system functions, and that consent to the Court's jurisdiction must be construed.[64]

Finally, consent may be given post hoc (namely the practice of *forum prorogatum*).[65] This is the ability of a respondent State to accept the jurisdiction of a court after a unilateral claim (without jurisdiction) has been submitted to it. Pure examples

[58] *Whaling in the Antarctic (Australia v Japan: New Zealand Intervening)* [2014] ICJ Rep 226.

[59] *Certain Phosphate Lands in Nauru (Nauru v Australia) (Preliminary Objections)* [1992] ICJ Rep 240; Order of 13 September 1993 [1993] ICJ Rep 322 (discontinuance).

[60] *Fisheries Jurisdiction Case (Spain v Canada)* [1998] ICJ Rep 432.

[61] See generally Y Shany, *Questions of Jurisdiction and Admissibility before International Courts* (Cambridge, Cambridge University Press, 2015).

[62] For some, this went further than ensuring a narrow reading of the reservation, but granting significant deference to the State's intention. See, eg, the separate opinion of Judge Oda in *Fisheries Jurisdiction Case (Spain v Canada)* (n 60) 479–80: 'Once Canada had excluded from the Court's jurisdiction certain disputes – namely, "disputes arising out of and concerning conservation and management measures" – the meaning of the reservation should, as I have explained above, be interpreted according to the intention of Canada. I am at a loss to understand why the Court should have felt it necessary to devote so much time to its interpretation of the wording of that reservation.'

[63] G Scott and C Carr, 'The ICJ and Compulsory Jurisdiction: The Case for Closing the Clause' (1987) 81 *American Journal of International Law* 57.

[64] See *Fisheries Jurisdiction Case (Spain v Canada)* (n 60) 509–10.

[65] See S Yee, '*Forum Prorogatum* in the International Court' (1999) 42 *German Yearbook of International Law* 147.

of this remain rare in international adjudication and for understandable reasons. Unless there is strong cause to the contrary, most States will not entertain a late encounter before an international tribunal. No environmental case has reached the International Court as yet by this route. The first 'true' dispute to do so was *Certain Criminal Proceedings in France (Republic of the Congo v France)* (2002),[66] followed a few years later by *Certain Questions of Mutual Assistance in Criminal Matters (Djibouti v France)* (2008).[67] Moreover, as the more recent judgment of the International Court in *Obligations Concerning Negotiations Relating to Cessation of the Nuclear Arms Race and to Nuclear Disarmament (Marshall Islands v United Kingdom)*[68] – which prima facie fell under the Court's jurisdiction by way of Article 36(2) – highlights, the majority of the Court now feel that a pre-existing awareness of a dispute by the respondent State is a prerequisite requirement.[69] Though not material to *forum prorogatum* per se (as post hoc consent would render admissible that which was not otherwise), the reasoning in the case nevertheless underlines more generally both the extreme sensitivity States often demonstrate in finding themselves before an international court when they have no desire to be so and the International Court's caution in so finding.[70]

Nothing said so far is exceptional to environmental disputes.[71] To that extent, ensuring environmental disputes are brought before international courts and tribunals raises similar issues to those posed by much of the rest of general international law. Of course, there are likely to be numerous matters – procedural, evidential and in terms of applying the substantive law, which are likely to be bespoke – but at its heart, international environmental dispute settlement benefits from, and is constrained by, those principles derived from the general international framework. To that extent, the current system might be said to achieve its desired result. If one, for instance, considers two (rather random) examples, one can see how the general system works reasonably well when States are willing to engage, either because or despite of their differences. In *Land Reclamation by Singapore in and around the Straits of Johor (Malaysia v Singapore)* (2005),[72] for instance, a dispute

[66] *Certain Criminal Proceedings in France (Republic of the Congo v France)* (Application Instituting Proceedings) General List No 129 [2003]; (Order of 16 November 2010) [2010] ICJ Rep 635 (discontinuance).

[67] *Certain Questions of Mutual Assistance in Criminal Matters (Djibouti v France)* [2008] ICJ Rep 177.

[68] *Obligations Concerning Negotiations Relating to Cessation of the Nuclear Arms Race and to Nuclear Disarmament (Marshall Islands v United Kingdom)* [2016] ICJ Rep 833. See generally V-J Proulx, 'The World Court's Jurisdictional Formalism and its Lost Market Share: The *Marshall Islands* Decisions and the Quest for a Suitable Dispute Settlement Forum for Multilateral Disputes' (2017) 30 *Leiden Journal of International Law* 925.

[69] Proulx (n 68) 854.

[70] Indeed, there is some suggestion that the Court is becoming ever more cautious: 'Whilst the accumulated wisdom of nearly a century of institutionalized state-to-state dispute settlement clearly suggests substance over form, a shift occurred in the Court's recent jurisprudence on contentious jurisdictional issues' (ibid 926).

[71] On specific issues germane to international environmental dispute settlement, see C Romano, 'International Dispute Settlement' in Bodansky et al (n 12) 1036–56.

[72] *Case Concerning Land Reclamation by Singapore in and around the Straits of Johor (Malaysia v Singapore)* (Award on Agreed Terms of 1 September 2005) PCA Case No 2004–05.

arising under the UNCLOS dispute settlement process, Malaysia complained of land reclamation activities by Singapore, which as well as damaging the environment had other negative consequences, including potential infringement of navigation under the Law of the Sea. Following on from provisional measures issued by ITLOS,[73] the parties were able through a joint study to reach a settlement and the arbitral tribunal was thus able to enter an award in the terms of the settlement agreement. The dispute was resolved and the formal mechanisms had played a small yet important component role.

More recently, the International Court has had occasion to consider for the first time the matter of compensation for environmental harm in *Certain Activities Carried out by Nicaragua in the Border Area (Costa Rica v Nicaragua) (Compensation Owed by the Republic of Nicaragua to the Republic of Costa Rica)* (2018).[74] Despite the strained relationship between these two States in recent years, evidenced by several cases brought before the International Court on a range of territorial and boundary questions, the Court has been able to assist the States to clarify their legal relations on a case-by-case basis. Nicaragua informed the Court that on 8 March 2018, barely five weeks after the compensation judgment and well within the deadline set by the Court of April 2018 for interest to start accruing, it had transferred to Costa Rica the total amount of compensation awarded to the latter. The quantum awarded was notably smaller than that requested,[75] which may in part explain the speedy transfer(!), and yet the principle of peaceful settlement of disputes worked. It is perhaps important to recognise that jurisdiction here was based both on an ante hoc provision of a regional dispute settlement treaty (namely, Article XXXI of the Pact of Bogotá, as was relied on in *Aerial Herbicide*) and optional declarations under Article 36.2 of the ICJ Statute.

Thus, inter-State environmental disputes remain very much to be decided within the traditional mould. As noted above, there is little appetite for an environmental court, and even if there were, it is not clear that its constitutional status or operation would differ that much from the courts or tribunals that presently exist, or at least not in any radical sense. Nevertheless, there is one – admittedly putative – feature in environmental law worth mentioning, which does have a direct bearing on the issue of the consensual jurisdiction of the court or tribunal in the dispute resolution process. This is the issue of the material locus of the dispute and the question of standing to be able to enforce a violation. As environmental disputes, by their nature, sometimes cross (or do not involve) statist boundaries – for instance, where it is an area of global commons – it has meant that such disputes have been at the forefront of debates over the *erga omnes* nature of international law rules[76] and the controversial assertion that one State (or a few States) can act in

[73] (Order of 8 October 2003) ITLOS Reports 2003, 10.

[74] *Certain Activities Carried out by Nicaragua in the Border Area (Costa Rica v Nicaragua)* (Judgment of 2 February 2018) [2018] ICJ Rep 15.

[75] Whereas Costa Rica had demanded US$6,711,685.26 plus pre-judgment interest of US$501,997.28, the Court awarded just US$238,740.55.

[76] See generally M Ragazzi, *The Concept of International Obligations* Erga Omnes (Oxford, Clarendon Press, 1997).

actio popularis for the perceived benefit of all.[77] As is well known, the International Court has been clear that it considers that 'the *erga omnes* character of a norm and the rule of consent to jurisdiction are two different things'.[78] As a matter of general law, this would still seem to be true; yet, as French and Scott have noted as regards multilateral treaty obligations: 'By contrast however, the issue of standing appears to be unproblematic as between the parties to a MEA in respect of obligations *erga omnes partes*.'[79]

Putting the issue of standing to one side for one moment, there is a wider point; namely, that in deciding whether (or not) to accede to jurisdiction in such a case, a court is deciding more than just determining its own competence to adjudicate the case; it is altering the balance of power within the international system, both between affected and (supposedly) non-affected States, and between States and the international judicial system. In short, though the narrow issue is one of consent to adjudicate, it touches upon the broader theme of bilateralism versus communitarianism.[80] Recent developments, notably by the International Law Commission[81] and the Seabed Disputes Chamber on this issue,[82] have opened up the possibility not just of standing for the purposes of enforcing the global interest, but also larger questions of responsibility and who is accountable to *whom* for *what*. And yet this is far from a settled area of law and goes to the heart of what role dispute settlement is to have in the international system, an issue that will be picked up in the next section.

Conversely, transboundary environmental disputes – when they do reach an international court or tribunal – often raise fewer jurisdictional questions, and the focus is more often than not on the substance of the primary law and issues of

[77] D French and KN Scott, 'International Environmental Law' in M Bowman and D Kritsiotis (eds), *Conceptual and Contextual Perspectives on the Modern Law of Treaties* (Cambridge, Cambridge University Press, 2018) 682.

[78] *East Timor (Portugal v Australia)* [1995] ICJ Rep 90, 102.

[79] French and Scott (n 77) 682. See, eg, *Application of the Convention on the Prevention and Punishment of the Crime of Genocide (The Gambia v Myanmar)* (Request for the Indication of Provisional Measure: Order of 23 January 2020) General List No 178 [2020], para 41: 'In view of their shared values, all the States parties to the Genocide Convention have a common interest to ensure that acts of genocide are prevented and that, if they occur, their authors do not enjoy impunity … It follows that any State party to the Genocide Convention, and not only a specially affected State, may invoke the responsibility of another State party with a view to ascertaining the alleged failure to comply with its obligations *erga omnes partes*, and to bring that failure to an end.'

[80] See generally U Fastenrath et al (eds), *From Bilateralism to Community Interest: Essays in Honour of Bruno Simma* (Oxford, Oxford University Press, 2011).

[81] See art 48 of the International Law Commission (ILC), 'Draft Articles on Responsibility of States for Internationally Wrongful Acts' (2001) UN Doc A/56/10, which permits the invocation of responsibility by a State where the obligation is owed to the international community as a whole and allows that State to demand that the State in breach cease the wrongful conduct and provide appropriate reparation to injured States.

[82] It is notable that in Advisory Opinion No 17, the Seabed Disputes Chamber of the International Tribunal for the Law of the Sea relied on art 48 of the ILC Draft Articles on State Responsibility when it stated that: 'Each State Party may also be entitled to claim compensation in light of the *erga omnes* character of the obligations relating to preservation of the environment of the high seas and in the Area' (*Responsibility and Obligations of States Sponsoring Persons and Entities with Respect to Activities in the Area* (Advisory Opinion of 1 February 2011) ITLOS Reports 2011, 10, 54).

fact. Nevertheless, even where parties show a willingness to resolve the dispute (for instance, by means of a *compromis* adopted after the dispute has arisen), fundamental legal arguments can arise on such matters as the scope of the applicable law, provisional measures and requested remedies. And though consent to jurisdiction may not be a matter of contention in that *particular* case, when one takes a longer-term view of the utility of international adjudication, how courts operate in one case and how far States are then willing to engage with them *in the future* are inextricably linked; State confidence in international courts and tribunals is the lifeblood of their continued existence.[83] As there have been relatively few international cases seeking to resolve transboundary and commons environmental disputes and almost zero attempts by States to challenge, through international courts, other States' domestic environmental abuses where they are of global relevance,[84] the question then becomes would a form of compulsory jurisdiction strengthen environmental dispute resolution?

IV. 'Compulsory Jurisdiction': Meanings, Misunderstandings and False Utopias

It is within the context of both perceived inefficacies of international dispute resolution (certainly in the face of the challenges of the Anthropocene) and concurrently the relatively low level of State engagement with the formal mechanisms that arguments are aired that inter-State dispute resolution should in some way be made 'compulsory'. Such arguments seemingly become more convincing and urgent when the objective to be achieved is perceived as being of global importance. The main rationale would be that individual discretion – ie, State sovereignty – be subjugated to the wider needs of the international community. As the anticipation of the Anthropocene arises, so does the need for action, though what that action might be is often constrained to just an enhanced variant on the *status quo*. As Kotzé notes:

> In time it will be necessary, however, to create judicial bodies where they do not exist or strengthen existing ones; expand the jurisdictions of these bodies; and create specialised environmental units within each to deal with highly technical and specialised environmental issues.[85]

For those who view the status quo as inadequate and fundamentally flawed, it requires more than tinkering at the edges; it requires setting aside traditional

[83] The response of the Global South to the *South West Africa* litigation is well known.

[84] *cf* the arbitral tribunal in *The South China Sea Arbitration (The Republic of the Philippines v The People's Republic of China)* remarked that the jurisdictional reach of the dispute settlement processes extended to environmental harm within a State's territorial sea as the 'environmental provisions of the Convention impose obligations on States Parties including in the territorial sea': (*Award on Jurisdiction and Admissibility of 29 October 2015*) PCA Case No 2013-19, para 408(a).

[85] L Kotzé, 'Global Environmental Constitutionalism in the Anthropocene' in Kotzé (n 3) 210.

doctrinal restraints. At the heart of such arguments is the belief that transboundary and commons environmental harm is so obviously per se an international bad that holding States to account for violations of international environmental law must invariably be seen as a good worth pursuing, regardless of institutional and normative barriers. Neglecting for the moment whether traditional dispute settlement should be seen either as the principal or the most effective means of holding States to account, the premise is that the current system is weak because States, unless they already have agreed to do so, can opt in to dispute resolution at their discretion.

How can such a system be effective when the world is faced with such global-level pressures? It cannot simply be a case of more of the same if the 'more' still relies on the same limiting principles of consent and consensual jurisdiction. In one sense, it is nothing more than a more updated version of the criticisms of international law of John Austin, and realists ever since. International law lacks effective enforcement mechanisms, and no reform of the current system can remedy that which is still reliant on the limitations of the status quo. This, of course, confuses dispute resolution and compliance – an important distinction that international environmental law has done much to demarcate;[86] nevertheless, as noted above, inter-State dispute resolution is still perceived as being at the apex of the enforcement pyramid, and from this perspective, it is simply not working well enough.

Other scholars have come to similar conclusions from different perspectives, notably the effectiveness of regional (ie, EU) law, the primacy of rights within a liberal order and the need for the international community to accept an increased constitutionalism. Perhaps it was most stridently brought together by Petersmann under the heading 'Need for Compulsory International Adjudication', in which he argues: 'WTO law and European integration law are based on the constitutional insight that protection of individual rights and the rule of law require compulsory judicial protection at the national and international level. Without access to impartial courts, human rights and the rule of law cannot prevail.'[87] Thus, at one level, the allure of compulsory dispute settlement as part of a broader argument for enhanced global governance would seem to be not only appealing but almost inevitable. For those willing to entertain such arguments, reasoning such as Judge Weeramantry's, who in the *Fisheries Jurisdiction Case* talked of 'the integrity of the entire system of international law, which is a seamless web',[88] begins to take on a new meaning. As Kotzé and French have noted:

> [A] full-scale transition from anthropocentrism to ecocentrism … and the way they are used to mediate the human-environment interface in the Anthropocene, would be

[86] R Mitchell, 'Compliance Theory: Compliance, Effectiveness, and Behaviour Change in International Environmental Law' in Bodansky et al (n 12) 893–921.

[87] E-U Petersmann, 'Constitutionalism and International Adjudication: How to Constitutionalize the UN Dispute Settlement System' (1999) 31 *New York University Journal of International Law and Politics* 780.

[88] *Fisheries Jurisdiction Case* (n 60) 510.

> fraught with several, seemingly insurmountable challenges … Despite or because of these challenges, the need for the world's regulatory institutions to transition into more ecocentric manifestations becomes all the more pronounced.[89]

States should not be allowed to rely on the very sovereignty that in many cases permitted the environmental misuse to take place in the first place. Ensuring enforcement would reinforce the proposition that there is an all-encompassing international rule of law under which States are expected to act; one might even begin to talk of an emerging ecological, or ecocentric, rule of law.[90]

Nevertheless, the possibility of something more ambitious should always be carefully scrutinised; it is easy to propose something in international law when the consequences are not fully considered. To begin with, precisely what 'compulsory dispute resolution' might mean needs to be acknowledged as rather vague. Taken at its most straightforward, it is the argument that States should not be able to prevent a court or tribunal from possessing jurisdiction when a dispute is brought before it. Of course, *in extremis*, this is patently nonsense if it conflates a State's consent to jurisdiction with a court or tribunal's authority to exercise jurisdiction over the matter. Though linked, the two are very different. Removing the requirement of the former is seen as preventing a State from determining for itself whether or not to be subject to international adjudication when it has violated international law. The argument – often derived from the hierarchical nature of domestic law[91] – revolves around the question of why should a State be able to exclude third-party resolution to protect its own interests? The chapter will return to this issue shortly.

On the other hand, assuming that the court or tribunal has jurisdiction over the matter in the first place is an altogether different question. It raises broader institutional challenges – some might rightly say naïveté – as to how international law operates. Of course, a court like the International Court of Justice does indeed have potential plenary jurisdiction over any matter of dispute – any 'question of international law'[92] – between States, the principal limitations being whether consent has appropriately been bestowed and whether the Court itself discovers any reason to find the matter inadmissible. But as a matter of course, no other international court has authority over such a general range of matters;[93] instead, the jurisdictional authority of a court or tribunal is set by its constitutive instrument and is invariably subject-specific and party-specific. To ascribe to a court or

[89] L Kotzé and D French, 'The Anthropocentric Ontology of International Environmental Law and the Sustainable Development Goals: Towards an Ecocentric Rule of Law in the Anthropocene' (2018) 7 *Global Journal of Comparative Law* 30.

[90] ibid 32.

[91] See R Bilder, 'Some Limitations of Adjudication as an International Dispute Settlement Technique' (1982–83) 23 *Virginia Journal of International Law* 1.

[92] As worded in art 36(2)(b) of the Statute of the International Court of Justice. The wording in art 36(1) of the Statute is even broader: 'all cases which the parties refer to it and all matters specially provided for in the Charter of the United Nations or in treaties and conventions'.

[93] *cf* Dupuy (n 57) 791: '[The International Court] is still the judicial body that, at the universal level, possesses the largest jurisdiction.'

tribunal a jurisdiction *ratione personae* or *ratione materiae* that it does not possess would not make the system more effective; it would simply raise questions over its legitimacy. How would it be properly constituted if not by States?

The current situation, for instance, as regards the expansion of its powers by the Inter-American Commission of Human Rights against States that have not accepted its authority in this regard, notably the US, is a telling controversy as to how far non-State bodies can and should go, and can and should not go, as regards the imposition of third-party scrutiny and overview.[94] A similar, if not more strenuous response would be forthcoming if a court sought to try the same approach. Indeed, it would seem that the Inter-American Court of Human Rights has begun to approach its jurisdiction in quite the same way.[95] One might ask the following question: if such expansion of jurisdiction is illegitimate, is any form of compulsory jurisdiction without State consent any different?[96]

It is therefore obvious that a much more nuanced approach is necessary than a mere wholesale removal of the requirement of consent. Specifically, as sovereignty will continue to underpin the fundamental features of any system,[97] it then becomes necessary to view consent as more than just an unnecessary obstacle to be removed at a whim, but rather to reflect how consent is currently bestowed, and to review the pros and cons of strengthening models of dispute settlement. On considering the present array of dispute regimes currently in existence, there is a broad array of approaches. These range from those which might be termed 'integral' and 'comprehensive' regimes right through to methods that are completely voluntary and ad hoc (on which, see above). It is the former that are now of interest. Such terms are, of course, debatable and rather contentious, yet undoubtedly for those regimes with a complicated scheme of dispute settlement, they invariably reflect a certain ambition in institutional design. Moreover, as the mechanisms employed ensure that a complete, or particularly broad, set of disputes fall within their respective jurisdictional nets, they perhaps come as close to 'compulsory' as treaty law presently provides. Of course, formal consent is preserved at ratification, and yet the possibility of being subject to third-party resolution of a dispute is notably increased.

[94] See Response of the US Government to the Inter-American Commission on Human Rights' Report 85/00 of October 23, 2000 (November 2001): 'the Declaration does not create legally-binding obligations and therefore cannot be "violated"'. See also C Gonzales, 'Environmental Racism, American Exceptionalism, and Cold War Human Rights' (2017) 26 *Transnational Law and Contemporary Problems* 281.

[95] G Neuman, 'Import, Export, and Regional Consent in the Inter-American Court of Human Rights' (2008) 19 *European Journal of International Law* 117.

[96] There are alternatives in the international system, however imperfect, including 'the importance of identifying creative solutions in this context, suggesting the United Nations General Assembly (UNGA) as a law-making facilitator and the UN Security Council (UNSC) as an alternate dispute settlement forum to tackle multilateral disputes with global security implications': Proulx (n 68) 928.

[97] See, eg, the strong wording in *Dispute Concerning Access to Information under Article 9 of the OSPAR Convention (Ireland v United Kingdom)* (Award of 2 July 2003) 23 RIAA 59, para 102, in which it was noted that: 'A treaty is a solemn undertaking and States Parties are entitled to have applied to them and to their peoples that to which they have agreed and not things to which they have not agreed.'

An 'integral' regime would indicate the acceptance by States of formal dispute resolution as being integral to the acceptance of the primary treaty obligations themselves, perhaps best encapsulated within the framework of the WTO dispute settlement regime,[98] which coincidentally also contains important and generally effective post-award implementation mechanisms. Somewhat similar in nature has been the investor-State dispute settlement system under bilateral and regional investment regimes.[99] On the other hand, a 'comprehensive' approach might describe a similarly broad ante hoc approach to jurisdiction, yet with important caveats, either in terms of court choice or with important jurisdictional limitations. A very good example of such a regime would be the dispute settlement system under UNCLOS,[100] which is comprehensive in many respects,[101] yet not as overarching as the WTO system.

Whilst not as complete as the WTO regime, it is also important to recognise certain innovative aspects of the UNCLOS framework, including where ITLOS has default ('compulsory') jurisdiction, namely on provisional measures[102] and the prompt release of vessels.[103] This would suggest that States are willing to negotiate instances where State choice is secondary to other imperatives, for instance, for reasons of expediency and urgency. Just as the integrity of the WTO dispute system is ultimately premised on non-legal reasons of reciprocity of all parties being held equally to account, these particular instances within UNCLOS suggest that there are also occasions when overt State sovereignty considerations will be made secondary to broader considerations. And staying with UNCLOS, of particular note is the jurisdiction of the Seabed Disputes Chamber (SDC)[104] and the much tighter considerations placed on State discretion as regards its jurisdiction, again reflecting the perceived need for a more obligatory requirement because of the objective being sought to be achieved. Of course, as noted above, formal State consent is preserved, given at ratification or accession, and yet both as regards the special procedures of ITLOS and as regards the SDC, it reveals the capacity

[98] T Schoenbaum, 'WTO Dispute Settlement: Praise and Suggestions for Reform' (1998) 47 *International and Comparative Law Quarterly* 648: 'There is compulsory jurisdiction; disputes are settled largely by applying rules of law; decisions are binding upon the parties; and sanctions may be imposed if decisions are not observed.'

[99] As regards recent proposals to replace the present approach with an international court system, see P Bernardini, 'Reforming Investor–State Dispute Settlement: The Need to Balance Both Parties' Interests' (2017) 32 *ICSID Review* 38.

[100] See – noting the title of the piece in particular – R Churchill, 'Trends in Dispute Settlement in the Law of the Sea: Towards the Increasing Availability of Compulsory Means' in French et al (n 51) 143–71.

[101] See, in particular, art 297 (limitations on applicability) and art 298 (optional exceptions) UNCLOS. As Churchill and Lowe (n 33) 454–55 note: 'The exceptions are designed to take out of the compulsory settlement process certain categories of dispute that touch upon vital interests of the State … Certain exclusions are prescribed by the Convention itself.'

[102] UNCLOS, art 290(5).

[103] ibid art 292.

[104] ibid art 187; *cf* art 189 (limitation on jurisdiction with regard to decisions of the International Seabed Authority).

through clever institutional design (and political will) to maximise State participation in dispute settlement towards what many might call the obligatory.

It would therefore seem axiomatic that the ante hoc bestowal of consent is to be preferred if the objective is to ensure greater third-party adjudication. Ad hoc and post hoc consent is more arbitrary and dependent on the political wishes of the governing interests at the time. Ante hoc consent on the other hand often removes that obstacle. The historically high caseload in the WTO and the increasing number of UNCLOS cases would both be apparent testament to this. And yet, consent bestowed (well) in advance is always subject to the risk of some level of contestation, and even if the consent itself cannot genuinely be questioned – for instance, within the WTO – it can still raise the dichotomy, identified above, between consent and willingness.[105] Much more telling of course is when a State denies that it has given consent or, more likely, that its consent does not extend to the particular dispute in question. Twice recently, this has happened in UNCLOS proceedings; Russian objections in *The Arctic Sunrise Arbitration (The Netherlands v Russia)*[106] and Chinese rejection of the legality and authority of the UNCLOS arbitral tribunal as regards the *South China Sea* dispute.[107] In both cases, not only was consent said by the respondent State not to extend to the dispute in question, but the State evidenced this lack of consent by its non-attendance at the hearings and political non-acceptance of the Award.[108] Few cases actually result in non-participation, but especially in the case of the *South China Sea* dispute, the procedural and evidential difficulties that this then creates for the tribunal and the political reality of the non-acceptance of the Award all speak to difficulties which a move towards compulsory jurisdiction – in whatever form – would invariably create.

Of course, over time, the non-accepting State may in some form accept the ruling (if never the process undergone), but there is no certainty of this. It also places the arbitral tribunal in a supremely powerful – if unenviable – position at the jurisdictional stage to decide on objections to jurisdiction and whether it has the consent to proceed. Should a tribunal interpret its jurisdiction broadly and narrow down reservations to consent? To do so would seemingly promote that 'haven of legality within the international system',[109] which Weeramantry talked

[105] This places other challenges on the system, and the recent political deadlocks within the WTO on Appellate Body membership is a reminder of the enduring power of (the most influential) States – which need to be seen within the context of any easy move to so-called compulsory jurisdiction. See 'Contemporary Practice of the United States: United States Blocks Reappointment of WTO Appellate Body Member' (2016) 110 *American Journal of International Law* 573–79. See also T Payosova, GC Hufbauer and JJ Schott, 'The Dispute Settlement Crisis in the World Trade Organization: Causes and Cures', available at www.piie.com/publications/policy-briefs/dispute-settlement-crisis-world-trade-organization-causes-and-cures.

[106] *The Arctic Sunrise Arbitration (The Netherlands v Russia)* (Award on the Merits of 14 August 2015) PCA Case No 2014-02.

[107] K Parlett, 'Jurisdiction of the Arbitral Tribunal in Philippines v China under UNCLOS and in the Absence of China' (2016) 110 *AJIL Unbound* 272.

[108] *Arctic Sunrise Arbitration* (n 106) para 8.

[109] *Fisheries Jurisdiction Case* (n 60) 510.

about in relation to Article 36(2), but applies arguably as meaningfully here, yet it is not without its long-term implications.[110] If the ultimate objective is to seek (early) resolution of the dispute, preliminary disputes over consent are rarely a positive sign of willing engagement. More worryingly for the system as a whole, a tribunal which is viewed as finding jurisdiction too liberally may itself be challenged both legally and extra-judicially going forward by wider sections of the international community.

For both doctrinal and realist scholars of international law, it is no surprise that any form of compulsory jurisdiction is a false start – a utopian panacea to circumvent State refusal to consent to jurisdiction. Nevertheless, even where consent is formally given, willingness may not follow if States feel aggrieved at the jurisdictional decision. However, this must be counter-balanced by the fact that whether a State politically accepts the jurisdiction of the tribunal is irrelevant as a matter of law. It also makes no difference whether the respondent party is a permanent member of the UN Security Council or not. Indeed, if it is, it sends an even more powerful message as to the coverage of the rule of law. Take the *South China Sea* arbitration, for instance. Here is a strongly worded Award on important questions of law of the sea and marine environmental protection, which provides key determinations on hugely contested *legal* questions[111] and, just as importantly, moves the law generally forward for the international community as a whole and the region in question in particular.[112] From an environmental perspective in particular, the Award is notably progressive and stronger in tone than many would have expected.[113] The wording is not just for China alone. It sends strong norm-signals to the rest of the international community as to their responsibilities under both treaty and customary international law. It is to be hoped that China will come to respect the Award, but that does not nullify the existence or legality of the Award in any formal sense.

So, what of compulsory jurisdiction? In its extreme form, of course, it exists in a fantasy realm of global governance where State sovereignty is easily disregarded. More importantly, it risks ignoring genuine real-world issues beyond the dispute itself, both in terms of the likely implementation of any judgment and the perceived future integrity and value of the dispute settlement system – what I previously referred to as the lifeblood of any court. But that is 'compulsory' jurisdiction at its extreme. Nonetheless, there are shades of meaning here. Notwithstanding challenges in the provision of ante hoc consent in particular, it remains a principled

[110] *cf* T Schoenbaum, 'The South China Sea Arbitration Decision: The Need for Clarification' (2016) 110 *AJIL Unbound* 295: 'The Tribunal's one-sided rulings are unlikely to contribute to resolving the dangerous disputes in the South China Sea.'

[111] On the particularly controversial issue of the determination of the nature of the physical features, see L Reed and K Wong, 'Marine Entitlements in the South China Sea: The Arbitration between the Philippines and China' (2016) 110 *American Journal of International Law* 746.

[112] See D French, 'In the Matter of the South China Sea Arbitration: Republic of Philippines v People's Republic of China, Arbitral Tribunal Constituted under Annex VII to the 1982 United Nations Law of the Sea Convention' (2017) 19 *Environmental Law Review* 55.

[113] ibid: 'the Award is particularly strong on holding States to account for environmental damage, in a way that few Law of the Sea cases have yet done'.

and strong means by which disputes can arrive at the doors of an international court or tribunal, without the contemporary consent of the respondent State.

And in relation to environmental disputes, it certainly would be advantageous if multilateral environmental agreements had rather stronger compromissory clauses; the regimes would undoubtedly be strengthened if at least key provisions were potentially subject to 'compulsory' dispute settlement, even if like UNCLOS they excluded particularly sensitive areas of State discretion. The *Whaling in the Antarctic* case reveals a putative appetite for *erga omnes partes* actions and, importantly, the Court found no cause to question that as a basis for Australia's standing. It is not a true *actio popularis*, of course, and requires an *inter partes* relationship to exist, but beyond this, can one foresee compulsion in *general* inter-State adjudication? The Seabed Disputes Chamber's 2011 Advisory Opinion gives some cause for optimism, and the ICJ has certainly not shut the door on the matter, though its judgment in the *Marshall Islands* case is arguably unduly formalistic in this regard. Thus, perhaps rather than seeking a universal truth, which the complexity of the international system does not encourage, it is better to embrace the traditional Chinese proverb: 'let a thousand flowers bloom'. Diversity rather than uniformity may be the preferred option here. The mechanics, of course, of *how* to improve the present processes and regimes will need to be reserved for another work.[114] And yet, nothing will be achieved without the necessary political will to respond to the challenges of the Anthropocene.

V. Beyond Dispute Resolution: Towards a *Lex Anthropocenae*?

In writing on law and the Anthropocene, Stephens has noted the paradox that:

> [I]nternational environmental law must therefore achieve a delicate (and quite conceivably impossible) balance in the Anthropocene. It must become more pragmatic, less focused on the local and more oriented towards protecting globally integrated environmental systems in order to sustain human civilisation. Yet at the same time it must not succumb to a technocratic temptation towards 'quick fixes'.[115]

This is as challenging for the particular as it is for the general, and there is no reason not to locate this chapter's focus on dispute resolution within this broader narrative of normative ambition and political despair. The 'technocratic temptation' Stephens very pointedly refers to is to such schemes as climate geoengineering, and yet arguably the same point holds for other 'quick fixes' such as that crafted

[114] For instance, as Harrison ((n 6) 506) notes: 'states wishing to bring actions to promote environmental protection may be left trawling through the patchwork of jurisdictional provisions in various treaties in order to identify an appropriate foundation for a legal claim. We are therefore a long way from all environmental disputes coming to court, even if that were desirable'.

[115] Stephens (n 31) 53.

by other instruments available to human society, including law. The context for all societal endeavours is both cultural and complex. As Bosselmann notes: 'The narratives that shape our lives, attitudes and behaviours urgently need changing … The narrative will, of course, also be influenced by the experiences of our children and grandchildren, to whom we have bequeathed a planet very different to the one enjoyed by humanity during the Holocene.'[116] A system of law devised in a previous era will take time and prove difficult to adjust; political will, not false panaceas, is ultimately what is required.

Thus, it is clear that whether one takes a narrow or a broader perspective on these things, dispute resolution, be it incremental change or radical compulsion, can only ever be one element of a much more complex normative and political response to the forthcoming challenges of the Anthropocene. And whether such impending events – 'crises' still seems hyperbolic – are seen as an opportunity to revisit global theory or merely to update, in a more evolutionary way, classic international legal rules, legal reform is a *sine qua non* response to what now confronts us. And yet I am left wondering whether our ambition for such reform is itself framed by the limitations of our own experience, mine as much as anyone's. Namely, it is the often unspoken truism that what we can imagine is often restricted to what we think is imaginable. The mere fact that the word 'crises' seemed too emotive a few sentences ago is itself surely testimony to my own literary and methodological constraints.

However, not all are so encumbered. Even within the mainstream legal literature – as compared to the works of cosmopolitan international relations scholars, futurists or, even more outlandishly, science-fiction novelists – there are glimmers of a broader consciousness. The work of Philip Allott is one of the most well-known examples, though perhaps the paucity of others writing at a similar level and in a similar way suggests a general unwillingness to grapple with the bigger questions. I am reminded of what he said in *Eunomia*, which I quoted in my PhD under the supervision of Professor Robin Churchill, to whom this chapter, and this edited collection, is dedicated – 'law which was not adequate to a less complex condition of society will be still less adequate to a greatly more complex condition of society'.[117]

Thus, while it is absolutely right to focus on the doctrinal (and some would say the minutiae) aspects of the law – as much of this chapter has done – and nothing I now say in this conclusion undermines my earlier plea to focus on the *transition* to the Anthropocene as a more practicable and realistic option than trying to grapple with the enormity of when things have already and irreversibly changed, counter-intuitively I am led to recognise the limitations of my own focus. If the ecological and societal challenges presented to us are half as great as is feared, we must not

[116] K Bosselmann, 'The Imperative of Ecological Integrity: Conceptualising a Fundamental Legal Norm for a New "World System" in the Anthropocene' in Kotzé (n 3) 265.

[117] P Allott, *Eunomia: A New Order for a New World* (Oxford, Oxford University Press, revised paperback edn, 2001) 298.

be resistant to challenge ourselves as to what law is required in the longer term. This volume has sought to identify the achievements of international law, but these do not remain static, and the discipline of law is only as effective as its capacity to tackle future problems.

And here I conclude by merely suggesting the importance of further research; benefiting from the invariable aspiration that writing in a *festschrift* permits. Namely, to consider what a *lex anthropocenae*, an Anthropocene law, might look like; a body of law that works within the constraints of our ecological reality, and the social and economic consequences arising therefrom. Not rejecting, but equally not being constrained by, traditional dichotomies of law – public/private international law, global/domestic, constitutional and administrative/private and transactional law etc – but rather seeing these as descriptors of a wider law, being supported and supplemented by other normative forms: transnational rules, customary norms and, indeed, new ways of governing.

There are no easy answers; it certainly could neither be the *lex mercatoria* of old, which broadly eschewed State regulation, on the one hand, nor the global government of cosmopolitan dreaming, on the other. A purposeful *lex anthropocenae* could not be either so limiting or so impractical. Moreover, I would suggest that the normative scope of such a body of law could not – and should not – be capable of precise delimitation, as delimitation then begins to create exclusionary silos, both of which have always been a significant part of the problem of the past. Rather, *lex anthropocenae* would provide a freedom for imagining both the *process* and *purpose* of reform beyond that which our present normative restrictions ordinarily permit.

And new ways of law-making will invariably prompt new ways to think about dispute settlement, the (re)design of the former invariably impacting upon the operation and effectiveness of the latter. Moreover, as this chapter on the present requirement of consensual jurisdiction in inter-State dispute resolution has hopefully shown – in many ways, one corner of one issue – creative and imaginary thinking is essential to awaken the 'infinite complacency' of peoples and States (humanity in all its complexity) from being 'serene in their assurance of their empire over matter'. It is this ability to adapt that will allow international law to tackle society's challenges and the wider community's needs. Perhaps – just perhaps – we can then begin 'to see that international law, old and new together, forms part of an emerging universal legal system which transcends the imaginary frontier between the national and the international'.[118]

[118] ibid xv–xvi.

PART IV

International Environmental Law

10

The Challenge of Effective Compliance and Enforcement with International Environmental Law

CATHERINE REDGWELL

Abstract: International environmental law is often considered to have an absence of effective compliance and enforcement mechanisms. This chapter outlines the parlous state of the global environment, notwithstanding extensive international environmental law-making over the past few decades, and considers the inadequacies of traditional dispute settlement for the enforcement of international environmental obligations. It also addresses the innovative role of implementation monitoring and compliance under multilateral environmental agreements, particularly in reference to biodiversity-related treaties. The chapter concludes that notwithstanding these innovations, the accelerating deterioration of the environment and the failure to comply with procedural and substantive environmental treaty obligations continues to undermine efforts at nature conservation.

I. Introduction

International environmental law (IEL) is often lamented to contain a 'soft underbelly'[1] owing to the absence of effective compliance and enforcement.[2] This frailty is particularly, though by no means exclusively, evident in species and habitat protection,[3]

[1] Criticism may also be made of the weakness of the substantive rules, which not even full compliance can redress: RB Mitchell, 'Compliance Theory: Compliance, Effectiveness, and Behaviour Change in International Environmental Law' in D Bodansky, J Brunnée and E Hey (eds), *Oxford Handbook of International Environmental Law* (Oxford, Oxford University Press, 2007) 893.

[2] Enforcement is part of the wider compliance process and generally refers to steps taken once there has been a violation of an international environmental obligation, whether that obligation is procedural (eg, reporting obligations) or substantive (eg, obligation to protect and preserve the marine environment) in character. See further EB Weiss, 'Understanding Compliance with International Environmental Agreements: The Baker's Dozen Myths' (1999) 32 *University of Richmond Law Review* 1555, 1562–63 (noting, inter alia, that implementation, compliance, enforcement and effectiveness are not synonymous).

[3] The principal examples drawn on in this chapter are from the 'big five' of multilateral species and habitat treaties, namely, the 1971 Ramsar Convention on Wetlands of International Importance

where the harm caused – eg, species extinction – may be irremediable and non-compensable, and intergenerational in its impacts. Yet treating non-compliance as a breach of international law and with the legal effect of terminating the non-complying State's participation in the treaty is an inappropriate response here for several reasons, not least of which is that the purpose of many multilateral environmental agreements (MEAs) is to protect the global and/or regional environment through participation in and compliance with the terms of the treaty.[4] An oft-cited example is Russia's non-compliance with the Montreal Protocol on Substances that Deplete the Ozone Layer, which was not treated by the parties as a breach terminating its participation in that agreement, but rather as a question of non-compliance addressed from within the regime.[5] As this example underscores, ousting from the treaty is distinct from suspension of the benefits of participation whilst within it, a compliance tool also used, inter alia, under CITES. It is no coincidence that these examples are drawn from MEAs employing trade-related environmental mechanisms where the compliance enforcement tool of suspending trading 'privileges' is available.[6] CITES, and the Protocols on Biosafety and on Access and Benefit Sharing to the CBD,[7] are the only biodiversity-related treaties[8]

Especially as Waterfowl Habitat (Ramsar Convention) (adopted 2 February 1971, entered into force 21 December 1975) 996 UNTS 245; the 1972 UNESCO Convention Concerning the Protection of the World Cultural and Natural Heritage (WHC) (adopted 16 November 1972, entered into force 17 December 1975) 1037 UNTS 151; the 1973 Convention on International Trade in Endangered Species of Wild Fauna and Flora (CITES) (adopted 3 March 1973, entered into force 1 July 1975) 993 UNTS 243; the 1979 Bonn Convention on the Conservation of Migratory Species of Wild Animals (CMS) (adopted 23 June 1979, entered into force 1 November 1983) 1651 UNTS 333; and the 1992 Convention on the Conservation of Biological Diversity (CBD) (adopted 5 June 1992, entered into force 29 December 1993) 1760 UNTS 79. See generally M Bowman, P Davies and C Redgwell, *Lyster's International Wildlife Law*, 2nd edn (Cambridge, Cambridge University Press, 2010); A Wiersema, 'Wildlife Law' in J Peel and L Rajamani (eds), *The Oxford Handbook of International Environmental Law* (Oxford, Oxford University Press, 2021); and A Boyle and C Redgwell, *International Law and the Environment*, 4th edn (Oxford, Oxford University Press, 2021) ch 11. As these references underscore, both terrestrial and marine species and habitat protection are also sometimes considered under the rubric of 'international wildlife law', which 'is concerned with 'conserving and avoiding the extinction of species of wild animals and plants': see further Wiersema, 'Wildlife Law'.

[4] Boyle and Redgwell (n 3) 474.

[5] *Montreal Protocol Non-compliance Procedures*, Dec IV/5 UNEP, 1992, UNEP/OzL.Pro.4/15, amended by Dec X/10, UNEP, 1998, UNEP/OzL.Pro.10/9. This was the first compliance mechanism to be established under an MEA. See further M Fitzmaurice and C Redgwell 'Environmental Non-compliance Procedures and International Law' (2000) XXXI *Netherlands Yearbook of International Law* 35; Boyle and Redgwell (n 3) ch 6, s 3(3).

[6] And not without controversy: see further J Werksman, 'Compliance and Transition: Russia's Non-compliance Tests the Ozone Regime' (1996) 36 *ZAÖRV* 750; see also M Koskenniemi, 'Breach of Treaty or Non-compliance? Reflections on the Enforcement of the Montreal Protocol' (1992) 3 *Yearbook of International Environmental Law* 123.

[7] 2000 Cartagena Protocol on Biosafety to the CBD 39 ILM 1027 and Nagoya-Kuala Lumpur Supplementary Protocol on Liability and Redress to the Cartagena Protocol; and the 2010 Nagoya Protocol on Access to Genetic Resources and the Fair and Equitable Sharing of Benefits Arising from Their Utilisation to the CBD.

[8] Nearly 20 MEAs spanning marine living resources, pollution, hazardous waste and biodiversity-related treaties contain trade-related measures: see Note by the WTO Secretariat, *Matrix on Trade-Related Measures Pursuant to Selected Multilateral Agreements* WT/CTE/W/160/Rev.8, 9 October 2017. Each MEA entry includes separate consideration of its non-compliance and dispute settlement mechanisms.

to contain such mechanisms,[9] and the Secretariats of both CITES and the CBD are permanent observers to the World Trade Organization (WTO)'s Committee on Trade and Environment. For most global and regional treaties addressing nature conservation, other compliance tools, whether wielded as 'sticks' or 'carrots', must be employed.

As this chapter explores, one of the achievements of IEL has been substantially to develop the toolbox of compliance approaches and mechanisms which operate alongside traditional dispute settlement. It starts with a brief overview of the parlous state of the global environment, notwithstanding extensive international environmental law-making over the past decades (section II) and considers the inadequacies of traditional dispute settlement for enforcement of international environmental obligations (section III), before turning to the innovative role of implementation monitoring and compliance under multilateral environmental agreements (MEAs) with particular reference to biodiversity-related treaties (section IV). The growth in IEL rules and standards, with MEAs 'an especially prominent means of developing IEL and regulating environmental risks and sustainable use of natural resources',[10] has rendered effective compliance with this growing body of law a matter of pivotal concern. Such concern is undoubtedly reflected in the growth of treaty-based compliance mechanisms, in part a response to the perceived inadequacies of traditional enforcement mechanisms in the environmental context, while reflecting that treaty non-compliance procedures can serve the same purpose of 'determining conformity with behaviour and changes that are required to promote compliance'.[11] The chapter concludes that notwithstanding these innovations and some limited success stories, the accelerating deterioration of the environment and the failure to comply with procedural and substantive environmental treaty obligations continues to undermine efforts at nature conservation.

II. The Declining State of the Global Environment

Developments over the last several decades have transformed IEL, from its early origins concerned primarily with regulating the transboundary environmental

[9] For general overview, see T Treves et al (eds), *Non-compliance Procedures and Mechanisms and the Effectiveness of International Environmental Agreements* (The Hague, TMC Asser Press, 2009); J Klabbers, 'Compliance Procedures' in Bodansky et al (n 1) 995; M Fitzmaurice, 'Compliance with Multilateral Environmental Agreements' (2007) *Hague Yearbook of International Law* 19; and, on compliance with soft law, D Shelton (ed), *Commitment and Compliance: The Role of Non-binding Norms in the International Legal System* (Oxford, Oxford University Press, 2000).

[10] Boyle and Redgwell (n 3) 473.

[11] A Nollkaemper, 'Compliance Control in International Environmental Law: Traversing the Limits of the National Legal Order' (2002) 13 *Yearbook of International Environmental Law* 165. See also AE Boyle, 'Progressive Development of International Environmental Law: Legislative or Litigate?' (2020) 62 *German Yearbook of International Law* 305.

effects of human activities to holistic regulation of global issues of common and intertemporal concern reaching both within and beyond the State.[12] There is now no shortage of law, and even some success stories such as the near-elimination of the hole in the ozone layer through substitution of ozone-depleting substances[13] and the significant environmental recovery of some regional seas.[14]

However, outweighing the success story side of the equation is a multitude of failures, the most notable of which are the ongoing climate emergency, 'the most significant environmental challenge of our time'[15] and the continuing decline of biological diversity. The rate of species extinctions is accelerating, with around one million animal and plant species now threatened with extinction, many within decades.[16] And these are undoubtedly linked since climate change is one of the direct drivers of biodiversity loss,[17] along with other anthropogenic impacts resulting in habitat change, overexploitation, pollution and the introduction of invasive species,[18] with grave impacts of such loss on humanity around the world now likely.[19]

This parlous environmental state has led, amongst other things, to increased concern to improve the implementation and enforcement of existing IEL and to secure greater buy-in to, and compliance with, existing obligations. Implementation and compliance are frequently described as lying on a continuum, from reporting on and monitoring of implementation to compliance and enforcement. In practice, however, the picture is neither linear nor unidimensional: for example, those treaties that have established compliance mechanisms frequently find that the bulk of the instances of non-compliance, at least initially, arise through non-reporting

[12] C Redgwell, 'International Environmental Law' in M Evans (ed), *International* Law, 5th edn (Oxford, Oxford University Press, 2018) 711.

[13] Pursuant to the 1987 Montreal Protocol on Substances that Deplete the Ozone Layer (adopted 16 September 1987, entered into force 1 January 1989) 1522 UNTS 3.

[14] See, for example, the improved environmental state of the Baltic Sea pursuant to measures adopted under the Helsinki Convention on the Protection of the Marine Environment of the Baltic Sea Area (adopted 22 March 1974, entered into force 3 May 1980, revised in 1992) 2009 UNTS 19. For 'State of the Baltic Sea' assessments, see www.helcom.fi. An action plan was adopted in 2007 with the objective of restoring the Baltic marine environment by 2021. See further M Fitzmaurice, 'Enhanced Marine Environmental Protection: A Case Study of the Baltic Sea' in J Barrett and R Barnes (eds), *The Law of the Sea: UNCLOS as a Living Treaty* (London, British Institute of International and Comparative Law, 2016) 293.

[15] Boyle and Redgwell (n 3) 684.

[16] Intergovernmental Science-Policy Platform on Biodiversity and Ecosystem Services (IPBES), *Global Assessment Report on Biodiversity and Ecosystem Services – Summary for Policymakers*, IPBES/7/10/Add.1, 29 May 2019, 4. See also UN Secretariat of the Convention on Biological Diversity, *Global Biodiversity Outlook 5* (Montreal, 2020).

[17] Millennium Ecosystem Assessment, *Ecosystems and Human Well-Being: Biodiversity Synthesis* (2005), 49.

[18] *Global Biodiversity Outlook 3*, 9; *Global Biodiversity Outlook 4*, 9; UN Secretariat (n 16) x; IPBES (n 16) 5.

[19] One such grave impact is the COVID-19 pandemic, which has been linked to human encroachment on habitat and trade in wildlife: see eg, G Ceballos, PR Ehrlich and PH Raven, 'Vertebrates on the Brink as Indicators of Biological Annihilation and the Sixth Mass Extinction' (2020) 117(24) *Proceedings of the National Academy of Sciences of the United States of America* 13596.

and other procedural failings.[20] One reason for this is that compliance with a reporting obligation is concrete and measurable, whilst compliance with aspirational treaty goals (eg, 'as far as possible and as appropriate' under the CBD) are more difficult to measure in concrete terms. It is for this reason that subsequent implementation measures under MEAs are crucial for the establishment of (measurable) obligations, such as targets and timetables, to serve as benchmarks against which to assess compliance.

To return to the examples of the climate change and biodiversity regimes, the contrast here is stark. The former developed from the broad obligations of the 1992 United Nations Framework Convention on Climate Change to the 1997 Kyoto Protocol[21] with its top-down approach establishing concrete internationally agreed targets and timetables for greenhouse gas emission reductions by Annex I parties.[22] The latter is replaced by the 2015 Paris Agreement with its common core obligations and nationally determined contributions subject to a degree of international oversight through global stocktaking with the expectation of progress over time.[23] A notable feature of the Kyoto Protocol is the robust compliance mechanism it established, with facilitative and enforcement branches reflecting its design to 'facilitate, promote and enforce compliance'.[24] This has not been replicated in the Paris Agreement compliance mechanism, which is designed to be facilitative, non-adversarial and non-punitive.[25] Thus, the Kyoto Protocol 'remains the most ambitious and elaborate of the … MEA compliance regimes in operation today'.[26]

As such, it constitutes a stiff comparison for the 1992 CBD.[27] Conservation of biological diversity and biological resources is its prime objective, but the requirements in this regard are stated in broad and often hortatory terms. The most significant obligations placed on parties concern in situ[28] and, to a lesser extent, ex

[20] See further section IV below (CITES, Ramsar and the CMS).

[21] UNFCCC (adopted 9 May 1992, entered into force 21 March 1994) 1771 UNTS 107; and Kyoto Protocol 37 ILM 22.

[22] The negotiation, adoption and operationalisation of the Kyoto Protocol was the third, 'regulatory' phase in the development of the UN climate regime; see D Bodansky, J Brunnée and L Rajamani, *International Climate Change Law* (Oxford, Oxford University Press, 2017) 96.

[23] FCCC/CP/2015/10/Add. 1. See ibid 210; see also D Klein et al (eds), *The Paris Agreement on Climate Change: Analysis and Commentary* (Oxford, Oxford University Press, 2017).

[24] Kyoto Protocol, art 18. On the implementation and compliance mechanisms of the UNFCCC, see Bodansky et al (n 22) 148–54; on the Kyoto Protocol, see ibid 195–200. The UNFCCC also contains a dispute settlement clause (art 14) which, consistent with the experience under other MEAs, has never been used.

[25] Article 15 of the Paris Agreement is a skeletal provision which has taken some time to operationalise, with the Paris Agreement Implementation and Compliance Committee (PAICC) holding its first formal meeting in 2020.

[26] Bodansky et al (n 22) 196.

[27] As noted above (n 7), two protocols have been concluded to the CBD and utilise its institutional arrangements. While piggy-backing on the CBD's institutional arrangements, unlike their parent treaty, both protocols have established a non-compliance mechanism: see Decision BX-I/7 and Decision NP/3-2; and the discussion below (see section IV).

[28] Article 8 CBD. 'In situ conservation' means 'the conservation of ecosystems and natural habitats and the maintenance and recovery of viable populations of species in their natural surroundings, and in the case of domesticated or cultivated species in the surroundings where they have developed their distinctive properties' (art 2).

situ conservation.[29] Parties must adopt national strategies, plans or programmes for their conservation and sustainable use, integrate these and sustainable use into their national sectoral or cross-sectoral plans, programmes and policies, monitor identified components of biodiversity, and identify processes and categories of activities impacting adversely upon it.[30] Adopting and reporting on national biodiversity strategies and action plans (NBSAPs) is a key implementation element of the Convention.[31] These strategies and action plans are adopted within the framework of Strategic Plans and global Biodiversity Targets established by the COP.[32] This softer global target-setting approach of the CBD that is reliant on voluntary implementation is unsurprisingly not bolstered by any compliance mechanism.[33]

III. Breach of International Environmental Obligations and State Responsibility: Leaving Nature Behind?

Clearly there is no 'one size fits all' in terms of compliance and enforcement. Generally speaking, pollution treaties are much more developed in terms of adopting compliance mechanisms, and compensation and liability regimes directed towards the non-State culprits in pollution incidents (for example, the ship and cargo owners in the event of an oil pollution casualty.[34] or nuclear operators where there is a nuclear incident),[35] and where attempts have even been made to quantify

[29] ibid art 9.'Ex situ conservation' means 'conservation of components of biological diversity outside their natural habitats' (ie, removing specimens or parts thereof from the wild and keeping them in a viable condition elsewhere; generally in zoos, aquaria and wildlife parks) (art 2). It is predominantly to be used for the purpose of complementing in situ measures and preferably to be taken in the country of origin of such components.

[30] ibid arts 6 and 7, respectively.

[31] See COP Decisions IX/8 and X/2, and Aichi Biodiversity Target 17.

[32] See eg, the Biodiversity Strategic Plan for 2011–20 and 20 Aichi Biodiversity Targets, CBD COP Decision X/2. However, apart from two protocols (n 7), 'there has been little in the way of development of further legal norms to strengthen or supplement the obligations contained in the Convention': P Sands and J Peel, *Principles of International Environmental Law*, 4th edn (Cambridge, Cambridge University Press, 2018) 405. See also SR Harrop and DJ Pritchard, 'A Hard Instrument Goes Soft: The Implications of the Convention on Biological Diversity's Current Trajectory' (2011) 21 *Global Environmental Change* 474.

[33] See further section III below.

[34] See eg, the 1969 Convention on Civil Liability for Oil Pollution Damage (adopted 29 November 1969, entered into force 19 June 1975) 973 UNTS 3; and the 1971 Convention on the Establishment of an International Fund for Compensation for Oil Pollution Damage (adopted 18 December 1971, entered into force 16 October 1978) 1110 UNTS 57 (CLC and Fund Conventions) as amended. See also the 2001 Convention on Civil Liability for Bunker Oil Pollution Damage and the 1996 Convention on Liability and Compensation for the Carriage of Hazardous and Noxious Substances by Sea (adopted 1 October 1996, not yet in force). However, treaty-based civil liability schemes have their own drawbacks and deficiencies and are not a complete replacement for international claims; see Boyle and Redgwell (n 3) 472.

[35] For example, the regional 1960 Paris Convention on Third Party Liability in the Field of Nuclear Energy (adopted 29 July 1960, entered into force 1 April 1968) 956 UNTS 25; and the global 1963

ecological damage.[36] Such liability regimes sidestep the necessity to rely on the route of inter-State claims and can plug the gap where transboundary damage occurs that is either not attributable to the source State or results from events that are either unforeseeable or unavoidable using reasonable due diligence.[37] While their development has been particularly marked for activities with significant transboundary consequences, they have also developed for the protection of common spaces (eg, Antarctica[38] and the deep seabed).[39]

While it might be thought that pollution treaties would be more amenable to claims for transboundary damage, it is indisputable that 'no modern pollution disaster, including Chernobyl,[40] Sandoz or *Amoco Cadiz*, has resulted in the adjudication of an international claim for transboundary damage against the state concerned'.[41] If the principal measure of 'effective enforcement' is an unequivocal determination of State responsibility for environmental damage in international law, the precedents are few.[42] This is partly owing to the barriers to international litigation addressing transboundary environmental disputes, including the lack of a forum with universal compulsory jurisdiction, the need to show a breach of

Vienna Convention on Civil Liability for Nuclear Damage (CLC), 1063 UNTS 26. However, as Chernobyl underscores, treaty-based civil liability schemes have their own drawbacks and deficiencies, and are not a complete replacement for the option of pursuing international claims; see Boyle and Redgwell (n 3) 472 and ch 9.

[36] For example, art 2 of the 1992 Protocol to the CLC defines 'pollution damage' to include compensation for impairment of the environment, other than loss of profit from such impairment, but excluding hypothetical damage (recovery is limited to 'costs of reasonable measures of reinstatement actually undertaken or to be undertaken').

[37] See eg, AE Boyle, 'Globalising Environmental Liability: The Interplay of National and International Law' (2005) 17 *Journal of Environmental Law* 3, 5. Sidestep but not avoid, as these instruments also provide for inter-State claims, even if these are not pursued.

[38] See eg, liability arising from environmental emergencies in Antarctica under the 2005 Annex to the 1991 Environmental Protocol to the 1959 Antarctic Treaty, 30 ILM 1461 (1991).

[39] See the responsibility and liability of seabed contractors for environmental damage in the 2000 regulations on prospecting and exploring for polymetallic modules promulgated by the International Seabed Authority under the 1982 UNCLOS.

[40] The release of radioactive material to the atmosphere caused by the Fukushima Dachai nuclear accident was 10 per cent that of Chernobyl, and neither the atmospheric nor marine discharges from the accident gave rise to an international claim, with compensation for nuclear damage governed exclusively by Japanese law. See A Morishima, 'The Impacts of the Fukushima Nuclear Accident on the International Nuclear Legal Regime' in R Beckman (ed), *Transboundary Pollution: Evolving Issues of International Law and Policy* (Singapore, NUS, 2014). The *Financial Times* reported on 26 March 2016 that the disaster has cost Japanese taxpayers in excess of $100 billion.

[41] Boyle and Redgwell (n 3) 421.

[42] See Certain Activities Carried out by Nicaragua in the Border Area (*Costa Rica v Nicaragua*) and Construction of a Road in Costa Rica along the San Juan River (*Nicaragua v Costa Rica*), Judgment [2015] ICJ Rep 665. Along with UN Security Council Resolution 687, adopted following Iraq's invasion and occupation of Kuwait in 1991, this is a rare example of an unequivocal determination of State responsibility for environmental damage in international law; Boyle and Redgwell (n 3) 422–23. See generally N Klein, 'International Environmental Law in International Courts and Tribunals' in L Rajamani and J Peel (eds), *The Oxford Handbook of International Environmental Law*, 2nd edn (Oxford, Oxford University Press, 2021); and J Harrison, 'Reflections on the Role of International Courts and Tribunals in the Settlement of Environmental Disputes and the Development of International Environmental Law' (2013) 25 *Journal of Environmental Law* 501.

due diligence by the State, and the reluctance of States to deal with environmental disputes in this way.[43]

The prohibition on causing significant harm to the territory of another State, elaborated upon in the *Trail Smelter* case,[44] very much fits within the traditional legal framework of the 'injured State' seeking reparation in the event of environmental damage caused by pollution. It is frequently cited as one of the first environmental cases and 'a pivotal – and indeed, foundational – moment in the development of international environmental law'.[45] Not only is it an early example of a successfully resolved inter-State environmental dispute,[46] but it remains the only decided international case on transboundary air pollution.[47] Here the bilateral character of the dispute facilitated the application of traditional rules on State responsibility and reparation for the pollution damage caused to economic interests in the US state of Washington. It is an illustration of how '[i]nternational law originally responded to environmental harm in the same way as it would for any other kind of injury, through the application of state responsibility'.[48]

However, while the specific focus was on responsibility for transboundary air pollution, it has subsequently developed into a more general principle of customary international law pursuant to which States have a duty to prevent, reduce and control pollution and significant transboundary environmental harm arising from activities within their territory, jurisdiction or control.[49] It has been enunciated in soft law declarations,[50] endorsed inter alia by the General Assembly[51] and the International Law Commission,[52] and in various multilateral environmental

[43] Boyle (n 11).

[44] *Trail Smelter Arbitration (United States v Canada)* (1939) 33 AJIL 182 and (1941) 35 AJIL 684; see also Principle 21 of the Stockholm Declaration and Principle 2 of the Rio Declaration.

[45] See D French, 'Trail Smelter' in E Bjorge and C Miles (eds), *Landmark Cases in Public International Law* (Oxford, Hart Publishing, 2017) 159; R Bratspies and R Miller (eds), *Transboundary Harm in International Law: Lessons from the Trail Smelter Arbitration* (Cambridge, Cambridge University Press, 2006).

[46] T Stephens, *International Courts and Environmental Protection* (Cambridge, Cambridge University Press, 2009) 124.

[47] Ecuador's claim against Uruguay for transboundary air pollution damage was settled without a hearing before the ICJ in the *Aerial Herbicide Spraying Case* and concerned not industrial emissions, but the transboundary drift of aerial herbicide spray: see Order of 13 September 2013 (Removal from List).

[48] L-A Duvic-Paoli, *The Prevention Principle in International Environmental Law* (Cambridge, Cambridge University Press, 2018) 15.

[49] Many international instruments refer to the need to take measures 'to prevent, reduce and control' pollution (see, eg, UNCLOS, art 194(1); the 1997 Convention on the Law of the Non-navigational Uses of International Watercourses (adopted 21 May 1997, entered into force 17 August 2014) 36 ILM 700, art 21) and the significant adverse transboundary environmental impact from proposed activities (see, eg, Convention on Environmental Impact Assessment in a Transboundary Context (adopted 25 February 1991, entered into force 10 September 1997) 30 ILM 1461 (1991), art 2(1)).

[50] See, eg, 1972 Stockholm Declaration, Principle 21; 1992 Rio Declaration, Principle 2.

[51] 1974 Charter of Economic Rights and Duties of States, GA Res 3281, UNGAOR, 29th Sess, Supp No 31, UN Doc A/9631 (1974) 50, art 30.

[52] See 'Draft Articles on Prevention of Transboundary Harm from Hazardous Activities, with Commentaries 2001' (UN Doc A/56/10) in *Yearbook of the International Law Commission 2001*, vol II, Part Two (UN, 2001).

agreements[53] and judicial decisions.[54] Thus, for example, in the *Pulp Mills* case, which involved the siting of a pulp mill on a shared watercourse, the River Uruguay, the International Court of Justice (ICJ) observed that: 'A State is … obliged to use all the means at its disposal in order to avoid activities which take place in its territory, or in any area under its jurisdiction, causing significant damage to the environment of another State.'[55] The obligation to prevent significant transboundary harm is widely viewed as imposing an obligation of due diligence.[56]

Yet these rules are of only limited assistance in the environmental field for several reasons. One is that responsibility rules generally operate once damage has already occurred rather than to prevent it from occurring in the first place – which in the case of environmental harms, such as species extinction or habitat destruction, may be irremediable.[57] That said, preventive measures may be sought, for example, by way of provisional measures of protection which, even in the conventional responsibility context, may serve to avoid or reduce harm.[58] A second difficulty, illustrated particularly well by the climate change example, is that harm may be incremental and difficult to link to the specific actions or omissions of another State. Problems of causation and proof will loom large.[59] The generally non-reciprocal character of international environmental obligations will also render it difficult to meet the requirement of breach of an obligation owed to another State. Both the *Trail Smelter* case[60] and the *Gabčíkovo-Nagymaros Dam* dispute between Hungary and Slovakia[61] saw the application of traditional rules on State responsibility because of the bilateral character of the dispute and of the parties' obligations. Had it proceeded to the merits, the ICJ case brought in 1974 against France by Australia and New Zealand regarding French atmospheric nuclear testing in the South Pacific would have likewise largely fit within this bilateral model.[62] So too does the

[53] See, eg, the UNFCCC and the CBD.

[54] See, eg, *Legality of the Threat or Use of Nuclear Weapons*, Advisory Opinion [1996] ICJ Rep 226, para 29.

[55] *Case Concerning Pulp Mills on the River Uruguay (Argentina v Uruguay)* [2010] ICJ Rep 14, para 101. See also the Draft Articles on Prevention (n 52) 152, which accurately reflect the current state of international law in this regard. And, as noted by the ICJ in *Legality of the Threat or Use of Nuclear Weapons* (ibid), States have a general obligation to ensure that activities within their jurisdiction and control respect the environment of other States.

[56] 'The obligation of the State of origin to take preventive or minimization measures is one of due diligence': Commentary to Article 3, Draft Articles on Prevention (n 52) para (7).

[57] On prevention, see Duvic-Paoli (n 48), especially pt I, 'From Reparation to Prevention'.

[58] Provisional measures were sought, for example, in the *Nuclear Tests*, *Pulp Mills* and *Border Activities Cases*. On their mixed record in the environmental context, see Klein (n 42) ('it may thus appear that development or economic imperatives implicitly weigh against environmental protection').

[59] See further C Redgwell, 'The Wrong Trousers: State Responsibility and International Environmental Law' in P Koutrakos and M Evans (eds), *The International Responsibility of the European Union – European and International Perspectives* (Oxford, Hart Publishing, 2013) 257.

[60] *Trail Smelter Arbitration* (n 44).

[61] *Case Concerning the Gabcikovo-Nagymaros Project (Hungary/Slovakia)* [1997] ICJ Rep 7.

[62] *Nuclear Tests (Australia v France)*, Interim Protection, Order of 22 June 1973 [1973] ICJ Rep 99; Judgment, [1994] ICJ Rep 253; *Nuclear Tests (New Zealand v France)*, Interim Protection, Order of 22 June 1973, [1973] ICJ Rep 135; Judgment, [1994] ICJ Rep 457.

Border Activities/San Juan River Cases.[63] Even the *Whaling Case* was couched in terms of a dispute over the interpretation and application of the International Whaling Convention, with *erga omnes* arguments very much muted.[64]

But what of the example of a breach by a State of its obligation to conserve biological diversity, expressly acknowledged as 'the common concern of humankind'?[65] A complainant State is required to show that the obligation is owed to it and (usually) that injury has resulted to it in order for standing requirements to be satisfied; there is no such thing (yet) under international law as an *actio popularis* whereby a State may bring an action on behalf of the international community.[66] There are glimmers of such an approach in Articles 42 and 48 of the 2001 Articles on State Responsibility drafted by the International Law Commission, wherein the possibility exists for a State Party to a multilateral treaty to complain of breach of a multilateral obligation by another State Party. While there has not yet been explicit international judicial recognition of this possibility in the environmental context, in the 2012 *Obligation to Prosecute or Extradite* case (*Belgium v Senegal*), the ICJ recognised that the Convention against Torture imposed obligations *erga omnes partes* giving rise to a common interest in compliance and 'the entitlement of each State party to the Convention to make a claim concerning the cessation of an alleged breach by another State party'.[67]

IV. Compliance Review in Nature Conservation Treaties

There are several consequences for IEL of the inadequacies of the traditional rules of State responsibility applied via the dispute settlement route. Not all of these are negative and indeed some illustrate the nimbleness of international law and institutions in responding to roadblocks to effective compliance, even if not within the classic mode of 'enforcement'. The first generation of nature conservation treaties

[63] Certain Activities Carried out by Nicaragua in the Border Area (*Costa Rica v Nicaragua*) and Construction of a Road in Costa Rica along the San Juan River (*Nicaragua v Costa Rica*), Judgment (n 42).

[64] *Whaling in the Antarctic (Australia v Japan, New Zealand Intervening)* [2014] ICJ Rep 226. There was the implicit assumption by all parties – and the ICJ – that Australia had standing to challenge Japan's non-compliance with art 8 ICRW; see further C Gray, 'Current Development: *Whaling in the Antarctic*' (2015) 109 *AJIL* 589; and, generally, M Fitzmaurice, *Whaling and International Law* (Cambridge, Cambridge University Press, 2015). See also the comments by Judge Cancade Trindade that: 'The [ICRW] concerns a matter of general or common interest, and is to be implemented collectively by State Parties, thus contributing to the public order of the oceans.' *Whaling* case, *Declaration of Intervention by New Zealand*, Order of 6 February 2013, Separate Opinion, para 71.

[65] CBD, Preamble.

[66] *South West Africa*, Second Phase, Judgment, [1966] ICJ Rep 6. See generally F Ahmadov, *The Right of Actio Popularis before International Courts and Tribunals* (Leiden, Brill/Nijhoff, 2018).

[67] *Questions Relating to the Obligation to Prosecute or Extradite (Belgium v Senegal)*, Judgment of 20 July 2012, para 69.

rarely provided for any degree of monitoring or oversight of national implementation. Increasingly, however, modern environmental treaties provide for a comprehensive feedback loop, from implementation, monitoring and reporting to international review and non-compliance mechanisms. This underscores the evolutionary nature of many such treaty instruments and the dynamic effect of decision-making by the conference of the parties (COP), as well as the impact of the work of treaty subsidiary bodies and secretariats. Perhaps the most striking example of monitoring and reporting obligations giving rise to new prescriptions is the evolution of the Convention on Migratory Species (CMS), a major framework agreement with a number of 'daughter' agreements addressed to specific species, one of which (the Agreement on the Conservation of Populations of European Bats (EUROBATS)) is already 'second generation'.[68] Under most MEAs, States Parties not only have the obligation to implement but also have an express obligation to report upon such implementation. Through reporting, it is possible to obtain a snapshot of overall implementation and enforcement patterns. Such reporting obligations might include supplying the text of implementing laws and measures (eg, the CMS); transmission of specimens of the documentation employed when implementing the permitting or certification system required (eg, CITES); supplying the results of monitoring environmental conditions (eg, the 1991 Environmental Protocol to the Antarctic Treaty (AT)); and the publication of records kept, and of the results of monitoring, as well as the compilation of official reports, or summaries thereof, reflecting the application and enforcement of the treaty (eg, CITES). A number of nature conservation treaties have had, and continue to have, problems with non-submission of reports[69] and inaccuracies in them.[70] Non-State actors can play an important role here, as a source of additional information on national implementation, eg, TRAFFIC under CITES and BirdLife International under Ramsar.

The link between reporting, implementation and compliance has also given rise to a relatively new phenomenon in the context of national implementation of international environmental obligations, and that is compliance review. This type of review occurs through scrutiny of implementation performance by a standing (or implementation or compliance) committee (eg, the 1991 Alps Convention and Protocols, the 2000 Cartagena Biosafety Protocol, the 'files' procedure of the Bern Convention and the role of the World Heritage Committee under the WHC) and/or by the COP (eg, CITES). Some more recent instruments make provision for the future establishment of an implementation review procedure, such as the compliance mechanism under the 2000 Cartagena Protocol to the 1992 CBD. Typically, compliance procedures are designed to ensure a return to compliance through a

[68] And the Siberian Crane MoU substantially revised: see further Boyle and Redgwell (n 3) ch 11, s 3(3).

[69] See, for example, compliance review of non-reporting under CITES, discussed below.

[70] A Chayes and A Handler Chayes, *The New Sovereignty; Compliance with International Regulatory Agreements* (Cambridge, MA, Harvard University Press, 1995) 155.

range of techniques, including the possibility of facilitative and/or coercive measures (eg, access to facilitative financing or the suspension of trading privileges if any).

Many obstacles to effective implementation may arise[71] and come to be highlighted under treaty-based non-compliance or other (facilitative) procedures. Under CITES, Ramsar, and the CMS, for example, numerous non-compliance cases have arisen from an inability of States to effectively carry out their reporting obligations. For a developing country, this can often be as a result of the lack of financial resources and technical expertise. Harmonising of reporting obligations, as has occurred under Ramsar, is one method for streamlining the reporting burden and enhancing compliance. Lack of scientific knowledge and expertise is another issue, which is evident, for example, in the implementation of the CBD, where especially developing country parties are hampered by inadequate scientific knowledge of the full extent of biodiversity contained within their borders. This is exacerbated by the fact that much of the taxonomic research is carried out by developed countries, a fact recognised and sought to be redressed by the treaty bodies through the Global Taxonomic Initiative.[72] In situ conservation obligations under the CBD may require the designation of protected areas, with the consequent need to enforce such designation, an issue also under a number of other nature conservation treaties. CITES is dependent on the issuance of certificates and careful monitoring of points of entry for illegally traded flora and fauna, as indeed is the 2000 Cartagena Protocol to the CBD regulating the transboundary movement of living modified organisms.

As this brief overview underscores, there is a considerable range of compliance approaches and mechanisms found in MEAs. Since '[t]he foundation of compliance strategy is the normative framework provided by the treaty',[73] the following sections explore in more detail the approach of the 'big five' biodiversity-related treaties to compliance and enforcement.

A. Compliance and Enforcement under the 1992 CBD

As observed above, the CBD makes no provision for enforcement in the sense of establishing an international inspection or observer system; indeed, that would

[71] In general, six types of obstacles to national implementation may be identified, and which may operate individually or collectively: (i) financial; (ii) technical; (iii) scientific; (iv) legal and administrative; (v) political; and (vi) textual (ie, the treaty text itself may be insufficiently clear and precise to give rise to precise obligations for national implementation): C Redgwell, 'National Implementation' in D Bodansky, J Brunnée and E Hey (eds), *The Oxford Handbook of International Environmental Law* (Oxford, Oxford University Press, 2008).

[72] See J Troudet et al, 'Taxonomic Bias in Biodiversity Data and Societal Preferences' (2017) 7(1) *Scientific Reports* 9132. The Global Taxonomic Initiative under the CBD aims at closing the developing country knowledge gap in respect of biological diversity through species identification. It is also designed to fill the general scientific knowledge gaps which exist regarding the nature and extent of biological diversity; the Global Register of Migratory Species (GROMS) system under the CMS is a further example of capacity-building of general scientific knowledge.

[73] Chayes and Handler Chayes (n 70) 110.

be an impossibility for a convention of this kind, which provides a broad framework of 'soft' obligations and requires domestic implementation through national legislation for its efficacy. As the majority of the areas and species concerned are found within national jurisdiction, enforcement *strictu sensu* is therefore a matter for national authorities. But, as the conservation of biodiversity is 'the common concern of humankind', the efficacy with which its Contracting Parties fulfil this obligation is potentially subject to international overview and criticism. The effectiveness of this criticism largely depends on the institutional structures available for voicing it both within the Convention's structure and in the wider international community. While reporting procedures for complaints with overview and comment from treaty bodies are a feature of some of the other MEAs considered below, they are not yet a feature under the Biodiversity Convention (but see the Cartagena Protocol below). However, the CBD does require each party to present to the COP reports on measures taken by it to implement the Convention and their effectiveness in meeting the objectives of the Convention.[74] This provides an opportunity for the COP to gain an overview of these reports and to comment on any weaknesses or failures of parties in this respect. Notwithstanding the primary importance of in situ conservation and other measures of national implementation under the CBD, the parties did not establish a Committee on Implementation until 2012.[75] However, in a development typical of the CBD, it was initially toothless and indeed continues to fall short of a robust review mechanism; for example, there is no provision for a mechanism analogous to that under the Paris Agreement to enhance the level of ambition in national targets to ensure that agreed global biodiversity targets are achieved. That this is needed is vividly underscored by the 2020 assessment of National Biodiversity Strategies and Action Plans (NBSAPs) and national reports that concludes that both ambition and effort 'have been insufficient to reach the level of ambition set out in the Aichi [Biodiversity] Targets' and 'progress is not sufficient to stem the direct and indirect drivers of nature deterioration. It is therefore likely that most of the Aichi Biodiversity Targets for 2020 will be missed'.[76]

i. The Cartagena Biosafety Protocol to the CBD

Owing to the subject matter of the Biosafety Protocol – regulation of the transboundary movement and the use of LMOs which may have an adverse effect on the conservation and sustainable use of biodiversity – it is unsurprising to find

[74] Article 26.

[75] CBD COP Decision XII/26. The Subsidiary Body on Implementation (SBI) replaced an Ad Hoc Open-Ended Working Group on Review of Implementation of the Convention, and to date has met twice (2016 and 2018). The four functions and core areas of work of the SBI comprise: (a) review of progress in implementation; (b) strategic actions to enhance implementation; (c) strengthening means of implementation; and (d) operations of the Convention and the Protocols.

[76] As quoted in CBD/SBI/3/2/Add.2, 16 March 2020, para 81.

that, unlike its parent Convention, provisions were included providing for the subsequent elaboration of rules and procedures on liability and redress (Article 27) and the conclusion of a compliance mechanism (Article 34). A facilitative compliance mechanism has been established, though in common with the mechanisms established under other treaty instruments, the Compliance Committee spent its first meetings elaborating rules of procedures, aided by an assessment of the practice of other environmental agreements' compliance procedures. This process was necessitated by the political compromises embedded in this weak compliance mechanism adopted in 2004, with further elaboration necessary. It is now established that the Compliance Committee may take a number of measures with a view to promoting compliance and addressing cases of non-compliance, including: (a) providing advice or assistance to the party concerned; (b) making recommendations to the COP-MOP (Meeting of the Parties) regarding the provision of financial and technical assistance, technology transfer, training and other capacity-building measures; and (c) requesting or assisting the party concerned to develop a compliance action plan regarding the achievement of compliance with the Protocol within a timeframe to be agreed upon between the Committee and the party. It is for the COP-MOP to take decisions on one of more specific measures, upon the recommendations of the Compliance Committee, such as the provision of financial and technical assistance or issuing a caution to the concerned party. While it has now considered some specific instances of party non-compliance submitted to it,[77] the bulk of the Committee's activities have related to general review, including: compliance with the obligation to designate national focal points and identify competent national authorities, based on the information available on the Biodiversity Clearing House;[78] the operation of the Protocol based on the national reports submitted by the parties;[79] and a general overview of compliance with the obligation to submit such reports.[80] This relatively slow uptick in 'business' is a reflection of the slow rate of implementation of the Protocol, hinging in part on disagreement over key aspects such as risk assessment and, until recently, lack of progress on liability and redress.[81]

[77] Any party may make a compliance submission in respect of itself, or any party 'which is affected or likely to be affected, with respect to another Party'. For the most recent overview of individual submissions, see CBD/CP/CC/17/5 17 February 2020 (Note by the Executive Secretary) and CBD/CP/CC/17/6, 17 April 2020.

[78] See Review of General Issues of Compliance, CBD/CP/CC/17/4 (2020).

[79] See, for example, the Report of the Compliance Committee submitted to COP-MOP 4 (2008) at UNEP/CBD/BS/COP-MOP/4/2; for pertinent decisions of the COP/MOP, see Decisions BS-I/7, BS-II/1, BS-III/1 BS-IV/1.

[80] CBD/CP/CC/17/2, 16 March 2020.

[81] An Ad Hoc Working Group on Liability and Redress was established pursuant to Decision BS-I/8 and met five times between 2005 and 2008. In 2010, the Nagoya–Kuala Lumpur Supplementary Protocol on Liability and Redress to the Cartagena Protocol on Biosafety was duly adopted and entered into force on 5 March 2018.

B. Compliance and Enforcement under CITES

CITES controls the import and export of endangered species and products on a global scale through a permitting system operated by designated national authorities, with species listed in three Appendices: Appendix I prohibits trade in the listed species, while trade in Appendix II species is subject to restrictions, and Appendix III listing buttresses national measures through international cooperation in controlling external trade. The compliance review process is based on infraction reports by the Secretariat to the COP with the effective sanction for non-compliance being temporary suspension of trade in specimens of CITES-listed species with the non-complying party.[82] Presently there are 25 (developing) States subject to one or more recommendations to suspend trade in certain species owing to 'significant trade' in contravention of CITES, many within the last five years, though the longest 'temporary' suspensions have applied for 25 years to Madagascar and the Solomon Islands. A recommendation to suspend all trade, or all commercial trade, may be made where non-compliance affects the implementation of CITES as a whole, namely the failure to: provide timely annual reports (eg, Afghanistan, Djibouti and Grenada); enact the appropriate national legislation (eg, Djibouti, Liberia and Somalia); and ensure effective compliance and enforcement (eg, Guinea). Recommendations can cover non-parties (eg, Haiti for significant trade in the Queen conch since 2003).

In practice, this has been a potent tool for ensuring the proper national implementation of the obligations of CITES to enact legislation, develop work plans, control legal/illegal trade and/or improve the basis for government decision-making.[83] It has also encouraged participation in CITES, with some accessions by States previously subject to trade suspensions while non-parties (Bahrain, Iraq and Tajikistan). However, empirically it is difficult to know how much the existence of CITES has made a difference to illegal wildlife trade[84] and views are divided on its effectiveness.[85] While regulated trade may help with species conservation and assist local communities to benefit from their sustainable utilisation, achieving it is fraught with uncertainties in ascertaining a sustainable level

[82] Article XIII. See generally R Reeve, *Policing International Trade in Endangered Species: The CITES Treaty and Compliance* (London, Earthscan, 2002); W Wijnstekers, *The Evolution of CITES*, 11th edn (Budapest, CIC, 2018) ch 16.

[83] N Yeater and J Vasquez, 'Demystifying the Relationship between CITES and the WTO' (2002) 10(3) *Review of European Community and International Environmental Law* 271.

[84] Wiersema (n 3) 9.

[85] Contrast, for example, Bowman et al (n 3) ch 16 and D Favre, *Convention on Trade in Endangered Species* (Dordrecht, Springer, 1990). Baker sees much room for improvement on compliance: see J Baker, 'A Substantive Theory of the Relative Efficiency of Environmental Treaty Compliance: The Case of CITES' (1999) 2 *Journal of International Wildlife Law & Policy* 1; see also G Wandesforde-Smith, 'Looking for Law in All the Wrong Places? Dying Elephants, Evolving Treaties and Empty Threats' (2016) 19 *Journal of International Wildlife Law & Policy* 365 and in reply A Wiersema, 'CITES and the Whole Chain Approach to Combating Illegal Wildlife Trade' (2017) 20 *Journal of International Wildlife Law & Policy* 207.

of exploitation for particular species,[86] and whether demand can be sufficiently controlled to avoid overexploitation and increased killing.[87] Sustainable utilisation of certain species– eg, charismatic mega-fauna – may be opposed even if trade in other animals and plants is not, or there may be ethical objections to any trade in any species. This is indeed 'an area riven both by uncertainty and fundamental value disagreements'.[88]

C. Compliance and Enforcement under the CMS

The potential of the 1979 CMS for comprehensive protection of migratory species is far from fully realised. Recognising the need to improve implementation and strengthen compliance with the Convention, in 2017 the Contracting Parties adopted a review mechanism intended as a 'supportive, non-adversarial and facilitative' process to provide support for parties experiencing difficulties in implementing the Convention.[89] However, no reports had been received by the Secretariat by the time of COP13 in 2020. It is thus not yet possible to evaluate the success of this process in contributing to the effectiveness of the CMS, other than to make two observations. The first is that the CMS has joined the ranks of most major multilateral environmental agreements in establishing a process for facilitating implementation, recognising that compliance with Convention obligations and the effectiveness of implementation measures are critical to the conservation and management of migratory species.[90] The second is that while the basis for review by the Standing Committee is wide – it may be 'triggered' not only by self-reporting, but by other parties, the CMS institutions (the Secretariat or the Standing Committee) and by '[a]ny body or agency technically qualified in protection, conservation and management of migratory species', such as an accredited non-governmental organisation (NGO) – the possibility for the submissions of the party concerned to remain confidential has obvious implications for the transparency of the process.[91] In keeping with the facilitative nature of the review process, the response of the Standing Committee when an 'implementation matter' has been identified is first and foremost to give the party concerned 'every opportunity to correct them within a reasonable time frame', failing which further measures ranging from further advice and assistance, technical and verification missions to a warning and request an implementation action are available. There is no

[86] Although listing decisions are intended to be based on science, it has frequently been observed that many voting decisions and CITES COPS are 'extremely political': Wiersema (n 3) 10.

[87] ibid.

[88] ibid.

[89] Specifically, arts III.4, III.5, III.7 and VI.2: UNEP/CMS Resolution 12.9 and Decisions 12.6–12.9 (2017). Two agreements within the CMS family already had review mechanisms: the Agreement on the Conservation of African-Eurasian Migratory Waterbirds (AEWA) and the Agreement on the Conservation of Cetaceans of the Black Sea, Mediterranean Sea, and Contiguous Atlantic Area (ACCOBAMS).

[90] As acknowledged in the preamble to UNEP/CMS/Resolution 11.7 (2014), indents 2 and 4.

[91] UNEP/CMS/Resolution 12.9 (2017), part B.

equivalent of the Montreux Record (Ramsar) or the Danger List (World Heritage Convention) discussed below, though conceivably reporting by the Standing Committee to the COP of actions taken might come to serve a similar purpose.

That urgent action is required is underscored by the preliminary review of the status of CMS listed species presented at COP13 (2020),[92] which reveals alarming declines in populations of most listed species. Highlighted as of 'global concern' is the conservation status of 87 per cent of endangered species listed in Appendix I and 56 per cent of the species with 'unfavourable conservation status' listed in Appendix II. Population trends are decreasing for 73 per cent of Appendix I species and 48 per cent of Appendix II species. While fish are the more rapidly declining taxa, more than 90 per cent of CMS-listed species are impacted by biological resource use,[93] and three out of four Appendix 1 species are impacted by intentional use,[94] with about 20 per cent subject to forms of persecution and control.[95] That stable or increasing population trends have been observed for only 14 per cent of Appendix I species and 18 per cent of Appendix II species is scant comfort.

D. Compliance and Enforcement under Ramsar

The Ramsar Convention is the only global environmental treaty addressed to a particular ecosystem, the conservation and wise use of wetlands primarily as a habitat for wild birds, and it is acknowledged to 'take the lead on wetlands biodiversity'.[96] To become a party, it is necessary to designate at least one wetland of international importance, though in practice many Ramsar parties have exceeded the minimum legal requirement of one site designation. However, both distribution and size of areas covered requires further enlargement to achieve the conservation purposes under the Ramsar Convention. Once designated, Ramsar sites are to be protected under national law, but they also acquire conservation significance for the international community as a whole. Thus, while it is estimated that nearly half of Ramsar-listed sites do not have a management plan,[97] the requirement to submit triennial reports on the implementation of the treaty to

[92] UNEP/CMS/COP13/Doc.24.

[93] 'Defined in the IUCN – CMP Unified Classification of Direct Threats as "Threats from consumptive use of 'wild' biological resources including both deliberate and unintentional harvesting effects; also persecution or control of specific species"': UNEP/CMS press release, 'CMS to Present Preliminary Review of the Conservation Status of Migratory Species', 19 February 2020.

[94] 'With reference to the IUCN classification of threats, this includes hunting and collecting terrestrial animals and fishing and harvesting aquatic resources at both small and large scales, when the species being assessed is the target.' ibid.

[95] 'Examples of persecution/control include wolf control, pest control, persecution of snakes because of superstition, beach protection with shark nets, sharks and seals killed because they eat commercial fish species, etc.' ibid.

[96] See, for example, Ramsar Resolution 5.1 (1993).

[97] 'According to the Ramsar Sites Information Service, 48% of the current 2,315 designated Ramsar Sites (1,120) have a management plan, and it is reported as effectively implemented at 37% (860) of the Sites.' *Report of the Secretary-General on the Implementation of the Convention*, COP13 Doc.11.1(2018), para 36.

the Contracting Parties provides an opportunity for the review of national implementation by other parties.

Failure to promote conservation and wise use of wetlands may lead to inclusion on the 'Montreux Record of Ramsar sites requiring priority attention', which highlights threats to designated sites.[98] This may not occur without the consent of the State concerned. There are currently 49 sites which have been added to the Montreux Record with consent.[99] Since failure to conserve wetlands may result, inter alia, from lack of capacity, a Small Grants Fund for Wetland Conservation and Wise Use was also established in 1990 with the express purpose of facilitating compliance, along with other forms of technical assistance. The Ramsar Advisory Mission was established as a technical assistance mechanism to provide advice to States on problems or threats which have caused Montreux listing to be contemplated. Site visits are an integral part of this mechanism and, as with the Montreux listing procedure itself, are conditional upon the agreement of the Contracting Party concerned. As of November 2019, the Ramsar Advisory mechanism had been applied on 93 occasions, most recently in Russia (the Kurgalsky Peninsula). For sites covered by both Ramsar and the World Heritage Convention, such visits may be requested and carried out jointly, as, for example, when Ichkeul National Park in Tunisia was listed on both the Montreux Record and the WHC Heritage in Danger List.[100] In practice, conservation efforts may be assisted by listing on the Montreux Record with consequent access to technical assistance and facilitative financing under the Convention and elsewhere – for example, the listing of the Azraq Oasis in Jordan assisted in obtaining funding from the Global Environmental Facility and of the Austrian Donau-March-Thaya-Auen in obtaining European Commission funding. The ultimate sanction is delisting because of the irremediable loss of the values which led to Ramsar listing in the first instance. This has never occurred; nor have any sites been deleted owing to 'urgent national interests' as also provided for in the Convention.[101]

These efforts notwithstanding, according to the Ramsar Convention's 2018 Global Wetland Outlook – the first global report specifically on the status of wetlands and the services they provide – wetlands are lost three times faster than natural forests, with an estimated 87 per cent of wetland resources lost since 1700.[102] While the total wetlands remaining today are estimated to exceed the size of

[98] See Resolutions 5.4 (1993) and VIII.8 (2002).

[99] For the complete list, see www.ramsar.org.

[100] In fact, the Park is one of a few sites which are protected by listing under three agreements: Ramsar (1980), the WHC (1979), and the Biosphere Reserve (1977). Details of listings can be found on the Ramsar website: www.ramsar.org. It was removed from the WHC Danger List in 2006 and from the Montreux Record in 2016, owing to improvements in the ecological character of the site. While designated, it received significant financial and technical support from both conventions in making these improvements.

[101] Article 2(5). Parties have invoked the 'urgent national interest' clause to *restrict* the boundaries of a Ramsar site on three occasions only: Belgium in the 1980s, Australia in 1997 (though not ultimately implemented) and Germany in 2000. Further guidance on the implementation of art 2(5) can be found in Resolution VIII.20 (2002).

[102] N Dudley (ed), *Global Wetland Outlook: State of the World's Wetlands and Their Services to People* (Gland, Ramsar Convention Secretariat, 2018) 3.

Canada, as with the state of biological diversity conservation more broadly, the message is one of accelerated decline.[103] Although the site network continues to grow, effective planning and integrated management of Ramsar sites shows no real progress, threats continue to increase, progress on restoration is declining, and assistance from the UN and other global or regional bodies is also declining.[104]

E. Compliance and Enforcement under the WHC

The purpose of the WHC is the identification, protection, conservation, presentation and transmission to future generations of cultural and natural heritage of outstanding universal value. The WHC is thus unusual in its express linking of nature conservation and preservation of cultural properties, seeking to achieve a balance between the two. Protection of designated natural and cultural heritage is conferred by inscription on the World Heritage List of natural and cultural sites satisfying the inscription criteria under the Convention.[105] As such, it has one important characteristic in common with the Ramsar Convention, which is that it works on the basis of maintaining a list of protected sites ('properties' under the WHC). At present, there are 1,121 properties on the list, 869 cultural, 213 natural and 39 mixed properties in 167 States Parties.[106] However, unlike under the Ramsar Convention, it is not necessary to have a site listed to become a full participating party to the WHC.[107] The World Heritage Fund provides an incentive for developing States to list sites, and with 193 States Parties, it enjoys participation by virtually all States vital to global conservation of outstanding natural sites.

In addition to stipulating the criteria for listing, published in the Operational Guidelines, the World Heritage Committee is also responsible for establishing the 'List of World Heritage in Danger', the latter designation signalling that major operations are necessary for conservation of the property and for which assistance has been requested under the Convention. Threats to the outstanding universal value of World Heritage properties are the familiar human-induced impacts ranging from incompatible development projects to poaching and armed conflict, as well as threats from 'sudden ecological and geological events' such as tsunamis and earthquakes, and 'management and institutional frameworks' such as gaps in the legal framework and governance deficiencies.[108] Unlike Ramsar, listing does not

[103] ibid.

[104] ibid.

[105] The inscription criteria of outstanding universal value and representativeness take precedence over geographical distribution: 47 per cent of listed properties are located in Europe and North America, and only 8 per cent in Arab States and 9 per cent in Africa (these are the geographical regions employed by UNESCO).

[106] Out of this total, 39 are transboundary properties shared by two or more States, such as the Mount Nimba Strict Nature Reserve (Côte d'Ivoire and Guinea) and Waterton-Glacier (Canada and the US).

[107] For a full list by country and property, see http://whc.unesco.org.

[108] See the 2008 'List of Factors Affecting Properties' identifying 14 primary factors and numerous secondary factors based on analysis of the 'state of conservation reports' by the parties.

require the consent of the State concerned, though considerable emphasis is placed on cooperation with it. 'Requested assistance' is broadly interpreted and may be requested by any member of the World Heritage Committee, or the Secretariat, and 'assistance' includes expressions of concern by the Committee and inscription on the List of World Heritage in Danger itself.[109] Under this List, the property must be threatened by 'serious and specific danger' (Article 11(4)), which under the Guidelines may be ascertained or potential danger. For ascertained danger, it must be 'specific and proven imminent danger', for example, that there is a threat of a serious decline in the population of an endangered species or 'severe deterioration of the natural beauty or scientific value of the property', or it is under 'major threats which could have deleterious effects on its inherent characteristics', such as a development project.[110] Threats must be correctable by human action. At present, there are 53 properties (36 cultural and 17 natural) in 33 States Parties on the World Heritage in Danger List, with Syria (six properties) and the Democratic Republic of the Congo and Libya (five properties each) reflecting the disproportionate presence of Arab (40 per cent) and African States (30 per cent) on the List.

In certain circumstances, properties that have deteriorated to such an extent as to lose the characteristics qualifying them for inclusion in the List of threatened sites may be removed from the List; this is the ultimate consequence of a State's failure to fulfil its obligations under the Convention. Unlike the Ramsar Convention, there have been deletions from the World Heritage List. This happened for the first time in 2007 with the removal of the Oman Arabian Oryx Sanctuary from the List after numbers of this endangered species tumbled to a mere four viable breeding pairs and the sanctuary was reduced by 90 per cent in size, a downgrading the World Heritage Committee considered to be incompatible with the values for which the natural heritage site was inscribed in 1994. The second occasion was in 2009 with the removal of the Dresden Elbe Valley in Germany from the List of the cultural landscape,[111] owing to the construction of a bridge over the River Elbe.

Danger listing may be perceived either as a form of 'naming and shaming' or as a means of highlighting to the international community difficulties in conserving heritage values and seeking assistance in addressing them. Indeed, as under the Ramsar Convention, there has been a concerted effort to underscore the implications and benefits of Danger Listing and remove the perceived stigma.[112] Whatever

[109] 2019 Guidelines, para 177.

[110] ibid, para 180.

[111] In 1992, the WHC became the first convention to recognise and protect cultural landscapes, with 114 properties now inscribed on the World Heritage List under the cultural landscape criteria: see generally N Mitchell, G Rössler and P-M Tricaud, *World Heritage Cultural Landscapes: A Handbook for Conservation and Management*, World Heritage Papers 26 (2009).

[112] See Decision 40 COM 7, para 27. An example of the benefits is the Florida Everglades, inscribed in 1979 and on the Danger List from 1993 to 2007 and again from 2010 to the present, owing to the impact of pollution, encroaching human development and high levels of tourism. Danger Listing has provided an important stimulus to significant Federal and State allocations of financial and human resources to assist with conservation and restoration measures.

the perception, the clear expectation upon Danger Listing is that steps will be taken by the State Party concerned to reduce and/or eliminate the danger posed to world cultural and natural heritage, often in consultation with the key stakeholders in the site and in the activities related to it, and with access to technical and financial assistance. Improvements in conservation will lead to removal from the Danger List, as had occurred for 40 properties up to 2019.[113] Success may also come in averting threats before Danger Listing becomes necessary.[114] This has been facilitated by the evolution of 'reactive monitoring' under the Convention, which supplements the periodic (every six years) reporting by the Contracting Parties required under Article 29 of the Convention on the legislative and administrative measures adopted for the application of the Convention and the state of conservation of inscribed properties.[115] This ad hoc form of institutional oversight is now formalised in the Operational Guidelines and is the most comprehensive monitoring system of any of the site-based biodiversity-related conventions.[116] It comprises reporting by the Secretariat, other sectors of the United Nations Educational, Scientific and Cultural Organization (UNESCO) and the Advisory Bodies to the World Heritage Committee on the state of World Heritage properties that are under threat, in cooperation with the States Parties concerned upon whom the obligation to protect cultural and natural properties continues primarily to rest.[117] A range of steps may result, from no action or the provision of technical assistance to inscription on the Danger List or removal entirely from the List (with prior notice to the State Party concerned).[118]

V. Conclusion

Ensuring compliance with environmental treaty obligations is achieved through formal and informal methods of compliance and enforcement. As we have seen, these methods include the invocation of formal dispute settlement machinery (rare);[119]

[113] Recent natural heritage examples are Comoé National Park in Côte d'Ivoire, Simien National Park in Ethiopia in 2017 and the Belize Barrier Reef Reserve System in 2018.

[114] Frequently highlighted examples include: the cancellation of a river diversion project owing to adverse impacts on the Royal Chitwan National Park in Nepal, one of the last remaining refuges of the Bengal tiger and one-horned Asiatic rhinoceros; relocation of an aluminium plant which would have affected the archaeological site of Delphi in Greece; and refusal of permission to extend to commercial scale saltworks in El Vizcaino Bay in Mexico, the last pristine reproduction lagoon for the Pacific grey whale.

[115] 2019 Operational Guidelines, ch IV.A (reactive monitoring) and ch V (periodic reporting). Further 'success stories' are cited in UNESCO Reactive Monitoring Review Team, *Strengthening the Effectiveness of the World Heritage Monitoring Process* (Final Report, 31 August 2019) 16–17.

[116] UNESCO Reactive Monitoring Review Team (n 115) para 18.

[117] 2019 Operational Guidelines, para 169.

[118] ibid para 176.

[119] Few dispute settlement clauses in MEAs provide for compulsory third-party settlement of inter-State claims. Sparse examples include the Ozone Layer Convention and the Montreal Protocol, and the UNFCCC and the Kyoto Protocol. Such provision is practically unheard of in relation to nature conservation treaties. And even if such provisions were widespread, as noted above, there would be no great appetite for recourse to them.

oversight by treaty supervisory bodies, including the COP[120] (ubiquitous); and non-compliance procedures (increasingly widespread). Having achieved a position where many environmental treaties now provide for a compliance procedure,[121] increased attention on the role of international compliance in the effective implementation and enforcement of international environmental treaties is unsurprising. As we have seen, the primary objective in establishing compliance procedures is to provide, within a multilateral context, encouragement to States to comply with their treaty obligations and, in the event of non-compliance, to provide a generally 'softer' and more responsive system to address non-compliance than that afforded by traditional dispute settlement procedures under general international law.[122] The function of compliance facilitation is not merely a response to threatened or actual non-compliance with obligations, but rather a complex and ongoing question of ensuring that States 'buy into', and are able to achieve, treaty and/or soft law objectives.[123]

For biodiversity-related agreements – even as we have seen some of those employing trade-related mechanisms – there has been little appetite for the operation of robust compliance mechanisms, whether envisaged in the treaty or subsequently developed. Instead, there has been a marked preference for softer forms of oversight and compliance commensurate with the 'softer' obligations contained within them. Yet even here, generalisations are apt to mislead: the transparency of listing and danger listing (or Montreux Record) under the WHC and Ramsar – and even delisting in extreme cases under the WHC – imitate the facilitative and coercive elements of the compliance procedures of the Montreal and Kyoto Protocols. Yet practice under the former reveals a particular reliance on facilitative approaches,[124] while the more robust coercive approach of the Kyoto Protocol was not replicated in the Paris Agreement mechanism. The Kyoto Protocol remains the 'high water mark' for a compliance mechanism wielding coercive as well as facilitative tools. Moreover, both the WHC and Ramsar have sought to downplay any stigma attached to Danger Listing, with access to technical and financial assistance associated with 'Danger Listing' under the WHC and Ramsar further evidence of the greater appetite for compliance facilitation over (non-)compliance sanctions.

[120] As has been the case under CITES, for example, discussed above. See also S Biniaz, 'Remarks about the CITES Compliance Regime' in U Beyerlin, PT Stoll and R Wolfrum (eds), *Ensuring Compliance with Multilateral Agreements* (Leiden, Martinus Nijhoff, 2006) 89.

[121] In addition, 'subsidiary bodies for operating non-compliance mechanisms could also be established without an explicit provision in the [multilateral environmental agreement] on the basis of "implied powers"'. RR Churchill and G Ulfstein, 'Autonomous Institutional Arrangements in Multilateral Environmental Agreements: A Little-Noticed Phenomenon in International Law' (2000) 94 *American Journal of International Law* 644.

[122] See generally M Fitzmaurice and C Redgwell, 'Environmental Non-compliance Procedures and International Law' (2000) XXXI *Netherlands Yearbook of International Law* 35.

[123] On 'managing compliance' see Chayes and Handler Chayes (n 70); on compliance with soft law, see further Shelton (n 9).

[124] Fitzmaurice and Redgwell (n 122).

The stark reality remains that notwithstanding the significant achievement of developing some innovative compliance approaches and even some rare success stories, the failure to comply with procedural and substantive environmental treaty obligations continues to undermine efforts at nature conservation. While it is difficult to know whether the instruments considered here would have been 'less effective' in the absence of these largely facilitative compliance procedures – counterfactuals of necessity being difficult to substantiate – there is little doubt that the 'soft underbelly' of traditional enforcement is also found with these innovative mechanisms. While this might be argued to be the point – to facilitate, to cajole, to influence – the end result is an accelerated and irrevocable loss of species and habitat. Ultimately the problem lies not just with the fitness for purpose of compliance and enforcement tools, but in the degree of robustness of the conservation obligations they address.

11

Where's the Catch? Shifting Stocks, International Fisheries Management and the Climate Change Conundrum

RICHARD CADDELL

Abstract: It is increasingly evident that many fish stocks are exhibiting unprecedented shifts in distribution, caused primarily by the impacts of climate change and associated processes on oceanic conditions. These trends have significant implications for future international fisheries management, with States prospectively losing important natural resources, while other States are keen to exploit a new biomass windfall. The aim of this chapter is to evaluate how international law has responded to this phenomenon to date, and whether current regulatory trends and philosophies are sufficient to address the future problems posed by the changing distributions of valuable marine living resources.

'[I]t is a well-established principle of the law of nations that the state of things that actually exists and has existed for a long time should be changed as little as possible.'[1]

'[F]isheries face a serious new challenge as climate change drives the ocean to conditions not experienced historically.'[2]

I. Introduction

The divergent subjects of multilateral regulation represented within this volume stand as a formidable testament to the breadth of the contribution made by Robin Churchill to the study of international law over the course of the past five decades.

[1] *The Grisbådarna Case* (*Norway v Sweden*), Award of 23 October 1909 [1909] 11 RIA 155, 161.
[2] M Pinsky et al, 'Preparing Ocean Governance for Species on the Move' (2018) 360 *Science* 1189, 1189.

It may nevertheless be suggested that his extensive and enduring legacy of scholarship is most prominently and thematically associated with the Law of the Sea and international environmental law. Within this context, and positioned at one of the many points of the porous frontier at which these two broad areas of international law intersect and commingle, Churchill's work has been of particular value in advancing the literature on the law of international fisheries, which continues to occupy a central concern in the regulation of marine resources. This chapter accordingly examines the contemporary management of global fish stocks as a fitting achievement of international law, albeit one that reflects many of the inherent strengths and frailties of multilateral governance canvassed elsewhere in this book.

Viewed panoramically, Churchill's work on these issues has encapsulated three broad themes. In the first instance, he has engaged strongly with the perennial difficulties encountered in securing compliance with important unifying obligations. A clear sense of fair play has long permeated Churchill's writings and, while pragmatic as to the drivers and incentives that tempt individual operators to disregard the law, he has maintained a firm belief that cherry-picking compliance with international commitments should not be tacitly accepted as the cost of doing multilateral business.[3] Moreover, and allied to this, he has also concentrated on the role that dispute resolution can – and should – play in these endeavours, both as a means of promoting compliance and in advancing a workable and consistent interpretation of key instruments.[4] Second, the coherence of international governance structures has also been a core consideration, notably in promoting institutional efficiency and in securing the legitimacy of multilateral machinery.[5] Third, Churchill's work has retained a foundation of concern for the health of the (marine) environment and the role that law can play in facilitating its long-term protection, while also remaining acutely mindful of its structural and normative limitations.[6]

Arguably the most pressing current issue that prospectively unites these common themes is the threat posed to marine ecosystems by climate change. One of the cornerstone accomplishments of modern international law has been the further codification of the Law of the Sea, primarily through the adoption of the United Nations Convention on the Law of the Sea 1982.[7] This framework has had a profound impact upon the governance of ocean space and has brought a considerable degree of normative clarity to the politically charged question of entitlements

[3] See, for instance, R Churchill, 'The Persisting Problem of Non-compliance with the Law of the Sea Convention: Disorder in the Oceans' (2012) 27 *International Journal of Marine and Coastal Law* 813, 815.

[4] R Churchill, 'The Jurisprudence of the International Tribunal for the Law of the Sea Relating to Fisheries: Is There Much in the Net?' (2007) 22 *International Journal of Marine and Coastal Law* 383, 423–24.

[5] R Churchill and G Ulfstein, 'Autonomous Institutional Arrangements in Multilateral Environmental Agreements: A Little-Noticed Phenomenon in International Law' (2000) 94 *American Journal of International Law* 623.

[6] R Churchill, 'The LOSC Regime for Protection of the Marine Environment: Fit for the Twenty-First Century?' in R Rayfuse, *Research Handbook on International Marine Environmental Law* (Cheltenham, Edward Elgar, 2015) 3–30.

[7] 1833 UNTS 3 ('UNCLOS').

to marine living resources. Nevertheless, the maturation of international fisheries law has not provided a panacea to the problems facing global fish stocks,[8] which remain in a troubling state and with concerns consistently raised by overfishing, excessive capacity, environmental damage and serial non-compliance. These regulatory shortcomings are compounded by the present and future impacts of climate change and associated processes upon fisheries resources,[9] which will exacerbate current management deficiencies and exert unprecedented pressures upon long-standing legal structures. One particularly pressing new challenge in this respect pertains to the changing distributional patterns of many fish and interdependent species, influenced by rising sea temperatures and ocean acidification, with current projections indicating their eventual displacement to deeper waters and the polar regions. This will inevitably have profound implications for future fisheries management, as some States experience an influx of new stocks while others endure a net loss of resources. While international law has brokered a series of solutions to past problems of access and allocation, the challenges posed by climate change threaten to undermine these hard-won achievements. The future success of international fisheries management will therefore hinge upon the development of far-sighted legal and management solutions to mitigate these impacts, in a context of scientific and political uncertainty, and demands for increased flexibility in the regulation of marine living resources.

This chapter therefore considers how international law has responded to climate-induced shifts in fish stocks, an issue that will become increasingly exigent over the course of the coming decades. To this end, the chapter first outlines current and prospective trends in the distribution of commercially significant fish stocks and the limitations of current legal instruments in confronting these shifts. It then examines some of the more promising achievements of international law in promoting the anticipatory management of shifting fisheries. Subsequently, it evaluates the current unsatisfactory treatment of climate change concerns by regional fisheries management organisations (RFMOs) before considering the scope to mitigate conflicts caused by the impacts of climate change upon global fish stocks.

II. Shifting Fish Stocks and the Limits of Current Legal Frameworks

The elaboration of a framework for the governance of international fisheries resources under UNCLOS and associated instruments may be rightly considered

[8] As noted by the UN Food and Agriculture Organization (FAO) in its biennial review of global fisheries trends, '[t]he state of marine fishery resources, based on FAO's monitoring of assessed marine fish stocks, has continued to decline': *The State of World Fisheries and Aquaculture 2018 – Meeting the Sustainable Development Goals* (Rome, FAO, 2018) 6.

[9] For a sobering overview, see W Cheung, V Lam, Y Ota and W Swartz, 'Modelling Future Oceans: The Present and Emerging Future of Fish Stocks and Fisheries' in R Caddell and E Molenaar (eds), *Strengthening International Fisheries Law in an Era of Changing Oceans* (Oxford, Hart Publishing, 2019) 13, 15–17.

to be a distinct achievement of international law, albeit one that is qualified by ambiguity and persisting lacunae. Fisheries are addressed within two separate parts of UNCLOS, engaging rights and duties of States within their exclusive economic zones (EEZs) and on the high seas respectively. With regard to the EEZ, coastal States exercise sovereign rights for the purpose of exploring and exploiting, conserving and managing natural resources, including fisheries.[10] Nevertheless, these rights are tempered by a series of obligations aimed at conserving stocks of marine living resources and promoting their optimal utilisation. Under Article 61(1) a coastal State is charged with determining the total allowable catch (TAC) of fish in its EEZ and is required, 'taking into account the best scientific evidence available to it', to institute proper conservation and management measures to ensure that stocks are not endangered by overexploitation.[11] Such measures are intended to maintain or restore populations at levels that are capable of supporting exploitation at maximum sustainable yield (MSY), specifically taking into account 'relevant environmental and economic factors' as well as fishing patterns, the interdependence of stocks and 'generally recommended international minimum standards',[12] while also considering the effects of harvesting on those species that are associated with or dependent upon the target stock.[13]

Article 62 obliges coastal States to promote the objective of optimal utilisation without prejudice to these preceding criteria.[14] To this end, coastal States are to determine their capacity to harvest the fish stocks located within these waters and grant access to other States to any surplus,[15] an often lucrative application of EEZ entitlements. Allocative decisions in this respect are considered to be an exercise of the sovereignty of the coastal States over the natural resources of its EEZ and are in principle non-justiciable, lying outside the broad framework of compulsory dispute resolution elaborated under UNCLOS,[16] subject to rather limited requirements to consider the interests of landlocked and geographically disadvantaged States in the process[17] and the need to minimise economic dislocation for those constituents that had played a key role in the development of the fishery in question.[18] In accessing the surplus, foreign fishers must comply with pertinent conditions and regulations that may be elaborated[19] and enforced[20] by the coastal

[10] Article 56(1)(a).
[11] ibid art 61(2).
[12] ibid art 61(3).
[13] ibid art 61(4).
[14] ibid art 62(1).
[15] ibid art 62(2).
[16] ibid art 297(3)(a). However, the position of transboundary stocks is rather more nuanced, with disputes concerning the high seas appearing to fall outside this exception: see Churchill (n 4) 389–90; and A Boyle, 'Problems of Compulsory Jurisdiction and the Settlement of Disputes relating to Straddling Fish Stocks' (1999) 14 *International Journal of Marine and Coastal Law* 1.
[17] Articles 69 and 70.
[18] ibid art 62(3); see further below.
[19] Article 62(4) prescribes a non-exhaustive list of elements that may be prospectively regulated by the coastal State in respect of foreign fleets within the EEZ.
[20] Article 73.

State. With a modest volume of catches occurring solely on the high seas,[21] these provisions are thus of enduring significance in framing international rights and responsibilities over the exploitation of fish.

Beyond the confines of national jurisdiction, fishing has long been recognised as one of the fundamental freedoms of the high seas, a position currently enshrined in Article 87(1), albeit tempered by the requirement to exercise 'due regard' for the interests of other States and rights pertaining to the International Seabed Area.[22] This is further constrained in principle by the need to adhere to pertinent obligations applied within[23] and beyond the letter of UNCLOS. As far as the 1982 Convention is concerned, States have a duty to take – either individually or in cooperation with others – such measures as may be necessary for the conservation of the living resources of the high seas.[24] While nebulously drawn, these requirements substantively mirror the core elements of the EEZ regime and aim to secure a consistent harvest of fish at MSY, taking into consideration the ecological coexistence of fish stocks and their wider ecosystems.[25] Although fishing on the high seas is technically open to all States, irrespective of their capacity or coastal presence, such fisheries have been the preserve of a relatively small number of States in practice.[26]

Nevertheless, fish have little respect for presumptive human-drawn boundaries. Few commercially significant stocks are 'discrete', in that they are confined purely to the high seas[27] or are located exclusively within the jurisdictional waters of a lone coastal State. Fish are predominantly either transboundary in nature, in that they regularly move between the EEZs of two or more coastal States, or are straddling stocks that transit between at least one EEZ and the high seas, while others pursue extensive migratory routes that see them traverse a series of maritime boundaries, both within and beyond areas of national jurisdiction. Collectively, these species are addressed under the rather insipid wording of Article 63, which requires States to 'seek, either directly or through appropriate sub-regional or regional organisations to agree on the measures necessary' for the conservation of such stocks. Similarly perfunctory obligations are established under Article 64 in respect of highly migratory species, for which States are to 'cooperate … with a view to' ensuring the conservation and management of 16 named families of species, primarily tunas, defined as such in Annex I to the Convention. In principle, the small number of species currently designated 'highly migratory' could be extended, although in practice the protracted amendment processes of UNCLOS

[21] U Sumaila et al, 'Winners and Losers in a World Where the High Seas is Closed to Fishing' (2015) 5 *Scientific Reports* 8481.

[22] Article 87(2).

[23] Specifically arts 63(2) and 64–67, addressing highly migratory species, marine mammals and anadromous and catadromous stocks respectively: art 116(b).

[24] ibid arts 117–19.

[25] ibid art 119(1).

[26] Sumaila (n 21). This is mainly attributed to a lack of nutritional imperative to fish on the high seas, as well as logistical and commercial constraints.

[27] ibid (noting that less than two per cent of currently fished species are discrete high seas stocks).

appear unlikely to be successfully pursued[28] and the list is thus expected to remain closed to other species, irrespective of biological behaviour. The tone of Article 64 appears oriented towards the regulation of specific fish, although its interpretation has been muddied by its lingering application to a small number of marine mammals due to complexities in its drafting process.[29] Ultimately, these ambiguities illustrate an overarching trend, noted with gentle understatement by Churchill, that 'many of the fisheries provisions of the LOSC are broadly drawn and lacking in precision'.[30]

The deficiencies of Articles 63 and 64 have been addressed to a considerable extent by the adoption of a specific Implementation Agreement to further elaborate guiding principles and commitments regarding these important fish species.[31] The UNFSA, which provides normative supplementation to the fisheries regime of UNCLOS yet remains a self-standing treaty,[32] has been of significant operative value in advancing international fisheries management. The UNFSA does not prescribe specific management measures for fisheries; instead, its value lies in its articulation of overarching governance expectations for current and future RFMOs, notably through enhanced transparency, participatory and administrative practices.[33] It has also been instrumental in promoting the ecosystem-based[34] and precautionary[35] approaches to fisheries that had been broadly absent from preceding instruments, elaborating expectations for securing compatibility between conservation measures adopted in respect of the high seas and areas under national jurisdiction,[36] as well as elucidating enforcement duties[37] and dispute resolution[38] requirements. Most significantly, the UNFSA has provided a regulatory template for the constituent treaties of new RFMOs to follow,[39] while also inspiring older structures to 'retro-fit' clearer environmental obligations

[28] Article 312. On the difficulties of amending the Convention, see A Boyle, 'Further Development of the Law of the Sea Convention: Mechanisms for Change' (2005) 54 *International and Comparative Law Quarterly* 563. Alternatively, the constituent treaties of some RFMOs have elaborated more nuanced definitions of the highly migratory species covered by their mandates in order to address a fuller range of species: D Owen, 'Annex I' in A Proelss (ed), *United Nations Convention on the Law of the Sea* (Oxford, Hart Publishing, 2017) 2049, 2064.

[29] C Jefferies, *Marine Mammal Conservation and the Law of the Sea* (Oxford, Oxford University Press, 2016) 176–83. Article 65 exempts marine mammals from the expectations of optimal utilisation inherent in the EEZ regime, a provision drafted concurrently with art 64. Contemporary accounts suggest that marine mammals were intended to be addressed separately, yet a small number of cetaceans remain listed on Annex I, to the interpretive detriment of these provisions.

[30] Churchill (n 4) 387.

[31] Agreement for the Implementation of the Provisions of the United Nations Convention on the Law of the Sea of 10 December 1982 Relating to the Conservation and Management of Straddling Fish Stocks and Highly Migratory Fish Stocks, 2167 UNTS 3 ('UNFSA').

[32] UNFSA, art 4.

[33] See especially ibid arts 8–14.

[34] ibid art 5.

[35] ibid art 6.

[36] ibid art 7.

[37] ibid arts 18–23.

[38] ibid arts 30–32.

[39] R Caddell, 'International Fisheries Law and Interactions with Global Regimes and Processes' in Caddell and Molenaar (n 9) 133, 147–48.

into their respective mandates,[40] thereby entrenching these requirements as core expectations of rational governance for transboundary stocks. Indeed, as Harrison observes, the principles established under the UNFSA 'not only provide a checklist for evaluating the functioning of fisheries cooperation, but they also provide an important baseline for states when negotiating the establishment of new cooperative mechanisms, whether they apply to straddling and highly migratory stocks or discrete high seas stocks'.[41]

Notwithstanding these developments, the fisheries provisions of UNCLOS – and indeed those of the UNFSA – operate largely on the assumption that fishing grounds will remain fundamentally static and predictable, and that fish stocks will continue to provide a perpetual bounty of resources at MSY. However, it is has become increasingly evident that the impacts of climate change and associated processes are challenging these assumptions. Rising sea temperatures and ocean acidification are influencing the current and projected distribution patterns of fish species, with many stocks now 'undergoing phenological and geographical shifts as a result of warming'.[42] These shifts are gradual, but they are not negligible, with fish and other interdependent marine species moving into new areas at a rate of up to 70 km a decade.[43] Current predictions indicate a general trend towards the eventual displacement of numerous fish species to deeper ocean waters and the polar regions,[44] with a corresponding reduction in catch potential in the Tropics.[45] Indeed, warm-water species have been represented in elevated numbers in global catches in recent years,[46] a trend that has been primarily attributed to the increased geographical range of these fish caused by rising ocean temperatures.[47] Distributional shifts are becoming apparent on a regional basis for particular species,[48] but their impacts have been most keenly felt at a more national level, with temperature spikes and localised heatwaves having prompted the displacement of substantial volumes of biomass in a number of key fishing locations,[49]

[40] Z Scanlon, 'The Art of "Not Undermining": Possibilities within Existing Architecture to Improve Environmental Protections in Areas beyond National Jurisdiction' (2018) 75 *ICES Journal of Marine Science* 405, 410.

[41] J Harrison, 'Key Challenges Relating to the Governance of Regional Fisheries' in Caddell and Molenaar (n 9) 79, 80–81.

[42] J-P Gattuso et al, 'Contrasting Futures for Ocean and Society from Different Anthropogenic CO2 Emissions Scenarios' (2015) 349 *Science* 39, 39.

[43] E Poloczanska et al, 'Global Imprint of Climate Change on Marine Life' (2013) 3 *Nature Climate Change* 923.

[44] A Perry et al, 'Climate Change and Distribution Shifts in Marine Fishes' (2005) 308 *Science* 1912, 1912–15.

[45] M Pinsky et al, 'Marine Taxa Track Local Climate Velocities' (2013) 341 *Science* 1239.

[46] U Sumaila et al, 'Climate Change Impacts on the Biophysics and Economics of World Fisheries' (2011) 1 *Nature Climate Change* 449, 451.

[47] W Cheung, R Watson and D Pauly, 'Signature of Ocean Warming in Global Fisheries Catch' (2013) 497 *Nature* 365, 365–66.

[48] I Montero-Serra, M Edwards and M Genner, 'Warming Shelf Seas Drive the Subtropicalization of European Pelagic Fish Communities' (2015) 21 *Global Change Biology* 144, 149–50.

[49] W Cheung and T Frölicher, 'Marine Heatwaves Exacerbate Climate Change Impacts for Fisheries in the Northeast Pacific' (2020) 10 *Scientific Reports* 6678.

which has considerable socio-economic implications for particular constituencies in both developed[50] and developing[51] countries.

Significant adjustments to the compositions of national EEZs are likely to result from climate-induced shifts in the mid- to long-term future. Much depends upon the ultimate rate of warming,[52] but permanent changes to the distribution of marine species are expected even if there is full and universal compliance with the more ambitious elements of current climate change targets.[53] The displacement, at least to some degree, of stocks previously present in the national EEZ of one State into that of another is projected to occur in up to 35 per cent of all present EEZs by 2100.[54] These re-adjustments will have profound consequences for economic, social and international relations. Inevitably, shifting stocks will present inviting commercial possibilities for coastal States gaining an influx of new resources, particularly in more temperate and northerly waters.[55] This will nevertheless come at the expense of jurisdictions that can often ill-afford such losses, either nutritionally,[56] economically,[57] industrially[58] or biologically.[59] Indeed, such adjustments are projected to be most acute in the Tropics,[60] South Pacific[61] and East Asia.[62] As Dubik et al observe, the 'geographic movement of resources across political boundaries has important implications for whether and how fishers "follow the fish", the potential social impacts of fish and fishery shifts, and governance response'.[63] In this respect, concerns have already been raised over the scope for both legal[64] and physical[65] conflict over shifting fisheries resources.

Despite these present and future trends, the core framework of the Law of the Sea provides few clear answers to the governance challenges posed by shifting

[50] M Pinsky and M Fogarty, 'Lagged Social-Ecological Responses to Climate and Range Shifts in Fisheries' (2012) 115 *Climatic Change* 883.

[51] R Blasiak et al, 'Climate Change and Marine Fisheries: Least-Developed Countries Top Global Index of Vulnerability (2017) 6 *PLoS One* e0179632.

[52] V Lam et al, 'Projected Change in Global Fisheries Revenues under Climate Change' (2016) 6 *Scientific Reports* 32607.

[53] W Cheung, G Reygondeau and T Frölicher, 'Large Benefits to Marine Fisheries of Meeting the 1.5°C Global Warming Target' (2016) 354 *Science* 1591.

[54] Pinsky et al (n 2) 1190.

[55] Cheung, Watson and Pauly (n 47).

[56] C Golden et al, 'Fall in Fish Catch Threatens Human Health' (2016) 534 *Nature* 317.

[57] E Allison et al, 'Vulnerability of National Economies to the Impacts of Climate Change on Fisheries' (2009) 10 *Fish and Fisheries* 173.

[58] L Teh and U Sumaila, 'Contribution of Marine Fisheries to Worldwide Employment' (2013) 14 *Fish and Fisheries* 77.

[59] M Barange et al, 'Impacts of Climate Change on Marine Ecosystem Production in Societies Dependent on Fisheries' (2014) 4 *Nature Climate Change* 211.

[60] W Cheung et al, 'Large-Scale Redistribution of Maximum Fisheries Catch Potential in the Global Ocean under Climate Change' (2010) 16 *Global Change Biology* 24, 30–31.

[61] Blasiak et al (n 51).

[62] C Free et al, 'Impacts of Historical Warming on Marine Fisheries Production' (2019) 363 *Science* 979.

[63] B Dubik et al, 'Governing Fisheries in the Face of Change: Social Responses to Long-Term Geographic Shifts in a US Fishery' (2019) 99 *Marine Policy* 243, 244.

[64] Pinsky et al (n 2); J Spijkers and WJ Boonstra, 'Environmental Change and Social Conflict: The Northeast Atlantic Mackerel Dispute' (2017) 17 *Regional Environmental Change* 1835.

[65] J Spijkers et al, 'Marine Fisheries and Future Ocean Conflict' (2018) 19 *Fish and Fisheries* 798.

stocks. There is an evident disconnect between legal regimes concerned with climate change on the one hand and oceans governance on the other. Interactions between these two frameworks have been 'muted at best'[66] and primarily confined to the realms of soft law,[67] while the marine sphere has been regularly marginalised in multilateral efforts to confront climate change.[68] Similarly, as products of their respective eras, climate change and associated processes such as acidification are not directly considered within the terms of UNCLOS or its current Implementation Agreements. This is particularly true of the UNFSA, whose provisions make no express mention of climate change, while as noted below, RFMOs have also proved slow to embrace this as a core concern. Nevertheless, certain provisions of the UNFSA could be read expansively to promote a degree of further attention towards these issues. Notably, parties recognise the need to 'assess impacts of fishing, other human activities and environmental factors on target stocks'[69] as an operative principle, while in applying the precautionary approach to fisheries, States are to take into account 'existing and predicted oceanic, environmental and socio-economic conditions'[70] in reviewing uncertainties related to fishing. These are nevertheless permissively and vaguely framed and provide little compulsion to address stock shifts as a regulatory priority. Ultimately, even the most activist interpretations of the UNFSA acknowledge that there are formidable obstacles to its ability to promote greater accountability and mitigative relief for the impacts of climate change,[71] and strong reservations remain over the ability of such instruments to be manipulated into more ecologically crusading territory.[72]

Likewise, UNCLOS is essentially silent on this issue, although its environmental provisions are being (re-)interpreted with increasing dynamism to integrate climate change concerns more explicitly within the mandate of a living instrument.[73] Of its specific fisheries provisions, only Article 62(3) offers – albeit indirectly – a potential basis to address a prospective change in the location of fisheries resources by requiring a coastal State to consider 'all relevant factors,

[66] C Redgwell, 'Treaty Evolution, Adaptation and Change: Is the UNCLOS "Enough" to Address Climate Change Impacts on the Marine Environment?' (2019) 34 *International Journal of Marine and Coastal Law* 440, 453.

[67] K Scott, 'Ocean Acidification: A Due Diligence Obligation under the UNCLOS' (2020) 35 *International Journal of Marine and Coastal Law* 1, 25.

[68] R Rayfuse, 'Addressing Climate Change Impacts in Regional Fisheries Management Organizations' in Caddell and Molenaar (n 9) 247–48.

[69] UNFSA, art 5(d).

[70] ibid art 6(3)(e). Parties may also contemplate emergency measures where a 'natural phenomenon has a significant adverse impact on the status of straddling fish stocks or highly migratory fish stocks' (art 6(7)), although such measures must be temporary and it remains questionable whether anthropogenically driven climate change constitutes a 'natural phenomenon' under this construction.

[71] W Burns, 'A Voice for the Fish? Climate Change Litigation and Potential Causes of Action for Impacts under the United Nations Fish Stocks Agreement' (2008) 11 *Journal of International Wildlife Law and Policy* 30, 55–62.

[72] J Grote Stoutenberg, 'Through the Back-Door: The Limits of the UN Law of the Sea Convention's Usefulness as a Tool to Combat Climate Change' in C Scofield, S Lee and M-S Kwon (eds), *The Limits of Maritime Jurisdiction* (Leiden, Brill, 2014) 679, 685–86.

[73] A Boyle, 'Litigating Climate Change under Part XII of the LOSC' (2019) 34 *International Journal of Marine and Coastal Law* 458, 463–69; on UNCLOS as an organic regime, see J Barrett, 'The UN

including, inter alia … the need to minimize economic dislocation in States whose nationals have habitually fished in the zone or which have made substantial efforts in research and identification of stocks'. This commitment was originally intended to mitigate the impact upon fleets that had regularly fished in locations that, prior to the recognition of the EEZ concept under UNCLOS, had constituted areas of the high seas and had now been repatriated as a new zone of national jurisdiction. In principle, Article 62(3) balances the 'loss' of these fish to the global community by requiring the coastal State to share that portion of the TAC that is surplus to its domestic nutritional requirements. In so doing, this provision applies non-exhaustive and non-hierarchical criteria to guide the allocation of any surplus, although few clear principles beyond the economic self-interest of the coastal State appear to have influenced the national application of Article 62(3) in practice.

The malleability of Article 62(3) in addressing changing fishing patterns has received little consideration to date. The current direction of judicial travel suggests a narrow interpretation of the coastal State's obligations towards interested foreign fishers, at least in the context of those claiming to have fished 'habitually' within the EEZ.[74] Even so, there are indications that individual coastal States may be prepared to interpret this obligation in a more inclusionary manner, albeit guided by financial or political advantage. One notable context is the post-Brexit position of fishing vessels flagged to the remaining EU Member States, which can demonstrate a long-standing presence in the EEZ of the UK through their participation in the Common Fisheries Policy and may thus advance a tenable case for having met the requirements of this provision. Although fisheries negotiations in the Brexit process are likely to remain a complex and inflammatory issue, the UK government suggested at an early stage that it was receptive to this interpretation of Article 62(3), which has been advanced by a number of EU fishing interests.[75] Nevertheless, this may be alternatively viewed as reflecting a sense of realpolitik, where a coastal State accustomed to making accommodations for particular fishers chooses to maintain access to its EEZ in the unique context of withdrawal from a regional economic integration organisation and with fishing entitlements leveraged against a series of broader negotiating objectives. Moreover, this is not reflective of the position of States attempting to gain access to a stock that has translocated into a neighbouring area of national jurisdiction.

Convention on the Law of the Sea: A "Living" Treaty?' in J Barrett and R Barnes (eds), *Law of the Sea: UNCLOS as a Living Treaty* (London, British Institute of International and Comparative Law, 2016) 1.

[74] *South China Sea Arbitration (The Philippines v China)*, Award of 12 July 2016, para 804 (noting that the EEZ regime of UNCLOS has essentially rescinded previous entitlements, hence a coastal State's decision to allow access on the basis of national legislation, bilateral arrangements or through an RFMO would be 'commendable' but not obligatory).

[75] House of Lords European Union Committee, *Eighth Report of Session 2016–17; Brexit Fisheries* (available at https://publications.parliament.uk/pa/ld201617/ldselect/ldeucom/78/78.pdf). However, this may be further complicated by jurisdictional turf wars between the various devolved administrations of the UK in exercising their respective fisheries competences within those parts of the UK EEZ under their respective control: see R Churchill, 'They're Scotland's Fish! Implications of Brexit for Scots Fisheries Law' (2018) 22 *Edinburgh Law Review* 110.

The *South China Sea* award only addressed the position of pre-existing fishing activities. The second and alternative prong of Article 62(3), concerning those who have materially contributed to the development of a fishery, would appear to offer more assistance to a State seeking access to a stock that has started to shift out of its own EEZ and into that of another. In this instance, it would be open to the State losing fish to argue that it had made the requisite efforts in researching and identifying the stock by previously managing those resources in its own jurisdictional waters. In such a case, the State gaining fish would in principle be required to consider this in determining access to any surplus. However, this does not guarantee access to the displaced fish: there may be no surplus to distribute, a shifting stock that has been previously unfished in these waters might instead be treated as a 'new' fishery (which, as observed below, would be subject to minimal catches and more restrictive oversight), and there may be little commercial interest in permitting access or, indeed, the relevant authorities may validly consider that any economic dislocation has ultimately been minimal. States seeking a more privileged degree of access to fish based on the circumstances of Article 62(3) therefore appear best advised to pursue a distinct bilateral arrangement with the other State in question.[76] Ultimately, this scenario will be optimally resolved through far-sighted and adjustable allocative arrangements between the States in question,[77] although, as noted below, relatively few successful examples exist at present.

III. Shifting Stocks and the Pre-emptive Management of Fisheries Resources

Notwithstanding concerns over the lack of express consideration for the implications of climate change within the broad fisheries framework of UNCLOS, particular legal instruments and regimes have developed proactive and valuable mechanisms to address some of the issues raised by distributional shifts in fish stocks. In this regard, two broad contexts are especially relevant. First, an array of provisions and policies have been elaborated to regulate the establishment of 'new' fisheries, which provides a precautionary and graduated basis to manage a potential influx of commercially attractive new species. Second, States have demonstrated their capacity to negotiate pioneering legal instruments and approaches to govern areas in which commercial fishing remains a theoretical proposition at present, but may become more tenable in future decades due to climate-driven stock shifts.

[76] S Allen, 'The Jurisprudence of Artisanal Fishing Revisited' in S Allen, N Bankes and Ø Ravna (eds), *The Rights of Indigenous Peoples in Marine Areas* (Oxford, Hart Publishing, 2019) 97, 116.

[77] Pinsky et al (n 2); K Oremus et al, 'Governance Challenges for Tropical Nations Losing Fish Species Due to Climate Change' (2020) 3 *Nature Sustainability* 277.

A. The Regulation of New Fisheries

Fish stocks that have been displaced across international boundaries due to changing ocean conditions may represent a resource that has been previously unexploited within that jurisdictional area. Individual States are now increasingly able to contemplate the sustained harvesting of species that have historically had a fleeting or inconsistent presence in their national waters or were not formerly available in sufficient numbers to constitute an economically viable fishery.[78] Traditionally, international law has been slow to restrain a collective frontier mentality towards unregulated marine living resources,[79] which has inflicted considerable damage upon fish stocks in locations subject to previously limited oversight, notably in areas beyond national jurisdiction[80] and the deep-sea environment.[81] Prior to the adoption of the UNFSA, the pursuit of new fishing opportunities had also been subject to minimal regulation. However, since the mid-1990s, a discernible set of rules and principles has emerged to regulate new fisheries,[82] which has provided a valuable management tool to address adjustments in fishing patterns and practices caused inter alia by shifting stocks.

The regulation of emerging fisheries is now an integral part of the precautionary approach to fisheries management promoted under the UNFSA. At a preliminary stage in the negotiations of the UNFSA, it was recognised that there was a strong commercial and nutritional interest in promoting alternative fishing opportunities, although such activities came with a significant degree of attendant scientific uncertainty and ecological risk.[83] Historically, new fisheries were initiated with little data – or thought – as to the prospective impacts of fishing on the target stock, non-target species and associated ecosystems, frequently resulting in a pattern of boom and bust as lasting damage was inflicted upon finite resources before meaningful regulation could be applied to these activities. The UNFSA fills this lacuna by imposing restrictions upon the parameters of intended new

[78] W Cheung et al, 'Review of Climate Change Impacts on Marine Fisheries in the UK and Ireland' (2012) 22 *Aquatic Conservation: Marine and Freshwater Ecosystems* 368, 374 (noting lucrative new fishing opportunities for stocks such as John Dory, anchovy and red mullet that have expanded their distribution into UK waters due to changing ocean conditions).

[79] A Merrie et al, 'An Ocean of Surprises: Trends in Human Use, Unexpected Dynamics and Governance Challenges in Areas beyond National Jurisdiction' (2014) 27 *Global Environmental Change* 19, 26.

[80] E Molenaar, 'Addressing Regulatory Gaps in High Seas Fisheries' (2005) 20 *International Journal of Marine and Coastal Law* 533.

[81] R Caddell, 'Deep-Sea Bottom Fisheries and the Protection of Seabed Ecosystems: Problems, Progress and Prospects' in C Banet (ed), *The Law of the Seabed: Access, Uses, and Protection of Seabed Resources* (Leiden, Brill, 2020) 255.

[82] See further R Caddell, 'Precautionary Management and the Development of Future Fishing Opportunities: The International Regulation of New and Exploratory Fisheries' (2018) *33 International Journal of Marine and Coastal Law* 199.

[83] FAO, *The Precautionary Approach to Fisheries with Reference to Straddling Fish Stocks and Highly Migratory Fish Stocks*; Document A/CONF.164/INF/8, 26 January 1994, para 90; reproduced in J-P Lévy and GG Schram, *United Nations Conference on Straddling Fish Stocks and Highly Migratory Fish Stocks: Selected Documents* (The Hague, Kluwer, 1996) 574.

fisheries, envisaging that conservation measures will be applied and subsequently eased as a fuller picture of the impacts of such fisheries progressively emerges. To this end, Article 6(6) provides:

> For new and exploratory fisheries, States shall adopt as soon as possible cautious conservation and management measures, including, inter alia, catch limits and effort limits. Such measures shall remain in force until there are sufficient data to allow assessment of the impact of the fisheries on the long-term sustainability of the stocks, whereupon conservation and management measures based on that assessment shall be implemented. The latter measures shall, if appropriate, allow for the gradual development of the fisheries.

The concept of a 'new' or an 'exploratory' fishery is not elaborated further within the UNFSA and indeed remains definitionally inconsistent across a range of regulatory bodies. Article 6(6) was heavily influenced by the contemporaneous elaboration of parallel policies by the Commission on the Conservation of Antarctic Marine Living Resources (CCAMLR), which remains the most prominent regulator of these specific fisheries. CCAMLR's more ostensible ecosystem-based mandate[84] renders it unique within the firmament of international fisheries regulators[85] and prior to the adoption of the UNFSA, it was arguably the only body with the requisite authority to pioneer a more conservation-oriented approach to fisheries.[86] While the UNFSA provides little guidance on the implementation of this requirement, its value lies in its guiding influence as a template for the competences of subsequent RFMOs. In this respect, the post-UNFSA RFMOs have included express provision for the regulation of new and exploratory fisheries within their constituent treaties – notably the Western and Central Pacific Fisheries Committee (WCPFC),[87] the South-East Atlantic Fisheries Organisation (SEAFO),[88] the Southern Indian Ocean Fisheries Agreement (SIOFA),[89] the South Pacific Regional Fisheries Management Organisation (SPRFMO)[90] and the North Pacific Fisheries Commission (NPFC)[91] – which may not have occurred as readily otherwise.

[84] Convention for the Conservation of Antarctic Marine Living Resources, 1329 UNTS 47 (art II).

[85] With a far broader ecological mandate than most classical fisheries bodies, CCAMLR is considered to be 'more than an RFMO'; see R Billé et al, *Regional Oceans Governance: Making Regional Seas Programmes, Regional Fishery Bodies and Large Marine Ecosystem Mechanisms Work Better Together* (Nairobi, UNEP, 2016) 29–34.

[86] See further E Molenaar, 'CCAMLR and Southern Ocean Fisheries' (2001) 16 *International Journal of Marine and Coastal Law* 465.

[87] Convention on the Conservation and Management of Highly Migratory Fish Stocks in the Western and Central Pacific Ocean 2000, 2275 UNTS 43 (art 6(5)).

[88] Convention on the Conservation and Management of Fishery Resources in the South-East Atlantic Ocean 2001; 2221 UNTS 189 (Art 20).

[89] Southern Indian Ocean Fisheries Agreement 2006, art 6, www.fao.org/fishery/rfb/siofa/en.

[90] Convention on the Conservation and Management of High Seas Fishery Resources in the South Pacific Ocean 2009, [2012] ATS 28, article 22.

[91] Convention on the Conservation and Management of High Seas Fisheries Resources in the North Pacific Ocean 2011, arts 3 and, http://npfc.r-cms.jp/About_Convention.

The first formal regulatory expectations for States seeking to develop new fisheries beyond national jurisdiction were formulated by CCAMLR in 1991,[92] which applied to fisheries for which 'information on distribution, abundance, demography, potential yield and stock identity from comprehensive research/surveys or exploratory fishing' or catch and effort data had not been submitted. Where a new fishery is proposed, the member in question is required to provide notice of its intent to fish three months in advance of the next regular CCAMLR meeting.[93] The applicant is also required to submit a Fishery Operation Plan, including a full outline of the nature of the new fishery, its location, target species, gear to be used and proposed minimum catch levels, alongside biological information on the target species, potential by-catches, comparable data from similar fisheries and possible impacts upon vulnerable marine ecosystems, especially benthic communities.[94] Proposals are contingent upon a commitment to implement a Data Collection Plan that may be established for that fishery by the CCAMLR Scientific Committee; such fishing opportunities may then only be undertaken by vessels that are suitably equipped and configured to comply with all relevant conservation measures. Once a new fishery has been instituted, it becomes an 'exploratory fishery' in subsequent years. Exploratory fisheries retain this status unless and until sufficient information is forthcoming to evaluate the distribution, abundance and demography of the target species so as to provide an estimate of the fishery's potential yield, to review the impacts of the fishery upon dependent and related species, and to allow the Scientific Committee to formulate and provide advice to the Commission on appropriate harvest catch levels, as well as effort levels and fishing gear, where appropriate.[95]

New and exploratory fisheries therefore operate on a quid pro quo basis, whereby a limited degree of fishing is permitted in exchange for the assiduous collection of agreed data on both the stock structure and the ecosystem impacts of fishing. Participation in new and exploratory fisheries in the CCAMLR Area is conditional upon a record of good conduct, with access denied to any vessel that has been listed as having participated in illegal, unreported or unregulated (IUU) fishing,[96] while exploratory privileges do not appear to generate preferential access to these resources if the fishery is later recategorised as a commercial enterprise.[97]

Seven exploratory fisheries are currently active within the CCAMLR Area, most having been established in the late 1990s, although none has graduated through the Article 6(6) process and transitioned into a commercial fishery. Although compliance with the broad requirements of new and exploratory fisheries has generally been high, meeting the data collection requirements incumbent

[92] CM 31/X; this was subsequently reformulated as CM 21-01, which applies today.
[93] CM 21-01; article 3(i).
[94] ibid art 3(ii).
[95] CM 21-02, para 1(ii).
[96] CM 21-01, para 9; and CM 21-02, para 13.
[97] Caddell (n 82) 223–26.

in the CCAMLR rules has proved to be a protracted and challenging process. Participation in these endeavours has been variable and relatively few vessels have yet returned the volumes of data conducive to a relaxation of these conditions.[98] This is partly attributable to the operational and financial difficulties inherent in undertaking developmental fishing in remote and hostile areas of the Southern Ocean, although concerns have been expressed that fishers have prioritised the collection of commercially oriented data concerning stock structures over the environmental impacts of harvesting or have failed to return necessary data from these activities.[99] CCAMLR has traditionally declined to punish poor data collection practices within exploratory fisheries, although this has clearly tested the patience of individual participants who have advocated a more punitive approach.[100] Only one such fishery, located in the Ross Sea, has approached the threshold requirements for a review of its exploratory status, although political approval has proved to be more elusive. Moreover, considerable scientific misgivings have been expressed as to the lack of adaptive capacity of the system and deficiencies in ecosystem monitoring,[101] and any eventual transition to commercial management would seemingly involve little easing of the current regulatory conditions.

These shortcomings aside, the approach taken to new and exploratory fisheries has provided a practical mechanism to help mitigate the scientific uncertainty inherent in shifting distributional patterns and an extension of fishing effort into new areas. The CCAMLR model has been incorporated largely verbatim into the practices of other RFMOs,[102] while similar approaches have been adopted in national policies, applying principles – if not necessarily terminology – reminiscent of the Antarctic arrangements.[103] This provides a precautionary basis for addressing new stocks that may be unfamiliar to the RFMO in question – an issue of particular pertinence to the high seas, where less than five per cent of fish species are currently subject to scientific assessment[104] – and can plug a potential regulatory vacuum pending more measured consideration.[105] Indeed, the regime of exploratory fisheries has provided a helpful mechanism to partially manage the ingress of particular species – and fishers – across the jurisdictional boundaries of RFMOs pending more formalised cooperation between governing bodies, as

[98] ibid 228–34.

[99] CCAMLR, *Report of the Thirty-Fourth Meeting of the Commission (CCAMLR-XXXIV)*, para 9.19.

[100] Notably the US: CCAMLR, *Report of the Twenty-Ninth Meeting of the Commission (CCAMLR-XXIX)*, para 12.37.

[101] P Abrams et al, 'Necessary Elements of Precautionary Management: Implications for the Antarctic Toothfish' (2016) 17 *Fish and Fisheries* 1, 14–17.

[102] Notably SPRFMO, which borders the CCAMLR Area and has sanctioned exploratory fishing in adjacent areas essentially conducted by the same operators, and SEAFO.

[103] See the New Emerging Fisheries Policy of Canada, first instituted in 1996.

[104] G Ortuño Crespo et al, 'High-Seas Fish Biodiversity is Slipping through the Governance Net' (2019) 3 *Nature Ecology and Evolution* 1273, 1275.

[105] Rayfuse (n 68) 254.

illustrated by the relationship between CCAMLR and the Commission for the Conservation of Southern Bluefin Tuna (CCSBT) that is discussed further below.

B. Pre-emptive Fisheries Management

As noted above, projections overwhelmingly indicate a concerted Poleward shift of marine living resources due to climate change. A number of northerly States have experienced an influx of fish and other marine species in recent years, raising expectations that the Arctic may constitute the ultimate destination for a number of displaced stocks.[106] While the extent of this potential biomass windfall remains uncertain – indeed, changing ocean conditions may ultimately create as many new biological impediments to Arctic colonisation as they remove[107] – this phenomenon has played out against a backdrop of increasing industrial ambition for the Arctic, as the receding ice coverage has generated tantalising economic opportunities and attracted the attention of a growing number of enterprising States from within and beyond the region.

Arguably the most ambitious regulatory initiative towards addressing shifting fish stocks has been the development of arrangements towards managing future commercial fisheries in the Central Arctic Ocean. A universally accepted definition of the 'Arctic' remains elusive[108] and the array of States most appropriately entitled to drive regulatory processes for these waters remains subject to enduring controversy.[109] Although a series of bodies technically exercise fisheries competence within parts of the areas beyond national jurisdiction in the Arctic region, this location has remained studiously unregulated to date.[110] Between 2008 and 2015, the coastal States comprising the 'Arctic Five' (Canada, Denmark, Norway, Russia and the US) convened a series of meetings on the prospective regulation of Arctic fisheries, resulting in a Declaration Concerning the Prevention of Unregulated High Seas Fishing in the Central Arctic Ocean,[111] pledging to apply the precautionary approach to develop interim measures to deter unregulated fishing.[112]

[106] See M Wisz et al, 'Arctic Warming Will Promote Atlantic-Pacific Fish Interchange' (2015) 5 *Nature Climate Change* 261, 262; and J Christiansen, C Mecklenburg and O Karamushko, 'Arctic Marine Fishes and Their Fisheries in the Light of Global Change' (2014) 20 *Global Change Biology* 352, 354–56.

[107] V Lam, W Cheung and U Sumaila, 'Marine Capture Fisheries in the Arctic: Winners or Losers under Climate Change and Ocean Acidification?' (2016) 17 *Fish and Fisheries* 335, 348–49.

[108] A Oude Elferink, E Molenaar and D Rothwell, 'The Regional Implementation of the Law of the Sea and the Polar Regions' in EJ Molenaar, AG Oude Elferink and DR Rothwell (eds), *The Law of the Sea and the Polar Regions: Interactions between Global and Regional Regimes* (Leiden, Brill, 2013) 1, 9–11.

[109] K Dodds, '"Real Interest"'? Understanding the 2018 Agreement to Prevent Unregulated High Seas Fisheries in the Central Arctic Ocean' (2019) 10 *Global Policy* 542.

[110] E Molenaar, 'International Regulation of Central Arctic Ocean Fisheries' in MH Nordquist, JM Moore and R Long (eds), *Challenges of the Changing Arctic: Continental Shelf, Navigation, and Fisheries* (Leiden, Brill, 2016) 429, 432–33.

[111] Reproduced at https://www.regjeringen.no/globalassets/departementene/ud/vedlegg/folkerett/declaration-on-arctic-fisheries-16-july-2015.pdf.

[112] V Schatz, A Proelss and N Liu, 'The 2018 Agreement to Prevent Unregulated High Seas Fisheries in the Central Arctic Ocean: A Critical Analysis' (2019) 34 *International Journal of Marine and Coastal Law* 195, 204–09.

Between 2015 and 2018, they were joined by China, the EU, Iceland, Japan and South Korea in a 'Broader Process' of negotiations towards elaborating a more formalised basis to pursue this objective, culminating in the conclusion of the Agreement to Prevent Unregulated High Seas Fisheries in the Central Arctic Ocean on 3 October 2018.[113]

The CAOFA is a concise document that recognises that although 'commercial fishing is unlikely to become viable in the high seas portion of the central Arctic Ocean in the near future', the ecosystem is changing 'due to climate change and other phenomena', thereby justifying precautionary consideration of the present and prospective fish stocks of the region.[114] The objective of the Agreement is therefore to 'prevent unregulated fishing in the high seas portion of the central Arctic Ocean through the application of precautionary conservation and management measures as part of a long-term strategy to safeguard healthy marine ecosystems and to ensure the conservation and sustainable use of fish stocks'.[115] The CAOFA is projected to apply to all fish other than sedentary species recognised under Article 77 UNCLOS[116] in the waters of the Arctic beyond which States exercise fisheries jurisdiction.[117] It is scheduled to remain in force for an initial period of 16 years and is extendable for five-year periods thereafter, until replaced with a more permanent regional fisheries body if required.[118] Participation in the COAFA is currently restricted to the 10 initial negotiating parties, although other States with a 'real interest' may be invited at a later point.[119]

The CAOFA restricts all commercial fishing activities in these waters pending the elaboration of interim measures or the adoption of specific conservation and management measures by any 'regional or subregional fisheries management organizations or arrangements, that have been or may be established and are operated in accordance with international law to manage such fishing in accordance with recognized international standards'.[120] The parties also commit to instituting a Joint Program of Scientific Research and Monitoring (JPSRM) 'with the aim of improving their understanding of the ecosystems of the Agreement Area and, in particular, of determining whether fish stocks might exist in the Agreement Area now or in the future that could be harvested on a sustainable basis and the possible impacts of such fisheries on the ecosystems of the Agreement Area'.[121] While commercial activities are currently precluded, the parties nonetheless contemplate the pursuit of two distinct categories of fishing in these waters. In the first instance,

[113] Reproduced at http://publications.europa.eu/resource/cellar/f075cd03-46f3-11e9-a8ed-01aa75ed71a1.0006.03/DOC_1 ('CAOFA').

[114] ibid Preamble.

[115] ibid art 2.

[116] ibid art 1(b).

[117] ibid art 1(a). This somewhat unusual formulation represents an acknowledgement of the contested fisheries sovereignty in the waters around the Svalbard archipelago.

[118] ibid art 13.

[119] ibid arts 9 and 10.

[120] ibid art 3(1). This construction recognises that existing fisheries bodies may have a future role to play in this respect.

[121] ibid art 4(2).

a volume of exploratory fishing may be conducted under specific conservation and management measures to be elaborated by the parties.[122] Alternatively, the parties 'are encouraged to' undertake research fishing under the JPSRM, provided that it 'does not undermine the prevention of unregulated commercial and exploratory fishing and the protection of healthy marine ecosystems', with the parties further encouraged to inform each other of such activities.[123] Concerns have nevertheless been raised that this provision could be abused in a manner reminiscent of the problems experienced with scientific whaling.[124] Indeed, the distinction between 'research' and 'exploratory' fishing is fundamentally artificial – both involve restricted fishing activities with specified methodologies and the reporting of an agreed volume of scientific data – although there has been a recent trend within RFMOs towards maintaining multiple nomenclature,[125] to the interpretive detriment of policies towards non-commercial fisheries.

Given that the CAOFA has not yet entered into effect, fishing arrangements in these waters remains a point of conjecture. It is likely that the regulation of non-commercial fishing will mirror that of CCAMLR to at least some degree, given its long-standing experience in managing such fisheries in analogous polar waters, its influence on such policies in other RFMOs and that most of the prospective CAOFA parties are also seasoned CCAMLR participants. Conversely, the challenges experienced in regulating non-commercial fisheries in the Antarctic are also likely to be replicated in these waters. Even so, the CAOFA represents a unique approach to changing marine ecosystems by elaborating pre-emptive controls and imposing a precautionary ethos ab initio. It is also one assisted by the current lack of entrenched interests[126] and formidable commercial and biological barriers to large-scale fishing, which are not widely replicated in other areas of the ocean. Nevertheless, the economic temptations of shifting stocks in the long-term future may represent a significant challenge to this regulatory approach. Indeed, notwithstanding these arrangements, Russia has recently announced its intention to establish a commercial fishery for pollock within the Chukchi Sea, with biomass having expanded dramatically in these waters due to climate change,[127] which suggests that future commercial ambition will increasingly chafe against laudably professed pre-emptive intentions.

[122] ibid art 3(3). Exploratory fishing is defined as 'fishing for the purpose of assessing the sustainability and feasibility of future commercial fisheries by contributing to scientific data relating to such fisheries' (art 1(e)).

[123] ibid art rt 3(4).

[124] Schatz, Proelss and Liu (n 112) 226.

[125] Caddell (n 82) 233–34.

[126] R Rayfuse, 'Regulating Fisheries in the Central Arctic Ocean: Much Ado about Nothing?' in N Vestergaard, BA Kaiser, L Fernandez and JN Larsen (eds), *Arctic Marine Resource Governance and Development* (Heidelberg, Springer, 2018) 35, 48–49.

[127] Y Rosen, 'Russia is Poised to Open the First-Ever Commercial Pollock Fishery in Chukchi Sea', *The Barents Observer* (25 June 2020).

IV. RFMOs and Climate Change

RFMOs remain the preferred vehicle through which the conservation and management of fish stocks, especially straddling and highly migratory stocks, is to be pursued.[128] To date, a loose constellation of fisheries management bodies has been established in many – but by no means all – areas of the global oceans to regulate particular stocks. However, despite this coverage, consideration of climate change impacts upon fisheries resources has been patchy and underwhelming. Indeed, climate change has generally transpired to be a peripheral concern for most bodies and even the most ecologically prominent fisheries actors have struggled to find the far-sighted political consensus necessary to address these problems proactively.

A. Shifting Stocks and RFMO Interactions

Mirroring current concerns over the propensity for changing ocean conditions to displace fish stocks across the boundaries of coastal States, RFMOs may also receive an influx of prospective new species into areas under their competence or, conversely, experience a steady displacement of stocks into the waters of a neighbouring RFMO or an unregulated area of high seas. As with individual States, stocks that are redistributed across frontiers of legal responsibility face the risk of overexploitation and dysfunctional oversight due to managerial turf wars between regulatory regimes. Nevertheless, while analogous to a transboundary shift between EEZs, distributional adjustments of stocks across the frontiers of RFMOs raise markedly different legal issues. Indeed, as astutely outlined in this context by EU fisheries representatives, a proprietary interest in the stock is absent given that RFMOs are forums that provide a foundation for their members to discharge their cooperation and conservation obligations prescribed under UNCLOS rather than 'entities with original exclusive rights similar to the ones enjoyed by sovereign States in sea areas under national fisheries jurisdiction'.[129]

The regulatory difficulties inherent in distributional shifts of commercially significant fish stocks were first encountered in the North Atlantic in the late 1990s in the context of oceanic redfish, a deep-sea fish that had been managed exclusively by the North-East Atlantic Fisheries Commission (NEAFC) since 1982.[130] By the

[128] UNFSA, arts 8–14. This position has been reinforced by successive Resolutions of the UN General Assembly as the primary means through which States give effect to the duty of cooperation established under UNCLOS and the UNFSA: Y Takei, *Filling Regulatory Gaps in High Seas Fisheries: Discrete High Seas Fish Stocks, Deep-Sea Fisheries and Vulnerable Marine Ecosystems* (Leiden, Brill, 2013) 67.

[129] NAFO, *Report of the NAFO/NEAFC Working Group on Oceanic Redfish*, Document NAFO/FC/Doc.01/3, 10.

[130] Redfish nevertheless raised regulatory complications, since the commencement of this fishery and a combination of scientific uncertainty and economic demand meant that catches have long been considered unsustainable: R Churchill, 'Managing Straddling Fish Stocks in the North-East Atlantic: A Multiplicity of Instruments – But How Effective a Management?' in O Stokke (ed), *Governing High Sea Fisheries: The Interplay of Global and Regional Regimes* (Oxford, Oxford University Press, 2001) 235, 255–62.

late 1990s, it was apparent that warming waters had displaced a sizeable contingent of redfish into the neighbouring area of competence of the North Atlantic Fisheries Organisation (NAFO), and a number of enterprising States sought to avail themselves of opportunities to maximise access to the stock.[131] While it remained unclear at the time whether this displacement was a temporary aberration or a more permanent shift, in 2001 the two bodies agreed on a pre-emptive system of joint management whereby NEAFC has continued to set the TAC, of which a portion is allocated to NAFO to be distributed among its membership. In this manner, the parties to two RFMOs with broadly similar memberships and conservation obligations were able to broker a pragmatic solution to a then-unprecedented issue, which has subsequently facilitated further collaboration on common operational matters.[132]

More recently, concerns have been raised by the changing distribution patterns of tuna, which have shifted Poleward 6.5 km per decade in the northern hemisphere and 5.5 km Poleward in the southern hemisphere.[133] Tuna have historically attracted the most sustained degree of regional regulation and opportunities for collaboration have been pursued under the Kobe Process between the array of RFMOs responsible for these species, even if these bonds are considerably looser than the clustering arrangements and policy alignments characteristic of multilateral environmental agreements.[134] As was initially mooted in the redfish saga, tuna RFMOs may be better placed to address stock shifts given the 'acquiescence of a regulatory priority for the organisation within which the bulk of a tuna stock occurred'.[135] This is most clearly exemplified by the CCSBT, whose constituent treaty applies to the entirety of the migratory range of this species rather than to specified geographical coordinates[136] and for which other tuna RFMOs have recognised its 'prime responsibility' over any stocks located within their areas of operation.[137] However, the precise arrangements for the regulation of southern bluefin tuna in areas under the competence of non-tuna RFMOs have required further negotiation. In 2005, southern bluefin tuna – and, more specifically, the fishing vessels pursuing these fish – were reported in increasing numbers within the CCAMLR

[131] A Thomson, 'The Management of Redfish (*Sebastes mentella*) in the North Atlantic Ocean: A Stock in Movement' in *FAO Fisheries Report No 695* (FAO 2003) 192, 196.

[132] O Stokke, 'Management Options for High Seas Fisheries: Making Regime Complexes More Effective' in Caddell and Molenaar (n 9) 51, 68.

[133] M Erauskin-Extramiana et al, 'Large Scale Redistribution of Tuna in a Warming Ocean' (2019) 25 *Global Change Biology* 2043.

[134] Harrison (n 41) 99; on these latter approaches, see Churchill and Ulfstein (n 5).

[135] NAFO (n 129) 11.

[136] Convention for the Conservation of Southern Bluefin Tuna 1993, 1819 UNTS 359 (art 1).

[137] As specified, for instance, by the Indian Ocean Tuna Commission (IOTC) at a preliminary stage in its operation: *Report of the First Special Session of the IOTC*, para 31. See also IOTC Resolution 98/03 on Southern Bluefin Tuna, which reinforces deference to the CCSBT on the management of these stocks within the IOTC Area, and the WCPFC, which, in its Memorandum of Understanding with the CCSBT, acknowledges that the CCSBT 'is the appropriate body to develop and implement southern bluefin tuna conservation and management measures': reproduced at https://www.wcpfc.int/doc/wcpfc-ccsbt-memorandum-understanding.

Area,[138] seemingly operating under the misconception that the management policies of the CCSBT overrode those of other organisations regarding such species,[139] a mindset that CCAMLR wished to dispel in a friendly but firm manner.

Particular concerns were raised that an influx of tuna vessels could encourage an expansion in IUU fishing, an already grievous concern within CCAMLR waters, while also promoting fishing practices that are not in compliance with CCAMLR standards.[140] In response, the CCSBT contacted CCAMLR seeking formal recognition of the primacy of the CCSBT over tuna stocks where they occurred within the Southern Ocean.[141] CCAMLR in return considered that a clearer demarcation of responsibilities ought to be established through an agreement between the two bodies, notably concerning which organisation's conservation and management measures should be prioritised. In this regard, CCAMLR appears to have been particularly concerned by the scope for seabird by-catches, for which extensive mitigation measures have been developed under its auspices. This was a point of contention for certain CCSBT parties, which argued that compliance with these requirements was disproportionately burdensome given the modest volume of fishing effort for tuna pursued in these waters.[142] CCAMLR nevertheless stood firm on this point,[143] a position that seems to have prolonged the endorsement of an agreement that was proposed in 2009, concluded in 2012 and renewed in 2015 and 2019. Pointedly, CCAMLR has insisted upon compliance with its conservation measures,[144] although the most recent iteration of the Agreement adopts a more collaborative approach, with both bodies pledging to exchange data on fishing effort and practices.[145] In the interim, tuna fishing in the Southern Ocean was addressed under a hybrid system in which participants in both organisations have agreed to pursue these allocations through the CCSBT, with catches in the CCAMLR Area most appropriately addressed under its regime on new and exploratory fisheries.[146]

[138] CCAMLR, *Report of the Twenty-Fourth Meeting of the Commission (CCAMLR-XXIV)*, para 15.21.

[139] A Serdy, 'Antarctic Fisheries Management' in Molenaar, Oude Elferink and Rothwell (n 108) 217, 236.

[140] R Rayfuse, 'Climate Change and Antarctic Fisheries: Ecosystem Management in CCAMLR' (2018) 45 *Ecology Law Quarterly* 53, 79.

[141] CCSBT, *Report of the Extended Commission of the 12th (2005) Annual CCSBT Meeting*, para 126; see A Hemmings, 'Regime Overlap in the Southern Ocean: The Case of Southern Bluefin Tuna and CCSBT in the CCAMLR Area' (2006) 3 *New Zealand Yearbook of International Law* 207, 210–13.

[142] CCSBT, *Report of the 14th Annual CCSBT Meeting*, paras 199–200. Tellingly, the CCSBT considered that CCAMLR's divergent approach was attributable to 'a purpose more associated with the protection of a unique environment than the CCSBT, where the purpose of its creation related more to the commercial international exploitation of a high seas fishery': Document CCSBT-EC/0710/12: Relationship with CCAMLR.

[143] CCAMLR, *Report of the Thirty-First Meeting of the Commission (CCAMLR-XXXI)*, para 9.15.

[144] ibid.

[145] Agreement between the Commission for the Conservation of Southern Bluefin Tuna and the Commission for the Conservation of Antarctic Marine Living Resources, https://www.ccamlr.org/en/system/files/CCSBT_2.pdf.

[146] CCAMLR, *Report of the Twenty-Fifth Meeting of the Commission (CCAMLR-XXV)*, para 16.40.

B. RFMOs and the Management of Shifting Stocks

While RFMOs have managed to broker collaborative arrangements between each other that provide a basis for information sharing and wider commitments towards cooperation – which could prospectively engage issues of future stock shifts and an exchange of pertinent scientific data to aid decision-making processes – few specific policies have emerged under their collective auspices to directly address wider distributional uncertainties created by climate change. Few RFMOs have sought to address climate change as a direct and holistic consideration. This may be partly attributable to a lack of homogeneous terminologies between organisations which have different means of articulating climate-induced management challenges, with the phrase 'climate change' panoramically considered to refer 'to more general climatic variance than to climate change as a specific phenomenon'.[147] Indeed, only CCAMLR has adopted a targeted Resolution on climate change to date, a position reflective of its status as 'more than' an RFMO and with a far broader ecological mandate than other fisheries bodies. In 2009, the CCAMLR members adopted Resolution 30/XVIII on climate change, declaring global climate change to be 'one of the greatest challenges facing the Southern Ocean' and calling for increased consideration of climate change impacts to better inform CCAMLR's management decisions.

However, to date, this appears to have had a limited impact upon fisheries management under CCAMLR. On the one hand, Resolution 30/XVIII has inspired new regulatory developments that demonstrate a far-sighted approach to fisheries management, albeit in highly specific contexts. One such example is the regulation of fisheries within 'newly-exposed marine areas', whereby new areas of the sea have become accessible following the collapse of segments of the Antarctic ice shelf. In 2017, CCAMLR established a process for the designation of time-limited Special Areas for Scientific Study in segments of the Agreement Area most vulnerable to ice-melt, based on the regulatory impetus of Resolution 30/XVIII.[148] Under these arrangements, a limited degree of research fishing may be prospectively pursued subject to broadly similar restrictions to CCAMLR's research and exploratory fisheries conditions.[149]

Nevertheless, further advancements have proved to be a difficult political proposition. This is exemplified by the protracted process towards the establishment of CCAMLR's cornerstone marine protected area (MPA) in the Ross Sea,[150] which also established time-limited restrictions on fishing activities, albeit after numerous years of tortuous negotiations.[151] More recently, various members have sought to integrate climate change considerations more centrally within Antarctic

[147] Rayfuse (n 68) 259.
[148] CM 24-04.
[149] ibid para 14.
[150] CM 91-05.
[151] Rayfuse (n 140) 68–72.

fisheries management, as recommended by the most recent Performance Review of CCAMLR in 2017.[152] However, this recommendation remains essentially unfulfilled: the submission of climate change data within the annual Fishing Reports returned by the members is considered a 'useful addition', but a strictly voluntary one.[153] Attempts to update Resolution 30/XVIII in a more ecologically robust manner appear to have met stern political resistance at the most recent CCAMLR Meeting.[154] The inability of CCAMLR, the international fisheries actor with the clearest ecological priorities, to broker the requisite political momentum to adopt far-sighted fisheries management in the face of global climate change suggests little cause for optimism for the policies of other RFMOs.[155]

Such a pessimistic outlook appears eminently justified. More broadly, the periodic Review Conference of the UNFSA has accorded little priority to climate change concerns. Climate change was not even tangentially considered at the first meeting of the Review Conference in 2006, while its subsequent instalments in 2010[156] and 2016[157] viewed this issue in largely unfocused terms, highlighting a general need to further understanding the risks posed to fish stocks by climate change. Similarly, despite a broad trend towards increased cooperation between RFMOs on an individual and collective basis, shifting stocks have received little attention to date. Indeed, the meetings of the Kobe Process have not yet considered this issue at all.[158] Certain participants have at least noted that this ought to be part of future collective discussions[159] – and the Kobe Process provides intriguing possibilities to promote cross-RFMO collaborations, with discernible progress having been made through joint working groups on by-catch mitigation and IUU fishing – although it remains to be seen whether this will ultimately translate into tangible activity.

Stock shifts may not yet have unduly occupied the regulatory attentions of RFMOs, but this issue has been independently identified as an issue for future concern within some of the more recent Performance Reviews of these organisations. These processes, conducted by critical friends of the RFMO in question, have resulted in a series of recommendations for governance and management improvements. This is no mere paper exercise, with the outcomes taken seriously by RFMOs, which have subsequently sought to implement meaningful adjustments to their working practices.[160] For instance, following its second Performance Review,

[152] CCAMLR, *Second Performance Review of CCAMLR – Final Report of the Panel*, Recommendation 6.

[153] CCAMLR, *Report of the Thirty-Seventh Meeting (CCAMLR-XXXVII)*, para 8.4.

[154] CCAMLR, *Report of the Thirty-Eighth Meeting (CCAMLR-38)*, para 8.14. These evidently divergent views were nevertheless reported with the traditional diplomatic understatement associated with the Antarctic Treaty System.

[155] Rayfuse (n 140) 81; MR Wendebourg, 'Southern Ocean Fishery Managemen: Is CCAMLR Addressing the Challenges Posed by a Changing Climate?' (2020) 118 *Marine Policy* 103647.

[156] A/CONF.210/2010/7, Outcome I(n).

[157] A/CONF.210/2016/5, Outcome 4.

[158] See further www.tuna-org.org/meetingspast.htm.

[159] CCSBT, *Performance of the CCSBT 2009–2013*, 80.

[160] B Haas et al, 'The Influence of Performance Reviews on Regional Fisheries Management Organizations' (2019) 76 *ICES Journal of Marine Science* 2082, 2089.

the General Fisheries Commission for the Mediterranean (GFCM) convened an extensive workshop on climate change implications for Mediterranean and Black Sea fisheries in 2017, which identified climate-induced shifts in fish distribution as a future challenge, both from the standpoint of broader governance issues as well as in the specific context of addressing invasive species.[161] Similarly, reviews of NAFO and NEAFC – mindful of their previous and current experiences with shifting stocks – have also identified this issue as a matter of future concern. In the context of NAFO, for instance, it was observed that 'climate change may have an impact on distribution patterns of fish stocks with subsequent challenges concerning allocation arrangements of those stocks straddling between Exclusive Economic Zones and the high seas',[162] for which the Review Panel recommended revisiting the current allocation of new fishing opportunities 'should a change in circumstances justify it'.[163] The Review Panel of NEAFC also observed that '[m] any of the species regulated by NEAFC appear to be sensitive to climate effects, not only in recruitment variability but species distributions and species overlaps … controversies regarding changing spatial distributions of migratory species stem in part from fishes responses to climate variations',[164] recommending that climate effects be considered more explicitly in developing its management programme and that the scientific basis for such approaches be improved.[165]

Identifying the problems associated with climate change and subsequently implementing meaningful outcomes nevertheless remains a significant challenge. Stock shifts and environmental changes are multifaceted phenomena and 'in many situations it remains difficult to disentangle the effects of climate change with those of other anthropogenic influences',[166] which may inhibit the recognition of such impacts as an operative priority. Meanwhile, it remains highly questionable as to whether RFMOs have the requisite mandate or institutional dynamism to respond swiftly and effectively to projections of future climate-induced management problems.[167] Ultimately, the most telling response is that suggested by the second Performance Review of the CCSBT, which recommended that the difficulties presented by shifting stocks of fish would be best addressed by 'developing an alternative approach to dispute settlement/conflict resolution to avoid the potential for future stalemates that could significantly compromise the conservation and management' of these stocks.[168] This approach suggests that RFMOs

[161] FAO, *Report of the Expert Meeting on Climate Change Implications for Mediterranean and Black Sea Fisheries* (Rome, FAO, 2018) 15.

[162] NAFO, *NAFO Performance Review Panel Report 2018*, 23.

[163] ibid 24.

[164] NEAFC, *Report of the Performance Review Panel 2014*, 39–40.

[165] ibid 40.

[166] JA Nye et al, 'Changing Spatial Distribution of Fish Stocks in Relation to Climate and Population Size on the Northeast United States Continental Shelf' (2009) 393 *Marine Ecology Progress Series* 111, 111.

[167] B Pentz and N Klenk, 'The "Responsiveness Gap" in RFMOs: The Critical Role of Decision-Making Policies in the Fisheries Management Response to Climate Change' (2017) 145 *Ocean and Coastal Management* 42, 49.

[168] CCSBT (n 159) Recommendation PR-2014-53.

are resignedly pragmatic as to their ability to address and mitigate distributional shifts, beyond providing supportive mechanisms to umpire the inevitable disputes between States over this issue, to which this chapter now turns.

V. Participatory Challenges and Contested Mobile Resources

Fisheries are frequently considered illustrative of the classic ecological conundrum of the 'tragedy of the commons',[169] where a shared resource becomes depleted due to users increasing their utilisation of a shared resource, thus promoting vested self-interest over that of the common good. While not always an accurate depiction of fishing practices,[170] it is nevertheless also true that those in possession of access rights to fish have generally behaved uncharitably towards purported newcomers. Complaints of 'quota-hoarding' are rife in a domestic context,[171] with fishers unwilling even to relinquish habitually unused allocations without executive or judicial intervention.[172] Similarly, behavioural science models predict that those States that are in the process of 'losing' fish through distributional shifts are more likely to exploit the stock unsustainably,[173] driven by (well-founded) fears over a prospective future inability to freely access the resource.[174]

This bleak management prognosis stems from long-standing concerns over access to fisheries under current arrangements. International fisheries law has facilitated a cartel mentality towards fishing entitlements, in a manner that does not bode well for States seeking access to shifting stocks. As noted above, the stewardship of shared fish resources is subject to copious obligations of cooperation. In the context of straddling and highly migratory species, the UNFSA envisages that States fishing on the high seas and 'relevant coastal states' will discharge this obligation either by becoming members or participants in a regional fisheries management organisation or arrangement for those waters, or by agreeing to apply the resultant conservation and management measures adopted by that organisation or arrangement,[175] with the ability to fish contingent upon adherence to these measures.[176] Under Article 8(3), other States exhibiting a 'real interest' in

[169] G Hardin, 'The Tragedy of the Commons' (1968) 162 *Science* 1243.
[170] F Berkes, 'Fishermen and the Tragedy of the Commons' (1985) 12 *Environmental Conservation* 199; for a more modern view, see A Serdy, *The New Entrants Problem in International Fisheries Law* (Cambridge, Cambridge University Press, 2016) 10–42.
[171] Dubik et al (n 63) 247.
[172] Aptly illustrated in a UK context in *R (United Kingdom Association of Fish Producer Organisations) v Secretary of State for the Environment, Food and Rural Affairs* [2013] EWHC 1959 (Admin).
[173] F Diekert and E Nieminen, 'International Agreements with a Shifting Stock' (2017) 7 *Dynamic Games and Applications* 185, 200–02.
[174] Oremus et al (n 77) 277.
[175] UNFSA, art 8(3).
[176] ibid art 8(4).

the stock – a term that, alongside a 'relevant coastal state', was undefined in the UNFSA[177] – should be able to become members or participants in this organisation or arrangements, without being impeded or discriminated against by existing constituents.

Nevertheless, the principle of *pacta tertiis* does not bind other States to such measures and essentially allows them to access the resource without participating in a regional management regime and accepting these constraints.[178] In turn, existing participants have imposed increasingly stringent requirements for admission to RFMOs and arrangements in order to protect their share of the resource from new entrants,[179] a trend that further disincentivises active cooperation by third States.[180] In response, and with an understandable reluctance to feed the hand that bites them, members of RFMOs and arrangements become even less inclined to share a diminishing resource.[181] Against this backdrop – and the lack of clear criteria by which States that are either losing or gaining fish may be considered 'relevant' or to have a 'real interest' in participating – unsustainable rates of fishing have been engendered as States seek to avail themselves of a resource windfall or maintain access to a moving stock.

This has been most recently illustrated in the so-called 'mackerel war' of 2013, an episode that exemplifies the tragedy of the commons with dispiriting ease. Throughout much of the latter part of the twentieth century, the distribution of commercially valuable stocks of Atlanto-Scandian herring and North-East Atlantic mackerel had exhibited subtle shifts, raising potential conflicts between interested States. The herring stock initially collapsed due to rampant overfishing in the 1960s before rallying and, in the process, changing its migratory route to remain largely confined to Norwegian waters.[182] A similar pattern appears to have

[177] See further E Molenaar, 'The Concept of "Real Interest" and Other Aspects of Co-operation through Regional Fisheries Management Mechanisms' (2000) 15 *International Journal of Marine and Coastal Law* 475.

[178] On these difficulties, see A Serdy, '*Pacta Tertiis* and Regional Fisheries Management Mechanisms: The IUU Fishing Concept as an Illegitimate Short-Cut to a Legitimate Goal' (2017) 48 *Ocean Development and International Law* 345.

[179] For instance, NAFO and NEAFC have advised prospective new participants that, 'presently and for the foreseeable future', their respective stocks have been 'fully allocated', with fishing opportunities for new members therefore likely to be restricted to new fisheries: see NAFO Resolution 1/99 of 17 September 1999 to Guide the Expectations of Future New Members with Regard to Fishing Opportunities in the NAFO Regulatory Area and the parallel *Guidelines for the Expectation of Future New Contracting Parties with Regard to Fishing Opportunities in the NEAFC Regulatory Area*, adopted at the Twenty-Second Annual Meeting of NEAFC in 2003. As noted above, some acknowledgement of the difficulties created by this stance in the context of distributional shifts has been acknowledged by NAFO (n 162).

[180] Serdy (n 170) 43–140.

[181] On the spiralling problems of this mindset, see A Serdy, 'Postmodern International Fisheries Law, or We are All Coastal States Now' (2011) 60 *International and Comparative Law Quarterly* 387.

[182] E Sissener and T Bjørndal, 'Climate Change and the Migratory Pattern for Norwegian Spring-Spawning Herring: Implications for Management' (2005) 29 *Marine Policy* 299, 300–05.

characterised the mackerel stock, which followed a familiar trend of boom and bust, before rebooming along a different geographical pathway.[183]

A series of significant distributional shifts, largely attributed to climate change, nevertheless began to create management and political difficulties in relation to both stocks. Until 2009, mackerel was primarily apportioned trilaterally between the EU, Norway and the Faroe Islands, and bilaterally between the EU and Norway as 'relevant' coastal States, albeit excluding Iceland, which had begun to exploit the increasing volumes of fish now displaced into its EEZ.[184] These participants subsequently failed to establish mutually acceptable allocations until a five-year agreement was brokered in 2014,[185] granting additional entitlements to the Faroe Islands, but omitting other interested – and arguably 'relevant'[186] – coastal States, much to the chagrin of Iceland.

In the context of herring – which ultimately constituted the main prize at stake in the perhaps inaptly named 'mackerel war' – matters came to a head in 2013, following the steady displacement of an increasing proportion of the stock into the EEZ of the Faroe Islands. The quota for herring has been historically apportioned between the EU, Faroe Islands, Iceland, Norway and Russia pursuant to the Atlanto-Scandian Management Arrangements (ASMA). As with many arrangements in which the EU is an assertive participant,[187] management decisions are taken in line with its favoured principle of relative stability,[188] which is based primarily on historical catches rather than zonal attachment, which proceeds more in line with the current location of the fish. Under the ASMA, the Faroe Islands received an agreed share of 5.16 per cent of the stock, an allocation that was increasingly meagre in proportion to the distributional pattern of the fish.[189] These circumstances prompted the Faroe Islands to agitate for a higher entitlement, leveraged against the physical presence of the stock within its national waters. Nevertheless, with scientific advice in 2012 recommending a 26 per cent reduction in TAC, and with the other participants loath to correspondingly reduce their respective entitlements, the Faroe Islands withdrew from the Arrangements and unilaterally set a catch limit of 17 per cent of the TAC within its EEZ, representing a threefold increase in catches.[190] The EU accordingly designated the Faroe

[183] T Jansen, 'Pseudocollapse and Rebuilding of North Sea Mackerel (*Scomber scombrus*)' (2014) 71 *ICES Journal of Marine Science* 299.

[184] For an excellent survey of these developments, see P Ørebech, 'The "Lost Mackerel" of the North East Atlantic: The Flawed System of Trilateral and Bilateral Decision-making' (2013) 28 *International Journal of Marine and Coastal Law* 343.

[185] See https://ec.europa.eu/fisheries/sites/fisheries/files/docs/body/2014-2018-agreed-record-eu-faroe-islands-norway-mackerel_en.pdf.

[186] Ørebech (n 184) 362.

[187] See R Churchill, 'The EU as an International Fisheries Actor: Shark or Minnow?' (1999) 4 *European Foreign Affairs Review* 463.

[188] R Churchill and D Owen, *The EC Common Fisheries Policy* (Oxford, Oxford University Press, 2010) 149–54.

[189] Regulation (EU) No 793/2013 of 20 August 2013 establishing measures in respect of the Faeroe Islands to ensure the conservation of the Atlanto-Scandian herring stock [2013] OJ L223/1.

[190] ibid recitals 7–9.

Islands as a 'country allowing non-sustainable fishing' and imposed a series of trade restrictions and access limitations to EU ports.[191] In response, Denmark (as the overarching administrative authority) initiated arbitration proceedings under Annex VII of UNCLOS,[192] as well as a request for consultations before the World Trade Organization (WTO).[193]

These proceedings were ultimately discontinued by Denmark once revised arrangements with other coastal States in favour of the Faroe Islands were forthcoming.[194] Nevertheless, while judicial intervention was averted, significant concerns may be expressed over the manner in which this dispute was ultimately resolved. The settlement resulted only in a recasting of entitlements that were numerically acceptable to the existing protagonists, without measured thought as to the long-term future of the fishery. Moreover, it served to marginalise other interests in the stock, which are legitimately entitled to pursue these fish within their national waters,[195] for which the outcome will be an inevitably unsustainable volume of combined catches. A more surgical reappraisal of entitlements, based predominantly on zonal attachment and on a real-time understanding of a stock distribution in flux is unlikely to materialise, given the long-standing vested interest of the current participants, notwithstanding its conceptual attractions.[196] Instead, the 'mackerel war' suggests that the most effective political solution to stock shifts will be a sustained period of brinkmanship followed by a concerted volume of overfishing.

Nevertheless, more constructive approaches have emerged, albeit on a more localised level, that have increasingly moved away from relatively stability – or have adopted a more flexible understanding of this concept – as an underlying model for fisheries allocations. Indeed, many long-standing fisheries arrangements, and the historical catches on which such understandings are based, were developed when the stock in question inhabited a markedly cooler ocean and was dispersed in more southerly locations.[197] Nationally, fisheries managers have recognised that meaningful consultations with those most closely affected, while also adopting flexible approaches to landings, may mitigate the sensitivities inherent in transitioning away from an emphasis upon relative stability in addressing stock shifts.[198]

[191] ibid art 5.

[192] *The Atlanto-Scandian Herring Arbitration (The Kingdom of Denmark in Respect of the Faroe Islands v The European Union)*, PCA Case No 2013-30.

[193] *European Union – Measures on Atlanto-Scandian Herring*, WT/DS469, https://www.wto.org/english/tratop_e/dispu_e/cases_e/ds469_e.htm.

[194] *The Atlanto-Scandian Herring Arbitration (The Kingdom of Denmark in Respect of the Faroe Islands v The European Union)*, Termination Order of 23 September 2014. The WTO dispute was terminated on 21 August 2014.

[195] Ørebech (n 184) 365–69.

[196] ibid 371.

[197] P Gullestad, S Sundby and OS Kjesbu, 'Management of Transboundary and Straddling Fish Stocks in the Northeast Atlantic in View of Climate-Induced Shifts in Spatial Distribution' (2020) 21 *Fish and Fisheries* 1008, 1013.

[198] Dubik et al (n 63) 247–49; T Young et al, 'Adaptation Strategies of Coastal Fishing Communities as Species Shift Poleward' (2020) 76 *ICES Journal of Marine Science* 93, 99–101.

This is more challenging to implement beyond the domestic sphere, but is by no means impossible to achieve. On a bilateral level, States have demonstrated that they are prepared to phase out a reliance upon historical catches and to integrate a more nuanced series of allocative practices based on the physical location of the fish. This has been exemplified by far-sighted arrangements between the US and Canada over multiple stocks of groundfish (including commercially significant stocks of cod and haddock) in the Georges Bank where, in a seven-year transitional period between 2003 and 2010, the weighting accorded to historical landings steadily diminished from 40 per cent to 10 per cent.[199] However, this approach is not without its trade-offs. While providing a transparent mechanism to remodel allocations for a shifting stock, this has inevitably led to fisheries management on a single-species basis rather than the ecosystem-based management to which fisheries regulation broadly aspires to pursue.[200]

Elsewhere, other collegiate approaches to stock fluctuations have emerged. One example that has been promoted as a means of prospectively addressing climate change impacts on fisheries is the Vessel Day Scheme (VDS),[201] adopted under the Palau Arrangement, an Implementing Agreement to the Nauru Agreement Concerning Cooperation in the Management of Fisheries of Common Interest 1982,[202] which allows for the transfer of fishing days between the participants in order to mitigate the stock fluctuations. Nevertheless, this programme has not been extended further under the wider auspices of the WCPFC[203] and doubt has been cast upon its broader feasibility without extensive side payments to discourage the 'race-to-fish' habitually experienced with stock shifts.[204] Ultimately, current practices clearly demonstrate that habitual fishers of a stock now exhibiting distributional shifts will retain a strong proprietorial mentality towards this resource, even as it gradually relocates from its traditional locus of concentration, which will have to be recognised and financially accommodated in any resultant recasting of allocative entitlements.

VI. Conclusions

Climate change has been evocatively portrayed as a 'legally disruptive' phenomenon that will continue to stress-test laws and institutions in a series of unprecedented

[199] EJ Pudden and DL VanderZwaag, 'Canada–United States Bilateral Fisheries Management in the Gulf of Maine: Struggling towards Sustainability under the Radar Screen' in DA Russell and DL VanderZwaag, *Recasting Transboundary Fishery Management Arrangements in the Light of Sustainability Principles: Canadian and International Perspectives* (Leiden, Martinus Nijhoff, 2010) 177, 183–85.

[200] ibid 198–99.

[201] T Aqorau, J Bell and JN Kittinger, 'Good Governance for Migratory Species' (2018) 361 *Science* 1208.

[202] See https://www.ffa.int/nauru_agreement ('Nauru Agreement').

[203] Serdy (n 170) 334–35.

[204] Oremus et al (n 77) 279.

and unforeseen ways.[205] This is particularly apparent in the context of marine living resources, for which regulatory regimes have traditionally favoured largely static management, underpinned by a working hypothesis that stocks are unlikely to exhibit vast shifts in historical coverage and habitat preferences. Rapidly altering oceanic conditions, increasingly driven by climate change and associated impacts, are nevertheless exposing the flaws inherent in these continued assumptions. Thus far, the scholarship on the impacts of climate change upon the central tenets of the Law of the Sea has predominantly considered coastal erosion and the potentially ambulatory nature of national baselines.[206] However, it is increasingly evident that the most significant and contested implications of climate change on marine entitlements will involve shifting marine living resources rather than a subtle reconfiguration of jurisdictional waters.

Climate change exhibits ample scope to disrupt long-standing achievements and certainties in international law, particularly in the context of fisheries. In extreme cases, a stock shift could prove so dramatic as to eventually render a single-species RFMO functionally redundant,[207] or prompt States to seek to renegotiate jurisdictional boundaries associated with fisheries entitlements.[208] The shifting distribution of marine living resources may even gain some traction in future boundary delimitations as a 'catastrophic repercussion' requiring corrective equity,[209] although it remains to be seen whether this would be sufficient to overcome the traditional ambivalence accorded to fisheries in such processes,[210] even where fish stocks are a central element of national claims.[211] Meanwhile, changing ocean conditions remain a particularly pervasive environmental stressor that will exacerbate existing challenges facing fisheries managers at all tiers of governance,[212] while the socio-economic implications of shifting stocks have

[205] E Fisher, E Scotford and E Barritt, 'The Legally Disruptive Nature of Climate Change' (2017) 80 *Modern Law Review* 173.

[206] Although this reveals that the loss of jurisdictional entitlements through climate change are not necessarily as automatic as may be popularly presumed; see K Purcell, *Geographical Change and the Law of the Sea* (Oxford, Oxford University Press, 2019) 260–86.

[207] Rayfuse (n 68) 268.

[208] S Árnadóttir, 'Ecological Changes Justifying Termination or Revision of EEZ and EFZ Boundaries' (2017) 84 *Marine Policy* 287.

[209] *Case Concerning Delimitation of the Maritime Boundary in the Gulf of Maine Area (Canada v United States of America)*, Judgment of 12 October 1984 [1984] ICJ Rep 340, para 237.

[210] See further R Churchill, 'Fisheries Issues in Maritime Boundary Delimitation' (1993) 17 *Marine Policy* 44, 53; and R Churchill, 'The Greenland-Jan Mayen Case and its Significance for the International Law of Maritime Boundary Delimitation' (1994) *9 International Journal of Marine and Coastal Law* 1, 21–22

[211] *Gulf of Maine Case* (n 209); *Maritime Delimitation in the Area between Greenland and Jan Mayen (Denmark v Norway)*, Judgment of 14 June 1993 [1993] ICJ Rep 38. On the general treatment of fisheries, see M Evans, 'Relevant Circumstances' in AG Oude Elferink, T Henriksen and SV Busch (eds), *Maritime Boundary Delimitation: The Case Law. Is it Consistent and Predictable?* (Cambridge, Cambridge University Press, 2018) 222, 253–56; and Y Tanaka, *Predictability and Flexibility in the Law of Maritime Delimitation* (Oxford, Hart Publishing, 2019) 370–93.

[212] Free (n 62) 979.

the propensity to generate considerable discord between interested States and to aggravate pre-existing geopolitical fractures.[213]

Thus far, international law has proved slow to respond to these challenges, although individual examples of far-sighted practices are nevertheless apparent. Most recently, a strikingly novel approach has been adopted to frame future fisheries management in the Arctic, pre-empting a prospective influx of new fish species into these waters and elaborating a highly precautionary new regime to address such stocks, if and when commercial and biological conditions are conducive to concerted fishing activities. In Antarctica, a series of mechanisms have been developed to establish precautionary limits on the fishing of new stocks, with these principles having also been exported to other RFMOs, and in new marine areas created by climate change. RFMOs have adopted a series of collaborative practices that provide a basis for cooperation in the event of displaced stocks, and in some instances have developed pragmatic solutions to managerial overlaps. Individual States have also brokered arrangements to reallocate fishing entitlements for shifting species in a manner that is more reflective of prevailing distributions, yet sensitive to those with a historical interest in the stock.

Nevertheless, these burgeoning achievements remain the exception rather than the rule. The pioneering Arctic arrangements are fundamentally untested, with indications that commercial opportunity may ultimately trump precautionary aspiration. Similarly, RFMOs have generally lacked the mandate, resources, political consensus and arguably the inclination to address the broader challenges associated with climate change, including distributional shifts. Moreover, the 'mackerel war' vividly illustrates the problems inherent in confronting the management challenges posed by shifting stocks: the current position largely disincentives States to relinquish historical entitlements over fish that are now eminently exploitable by other States, which in turn may find themselves excluded from participation in the fishery and must therefore resort to unilateralism. The likely solution to this conundrum appears to be a compensatory mechanism to encourage a rebalancing of allocative practices based more closely upon zonal attachment, although this has largely eluded the international community to date. Ultimately, shifting stocks will need to be addressed in an environmentally sensitive manner, based on meaningful cooperation between States and supported by effective institutional arrangements, with an emphasis upon effective dispute resolution and underpinned by a sense of realism as to the barriers presented by State interests, as aptly and amply demonstrated in the rich and enduring legacy of fisheries scholarship of Robin Churchill.

[213] J García Molinos et al, 'Climate Velocity and the Future Global Redistribution of Marine Biodiversity' (2015) 6 *Nature Climate Change* 83, 87 (observing that distributional shifts are occurring in areas encompassing 'some of the world's most vexing maritime territorial disputes', notably the East and South China Seas).

PART V

International Criminal Cooperation

12

The Influence of *Jus Cogens* on International Crimes

Have they made any Difference?

ROBERT CRYER*

Abstract: It is often thought that the concepts of *jus cogens* and international crimes walk hand in hand. After all, they both appear at least to be about protecting basic values of the international community of States. Some even go as far as to assert that international crimes are, per se, *jus cogens*. However, this chapter will argue that this goes too far. Although there is a fair amount of substantive overlap, international crimes can exist outside of violations of *jus cogens* and, indeed, pre-dated the acceptance of such a concept. Furthermore, through an evaluation of the jurisprudence of the ICJ and the ICTY, it will be argued that for the most part, no real additional consequences have been seen to flow from the *jus cogens* nature of violations of international criminal law, and where such consequences have been postulated (most notably in the *Furundjžia* case), these can be easily explained on other bases than *jus cogens*. It will conclude that in spite of frequent reference to the concept, especially in an academic context, it has not influenced States in any meaningful way.

I. Introduction

Jus cogens, as a concept, has been the darling of international lawyers for many years. It would be impossible to list the entirety of the literature on it, and it would not be advisable to attempt to do so.[1] It would be still more foolish, for a number

* For full disclosure, I ought to state Professor Robin Churchill gave me my first academic job, which was as a research assistant for the third edition of the standard reference on point: R Churchill and V Lowe, *The International Law of the Sea*, 3rd edn (Manchester, Manchester University Press, 1999).

[1] Some of the most important are A Verdross, 'Forbidden Treaties in International Law' (1937) 31 *American Journal of International Law* 571; A Verdross, '*Jus Dispositivum* and *Jus Cogens* in International Law' (1966) 60 *American Journal of International Law* 55; E Schwelb, 'Some Aspects of International *Jus Cogens*' (1967) 61 *American Journal of International Law* 946; J Sztucki, Jus Cogens *and the Vienna Convention on the Law of Treaties* (Vienna, Springer, 1974); P Weil, 'Towards Relativity in International

of reasons, to undertake the Sisyphean task of actually reading it all. The same could be said about the literature on international criminal law.[2] That said, there is surprising little on the interrelationship between the two that goes beyond a brief mention of the matter in other contexts. Therefore, it is the intention of this chapter to investigate the links between the two at both a conceptual and a practical level. It will begin with a description of the two areas of law before investigating the conceptual links between the two and then moving on to how *jus cogens* has added (or not) to the practical aspects of international crimes, both in the civil and criminal fields (as there have been numerous civil claims relating to international crimes). Finally, it will concentrate primarily on judicial decisions in the area as they have been fairly plentiful, or certainly more so than State practice in the area. To some extent, the investigation is designed to provide an answer to the question set some years ago by Professor Anthony D'Amato: 'what is the utility of a norm of *jus cogens* (other than its rhetorical value as a sort of exclamation point)?'[3] It concludes that in spite of the conceptual links between them, as it stands, the concept of *jus cogens* has not, despite a few exceptions, added a great deal to the legal nature of international crimes other than the symbolic value that attaches to the label, although that in itself is a benefit.

As such, the relationship between the concepts of *jus cogens* and international crimes is indicative of the promise of the concept of *jus cogens* and its limitations. In the words of Georg Schwarzenberger, it displays both the misery and grandeur of international law.[4] International law may be seen as being caught between these two poles – perceived universal ideals and perceptions of 'reality'. Such concepts may also be seen in terms of the dichotomy Martii Koskenniemi drew, very influentially, between apology and utopia.[5] In many ways this can be seen in Robin Churchill's work, which shows a clear, perspicuous and indeed prophetic understanding of the critical issues that face the world, and the extent to which law can

Law?' (1977) 73 *American Journal of International Law* 413; M Janis, 'Jus Cogens: An Artful Not a Scientific Reality' (1987–89) 3 *Connecticut Journal of International Law* 370; H Charlesworth and C Chinkin, 'The Gender of *Jus Cogens*' (1993) 15 *Human Rights Quarterly* 63; A Orakhelashvili, *Peremptory Norms in International Law* (Oxford, Oxford University Press, 2006); D Shelton, 'Normative Hierarchy in International Law' (2006) 100 *American Journal of International Law* 291.

[2] The main question here would be where even to begin. For overviews of the entire area, see MC Bassiouni (ed), *International Criminal Law Vols I–III*, 3rd edn (Leiden, Nijhoff, 2008); A Cassese et al, *Cassese's International Criminal Law*, 3rd edn (Oxford, Oxford University Press, 2013); R Currie and J Rikhof, *International and Transnational Criminal Law*, 2nd edn (Toronto, Irwin, 2013); R Cryer, D Robinson and S Vasiliev, *An Introduction to International and Criminal Law and Procedure*, 4th edn (Cambridge, Cambridge University Press, 2019).

[3] A D'Amato, 'It's a Bird, it's a Plane, it's *Jus Cogens*' (1990–91) 6 *Connecticut Journal of International Law* 1, 6.

[4] G Schwarzenberger, 'The Misery and Grandeur of International Law' (1964) 17 *Current Legal Problems* 184.

[5] M Koskenniemi, *From Apology to Utopia* (Cambridge, Cambridge University Press, 2005). For an insightful set of reflections on this, see W Werner, M de Hoon and A Galán (eds), *The Law of International Lawyers: Reading Martii Koskenniemi* (Cambridge, Cambridge University Press, 2017).

help in addressing issues such as pollution and the protection of the maritime environment.[6]

II. *Jus Cogens* and International Crimes: The Concepts and their Links

It should be noted that both the concepts of international crimes and *jus cogens* are not immutable, and are not necessarily agreed upon. Therefore, it is necessary to enter into some perhaps stipulative discussion. We will begin with international crimes and will then move on to *jus cogens*.[7]

A. International Crimes

What comes under the rubric of international crimes is, like so many things, in the eye of the beholder. There is no single authority that has set down its meaning in an authoritative lapidary fashion and there is unlikely to be one in the near (or distant) future.[8] For some, it is normative (ie, crimes that threaten the peace and security of humankind, as the International Law Commission (ILC) used to put it), while for others, it is purely descriptive. But this in itself assumes that there is a concept to describe, when in fact the whole area is subject to debate.[9]

At the outset, though one limitation can be made, for the purposes of this chapter, at the very least, the concept is limited to issues relating to individual liability. Therefore, the controversial concept of 'international crimes of States' introduced by the ILC in the (in)famous Article 19 of the draft Articles on State Responsibility in the 1970s is excluded from consideration here.[10] There are two reasons for this. The first is that, in the words of James Crawford, 'the language of "crime" and "delict" is not merely unnecessary, it is deceptive and misleading'.[11] The second is

[6] See, eg, R Churchill, 'Port State Jurisdiction Relating to the Safety of Shipping and Pollution from Ships: What Degree of Extra-territoriality?' (2016) 31 *International Journal of Maritime and Coastal Law* 442.

[7] See generally S Kadelbach, '*Jus Cogens*, Obligations *Erga Omnes* and Other Rules: The Identification of Fundamental Norms' in C Tomuschat and J-M Thouvenin (eds), *The Fundamental Rules of the International Legal Order* (Leiden, Brill, 2006).

[8] On the issue, see generally Cryer, Robinson and Vasiliev (n 2) ch 1.

[9] See, eg, G Schwarzenberger, 'The Problem of an International Criminal Law' (1950) 3 *Current Legal Problems* 263; C Kreβ, 'International Criminal Law' in R Wolfrum (ed), *Max Planck Encyclopaedia of Public International Law* (Oxford University Press, 2012) 717, 717–21.

[10] On which see G Gaja, '*Ius Cogens*, Obligations *Erga Omnes*, and International Crimes: A Tentative Analysis of Three Related Concepts' in J Weiler, A Cassese and M Spinedi (eds), *International Crimes of State: A Critical Analysis of Article 19 of the ILC's Draft Articles on State Responsibility* (Berlin, De Gruyter, 1989) 151; J Crawford, *State Responsibility: The General Part* (Cambridge, Cambridge University Press, 2014) 390–94.

[11] J Crawford, 'International Crimes of State' in J Crawford, A Pellet and S Olleson (eds), *The Law of International Responsibility* (Oxford, Oxford University Press, 2010) 405, 413.

that the concept must be considered, to all intents and purposes, dead and buried following its express rejection by the International Court of Justice (ICJ) in the *Bosnian Genocide* case.[12]

As a matter of positive law, two approaches seem dominant. The first is to include only those crimes which are directly criminalised by international law, ie, those that are covered by the famous statement of the Nuremberg International Military Tribunal that:

> [C]rimes against international law are committed by men, not abstract entities, and only by punishing individuals who commit such crimes can the provisions of international law be enforced … individuals have international duties which transcend the national obligations of obedience imposed by the individual state.[13]

There are four crimes that undoubtedly fall within this category: aggression, genocide, crimes against humanity and war crimes.[14] There are two controversial additions to this list, at least according to some:[15] a generalised offence of terrorism, and individual acts of torture, insofar as either does not fall under the rubric of the other direct liability international crimes.

The other approach is to include in the category of 'international crimes' conduct covered by the 'suppression treaties', which, rather than creating crimes in international law directly, create obligations on States to create domestic offences that are covered by the definitions they set out. These 'transnational' crimes are disparate, covering conduct ranging from cutting submarine cables to hijacking aircraft,[16] but their common feature is that international law does not directly create liability for individuals, but instead obligations on States.[17]

It ought to be made clear that the two types of crime are not hermetically sealed; torture, terrorism and enforced disappearances are the subject of transnational criminal law conventions, but in certain circumstances can also fall under the definitions of international crimes in the narrow sense, and there is nothing inherent in the conduct that requires one or the other method of criminalisation to occur. However, for the purposes of this chapter, the narrower definition will be followed for the most part, concentrating on the 'big four' international crimes, with one addition: torture. The reason for this is that although the case for individual acts of torture contrary to the 1984 Convention against Torture being international

[12] *Application of the Convention on the Prevention and Punishment of Genocide (Bosnia and Herzegovina v Serbia and Montenegro)* [2007] ICJ Rep 43, para 170.

[13] 'Nuremberg IMT: Judgment and Sentences' (1947) 41 *American Journal of International Law* 172, 221.

[14] Cryer, Robinson and Vasiliev (n 2) 3–5.

[15] Cassese et al (n 2) 132–35.

[16] Convention for the Protection of Submarine Telegraph Cables (signed 14 March 1884, entered into force 1 May 1888) 24 Stat 989, Treaty Series 380; Convention for the Suppression of Unlawful Seizure of Aircraft (Hijacking Convention) (signed 16 December 1970, entered into force 14 October 1971) 860 UNTS 105.

[17] On which see generally N Boister, 'Transnational Criminal Law?' (2003) 14 *European Journal of International Law* 953; N Boister, *An Introduction to Transnational Criminal Law*, 2nd edn (Oxford, Oxford University Press, 2018).

crimes per se (rather than the actus reus of a war crime, a crime against humanity or genocide) is shaky, as we will see, not only is torture contrary to *jus cogens*,[18] but it has also been treated as an international crime in a context directly on point in one of the most influential cases on *jus cogens* and international crimes, so it is worth sacrificing some level of doctrinal purity for the sake of empirical coverage.

B. *Jus Cogens*

The origins of *jus cogens* can traced back to the scholastic natural law era of international law;[19] however, this was based on a radically different understanding of the international legal order[20] and cannot be seen as a direct precedent for *jus cogens* in the modern era. The renaissance of the idea came first in the 1930s, in particular from Alfred Verdross and those who studied under him.[21] Again working within the natural law tradition,[22] Verdross developed a substantive conception of *jus cogens* that invalidated treaties contrary to the *mores* of society, as he put it in 1937:

> This prohibition, common to the juridical orders of all civilized states, is the consequence of the fact that every juridical order regulates the rational and moral coexistence of the members of that community. No juridical order can, therefore, admit treaties between juridical subjects, which are in obvious contradiction to the ethics of a certain community.[23]

Unfortunately, the definition he gave (those which 'restrict the liberty of one contracting party in an excessive or unworthy manner or which endanger its most important rights')[24] was somewhat Delphic, and the examples given (those

[18] Admittedly, the same could be said about enforced disappearances. See, eg, UNGA Res 61/177, 'International Convention for the Protection of All Persons from Enforced Disappearances' (12 January 2007) UN Doc A/RES/61/177, Annex; J Sarkin, 'Why the Prohibition of Enforced Disappearances Has Achieved the Status of *Jus Cogens* in International Law' (2012) 81 *Nordic Journal of International Law* 537. Yet there is very little practice to date on this to discuss for our purposes. Nevertheless, see AC Trindade, 'Enforced Disappearance of Persons as a Violation of *Jus Cogens*: The Contribution of the Jurisprudence of the Inter-American Court of Human Rights' (2012) 81 *Nordic Journal of International Law* 507.

[19] A Paulus, '*Jus Cogens* in a Time of Hegemony and Fragmentation: An Attempt at a Reappraisal' (2005) 74 *Nordic Journal of International Law* 297, 300.

[20] D Kennedy, 'Primitive International Law' (1986) 26 *Harvard International Law Journal* 1, 5–6; M Koskenniemi, 'International Law and *Raison d'etat*: Rethinking the Prehistory of International Law' in B Kingsbury and B Straumann (eds), *The Roman Foundations of the Law of Nations: Alberio Gentili and the Justice of Empire* (Oxford, Oxford University Press, 2010) 297, 298.

[21] See Verdross, '*Jus Dispositivum*' (n 1). However, as noted by Zemanek, Verdross was not the first to write on *jus cogens* in this era – in fact, it was one of his protégés: K Zemanek, 'The Metamorphosis of *Jus Cogens*: From an Institution of Treaty Law to the Bedrock of the International Legal Order?' in E Cannizzaro (ed), *The Law of Treaties Beyond the Vienna Convention* (Oxford, Oxford University Press, 2011) 381–82.

[22] Verdross, 'Forbidden Treaties' (n 1) 576: 'A truly realistic analysis of the law shows us that every positive juridical order has its roots in the ethics of a certain community, that it cannot be understood apart from its moral basis.'

[23] ibid 573.

[24] ibid 574.

which restrict police and courts to a low level of intervention, prevent self-defence, prevent the protection of nationals abroad, or expose its population to distress) are neither clear nor in some instances non-ideological.[25] However, in the interwar period, Verdross was very much in the minority, and the concept gained little traction. There was a hint of an idea at least linked to *jus cogens* in the *High Command* case, in which it was suggested that an agreement to permit prisoners of war to undertake work that would be otherwise prohibited would be void, but since no such agreement was proved to have existed, the issue did not arise.[26]

The positivisation of the concept of *jus cogens* had to wait until the 1960s and the drafting of the Vienna Convention on the Law of Treaties.[27] At this point in time, a broad but not unanimous scholarly consensus emerged that such a concept existed in positive law.[28] The coronation of the concept probably came in the Vienna Convention, Article 53 of which reads:

> A treaty is void if, at the time of its conclusion, it conflicts with a peremptory norm of general international law. For the purposes of the present Convention, a peremptory norm of general international law is a norm accepted and recognized by the international community of states as a whole as a norm from which no derogation is permitted and which can be modified only by a subsequent norm of general international law having the same character.

That said, there was no immediate consensus, to say the least. France in particular was a strong critic of the concept. Indeed, it was no surprise that one of the latest critiques of relative normativity in international law was published in the *Revue generale de droit international*, and the ICJ, even in the 2000s, did not refer to the concept until its (French) President Guillaume stood down,[29] and this was after the ILC had endorsed the concept in the 2001 Articles on State Responsibility,[30] although this aspect was not uncontroversial at that stage.[31]

Yet, one of the most enduring criticisms of the concept, which has not entirely gone away, is what norms have actually reached that status, owing to the lack of

[25] And the ideology was deeply troubling. On Verdross's links with Nazism, see B Simma, 'The Contribution of Alfred Verdross to the Theory of International Law' (1995) 6 *European Journal of International Law* 33, 36–38; A Carty, 'Alfred Verdross and Othmar Spann: German Romantic Nationalism, National Socialism and International Law' (1995) 6 *European Journal of International Law* 78.

[26] *US v Krupp*, IX TWC (1949), 1395.

[27] Although some argue, with some justification, that the basis remains somewhat naturalistic: M Janis, 'The Nature of *Jus Cogens*' (1987–89) 3 Connecticut Journal of International Law 359, 361–62.

[28] See, eg, E Suy, 'Article 53' in O Corten and P Klein (eds), *The Vienna Convention on the Law of Treaties: A Commentary* (Oxford, Oxford University Press, 2011) 1224, 1227; J Crawford, *Brownlie's Principles of Public International Law*, 8th edn (Oxford, Oxford University Press, 2012) 594. A notable dissenter was Schwarzenberger (n 4) 167.

[29] It did not take too long for a majority opinion to utter the term; see below, n 116 and accompanying text.

[30] International Law Commission, 'Draft Articles on Responsibility of States for Internationally Wrongful Acts' (2001) UN Doc A/56/10, arts 26, 40 and 41. See below section III.C.

[31] See now A Paulus, '*Jus Cogens* in a Time of Hegemony and Fragmentation: An Attempt at a Reappraisal' (2005) 74 *Nordic Journal of International Law* 297; E Canniszzaro, 'A Higher Law for Treaties?' in Cannizzaro (n 21) 425, 426, who argues that the distinction between the treaty law implications and more general effects are more blurred than might be thought.

an adequate definition.[32] Therefore, it is necessary to examine the extent to which international crimes and *jus cogens* obligations overlap.

C. International Crimes and *Jus Cogens*

There are unquestionable theoretical links between international crimes and ideas of *jus cogens*. When Verdross was developing the concept in the 1960s, he went so far as to say that all 'rules of general international law created for a humanitarian purpose' were *jus cogens*.[33] It could be said that this statement was a little ahead of its time. Indeed, at a deeper level, there are other links between *jus cogens* and crime. Both share some concept of public order which they are intended to enshrine and, like *jus cogens*, a person cannot opt out of the criminal law.

Nevertheless, it would nonetheless be risky to attempt to read too much into this. International law, even more than law more generally, is not so deductive. That said, in Sir Humphrey Waldock's commentary on the draft Article 13 of the Vienna Convention on the Law of Treaties (which was the progenitor of Article 53), two of the three examples of *jus cogens* he identified related to international crimes *latto sensu* (the other being treaties procured by force). He identified *jus cogens* with treaties involving international crimes in the narrow sense, and those that States are required by international law to suppress and punish (ie, transnational crimes).[34] Large parts of the latter must be considered far in advance of international law both then and now. It would be difficult to say that, for example, the transnational crime of cutting undersea cables (subject to the 1884 Convention on Cutting Undersea Cables)[35] could reach *jus cogens* status anytime soon. However, as mentioned above, the position on torture is more complex.[36]

That said, Crawford, in relation to international crimes *stricto sensu*, has stated, with a considerable degree of authority,[37] that the prohibition of genocide, crimes against humanity and 'the basic rules of international humanitarian law' have reached this status.[38] For the sake of simplicity, we will take the first two as being as defined in Articles 6 and 7 of the Rome Statute of the International Criminal Court (ICC). The definition of genocide in Article 6 is drawn from Article II of the Genocide Convention, and there is ICJ jurisprudence to the effect that this definition reflects a *jus cogens* prohibition.[39] Although the definition of crimes

[32] U Linderfalk, 'The Effect of *Jus Cogens* Norms: Whoever Opened Pandora's Box, Did You Ever Think about the Consequences?' (2007) 18 *European Journal of International Law* 853, 854.

[33] Verdross, '*Jus Dispositivum*' (n 1) 59

[34] UN Doc A/CN.4/156 and Add 1–3. See Suy (n 28) 1226–67.

[35] Convention for the Protection of Submarine Telegraph Cables (n 16).

[36] Piracy and slavery fall outside the scope of this chapter.

[37] Lest we forget, the project to deal with the law in this area was brought in the ILC to fruition by Professor Crawford. See, eg, R Kolb, *The International Law of State Responsibility: An Introduction* (Cheltenham, Edward Elgar, 2017) 27–30.

[38] Crawford (n 10) 380.

[39] *Case Concerning Armed Activities on the Territory of the Congo (New Application: 2002) (Democratic Republic of the Congo v Rwanda) (Jurisdiction and Admissibility)* [2006] ICJ Rep 6, 32. Indeed, this was the first time the ICJ ever used the term in a majority opinion.

against humanity in Article 7 of the Rome Statute is probably a little narrower than customary law in some respects,[40] few would now deny that it is at least the base level of what is encompassed by the *jus cogens* prohibition of those crimes.[41] When it comes to war crimes, the position is a little more complex, in that although the ICJ has said that the basic rules have achieved the standard of *jus cogens*,[42] exactly which rules have reached this status is not entirely clear. However, these certainly include common Article 3 of the 1949 Geneva Conventions, which were described by the ICJ more than half a century ago as reflecting the 'elementary considerations of humanity'.[43]

There are certainly rules more than this and the ICJ has gone a little further in the *Jurisdictional Immunities* case willing to assume that certain prohibitions of war crimes (especially the murder of civilians, the imposition of slave labour and deportations to such labour) were contrary to *jus cogens* as long ago as the Second World War.[44] Even so, not all norms of humanitarian law are *jus cogens* or even customary.[45] Article 8 of the Rome Statute, whilst helpful, is not a complete list of

[40] See R Cryer, *Prosecuting International Crimes: Selectivity and the International Criminal Law Regime* (Cambridge, Cambridge University Press, 2005) 247–62. See also art 10 of the Rome Statute of the International Criminal Court (adopted 17 July 1998, entered into force 1 July 2002) 2187 UNTS 3, which comprises a 'savings clause' that says that the definitions in the Statute do not affect existing or developing custom, on which see W Schabas, *The International Criminal Court: A Commentary on the Rome Statute*, 2nd edn (Oxford, Oxford University Press, 2016) 34–38.

[41] MC Bassiouni, *Crimes against Humanity: Historical Evolution and Contemporary Application* (Cambridge, Cambridge University Press, 2011) 12; Crawford (n 10) 380; A Orakhelashvili, *Akehurst's Modern Introduction to International Law*, 8th edn (Abingdon, Routledge, 2019) 54. However, it should be noted that in the context of the ILC's work on crimes against humanity, five States (China, France, Iran, Turkey and the UK) sought to delete a preambular reference in the draft Articles to the *jus cogens* status of crimes against humanity, although it remains in the text adopted by the ILC, 'Texts and titles of the draft preamble, the draft articles and the draft annex provisionally adopted by the Drafting Committee on second reading' (15 May 2019) UN Doc A/CN.4/L935.

[42] *Legality of the Threat or Use of Nuclear Weapons (Advisory Opinion)* [1996] ICJ Rep 226, 257. On this aspect, see J Werksman and R Kalatschi, 'Nuclear Weapons and *Jus Cogens*: Peremptory Norms and Justice Preempted?' in LB de Chazournes and P Sands (eds), *International Law, the International Court of Justice and Nuclear Weapons* (Cambridge, Cambridge University Press, 1999) 181, especially 194–96.

[43] *Corfu Channel Case (United Kingdom v Albania)* [1949] ICJ Rep 4, 22. See also M Zagor, 'Elementary Considerations of Humanity' in K Bannelier, T Christakis and S Heathcote (eds), *The ICJ and the Evolution of International Law: the Enduring Impact of the Corfu Channel Case* (Abingdon, Routledge, 2012) 264.

[44] *Jurisdictional Immunities of the State (Germany v Italy: Greece Intervening)* [2012] ICJ Rep 99, 140–42. See O Sender and M Wood, 'Jurisdictional Immunities of the State' in E Bjorge and M Jackson (eds), *Leading Cases in International Law* (Oxford, Hart Publishing, 2017) 563, 572, which describes the Italian course use of *jus cogens* reasoning to trump immunity as leaving it as the 'single (and misbegotten) outlier'.

[45] R Neito-Navia, 'International Peremptory Norms (*Jus Cogens*) and International Humanitarian Law' in LC Vohrah et al (eds), *Man's Inhumanity to Man: Essays in Honour of Antonio Cassese* (Leiden, Njjhoff, 2003) 595, 633–35 notes that the fact that the 1949 Geneva Conventions may be denounced implies that not all of the norms they contain are necessarily *jus cogens*. The point is a bit more complex, in that *jus cogens* exist separately to treaties, but the point is well taken. On the customary status of Additional Protocol I, see, eg, C Greenwood, 'Customary Status of the 1977 Geneva Protocols' in AJM Delissen and GJ Tanja (eds), *Humanitarian Law of Armed Conflict: Challenges Ahead* (Leiden, Nijhoff, 1991) 93. For a broader view, see, eg, J-M Henckaerts and L Doswald-Beck, *Customary International Humanitarian Law* (Cambridge, Cambridge University Press, 2005). On the links, see R Cryer,

war crimes in international law, still less than those which reflect *jus cogens*, and nor was it intended to be.[46]

Fortunately, it is not necessary here to enter into a detailed discussion of the precise norms of international humanitarian law which have reached this status. For the purposes of this chapter, the term 'war crimes' will be taken to mean those that have reached *jus cogens* status. Identification of the precise norms that have done so must wait for another day – suffice it to say that there is a core of norms of humanitarian law that have reached this status. This provisional identification also deals with the vexed issue of aggression.

It is clear that the prohibition of the use of force in Article 2(4) of the UN Charter has the standing of a *jus cogens* norm.[47] However, the definition of the crime of aggression, which relies upon Article 2(4), is (and has been) a matter of considerable controversy, even after the 2010 Kampala Amendments to the Rome Statute that created a definition of this crime for the purposes of the ICC.[48] It was not necessarily intended to be reflective of customary law and even less so *jus cogens*.[49] But there is a core of the criminal prohibition of aggression which does reflect such a norm, to which references in this chapter will thus refer. What is important to take from this is that, as Cherif Bassiouni has said:

> Since not all international crimes rise to the level of *jus cogens* the source of legal obligation differs with respect to different categories of international crimes. Also in the era of globalization more international crimes which have not so far been deemed part of *jus cogens* like 'terrorism' have risen to a higher level of international concern, which may lead to their inclusion in the category of *jus cogens* international crimes.[50]

Bassiouni adopts a broader version of international crimes than this chapter does, but the general point stands. What is important to look for is the specific consequences that follow from that status rather than those that arise from the nature of the norms as *erga omnes* obligations or from the concept of individual liability under international law. It will be contended that most of the purported consequences that are said to come with the status of some international crimes having reached the exalted status of *jus cogens* can be more simply explained by reference

'War Crimes' in ND White and C Henderson (eds), *Research Handbook on Conflict and Security Law* (Cheltenham, Edward Elgar, 2013) 467, 479–81.

[46] H von Hebel and D Robinson, 'Crimes within the Jurisdiction of the Court' in RS Lee (ed), *The International Criminal Court: The Making of the Rome Statute* (The Hague, Kluwer, 1999) 79, 103–39, 122.

[47] *Military and Paramilitary Activities in and against Nicaragua (Nicaragua v United States of America)* [1986] ICJ Rep 14, 100–01.

[48] Annex II to Res RC/Res.6 (adopted 11 June 2010). See C Kreβ and S Barriga (eds), *The Crime of Aggression, Vols I and II* (Cambridge, Cambridge University Press, 2017). From a UK point of view, the customary status of the crime of aggression has been confirmed in *R v Jones and Others* [2006] UKHL 1; *Ayliffe and Others v Director of Public Prosecutions; Swain v Director of Public Prosecutions* [2006] 2 All ER 741.

[49] Article 8 *bis* of the Rome Statute stated that the definition is specifically stated to be 'for the purposes of this Statute'.

[50] MC Bassiouni, *An Introduction to International Criminal Law*, 2nd edn (Leiden, Nijhoff, 2013) 499–500.

to the former two concepts rather than the *jus cogens* doctrine. Ockham's razor[51] tells us that this would be the best way to proceed. Such a concept is especially pertinent in a diverse international legal order.[52]

III. The Consequences of a Violation of a *Jus Cogens* Norm: General and Particular, the ILC View and Beyond

To understand the nature of the relationship between international crimes and *jus cogens*, and the consequences of both, it is necessary first to look at the general consequences of a violation of *jus cogens* norms and then to look at the specifics of how these are and have been asserted to apply in the specific context of international crimes.[53] The discussion will then go on to look at how judicial and State practice has looked at the matter. It should be noted that the coverage here will be largely limited to the additional consequences that *jus cogens* add; it is not intended as a general *excursus* on the duties of States to respond to international crimes more generally, and their liability for their conduct in relation to these under the general law of State responsibility.

A. The General International Law on Responsibility for Violations of *Jus Cogens* Norms

This chapter has already noted how the Vienna Convention on the Law of Treaties deals with treaties that contradict *jus cogens* norms, ie, that they are void (whether in whole or in part). More general aspects of the legal results of violations of *jus cogens* norms may usefully be investigated by reference to the semi-authoritative ILC Articles on State Responsibility, which were adopted in 2001.[54] Whilst the

[51] This is: 'A methodological principle dictating a bias towards simplicity in theory construction, where the parameters of simplicity vary from kinds of entity to the number of presupposed axioms.' MM Adams, 'Ockham's Razor' in T Honderich (ed), *The Oxford Companion to Philosophy* (Oxford, Oxford University Press, 1995) 633.

[52] See, eg, O Yasukai, *International Law in a Transcivilizational World* (Cambridge, Cambridge University Press, 2017).

[53] It is not the purpose of this chapter to enter into the debate of whether or not the concept involves a constitutionalisation of the international legal order; its focus is more practical than that. Still, see K Zemanek, 'The Metamorphosis of *Jus Cogens*: From an Institution of Treaty Law to the Bedrock of the International Legal Order?' in Cannizzaro (n 21) 381, 409.

[54] On their authority, see DD Caron, 'The ILC Articles on State Responsibility: The Paradoxical Relationship between Form and Authority' (2002) 96 *American Journal of International Law* 857; Crawford (n 10) 42–44; Kolb (n 37) 29–30. On the particular Part (III), see J Crawford, *The International Law Commission's Articles on State Responsibility: Introduction, Text and Commentaries* (Cambridge, Cambridge University Press, 2002) 35–43. For an overview of the entire area, see Daniel Costelloe, *Legal Consequences of Peremptory Norms in International Law* (Cambridge, Cambridge University Press, 2017).

primary focus of this chapter is individual responsibility, it ought to be remembered that where international crimes are committed by those whose conduct is attributable to a State, the issue of State responsibility also arises.[55] Given that the paradigmatic examples of international crimes tend to be committed by State agents,[56] it is worth looking into this analogous area to individual responsibility.

We will begin with the substantive impact that the status of a norm as a *jus cogens* norm has on the substance norms involved, before moving on to the procedural aspects of it as a concept and then the question of what follows from the status in the procedural arena(s). It is true that the distinction between the two areas is one which is porous and not without its own ideological implications,[57] but as Stefan Talmon has said, it is one that comes rather naturally to lawyers.[58] So, as a shortcut and as a means of ordering the material, the distinction will be adopted, but with an eye on the fact that it can be reductive.

B. Substance

The first time that the draft ILC Articles on State Responsibility allude to *jus cogens* is in relation to 'circumstances precluding wrongfulness' in Part One, Chapter V. This occurs in Article 26, which reads: 'Nothing in this chapter precludes the wrongfulness of any act of a State which is not in conformity with an obligation arising under a peremptory norm of general international law.'

This is an article that raises many questions, not least as it seems to mix questions of the status of the norm and its ambit.[59] The Articles refer to various circumstances such as necessity and self-defence, which has caused controversy.[60] Nevertheless, it should be noted that in spite of the fact that the majority of crimes in the Rome Statute are contrary to *jus cogens* norms, this did not prevent the drafters of that treaty from including detailed provision for defences, including

[55] *Application of the Convention on the Prevention and Punishment of the Crime of Genocide (Bosnia and Herzegovina v Serbia and Montenegro)* (Judgment of 26 February 2007) [2007] ICJ Rep 43, paras 377–415. See M Milanović, 'State Responsibility for Genocide: A Follow-up' (2007) 18 *European Journal of International Law* 669; P Gaeta, 'On What Conditions Can a State Be Held Responsible for Genocide?' (2007) 18 *European Journal of International Law* 631; A Cassese, 'On the Use of Criminal Law Notions in Determining State Responsibility for Genocide' (2007) 5 *Journal of International Criminal Justice* 875; P Gaeta, *The UN Genocide Convention: A Commentary* (Oxford, Oxford University Press, 2009) pt V. See more generally A Nollkaemper, 'Concurrence between Individual Responsibility and State Responsibility in International Law' (2003) 52 *International and Comparative Law Quarterly* 615; A Bianchi, 'State Responsibility and Criminal Liability of Individuals' in A Cassese (ed), *The Oxford Companion* (Oxford, Oxford University Press, 2010) 16; B Bonafè, *The Relationship between State and Individual Responsibility for International Crimes* (Leiden, Brill, 2009).

[56] See Cryer, Robinson and Vasiliev (n 2) 16–17.

[57] D Kennedy, 'Form and Substance in Private Law Litigation' (1976) 89 *Harvard Law Review* 1685.

[58] S Talmon, '*Jus Cogens* after *Germany v Italy*: Substantive and Procedural Rules Distinguished' (2012) 25 *Leiden Journal of International Law* 979, 983.

[59] See generally Crawford (n 54) 187–88; Crawford (n 10) ch 9, especially 315–18; Kolb (n 37) 135–36.

[60] P Allott, 'State Responsibility and the Unmaking of International Law' (1988) 29 *Harvard Journal of International Law* 1, 17–22; Kolb (n 37) 57.

self-defence and necessity in Article 31[61] and superior orders (for war crimes) in Article 33.[62] Hence, the status of a norm may not have the implications for individual criminal responsibility that the ILC has said apply to State responsibility, so perhaps the peremptory status of a rule may have different consequences in this respect.

That said, in one case, a State has made an argument that one of the defences was made on one of the rare occasions in which States have used *jus cogens* status to draw conclusions on substantive norms. This was the statement of Belgium on ratifying the Rome Statute, which in its view provided as follows: 'According to Article 2(1)(1)(b) of the Statute, and taking into consideration the rules of international humanitarian law from which no departure is allowed, the Belgian Government considers that Article 31(1)(c) can be applied and interpreted only in compliance with these rules.'[63]

No other State has made a similar declaration and it should be stated that not only is this not a reservation, but it also does not limit the authority of the ICC to interpret its own Statute as it sees fit.[64] It is carefully framed in terms of the applicable law for the ICC (ie, Article 21 of the Rome Statute),[65] so it is unlikely to have a broad effect. Nonetheless, it does represent an interesting, albeit isolated example of State practice where *jus cogens* reasoning seems to have been relied upon to draw conclusions about the substantive law. This declaration did not appear to have influenced the International Criminal Tribunal for the former Yugoslavia (ICTY) in the *Kordić and Čerkez* decision, where it declared that Article 31(1)(c) reflected customary international law,[66] and also remains a largely forgotten outlier in terms of practice.

C. Process

When it comes to the consequences of a violation of a *jus cogens* norm, the ILC Articles are rather more forthcoming than they are in relation to substance. The history of the provisions in question is related to the controversy regarding the concept itself. This controversy helps explain the deletion of the concept of international crimes of State noted above.

[61] See, eg, A Eser, 'Article 31' in O Triffterer and K Ambos (eds), *The Rome Statute of the International Criminal Court: A Commentary*, 3rd edn (Oxford, Hart Publishing, 2017) 1125.

[62] O Triffterer and S Bock, in Triffterer and Ambos (n 61) 1183. See generally Cryer, Robinson, and Vasiliev (n 2) ch 16.

[63] *Moniteur Belge* of 1 December 2000, 40423. The translation is that provided in E David, 'Belgium: Correspondent's Report' (2000) 3 *Yearbook of International Humanitarian Law* 426, 427. As he notes, this seems to have been influenced by academic critique. There was later judicial confirmation of the position in the Belgian courts.

[64] David (n 63) 427–28.

[65] See, eg, Schabas (n 40) 511–35.

[66] *Prosecutor v Kordić and Čerkez* (Judgment) IT-95-14/2-T (26 February 2001), para 449.

As a quid pro quo for the deletion of the concept, the ILC drew upon related norms, especially obligations *erga omnes* and *jus cogens*. The ILC was careful (and was probably right to be careful) to explain that there is a relation between the two, whilst holding back from conflating them. As it said in its commentary on the relevant provisions (which will be discussed below):

> [I]t is necessary for the articles to reflect that there are certain consequences flowing from the basic concepts of peremptory norms of general international law and obligations to the international community as a whole within the field of State responsibility ... there is at least a difference in emphasis. While peremptory norms of general international law focus on the scope and priority to be given to a certain number of fundamental obligations, the focus of obligations to the international community as a whole is essentially on the legal interest of all States in compliance.[67]

As we will see when we look at the case law, this was a sensible distinction to draw, although the relationship between the two may become closer as time passes.[68]

The (inter)relationship between the two concepts is further elaborated upon later on in the Articles:

Article 40

1. This chapter applies to the international responsibility which is entailed by a serious breach by a State of an obligation arising under a peremptory norm of general international law.
2. A breach of such an obligation is serious if it involves a gross or systematic failure by the responsible State to fulfil the obligation.[69]

Article 41

1. States shall cooperate to bring to an end through lawful means any serious breach within the meaning of article 40.
2. No State shall recognize as lawful a situation created by a serious breach within the meaning of article 40, nor render aid or assistance in maintaining that situation.[70]
3. This article is without prejudice to the other consequences referred to in this Part and to such further consequences that a breach to which this chapter applies may entail under international law.

[67] Crawford (n 54) 244.

[68] For a sceptical view, see P Picone 'The Distinction between *Jus Cogens* and Obligations *Erga Omnes*' in Cannizzaro (n 21) 411.

[69] For the commentary on this, see Crawford (n 54) 245–48. It is not necessary for our purposes to enter into the debate on the details of the definition in art 40, as the purpose of this chapter is to look to the outcome rather than the substance of the primary norms.

[70] See ibid 381–86; S Talmon, 'The Duty Not to "Recognize as Lawful" a Situation Created by the Illegal Use of Force or Other Serious Breaches of a *Jus Cogens* Obligation: An Obligation without Real Substance?' in Tomuschat and Thouvenin (n 7) 99.

This is added to by Article 48 of the ILC Articles, which provides that:

> 1. Any State other than an injured State is entitled to invoke the responsibility of another State in accordance with paragraph 2 if:
>   (a) the obligation breached is owed to a group of States including that State, and is established for the protection of a collective interest of the group; or
>   (b) the obligation breached is owed to the international community as a whole.
> 2. Any State entitled to invoke responsibility under paragraph 1 may claim from the responsible State:
>   (a) cessation of the internationally wrongful act, and assurances and guarantees of non-repetition in accordance with article 30; and
>   (b) performance of the obligation of reparation in accordance with the preceding articles, in the interest of the injured State or of the beneficiaries of the obligation breached.[71]

It is true that, as Robert Kolb has said, the Articles are brief and leave much to be determined, not least in that they do not identify the core and periphery of specific rules subject to this regime, and the results that flow from violations of the various aspects of each rule,[72] a matter to which we will return below. Nor do they spell out as clearly as possible what the consequences are or steep themselves in State practice as much as might be desirable.[73] Nevertheless, they provide a useful locus of debate on point, although it is the intention of this chapter to go a little further than the Articles themselves, as some other scholars have also done.[74]

So, let us turn to the first aspect of Article 41.[75] This is the duty to cooperate in bringing to an end the situation brought about by the contravention of a peremptory norm. The relationship of this to international crimes is not always clear; much of this simply follows from the nature of direct liability under international law rather than having to relate to *jus cogens* and their consequences. It is also the case that the Articles, as noted by Kolb, do not elaborate on what ought to be done.[76] As the Commentary itself states: 'Because of the diversity of circumstances which could possibly be involved, the provision does not prescribe in detail what form this cooperation should take.'[77]

However, it seems that the obligation as identified is a broad one, relating to all aspects of the illegality, including those that even imply the recognition of the legality of the conduct at issue.[78] Exactly how this would relate to international

[71] See generally Crawford (n 10) 380–81.
[72] Kolb (n 37) 57–58. For a very detailed study on point, see Martin Dawidowicz, *Third Party Countermeasures in International Law* (Cambridge, Cambridge University Press, 2017).
[73] ibid 58–59.
[74] Perhaps most notably Orakhelashvili (n 1) especially 288–319.
[75] Crawford (n 10) 381 includes invalidity, but this may be considered simply axiomatic and it is not expressed in the Articles per se.
[76] Kolb (n 37) 58–59.
[77] Crawford (n 54) 249.
[78] Orakhelashvili (n 1) 282; Crawford (n 10) 382.

crimes specifically is unclear, as all the practice referred to in the Commentary to Article 41(1) refers to collective responsive activity rather than individual criminal responsibility.[79] The Commentary itself admits that this collective obligation may relate to progressive development of the law rather than a simple codification.[80]

There is little if any practice relating to international crimes specifically that is referable to Article 41(1), and as such cannot be considered to have made any serious impact on practice on individual criminal liability. It is possible that an argument could be made that an obligation to prosecute offences or cooperate in such prosecutions could be inferred from this, but this seems a stretch too far. There is nothing in the Commentary to Article 41 that even implies such an expansive view of the obligations that the Articles reflect.[81]

Yet, in addition, there is the duty of cooperation to bring an end to any situation that has arisen as a result of the violation of the relevant norm. Again, this is something subject to a wide interpretation,[82] but does not identify precisely in what manner this duty may be fulfilled.[83] However, the practice identified in the Commentary to this provision relates to collective action and, whilst dealing with issues relating to international crimes, none of the practice makes mention of individual criminal responsibility.[84] Although the Articles relate to State rather than individual liability, it is notable that elsewhere in the Commentary, the ILC did not shy away from using such analogies.[85] The discussion in the Commentary to Article 41 relates primarily to collective non-recognition rather than anything else.[86] Nevertheless, as a counterpoint, there are certain comments that are included in the Commentary that (as we will see below) do have relevance with respect to international crimes, although they were not the focus of the comments directly:

> Under article 41, paragraph 2, no State shall recognize the situation created by the serious breach as lawful. This obligation applies to all States, including the responsible State ... since the breach by definition concerns the international community as a whole, waiver or recognition induced from the injured State by the responsible State cannot preclude the international community interest in ensuring a just and appropriate settlement.[87]

As such, there is more than a hint here that the nature of violations of peremptory norms are not simply bilateral and that all States, and the international community as a whole, have separate rights that cannot be abolished by unilateral or bilateral action. When we look at the relevant jurisprudence, all have an interest in the

[79] Crawford (n 10) 382–85.
[80] Crawford (n 54) 249.
[81] Other views on point will be canvassed below.
[82] Crawford (n 10) 386.
[83] ibid 383–85.
[84] Crawford (n 54) 250–51.
[85] ibid 243–44.
[86] ibid.
[87] ibid 251.

protection of the values that peremptory norms encapsulate. However, this can again be referred to the nature of individual liability in international law rather than the *jus cogens* concept more generally. This will be elaborated upon further when the jurisprudence on these issues is discussed in the next section.

Overall, though, there is not a great deal that can be drawn from the Articles on this specific to international crimes. States have certainly not considered this obligation to require them to cooperate to create international criminal tribunals, nor have they used the Articles as a basis upon which to rely in order to provide mutual legal assistance in relation to or the extradition of international criminals on the basis of the obligation postulated in the Articles.[88]

Moving on to the obligation of non-assistance, this includes an obligation not to assist in maintaining the situation brought about by the relevant violation. This may implicate issues relating to the granting of immunity for international crimes.[89] This is particularly the case as the concept of aid or assistance includes such conduct after the fact, which applies even if the violation is not one of a continuing nature.[90] Yet again, and consistently with the integrated nature of the three obligations identified in Article 41,[91] there is little detail on what this amounts to, and the examples used relate to collective action rather than to individual responsibility, although this is understandable.

D. Beyond Article 41

As is made clear by Article 41(3) of the ILC Articles, the Articles are not exhaustive of the consequences that come about as a result of a violation of a peremptory norm.[92] First, all of the standard results and secondary obligations that are applicable to violations of all obligations, irrespective of the nature of the norm, apply to violations of peremptory norms.[93] Hence, the extent to which States are obliged to prosecute international crimes on the basis of their human rights obligations, and the obligation to provide satisfaction in spite of suggestions to the contrary[94]

[88] There are some General Assembly Resolutions that are relevant, but they are not taken to have created a legal obligation; see Cryer (n 40) 105–10.

[89] Crawford (n 10) 385ff.

[90] Crawford (n 54) 252. Some violations of international criminal law are of that nature (see, eg, R Rastan and ME Badar, 'Article 11' in Triffterer and Ambos (n 61) 657, 663–69), although given the above, it is unnecessary to pursue the matter further at this point.

[91] Crawford (n 54) 252.

[92] ibid 253: 'The fact that such further consequences are not expressly referred to in chapter III does not prejudice their recognition in present-day international law, or their further development. In addition, paragraph 3 reflects the conviction that the legal regime of serious breaches is itself in a state of development. By setting out certain basic legal consequences of serious breaches in the sense of article 40, article 41 does not intend to preclude the future development of a more elaborate regime of consequences entailed by such breaches.' See also Costelloe (n 54) ch 3.

[93] Crawford (n 54) 252.

[94] Orakhelashvili (n 1) 264–65.

are not directly related to the status of the norm that has been violated; rather, such obligations arise directly from treaty or general international law.[95]

Other suggestions have been made that outside of the ILC regime, the *jus cogens* status enjoyed by many rules of international criminal law creates a duty to prosecute those violations. Perhaps the most strident advocate of such a position is Cherif Bassiouni, who took the view that the development of international society had reached a communitarian level from which a duty to prosecute international crimes may be deduced from principle alone.[96] Even Bassiouni accepted that this was controversial,[97] and given the ambivalent nature of the case law discussed below, the jurisprudence cannot be considered to support such a strong conclusion, one that was reached by Bassiouni's co-author on the book in which he first made that assertion.[98]

A more sophisticated, arguably 'Grotian' position[99] is adopted by Alexander Orakhelashvili, who mixes practice (in particular treaty law), some jurisprudence and deductive reasoning from the nature of *jus cogens* to establish not only a right for States to assert universal jurisdiction, but a duty to do so.[100] Although elegant, the evidence does not quite bear the weight of the (proposed) argument. The treaty law is subject to an analogous argument to the Baxter paradox,[101] in that the feeling on the part of States that they have to make it clear in treaties relating to international crimes that they may create mandatory universal jurisdiction is open to an *a contrario* argument. This analogous argument would be that the drafters felt that even where the relevant norms may implicate *jus cogens* issues, it was and is necessary to provide for the consequences needed to be addressed directly in the relevant treaties.

The most important case law is dealt with below; as will be seen, it is at best ambivalent or not well-reasoned (although national case law may amount to State practice where it is the emanation of a national court).[102] The influence of international decisions, outside of their binding force between contentious litigants, is not binding. Advisory opinions by their very nature are precisely that, but, as with contentious litigation, the decisions of international courts, especially the ICJ, have a far broader impact than Article 38(1)(d) of the ICJ Statute might imply.[103]

[95] Cryer (n 40) 102–10.

[96] See MC Bassiouni and E Wise, Aut Dedere Aut Judicare: *The Duty to Extradite or Prosecute in International Law* (Leiden, Nijhoff, 1995) 49–50. For an elaboration on this, see ibid 110–12. For a sophisticated discussion, see Orakhelashvili (n 1) 288–319.

[97] Bassiouni and Wide (n 96) 26–37.

[98] EM Wise, '*Aut Dedere aut Judicare*: The Duty to Extradite or Prosecute' in MC Bassiouni (ed), *The International Criminal Court* (Chicago, Erès, 1997) 27–28.

[99] H Lauterpacht, 'The Grotian Tradition in International Law' (1946) 23 *British Yearbook of International Law* 1.

[100] Orakhelashvili (n 1).

[101] R Baxter, 'Treaties and Custom' (1970) 129 *Recueil des Cours* 64, 64; J Crawford, *Chance, Order, Change: The Course of International* Law (Leiden, Brill/Nijhoff, 2014) ch IV.

[102] For a brief comment, see Orakhelashvili (n 41) 47.

[103] See, eg, M Shabuddeen, *Precedent in the World Court* (Cambridge, Cambridge University Press, 1996); A Pellet, 'Article 38' in A Zimmermann et al (eds), *The Statute of the International Court of Justice: A Commentary*, 2nd edn (Oxford, Oxford University Press, 2012) 731, 854–68.

Much depends on the quality of their reasoning.[104] When it comes to deductive, conceptual reason, much of this is a matter of taste in terms of jurisprudential style (and it ought to be said that Orakhelashvili does not place the strong normative reliance on concepts that Bassiouni does) and there are risks in top-down reasoning. The concepts that exist in international law, for better or worse, come from States, and at best exist in a reflexive relationship with what States are willing to accept and their practice in relation to any particular rule. To go too far one way would, in Koskenniemi's well-known terms, be apologetic, the other utopian.[105]

So far, in spite of the sterling efforts of academics to push the debate forward,[106] States remain far more aligned to their own practice rather than conceptual analysis being determinative.[107] As Kai Ambos has noted, in relation to the idea that a duty to prosecute international crimes can be directly derived from the *jus cogens* nature of the prohibitive norm that some of the strictures of international criminal law impose:

> It is sometimes argued that a duty to prosecute serious crimes … may be inferred from the character of those crimes as *jus cogens* since this generates a duty *erga omnes*. However, the *jus cogens* nature of certain crimes does not, automatically, entail a duty to prosecute such crimes. It only means that the underlying prohibition and the ensuing criminalization cannot be derogated, and that States may prosecute these crimes domestically even if there exists no jurisdictional link.[108]

As a matter of doctrine and positive international law, it is difficult to fault this conclusion, although there is some case law that implies the contrary.[109]

Finally, and briefly, as the Commentary makes clear, Article 48 is based on the concept of *erga omnes* obligations rather than *jus cogens* obligations per se.[110] Hence, little needs to be said as to how the two concepts differ: *jus cogens* norms are a sub-set of *erga omnes* rules, and the focus here is on what makes the former differ from the latter.[111] As with many of the areas we have covered here, though State practice is still rather scant, what seems to be clear concerning States' international obligations is that most exist without reliance on *just cogens* as a concept.[112]

[104] G Schwarzenberger, 'The Inductive Approach to International Law' (1947) 60 *Harvard Law Review* 539, 552–54; C Parry, *The Sources and Evidences of International Law* (Manchester, Manchester University Press, 1965) 91–94.

[105] Koskenniemi (n 5).

[106] On their influence, see generally S Sivakumaran, 'The Influence of Teachings of Publicists on the Development of International Law' (2017) 66 *International and Comparative Law Quarterly* 1.

[107] C Focarelli, 'Promotional *Jus Cogens*: A Critical Appraisal of *Jus Cogens*' Legal Effects' (2008) 77 *Nordic Journal of International Law* 429, 445. For another deductive argument, see A Paulus, '*Jus Cogens* in a Time of Hegemony and Fragmentation: An Attempt at a Reappraisal' (2005) 74 *Nordic Journal of International Law* 297, 309.

[108] K Ambos, 'Principle 19' in F Haldemann and T Unger (eds), *The United Nations Principles to Combat Impunity: A Commentary* (Oxford, Oxford University Press, 2018) 205, 209.

[109] The same applies in relation to immunity; see sections IV.B–IV.D below; and Costelloe (n 54) 259–85.

[110] Although it deliberately avoids the term; Crawford (n 54) 278.

[111] Shelton (n 1) 318 expresses the point clearly: 'Not all obligations *erga ommes* have been described as international crimes.'

[112] ibid 304.

IV. *Jus Cogens* and International Crimes: The Case Law

As a result of the comparative lack of State practice in relation to the relationship between *jus cogens* and international crimes, it has often fallen to courts to stake out new claims with regard to the relationship between *jus cogens*, international crimes and the obligations of States. Due to space constraints, the general focus here will be on the decisions of international courts and tribunals, as they tend to have greater 'ripple' effects than those of domestic courts, although where they have had an impact, this will be noted. As discussed above, much will depend on the quality of the reasoning in the specific case rather than its formal authority For similar reasons, the case law of human rights bodies and domestic decisions relying upon it will, sadly, not be covered.

As stated above, the selection of cases given below is not comprehensive, but, it is to be hoped, emblematic, owing to the fact that the law has been in a consistent state of flux and development. For the same reason, the coverage here will limit itself, for the most part, to cases that have directly related to the status of a *jus cogens* violation as an international crime. As the next section will show, at times, it is necessary to investigate the relationship between a violation of a norm which is *jus cogens* and an international crime. The discussion will concentrate on those aspects of the relationship that do not relate to civil immunities. There is an enormous literature on civil immunities and the matter falls outside of the scope of this chapter.

A. The Beginning: The *Barcelona Traction* Case

The concept of community obligations from which specific legal consequences could be derived can, as a matter of international judicial practice, be traced back to the ICJ's dictum in the *Barcelona Traction* case.[113] The case is generally considered a belated apology for the ICJ's legitimacy demolishing opinion in the *South West Africa* case,[114] in which Ethiopia and Liberia were refused the standing to bring South African policies of apartheid to court on the basis that:

> [A]n essential distinction should be drawn between the obligations of a State towards the international community as a whole, and those arising vis-à-vis another State in the field of diplomatic protection. By their very nature the former are the concern of all States. In view of the importance of the rights involved, all States can be held to have a legal interest in their protection; they are obligations *erga omnes*.[115]

[113] *Barcelona Traction, Light and Power Company, Limited (Belgium v Spain) (New Application: 1962)* [1970] ICJ Rep 3. See G Gaja, '*Barcelona Traction, Light and Power Company*' in Bjorge and Jackson (n 44) 307, 309–11.

[114] On which see J Crawford and P Mertenskötter, 'The *South West Africa* Cases' in Bjorge and Jackson (n 44) 263.

[115] *Barcelona Traction* (n 113) 32.

This decision, which came hot on the heels of the 1969 Vienna Convention of the Law of Treaties, was careful to acknowledge the existence of communitarian obligations, which all States may have an interest in vindicating, but the terminology of *jus cogens* was studiously avoided. It may even be postulated that the concept of *erga omnes* obligations was created in the *Barcelona Traction* case as a compromise between the embarrassment the Court felt about the *South West Africa* case and a concern that it would overreach itself if it were to adopt a full-blooded concept of *jus cogens*, which was by no means accepted at this point.[116]

To attempt to square this particular circle, the Court apparently opted for a halfway house between the old and the new approaches to the hierarchy of norms in international law, whilst doing so without allowing it to alter its decision on the case before it. Yet, what this decision did do was to create an interstitial position between traditional notions of *jus dispositivum* and *jus cogens*. Given that this was not key to the decision, the effects of the distinction the Court drew at the time had no substantive impact. This impact-free approach to the notion of *erga omnes* norms was consolidated in the *East Timor* case, in which the right of self-determination, despite its *erga omnes* character, did not trump the *Monetary Gold* principle.[117]

This is something that was later expanded out to *jus cogens* norms in the *Armed Activities (DRC v Rwanda)* case. Here, although the ICJ determined that the prohibition of genocide was contrary to a *jus cogens* norm, this determination did not alter the fundamental condition of consent to establish the jurisdiction of the Court:

> The same [consent-based approach] applies to the relationship between peremptory norms of general international law (*jus cogens*) and the establishment of the Court's jurisdiction: the fact that a dispute relates to compliance with a norm having such a character, which is assuredly the case with regard to the prohibition of genocide, cannot of itself provide a basis for the jurisdiction of the Court to entertain that dispute. Under the Court's Statute that jurisdiction is always based on the consent of the parties

Finally, the ICJ deemed it necessary to recall that the mere fact that rights and obligations *erga omnes* or peremptory norms of general international law (*jus cogens*) are at issue in a dispute cannot in itself constitute an exception to the principle that its jurisdiction always depends on the consent of the parties.[118]

As is clear from the above, the ICJ, whilst finally accepting the existence of the concept of *jus cogens*, gave with one hand and took away with the other by denying any normative impact of the recognition of that status. Hence, there has been no case to date before the ICJ in which *jus cogens* has played any normative role.[119]

[116] As implied above, it took another 35 or so years before the ICJ dared to use the term 'jus cogens' in *Case Concerning Armed Activities on the Territory of the Congo (New Application: 2002) (Democratic Republic of the Congo v Rwanda)* [2006] ICJ Rep 6, para 64.

[117] *Monetary Gold Removed from Rome in 1943 (Italy v France, United Kingdom of Great Britain and Northern Ireland and United States of America) (Preliminary Question)* [1954] ICJ Rep 19.

[118] *Armed Activities* case (n 116) paras 64–65.

[119] Focarelli (n 107) 430.

B. The High Water Mark: The ICTY in the *Furundžia* Case

In contrast to the ICJ, the ICTY, under the inspirational leadership of Antonio Cassese,[120] took a far more assertive approach to the results that arose, *ipso jure*, on the basis of the decision of the Trial Chamber (over which Cassese presided) that the prohibition of torture was contrary to *jus cogens*.[121] This was in itself not such a controversial finding, and one that has been confirmed by the ICJ in the *Habré* case[122] (on which, see below). More difficult, though, were the conclusions that the Trial Chamber came to on the basis that torture was prohibited by a *jus cogens* norm,[123] as well as being a norm applicable *erga omnes*.[124]

Yet, at the outset, it is only right to issue a caveat: the decision has been gently described as 'generous' in its interpretation of the normative consequences from determining that torture is prohibited by a *jus cogens* norm. Many if not all of the Trial Chamber's conclusions can be explained on bases that are firmer than conceptual derivation from the *jus cogens* concept. Ockham's razor returns to inform the following analysis. There is little use in lavish reasoning to bolster conclusions that can be reached in a far more direct manner.

The Opinion begins in the relevant part with a statement that few would disagree with. This is that torture is now considered to be contrary to a *jus cogens* norm.[125] The Trial Chamber began on fairly strong ground, stating that:

> Because of the importance of the values it protects, this principle has evolved into a peremptory norm *or jus cogens*, that is, a norm that enjoys a higher rank in the international hierarchy than treaty law and even 'ordinary' customary rules. The most conspicuous consequence of this higher rank is that the principle at issue cannot be derogated from by States through international treaties or local or special customs or even general customary rules not endowed with the same normative force.[126]

As such, the Opinion argues, in a more subtle manner than might initially be thought on first reading, that:

> At the inter-state level, it serves to internationally de-legitimise any legislative, administrative or judicial act authorising torture. It would be senseless to argue, on the one hand, that on account of the *jus cogens* value of the prohibition against torture, treaties or customary rules providing for torture would be null and void *ab initio*, and then be

[120] Upon whom, in this regard, see T Hoffman, 'The Gentle Civilizer of Humanitarian Law: Antonio Cassese and the Creation of the Customary Law of Non-international Armed Conflict' in C Stahn and L van den Herik (eds), *Future Perspectives in International Criminal Justice* (The Hague, Asser, 2009) 58.

[121] It is not entirely clear whether the Trial Chamber was discussing torture contrary to the 1884 Convention (which is a transnational crime) or as a way in which a war crime or a crime against humanity may be committed. See Cassese et al (n 2) 131–35.

[122] *Questions Relating to the Obligation to Prosecute or Extradite (Belgium v Senegal)* (Judgment) [2012] ICJ Rep 422, para 99.

[123] *Prosecutor v Anto Furundžia* (Judgment) IT-95-17/1-T (10 December 1998), paras 153–54.

[124] ibid paras 151–52.

[125] ibid para 155.

[126] ibid para 153.

> unmindful of a State say, taking national measures authorising or condoning torture or absolving its perpetrators through an amnesty law.[127]

The result may be easily agreed with, but it is not necessary to resort to *jus cogens* reasoning to reach this agreeable position.[128] Any domestic law that condoned or amnestied acts of torture would simply be a matter of domestic legislation, which, of course, would not bind any other State wishing to exercise jurisdiction.[129] This further flows from the fact that liability which arises directly under international law and its absolution simply does not lie within the gift of any one State to give. The liability does not arise from its domestic legal order, as the Nuremberg International Military Tribunal made clear,[130] and therefore, if for no other reason than the general principle of *nemo dat quod non habet* (very roughly translated as 'one cannot give what one does not have')[131] nor can one give away what is not within one's power to give away.

This seemed to be accepted by the ICTY in the *Furundžia* case, where it averred that:

> [P]erpetrators of torture acting upon or benefiting from those national measures may nevertheless be held criminally responsible for torture, whether in a foreign State, or in their own State under a subsequent regime. In short, in spite of possible national authorisation by legislative or judicial bodies to violate the principle banning torture, individuals remain bound to comply with that principle. As the International Military Tribunal at Nuremberg put it: 'individuals have international duties which transcend the national obligations of obedience imposed by the individual State'.[132]

Against the backdrop of this statement, it can reasonably be questioned whether the *jus cogens* concept adds anything, as the statement from Nuremberg did not rely on such a construct, but on direct liability under international law, which no one State has the right to wish away. The conceptual work is not being done by the ideas behind *jus cogens*, which were not only a questionable foundation, but also an unnecessary one. Instead, basic principles of jurisdiction may provide a convincing answer.[133]

It is also worth bearing in mind that owing to the fact that liability for international crimes arises from the fact that direct liability for such offences comes from international rather than domestic law, no one State's domestic law can extinguish

[127] ibid para 155. For a broad interpretation, see IM Siatistsa and M Wierda, 'Principle 24' in Haldeman and Unger (n 108) 258, 264.

[128] The literature on amnesties is vast. For an overview, see Cryer, Robinson and Vasiliev (n 2) ch 22.

[129] The position adopted here by the ICTY seemed at times to have been adopted by the Special Court for Sierra Leone in, eg, *Prosecutor v Kallon and Kamara (Decision on Jurisdiction: Lomé Accord Amnesty)* (13 March 2004) Case No SCSL-2001-14-AR72(E), para 71.

[130] 'Nuremberg IMT: Judgment and Sentences' (n 13).

[131] On the place of this principle in international law, see Crawford (n 10) 213.

[132] *Furundžia* (n 123) para 155.

[133] Along similar lines, albeit dealing with the linked issue of immunities, see D Akande and S Shah, 'Immunity of State Officials, International Crimes and Foreign Domestic Courts' (2011) 21 *European Journal of International Law* 815.

that liability on the *nemo dat* basis mentioned above. The same applies to the statement of the ICTY that the *jus cogens* status of the prohibition of torture (however defined) means that 'every State is entitled to investigate, prosecute and punish or extradite individuals accused of torture, who are present in a territory under its jurisdiction'.[134]

This may well be correct, but need not rely on the broader claim that the prohibition of torture has reached *jus cogens* status. It can easily be defended on the basis of the fact that, *pace* the *Barcelona Traction* case, *erga omnes* obligations, whilst linked to *jus cogens* norms in many ways, relate to the right of any State to assert a legal right in relation to locus standi, that is, a closer tie to the broader claim of the overall consequences of the *jus cogens* prohibition of torture. The same may be said about the ICTY's pronouncement that: 'It would seem that other consequences include the fact that torture may not be covered by a statute of limitations.'[135]

The statement in the same paragraph that torture 'must not be excluded from extradition under any political offence exemption' must be taken with a little more circumspection, in that it does not refer to any authority that relates to the *jus cogens* concept in and of itself, and as such must be treated with a considerable degree of caution, unless one accepts the deductive approach (as some do)[136] rather than inducting the consequences from what States or, in the terminology of the ILC, the 'international community as a whole' do.[137]

As a result, it is fair to say that the interpretation of the relation of *jus cogens* and international crimes is not as simple as is often asserted, and the *Furundjžia* case was at most a 'generous' interpretation of the concept,[138] even if, on its own terms, it did fall a little short of asserting the direct effect of *jus cogens* norms in domestic law.[139]

C. The ICJ Post-*Furundjžia*

It is naturally the case that international tribunals, in the absence of specific provision, do not bind one another. Hence, it was no real surprise that the ICJ, which had been so chary of discussing *jus cogens*, even post-*Furundjžia*, chose to abjure any discussion of *jus cogens*, making no reference to the concept at all, never mind its legal consequences.

The *Yerdoia* case is one that is well known to most international lawyers, whether it is considered famous or infamous. The majority judgment notably

[134] *Furundjžia* (n 123) para 156.
[135] ibid para 157.
[136] Orakhelashvili (n 1).
[137] Admittedly a broader concept, but the matter remains 'up in the air' at the moment.
[138] Focarelli (n 107) 429.
[139] Paulus (n 107).

decided not to discuss matters relating to *jus cogens*, simply passing over them on the basis that they did not affect the outcome of the case:

> [I]n its Application instituting these proceedings, the Congo originally challenged the legality of the arrest warrant of 11 April 2000 on two separate grounds: on the one hand, Belgium's claim to exercise a universal jurisdiction and, on the other, the alleged violation of the immunities of the Minister for Foreign Affairs of the Congo then in office. However, in its submissions in its Memorial, and in its final submissions at the close of the oral proceedings, the Congo invokes only the latter ground. As a matter of logic, the second ground should be addressed only once there has been a determination in respect of the first.[140]

This was criticised by two of the dissenting opinions in the case, such as Judge ad hoc van den Wyngaert, who noted that others had looked into the relationship between *jus cogens* and immunity in more detail and, as such, was uncomfortable with the result in the case. For her,[141] the failure of the majority opinion to deal with the issue of immunities and their relation to the *jus cogens* position of crimes against humanity in the international legal system was an abdication of their responsibility.[142]

Judge Al-Khasawneh went further, saying that the combating of grave crimes has arguably assumed a *jus cogens* character owing to the 'vital community interests and values it seeks to protect and enhance'. Therefore when this hierarchically higher norm comes into conflict with the rules on immunity, it should prevail'. There was little in Al-Khasawneh's opinion that provides a reason to simply accept his views other than a naturalistic form of reasoning,[143] which, as we will see, over time has been confined to dissenting opinions, albeit asserted more forcefully (or at least in greater depth) in later dissent.

However, this decision ought to be seen against the backdrop of the fact that at the time of the *Yerodia* decision, the ICJ had not even accepted the existence of *jus cogens* as a matter of international law; its first mention of the concept, as mentioned above, was in its 2006 decision in *DRC v Rwanda*,[144] in which, whilst agreeing that the prohibition on genocide was a *jus cogens* norm, it denied that any particular procedural consequences followed therefrom[145] – in particular, with echoes of the *East Timor* decision that the *erga omnes* nature of the obligations concerned (here those relating to self-determination) did not trump the necessarily consensual jurisdictional regime of the ICJ.[146]

[140] *Arrest Warrant of 11 April 2000 (Democratic Republic of the Congo v Belgium)* (Judgment) [2002] ICJ Rep 3, para 45.

[141] ibid, Dissenting Opinion of Judge van den Wyngaert, para 156.

[142] ibid.

[143] ibid, Dissenting Opinion of Judge Al-Khawnseh, para 7.

[144] *Armed Activities* case (n 116) para 64.

[145] ibid. There was discussion on point from Judge ad hoc Dugard (separate opinion, para 8ff). See Shelton (n 1) 308; yet, as Professor Shelton makes clear, Dugard did not assert that the *jus cogens* nature of the rules at issue made no difference (ibid 30–39).

[146] *Armed Activities* case (n 116) paras 64, 125.

The ICJ 'doubled down' on this regime in the *Jurisdictional Immunities* case, in which despite agreeing with the parties that the conduct in question, which involved the massacre of civilians in the Second World War,[147] was contrary to *jus cogens* norms (the temporal existence of which the ICJ carefully sidestepped by reference to the agreement of the parties on point).[148] It decided that irrespective of the status of the primary prohibitive norm (in this case, that of the war crime of killing civilians) having achieved *jus cogens* status, this did not directly impact on other rules of international law. The argument that *jus cogens* norms had such an impact was dismissed by the Court in firm terms.

This argument therefore depends upon the existence of a conflict between a *jus cogens* rule (or rules) and the rule of customary law, which requires a State to accord immunity to another State. However, in the opinion of the ICJ, no such conflict exists. Instead, the *jus cogens* rule, prohibiting war crimes, is one from which no derogation is permitted, but the rules which determine the scope and extent of jurisdiction and when that jurisdiction may be exercised do not derogate from the substantive rules which possess *jus cogens* status, nor is there anything inherent in the *jus cogens* concept which would require their modification or would displace their application.[149]

This was very thoughtfully elaborated upon by Judge Gaja in this case, who, with direct reference to the ILC's work in the area, as well as the opinions of domestic and other international courts (especially the European Court of Human Rights), determined that: 'It would be difficult to maintain that the obligation to provide reparation of a breach of an obligation under *jus cogens* is also set forth by a peremptory norm.'[150] Gaja's opinion is one which is closely reasoned and is grounded in both reason and authority, as might be expected. It supports the analysis expressed above in relation to the ILC's work that the status of a norm is separate from its consequences and, like the majority, Gaja, minimised, if not denied, that any particular consequences followed from the *jus cogens* status of any prohibitions other than those directly provided for in positive international law. The deduction of such results from the nature of *jus cogens* was thus not a line of enquiry that was of use to him.

The same cannot be said for judge Cançado-Trindade, who, in a characteristically naturalistic, lengthy and self-referential opinion, took the opposite view. For him, the Martens Clause, indicative, it would appear, of his view of the natural law that underlay it, meant that:

> Due attention had been taken not to leave anyone outside the protection granted by the *corpus juris gentium* – by conventional and customary international law – against

[147] The detailed toing and froing between Italy, Greece and Germany is usefully summarised in Sender and Wood (n 44).

[148] There are echoes here of the ICJ's position in relation to the status of the prohibition of the use of force as *jus cogens* in the *Nicaragua* case (n 47) para 190.

[149] *Jurisdictional Immunities of the State* (n 44), paras 92, 95. See also the discussion of practice in para 96.

[150] ibid, Separate Opinion of Judge Gaja, para 10.

> forced and slave work in [the] armaments industry. Such protection was extended by the *jus gentium* to human beings, well before the sinister nightmare and the horrors of the Third Reich.[151]

Judge Cançado-Trindade surveyed the pleadings of the parties and distinguished the approach of Germany, which maintained the distinction between the primary (*jus cogens*) prohibition of conduct and the secondary governing rules that resulted from it, with that of Italy and Greece, which argued the opposite – ie, that the two cannot be separated.[152] Yet, in a conclusionary manner, this did not deal with the substantive arguments, but instead looked out to policy considerations to say that: 'In my understanding, what jeopardizes or destabilizes the international legal order are the international crimes and not individual suits for reparation in the search for justice. In my perception, what troubles the international legal order are [*sic*] the cover-up of such international crimes.'[153] This understanding is, in the end, subject to the same critique that has been made of all naturalist approaches (including the critique that consequentialist policy arguments have mixed with conventional doctrinal reasoning).[154]

D. (Not) Dealing with the Issue: The ICJ in the *Habré* Case

The most important current pronouncement on the issue of *jus cogens* and charges that could amount to international crimes came in relation to the proceedings between Belgium and Senegal with respect to the prosecution of Hissène Habré, the former dictator of Chad. Belgium had issued an arrest warrant against Habré, in part on the basis of the ratification of all the parties of the Torture Convention, but also on the basis of general international law. However, in its plea to the ICJ as to its jurisdiction, Belgium relied on the parties' mutual ratification of the Torture Convention.[155]

However, the Court decided on jurisdictional grounds to deal with the matter on the basis of the clear jurisdictional basis of the Torture Convention.[156] Although the majority were clear that the prohibition of torture was one which had achieved *jus cogens* status, they decided that it was unnecessary to engage further in relation to the consequences of this, as they took their basis of jurisdiction to be based on the Torture Convention rather than more broadly.[157] As a result, they did not even pronounce on the issue of the general international law of *erga omnes* obligations, which, as was noted above, is not identical to the law on *jus cogens*. Instead, they decided that Belgium had standing to state its rights *erga omnes partes* (in other

[151] ibid, Separate Opinion of Judge Cançado-Trindade, para 117.
[152] ibid paras 121–28.
[153] ibid para 129.
[154] N Duxbury, *Patterns of American Jurisprudence* (Oxford, Oxford University Press, 1995) 191–99.
[155] *Belgium v Senegal* (n 122) paras 55, 63.
[156] ibid para 55.
[157] ibid. Judge Abraham would have broadened the issue to deny a customary right to prosecute. See Separate Opinion of Judge Abraham at paras 21–40.

words, as a party to the Torture Convention, Belgium was entitled to raise a claim against any other party to that treaty). This allowed them to avoid the broader issues that the Belgian claim raised. As a matter of judicial economy, this may be understandable, but it meant that some of the considerations relating to *jus cogens* that had been raised in the litigation were not given detailed analysis in the majority opinion.

Perhaps unsurprisingly, the same cannot be said of the opinion of Judge Cançado-Trindade, who placed his analysis firmly within his naturalistic approach to *jus cogens*.[158] Discussing the prohibition of torture (which was not a matter of contention between the parties) he opined that:

> Such absolute prohibition of torture finds expression at both *normative* and *jurisprudential* levels. The basic principle of humanity, rooted in the human conscience, has arisen and stood against torture. In effect, in our times, the *jus cogens* prohibition of torture emanates ultimately from the universal juridical conscience and finds expression in the *corpus juris gentium*.[159]

If there were any question as to the basis of Judge Cancado-Trindade's thinking, this is made clear later on in his opinion, where he states that his views are 'in line' with naturalist thinking.[160] However, what is interesting about his opinion, in addition to its jurisprudential foundation, is that contrary to the majority opinion, he was willing to draw broader normative conclusions from his determination that the prohibition of torture had reached the vaunted level of *jus cogens*. Hence, he argued that there was an obligation of result rather than conduct. Yet, precisely what he meant by this in the abstract rather than in the individual case (which after the judgment led to Habré's conviction before a special Senegalese court supported by the African Union) remains unclear.

There are statements in Cancado-Trindade's opinion that the rights of victims are a result of the *jus cogens* prohibition of torture and that there is a continuing violation of their rights.[161] This may be true, but the law relating to *jus cogens* does not do any normative work here. This is perhaps unsurprising, in that Cancado-Trindade's opinion is often difficult to decipher, in particular regarding the relationship between *jus cogens*, *erga omnes* obligations and *erga omnes partes* obligations. The conflation of them is made abundantly clear in paragraph 175 of his opinion, where it is stated that:

> The absolute prohibition of torture being one of *jus cogens* – as reckoned by the ICJ itself in the present Judgment – the obligations under a 'core human rights Convention' of the United Nations such as the Convention against Torture are not simple obligations of means or conduct: they are, in my understanding, obligations necessarily of result, as we are here in the domain of peremptory norms of international law, of *jus cogens*, generating obligations *erga omnes partes* under the Convention against Torture.[162]

[158] *Belgium v Senegal* (n 122), Dissenting Opinion of Judge Cançado-Trindade, para 82.
[159] ibid para 84.
[160] ibid para 176.
[161] ibid para 148.
[162] ibid para 175.

In contrast, it should be noted that Judge ad hoc Sur took an utterly contrary view, asserting that:

> [L]et us take the reference to *jus cogens* which appears in the reasoning, a reference which is entirely superfluous and does not contribute to the settlement of the dispute, as will be seen. The purpose of this obiter dictum is to acknowledge and give legal weight to a disputed notion, whose substance has yet to be established. Thus, the dispute is used for other ends, namely as a starting-point for further developments outside of its scope.[163]

Both of these outlying positions should not be given too much weight. They must stand or fall on their own quality of reasoning.[164] Neither of them is strong on this regard. Cançado-Trindade's opinion is an almost parodic example of naturalism, which is not the (rightly or wrongly) dominant form of discourse in international law, especially in a diverse world, with intercivilisational perspectives.[165] Judge ad hoc Sur's approach runs counter to the vast majority of opinion and perhaps reflects the earlier views of Prosper Weil in his extremely influential piece on relative normativity in international law.[166] Either way, both, like the majority, did not attribute any normative weight to *jus cogens* concepts. So, by hook or by crook, the normative relevance of the status of a norm as *jus cogens* has not, at the international level, carried much (if any) weight.

V. Conclusions

As this chapter has sought to show, as a matter of law, the concept of *jus cogens* has not added greatly to the idea of international crimes. Where there are alleged effects that follow from the *jus cogens* prohibitions of international crimes, the vast majority of them are more simply attributable to traditional principles of international law, such as the territorial reach of domestic laws, general principles of jurisdiction and the (slightly) narrower ideas of *erga omnes* obligations.

There have been assertions that broad consequences can be deduced from the concept of *jus cogens*, but for the most part, these have fallen on stony ground before international tribunals, with the exception of the ICTY and occasionally regional human rights courts.

It is notable that in the most recent decision of the ICC, denying immunity for (now former) President Al-Bashir from arrest relied on arguments (whether one

[163] ibid, Dissenting Opinion of Judge *ad hoc* Sur at para 4.

[164] A Boyle and C Chinkin, *The Making of International* Law (Oxford, Oxford University Press, 2007) 300–10.

[165] Yasukai (n 52).

[166] Weil (n 1), although in later works, Weil became more sanguine about community values. See P Weil, 'Le Droit international en quête de son identité. Cours général de droit international public' (1992) 237 *Recueil des Cours de l'Académie de Droit International* 1.

accepts them or not)[167] that related to an asserted customary rule that meant that immunities did not apply before international courts. There was no acceptance of *jus cogens* reasoning in the decision. This is perhaps telling.

This is not to say that the determination of something as a violation of a *jus cogens* norm is unimportant; if nothing else, it has a symbolic aspect that ought not to be ignored.[168] A similar matter of labelling something that is truly contrary to fundamentally agreed-upon norms as such was asserted by the ICTY in the *Krstić* appeal decision, where it stated that in relation to the Srebrenica massacre, 'the law condemns, in appropriate terms, the deep and lasting injury inflicted, and calls the massacre at Srebrenica by its proper name: genocide. Those responsible will bear this stigma, and it will serve as a warning to those who may in future contemplate the commission of such a heinous act'.[169]

In terms of the achievements of the law of *jus cogens* and their advocates, they remain, for the most part, at the rhetorical level rather having an impact than the ground level. However, their influence ought not to be underestimated either. The perlocutionary aspect of explaining conduct[170] as contrary to *jus cogens* does have an important effect, in that it can galvanise opinion that something is contrary to the basic standards that the (fragile) international society has set. However, this is perhaps cold comfort when the legal consequences of such a statement remain nebulous at best.[171]

[167] *Prosecutor v Al-Bashir (Judgment in the Jordan Referral re Al-Bashir Appeal)* ICC-02/05-01/09 OA2 (6 May 2019). The reasoning of the majority is set out in the Joint Concurring Opinion of Judges Eboe-Osuji, Morrison, Hofmánski and Bossa.

[168] A Bianchi, 'Human Rights and the Magic of *Jus Cogens*' (2008) 19 *European Journal of International Law* 491, 503–34. Similarly, see Paulus (n 107) 297.

[169] *Prosecutor* v *Krstić* (Judgment) IT-99-33-A (19 April 2004). See also D Luban, 'Calling Genocide by its Rightful Name: Lemkin's Word, Darfur and the UN Report' (2006) 7 *Chicago Journal of International Law* 33; P Akhavan, *Reducing Genocide to Law* (Cambridge, Cambridge University Press, 2012).

[170] On which, in international law, see F Kratochwil, *Rules, Norms and Decisions* (Cambridge, Cambridge University Press, 1989).

[171] It should be noted tha the ICC has referred to an obligation on States to cooperate in the suppression of international crimes that are violations of *jus cogens* norms (*Al-Bashir* (n 167) para 123), but, as with other decisions on point, it remains frustratingly unclear, and does not clearly delineate obligations with respect to *jus cogens*, *erga omnes* obligations and obligations under the Rome Statute.

13

The Achievements and Limits of Global Counter-terrorism Cooperation

JACQUES HARTMANN*

Abstract: This chapter investigates the importance of domestic law for international counter-terrorism cooperation. Terrorism requires action by State organs directed against the activities of non-State actors, and these actors – most notably individuals – have rights under domestic law that national authorities cannot breach. National law therefore provides a substantial limit on any international response to terrorism. This chapter seeks to illustrate both the achievements and limits of international law by focusing on global counter-terrorism cooperation. It highlights the incremental improvement in the protection of individual rights and the limits of transnational criminal law enforcement.

I. Introduction

This chapter investigates the importance of domestic law for international counter-terrorism cooperation. It highlights an important but often forgotten truism: that any response to terrorism requires action by State organs directed against activities of non-State actors, and these actors – most notably individuals – have rights under domestic law that national authorities cannot breach. National law therefore provides a substantial limit on any response to terrorism. This is true both of the conventional counter-terrorism system based on punitive measures, viz criminalisation and assertion of jurisdiction, and of the post-2001 regime established by the United Nations (UN) Security Council, which is essentially preventive, focusing on the freezing of assets and the listing of suspects. This chapter therefore seeks to illustrate both the achievements and limits of international law by focusing on global counter-terrorism cooperation. It is divided into three main sections. Section II provides an overview of the origins of transnational criminal

* Reader, School of Law, University of Dundee

law enforcement and some of the historical limitations of the criminal regime, focusing especially on extradition. Sections III and IV focus specifically on counter-terrorism cooperation before and after 2001, highlighting the incremental improvement in the protection of individual rights and the limits of transnational criminal law enforcement.

II. The Origins of Transnational Criminal Law Enforcement

States have long cooperated in ways we may today describe as transnational criminal law enforcement.[1] That is to say, as long as there have been sovereign rulers with defined territories, those rulers have been anxious to lengthen the arm of justice outside their territories, with the aim of securing the prosecution of criminals, rebels and other offenders.[2] One area of criminal cooperation in particular – the return of fugitives – has a long history.[3] The first recorded extradition treaty is generally considered to date back to 1280 BCE.[4] And as early as 1625, Hugo Grotius wrote:

> Since it is not customary for states to permit another state to enter its territory under arms for the sake of administering punishment, nor is it expedient, it follows that the state where the offender sojourns ought to do one of two things: either on demand it should punish the guilty party, or it should turn him over for trial to the state making the demand.[5]

Early cooperative arrangements in the seventeenth and eighteenth centuries were mainly used to facilitate the return of political offenders.[6] As soon as States consolidated their powers, they started to cooperate to protect themselves against dissidents.[7] For this purpose, secret agents were sent abroad to spy on those suspected of subversive activities. In addition, foreign monarchs and police chiefs were urged to exchange information, to keep track of subversives, and to arrest and extradite them.[8]

[1] The term 'transnational criminal law' may be defined as the 'indirect suppression by international law through domestic penal law of criminal activities that have actual or potential trans-boundary effects': N Boister, *An Introduction to Transnational Criminal Law*, 2nd edn (Oxford, Oxford University Press, 2018) 17.

[2] G Schwarzenberger, *A Manual of International Law* (London, Stevens, 1960) 108.

[3] For an overview, see G Gilbert, *Transnational Fugitive Offenders in International Law* (Leiden, Brill Nijhoff, 1998) 17–21.

[4] IA Shearer, *Extradition in International Law* (Manchester, Manchester University Press, 1971) 5.

[5] English translation in O Svarlien, *An Introduction to the Law of Nations* (New York, McGraw-Hill, 1955) 430.

[6] See, for example, the Anglo-French and Anglo-Dutch treaties of 1661 and 1662, respectively, referred to in CL Blakesley, 'The Practice of Extradition from Antiquity to Modern France and the United States: A Brief History' (1981) 4 *Boston College International and Comparative Law Review* 23, 45.

[7] P Andreas and EA Nadelmann, *Policing the Globe: Criminalization and Crime Control in International Relations* (Oxford, Oxford University Press, 2008) 64–75.

[8] See ibid for the emergence of criminal law enforcement cooperation in Europe.

This initial informal network of cooperation consolidated with the spread of anarchism towards the end of the nineteenth century. One of the most serious incidents was the failed attack on Napoleon III by an Italian refugee, Felice Orsini, in Paris in 1858. The revelation that the attack had been planned in England put intense diplomatic pressure on the UK government.[9]

Not unlike today, such pressure has, at times, forced otherwise unwilling governments to take action against foreign nationals within their territory. However, important differences between States often influenced the extent of such cooperation. Liberal States frequently combined public refusal to cooperate with more discreet efforts to secure international cooperation.[10] But even liberal States with strong popular support for political asylum sometimes gave in to political pressure from foreign powers to ensure the suppression of political dissidents. States were especially cooperative when violence threatened their own security.[11]

Cooperation after the attempt to assassinate Napoleon III was in many ways a precursor of modern counter-terrorism action. In particular, the so-called 'attentat clause', which was introduced after a second attempt to murder Napoleon III, demonstrated that States shared the view that attacks on their leaders were never legitimate and that there was no justification for not pursuing criminal cooperation.[12]

Not all States cooperated on equal terms. Liberal States tended to incorporate specific provisions in their criminal cooperation agreements, ensuring procedural safeguards and the protection of individual freedoms. For instance, the Jay Treaty concluded in 1794 between the UK and the US contained many of the features known in contemporary extradition treaties, such as the requirement of a prima facie case, and it is commonly regarded as the precursor of the UK's modern law on extradition.[13]

The requirement of a prima facie case and other forms of individual protection were fostered by a new way of viewing the relationship between the State and its subjects, initiated during the Enlightenment.[14] The ideas of the Enlightenment increasingly influenced the law of extradition. As Gilbert observes, 'nineteenth century's liberalism developed the details of the process we know now as extradition'.[15]

[9] H Hearder, 'Napoleon III's Threat to Break off Diplomatic Relations with England during the Crisis over the Orsini Attempt in 1858' (1957) 72 *English Historical Review* 474.

[10] The UK, for example, rarely extradited political dissidents: Andreas and Nadelmann (n 7) 70.

[11] See, for example, A Kimball, 'The Harassment of Russian Revolutionaries Abroad: The London Trial of Vlademir Burtsev in 1898' in *Oxford Slavonic Papers* (Oxford, Oxford University Press, 1973) 48–65.

[12] The clause excludes from the class of political offences any attempt against the life of a head of State or head of government. See C van den Wyngaert, *The Political Offence Exception to Extradition: The Delicate Problem of Balancing the Rights of the Individual and the International Public Order* (The Hague, Kluwer, 1980) 14.

[13] See Blakesley (n 6).

[14] See, for example, JS Mill, *On Liberty* (London, Penguin, 2006 [1859]).

[15] Gilbert (n 3) 20.

Thus, international criminal cooperation – predominantly in the form of extradition – arose from the development of the nation-State and equal sovereignty in Europe, and from an evolving convergence of perceptions as to which forms of conduct needed suppression and consequently necessitated international cooperation. This convergence was not absolute and cooperation was limited by divergent views on which conduct required criminalisation, and ultimately international cooperation, as well as on the legitimate treatment of individuals subject to transnational law enforcement measures. As will be seen in relation to the evolution of the modern counter-terrorism regime, these considerations are still the most significant impediments to transnational criminal cooperation.

III. Global Counter-terrorism Cooperation before 2001

States have long agreed that establishing an international definition of 'terrorism' could make the fight against this phenomenon more effective. Even so, they have long failed to settle on a comprehensive definition.[16] This is not for a lack of trying. The first international counter-terrorism instruments were developed in the late 1920s.[17] Later, the Council of the League of Nations took the initiative by establishing a committee with a view to drafting a proposal for an international counter-terrorism convention. This resulted in the 1937 Convention for the Prevention and Punishment of Terrorism, which never entered into force.[18] It was, as noted by Cassese, a 'complete failure'.[19] Ever since, various attempts have been made to secure agreement on a global definition of terrorism, but none of them has ever resulted in a comprehensive treaty.[20] A resolution at the 1998 Rome Conference, establishing the International Criminal Court, recommended that a review conference consider crimes of terrorism, but the recommendation was not taken up by the 2010 Kampala Conference.[21] In 2011, the Appeals Chamber of the Special Tribunal for Lebanon found that there was a customary crime of terrorism, but the finding was widely derided.[22] Instead of a comprehensive treaty,

[16] *cf* B Saul, *Defining Terrorism in International Law* (Oxford, Oxford University Press, 2008).

[17] TM Franck and BB Lockwood, 'Preliminary Thoughts towards an International Convention on Terrorism' (1974) 68 *American Journal of International Law* 69.

[18] It began as a study on the legal powers of aircraft commanders, initiated by the International Federation of Airline Pilots. *cf* RP Boyle and R Pulsifer, 'The Tokyo Convention on Offenses and Certain Other Acts Committed on Board Aircraft' (1964) 30 *Journal of Air Law and Commerce* 305.

[19] A Cassese, *Terrorism, Politics and Law: The Achille Lauro Affair* (Chichester, Wiley, 1991) 9.

[20] *cf* H Duffy, *The 'War on Terror' and the Framework of International Law*, 2nd edn (Cambridge, Cambridge University Press, 2015) 106–12.

[21] Resolution F to the Final Act of the United Nations Diplomatic Conference of Plenipotentiaries on the Establishment of an International Criminal Court (17 July 1998) UN Doc A/CONF.183/10.

[22] *The Prosecutor v Ayyash et al* (16 February 2011) STL AC, para 85. For criticism, see, eg, B Saul, 'Legislating from a Radical Hague: The United Nations Special Tribunal for Lebanon Invents an International Crime of Transnational Terrorism' (2011) 24 *Leiden Journal of International Law* 677;

individual instruments have focused on specific conduct that most States agreed constituted an impermissible form of violence, such as attacks on civil aviation, hostage-taking, nuclear terrorism or terrorism financing. These are commonly referred to as 'piecemeal' or 'sectoral' treaties.[23] Today, there are 19 sectoral treaties or protocols, which were drawn up between 1963 and 2010.[24] The sectoral treaties reflect the simple truism that any response to terrorism requires respect for individual rights. As will be illustrated below, the need to ensure the protection of individual safeguards was evident from the very beginning.

A. Human Rights Protection in the Sectoral Treaties

The first global counter-terrorism treaties concerned civil aviation. The precursor was the 1963 Convention on Offences and Certain Other Acts Committed on Board Aircraft. It was initiated in 1950.[25] At the time, most States had not extended their legislative jurisdiction to aircraft flying abroad. This created considerable uncertainty, especially over the high seas, where aircraft were described as 'flying oases of lawlessness'.[26] As the number of hijackings escalated throughout the world, the lack of jurisdiction became an issue of intense concern. The 1963 Convention was the first of several attempts to address the safety of civil aviation. The aim of the treaty was to secure international agreement on the powers of aircraft commanders and the right of States to exercise jurisdiction over aircraft overseas. It did not contain any obligation to enact a specific offence. Even so, a 'high element of protection' was included.[27] According to Article 13:

> Upon being satisfied that the circumstances so warrant, any Contracting State shall take custody or other measures to ensure the presence of any person suspected of [unlawful seizure of aircraft] … The custody and other measures shall be as provided in the law of that State but may only be continued for such time as is reasonably necessary to enable any criminal or extradition proceedings to be instituted.

It follows that any alleged offender must be detained in accordance with domestic law and only for such times as is necessary either to secure prosecution or effect extradition.

K Ambos, 'Judicial Creativity at the Special Tribunal for Lebanon: Is There a Crime of Terrorism under International Law?' (2011) 24 *Leiden Journal of International Law* 655.

[23] A Gioia, 'The UN Conventions on the Prevention and Suppression of International Terrorism' in G Nesi (ed), *International Cooperation in Counter-terrorism: The United Nations and Regional Organizations in the Fight Against Terrorism* (Abingdon, Routledge, 2016) 4.

[24] For an overview, see https://www.un.org/counterterrorism/international-legal-instruments.

[25] Boyle and Pulsifer (n 18) 308.

[26] See Report to the Royal Aeronautical Society, 'Crimes and Offences on Board Aircraft' (1962), reproduced in CJ Cheng, *Studies in International Air Law: Selected Works of Bin Cheng* (Leiden, Brill, 2017) 282.

[27] GF FitzGerald, 'Offences and Certain Other Acts Committed on Board Aircraft: The Tokyo Convention of 1963' (1964) 2 *Canadian Yearbook of International Law* 191, 201.

States quickly realised that the 1963 Convention was inadequate to respond to the surge of hijackings that occurred in the 1960s and adopted the 1970 Convention for the Suppression of Unlawful Seizure of Aircraft.[28] The drafting was prompted by the shortcomings of the 1963 Convention and by the transformation of hijacking from a 'relatively crude and amateurish affair to a violent and highly organised conduct'.[29]

The 1970 Convention introduced what was to become a familiar formula in global counter-terrorism instruments: parties agreed to a specific conduct that would be criminalised in domestic law, regardless of motive, and to provide mutual legal assistance to secure its suppression. This formula is known by its Latin name *aut dedere aut judicare* and is the main mechanism of the traditional counter-terrorism regime.[30] However, the Latin formulation is somewhat misleading as it seems to call for a full trial.[31] But trial is not mandatory. Nor do criminal proceedings even need to be initiated. All that the *aut dedere aut judicare* principle requires is that the relevant domestic authorities take their decision in the same manner as in the case of any ordinary offence of a serious nature under the law of that State. As pointed out by Judge Guillaume, the real option open to States is then *aut dedere aut prosequi* (extradite or prosecute).[32] But even this may be an overstatement.

In addition to the *aut dedere aut judicare* principle, States also agreed to wide-reaching jurisdictional provisions, including Article 7, according to which parties must 'take such measures as may be necessary to establish its jurisdiction over the offence in the case where the alleged offender is present in its territory and it does not extradite him'.[33] According to Judge Guillaume, the obligation to assert jurisdiction was a 'conscious turning-point' in the fight against terrorism.[34] From this point onwards, the obligation to prosecute was no longer conditional on the existence of jurisdiction; rather, jurisdiction itself had to be established in order to make prosecution possible.[35]

[28] For a list of aircraft hijackings, see AE Evans, 'Aircraft Hijacking: What is Being Done' (1973) 67 *American Journal of International Law* 641, 648. The Protocol Supplementary to the Convention for the Suppression of Unlawful Seizure of Aircraft (adopted September 2010, entered into force 1 January 2018) significantly expands the original scope.

[29] AE Evans, 'Aircraft and Aviation Facilities' in AE Evans and JF Murphy (eds), *Legal Aspects of International Terrorism* (Lexington, MA, Lexington Books, 1978) 1.

[30] On the principle, see generally ILC, 'Preliminary Report on the obligation to extradite or prosecute ("*aut dedere aut judicare*")' (7 June 2006) UN Doc A/CN.4/571; MC Bassiouni and EM Wise, Aut Dedere Aut Judicare: *The Duty to Extradite or Prosecute in International Law* (Leiden, Martinus Nijhoff, 1995).

[31] The term 'judicare' primarily means to 'to judge' or 'to try'. *cf* ibid 4.

[32] G Guillaume, 'Terrorisme et Droit International' *215 Hague Rec*, 287 (1989-III) 371.

[33] Convention for the Suppression of Unlawful Seizure of Aircraft (signed 16 December 1970, entered into force 14 October 1971) 860 UNTS 105, art 7.

[34] Separate Opinion of President Guillaume, *Case Concerning the Arrest Warrant of 11 April 2000 (Democratic Republic of Congo v Belgium)* (Judgment) [2002] ICJ Rep 3, 38 at para 7.

[35] ibid.

As under the 1963 Convention, the alleged hijacker must be treated in accordance with domestic law and detention must not be disproportionate to the aim of enabling prosecution or extradition.[36] And despite the conscious turning point, the obligation to take custodial or other measures was still applicable only when 'the circumstances so warrant', leaving considerable discretion to States Parties.[37] This wide discretion was a deliberate choice, as the majority of States involved in the drafting did not want to commit themselves unequivocally to taking measures against any alleged offender.[38]

Like its predecessor, the 1970 Convention soon proved to be inadequate. It only covered unlawful seizure of aircraft in flight and not interferences on or from the ground.[39] This 'gap' prompted the adoption of the 1971 Convention for the Suppression of Unlawful Acts against the Safety of Civil Aviation.[40] The aim of the 1971 Convention was to close the gap, but many of its provisions were modelled on its predecessor, including those on individual protection.[41]

The guarantees introduced in the early counter-terrorism treaties on aviation were also included in other sectoral treaties, which continued the evolution, incrementally raising the protection of individual safeguards. Thus, a provision of 'fair treatment' was introduced in the 1973 Convention on the Prevention and Punishment of Crimes against Internationally Protected Persons.[42] The expression 'fair treatment' was deliberately chosen for its generality as it was considered broader than expressions such as 'due process' and 'fair trial'.[43]

The already broad protection was again expanded in the 1979 International Convention against the Taking of Hostages, which, in addition to 'fair treatment' at all stages of the proceedings, added the key words 'including enjoyment of all the rights and guarantees provided by the law of the State in the territory of which he is present'.[44] Thus, the 1979 Convention clearly envisaged that any alleged offenders would be treated in accordance with domestic law – in the same way as any other criminal.

[36] Convention on Offences and Certain Other Acts Committed on Board Aircraft (signed 14 September 1963, entered into force 4 December 1969) 704 UNTS 219, art 13(2).

[37] ibid. *cf* JJ Lambert, *Terrorism and Hostages in International Law: A Commentary on the Hostages Convention 1979* (Cambridge, Grotius, 1990) 168.

[38] ibid 170.

[39] PS Dempsey, 'Aviation Security: The Role of Law in the War against Terrorism' (2002) 41 *Columbia Journal of Transnational Law* 649, 657.

[40] The Protocol for the Suppression of Unlawful Acts of Violence at Airports Serving International Civil Aviation, supplementary to the Convention for the Suppression of Unlawful Acts against the Safety of Civil Aviation (signed 24 February 1988, entered into force 6 August 1989) 1589 UNTS significantly expands the original scope of the 1971 Convention.

[41] *cf* GF FitzGerald, 'Towards Legal Suppression of Acts against Civil Aviation' (1971) 585 *International Conciliation* 42, 51–76.

[42] 1973 Convention on the Prevention and Punishment of Crimes against Internationally Protected Persons (adopted 14 December 1973, entered into force 20 February 1977) 1035 UNTS 167, art 9.

[43] United Nations, *Yearbook of the International Law Commission 1972*, vol II (United Nations, 1972) 320.

[44] 1979 International Convention against the Taking of Hostages (adopted 17 December 1979, entered into force 3 June 1983) 1316 UNTS 205, art 8(2).

This wording was partly echoed in the 1980 Convention on the Physical Protection of Nuclear Material, although it mainly concerns the security of nuclear material, and in the 1988 Convention for the Suppression of Unlawful Acts against the Safety of Maritime Navigation.[45] Article 10(2) of the 1988 Convention for the Suppression of Unlawful Acts against the Safety of Maritime Navigation obliges parties to ensure fair treatment, including all the rights and guarantees provided by law for criminal proceedings in the host State.[46] The 1988 Convention was the first counter-terrorism treaty to remove the political offence exception, which traditionally served as a humanitarian safeguard.[47] This traditional safeguard had been slowly eroded under growing pressure for more effective international cooperation.[48] The removal might be seen as an indication that States were willing to give up individual protection for the benefit of more effective criminal cooperation. This, however, was not the case. Instead, the removal was accompanied by stronger human rights protections and numerous reservations.[49] As Wyngaert notes:

> States' reluctance with respect to such an automatic duty to extradite is not only based on upon political consideration, but also originates from basic concerns for the individual, i.e. their wish to avoid being bound to extradite to all states without discretion, even to those who do not offer the minimum safeguards for fair trial.[50]

After the 1988 Lockerbie bombing, the 1991 Convention on the Marking of Plastic Explosives for the Purpose of Detection was adopted. Unlike most counter-terrorism treaties, it does not oblige parties to enact specific offences. But such an obligation was introduced by the 1997 International Convention for the Suppression of Terrorist Bombings. The 1997 Convention continued the gradual evolution in the protection of individual rights. Article 14 states:

> Any person who is taken into custody or regarding whom any other measures are taken or proceedings are carried out pursuant to this Convention shall be guaranteed fair treatment, including enjoyment of all rights and guarantees in conformity with the law of the State in the territory of which that person is present and applicable provisions of international law, including international law of human rights.

[45] See the Convention on the Physical Protection of Nuclear Material (signed 3 March 1980, entered into force 8 February 1987) 1456 UNTS 101, art 9.

[46] 1988 Convention for the Suppression of Unlawful Acts against the Safety of Maritime Navigation (adopted 10 March 1988, entered into force 1 March 1992) 1678 UNTS, art 10(2).

[47] Committee on Extradition and Human Rights, 'Second Report' in International Law Association Report of the 67th Conference (Helsinki, 1996) 216–25 and 236.

[48] *cf* N Boister, 'Human Rights Protections in the Suppression Conventions' (2002) 2 *Human Rights Law Review* 199, 201–03.

[49] See, eg, Belgium's previous reservation to art 11 of the International Convention for the Suppression of Terrorist Bombings (adopted 15 December 1997, entered into force 23 May 2001) 2149 UNTS 256. The reservation was withdrawn on 28 January 2008. See also Belgium's previous reservation to art 14 of the International Convention for the Suppression of the Financing of Terrorism (adopted 9 December 1999, entered into force 10 April 2002) 2178 UNTS 197. The reservation was withdrawn on 28 January 2008.

[50] Van den Wyngaert (n 12) 161. See also Lambert (n 37) 192.

The reference to 'human rights' was also included in the 1999 International Convention for the Suppression of the Financing of Terrorism and in the most recent counter-terrorism treaty, the 2010 Convention on the Suppression of Unlawful Acts Relating to International Civil Aviation.[51] These treaties cemented a long evolution in the protection of individual rights in counter-terrorism instruments.

As is clear from this overview, prior to 2001, terrorism was not treated differently from any other regime of international cooperation. The international approach depended on the formula introduced in the 1970 Convention, whereby heinous conduct was proscribed in domestic law and States cooperated to suppress it. The criminal law approach meant that States were obliged to attend to the human rights of those caught up in the investigatory and prosecutorial processes. In other words, putative terrorists were to be treated as ordinary criminals. The fact that human rights have played an increasingly crucial role, regardless of potential conflicts, illustrates the inherent limits of the conventional approach to transnational law enforcement, viz that any response to terrorism requires action by State organs directed against activities of non-State actors, and these actors – most notably individuals – have rights under domestic law that national authorities cannot breach.

IV. Global Counter-terrorism Cooperation after 2001

The 11 September 2001 attacks in the US brought about significant changes in international criminal cooperation. One such change was the characterisation of terrorism as a form of armed conflict.[52] Another crucial development was the unprecedented attribution of powers to the Security Council to elaborate and supervise global counter-terrorism efforts. The post-2001 counter-terrorism regime differs significantly from the treaty-based system, which had developed since the 1950s. The conventional system was essentially based on punitive measures, viz criminalisation and assertion of jurisdiction. By contrast, the post-2001 regime is principally preventive, focusing on the freezing of assets and the listing of suspects.[53]

[51] 1999 International Convention for the Suppression of the Financing of Terrorism, art 17; Convention on the Suppression of Unlawful Acts Relating to International Civil Aviation (adopted 10 September 2010, entered into force 1 July 2018), art 11.

[52] *cf* Duffy (n 20) 388–405.

[53] The classification of the post-2001 regime as simply 'preventive' is not uncontroversial, but in 2008, the Human Rights Committee said that: 'Although the sanctions regime has serious consequences for the individuals concerned, which could indicate that it is punitive in nature, the Committee considers that this regime does not concern a "criminal charge".' *Nabil Sayadi and Patricia Vinck v Belgium* (29 December 2008) UN Doc CCPR/C/94/D/1472/2006, para 10.11. For a discussion of the nature

Moreover, in formal legal terms, the participation of the Security Council introduced a new element in the response to terrorism. The Security Council has the power to make decisions binding on all Member States of the UN and those decisions have priority over other obligations.[54] Potentially therefore, the new regime established a vertical authority system through which States were obliged to cooperate with one another. Lack of compliance might even result in sanctions through the authorisation of measures, including forcible measures.[55] In practice, however, the cooperative element has remained strong. Despite the significant achievements of the new regime, the Security Council is still limited by the same truism as the conventional system: decisions by the Security Council are ultimately directed against the activities of non-State actors, and their implementation depends on the cooperation of State authorities, which are limited by domestic law.

A. The Origins of Security Council Counter-Terrorism Efforts

The Security Council has long been involved in international counter-terrorism cooperation, but the modes of this involvement fundamentally changed after 2001. Before 2001, the Security Council had an established tradition of condemning individual acts of terrorism. In 1948, for example, it condemned the murder of Count Folke Bernadotte who had been killed by a 'criminal group of terrorists' while on a peacekeeping mission in Jerusalem.[56] Two decades later – as the 1970 Convention was being signed – the Security Council called upon States to take all possible legal steps to prevent hijacking or any other interference with international civil aviation.[57] In 1985, two years after the entry into force of the 1979 Convention, the Security Council affirmed the obligation of all States to prevent hostage-taking and to take all appropriate measures to secure the safe release of hostages.[58] At times, it also intervened more directly in individual incidents.

of sanctions, see, among others, I Cameron, 'The European Convention on Human Rights, Due Process and United Nations Security Council Counter-terrorism Sanctions' (Athens, 13–14 September 2006) CAHDI (2006) 22, available at https://www.statewatch.org/media/documents/terrorlists/docs/Cameron-06.pdf; B Fassbender, 'A Study Commissioned by the UN Office of Legal Affairs and Follow-up Action by the United Nations' (2006) 3 *International Organizations Law Review* 437.

[54] Charter of the United Nations (signed 26 June 1945, entered into force 24 October 1945) 1 UNTS XVI, art 103.

[55] In accordance with art 39 of the 1945 Charter of the United Nations, the Security Council may determine the existence of any threat to the peace, breach of the peace or act of aggression, after which it may decide to take measures accordance with arts 41 and 42 to maintain or restore international peace and security.

[56] UNSC Res 57 (18 September 1948) UN Doc S/RES/57. Bernadotte was assassinated on 17 September 1948 by members of Lehi, a Jewish Zionist group also known as the 'Stern Gang'. The assassination led to the advisory opinion on *Reparation for Injuries in the Service of the United Nations* [1949] ICJ Rep 174.

[57] UNSC Res 286 (9 September 1970) UN Doc S/RES/286. See also UNSC Res 635 (14 June 1989) UN Doc S/RES/635.

[58] UNSC Res 579 (18 December 1985) UN Doc S/RES/579.

In 1988, for example, it demanded the immediate release of a US marine who had been taken hostage in Lebanon.[59] On none of these occasions did it invoke Chapter VII of the UN Charter and nor was 'terrorism' ever classified as a threat to international peace and security.

The rather timid response of the Security Council can partly be explained by the prevailing attitude among States that terrorism was a national problem, as opposed to an issue of international concern.[60] Most States therefore dealt with terrorist threats either on their own or with some help from their closest allies or immediate neighbours.[61] Moreover, the targeted States often chose not to bring any of these cases to the attention of the Security Council. States like India, Russia and the UK have, for example, all minimised the Security Council's involvement in Kashmir, Chechnya and Northern Ireland, respectively.[62] This does not mean that terrorism was contained within individual States. The adoption of the counter-terrorism instruments provides ample evidence that terrorism has long been considered a phenomenon of international concern. In spite of this, until the end of the Cold War, terrorism was never a major focus of the Security Council. This was particularly evident in the Security Council's tepid response to the 1972 Munich Olympics attack.[63] This restraint ended after the Cold War. In 1992, the Security Council dealt with the Lockerbie bombing and in 1996, it called upon Sudan to stop supporting terrorist activities and to extradite to Ethiopia three suspects wanted for attempting to assassinate President Hosni Mubarak of Egypt.[64] In 1999, it established the 1267 Committee, which was initially mandated with monitoring sanctions against the Taliban. But the change in the prevailing geopolitical environment facilitated the Security Council's radically different approach to terrorism after 2001.

B. Security Council Resolution 1373

After the events of 11 September 2001 (9/11), the Security Council adopted Resolution 1373.[65] The Resolution broke new ground at several levels. Despite its extensive scope, it was widely welcomed and few seemed concerned that the

[59] UNSC Res 618 (29 July 1988) UN Doc S/RES/618. See also UNSC Res 638 (31 July 1989) UN Doc S/RES/638. For details, see, eg, TL Friedmann, 'Hostage Situation Straining Washington's Ties to Israel', *New York Times* (17 August 1989).

[60] EC Luck, 'The Uninvited Challenge: Terrorism Targets the United Nations' in E Newman, RC Thakur and J Tirman (eds), *Multilateralism under Challenge? Power, International Order, and Structural Change* (New York, United Nations University Press, 2006) 19.

[61] M Chandler and R Gunaratna, *Countering Terrorism: Can We Meet the Threat of Global Violence?* (London, Reaktion, 2007) 86.

[62] Luck (n 60) 19.

[63] For a debate in the Security Council, see 'The Situation in the Middle East' UN Doc S/PV.1662 (1972). For a fuller account of the Security Council and the Cold War see EC Luck, 'Terrorism' in D Malone (ed), *The UN Security Council: From the Cold War to the 21st Century* (Boulder, Lynne Rienner Publishers, 2004) 85–95.

[64] UNSC Res 1044 (31 January 1996) UN Doc S/RES/1044.

[65] UNSC Res 1373 (28 September 2001) UN Doc S/RES/1373.

Security Council was acting in the manner of a global legislator.[66] Unlike the conventional approach, which was based on consent, Resolution 1373 obliged all UN Member States to cooperate in a wide range of areas, from combating the financing of terrorism to providing effective border control. In particular, Resolution 1373 obliged States to prevent and suppress the financing of terrorism, criminalise the wilful provision or collection of terrorist funds, and to freeze such funds without delay. Most obligations were modelled on the provisions of the 1999 Convention, which, at that time, had only been ratified by four States.[67] While its main focus was on the financing of terrorism, Resolution 1373 contained other extensive obligations, such as an open-ended obligation to 'take all necessary steps to prevent the commission of terrorism'.[68] In line with counter-terrorism conventions, it further required States to prevent the commission of terrorist acts, deny safe haven to terrorists, ensure that terrorists were brought to justice and ensure that terrorism be classified as a serious criminal offence in domestic law. The resolution further echoes counter-terrorism conventions obliging States to afford one another the 'greatest measure of assistance' in the fight against terrorism.[69] None of these obligations was confined to acts related to the events of 9/11. Resolution 1373 targeted all acts of terrorism universally and without any express time limitation or definition of the purported conduct.[70] In fact, Resolution 1373 is still in force.

The unprecedented authority seized by the Security Council was accompanied by a mechanism to supervise State compliance, viz the Counter-Terrorism Committee. The Counter-Terrorism Committee assumed very extensive and

[66] Turkey referred to it as 'groundbreaking'; see the statement by Turkey, UNGA Meeting Record (12 November 2001) UN Doc A/56/PV.48. Singapore greeted it as a 'landmark decision'; see the statement by Singapore, UNGA Meeting Record (12 November 2001) UN Doc A/56/PV.48. The UK welcomed it as an 'historic event'; see the statement by the UK, UNSC Meeting Record (12 November 2001) UN Doc S/PV.4413. See also the statements by France ('one of the most important resolutions in its history'), Spain (on behalf of the EU): 'Security Council Resolution 1373 (2001) is of historic significance') and Russia ('undoubtedly a major historic document'): UNSC Meeting Record (18 January 2002) UN Doc S/PV.4453 (Resumption 1). For comment, see PC Szasz, 'The Security Council Starts Legislating' (2002) 96 *American Journal of International Law* 901; S Talmon, 'The Security Council as World Legislature' (2005) 99 *American Journal of International Law* 175.

[67] Botswana (8 September 2000); Sri Lanka (2000); the UK (2001); and Uzbekistan (2001).

[68] UNSC Res 1373 (28 September 2001) UN Doc S/RES/1373, para 1(b). Before the UN Human Rights Committee, the UK reportedly invoked art 103 of the 1945 Charter of the United Nations to argue that its obligations under UNSC Res 1373 took precedence over its obligations to the UN Human Rights Committee. See Redress, 'Terrorism, Counter-terrorism and Torture: International Law in the Fight against Terrorism' (July 2004) 16, https://redress.org/wp-content/uploads/2018/01/July-TerrorismReport.pdf. Sweden specifically invoked UNSC Res 1373 before the UN Committee Against Torture (CAT) in regard to the extradition of two Egyptian nationals in 2001: CAT, *Attia v Sweden* (17 November 2003) Comm No 199/2002, para 4.4.

[69] UNSC Res 1373 (28 September 2001) UN Doc S/RES/1373, para 2(f).

[70] The fact that the Security Council has failed to adopt a definition of 'terrorism' has continuously been highlighted by the Special Rapporteur on the 'promotion and protection of human rights and fundamental freedoms while countering terrorism'. See most recently the Special Rapporteur's report on the 'impact of measures to address terrorism and violent extremism on civic space and the rights of civil society actors and human rights defenders' (3 September 2018) UN Doc A/73/361, para 19. For comments on UNSC Res 1566 (8 October 2004) UN Doc S/RES/1566, see para 34.

intrusive monitoring powers.[71] It further maintained the right to 'consider what action is needed to address failures to meet the requirements of resolution 1373'.[72] Neither the Security Council nor the Counter-Terrorism Committee has ever taken action against individual States for lack of compliance, although the Committee has publicised the names of States that failed to comply with their reporting obligations.[73] Many States have raised the issue of 'reporting fatigue' and the fact that the extensive reporting obligations took away essential resources that could otherwise have been spent on implementation.[74]

The work of the Counter-Terrorism Committee was initially divided in three stages.[75] First, Member States were required to enact laws to combat terrorism, covering all aspects of Resolution 1373.[76] During this stage, States were inter alia expected to enact laws to tackle money-laundering, tighten regulation of border controls and initiate the ratification of all international instruments relating to terrorism.[77] The second stage focused on the enforcement of legislation implemented under the first stage. This included the monitoring of police and intelligence structures, customs, immigration and border controls.[78] The third stage related to international cooperation.[79] In this last stage, the Counter-Terrorism Committee focused on bilateral, regional and international cooperation, for example, with regard to the exchange of information or judicial cooperation. In 2004, the Security Council approved a new structure, establishing a Counter-Terrorism Committee Executive Directorate as well as an Assessment and Technical Assistance Office and an Information and Administrative Office.

i. The 1267 Committee

The Counter-Terrorism Committee was not the only committee established by the Security Council. In 1999, following the Taliban regime's refusal to surrender

[71] See generally N Rostow, 'Before and after: The Changed UN Response to Terrorism since September 11th Symposium: Terrorism: The Legal Implications of the Response to September 11, 2001' (2001) 35 *Cornell International Law Journal* 475.

[72] UNSC Meeting Record (15 April 2002) UN Doc S/PV.4512.

[73] *cf* UNSC Letter from the Chairman of the Security Council Committee (29 June 2005) UN Doc S/2005/421. Rosand et al have argued that the reluctance of the Committee to ensure enforcement may stem from the UN members' general reluctance to single out other States, and the consensus-based practice under which the UN Committees normally operates: E Rosand, A Millar and J Ipe, *The UN Security Council's Counterterrorism Program: What Lies Ahead?* (Vienna, International Peace Academy, 2007) 10.

[74] See, eg, UNSC Meeting Record (20 December 2006) UN Doc S/PV.5601.

[75] See 'Work programme of the Counter-Terrorism Committee (28 September–31 December 2002)' (25 September 2002) UN Doc S/2002/1075, 3.

[76] ibid.

[77] See 'Work programme of the Counter-Terrorism Committee (1 January–31 March 2003)' (17 January 2003) UN Doc S/2003/72, 3.

[78] ibid.

[79] 'Report by the Chair of the Counter-Terrorism Committee on the problems encountered in the implementation of Security Council Resolution 1373 (2001)' (26 January 2004) UN Doc S/2004/70, 10–11.

Osama bin Laden, the Security Council passed Resolution 1267.[80] The Resolution was adopted under Chapter VII and obliged Member States to adopt various measures against the Taliban regime, including the denial of access to aircraft and the freezing of funds owned or controlled by the Taliban. To ensure the effective implementation of these sanctions, a special committee was set up to monitor implementation, viz the 1267 Committee. The 1267 Committee was mandated to consider instances of non-compliance, recommend appropriate action and make periodic reports on the impact of the measures imposed. In 2000, the Security Council expanded the list of sanctioned individuals to include Osama bin Laden and his associates. After the events of September 2001, the Committee's mandate was further modified and strengthened to complement the work of the Counter-Terrorism Committee.[81] In so doing, the 1267 Committee was given a mostly operative role, while the Counter-Terrorism Committee had a more legislative role.[82]

Individuals and entities targeted by the 1267 Committee were and are placed on the Consolidated List. The List contains names of people and other entities whose assets or freedom of movement should, according to the Security Council, either be frozen or limited – a process commonly referred to as 'blacklisting'.[83] In 2002, the Consolidated List was expanded by Resolution 1390, which renewed the Consolidated List and extended sanctions to cover travel and arms embargoes.[84] This later resolution was qualitatively different from previous resolutions, as there is no connection between the targeted group or individuals, and any territory or State.[85] Just as the *aut dedere aut judicare* principle was central to the old approach to counter-terrorism, so listing has been a vital tool in the Security Council's efforts against terrorism. However, this approach has not met with universal approval. As the Monitoring Team, established pursuant to Security Council Resolution 1263 in 1999, has highlighted numerous times, the Consolidated List has suffered from 'serious defects'.[86] A common problem was the absence of basic identifiers such as full names and dates of birth.[87] A further problem has been that many States have been reluctant to submit information.

The process of listing and delisting has been severely criticised, and support for the sanctions regime seems to have been eroded as a result of concerns regarding

[80] UNSC Res 1267 (15 October 1999) UN Doc S/RES/1267.

[81] Including UNSC Res 1333 (19 December 2000) UN Doc S/RES/1333; UNSC Res 1390 (16 January 2002) UN Doc S/RES/1390; UNSC Res 1455 (17 January 2003) UN Doc S/RES/1455; UNSC Res 1526 (30 January 2004) UN Doc S/RES/1526; UNSC Res 1617 (29 July 2005) UN Doc S/RES/1617; UNSC Res 1735 (22 December 2006) UN Doc S/RES/1735.

[82] Cameron (n 53) 4.

[83] See the United Nations Security Council Consolidated List, available at www.un.org/securitycouncil/content/un-sc-consolidated-list.

[84] UNSC Res 1390 (16 January 2002) UN Doc S/RES/1390.

[85] Cameron (n 53) 4.

[86] 'Report of the Analytical Support and Sanctions Monitoring Team pursuant to Resolution 1735 (2006) concerning Al-Qaida and the Taliban and associated individuals and entities' (14 May 2008) UN Doc S/2008/324, 12.

[87] ibid.

the quality of the information on the list and the absence of fully transparent procedures for adding and removing names.[88] Thus, even the procedure established by the Security Council has been met with the traditional resistance common to international criminal cooperation efforts: diverging opinions over what conduct should be suppressed and which rights apply to individuals caught up in the process. In numerous cases, national law has also hampered implementation.[89] In addition, the whole listing process raises several human rights concerns, most of which have been analysed in detail.[90] Not only are the procedural aspects of listing problematic, but sanctions themselves may also violate the human rights of those targeted. Travel restrictions may breach the right to freedom of movement and may affect the right to respect for private and family life, and even the right to life – for example, when a targeted subject needs foreign medical care.[91] Financial sanctions can interfere with a person's private and family life and the right to property. Questions of defamation may arise in domestic law.[92] In addition, any interference with human rights that cannot be appealed to an impartial and independent tribunal may violate the right of access to court, as well as the right to an effective remedy.

The Council's response is, in itself, problematic. In the past, Security Council sanctions have only been symbolically successful – if they have been successful at all.[93] Iraq's refusal to allow the weapons inspections required by Resolution 687 is a notable example.[94] Another is the doubtful persuasive powers of sanctions imposed against Libya for refusing to hand over the suspects of the Lockerbie bombing.[95]

[88] Rosand, Millar and Ipe (n 73) 3.

[89] Chandler and Gunaratna (n 61) 139.

[90] See, eg, Cameron (n 53); Fassbender (n 53) 437; TJ Biersteker and SE Eckert, 'Strengthening Targeted Sanctions through Fair and Clear Procedures: White Paper Prepared by the Watson Institute Targeted Sanctions Project Brown University' (2006); D Marty, 'United Nations Security Council and European Union Blacklists' (Committee on Legal Affairs and Human Rights 2007) Doc 11454; L van den Herik, 'The Security Council's Targeted Sanctions Regimes: In Need of Better Protection of the Individual' (2007) 20 *Leiden Journal of International Law* 797; Report of the Special Rapporteur, 'Promotion and Protection of Human Rights and Fundamental Freedoms While Countering Terrorism' (26 September 2012) UN Doc A/67/396; J Cockayne, R Brubaker and N Jayakody, *Fairly Clear Risks: Protecting UN Sanctions' Legitimacy and Effectiveness through Fair and Clear Procedures* (New York, United Nations University, 2018).

[91] Cameron (n 53).

[92] See, eg, *Zollman v United Kingdom (Inadmissible)* (27 November 2003) App No 62902/00. In this case, two Belgian diamond merchants sued for slander after a British Minister publicly accused them of breaching the UN targeted sanctions against the Angolan UNITA Party. The case was declared inadmissible due to parliamentary immunity. However, Cameron ((n 53) 11) argues that: 'If this limit had not existed, it is evident that the ECtHR would have considered the blacklisting to be an attack on one's reputation.'

[93] *cf* D Cortright, GA Lopez and TE McNamara, 'Unilateral and Strategies against State Sponsors of Terror: A Case Study of Libya' in D Cortright and GA Lopez (eds), *Uniting against Terror: Cooperative Nonmilitary Responses to the Global Terrorist Threat* (Cambridge MA, MIT Press, 2007) 83–122.

[94] UNSC Res 687 (2001) UN Doc S/RES/687.

[95] *cf* M Plachta, 'The Lockerbie Case: The Role of the Security Council in Enforcing the Principle *Aut Dedere Aut Judicare*' (2001) 12 *European Journal of International Law* 125.

For any preventative regime, such as that established by the Security Council, near-universal compliance is crucial. However, some sanctions regimes were too broad in their application and the Security Council therefore decided to target individual or particular entities. These so-called 'smart sanctions' have, in turn, created other problems, including allowing human rights challenges by those selected for punitive measures.[96] The Security Council was initially reluctant to uphold human rights standards.[97] Yet, allowing each State to fashion its own remedies would affect the comprehensiveness of the regime. This creates an unavoidable conflict with national law in most jurisdictions, which is essentially the same conflict that faced the counter-terrorism regime before 2001. As in the previous regime, smart sanctions are targeted against individuals and need to be carried out by national authorities according to domestic law.[98] However, the same law often also protects the right of the targeted individuals, thus creating an inherent conflict, as is evident with regard to the Consolidated List.

ii. The Consolidated List

In 2001, the Sanctions Committee published the first consolidated list of entities and persons subject to the freezing of funds. After 9/11, there was 'enormous goodwill and willingness to trust any name that the US submitted'.[99] In this atmosphere, hundreds of names were hastily listed.[100] The sanctions regime has since been modified and strengthened by subsequent resolutions.[101]

It quickly emerged that initial listing procedures lacked transparency and consideration for fundamental human rights.[102] Among other things, it was unclear who was entitled to submit listing requests and what type of information ought to be provided. The system also lacked any procedure for the notification of subjects who were named on the Consolidated List and it did not provide any humanitarian exemptions. Thus, until Resolution 1465 of 2002, listing had the effect of depriving targeted persons of all their resources.[103] Not only were their assets frozen, but the broad wording of Resolution 1373[104] and subsequent

[96] *cf* Cameron (n 53) 4.

[97] UNSC Meeting Record (18 January 2002) UN Doc S/PV.4453 (Resumption 1).

[98] The term 'smart sanctions' is used for sanctions targeted at responsible parties in the hope of minimising collateral damage. See generally D Cortright and GA Lopez (eds), *Smart Sanctions: Targeting Economic Statecraft* (Lanham, MD, Rowman & Littlefield, 2002).

[99] C Cooper, 'Shunned in Sweden: How the Drive to Block Funds for Terrorism Entangled Mr Aden', *Wall Street Journal* (6 May 2002).

[100] *cf* Eric Rosand, 'The Security Council's Efforts to Monitor the Implementation of Al Qaeda/Taliban Sanctions' (2004) 98 *American Journal of International Law* 745, 749.

[101] For an overview, see Cockayne, Brubaker and Jayakody (n 90).

[102] UNSC Res 1390 (16 January 2002) UN Doc S/RES/1390.

[103] UNSC Res 1465 (13 February 2003) UN Doc S/RES/1465.

[104] UNSC Res 1373 (28 September 2001) UN Doc S/RES/1373 essentially copied the wording of the 1999 International Convention for the Suppression of the Financing of Terrorism, which defines the term 'funds' as 'assets of every kind'.

resolutions also prevented their access to any funds, financial assets or economic resources.[105] Even access to social benefits and means of subsistence became a real problem.[106]

Despite States' appeals to protect the fundamental rights of those placed on the Consolidated List, the Security Council was initially reluctant to integrate any safeguards. The first Chairman said that: 'Monitoring performance against other international conventions, including human rights law, is outside the scope of the Counter-Terrorism Committee's mandate.'[107] Continued pressure resulted in a series of incremental improvements. In the first instance, improvements originated from a case concerning three Somali-born Swedish citizens.[108] The men were allegedly implicated in a Somali banking network, known as Al Barakaat, suspected of channelling money to terrorist groups. The evidence concerning these allegations was only presented to members of the 1267 Committee, which did not include Sweden. Consequently, the Swedish authorities did not have access to evidence on the facts of the case and had no way of verifying the allegations against the putative terrorists. As in all rule of law States, the absence of evidence made it impossible for the Swedish authorities to proceed. They therefore had little choice but to challenge the listing itself. The Swedish challenge provided a major impetus to a long campaign, led predominantly by European States, to heighten procedural safeguards. The campaign was in effect precipitated by the incompatibility of domestic legal standards with the listing system.

In response to repeated criticisms, in 2002 the Counter-Terrorism Committee adopted a set of guidelines for its work, providing criteria for both listing and delisting.[109] However, this minimal response was wholly insufficient. In 2004, the Security Council adopted Resolution 1526, which called upon States to provide information demonstrating association of listed persons with either Osama bin Laden, Al-Qaida or the Taliban.[110] The late inclusion of such a precaution may be regarded as a sign of the Counter-Terrorism Committee's lack of concern for protecting individual rights. Since 2004, the Security Council has included references to human rights.[111] More recently, it has started to incorporate wording which clarifies that 'effective counter-terrorism measures and respect for … the rule of law are complementary and mutually reinforcing' and are 'an essential part

[105] For the concrete consequences, see, eg, S Schmemann, 'A Nation Challenged: Sanctions and Fallout', *The New York Times* (26 January 2002).

[106] *R (on the Application of M) v HM Treasury* (C-340/08) [2010] 3 CMLR 31, [2011] All ER (EC) 68.

[107] UNSC Meeting Record (18 January 2002) UN Doc S/PV.4453 (Resumption 1).

[108] See generally Schmemann (n 105).

[109] See 'Statement of Chairman of 1267 Committee on De-listing Procedures' (16 August 2002), Press Release SC/7487-AFG/203. See also E Rosand, 'The Security Council's Role: Problems and Prospects in the Fight against Terrorism' in G Nesi (ed), *International Cooperation in Counter-terrorism: The United Nations and Regional Organizations in the Fight against Terrorism* (Abingdon, Routledge 2006).

[110] The Resolution only calls upon States to include such information to the 'greatest extent possible'. UNSC Res 1526 (30 January 2004) UN Doc S/RES/1526, para 17.

[111] See UNSC Res 1535 (20 March 2004) UN Doc S/RES/1535; UNSC Res 1456 (20 January 2003) UN Doc S/RES/1456, para 6; UNSC Res 1624 (14 September 2005) UN Doc S/RES/1624, para 4.

of a successful counter-terrorism effort'.[112] However, the Special Rapporteur on the promotion and protection of human rights and fundamental freedoms while countering terrorism has questioned the utility of such language without 'clear and explicit human rights guidance'.[113]

A group of like-minded States have continuously campaigned for improved standards. Among others, Denmark, Liechtenstein, Sweden and Switzerland insisted on a meaningful review system, advocating the establishment of a review panel within the Security Council.[114] As a result of such pressure, in 2005 Resolution 1617 introduced some important improvements.[115] In 2006, the Security Council adopted a new delisting procedure.[116] This included the setting up of a special organ by the Secretary-General to function as a 'focal point' for delisting requests.[117] One of the purposes of the organ was to receive requests from individuals or other entities. However, it was still national governments that submitted final petitions.[118] Thus, while individuals could contact the focal point directly, the mechanism did nothing more than forward the request to the listed person's State of nationality.[119] The mechanism was in effect a form of diplomatic protection.[120] Even with the described improvements, the existing safeguards were still grossly insufficient.[121]

This insufficiency was exposed in the seminal *Kadi* case. In this case, Yassin Abdullah Kadi and the Al Barakaat International Foundation had been listed under EC Regulation 881/2002. This Regulation gave effect to the Security Council's asset-freezing regime under Resolution 1267. The claimants challenged their

[112] See UNSC Res 2129 (17 December 2013) UN Doc S/RES/2129; UNSC Res 2170 (15 August 2014) UN Doc S/RES/2170; UNSC Res 2178 (24 September 2014) UN Doc S/RES/2178; UNSC Res 2395 (21 December 2017) UN Doc S/RES/2395; UNSC Res 2396 (21 December 2017) UN Doc S/RES/2396.

[113] Report of the Special Rapporteur, 'Promotion and protection of human rights and fundamental freedoms while countering terrorism' (3 September 2018) UN Doc A/73/361, para 37.

[114] See M Bothe, 'Discussion Paper on Supplementary Guidelines for the Review of Sanctions Committees' Listing Decisions: Explanatory Memorandum' (2007). See also Cockayne, Brubaker and Jayakody (n 90) 15.

[115] The Resolution introduced a non-exhaustive definition of 'association', as well as a requirement to describe the factual basis of any case proposed for listing. UNSC Res 1617 (29 July 2005) UN Doc S/RES/1617, paras 2 and 4. This latter requirement has further been clarified in UNSC Res 1735 (22 December 2006) UN Doc S/RES/1735.

[116] UNSC Res 1730 (19 December 2006) UN Doc S/RES/1730.

[117] In a letter of 30 March 2007, the Secretary-General informed the President of the Security Council that the focal point for delisting had been established. UNSC Letter from the Secretary-General (30 March 2007) UN Doc S/2007/178.

[118] UNSC Res 1730 (19 December 2006) UN Doc S/RES/1730, para 5.

[119] Pursuant to fn 1 of the annex to UNSC Res 1730 (19 December 2006) UN Doc S/RES/1730, a State can decide that as a rule, its citizens or residents should address their delisting requests directly to the focal point. By May 2008, only France had submitted such a request.

[120] The option for a State to initiate delisting procedures on behalf of its citizens was highlighted by the European Court of First Instance. See Joined Cases C-402/05 P and C-415/05 P *Kadi and Al Barakaat International Foundation v Council and Commission* [2008] ECR I-6351, paras 267–91 (*Kadi I*).

[121] Marty (n 90) para. 16. See also *Al-Dulimi and Montana Management Inc v Switzerland* App no 5809/08 (ECtHR, 21 June 2016), para 153.

listing under this Regulation, arguing that it breached their fundamental rights.[122] The Court of Justice of the European Union held that EU courts must ensure a full review of the lawfulness of all EU acts, including those designed to implement UN Security Council resolutions, and annulled Regulation 881/2002.[123]

The pressure created by this and other successful challenges, including the UN Human Rights Committee's opinion in *Sayadi and Vinck v Belgium*, led to renewed improvements.[124] With Resolution 1822 in 2008, the Security Council introduced a stronger review mechanism and obliged States to ensure that listed individuals and entities were notified of the actions taken against them. It also took unprecedented note of the importance of domestic legal standards. Thus, in addition to heightening due process standards, the Resolution repeatedly asserts that various measures have to be taken 'in accordance with domestic laws and practices'.[125] The reference to domestic law was a new development by the Security Council and reflected an increasing awareness of the importance of domestic standards.

Despite these improvements, the listing and delisting mechanisms were still subject to severe criticism and some States continued to argue that they did not comply with fundamental human rights standards. An independent and impartial Ombudsperson, who reviews requests from individuals, groups, undertakings or entities seeking to be removed from the Council's lists, was established in 2009 and the mandate has continually been renewed and extended.[126]

However, as they stand, the Security Council procedures are still incompatible with human rights protection, as they fail to include one of the most crucial human rights guarantees: the right to access an impartial and independent forum where individuals can prove their innocence.[127] This not only violates the right to a fair trial or an independent hearing, but also sets aside one of the most salient accomplishments of the human rights project: the standing of the individual in international law. Human rights law has largely displaced discarded diplomatic protection as a means of protecting individuals. It is therefore difficult to envisage a listing system compatible with human rights without an independent tribunal or other judicial body scrutinising it.[128] This was also the outcome of *Kadi II*.

[122] They argued that Council Regulation (EC) No 881/2002 [2002] OJ L139/9 violated their right to a fair hearing, their right to property and their right to effective judicial protection. See *Kadi I* (n 120) paras 49–50.

[123] ibid. In the first instance, the General Court only allowed a review of *jus cogens* violations.

[124] *Nabil Sayadi and Patricia Vinck v Belgium* (Comm No 1472/2006) (22 October 2008) UN Doc CCPR/C/94/D/1472/2006.

[125] UNSC Res 1822 (30 June 2008) UN Doc S/RES/1822, paras 17, 23, 33 and 34.

[126] The Office of the Ombudsperson was established by UNSC Res 1904 (17 December 2009) UN Doc S/RES/1904. The current mandate is contained in UNSC Res 2368 (20 July 2017) UN Doc S/RES/2368.

[127] The Monitoring Team has stated that: 'It is difficult to imagine that the Security Council could accept any review panel that appeared to erode its absolute authority to take action on matters affecting international peace and security, as enshrined in the Charter.' See 'Report of the Analytical Support and Sanctions Monitoring Team pursuant to resolution 1735 (2006) concerning Al-Qaida and the Taliban and associated individuals and entities' (14 May 2008) UN Doc S/2008/324, 17.

[128] Most commentators seem to agree. See, eg, Marty (n 90). See also Cameron (n 53); Biersteker and Eckert (n 90); Fassbender (n 53); Rosand, Millar and Ipe (n 73).

Following the judgment in *Kadi I*, the European Commission adopted Regulation 1190/2008, which maintained Kadi's listing. Kadi challenged this decision. On appeal, the Court of Justice of the European Union confirmed its previous findings and stated that EU courts:

> [M]ust … ensure the review, in principle the full review, of the lawfulness of all Union acts in the light of the fundamental rights forming an integral part of the European Union legal order, including review of such measures as are designed to give effect to resolutions adopted by the Security Council under Chapter VII of the Charter of the United Nations.[129]

Some see the decision of the EU General Court in *Al-Ghabra* as an indication that the present Ombudsperson offers sufficient protection.[130] It is true, as suggested by Judge Keller in *Al-Dulimi*, that adequate human rights protection at the UN level need not take the same form as in domestic criminal proceedings.[131] But the institution of the Ombudsperson still falls short of many of the criteria established in contemporary human rights law. And while no court has, to date, directly impugned the counter-terrorism regimes established by the Security Council after 9/11, the effect of several judgments has in effect been to render that regime unenforceable.[132] Thus, the European Court of Human Rights has, while citing *Kadi*, insisted that any listed person should be afforded 'a genuine opportunity to submit appropriate evidence to a court, for examination on the merits, to seek to show that their inclusion on the impugned lists had been arbitrary'.[133] Without such an opportunity, 'the very essence' of the right of access to a court will be impaired.[134]

V. Conclusion

Since its inception in the 1960s, the global counter-terrorism regime has made remarkable progress – a significant achievement. Until 2001, the regime was essentially based on punitive measures, viz criminalisation and assertion of jurisdiction. By contrast, the post-2001 regime is essentially preventive, focusing on the freezing of assets and the listing of suspects. The new regime is less focused on bilateral collaboration between individual States; rather, it is a global effort centralised under the supervision of the Security Council. Over the years, the

[129] Joined Cases C-584/10 P, C-593/10 P and C-595/10 P *Kadi and Al Barakaat International Foundation v Council and Commission* [2013], para 96 (*Kadi II*).

[130] Case T-248/13 *Mohammed Al-Ghabra v European Commission* [2016]. For comments, see Cockayne, Brubaker and Jayakody (n 90) 21.

[131] *Al-Dulimi* (n 121), Concurring Opinion of Judge Keller at para 23.

[132] In addition to *Kadi I* and *II*, see *Nada v Switzerland* App No 10593/08 (ECtHR, 12 September 2012) and ibid.

[133] *Al-Dulimi* (n 121) paras 150–51.

[134] ibid.

listing regime established by numerous resolutions has evolved in terms of its nature and scope to become a permanent tool of the UN global counter-terrorism apparatus, more closely resembling a system of international law enforcement than a temporary political measure. In formal legal terms, the participation of the Security Council introduces a novel element in the response to terrorism, but, despite the Security Council's extensive powers, the cooperative element has remained strong. Security Council decisions are ultimately directed against the activities of non-State actors, and their implementation depends on the cooperation of State authorities. Furthermore, actual resort to coercive measures against non-complying States is rare, and its use has been somewhat arbitrary. Some States have encountered difficulties in fulfilling some of the requirements laid out by the Security Council, especially those that authorise or demand action incompatible with national law or international human rights obligations. So, although there has been a formal change in the basis for counter-terrorism cooperation, many of the difficulties identified with relation to the conventional approach still arise. This is not to deny that there has been a fundamental change or that there are indeed advantages in the Security Council's involvement – notably, its capacity to create specific obligations, which are binding upon all States. Even so, inherent impediments to international cooperation are also evident in the post-2001 developments. As a result, the regime has been subject to frequent criticism for its failure to incorporate a mechanism of independent judicial review. In particular, a lack of procedural safeguards within the new system has meant that numerous States have found themselves in unsolvable legal dilemmas, in which they were forced to breach either their international obligations or domestic law. Such dilemmas have impeded cooperation and provide crucial lessons for any aspiration to replace the essentially horizontal character of the international legal order with one endowed with some vertical imposition of authority. Such lessons are equally valuable to other areas of international law and will continue to limit the possible achievements of the international legal system.

INDEX

Introductory Note: References such as '178–79' indicate (not necessarily continuous) discussion of a topic across a range of pages. Wherever possible in the case of topics with many references, these have either been divided into sub-topics or only the most significant discussions of the topic are listed. Because the entire work is about 'international law', the use of this term (and certain others which occur constantly throughout the book) as entry points has been minimized. Information will be found under the corresponding detailed topics.

www.ingramcontent.com/pod-product-compliance
Ingram Content Group UK Ltd.
Pitfield, Milton Keynes, MK11 3LW, UK
UKHW020231290926
15470UKWH00002B/481

9 781509 917372